The Blackwell Guide to Hegel's *Phenomenology of Spirit*

Blackwell Guides to Great Works

A proper understanding of philosophy requires engagement with the foundational texts that have shaped the development of the discipline and which have an abiding relevance to contemporary discussions. Each volume in this series provides guidance to those coming to the great works of the philosophical canon, whether for the first time or to gain new insight. Comprising specially commissioned contributions from the finest scholars, each book offers a clear and authoritative account of the context, arguments and impact of the work at hand. Where possible the original text is reproduced alongside the essays.

Published
1. The Blackwell Guide to Plato's *Republic*, edited by Gerasimos Santas
2. The Blackwell Guide to Descartes' *Meditations*, edited by Stephen Gaukroger
3. The Blackwell Guide to Mill's *Utilitarianism*, edited by Henry R. West
4. The Blackwell Guide to Aristotle's *Nicomachean Ethics*, edited by Richard Kraut
5. The Blackwell Guide to Hume's *Treatise*, edited by Saul Traiger
6. The Blackwell Guide to Hegel's *Phenomenology of Spirit*, edited by Kenneth R. Westphal

Forthcoming
The Blackwell Guide to Kant's Ethics, edited by Thomas E. Hill, Jr.
The Blackwell Guide to Heidegger's *Being and Time*, edited by Robert Scharff

THE BLACKWELL GUIDE TO
Hegel's *Phenomenology of Spirit*

EDITED BY KENNETH R. WESTPHAL

WILEY-BLACKWELL
A John Wiley & Sons, Ltd., Publication

This edition first published 2009
© 2009 Blackwell Publishing Ltd except for editorial material and organization © 2009 Kenneth R. Westphal

Blackwell Publishing was acquired by John Wiley & Sons in February 2007. Blackwell's publishing program has been merged with Wiley's global Scientific, Technical, and Medical business to form Wiley-Blackwell.

Registered Office
John Wiley & Sons Ltd, The Atrium, Southern Gate, Chichester, West Sussex, PO19 8SQ, United Kingdom

Editorial Offices
350 Main Street, Malden, MA 02148-5020, USA
9600 Garsington Road, Oxford, OX4 2DQ, UK
The Atrium, Southern Gate, Chichester, West Sussex, PO19 8SQ, UK
For details of our global editorial offices, for customer services, and for information about how to apply for permission to reuse the copyright material in this book please see our website at www.wiley.com/wiley-blackwell.

The right of Kenneth R. Westphal to be identified as the author of the editorial material in this work has been asserted in accordance with the Copyright, Designs and Patents Act 1988.

All rights reserved. No part of this publication may be reproduced, stored in a retrieval system, or transmitted, in any form or by any means, electronic, mechanical, photocopying, recording or otherwise, except as permitted by the UK Copyright, Designs and Patents Act 1988, without the prior permission of the publisher.

Wiley also publishes its books in a variety of electronic formats. Some content that appears in print may not be available in electronic books.

Designations used by companies to distinguish their products are often claimed as trademarks. All brand names and product names used in this book are trade names, service marks, trademarks or registered trademarks of their respective owners. The publisher is not associated with any product or vendor mentioned in this book. This publication is designed to provide accurate and authoritative information in regard to the subject matter covered. It is sold on the understanding that the publisher is not engaged in rendering professional services. If professional advice or other expert assistance is required, the services of a competent professional should be sought.

Library of Congress Cataloging-in-Publication Data

The Blackwell guide to Hegel's Phenomenology of Spirit / edited by Kenneth R. Westphal.
    p. cm. – (Blackwell guides to great works ; 6)
  Includes bibliographical references (p. 296) and index.
  ISBN 978-1-4051-3109-4 (hardcover : alk. paper) – ISBN 978-1-4051-3110-0 (papercover : alk. paper) 1. Hegel, Georg Wilhelm Friedrich, 1770–1831. Phänomenologie des Geistes.   2. Spirit. 3. Consciousness. 4. Truth. I. Westphal, Kenneth R.   II. Title: Guide to Hegel's Phenomenology of Spirit.
  B2929.B53   2009
  193–dc22
                                    2008026532

A catalogue record for this book is available from the British Library.

Set in 10 on 13pt Galliard
by SNP Best-set Typesetter Ltd., Hong Kong
Printed in Singapore by Fabulous Printers Pte Ltd

1   2009

To Henry Stilton Harris

Contents

Notes on Contributors   ix

References   xi

Introduction   xvi

1. Hegel's Phenomenological Method and Analysis of Consciousness   1
   Kenneth R. Westphal

2. Desire, Recognition, and the Relation between Bondsman and Lord   37
   Frederick Neuhouser

3. Freedom and Thought: Stoicism, Skepticism, and Unhappy Consciousness   55
   Franco Chiereghin

4. The Challenge of Reason: From Certainty to Truth   72
   Cinzia Ferrini

5. Reason Observing Nature   92
   Cinzia Ferrini

6. Shapes of Active Reason: The Law of the Heart, Retrieved Virtue, and What Really Matters   136
   Terry Pinkard

7. The Ethics of Freedom: Hegel on Reason as Law-Giving and Law-Testing   153
   David Couzens Hoy

8. Hegel, *Antigone*, and Feminist Critique: The Spirit of
    Ancient Greece   172
    Jocelyn B. Hoy

9. Hegel's Critique of the Enlightenment in "The Struggle of the
    Enlightenment with Superstition"   190
    Jürgen Stolzenberg

10. "Morality" in Hegel's *Phenomenology of Spirit*   209
    Frederick C. Beiser

11. Religion, History, and Spirit in Hegel's *Phenomenology of Spirit* 226
    George di Giovanni

12. Absolute Knowing   246
    Allegra de Laurentiis

13. Spirit and Concrete Subjectivity in Hegel's *Phenomenology
    of Spirit*   265
    Marina F. Bykova

General Bibliography   296

Index of Names   299

Subject Index   304

Table of Concordances   324

Notes on Contributors

Frederick C. Beiser is Professor of Philosophy at Syracuse University, New York. He specializes in the history of early modern philosophy and classical German philosophy from Leibniz to Weber. His most recent works are *German Idealism: The Struggle against Subjectivism: 1781–1801* (2002), *The Romantic Imperative: The Concept of Early German Romanticism* (2003), *Hegel* (2005), and *Schiller as Philosopher* (2005).

Marina F. Bykova is Professor of Philosophy at North Carolina State University and editor of the journal *Russian Studies in Philosophy*. She has written *The Mysteries of Logic and the Secrets of Subjectivity* (in Russian, 1996), *Hegel's Interpretation of Thinking* (1990), and (with A. Krichevsky) *Absolute Idea and Absolute Spirit in Hegel's Philosophy* (1993), and numerous articles on German Idealism in Russian, German, and English. She has edited a new Russian edition of Hegel's *Phenomenology of Spirit* (2000), with a new commentary.

Franco Chiereghin is Professor of Philosophy at the University of Padua. He specializes in German Idealism. His books include *Dialettica dell'assoluto e ontologia della soggettività* (1980), *Il problema della libertà in Kant* (1991), and *L'eco della caverna. Ricerche di filosofia della logica e della mente* (2004).

Cinzia Ferrini is a Researcher at the University of Trieste. She has written *Guida al "De orbitis"* (1995), *Scienze empiriche e filosofie della natura nel primo idealismo tedesco* (1996), *Dai primi hegeliani a Hegel* (2003), "Testing the Limits of Mechanical Explanation in Kant's Precritical Writings" (2000), and "Being and Truth in Hegel's Philosophy of Nature" (2004); she edited *Eredità kantiane (1804–2004): questioni emergenti e problemi irrisolti* (2004).

George di Giovanni is Professor of Philosophy at McGill University (Montréal), specializing in the late German Enlightenment and in German Idealism. His main publications include *Freedom and Religion in Kant and His Immediate Successors: The Vocation of Humankind, 1774–1800* (2005); with H. S. Harris (eds., trs.), *Between Kant and Hegel: Texts in the Development of Post-Kantian Idealism*

(2000); *Friedrich Heinrich Jacobi: The Main Philosophical Writings and the Novel Allwill* (tr.) with an Introductory Study (1994).

David Couzens Hoy is Professor of Philosophy and Distinguished Professor of Humanities at the University of California, Santa Cruz. His most recent works include *Critical Resistance: From Poststructuralism to Post-Critique* (2004) and *The Time of Our Lives: A Critical History of "Temporality"* (2009). Currently he is writing a study of the history of consciousness from Kant to the present.

Jocelyn B. Hoy is Lecturer in Philosophy at the University of California, Santa Cruz. Her publications include "Hegel's Critique of Rawls" (1981) and essays on Annette Baier, Philippa Foot, and Richard Wasserstrom in the *Dictionary of Modern American Philosophers* (2005).

Allegra de Laurentiis is Associate Professor at SUNY-Stony Brook and specializes in nineteenth-century German philosophy. Her publications include *Subjects in the Ancient and Modern World: On Hegel's Theory of Subjectivity* (2005), "The *Parmenides* and *De Anima* in Hegel's Perspective" (2006), and "Not Hegel's Tales" (2007). She is currently working on Hegel's "Anthropologie."

Frederick Neuhouser is Viola Manderfield Professor of German and Professor of Philosophy at Barnard College, Columbia University, New York. He is the author of *Fichte's Theory of Subjectivity* (1990), *The Foundations of Hegel's Social Theory: Actualizing Freedom* (2000), and *Rousseau's Theodicy of Self-Love (Amour-propre): Evil, Rationality, and the Drive for Recognition* (2008).

Terry Pinkard is Professor of Philosophy at Georgetown University, Washington, DC. His books include: *Hegel's Phenomenology: The Sociality of Reason* (1994), *Hegel: A Biography* (2000), and *German Philosophy, 1760–1860: The Legacy of Idealism* (2002).

Jürgen Stolzenberg is Professor of Philosophy at the Martin-Luther-Universität Halle-Wittenberg. His specialties include Kant, German Idealism, Neokantianism, theory of subjectivity, and aesthetics. He has published *Fichtes Begriff der intellektuellen Anschauung. Seine Entwicklung in den Wissenschaftslehren von 1793/94 bis 1801/02* (1986) and *Ursprung und System. Probleme der Begründung systematischer Philosophie im Werk Hermann Cohens, Paul Natorps und beim frühen Martin Heidegger* (1995).

Kenneth R. Westphal is Professor of Philosophy at the University of Kent, Canterbury, and Professorial Fellow at the University of East Anglia. He is author of *Kant's Transcendental Proof of Realism* (2004), *Hegel's Epistemology* (2003), and "Normative Constructivism: Hegel's Radical Social Philosophy," *SATS* (2007). He is completing a book, "Hegel's Critique of Cognitive Judgment: From Naïve Realism to Understanding."

References

Recent translations of the works of Kant and his successors contain pagination from their critical German editions. References to pages of English translations are only provided when the translation does not contain pagination from the relevant critical edition. Multi-volume editions are cited by volume:page numbers; when possible, they are cited by volume:page.line numbers. Works divided into numbered sections are cited by section (§) number.

Hegel's *Phenomenology of Spirit* is cited according to the critical edition in his *Gesammelte Werke*, vol. 9 (see below). Page numbers are also provided for A. V. Miller's translation, though contributors have either provided their own translations or have revised Miller's without notice. Two new, and doubtless much improved, English translations are now in preparation, which will indicate the pagination of the critical edition of Hegel's *Phänomenologie des Geistes*.

Hegel's *Encyclopedia of Philosophical Sciences* and *Philosophy of Right* are composed as lecture syllabi. They contain three distinct kinds of text: Main sections, Remarks Hegel appended to those main sections, and "*Zusätze*," lecture notes appended by Hegel's editors to Hegel's sections or remarks. Where Hegel's published remarks are cited, the section number is followed by the suffix 'R', as in '§345R'. Where student notes from Hegel's lectures are cited, the section number is followed by the suffix '*Z*', as in '§345*Z*'. Where both a main section and a remark or a lecture note are cited an ampersand is interposed thus: '§345 & R' or '§345 & *Z*'. (In no case are all three kinds of text cited together.)

Kant

Ak   *Kants Gesammelte Schriften*, 29 vols. Königlich Preußische (now Deutsche) Akademie der Wissenschaften. Berlin: G. Reimer, now De Gruyter, 1902–.

CPR   *Kritik der reinen Vernunft*: 1st ed., 1781 (A), Ak 4; 2nd ed., 1787 (B), Ak 3.

	The Critique of Pure Reason, tr. P. Guyer and A. Wood. Cambridge: Cambridge University Press, 1998.
Prol.	*Prolegomena zu einer jeden künftigen Metaphysik, die als Wissenschaftlich wird auftreten können* (1783), Ak 4.
	Prolegomena to Any Future Metaphysics, ed. Günter Zöller. Oxford: Oxford University Press, 2003.
MFNS	*Metaphysische Anfangsgründe der Naturwissenschaft* (1786), Ak 4.
	Metaphysical Foundations of Natural Science, ed. and tr. M. Friedman. Cambridge: Cambridge University Press, 2004.
CPrR	*Kritik der praktischen Vernunft* (1788), Ak 5.
	Critique of Practical Reason, tr. M. Gregor, in M. Gregor (ed., tr.), Immanuel Kant, *Practical Philosophy* (pp. 133–272). Cambridge: Cambridge University Press, 1997.
CJ	*Kritik der Urteilskraft* (1790), Ak 5.
	Critique of the Power of Judgment, ed. and tr. P. Guyer. Cambridge: Cambridge University Press, 2000.
MM	*Metaphysik der Sitten* (1797), Ak 6.
	Metaphysics of Morals, tr. M. Gregor, in M. Gregor (ed., tr.), Immanuel Kant, *Practical Philosophy* (pp. 353–604). Cambridge: Cambridge University Press, 1997.
	(Note: 'MM' *without* italics is used to designate Moldenhauer and Michel (eds.), *Werke in 20 Bänden*. Confusion is avoided by the context of the citation – one involves an attribution to Hegel, the other to Kant – and by the use or lack of italics.)
Rel.	*Die Religion innerhalb der Grenzen der bloßen Vernunft* (1793), Ak 6.
	Religion within the Boundaries of Mere Reason, tr. G. di Giovanni, in A. Wood and G. di Giovanni (eds., trs.), Immanuel Kant, *Religion and Rational Theology* (pp. 39–216). New York: Cambridge University Press, 1996.

Fichte

FNW	*Johann Gottlieb Fichtes nachgelassene Werke*, 3 vols., ed. I. H. Fichte. Bonn: Adolph-Marcus, 1834–35.
FSW	*Johann Gottlieb Fichtes sämtliche Werke*, 8 vols., ed. I. H. Fichte. Berlin: Veit, 1845–46.
FGA	*J. G. Fichte – Gesamtausgabe der Bayerischen Akademie der Wissenschaften*, ed. R. Lauth and H. Jacob. Stuttgart-Bad Cannstatt: frommann holzboog, 1965–.
SK	*The Science of Knowledge*, ed. and tr. P. Heath and J. Lachs. Cambridge: Cambridge University Press, 1982.
EPW	*Early Philosophical Writings*, ed. and tr. D. Breazeale. Ithaca, NY: Cornell University Press, 1988.

FTP	*Foundations of Transcendental Philosophy: Wissenscahftslehre novo methodo*, ed. and tr. D. Breazeale. Ithaca, NY: Cornell University Press, 1992.
IWL	*Introduction to the Wissenschaftslehre*, ed. and tr. D. Breazeale. Indianapolis, IN: Hackett, 1992.

Schelling

SW	*Schellings Werke*, ed. M. Schröter. München: Beck, 1958.
HKA	*Werke: Historisch-Kritische Ausgabe*, ed. W. G. Jacobs and W. Schieche. Stuttgart: frommann-holzboog, 1976–.
Heath	*System of Transcendental Idealism (1800)*, tr. P. Heath. Charlottesville: University Press of Virginia, 1978.
H&L	*The Science of Knowledge with the First and Second Introductions*, tr. P. Heath and J. Lachs. Cambridge: Cambridge University Press, 1982.

Hegel

GW	*Gesammelte Werke*, 21 vols. Deutsche Forschungsgemeinschaft, with the Hegel-Kommission der Rheinisch-Westfälischen Akademie der Wissenschaften and the Hegel-Archiv der Ruhr-Universität Bochum. Hamburg: Meiner, 1968–.
MM	*Werke in 20 Bänden*, ed. K. Moldenhauer and K. Michel. Frankfurt am Main: Suhrkamp, 1970.
	(Note: '*MM*' *with* italics is used to designate Kant's *Metaphysics of Morals*. Confusion is avoided by the context of the citation – one involves an attribution to Hegel, the other to Kant – and by the use or lack of italics.)
Diff.	"Differenz des Fichte'schen und Schelling'schen Systems der Philosophie," *Kritisches Journal der Philosophie* 1.1 (1801): 111–84; rpt. *GW* 4:3–92.
	The Difference between Fichte's and Schelling's System of Philosophy, ed. and tr. H. S. Harris and W. Cerf. Albany, NY: State University of New York Press, 1977.
Skept.	"Verhältniß des Scepticismus zur Philosophie, Darstellung seiner verschiedenen Modificationen, und Vergleichung des neuesten mit dem alten," *Kritisches Journal der Philosophie* 1.2 (1801): 1–74; rpt. *GW* 4:197–238.
	"Relationship of Scepticism to Philosophy, Exposition of Its Different Modifications and Comparison to the Latest Form with the Ancient One," tr. H. S. Harris, in H. S. Harris and G. di Giovanni (eds.), *Between Kant and Hegel: Texts in the Development of Post-*

Kantian Idealism (pp. 311–62). Rev. ed. Cambridge, MA: Hackett, 2000.

F&K "Glauben und Wissen oder die Reflexionsphilosophie der Subjectivität, in der Vollständigkeit ihrer Formen, als Kantische, Jacobische, und Fichtesche Philosophie," *Kritisches Journal der Philosophie* 2.1 (1802): 3–189; rpt. *GW* 4:313–414.

Faith and Knowledge, ed. and tr. W. Cerf and H. S. Harris. Albany, NY: State University of New York Press, 1977.

SEL *System of Ethical Life (1802/3) and first Philosophy of Spirit*, ed. and tr. H. S. Harris and T. M. Knox. Albany, NY: State University of New York Press, 1979.

Phil. Prop. "Kurse. Manuskripte und Diktate," *GW* 10:523–818. (Formerly designated "*Texte zur Philosophischen Propaedeutik (1801–13)*.")

The Philosophical Propaedeutic, ed. M. George and A. Vincent, tr. A. V. Miller. Oxford: Basil Blackwell, 1986.

L&M *The Jena System, 1804–5: Logic and Metaphysics*, ed. and tr. J. W. Burbidge, G. di Giovanni, and H. S. Harris. Kingston: McGill-Queen's University Press, 1986.

PS *Phänomenologie des Geistes* (1807). In: *GW* 9.

M *Phenomenology of Spirit*, tr. A. V. Miller. Oxford: Clarendon Press, 1979. (Cited by page, not paragraph, number; translations revised without notice.)

Phänomenologie des Geistes, ed. H.-F. Wessels and H. Clairmont, with an Introduction by W. Bonsiepen. Hamburg: Meiner, 2006. Based on *GW* 9; provides a page concordance among the standard German editions of Hegel's *Phenomenology* (pp. 621–7).

SL *Wissenschaft der Logik* (1st ed.: 1812–16, 2nd ed: 1832), 2 vols. *GW* 11, 12, 21 (Bk. 1, 2nd ed.).

Science of Logic, tr. George di Giovanni. Cambridge: Cambridge University Press, forthcoming. (Contains pagination from *GW*.)

PR *Grundlinien der Philosophie des Rechts. Naturrechtslehre und Politikwissenschaft im Grundrisse. GW* 14.

Elements of the Philosophy of Right, ed. A. Wood, tr. H. B. Nisbet. Cambridge: Cambridge University Press, 1991.

Enc. *Enzyklopädie der philosophischen Wissenschaften* (1st ed.: 1817, 2nd ed.: 1827, 3rd ed.: 1830), 3 vols., *GW* 13, 19, 20; cited by §, as needed with the suffix 'R' for Remark (*Anmerkung*), or 'Z' for *Zusatz* (addition from student lecture notes).

Hegel's Encyclopedia Logic (*Enc.* 1), tr. T. Geraets, W. Suchting, and H. S. Harris. Cambridge, MA: Hackett, 1991.

Hegel's Philosophy of Nature (*Enc.* 2), tr. A. V. Miller. Oxford: Clarendon Press.

Hegel's Philosophy of Nature (*Enc.* 2), 3 vols., ed. and tr. M. J. Petry. London: George Allen & Unwin; New York: Humanities Press, 1970.

Hegel's Philosophy of Mind (*Enc.* 3), tr. W. Wallace and A. V. Miller. Oxford: Clarendon Press, 1976.

Hegel's Philosophy of Subjective Spirit (*Enc.* 3, §§377–482), 3 vols., ed. and tr. M. J. Petry. Dordrecht: D. Reidel, 1978. (Also contains the 'Berlin *Phenomenology*'.)

VGP — *Vorlesungen über die Geschichte der Philosophie*, ed. P. Garniron and W. Jaeschke, Vorlesungen vols. 6–9. Hamburg: Meiner, 1986, 1984, 1996.

H&S — *Hegel's Lectures on the History of Philosophy*, tr. E. S. Haldane and F. H. Simson. New York: Humanities Press, 1955.

B/HP — *Lectures on the History of Philosophy: The Lectures of 1825–1826*, ed. R. F. Brown, tr. R. F. Brown and J. M. Stewart. Berkeley: University of California Press, 1990.

Briefe — *Briefe von und an Hegel*, 4 vols., ed. J. Hoffmeister. Hamburg: Meiner, 3rd ed., 1981.

B&S — *Hegel: The Letters*, tr. C. Butler and C. Seiler. Bloomington: Indiana University Press, 1984.

Introduction

The present volume celebrates the bicentennial of the publication of Hegel's *Phänomenologie des Geistes* in 1807. This bicentennial has occasioned many conferences and collections on Hegel's first masterpiece. Distinctive of the present volume is that it is a collective, sequential commentary on the entirety of Hegel's *Phenomenology of Spirit* composed by a diverse international group of experts, who, on the basis of one common influence – Hegel's book – provide a rich and cohesive interpretation of Hegel's *Phenomenology*. Contributors hail from Canada, England, Germany, Italy, Russia, and the United States.

The first print run of 750 copies of Hegel's *Phenomenology* quickly established his reputation as Germany's leading philosopher.[1] Though neglected in the later nineteenth and early twentieth centuries, post-war scholarship re-established Hegel's *Phenomenology* as a philosophical landmark. For example, anti-Cartesianism has become a major theme in recent analytical philosophy of mind, philosophy of language, and epistemology. Yet the first and still the most searching anti-Cartesian revolt in philosophy was Kant's, whose lessons were further developed by Hegel. On a surprising range of philosophical topics, Hegel has already been where we still need to go. For example, instead of fretting about which is more basic, individuals or social groups, Hegel argues that both options are mistaken because individuals and societies are mutually interdependent; neither is more basic than the other. The Enlightenment bequeathed to us the idea that if our knowledge is a social or historical phenomenon, then we must accept relativism. Hegel criticized this dichotomy too, arguing that a sober social and historical account of human reason and knowledge *requires* realism about the objects of knowledge and strict objectivity about practical norms.

There have been doubts about the status of Hegel's *Phenomenology* within his mature philosophical system, specifically: What is the proper introduction to Hegel's *Science of Logic* and thus to his philosophical system? Though Hegel provided various "introductions" to his *Science of Logic*, only one is designated by him as the "justification," "deduction," and "proof" (*Rechtfertigung, Deduktion, Beweis*) of its standpoint: the 1807 *Phenomenology of Spirit*.[2] (Hegel here uses the term 'deduction' in the legal sense brought into philosophy by Kant: the justification of an entitlement.) Though Hegel remarked that the *Phenomenology* was a creature of its time, before his death of cholera in 1831 he planned to publish a second, revised edition of the *Phenomenology*. Though the elder Hegel no longer claimed that the *Phenomenology* formed the first part of – that is, *within* – his philosophical system of Logic, Philosophy of Nature, and Philosophy of Spirit, he did not expunge his first masterpiece from his systematic philosophy.[3]

Hegel's *Phenomenology* is preceded by his famous Preface (*Vorrede*), "On Scientific Cognition." Written after the body of his text, Hegel's Preface ranges broadly across his anticipated system of *Logic, Philosophy of Nature*, and *Philosophy of Spirit*; it is not a preface to the *Phenomenology of Spirit* alone. We agree with Lauer (1993: 2) that Hegel's *Phenomenology* is best begun with the Introduction, and that Hegel's Preface is best read in conclusion. Central themes of Hegel's Preface are considered in chapter 13.

Hegel's scholars have puzzled about whether or how the *Phenomenology* is unitary. Our collective commentary develops a significant consensus about the integrity of Hegel's text and issues. This point is examined expressly in chapters 1, 12, and 13, while chapters 10 and 11 say much about it too. A first word on the unity of Hegel's *Phenomenology* may be offered here by reviewing the chapters to follow and their relations.

Hegel's *Phenomenology* is an imposing work. In it, Hegel proposes to explicate and justify his philosophy through the detailed, internal critique of alternative views, so that the oversights of each can be remedied while their insights can be incorporated into an adequate philosophical account. The large-scale structure of the *Phenomenology* is reflected by Hegel's critique of and response to the common presumption that priority must be given either to individuals or to social wholes. He argues instead that individuals and their communities are mutually interdependent for their existence and characteristics; neither is more basic than or 'prior to' the other. At the beginning of the fourth part of the *Phenomenology*, "Spirit," Hegel claims to have demonstrated to his readers that the first three parts, "Consciousness," "Self-consciousness," and "Reason," have examined individualistically our cognitive and practical capacities and abilities which are, in fundamental ways, socially grounded (*PS* 239.15–23/M 264). (Hegel's Table of Contents appears in outline form below, pp. 28–29). In "Spirit" Hegel first considers the Attic Greek polis as a form of communal spirit which is "immediate" because it lacks adequate rational resources to assess and to justify its fundamental normative principles, based on unwritten and on positive law. In this way Hegel argues that rational reflection and assessment are necessary for establishing adequate norms. He then reconsiders our cognitive and practical capacities with reference to their social context and grounds, although these social dimensions of our cognitive and practical lives are neglected, denied or distorted in various ways by the Modern and especially the Enlightenment forms of consciousness he considers in the remaining sub-sections of "Spirit," "Self-Alienated Spirit" and "Self-Certain Spirit." Hegel's critique of these individualist views purports to justify explicitly to Modern individualists that our reasoning and thus our justificatory capacities are fundamentally intersubjective and thus social. Thus does Hegel make the issue of our collective, communal self-understanding explicit *for* Modern individuals at the very end of "Spirit." "Religion" and its history, Hegel contends, represent humanity's most significant and expressly communal self-understanding of ourselves in relation to one another and to our universe. Though Hegel argues that religious deities are human projections – they are *Vorstellungen* (representations) rather than *Begriffe* (concepts) – he contends that religious representations express legitimate human needs and aspirations. The final form of religion, according to Hegel, is a post-Enlightenment form of "manifest religion" which, when combined with the rational resources of human cognition and action examined previously, enables us to understand that we know the world as it is and we know ourselves as we are. This is "Absolute Knowing," the final stage of Hegel's *Phenomenology of Spirit*. Hegel's "idealism" is a moderate holism, according to which wholes and parts are mutually interdependent for their existence and characteristics.[4] Accordingly, as we obtain ever more comprehensive knowledge of the world-whole, the world-whole obtains ever more comprehensive self-knowledge through us. We are, so to speak, the homunculi in *Geist*. Yet the world-whole is not simply there for us to pluck; there *is* only the present, though presently there are old objects, phenomena, and systems which persist into and continue to function or to deteriorate into the future. Only through our investigation, reconstruction, knowledge and understanding can the world-whole expressly exist as spirit. With this structure in mind, we may consider more closely the individual stages in Hegel's grand analysis.

In "Hegel's Phenomenological Method and Analysis of Consciousness" (chapter 1), Kenneth R. Westphal shows that Hegel is a major (albeit unrecognized) epistemologist: Hegel's Introduction provides the key to his phenomenological method by showing that the Pyrrhonian Dilemma of the Criterion refutes traditional coherentist and foundationalist theories of justification. Hegel then solves this Dilemma by analyzing the possibility of constructive self- and mutual criticism. "Sense Certainty" provides a sound internal critique of "knowledge by acquaintance," thus undermining a key tenet of Concept Empiricism, a view Hegel further undermines by showing that a series of non-logical *a priori* concepts must be used to identify any particular object of experience. Most importantly, Hegel justifies a semantics of singular cognitive reference with important anti-skeptical implications. "Perception" extends Hegel's criticism of Concept Empiricism by exposing the inadequacy of Modern theories of perception (and also sense data theories), which lack a tenable concept of the identity of perceptible things. Hegel demonstrates that this concept is *a priori* and integrates two counterposed sub-concepts, "unity" and "plurality." Hegel's examination of this concept reveals his clear awareness of what is now called the "binding problem" in neurophysiology of perception, a problem only very recently noticed by epistemologists. "Force and Understanding" exposes a fatal equivocation in the traditional concept of substance which thwarts our understanding of force and causal interaction. Hegel's disambiguation of that concept enables us to comprehend how relations can be essential to physical particulars. Hegel contends that Newtonian universal gravitation shows that gravitational relations are essential to physical particulars, and then criticizes a series of attempts – including the infamous "inverted world" – to avoid this conclusion. Hegel's cognitive semantics supports Newton's Fourth Rule of philosophizing, which rejects mere logical possibilities as counterexamples to empirical hypotheses. Finally, Hegel's cognitive semantics reveals a previously unnoticed link between Pyrrhonian and Cartesian skepticism and empiricist anti-realism about causality within philosophy of science: all three appeal to premises, hypotheses or mere logical possibilities which in principle lack fully determinate, cognitively legitimate meaning. Westphal concludes by summarizing Hegel's overarching epistemological analysis in the *Phenomenology*.

In "Desire, Recognition, and the Relation between Bondsman and Lord" (chapter 2), Frederick Neuhouser reconstructs the succession of configurations of consciousness that make up the first section of the *Phenomenology*'s second main part, "Self-Consciousness." Its central theme is how, through phenomenological experience, the self-conscious subject makes progress towards its goal of uniting into a coherent conception of self and world the two seemingly contradictory self-descriptions inherited from its experience in "Consciousness": as the essential, law-giving pole of the subject–object pair and as a subject that, at the same time, necessarily stands in relation to an object, to some reality other than itself. Neuhouser reconstructs Hegel's argument to show that a subject cannot satisfy its aspiration to achieve a self-sufficient existence in the world by relating to its objects in the mode of desire (by destroying an other that is taken not to have the status of a subject) and why its aspiration to embody self-sufficiency can be achieved only by seeking the recognition of its elevated standing from another being who it, in turn, recognizes as a subject. The chapter concludes with an extended analysis of the advances and shortcomings of the reciprocal though asymmetric pattern of recognition that characterizes a relation between lord and bondsman. The failure of these practical strategies for achieving self-sufficiency thus yield to a series of theoretical strategies for achieving it in the remainder of "Self-Consciousness."

In "Freedom and Thought: Stoicism, Skepticism, and Unhappy Consciousness" (chapter 3), Franco Chiereghin examines the second section of "Self-Consciousness," which Hegel subdivided into three figures: Stoicism, Skepticism, and Unhappy Consciousness. Hegel presents these as further specifications of the section's general theme, "Freedom of Self-Consciousness." In the introductory pages, Hegel presents his account of thought. The activity of thought expresses the unity of being and of knowledge, of the subject and the object, and the multiplicity of aspects into a totality which is articulated in itself and by itself – a view for which Hegel argued in "Consciousness." Now none of the three figures of Self-Consciousness realizes these features. The freedom of thought claimed by Stoicism is only the abstract thought of freedom. Skepticism is unable to escape a dialectic which is only negative and destructive. Finally, the Unhappy Consciousness is the cause of its own unhappiness since it separates from itself and ascribes to an unreachable "beyond" what is essential for itself and degrades itself to the most despicable nullity. Actualizing freedom of thought thus requires an entirely new strategy, exhibited by "Reason."

In "The Challenge of Reason: From Certainty to Truth" (chapter 4), Cinzia Ferrini examines Hegel's compressed, allusive, important, and surprising introduction to his lengthy chapter on "Reason," "The Certainty and Truth of Reason." The central issue is the proper significance of reason's idealism, as the abstract beginning of its certainty of being all reality. The dialectical movement of the section shows that although reason in truth, and by instinct, is only the universality of things, its attempt to possess itself directly *in natural things* is contradictory because its knowing takes natural things opposed to the 'I' and believes that truth lies in their sensible being. Ferrini challenges the standard view that this first appearance presents Fichte's 'I'. She contends that Hegel addresses the general Modern insight that thought progresses freely in its determinations, making these thought-determinations the intrinsic, objective substantiality of nature, and linking the principle of realism to the movement of absolute liberation of self-consciousness, a thought shared in common by the empirical side of rationalism, the idealistic side of "concrete" empiricism, and by subjective idealism, though subjective idealism seized upon only one side of this relation.

In "Reason Observing Nature" (chapter 5), Cinzia Ferrini shows that Hegel's central concern is to expose the contradiction between reason's belief and its actual procedure in scientific knowledge. In empirical sciences, reason in fact rises conceptually above the diversity of the sensible when it seeks to identify laws, forces, purified chemical matters, and genera. Ferrini retraces Hegel's objections to description, classification, and the quest for laws in contemporaneous mineralogical, biological, psychological, and phrenological literature, showing how Hegel both accounted for the methodological self-consciousness of working scientists and took active part in debates between rival scientific theories, publicly siding with some lines of contemporaneous natural science against others and providing for them a speculative justification and foundation. She shows that natural science and our understanding of natural science are central to Hegel's *Phenomenology of Spirit* and to his critique of Kant, and she details how Hegel's critique of explaining human beings scientifically as human bodies shows by *reductio ad absurdum* that understanding human beings requires examining individual human agency and behavior, Hegel's topic in the remainder of "Reason."

In "Shapes of Active Reason: The Law of the Heart, Retrieved Virtue, and What Really Matters" (chapter 6), Terry Pinkard shows that the puzzling nature of Hegel's chapter on "Reason" has an important, if not obvious, rationale. First, Hegel's chapter advances the thesis that all individualist accounts of authority experience a *partial* failure, which propels them towards more social accounts. Second, this sub-section sets the stage for Hegel's thesis that we best understand the failure of individualist accounts only if we understand the role of reason in history; specifically, once we understand that when history is understood from the point of view of ourselves as self-interpreting animals, what turns out to have been at stake in history is the very nature of normative authority itself. Third, Hegel contends that over historical time we have learned better how to identify what counts as normative authority, and that understanding what this requires of us amounts to "spirit's coming to a full self-consciousness," which is best characterized as an "absolute" point of view. This leads Hegel to propose that the best way to understand how a norm has its grip on us is to be found by looking at how accepted, "positive" norms *lose* their grip on us. This is why Hegel examines phenomenologically such norms as they are *at work*, or are "actual," *wirklich* (as Hegel says), in various *practices*. Once we understand normative governance in this way, we understand, Hegel contends, that reason itself must be also understood as social, and that in a very complicated, "dialectical" way, we hold ourselves responsible to the *world* only in holding ourselves in certain very determinate ways responsible to *each other*. The most obvious way to do this is by using Kant's tests of the Categorical Imperative, which Hegel considers in the final sub-section of "Reason."

In "The Ethics of Freedom: Hegel on Reason as Law-Giving and Law-Testing" (chapter 7), David Couzens Hoy reconsiders the last two sections of part five of the *Phenomenology*, "Reason." The next part is entitled, simply, "Spirit." These concluding sub-sections of "Reason," on "Reason as Lawgiver" and "Reason as Testing Laws," are thus the point at which Reason becomes aware of itself as Spirit. What do 'Reason' and 'Spirit' mean here? Reason is essentially individual reason, but individual reason projects itself as universal. Reason is the "I" that thinks that everybody else should know what it knows and agree with it. Spirit, in contrast, is the "We" that makes individual forms of Reason possible. Spirit provides the cultural and historical background that enables one to be who one is. These two concluding sub-sections are important, therefore, because they represent the moment when individual reason becomes moral. Morality implies seeing that one's own maxims for actions are the same for everyone else. The most famous version of this view is Kant's theory of practical reason. Hegel provides counter-examples to show the emptiness of Kant's famous procedure by which we can test our maxims to see if they can consistently be viewed as moral rules. Hoy contends that Hegel does not simply shift his narrative from the I to the We. Instead, he develops a stronger argument that there is no I without a We. Thus Hegel does not simply jump from Reason to Spirit; he provides an interpretive *explanation* of the transition from (individual) Reason to (collective) Spirit.

In "Hegel, *Antigone*, and Feminist Critique: The Spirit of Ancient Greece" (chapter 8) Jocelyn B. Hoy focuses on the appearance of Spirit in the world of ancient Greece. She first presents a brief account of the "story" of this appearance of Spirit in Hegel's examination of "True Spirit. Ethics." She reflects on Hegel's use of dramatic form, specifically Attic tragedy, to introduce us to Spirit, and then examines contemporary feminist interpretations of Hegel's account of *Antigone* in this section of the *Phenomenology*. Questions about sexist biases, literary figures, and historical examples, she shows, are not philosophically tangential or irrelevant. Exploring recent feminist critiques of this section gets to the heart of Hegel's phenomenological project, and may well support a general interpretation of Hegel's *Phenomenology* potentially fruitful for feminist and social theory as well as contemporary philosophy. Hegel argues that "human" and "divine" (or statutory and natural) law inevitably conflict within the "immediate" spirit of Attic Greek society because they are held to be distinct, though in fact they are mutually integrated. "Legal Status" resolves this conflict by jettisoning "divine" (or natural) law, focusing instead on positive, human law, a prelude to the rational individualist, though self-alienated spirit of modern times.

In "Hegel's Critique of the Enlightenment in 'The Struggle of the Enlightenment with Superstition'" (chapter 9), Jürgen Stolzenberg examines Hegel's most explicit assessment of the Enlightenment, in the sub-section "The Struggle of the Enlightenment with Superstition." Hegel develops his critique of the Enlightenment within the context of his theory of spirit. Hegel's provocative though obscure thesis is that the Enlightenment's critique of superstition is in fact an unwitting *self*-critique. Stolzenberg reconstructs Hegel's arguments for this thesis on the basis of Hegel's systematic development of the concept of spirit in the *Phenomenology*. Hegel defines spirit by the unity of its relation to itself and to another. This is to say, this "other" is only the objectification of spirit itself. At this stage Hegel's attention shifts from "forms of consciousness" to "forms of a world." Hegel's explication of the concept of spirit requires several stages. The first stage consists in the simple intentional relation to an object, with no awareness that this object is the objectification of spirit itself. This stage corresponds to the relation between the Enlightenment and Faith in the *Phenomenology*. In Hegel's reconstruction the Enlightenment thus has no awareness that its relation to Faith is in truth only its relation to itself. Hence the struggle of the Enlightenment with Faith is an unwitting struggle with itself. The Enlightenment focuses on its relation to spatio-temporal objects, though its individualism occludes how its relations to objects are a function of its collective, cultural self-understanding. Faith focuses on its relation to God within a religious community, while neglecting that these relations are functions of how it relates to spatio-temporal objects. Neither side correctly or fully understands the self-relations involved in relating to objects, nor the relations to objects involved in relating to oneself. Hence neither side can properly account for itself nor justify its claims and actions. These failings appear dramatically in the moral and political counter-part to Enlightenment deism, the French Reign of Terror.

In "Morality in Hegel's *Phenomenology of Spirit*" (chapter 10) Frederick C. Beiser examines how Hegel's treatment of "Morality" is a distinctive stage in the development of "Spirit," of the "I that is We, and We that is I." The world of morality is one of persons who, as individuals, express the universal will. This is a significant advance beyond forms of agency considered previously in the *Phenomenology*, though it represents spirit in its extreme of particularity and subjectivity. Hegel aims to show that this extreme must be integrated properly with the universality and substantiality of spirit. Here Hegel examines Kant's and Fichte's moral worldview, conscience, and finally the beautiful soul, which present three increasingly extreme versions of moral individualism. Central to the moral worldview is the division between and the dominance of morality over nature. Morality is thus both independent of nature but also dependent upon it as a source of obligations and as its context of moral action. However, human agents cannot renounce their claim to happiness, though happiness requires the cooperation of nature. This tension generates a series of contradictions within the Kantian account of moral agency, which generates a series of forms of dissemblance, none of which can resolve or occlude the original contradiction. Conscience claims to be the sole and sufficient basis for determining right action. It purports to avoid the problems of the moral worldview by revising its universality requirement, thus integrating pure duty with moral action. However, claiming to identify what is universally right to do in any situation on the basis of individual conviction is impossible, because particular circumstances defy the simplicity of conscience and because agents have different convictions about what is right to do on that occasion. A final attempt to retain moral individualism in the face of these difficulties is made by the moral genius of the beautiful soul, characterized by Goethe and Rousseau, which places itself above specific moral laws. This presumed moral superiority requires withdrawing from the world of moral action in order to live by its demands for honesty, openness, and authenticity. Yet, even if the beautiful soul withdraws into a tiny community with carefully chosen companions, living with other people drives it to hypocrisy, thus thwarting its own principles. The shortcomings of moral individualism thus justify reintegrating moral agents into their community, and justify Hegel's turn to "Spirit" in the conclusion of this chapter and in the remainder of the *Phenomenology*.

In "Religion, History, and Spirit in Hegel's *Phenomenology of Spirit*" (chapter 11), George di Giovanni shows that, although Hegel treats religion only in the penultimate chapter of the *Phenomenology*, the phenomenon is everywhere present in his analysis of forms of consciousness and forms of a world. Religion is so fundamental to human existence, and so pervasive, that *we* (the phenomenologist-readers) are capable of reflecting upon it only at the end, after we have understood Hegel's case, presented in "Reason" and in "Spirit," to show that the critical, justificatory resources of reason can only function properly when we each recognize that we are members of the human community who require one another's critical assessment in order to justify our own claims to knowledge, both in theory and in practice. Religion concerns the experience of an individual as "individual" and as "individual in society," an experience that works itself out at the interface between nature and spirit. This interface entails the two aspects of "cult" and "belief," each of which provides the emotional and representational means for transforming an otherwise purely natural world into a human home. Di Giovanni reformulates the issue of "faith" and "knowledge" in Hegel's philosophy by tracing this process of transformation from the *agere bellum* of Chapter IV ("Self-Consciousness") to the *agere gratias* at the end of Chapter VI ("Spirit"), that is, from an early culture where social identity is established through warfare under the aegis of the gods to a society of individuals who recognize the inevitability of violence but also their power to contain and redeem it, under the aegis of spirit, in confession and forgiveness. So understood, "manifest" religion provides the social and historical context for the mutual recognition among rational judges reached at the end of "Morality" in "Evil and Forgiveness" and for reconciling the conflicting claims of reason and faith which plagued the Enlightenment.

In "Absolute Knowing" (chapter 12), Allegra de Laurentiis presents Hegel's concluding chapter (Chapter VIII, "Absolute Knowing") as a response-in-progress to the problem of phenomenal knowledge "losing its truth" on the path to conceptual comprehension. She identifies in Hegel's chapter two critical recapitulations of consciousness's many relations to its object, relations Hegel now presents as preparatory to the speculative or "absolute relation" of thought and object. Hegel maintains for logical reasons that this speculative feature is present, though only implicitly, in all modes of knowing. She points out the (originally Aristotelian) metaphysical foundation for this claim, namely the necessary logical sameness (*Gleichheit*) of thought and its content. Going well beyond Aristotle, Hegel then explains the "absolute relation" as the fundamental logical structure of spirit in the form of Self (*selbstische Form*). De Laurentiis reconstructs this "absolute ground" of phenomenal consciousness and its connection to Hegel's understanding of spirit's movement toward selfhood. She then presents this dynamic conception of spirit as a process of simultaneous expansion and inwardization through space and time. This process is possible due to inferential, primarily syllogistic structures of judgment which enable us to know particular objects (of whatever scale or kind) by grasping the interrelations among their specific aspects and by grasping interrelations among objects. Understanding these relations and understanding how we are able to make such cognitive judgments is central to understanding our knowledge of the natural, social and historical aspects of our world, which in turn is central to our self-knowledge. It is likewise central to the self-knowledge of spirit as the world-system, which it achieves through us. De Laurentiis highlights how the famous metaphors which conclude the *Phenomenology* (spirit's "slothful movement" through and "digestion" of its own forms) anticipate the kind of knowing Hegel makes explicit in his philosophical system.

In "Spirit and Concrete Subjectivity in Hegel's *Phenomenology of Spirit*" (chapter 13), Marina F. Bykova analyses the central topic of subjectivity in Hegel's *Phenomenology*, emphasized in his Preface, by examining Hegel's discussion of individual (concrete) subjectivity and its development within the forms of the universal ("cosmic") spirit. Her approach differs significantly from the two traditional, prominent interpretations of Hegel's work. The traditional approaches overemphasize either the universal ("cosmic") or the individualistic aspects of the *Phenomenology* and thus represent incomplete, one-sided views that misconceive Hegel's project. Bykova shows that in the *Phenomenology* Hegel emphasizes both the broad scale of collective and historical phenomena and the specific dimension of the individuals who participate in those phenomena and, in Hegel's view, through whom alone broad-scale collective and historical phenomena occur. In the *Phenomenology*, we observe a double movement: the embodiment and realization of "cosmic" spirit in individuals and the development of individuals raising themselves to "cosmic" spirit. Both converse movements coincide historically and practically; only taken together can they reconstruct the real process of the historical development of human spirit captured in Hegel's *Phenomenology of Spirit*. This movement must be read in both directions at once. The individual self becomes who he or she is by absorbing spirit – in all the variety of its forms and appearances (*Gestalten*) in the world – into his or her own specific structures; conversely, spirit reaches its self-realization in and through its embodiment in individuals who interact with each other and the world. This complex process of mediation between collective spirit and individual spirits Hegel calls human history. He maintains that only taken as a mutual process of individual and communal development can we understand universality within human history and preserve the autonomy of its social agents. By reviewing key stages in the development of spirit, so understood, Bykova indicates how the philosophical and historical materials considered in the body of Hegel's *Phenomenology* (and throughout this commentary) fit into the accounts of the religious community and of absolute knowing provided by di Giovanni and de Laurentiis.

Henry S. Harris, to whom we dedicate this commentary, deeply touched and greatly enlightened generations of students and scholars interested in Hegel's philosophy. Those of us now working on Hegel's early views and on the *Phenomenology of Spirit* in particular are extremely fortunate to have been taught by his magnificent trio of *magna opera* – *Hegel's Development I: Towards the Sunlight 1770–1801* (Oxford, 1972), *Hegel's Development II: Night Thoughts (Jena 1801–1806)* (Oxford, 1983), and *Hegel's Ladder* (2 vols., Hackett, 1997) – and by his wealth of published articles. Particularly commendable is his use of careful and comprehensive reconstruction of Hegel's writings to determine how Hegel understood, assessed, and used his source materials. Harris paid equal attention to the frequent and often dramatic ways in which Hegel redeveloped or revised his previous themes, views or analyses in later, more mature works. Throughout, Harris fearlessly reassessed and revised the 'received wisdom' about Hegel's views. For example, *Night Thoughts* demonstrates that Hegel's realism and naturalism appear much earlier and are more deeply rooted in Hegel's philosophy than is generally recognized even now. *Hegel's Ladder* is a landmark. Hegel's texts are notoriously rich, compressed, systematic, and rife with allusions. Harris identified a wealth of Hegel's profuse sources and shows why and how Hegel used them; his commentary demonstrates the decompression and detailed explication Hegel's text deserves and requires. Yet Harris also acknowledged some of his limits, for example, that he did not know enough contemporaneous natural science to grasp properly Hegel's Jena *Naturphilosophie*. His very special combination of intellectual daring, patience with Hegel's materials and issues, and personal humility are and shall remain exemplary.

This collective commentary has been undertaken very much in the spirit of Harris' example. The staggering range of issues and materials Hegel incorporated within the *Phenomenology of Spirit* require a diverse range of expertise and philosophical sensibility, virtually demanding a collective philosophical undertaking, and indeed an international one because each regional research community contributes special, complementary strengths. From beginning to end Hegel's philosophy is Occidental philosophy, and he made the best use he could of the Oriental and Arabic materials available to him. The international character of philosophical inquiry was disrupted, to our great philosophical disadvantage, by World War II. Inquiry and scholarship cannot afford to remain regional. We hope this commentary exhibits the benefits of international cooperation and engagement with Hegel's issues and texts. If it is the first endeavor of this kind, we hope and trust it shall not be the last. If we have been more concise than Harris, we hope to have compensated by explicating the structure of Hegel's analysis in the *Phenomenology of Spirit*, the role of each section within it, and how Hegel's analyses bear on salient issues in the field, both historical and contemporary.

Acknowledgments

I am grateful to Blackwell's philosophy editors, Jeff Dean and Nick Bellorini, for kindly inviting me to edit this volume. It has been an honor and a great pleasure to work together with the contributors on this volume; it is truly a delight when all of an editor's top choices accept with alacrity and spontaneously agree on the proper division of labor. I am deeply grateful to them for their outstanding efforts, and – along with the editors – for their great forbearance when life interrupted philosophy, significantly delaying the completion of this volume. I am also very grateful to Cinzia Ferrini for her indispensable assistance in editing chapters 4 and 5. Finally, I wish to thank Liz Cremona at Wiley Blackwell and Valery Rose, my copy-editor, for their highly professional, efficient, and invaluable work on behalf of this volume.

Notes

1 Chronologies of Hegel's life are provided by Beiser (2005, xix–xx), Kaufman (1966, 21–5), and Pinkard (2000, 754–49); cf. Harris (1993).
2 *SL*, *GW* 11:20.5–18, 20.37–21.11, 33.5–13; 21:32.23–33.4, 33.20–34.1, 54.28–55.5. These passages occur both in the first and the second editions of Hegel's *Science of Logic* (1812, 1832 respectively).
3 The case for this has been best made by Fulda (1975). Hegel speaks positively about, draws from, and cites for justification the 1807 *Phenomenology* in many of his later writings; e.g., *SL* (2nd ed., 1832), *GW* 21:7.25–8.2, 37.27–32, 11:351.3–12, 12:36–198.11, 232.30–17, 6:544–5, *PR* §§35R, 57R, 135R, 140R & note, *Enc.* (3rd ed., 1831) §25.
4 Westphal (1989, 140–5).

References

Beiser, F. C. (2005) *Hegel*. London: Routledge.
Fulda, H.-F. (1975) *Das Problem einer Einleitung in Hegels Wissenschaft der Logik*, 2nd ed. Frankfurt am Main: Klostermann.
Harris, H. S. (1993) "Hegel's Intellectual Development to 1807," in F. C. Beiser (ed.), *The Cambridge Companion to Hegel* (pp. 25–51). Cambridge: Cambridge University Press.
Hegel, G. W. F. (1807) *System der Wissenschaft, Erster Theil, die Phänomenlogie des Geistes*. Bamberg and Würzburg: Goebhardt.

Kaufmann, W. A. (1966) *Hegel: Reinterpretation, Texts, and Commentary.* London: Weidenfeld & Nicolson.
Lauer, Q. (1993) *A Reading of Hegel's Phenomenology of Spirit*, 2nd rev. ed. New York: Fordham University Press.
Pinkard, T. (2000) *Hegel: A Biography.* Cambridge: Cambridge University Press.
Westphal, K. R. (1989) *Hegel's Epistemological Realism: A Study of the Aim and Method of the Phenomenology of Spirit.* Dordrecht: Kluwer.

1

Hegel's Phenomenological Method and Analysis of Consciousness

Kenneth R. Westphal

1 Introduction

Hegel's 1807 *Phenomenology of Spirit* has been widely interpreted in view of his Preface rather than his Introduction. This is unfortunate. Hegel's notoriously rich, ambitious, and exciting Preface is a Preface not only to the *Phenomenology* but to Hegel's projected philosophical system, which was to contain the *Phenomenology* as Part 1 and a second work as Part 2 which would cover logic, philosophy of nature, and philosophy of spirit. Hegel's Preface thus greatly surpasses the issues and aims of the *Phenomenology* itself.[1] As Hegel insists in his retrospectively written Preface, truth can only be obtained as the *result* of inquiry, not from initial projections.[2] Hegel's prospectively written Introduction contains invaluable information about Hegel's issues and methods, especially about epistemological issues addressed throughout the *Phenomenology*, which examines the possibility of "absolute knowing" or genuine knowledge of "what in truth is,"[3] that is, knowledge no longer qualified by any distinction between mere appearance and genuine reality.[4]

Hegel's texts yield richly to the traditional hermeneutical requirements that an adequate interpretation integrates complete textual, historical, and systematic (that is, issues-oriented philosophical) analysis of a text. Meeting these requirements leads to heterodox interpretations, yet also maximally justifies them. Such detailed analysis I have provided elsewhere; here I epitomize the central points of Hegel's Introduction (§2) and first three chapters, "Sense Certainty" (§3), "Perception" (§4), and "Force and Understanding" (§5). I then summarize Hegel's overarching analysis of human knowledge in the *Phenomenology* (§6).

2 Hegel's Introduction

2.1 Problems about knowledge and justification

One key epistemological problem Hegel poses in his Introduction is how legitimately to assess or to establish the truth or falsehood of competing philosophies (*PS* 55.12–31, 58.10–22/M 48, 52). Hegel recognized that settling controversy about claims to knowledge, whether commonsense, natural-scientific, or philosophical, requires adequate criteria for judging the debate, though the controversy often also concerns those criteria. This threat of vicious circularity and question-begging[5] was quintessentially formulated by Sextus Empiricus as the Dilemma of the Criterion:

> [I]n order to decide the dispute which has arisen about the criterion [of truth], we must possess an accepted criterion by which we shall be able to judge the dispute; and in order to possess an accepted criterion, the dispute about the criterion must first be decided. And when the argument thus reduces itself to a form of circular reasoning the discovery of the criterion becomes impracticable, since we do not allow [those who make knowledge claims]to adopt a criterion by assumption, while if they offer to judge the criterion by a criterion we force them to a regress *ad infinitum*. And furthermore, since demonstration requires a demonstrated criterion, while the criterion requires an approved demonstration, they are forced into circular reasoning. (Sextus Empiricus, *PH* 2:4 §20; cf. 1:14 §§116–17)

Hegel refers in passing to this Dilemma (henceforth: 'the Dilemma') in his 1801 essay on skepticism (*Skept.*, *GW* 4:212.9), though he then agreed with Schelling that only the "limited" claims of the understanding confronted this problem, which was surpassed by the "infinite" claims of reason obtained through intellectual intuition. A satirical critique of intellectual intuition led Hegel to realize that intuitionism in any substantive form,[6] including Schelling's, is cognitively bankrupt because it can only issue claims without justifying reasons, and "one mere claim is worth as much as another" (*PS* 55.21–24/M 49). Conflicting claims suffice to show that at least one of them is false, though none of them provide a basis for determining which are false and which, if any, are true.[7]

Hegel restates Sextus' Dilemma in the middle of the Introduction (*PS* 9:58.12–22/M 52). Hegel recognized that it is a genuine philosophical problem; that it disposes of both coherentist and foundationalist models of justification, and so disposes of the two traditional models of knowledge (*scientia* and *historia*), although this Dilemma does *not* ultimately justify skepticism about ordinary, scientific, or philosophical knowledge.

Against coherentism, the Dilemma raises the charge of vicious circularity. On the basis of coherence alone it is hard to distinguish in any principled way between genuine progress in our knowledge in contrast to mere change in belief. Coherentism's most able and persistent contemporary advocate, Laurence BonJour, has conceded that coherentism cannot meet this challenge.[8]

Foundationalist models of justification typically distinguish between *historia* and *scientia*. Historical knowledge (*historia*) derives from sensory and memorial data; rational knowledge (*scientia*) is logically deduced from first principles.[9] Both models involve justifying conclusions by deriving them unilaterally from basic foundations: justification flows *from* basic foundations *to* other, derived claims, not vice versa. This holds whether justificatory relations are strictly deductive or whether they involve other kinds of rules of inference (e.g., induction, abduction) or weaker forms of basing relations.

The Dilemma exposes foundationalist models of justification as dogmatic *and* question-begging because such models cannot be justified to those who fundamentally dispute either the foundations or the basing relations invoked by any foundationalist theory, or the foundationalist model itself, because this model understands justification *solely* in terms of derivation from first premises of whatever kind. In principle, foundationalism preaches to the (nearly) converted, and begs the question against those who dissent; once they are disputed, foundationalism cannot justify its criteria of truth or of justification.[10]

Hegel recognized that solving the Dilemma requires a fallibilist, pragmatic, socio-historical account of rational justification which is consistent with realism about the objects of knowledge (and with strict objectivity about normative principles). Hegel's account of rational justification is based in part in his phenomenological method, which is based on Hegel's account of the self-critical structure of consciousness, which is embedded in Hegel's account of forms of consciousness.

2.2 Forms of consciousness

A "form" (*Gestalt*) of consciousness comprises a pair of basic principles, applied by their ideal exponent to their intended domains.[11] One principle specifies the kind of knowledge that form presumes to have; the other specifies the kind of objects it presumes to know. Hegel calls these two principles a form of consciousness's "certainty" (*Gewißheit*). Put idiomatically, these principles specify what a form of consciousness is sure the world and its knowledge of it are like.

A form of consciousness, so specified, is neutral between an individual's view and a group's collective outlook, and between historically identifiable and merely possible views of human knowledge and its objects. Historical epochs and extant philosophies are, Hegel contends, variations on the forms of consciousness examined in the *Phenomenology*, because both forms of consciousness and historically identifiable views devolve from central characteristics of human consciousness. This is one point of Hegel's claim that the *Phenomenology* presents "the path of the soul which is making its way through the sequence of its own transformations as through waystations prescribed by its very nature . . ." (*PS* 55.36–39/M 49).

By grasping some aspect of its own nature as a cognizer, each form of consciousness adopts a particular principle concerning what knowledge is. This epistemic principle implies certain constraints on the objects of knowledge. Therefore the adoption of an epistemic principle brings with it a concomitant ontological principle. To take a pair of epistemic and ontological principles as a *form* of consciousness allows latitude for developing from less to more sophisticated versions. To consider such a pair of principles as a form of *consciousness* examines them only as they can be adopted and employed by consciousness in attempting to comprehend its intended objects.[12]

Hegel proposes to examine such concepts as 'subject', 'object', 'knowledge', and 'world'. These abstract terms specify little. Hence Hegel examines particular sets of specific versions of these conceptions by examining their ideal employment by each form of consciousness. To solve the Dilemma and to avoid *petitio principii*, Hegel's justification of his own views results from an internal, self-critical assessment of every form of consciousness (see below, §6). Examining the insights and oversights of each form of consciousness enables us, Hegel's readers, to understand the adequate specification of these abstract conceptions Hegel provides at the end of the *Phenomenology*.

2.3 The possibility of constructive self-criticism

Against "coherentist," "circular," or "dialectical" theories of justification, Sextus' Dilemma raises the trope of vicious circularity. However, this horn of the Dilemma is defeated, and is shown to be *merely* a skeptical trope, by Hegel's account of the possibility of constructive self- and mutual criticism. The key points in Hegel's account are these.

In the Introduction, Hegel analyses this unassuming claim about human consciousness:

> consciousness *distinguishes* from itself something to which it at the same time *relates* itself; or, as this is expressed, this something is something *for consciousness*. The determinate side of this *relation*, or the *being* of something *for a consciousness*, is *knowledge*. From this being for an other, however, we distinguish the *being in itself*; that which is related to knowledge is at the same time distinguished from it and is posited as *existing* also outside this relation. (*PS* 58.25–31/M 52)

Hegel analyzes this bit of common sense to distinguish the object itself from our conception of it, and ourselves as actual cognitive subjects from our *self-conception* as cognitive subjects. Hegel analyses our *experience* of an object and our experience of *ourselves* as cognitive subjects, as *resulting* from our use of our conceptions in attempting to know our intended objects: our experience of the object results from our use of our conception of the object in attempting to know the object itself. Likewise, our self-experience as cognizant beings results from our use of our cognitive self-conception in attempting to know ourselves in our cognitive engagements. Hegel distinguishes these aspects of consciousness as a cognitive relation to objects:

> A. Our conception of the object.
> B. Our experience of the object.
> C. The object itself.

> 1. Our cognitive self-conception.
> 2. Our cognitive self-experience.
> 3. Our cognitive constitution itself.

Accordingly, our experience of the object (B) is structured both by our conception of the object (A) *and* by the object itself (C). Likewise, our self-experience as knowers (2) is structured both by our cognitive self-conception (1) *and* by our actual cognitive constitution (3). Hegel's analysis entails that we have no concept-free empirical knowledge or self-knowledge, and also that we are not trapped within our conceptual schemes! Positively, our experience of the object (B) can correspond with the object itself (C) only if our *conception* of the object (A) also corresponds with the object itself (C). Likewise, our cognitive self-experience (2) corresponds with our actual cognitive capacities (3) only if our cognitive self-conception (1) also corresponds with our actual cognitive capacities (3). Conversely, insofar as our conception of the object (A) or likewise our cognitive self-conception (1) fail to correspond with their objects (C, 3), we can detect and correct this lack of correspondence through sustained attempts to comprehend our objects (C, 3) by using our conceptions (A, 1) in our experience of those objects (B, 2). So doing can inform us whether and how our conceptions (A, 1) can be revised in order to improve their correspondence with their objects (C, 3).

Additionally, our conception of the object (A) and our cognitive self-conception (1) must not merely be consistent, but must support each other. Likewise our experience of the object (B) and our cognitive self-experience (2) must support each other. Finally, our conception of the object (A) must render our cognitive self-experience (2) intelligible, and our cognitive self-conception (1) must render our experience of the object (B) intelligible, thus rendering our experience and our account of it more coherent, comprehensive, and better suited to assessing and justifying our epistemic and other cognitive commitments. Achieving this requires that our conceptions (A) and (1) correspond to their objects (C) and (3). At the broad level of epistemology, where different models of the objects of knowledge require different models of knowledge, this complex of correspondences is a sufficient criterion of the truth of an epistemology.

The nub of Hegel's reply to the trope of circularity is to show that, when assessing or reassessing any piece of justificatory reasoning by re-examining its basic evidence, principles of inference, and its use of these, we can revise, replace, or reaffirm as needed any component and any link among components within the justificatory reasoning in question. Because self-criticism and constructive mutual assessment are both fallible and (fortunately) corrigible, Hegel's account of rational justification is fundamentally fallibilist. Hegel recognized that fallibilism about justification is consistent with realism about the objects of empirical knowledge.

Cognitive justification requires mutual critical assessment because our rational capacities are finite: we lack omniscience and omni-competence and we can only base our judgments on information, principles, evidence, examples, and reasonings we actually use, although any claim we make has implications far exceeding what one person can experience. These manifold implications, together with our predilections to focus on some activities, issues, inquiries, or methods rather than others and the division of cognitive labor this generates, entail that others have information pertaining to the rational assessment and justification or revision of our own judgments which we lack.[13]

Part of Hegel's genius is his ability to identify the core principles of philosophical views, to take them absolutely literally, and to state exactly what follows from them. Often what follows is far from obvious; Hegel's statement of these implications can be puzzling. Hegel's point is to prompt us to reflect on what we have implicitly assumed and ascribed to that view which is not officially stated in its principles, but is required for them to appear plausible. Hegel's phenomenological method is designed to induce forms of consciousness to reflect more carefully on their initial principles (their "certainty"); it is likewise designed to induce readers to reflect more carefully on their own understanding, not only of any form of consciousness, but also on their own preferred principles and views. For all of these reasons, the possibility of constructive self-criticism is fundamental to Hegel's entire philosophy, and especially to the *Phenomenology*.[14]

2.4 Hegel's introductory anticipation of spirit

Hegel's internal critique of forms of consciousness is designed to identify both the insights and the oversights of each form of consciousness, so that the oversights can be corrected by successor forms of consciousness which ultimately integrate these insights into an accurate, comprehensive account of human knowing (see below, §6)

Controversy about the integrity of Hegel's *Phenomenology* requires noting that Hegel planned from the beginning to integrate within the *Phenomenology* both his "science of the experience of consciousness" and his "phenomenology of spirit," as he indicates in the closing lines of his Introduction and reiterates in "Absolute Knowing."[15]

3 Sense Certainty

3.1 The context and aims of "Sense Certainty"

In "Sense Certainty" Hegel seeks to justify his provisional claim in the Introduction that aconceptual "knowledge by acquaintance" is not humanly possible.[16] Hegel thus criticizes Concept Empiricism, the view that every meaningful term in a language is either a logical term, a name of a simple sensed quality, or can be exhaustively defined by additive combinations of these two kinds of terms. Hegel's critique addresses both aconceptual knowledge of particulars (naive realism) and of sense data (e.g., Hume's simple impressions of sense or Russell's sense data). More constructively, in "Sense Certainty" Hegel reconstructs and defends Kant's semantics of cognitive reference while liberating this semantics from Kant's transcendental idealism.

"Sense Certainty" divides into five main parts: an introduction (¶¶1–5), three analytical phases (¶¶6–11, 12–14, 15–19), and a conclusion (¶¶20–21).[17] Phases I and II focus on designating particulars by using tokens of types of demonstrative (indexical) expressions, such as 'this', 'that', 'I'; Phase III focuses on designating particulars by ostensive gestures. The transition from "Sense Certainty" to

"Perception" is based on *combining* linguistic expressions with ostensive gestures. Hegel's thesis is: singular semantic reference via tokens of demonstrative terms or via ostensive gestures are mutually interdependent, and only secure singular cognitive reference through conceptually structured determinate thoughts about the designated individual and the spatio-temporal region it occupies. *En passant* Hegel justifies the distinction between the 'is' of identity and the 'is' predication by reducing their presumed identity to absurdity. Initially Sense Certainty conflates these two senses of 'is'; this conflation is the premise of Hegel's *reductio* argument against their conflation.

Recent semantic theory has shown that part of the meaning of a token of an indexical type term is that a specific speaker designates a specific item within a determinate region of space and time.[18] Hegel argues for this thesis, which is the negation of sense certainty. Hegel shows that determining the origin of the relevant reference system (the speaker) and the scope of the spatio-temporal region of the designated particular is possible only by using concepts of 'space', 'spaces', 'time', 'times', 'I', and 'individuation', which can only be properly used by also using concepts of at least some of the designated item's manifest characteristics (properties designated by predicates). Hence neither ostensive designation nor singular cognitive reference are possible on the basis of concept-free "knowledge by acquaintance," i.e., sense certainty.

Sense Certainty maintains that our knowledge of sensed particulars is immediate, direct, and non-conceptual; its "certainty" is that we can and do have such knowledge (*PS* 63.1–5/M 58). To justify his counter-thesis Hegel must assess Sense Certainty strictly internally. Hence Hegel's main question is whether any object of alleged sense-certain knowledge in fact is and appears "immediately" to Sense Certainty. To be charitable to Sense Certainty, Hegel disregards descriptions or predicates and focuses on tokens of indexical expressions such as 'this', 'now', or 'here', which Sense Certainty uses as logically proper names in Russell's sense.

3.2 The three phases of "Sense Certainty"

Hegel's first example of "the now" is "the now is the night" (*PS* 64.32–33/M 60). Here 'is' purportedly expresses an identity. Hegel suggests that we can assess this first example by preserving it: by daybreak it is false. Hence Sense Certainty cannot grasp a simple truth about spatio-temporal particulars without indexing its claims temporally, as true within some period of time. Sense Certainty maintains only that the object it knows "is" (*PS* 63.28/M 58). However, Sense Certainty cannot reconcile its unrefined, undifferentiated use of 'is' with its own temporally limited and transitory experiences of particulars. Hence our knowledge of sensed particulars requires having and using concepts of 'time' and of determinable 'times', and analogously 'space' and 'spaces'. Hence any tenable analysis of human knowledge of sensed particulars must admit universal, determinable concepts.

In Phase II, Sense Certainty responds by acknowledging the context-dependence of its use of type and token indexical expressions, but claims that genuine sense certainty lies only within *its own* cognitive reference to an object:

> The truth of this certainty is in the object as *my* object, or in *my meaning*; it is, because *I* know of it. (*PS* 66.7–8/M 61)

Sense Certainty thus focuses on any one instance of sense certainty, e.g., "The Here is a tree" (*PS* 66.17/M 61). Yet someone else claims: "The Here is a House."[19] Is this a counter-example? Hegel's first point is that the mere *sensibility* of sense certainty (*PS* 66.12–13/M 61) cannot distinguish among cognitive subjects. Hegel shows, second, that the term 'I' is not a logically proper name; it too is an indexical expression that can only be used by distinguishing between its type and its tokens, because its tokens can only designate a particular speaker (on a particular occasion of use) through its context-dependent character or role.

In Phase III, Sense Certainty ascribes its previous difficulties to its use of language to export its sense-certain knowledge out of its immediate context by reporting it to others (*PS* 67.27–30/M 63). It now restricts immediate knowledge to the immediate context in which it grasps any one particular, which can only be pointed out ostensively (*PS* 67.19–27/M 63). Hegel's key point is that, by itself, no ostensive gesture determines the relevant spatial or temporal scope of what it purportedly designates. Any punctual 'here', 'now', 'this', or 'that' lacks temporal and spatial extension; hence it cannot contain, coincide with, or pick out any spatio-temporal particular. Any such particular can be designated ostensively only by determining the relevant volume of space it occupies during some relevant period of time. However, even an approximate specification of the relevant region of space and period of time requires using concepts of 'time', 'times', 'space', 'spaces', 'I', and 'individuation'. Regarding time, Hegel states:

> *Pointing out* is thus itself the movement which pronounces what the now is in truth, namely a result, or a plurality of nows taken together. (*PS* 68.18–20, cf. 68.22–29/ M 64)

We can only understand or rightly interpret any use of an ostensive gesture if we understand a presupposed system of spatial and temporal coordinates together with the specification of the spatio-temporal region of the designated individual. Mere sensation, mere sensibility is necessary, though not at all sufficient, for sensory knowledge of any spatio-temporal particular, because sensibility alone can neither identify nor ostensively specify *which* individual is purportedly known, whenever and wherever it may be known by whomever purports to know it. Hence our knowledge of individual sensory objects is neither immediate nor aconceptual.

In the concluding paragraph of "Sense Certainty" Hegel develops his main point. Defenders of immediate knowledge speak of

> the being of *outer* objects, which can be determined still more precisely as *actual*, absolutely *individual, utterly personal, individual* things, none of which has an exact duplicate . . . (*PS* 69.35–70.1/M 66)

Hegel notes that such talk cannot specify any concrete particular, because these terms equally describe any and every particular. Augmenting such vague terminology with explicit descriptions, however detailed, cannot solve this problem. However specific, no description by itself determines whether no corresponding individual exists, only one such individual exists, or more than one such individual exists. Which is so is equally a function of the contents of the world. Hence to *know* any one particular requires both describing it *and* locating it in space and time. Only through ostensive designation can we *ascribe* the predicates used in the description *to* any *one*, putatively located and known, particular. Hegel thus shows that predication is required for singular cognitive reference to any spatio-temporal particular, and that predication requires singular sensory presentation. Only through predication can anyone specify (even approximately) the relevant spatio-temporal region (putatively) occupied by the object one purports to designate. Only in this way can we determine *which* spatio-temporal region to designate, in order to grasp *this* (intended, ostended) individual.[20] In this way, Hegel demonstrates that "the 'is' of predication" is distinct from "the 'is' of identity," and that predication is fundamental in even the simplest cases of our knowledge of sensed particulars.

3.3 Anti-skeptical and ontological implications of Hegel's analysis

Hegel's semantics has an important ontological implication. One main Pyrrhonian trope is that we are incapable of knowing reality because all we experience is changing, variable, relative, and transitory. This inference presumes the Paramenidean conception of truth and being, according to which something is 'true' only if it is constant, unchanging, independent (non-relative), and therefore reliable and trustworthy. If so, we can have no knowledge of truth because everything we experience is transitory. Hegel's semantic point is that any concept can play a legitimate cognitive role only if it is referred to particulars. This holds of the concept 'being' (*PS* 65.1–19/M 60). However, because particulars and our experiences of them are variable and transitory, the Paramenidean conception of truth and being has no legitimate cognitive use. To presume it does is to suffer from cognitively transcendent illusion. This point has an important ontological implication because it concerns in part how we can legitimately conceive the object(s) of human knowledge and experience. These implications are important to Hegel's subsequent critique of skepticism and also to "Force and Understanding" (below, §5).[21]

4 Perception

4.1 Hegel's issues and aims in "Perception"

In "Perception" Hegel confronts an issue central to the Modern "new way of ideas" and to the sense data tradition: How can we perceive any one unitary object amidst the multitude of its (putative) sensed qualities? Hegel seeks to show three points: (1) demonstrative and observation terms do not suffice for human knowledge of the world, which also requires the legitimate use of substantive *a priori* concepts of 'perceptible thing' and 'force'; (2) the relation 'thing/property' cannot be defined, substituted, reduced to, or replaced by the relations 'one/many', 'whole/part', set membership, or 'ingredient/product'; (3) the *a priori* concept of the identity of perceptible things integrates two opposed quantitative sub-concepts, 'one' and 'many'. This is characteristic of what Hegel designates as genuine *Begriffe* (concepts) in contrast to *Vorstellungen*, that is, to universals which lack this kind of internal integration of counterposed sub-concepts. Hegel associates *Vorstellungen* with the "abstract, finite understanding" and *Begriffe* with "concrete, infinite reason." Any one *Vorstellung* is "limited" or finite because it is qualified by – and its use is inseparable from – its unacknowledged counterpart. The understanding's use of *Vorstellungen* is limited or "finite" because its use of any one *Vorstellung* requires implicitly relying upon its contrary. In contrast, *Begriffe* incorporate two counterposed sub-concepts; hence they are not limited in that way. Hence reason's use of *Begriffe* is unlimited or "infinite" because *Begriffe* grasp the counterposed aspects of what it knows and thus knows them truly.[22]

The main target of Hegel's critique in "Perception" is Hume's analysis of "body," that is, of our concept and perceptual knowledge of physical objects and their identity (*Treatise* 1.4.2–3). The "contradictions" Hume identifies in our belief in physical objects coincide with those Hegel identifies within Perception. Hegel's analysis exploits Hume's failure to account for our concept 'physical object' in accord with his own Concept Empiricism to show that our concept of the identity of perceptible things is *a priori*.

4.2 Perception as a form of consciousness

Once Sense Certainty shows that our use of token-indexical terms requires using universal conceptions ('space', 'spaces', 'time', 'times', 'I', 'thing', and 'individuation'), then descriptive concepts of any kind may be admitted into any relevantly human epistemology. Hence Perception purports to know perceptible objects by describing them with predicates and designating them with token-demonstrative terms.[23] This includes both 'I' to designate a human cognitive subject and 'object' to designate what is there to be known (*PS* 71.5–8/M 67), as well as predicates. A universal is variously instantiated, though it cannot be identified with any one nor with any set of its instances, and it contrasts with other such universals and their instances (*PS* 65.11–13/M 60). Perception is the appropriate and necessary successor to Sense Certainty because its epistemic principles admit the use of such universals, though only such universals, to know particular perceptible objects (*PS* 71.8–11, cf. 63.4–5/M 67, cf. 58). Hegel's gloss on 'universal' matches Hume's (*Treatise*, 1.1.7.18).

Hegel notes that the perceived object is itself in this sense a universal because the object combines its "moments," its perceptible qualities, into a unity; the object exists only in and through its qualities, though it cannot be identified with or reduced to them. Perception itself counts as universal because it differentiates, distinguishes, and also grasps together these "moments" of the object (*PS* 71.14–16/M 67). Perception regards itself as unessential; the object is essential (*PS* 71.22–25/M 67). Like Sense Certainty, perceptual consciousness begins by avowing realism.

Hegel notes this contrast between Sense Certainty and Perception:

> the sensuous is itself still present [in Perception], but not as it is supposed to be in immediate certainty, as the individual meant; but instead as the universal, or as that which will determine itself as a *property*. (*PS* 72.3–6/M 68)

Initially the thing's sensible qualities do not yet count as properties.[24] This qualification indicates a key issue: properties are not parts or ingredients of things. In order to comprehend a sensible object, we need more than just descriptive concepts and merely quantitative conceptions or designations.

The counterpart to the sensed qualities is "thinghood" (*PS* 72.23/M 68), Perception's conception of its object. An instance of this conception, i.e. an object, constitutes a "medium" in which various instances of sensed qualities occur. Thus far, this object is a region of space and time within which a plurality of sensible quality instances occur (*PS* 72.22–26/M 68).

Hegel's discussion seems inadequate to characterize a thing with many properties. This is his point: What exactly are the further conditions or presuppositions of a perceptible thing and of our perceptual knowledge of it? Hegel's initial description corresponds to Modern accounts of the concept of substance. In analogy to Descartes's wax, Hegel considers a grain of salt:

> This [bit of] salt is a simple here, and yet manifold as well. It is white, and *also* tart, *also* cubically formed, *also* of a determinate weight, and so forth. (*PS* 72.26–28/M 68)

The perceived thing has three aspects: (1) the "also" or the "indifferent passive medium" in which its various sensible qualities occur. The passivity and indifference of this "thinghood" provisionally hints at the role causality plays in the identity of perceptible things; this passivity marks an assumption of Hegel's *reductio* argument. (2) The "properties" collected in the thing are "rather *matters*." These "matters" are determinate stuffs, analogous to the "heat matter" or "magnetic matter" of contemporaneous physics. This analogy suggests how perceptual consciousness comes to regard the qualities of a thing as independent ingredients. Calling them "matters" stresses that, as ingredients of a thing, the perceived instances of universal qualities are not yet *proper* to the perceived thing. (3) The "unity" of the thing as one individual, distinct from others and excluding them from its region (*PS* 73.19–26/M 69).

A form of consciousness is "perceptual" if it conceives its object as a "thing" in the sense just specified. However, this conception does not account for how these three aspects of the object are related, especially in Perception's experience. Perception is aware of the plurality of properties of any possible object of perception and recognizes that it must properly combine the various qualities of an object with each other. Accordingly, it regards the object as "self-identical" and acknowledges that it may not properly combine the various qualities of an object when apprehending it (*PS* 74.1–11/M 70).

Acknowledging this suggests that the alleged passivity of perception is untenable and also suggests the questions noted above: How can we combine a particular group sensory qualities into the perception of some *one* object? What conception of the object is required for such combination? Perceptual consciousness is aware of the possibility of deception; accordingly, it uses "self-identity" as its criterion of truth. To achieve true knowledge of its object, Perception must preserve the thing's "self-identity" while apprehending its various qualities. Lack of self-identity indicates error.

Initially, perceptual consciousness has only the conceptions 'unity' (numerical identity) and 'plurality' (number) to conceive the identity of perceptible things. Hegel grants that 'identity' can only mean 'numerical identity' ('one and the same as' or '='); he aims to show that the concept of numerical identity only provides a tenable conception of the identity of perceptible things in conjunction with an integrated conception of the thing as a single thing with a plurality of characteristics. Such an *integrated* conception of the thing is not initially admitted by perceptual consciousness; it cannot admit it without rescinding its official cognitive passivity and its Concept Empiricism.

4.3 The three phases of Perception's self-examination

"Perception" again divides into five parts: an Introduction (¶¶1–6), three analytical phases (Phase I: ¶¶7–8, Phase II: ¶¶9–12, Phase III: ¶¶13–18), and a summary and conclusion (¶¶ 19–21).[25]

In Phase I Perception begins with a Humean idea: "The object that I take up presents itself as *purely one*" (*PS* 74.15–16/M 70; cf. *Treatise*, 1.4.2.26). Yet Perception is also aware of the plurality of the thing's many sensible qualities (or presumptive properties). Hegel aims to exhibit how its failure to integrate the three aspects of its object (noted above) leads Perception to use its conceptions of unity and plurality to reify the thing's qualities to the point of considering only their merely numerical diversity. Hence Perception is led into error and deception (*Täuschung*) by its own principles and standards. The deception mentioned in Hegel's subtitle to "Perception," "or the thing and deception," is this: Given Modern philosophical ideas about perception and its objects, we deceive ourselves by believing that we perceive physical objects at all, precisely Hume's conclusion. This is not a problem about indirect, representationalist theories of perception, but of a problem lurking at the core of Modern views of sensory ideas and sense data theories: If all we directly sense are various sensory qualities, how can we identify any one physical object at all?

Because Perception lacks a coherent conception of 'physical object', it conflates the identity of a physical object with purely quantitative unity. Perception thus commits itself to reducing the relation 'thing/property' to the relation 'one/ many' (or 'whole/part'). The inadequacy of Perception's conceptions emerges directly in Phase I of its self-examination: In trying to perceive *one* thing, Perception is led by its strictly quantitative conception of unity to distinguish among the thing's various sensed qualities, identifying each in turn as *one* (unitary) perceptible object. Hence Perception regards the presumed thing as simply a "medium" in which its various (putative) properties occur (*PS* 74.34, cf. 72.17–26/M 74, cf. 68). This fails to make sense of the unity of the perceived thing; hence the perceptible thing cannot be properly conceived even as a "medium" of its properties. Hence Perception fails to perceive any one thing amidst its (alleged) plurality of properties.

Obviously, something has gone badly wrong. Hegel's point is to make this manifest within Perception. The remedy lies in adopting Locke's view that each sensible quality of a thing enters our mind through our distinct sensory channels as a completely separate, simple, pure, and particular sensory idea (*Essay* 2.2.1, *PS* 75.35–39/M 72), a view also found in Hume's account of simple sensory impressions. Perception thus improves its conception of its perception, thus rescinding the belief in the utter passivity of perception by recognizing that perception involves some kind of mental processing.

These revisions are central to Perception's second strategy for sustaining its initial conception of the perceived object. In Phase II Perception divides the locus of the thing's unity and plurality. Initially it regards the perceived thing as unitary, but now ascribes the diversity of its perceived qualities to its own distinct sensory channels. Accordingly, Perception assumes the role of the "universal medium" in which a plurality of perceived qualities occurs, thus preserving Perception's conception that the perceived thing is unitary (*PS* 75.29–76.3/M 72-3).

The problem now is that any perceptible thing is only some one distinct and determinate thing because *it* has a variety of determinate characteristics which distinguish it from other things (and determine which region it occupies). Taking upon itself the diversity of the thing's properties thus violates Perception's initial thesis that it perceives determinate, identifiable, mutually distinct individual things (*PS* 76.4–23/M 72-3). To correct this error, Perception ascribes singularity to the perceived thing, not as an undifferentiated unity, but as a spatio-temporal region in which a plurality of "free matters" (in contemporary terms, 'tropes') occur. These revisions of Perception's view highlight its thoughtful, reflective, and hence active character. They also indicate that Perception sequentially ascribes unity to the thing and qualitative plurality to itself, and then conversely ascribes unity to itself and qualitative plurality to the perceived thing. Perception thus realizes through its experience that the perceived thing presents itself as unitary thing with a plurality of characteristics. Accordingly, Perception must devise a way of ascribing both of these aspects to the thing it perceives (*PS* 76.24–39/M 73-4).

In Phase III Perception ascribes both unity and a plurality of characteristics to the perceived object, while avoiding the contradiction between its unity and plurality by isolating them from each other. This it does by ascribing the plurality of the thing's characteristics to its relations (both similarities and differences) to other things, while ascribing unity to the thing in its isolation from other things (*PS* 77.13–32/M 74–7). Resolving the contradiction between the thing's unity and plurality requires granting primacy to one of these two aspects of the unitary, self-identical thing. Hence Perception posits the unity of the thing as essential and regards as inessential the plurality of its characteristics (*PS* 77.33–78.13/M 75).[26]

This strategy fails because emphasizing the sheer unity of any one perceived thing fails to grasp any *one* such thing because *any* perceived thing is essentially a unitary individual. This strategy reduces the concept of perceptible things to mere "thinghood." Any perceptible thing is only perceived, experienced, and identified as a particular individual due to its particular characteristics (by which alone we can specify the region it occupies). Hence the distinction Perception draws between the essential unity of the perceived thing and the unessential diversity of its characteristics proves to be merely nominal, not genuine (*PS* 78.14–79.2/M 75–6).

Hegel concludes that the concept of the identity of perceptible things requires an integrated concept of the internally complex thing, which integrates the quantitative sub-concepts 'unity' and 'plurality'. Hegel shows this by demonstrating that neither the unity of the thing can be understood without the plurality of its properties, nor can the plurality of its properties be understood without the unity of the thing.

This provides the basic point of Hegel's claim that the concept of identity of perceptible things contains an objectively valid contradiction. Michael Wolff has shown that Hegel's view of "dialectical" contradictions neither denies nor violates the law of non-contradiction. Instead, Hegel holds that certain important truths can only (or at least can best) be expressed by using what appears to be a formal contradiction.[27] In the present case, it can appear – as it did to Hume, and as it must to a concept empiricist – that the two quantitative partial concepts contained in the concept of the identity of perceptible things, namely unity and plurality, contradict each other. In the case of perceptible things and the thing/property relation, this is not the case. On the contrary, both aspects of any perceptible thing are mutually interdependent; there is no unitary perceptible thing without its plurality of properties, and, conversely, there are no *properties* without a unitary thing which they qualify. Hegel's point can be expressed using a biconditional statement: Something is a perceptible thing if and only if it unifies a plurality of properties – and vice versa, a plurality of qualities are properties if and only if they are unified in some one perceptible thing. An adequate concept of perceptible things integrates the two quantitatively opposed sub-concepts 'unity' and 'plurality'. Only with such an integrated concept of perceptible things can one grasp their identity.[28]

Two important, related points about the activity involved in cognition follow. First, we can perceive things only if we integrate the various sensations they cause in us; this is a cognitive activity on our part. Second, the concept of the identity of perceptible things required to integrate sensations or perceptions is *a priori*, because it cannot be defined or derived in accord with Concept Empiricism.

4.4 The binding problem

Hegel's central concern with the concept of the identity of perceptible things is philosophically significant. The question of what unites any group of sensations into a percept of any one object arises within each sensory modality, and across our sensory modalities; it arises synchronically within any momentary perception of an object, and diachronically as a problem of integrating successive sensations or percepts of the same object. These questions recur at an intellectual level: How can we recognize various bits of sensory information received through sensation to be bits of information about one and the same object, whether at any one moment or across any period of time? These problems about sensations lurk in the core of the Modern "new way of ideas" and within the sense data tradition, though they were recognized by only three Modern philosophers: Hume, Kant, and Hegel. They have been widely occluded by uncritical appeal to what we "notice." These problems with sensations recur today in neurophysiology of perception as versions of a set of problems now called the 'binding problem', which has only very recently garnered attention from epistemologists.[29]

5 Force and Understanding

5.1 Hegel's ontological revolution in "Force and Understanding"

Hegel's third chapter, "Force and Understanding," is notoriously obscure. One key issue is this: Hegel identifies a crucial equivocation in the traditional concept of substance, unchallenged from the Greeks up through Kant, concerning two senses of the term 'intrinsic' (or 'internal') used to characterize the properties of individual substances. In one sense a characteristic is 'intrinsic' if it is essential to a substance. In another sense, 'intrinsic' contrasts with 'relational'. In this sense, an 'intrinsic' characteristic is contained solely within the individual substance; it is non-relational. Conflating these two senses of 'intrinsic' generates the standard assumption that relational properties cannot be essential to individual substances – whence the (broadly) "atomistic" orientation of Occidental philosophy, that individuals are ontologically basic, whilst relations are derivative, because they depend on individuals, whereas individuals do not depend on their relations.

Hegel's central theses in "Force and Understanding" are these:

1 Forces are essential to matter, and thus to individual physical substances.
2 Forces are essentially interrelations (i) among the components of individual physical substances and (ii) among interacting individual physical substances.
3 (1) and (2.ii) are proven empirically by Newtonian universal gravitation.
4 The traditional ontological presumption that relational characteristics cannot be essential to individual substances thwarts our understanding causal necessity by making it impossible to conceive (1) and (2.ii) consistently.

5   Causal necessity can be understood properly only if the traditional conflation of the two senses of 'intrinsic' is rejected, so that we can recognize that relational characteristics can be essential to individual substances.

6   (1) and (2.ii) (and hence also (3) and (4)) can be proven by philosophical argument, in ways attempted in "Force and Understanding."

Thesis (1) is Kant's, though Hegel identified the key defects of Kant's proof and attempts a sound justification of it. Hegel defends thesis (2.i) by arguing that only causal forces and the concept 'cause' enable us to understand the identity of any one perceptible thing amidst its plurality of properties. Thesis (2.ii) marks Hegel's attempt to re-analyze and to justify philosophically Kant's thesis that all causal actions (within space and time) are causal interactions. One might distinguish "forces" as relations from the "powers" that give rise to them. Hegel argues that this distinction is nominal, not real, and is a rich source of misleading reifications. Very briefly, Hegel contends that dispositions cannot be monadic properties because dispositions are partly specified by triggering conditions (roughly, occasioning causes) which pertain to the dispositions of other objects or events. Hegel also contends that treating dispositions as monadic properties rests on conflating the two senses of 'intrinsic' he distinguishes.

5.2 Newtonian proof of theses (1) and (2.ii)

Hegel's third thesis is surprising; empiricism has made it a commonplace that no claims about essences can be justified by empirical methods. More surprising is Hegel's claim that Newton developed methods that justify some claims about empirical essences (not that Newton used the term). Still more surprising is that Hegel understood Newtonian methods better than empiricists and appreciated these surprising and significant results.[30] This is a complex issue, which fortunately may be epitomized briefly by considering Newton's debate with Robert Hooke and Christian Huygens about color and its proper scientific study.

Hooke (1667, 49–56, esp. 54) expressly defended Descartes's theory of light against Newton's. Referring to Hooke's work, Christian Huygens (Anon. 1673) likewise criticized Newton's theory of colors, arguing that yellow and blue are the two fundamental colors. He charged that Newton's account of refrangibility only analyzes an "accident" of light, albeit a "very considerable" one, although refrangibility is not quantitatively uniform in the way Newton's theory requires.

Newton (1673) replied that what appears to be white light can be produced by various combinations of colored light, so that white lights can have different constitutions (ibid., 6088–89). Additionally, the fact that combinations of any two colors of light may appear white cannot prove that any pair of colors are the sole "original" colors of which all other colors are composed (ibid., 6089). Newton then summarily stated his method for investigating the colors of light (ibid., 6090–91); this statement is very revealing for the present topic. Newton first defines 'homogenous' light in terms of its equal refrangibility and 'heterogeneous' light in terms of unequal refrangibility of its rays. He then reports finding that light rays differ only in their refrangibility, reflexibility, and color, and that any two sources of light which are the same in any one such regard are also the same in the other two. Newton avoided using metaphysical terms and distinctions such as 'essence' versus 'accident', though he expressly *defines* the homogeneity of colors of light in explicitly quantitative terms of exactly measured refrangibility and reflexibility. Cassirer (1971, 2:407) follows Bloch (1908, 353–6, 451–2), presenting Newton's view as concerning a "physical essence" of light.[31] Newton avoids such terms. However, Newton's concise statement of his method plainly indicates that the only qualities or characteristics of light subject to scientific investigation and comprehension are precisely quantifiable, and he criticized as "impracticable" Huygens's methods for the very difficult task of measuring these quantities (ibid., 6091). As Bloch notes, Newton reiterates these quantitative methods and their use for analyzing light in Query 31 of the *Opticks*.[32]

At first glance Hooke's and Huygens's replies to Newton's theory of colors, and his reply to them, may look like convinced advocates reasserting their views in the face of opposition because they disagree about whether or how to quantify physical inquiry and whether only to count as physical science an inquiry which provides exact quantification. Hence this scientific disagreement may appear to be yet another example of inevitable *petitio principii* due to fundamental disagreement about relevant criteria of justification, as discussed in Hegel's Introduction. This issue about criteria of justification bears on Newton's Rule Four of philosophizing:

> In experimental philosophy, propositions gathered from phenomena by induction should be considered either exactly or very nearly true notwithstanding any contrary hypotheses, until yet other phenomena make such propositions either more exact or liable to exceptions. (Newton 1999, 796)

Newton adds: "This rule should be followed so that arguments based on induction may not nullified by hypotheses" (ibid.). Harper (forthcoming) shows that Newton's Rule Four is anti-Cartesian because it rules out as scientifically illegitimate merely logically possible alternative 'hypotheses' and because it requires any genuinely scientific competing hypothesis to have, not merely empirical evidence, but sufficient evidence and precision either to make an accepted scientific hypothesis "more exact" or to qualify or restrict it by demonstrating actual "exceptions." Newton's Rule Four thus rejects the deductivist justificatory ideal of *scientia*, and with it mere logical possibility as a sufficient basis for a proposition to state either a scientific hypothesis or a scientifically legitimate objection to an hypothesis.

The anti-Cartesianism of Newton's Rule Four may appear simply to repudiate rationalism and to advocate empiricism about natural science. Empiricists generally tend to regard physical theories as involving only maximally precise measurements and precisely formulated mathematical descriptions of natural regularities, though without commitment to any specific causal ontology that generates measured regularities. Even the non-empiricist Ernst Cassirer mistook the Newtonian method of John Keill in this way.[33]

However, Harper shows that this deflationary view seriously misunderstands Newton's methods and achievement. Newton devised analytical methods for using the phenomena of planetary motions to measure with increasing precision the strength of the gravitational force produced by each planet. This increasing precision results from iterative use of the same explanatory resources to progressively eliminate various idealizations used in the initial approximations. The progressive increase in accuracy required by Newton's standards of theoretical adequacy significantly exceeds the requirements of other accounts of theoretical adequacy current among philosophers of science. Significantly, Newton's standards of theoretical adequacy apply to the shift from Newtonian to Einsteinian mechanics, and, on the basis of the relevant evidence, favor Einsteinian mechanics. This is only the briefest word about the method and aim of Newton's gravitational theory, which requires a stout book (such as Harper's *tour de force*) to explain.

In "Force and Understanding" Hegel argues that Newtonian gravitational theory, as revised on the basis of analysis (calculus), provides the sole and sufficient basis ascribing gravity as an essential characteristic to matter.[34] In this regard, Hegel contends that natural science *can* identify the essences of natural objects and events, where these essences are physical or material or, in a word, natural rather than supernatural or metaphysical. In this regard, Hegel argues on behalf of Newton in his debate, for example, with Hooke and Huygens about color and its scientific investigation. Hegel does this by justifying Newton's Rule Four by exploiting an important consequence his semantics of cognitive reference defended in "Sense Certainty."

5.3 Hegel's semantic support for Newton's Rule Four

Kant's rejection of pre-Critical metaphysics is rooted in his cognitive semantics. Kant's cognitive semantics grants that *a priori* concepts can have content or meaning unto themselves, but also requires that determinate, genuinely cognitive content for any proposition or judgment using *a priori* concepts requires another constituent of meaning provided by referring those propositions or judgments to spatio-temporally identified (located) particulars. The semantic requirement of reference to particulars thus achieves the empiricist aim of restricting our cognitive claims to the realm of what we can experience, while dispensing with untenable verificationist theories of meaning.

Hegel recognized that Kant's semantics of cognitive reference also has important implications for judgments or propositions formulated with empirical concepts: to have determinate and cognitively legitimate meaning, they too require being referred to spatio-temporally identified (located) particulars. *Voilà!* The direct implication is that the mere logical consistency of a presumed alternative to a natural-scientific theory or hypothesis does not suffice for its cognitive legitimacy! To be cognitively legitimate, an alternative must also be referred (and not merely be "refer*able* in principle") to spatio-temporally identified (located) particulars. Hegel's cognitive semantics thus rules out the deductivist model of *scientia* for empirical justification, and so rules out mere logical possibilities as counterexamples to empirical – or to philosophical – claims.

Hegel's pro-Newtonian cognitive semantic is important for understanding one of the most important and puzzling statements in "Force and Understanding." Hegel recognized that Newton's theory provides adequate grounds for ascribing gravitational force directly to matter; matter is "essentially heavy" in the sense that material bodies inherently tend – they gravitate – towards one another (*Enc.* §§262, 269). So far as logical or metaphysical necessities are concerned, natural phenomena could instantiate any mathematical function whatsoever, various mathematical functions on different occasions, or *no such function at all*. However, the fact that a natural phenomenon regularly exhibits a precise mathematical function indicates, as nothing else can, that something in that phenomenon is structured in accord with that mathematical function. That "something" is the causal structure of the phenomenon, the structure of the basic causal powers or disposition(s) which generate the phenomenon in question. Bringing various specific phenomena under a common general law (not merely a common mathematical function) formulated in terms of common explanatory factors (such as gravity) shows that these phenomena are interrelated; they are not mutually independent, self-sufficient objects or events (*PS* 92.23–26/M 91–2). Hence the concepts 'law-like relation' and 'force' require interdefined factors into which the phenomena can be analyzed (*PS* 93.7–94.28/M 92–4). In sum:

the force is constituted exactly like the law. (*PS* 95.12–13/M 95, original emphasis)

This statement indicates Hegel's concern to show that adequate scientific explanation provides sufficient basis for determining the essential, and essentially causal, characteristics of natural objects and events. Comprehending their essential characteristics provides explanatory insight.[35]

The standard objection to this claim is that the "underlying" causal factors giving rise to any natural regularity, however precisely measured and described mathematically, may be structured very differently than is stated or suggested by our formulation of natural laws. This is Cartesianism speaking, pure and simple! Yes, there's a "logical" gap between any statement of a law of nature and whatever generates the regularity specified by that statement. However, this logical gap does not entail a *cognitive* gap between a well-grounded causal law and the causal structure generating the regular natural phenomenon described by that law. To suppose that a "logical" gap entails a cognitive gap un-Critically presupposes the pre-Newtonian, Cartesian deductivist ideal of justification as *scientia*. To the contrary, any discrepancies between our best-justified causal laws and the actual causal structure(s) of natural phenomena can only be discovered by extended scientific investigation. Deductivist cavils of empiricist philosophers are, Hegel's anti-Cartesian cognitive semantics shows, cognitively transcendent idle speculations.

5.4 Hegel's transcendental support for his cognitive semantics

These consequences place a considerable burden of proof on Hegel's cognitive semantics. "Sense Certainty" provides powerful – I have argued elsewhere, sound – justification of Hegel's cognitive semantics. Hegel's *Phenomenology* also purports to offer a genuinely transcendental proof of realism which supports his cognitive semantics. By 1802 Hegel recognized that Kant's transcendental idealism was subject to internal critique which shows that genuinely transcendental proofs do not require transcendental idealism, and that one such proof demonstrates mental content externalism, the thesis that at least some of our 'mental' contents can only be defined and understood in terms of extra-mental objects or events. Indeed, Hegel argues that we human beings cannot be self-conscious and cannot be aware of *any* 'mental' contents *unless* we are conscious of and identify at least some features of objects or events within our surroundings, which are what they are regardless of what we say, think, or believe about them.[36] Hegel made these discoveries before writing the *Phenomenology*, and incorporated them into it.

Very briefly, Hegel aims in the first three chapters, "Consciousness," to prove that we can be conscious of objects in the world around us only if we are self-conscious. In the second main section, "Self-Consciousness," Hegel aims to prove that we can be self-conscious only if we are conscious of objects in the world around us. In this way, Hegel's *Phenomenology* aims to re-establish the conclusion to Kant's "Refutation of Idealism," though without appeal to transcendental idealism. If Hegel can establish these claims, then he provides genuinely transcendental proof of realism which also supports his cognitive semantics, which is required for our determinate consciousness of any particulars at all. The implication for Newton's Rule Four is that Hegel's cognitive semantics rules any alleged hypothesis lacking supporting evidence out of legitimate cognitive, hence also scientific, bounds. By establishing that positive empirical support is required for any determinate, cognitively significant hypothesis, Hegel's cognitive semantics unloads much of the justificatory onus from Newton's Rule Four, which (in view of Hegel's cognitive semantics) very reasonably requires that to be a legitimate counter-hypothesis, an hypothesis must have sufficient empirical support to render an established hypothesis either "more exact" or to restrict its scope by identifying "exceptions" to it.[37]

5.5 "Force and Understanding" in brief

"Force and Understanding" is ungainly, though it too has an introduction (¶¶1–4), three analytical phases (I: ¶¶5–10, II: ¶¶11–17, III: ¶¶18–30), and conclusion (¶¶32–34).[38] Whereas all three phases of Perception sought to isolate the unity of the thing from the plurality of its characteristics by reifying them into distinct, mutually independent aspects of the perceived thing, all three phases of

Understanding seek to isolate the relatta of causal relations by reifying them into distinct, mutually independent entities.

By the end of "Perception," Perception became "perceptual understanding" by developing and using an unconditioned universal concept, that is, a concept integrating two counterposed sub-concepts (*PS* 79.24/M 77). The main problem confronting Understanding (as a form of consciousness) is that it does not grasp how the unity of the thing is integrated with its plurality of properties (*PS* 83.4–6/M 80). The general solution to this problem, in Phase I, is to introduce the concept of force. So doing is warranted by the reciprocal relations between any one perceptible thing and its plurality of properties, and by how these reciprocal relations are manifest in relations among perceived particulars (*PS* 83.31–85.8/M 81–3). Understanding distinguishes between "repressed" and "expressed" (or potential and actual) force and ascribes potential forces to mutually independent particulars. This invokes a substantival (rather than relational) conception of force, which includes the asymmetrical or unilateral notions of force inherent in pre-Newtonian mechanical models of causality (*PS* 85.9–13/M 83). The sharp contrast thus drawn between (allegedly) "real" potential force and the manifest appearances of its actualization requires that any individual force is triggered into expressing itself by other, intervening objects which "solicit" that force into activity (*PS* 85.9–30/M 83).

The term "solicitation" was used by both Leibniz and Kant in their dynamic theories. However, the target of Hegel's critique is what Herder made of their views. Herder advocated the thesis that "things" are the unsensed causes of our sensory experience, a notion found in Protagoras, Pyrho, Sextus Empricus, Locke, Kant and in some of Putnam's arguments for 'internal realism'.[39] Herder sought to justify this thesis, or at least to make it unassailable by advocates of science, by reifying the aspects of causal interaction into distinct, intervening entities, so that (purportedly) we only can observe the manifestations of any real force, though we cannot identify either its locus or its genuine, intrinsic character. Herder's antiscientific skepticism welcomed the infinite regress apparently generated by positing forces of solicitation, which themselves require solicitation by yet other forces of solicitation, ad infinitum.

Briefly, Hegel's analysis of force responds to this view by showing that introducing reified "solicitations" (so to speak) does not avoid the original relations of force-interaction for which they purportedly substitute; instead, each "solicitation-event" (so to speak) requires causal interaction (that is, causal relation) between two particulars, including, *ex hypothesi*, "solicitations." Hence multiplying particulars to avoid analyzing causal interactions by introducing "solicitations" fails to come to terms with the original phenomenon of causal interaction which this line of objection presupposes rather than eliminates. This failure to eliminate basic causal interaction between particulars underscores that forces essentially consist in causal interactions. Causal interaction involves (roughly) two or more particulars triggering each other's potentials (dispositions) to manifest themselves actively. This requires that each particular is both unitary and that it generates a plurality of active, occurrent, *relational* qualities (*PS* 86.12–87.8/M 84–5). Hegel's interim result is: forces are actual only in causal interactions among particulars. Unto themselves, dispositions as such are only potentially forces; to regard them as 'potential forces' is an unwarranted reification (*PS* 87.9–39/M 85–6).

Not yet prepared to concede Hegel's interim conclusion, in Phase II (¶¶12–18) Understanding ascribes unitary, intrinsic force-centers to a supersensible realm and ascribes their manifold manifestations to the realm of appearances (*PS* 88.1–89.3/M 86–8). This universalizes Herder's view. The object "in itself" is supersensible; "for us" are only its (purportedly causal) manifestations. Though clearly alluding to Kant's "thing in itself," Hegel aims to show that no distinction between things "for us" and things "in themselves" contributes to understanding forces, regardless of whether this distinction is drawn empirically or transcendentally.

The realm of appearance thus intervenes between us and things in themselves; appearances are their sole effects on us, and they provide our sole access to real, supersensible objects (*PS* 89.4–15/M 87–8). Hegel first points out that this supersensible realm is our own projection. The contrast between it and appearances is made in such a way that in principle appearances can provide no basis for any determinate ascription of characteristics to (purported) supersensible objects. Hence our utter ignorance of supersensible entities shows nothing about such entities, nor about the limits of human cognition, but only how this distinction between appearances and the supersensible has been devised by its advocates (*PS* 89.16–90.7/M 88–9). Thus distinguishing broadly (whether empirically or transcendentally) between the realms of appearance and of things in themselves contributes nothing to comprehending manifest causal interactions. Second, Hegel notes, our only possible basis for supposing there is a supersensible realm, or that it is characterized in one way rather than another, is the realm of appearances. However, the distinction between them is devised to block any determinate inference from appearances to the supersensible.

To remedy this situation, in Phase III (¶¶19–31) Understanding seizes upon the determinate specification of causal forces in the form of "laws of force" (*PS* 90.32–91.26/M 89–91). Causal laws now provide a determinate content for the Understanding, which posits these laws in a peaceful supersensible realm, in contrast to the plethora of ceaseless changes among appearances governed by these laws (*PS* 91.27–30/M 90–1). The problem with distinguishing in this way between a supersensible realm of causal laws and the ceaseless changes manifest in nature is that appearances are essential to the specific manifestations of causal laws because any causal law manifests itself differently in different conditions (*PS* 91.33–35/M 91), now called 'triggering conditions'. Accommodating these conditions multiplies particular causal laws, which must then be explanatorily integrated under more general laws, such as Newton's law of universal gravitation (*PS* 92.8–10/M 91). Hegel claims Newton's law is

> of great importance insofar as it is directed against the thoughtless *representation* (*Vorstellung*), according to which everything presents itself in the form of contingency, and determinateness has the form of sensible self-sufficiency. (*PS* 92.23–25/M 91)

The "form of sensible self-sufficiency" Hegel here criticizes is the presumptive ontological atomism according to which spatio-temporal particulars are mutually independent, hence self-sufficient unto themselves and only contingently related to one another. Hegel here claims that Newtonian gravitational theory belies this apparently obvious, commonsense atomism by showing that physical particulars are fundamentally interrelated by gravitational forces which are intrinsic to matter even though they are relational, though his statement of this key conclusion is provisional.[40]

The Understanding now ascribes all particular laws to the realm of appearances while the pure form of law, that "everything exhibits a constant difference to everything else," is ascribed to the supersensible realm (*PS* 92.26–95.17/M 92–5). This approach generates the "covering law" or "hypothetico-deductive" model of scientific explanation, which Hegel deftly shows is circular and explanatorily vacuous (*PS* 94.26–95.24/M 94). The Understanding thus loses its presumed grasp of the very happening of events it proposed to comprehend with causal laws (*PS* 95.24–39/M 95). Hence the Understanding modifies its account of the supersensible realm by introducing into it a "law of pure change" and explaining the apparent world of manifest change on the basis of a very different supersensible realm consisting in the opposites of all apparent, occurrent qualities. For example, manifest sweetness is generated by supersensible sourness, manifest black is generated by supersensible white, etc. Hence this very different version of the supersensible world is the inversion of the manifest world of appearances (*PS* 96.1–97.35/M 95–8). Understanding's strategy thus attempts to analyze causal necessity in terms of logical exclusion relations. (This view in some regards resembles Brandom's inferentialism.)

Philosophically, this new supersensible world is equally a perversion of the realm of appearances and of causal concepts altogether. Now that the Understanding identifies relevant contrasts between positive and negative electricity, or the oxygen and hydrogen poles of an electrolytic cell, or the two poles of a magnet, its key distinctions, 'inner/outer' and 'appearance/supersensible', are simply useless because the polar phenomena it identifies cannot be justifiably distributed among any two substances, whether they are distinguished numerically or metaphysically, not at least without reverting to the reifying strategies of Perception critically rejected previously. Such a supersensible world is merely a projected converse sensible world, which in principle cannot itself be sensed at all (*PS* 97.39–98.10/M 98).

Once these atomizing and reifying tendencies collapse, we can appreciate that what produces a North magnetic pole produces the South pole of the same magnet, and likewise for other polar phenomena, which Hegel thinks is typical for causal relations: the terms of these relations are mutually interdefined in ways that reflect the interdependent identity conditions of particulars which stand in causal relations. Hegel thinks this also holds for space and time and for distance and velocity, which are interdefined as aspects of any gravitational motion (*PS* 99.15–21/M 99). If Hegel describes this kind of mutual interrelation in terms of "contradiction" (*PS* 98.33/M 99), this is because such relations must appear to any atomist as contradictions, in part due to the once-pervasive assumption that the logical law of identity entails an atomistic ontology. This assumption is false, and Hegel's use of the term "contradiction" does not violate the logical law of non-contradiction.[41]

In sum, Hegel's thesis that the causal characteristics of things are central to their identity conditions, and that their identity conditions are mutually interdefined due to their essential causal relations, is justified by exhibiting the futility of atomistic, reifying strategies to avoid this conclusion in the face of Newtonian universal gravitation.[42] Furthermore, the relevant interdefined aspects of causal phenomena, Hegel contends, cannot be specified by armchair philosophical reflection, but only by empirical, natural-scientific investigation of causal phenomena.[43] Natural science is thus essential (necessary, if not fully sufficient) to identifying and justifying the relevant conceptual distinctions.

6 Hegel's Epistemological Analysis in the *Phenomenology of Spirit*

6.1 One unifying armature of the *Phenomenology of Spirit*: epistemology

Hegel's overarching epistemological analysis in the *Phenomenology* may be summarized briefly. In "Sense-Certainty" Hegel argues by *reductio ad absurdum* against naive realism, that our conceptions of 'time', 'times', 'space', 'spaces', 'I', and 'individuation' are *a priori* because they are necessary for identifying and knowing any particular object or event, on the basis of which alone we can learn, define, or use any empirical concept. Hence these concepts are presupposed rather than defined by Concept Empiricism. Hegel further argues that localizing a particular object or event in space and time and ascribing characteristics to it are mutually complementary components of predication, which is required for singular cognitive reference, which requires singular sensory presentation. Hence aconceptual "knowledge by acquaintance" or sense certainty is humanly impossible.

In "Perception" Hegel further argues against Concept Empiricism that observation terms plus logic do not suffice for empirical knowledge because our concept 'physical object' cannot be defined in accord with Concept Empiricism, it is *a priori* and is necessary for identifying and knowing any particular object or event. More specifically, Hegel argues that the 'thing/property' relation cannot be reduced to or adequately analyzed in terms of the relations 'one/many', 'whole/part', set membership, or 'ingredient/product' because the concept of the identity of a perceptible thing integrates the two opposed quantitative sub-concepts 'unity' and 'plurality'.

In "Force and Understanding" Hegel argues that our conception of 'cause' is pure *a priori* and is necessary for identifying and knowing any object or event;

that statements of laws of nature are conceptual and express actual structures of nature; that the identity conditions of spatio-temporal particulars are mutually interdefined on the basis of their essential causal relations; and that our consciousness of objects is possible only if we are self-conscious.

In the introductory discussion to "Self-Consciousness," Hegel argues that biological needs involve classification and thus entail realism about objects meeting those needs. In "Lord and Bondsman" Hegel argues that the natural world is not constituted by will, a second important lesson in realism. In "The Freedom of Self-consciousness," Hegel argues that the contents of consciousness are derived from a public world, and that self-consciousness is humanly possible only if we are conscious of mind-independent objects. The first two major sections of Hegel's *Phenomenology*, "Consciousness" and "Self-consciousness," thus replace Kant's "objective" Deduction of the Pure Concepts of the Understanding, his proof that we can and must use *a priori* concepts in legitimate cognitive judgments about spatio-temporal objects and events. Hegel's justification of Kant's conclusion to his "Refutation of Idealism," that "inner experience in general is only possible through outer experience in general" (*CPR* B277, cf. B275), does not rely on Kant's transcendental idealism.

In "The Certainty and Truth of Reason," Hegel argues that classificatory thought presupposes natural structures in the world which must be discovered (rather than created or legislated) by us. In "Observing Reason" he argues that classificatory, categorial thought is not merely a *natural* phenomenon. In the two subsequent sections of "Reason," "The Actualization of Rational Self-Consciousness by Itself" and "Individuality That Is Real in and for Itself," Hegel argues that categorial thought is not merely an *individual* phenomenon. The implicit epistemological result of these *reductio* arguments in "Reason" is that individual thinkers are who they are only within a natural and social context. Hegel's express result is that each of the preceding sections of the *Phenomenology* has analyzed different aspects of one concrete social whole, including its natural environment.

In "Spirit" Hegel analyses the tension and interaction between individual reasoning and customary practice. In "True Spirit, Ethics," Hegel argues that categorial and justificatory thought are not constituted or justified merely by *custom* or *fiat*. In "Self-Alienated Spirit" and in "Self-Certain Spirit, Morality," Hegel argues that categorial and justificatory thought are not corrigible merely *a priori* (and so individualistically). In the concluding section of "Spirit," "Evil and Forgiveness," Hegel argues that the corrigibility of categorial and justificatory thought is a *social* phenomenon, and yet is consistent with realism about the objects of human knowledge (and strict objectivity about practical norms).

This is precisely the point reached by the two moral judges Hegel analyses in "Evil and Forgiveness." Here an agent and an observer dispute who has proper, legitimate authority to judge the agent's behavior. After struggling over this issue in various ways, these two moral judges finally each rescind the presumed supremacy and self-sufficiency of their own antecedent convictions and standpoint, and recognize that they are both equally fallible *and* equally competent to judge particular acts (whether their own or others'), and that each of them requires the other's assessment in order to scrutinize and thereby to assess and to justify his or her own judgment regarding any particular act.[44] With this insight, the two judges become reconciled to each other, and to the fundamentally social dimensions of genuine rational, justificatory judgment. Expressly, this is the first instance of genuine mutual recognition in Hegel's *Phenomenology of Spirit*.[45]

Significantly, Hegel also indicates that this achievement *is* the advent of "absolute spirit":

> The word of reconciliation [between the two judges] is the *extant* spirit, which beholds the pure knowledge of itself as *universal* essence in its opposite, in the pure knowledge of itself as the absolute *individuality* existing in itself – a reciprocal recognition which is *absolute spirit*. (*PS* 361.22–25/M 408)

The "universal essence" mentioned here is the knowledge, principles, practices, and context of action (both social and natural) shared within a social group. All of this is required, and understanding of all this is required, in order rationally to *judge* that "I judge," and not merely to utter the words "I judge," thereby only feigning rationality.[46]

In "Religion" Hegel contends (very roughly) that the history of religion is the initial, allegorical, premature recognition of the social and historical bases of our categorial comprehension of the world. These three major sections of the *Phenomenology*, "Reason," "Spirit," and "Religion," thus form Hegel's replacement for Kant's "subjective" Deduction of the Categories, which explains *how* we are able to make the kinds of legitimate, justifiable judgments analyzed in his prior Objective Deduction (in "Consciousness" and "Self-Consciousness"), which shows *that* we can make such judgments, because if we couldn't, we could not be self-conscious.

Hegel draws these strands together in his concluding chapter, "Absolute Knowing," in which he highlights how the *Phenomenology* provides us with reflective conceptual comprehension of the social and historical bases of our categorial comprehension of the world. This result is a sophisticated version of sociohistorically based epistemological realism.[47]

6.2 The structure of Hegel's epistemological argument in the *Phenomenology of Spirit*

The structure of Hegel's epistemological analysis is easily mapped onto Hegel's Table of Contents. So doing provides a useful summary of Hegel's epistemology in the *Phenomenology* and may also help orient the reader for the subsequent chapters of this collective commentary; see below, pp. 28–29.

7 Conclusion

Like other philosophers, epistemologists must heed the 'Kiss principle': Keep it simple, stupid. Yet epistemologists have not often heeded Einstein's explication of Ockham's Razor: "Everything must be made as simple as possible, but not any simpler."[48] The scope, issues, and content of Hegel's epistemological analysis in the *Phenomenology* are vast and unparalleled. If Hegel is right that both Concept Empiricism and transcendental idealism are false, that the Dilemma of the Criterion puts paid to both coherentism and foundationalism (either as *scientia* or *historia*), that epistemology must heed our cognitive finitude and our mutual interdependence as cognizant beings, that epistemology is closely linked to natural science, and that (to avoid *petitio principii* and to solve the Dilemma) positive theses must be justified by strictly internal critique of all relevant alternatives, then an epistemological project like Hegel's *Phenomenology* must be undertaken.[49]

It is a major contribution to epistemology to identify, as Hegel does in his first three chapters, a previously unnoticed though central link between Pyrrhonian and Cartesian skepticism also shared by empiricist objections to causal realism within philosophy of science: In principle, none of their key premises or hypotheses have legitimate cognitive significance because none of them are referred to identified particulars located in space and time. The Paramenidean conception of changeless truth and being lacks such referrability in principle, Cartesian skeptical hypotheses are designed to lack such referrability, while empiricist objections to causal realism based on mere logical possibilities of justificatory gaps or alternative causal scenarios all lack such referrability. These results underlie Hegel's subsequent analysis of how skepticism (and ultimately relativism, too), in whatever forms, involves fundamental alienation from our natural and social world rooted in self-alienation from human knowledge. Hegel considers these issues directly in the second part of "Self-Consciousness," they are at least implicit in "Observing Reason," and they come to the fore in "Self-Alienated Culture." This theme links Hegel's epistemology to his ensuing *Kulturkritik*.[50]

A second major contribution to epistemology is to solve the Dilemma of the Criterion; a third is to show that genuine transcendental proofs can be provided without appeal to Kant's transcendental idealism and can be used to justify realism, in part by justifying mental content externalism. Hegel's fourth contribution is to support Newton's Rule Four with his cognitive semantics. Finally, lingering suspicion of causal notions among philosophers of science – because causal relations cannot be "perceived" – is a relic of Hume's concept empiricism and theory of perception. Hegel's trenchant critique of these two views shows how ill founded such suspicions are. Notorious allegations about Hegel's neglect of epistemology or misunderstanding of natural science reflect ignorance of Hegel's actual views; such allegations do not survive scrutiny. Hegel's epistemology is more vital today than ever; it behooves us to mine its philosophical riches.[51]

Structure of Hegel's Epistemological Contents of Hegel's *Phenomenology of Spirit*

A **Consciousness**	I	*Sense-Certainty; The 'this' and meaning.*		
	II	*Perception; The thing and deception.*		
	III	*Force & Understanding; Appearance & the super-sensible world.*		
B **Self-Consciousness**	IV	*The Truth of Self-Certainty [Life & Desire].*		
	IVA	*Self-Sufficiency & Self-Insufficiency of Self-consciousness; Mastery & Servitude.*		
	IVB	*Freedom of Self-Consciousness.*	a	Stoicism.
			b	Skepticism.
			c	Unhappy Consciousness.
C/AA/V **Reason**	\multicolumn{4}{l	}{Certainty & Truth of Reason.}
	VA	*Observing Reason.*	a	Observation of Nature.
			b	Observation of Self-consciousness I: Logic & Psychology.
			c	Observation of Self-consciousness II: Physiognomy & Phrenology.
	VB	*The Actualization of Rational Self-consciousness through Itself.*	a	Pleasure & Necessity.
			b	Law of the Heart & the Insanity of Conceit.
			c	Virtue & the Way of the World.
	VC	*Individuality which is Real In & For Itself.*	a	The Animal Kingdom of the Spirit & Humbug.
			b	Legislative Reason.
			c	Law-testing Reason.
C/BB/VI **Immediate Spirit**	VIA	*True Spirit; Ethics.*	a	The Ethical World: Human & divine law; man & woman.
			b	Ethical Action: Human & divine knowledge, guilt & fate.
			c	Legal Status.
	VIB	*Self-Alienated Spirit; Enculturation.*	a	The world of self-alienated spirit. i Enculturation & its realm of actuality. ii Faith & pure insight.
			b	The enlightenment. i The enlightenment *vs.* superstition. ii The truth of the enlightenment.
			c	Absolute freedom & the terror.
	VIC	*Self-Certain Spirit; Morality.*	a	The Moral Worldview.
			b	Dissemblance.
			c	Conscience; the beautiful soul, evil & its forgiveness.
C/CC/VII **Religion**	VIIA	*Natural Religion.*	a	The Light-being.
			b	Plants & Animals.
			c	The Artificer.
	VIIB	*Art-Religion.*	a	The Abstract Work of Art.
			b	The Living Work of Art.
			c	The Spiritual Work of Art.
	VIIC	*Manifest Religion.*		
C/DD/VIII **Absolute Knowing**				

Argument in the *Phenomenology of Spirit*

Main Epistemological Theses Hegel Defends in the *Phenomenology*[52]

t.s.: (1) Our conceptions of 'time', 'times', 'space', 'spaces', 'I', and 'individuation' are pure *a priori* and (2) are necessary for identifying and knowing any particular object or event.

t.s.: (1) Observation terms alone do not suffice for empirical knowledge; (2) our conception 'physical object' is pure *a priori*, (3) it integrates the two opposed sub-concepts 'unity' and 'plurality' and (4) it is necessary for identifying and knowing any particular object or event.

t.s.: (1) We can only properly conceive causal forces by recognizing that essential properties can be relational; (2) Statements of laws of nature are conceptual and express actual structures of nature; (3) Our consciousness of objects is possible only if we're self-conscious.

t.s.: Biological needs involve classification, which entails realism about objects meeting those needs.

t.s.: The natural world is not constituted at will: a lesson in realism.

t.s.: (1) The contents of consciousness are derived from a public world;
(2) Self-consciousness is possible only if we're conscious of objects.

(Consciousness + Self-Consciousness = Hegel's replacement for Kant's Objective Deduction of the Categories.)

t.s.: Classificatory thought presupposes natural structures in the world which must and can be discovered.

t.s.: Classificatory, categorial thought is not merely a *natural* phenomenon.

t.s.: Categorial and justificatory thought are not merely *individual* phenomena.

(Implicit results of Reason: (1) Individual thinkers are who they are only within a natural and social context; (2) Each of the preceding sections has analyzed different aspects of one concrete social whole.)

t.s.: Neither *custom* nor *fiat* suffice to constitute genuine categorial or justificatory thought.

(Analysis of the tension and interaction between individual reasoning and customary practice runs throughout 'Immediate Spirit'.)

t.s.: Categorial and justificatory thought are not corrigible merely *a priori*.

t.s.: Kant's individualist theory of moral judgment and action is inadequate.

t.s.: (1) Individual judgment, required for rational justification of all kinds, is social, because we can only judge fully rationally by recognizing our own fallibility, so that we require the constructive criticism of others (and they require ours) in order to assess and to sustain our own rational judgment; hence (2) The corrigibility of categorial and justificatory thought is a *social* phenomenon.

t.s.: Religion is the initial, allegorical, premature, collective recognition of the social and historical bases of categorial comprehension of the world.

(Reason + Spirit + Religion = Hegel's socio-historical replacement for Kant's 'Subjective Deduction' of the Categories.)

t.s.: Through the *Phenomenology*, we gain reflective conceptual comprehension of the social and historical bases of categorial comprehension of the world (= socio-historically grounded epistemological realism).

Notes

1 Central issues from Hegel's Preface are discussed below, chapter 13. – *Ed.*
2 *PS* 19.12–23, 19.34–20.4/M 11, 12.
3 This is how Hegel initially defines 'the absolute' (*PS* 53.1–2/M 46). Note: Single quotes are used to mention terms which are not used in their present context.
4 All translations are by the author.
5 'Question-begging' or 'begging the question' name the logical fallacy of *petitio principii*.
6 Omitted is intuitionism in logic or mathematics.
7 The problem of assessing and resolving conflicting assertions raises key issues about the normative adequacy of individual rational judgment; it recurs throughout the *Phenomenology*, e.g., in "Lord and Bondsman," "Skepticism," "Observing Reason," "The Law of the Heart," "The Animal Kingdom of the Spirit," Antigone *vs.* Creon, Enlightenment *vs.* Faith, and "Conscience." See below, pp. 2–3, 17–18, 25–26, 37–53 *passim*, 60–64, 178–80, 229–30, 239–40. – *Ed.*
8 BonJour (1997, 14–15). Unwittingly, BonJour concedes the very point already made by von Juhos and Ayer against Hempel; see Westphal (1989, 56–7).
9 Common from Aristotle through the Modern period, this distinction remains influential today, as is evident from the extent to which analytical philosophers continue to distinguish in kind between "conceptual" and "empirical" issues.
10 Externalist accounts of epistemic justification, such as reliabilism or information-theoretic epistemology, are designed to scuttle internalist worries about justification. However, externalist accounts of justification only pertain to sensory knowledge, while identifying and justifying our claims about principles, whether epistemic or moral, raises these issues again. Hegel's theory of perceptual knowledge includes reliabilism about our perceptual neuropsychology.
11 Other contributors translate Hegel's term '*Gestalt*' differently, e.g., by 'shape' or 'figure'. – *Ed.*
12 Hegel indicates this in stating that, "the moments of truth present themselves, not as abstract, pure moments, but in the peculiar determinateness of being as they are for consciousness, or as consciousness itself appears in relationship to them" (*PS* 61.33–36/M 56).
13 On Hegel's further discussion of skepticism in the Introduction, see pp. 60–64. – *Ed.*
14 Recall Hegel's aphorism in the Preface: "in general what is familiar (*bekannt*), precisely because it is *familiar*, is not known (*erkannt*)" (*PS* 26.21/M 18); cf. MM 20:352, H&S 3:444, B/HP 3:237.
15 Hegel states: "at that point where its appearance becomes identical to its essence, consciousness' presentation will thus converge with this very same point in the science of spirit proper. And, finally, since consciousness itself grasps this its essence, it will indicate the nature of absolute knowing itself" (*PS* 61.31–62.5/M 56–7; cf. *PS* 431.36–432.1, 432.14–16/M 490, 491).
16 "Sense Certainty" designates Hegel's chapter, Sense Certainty (without quotes) designates the form of consciousness examined in this chapter, sense certainty (without capitals) designates the philosophical view, the key ideas, of Sense Certainty – and analogously for Hegel's next two chapters.
17 These paragraph numbers indicate paragraphs within Hegel's chapter; they do not correspond to Miller's paragraph numbering. Introduction: *PS* 63–64.28/M 58–9, Phase I: *PS* 64.29–66.11/M 59–61, Phase II: *PS* 66.12–67.8/M 61–2, Phase III: *PS* 67.9–68.33/M 62–4, Conclusion: *PS* 68.34–70/M 64–6.
18 See Evans (1982, chapter 6); Kaplan (1989); Perry (1979). A 'token' is a specific instance, a specific use of a repeatable word ('type').

19 *PS* 66.18–19/M 61. Hegel's examples are deliberate. "Tree" and, less frequently, "house" run through the modern Empiricists as obvious examples of commonsense physical objects, or particulars. Both Locke and Berkeley use "tree" as an obvious example of what is meant by a physical substance (Locke 1975, 174, 330, cf. 409); (Berkeley 1975, 23, 77, 173, 180, 186). Most significant in the present context, "tree" and "house" are two of Hylas's key examples of physical objects that obviously exist without the mind, against which Philonous argues on behalf of Berkeley (Berkeley 1975, 158). Hume (1975, 152) then uses these same examples to endorse this argument from Berkeley. (Cinzia Ferrini kindly reminded me of Hylas's use of these examples.)
20 Here Hegel's analysis coincides with Evans (1975); see Westphal (2006).
21 On Hegel's critique of skepticism, see below, pp. 60–64. – *Ed.*
22 Hegel's contrast between representations and concepts (*Begriffe*) is central to his contrast between "Understanding" and "Reason" and to his transition from "Religion" to "Absolute Knowing" (*PS* 422.3–10/M 479); see below, pp. 23–24, 55–58, 77–78, 249–250, 254–255. – *Ed.*
23 "The riches of sensuous knowledge belongs to perception, not to immediate certainty, ... for only perception has *negation*, difference or manifoldness within its essence" (*PS* 71.30–33/M 67). These last three characterizations all stem from admitting general concepts in order to comprehend general properties of things.
24 Although Hegel speaks of "properties" (*PS* 72.12–14/M 68), he immediately adds: "these *determinatenesses* ... strictly are properties only insofar as they first receive a further determination ..." (*PS* 72.14–16/M 68).
25 Introduction: ¶¶1–6 *PS* 71–74.11/M 67–70; Phase I: ¶¶7–8, *PS* 74.12–75.28/M 70–2; Phase II: ¶¶9–12, *PS* 75.29–77.12/M 72–4; Phase III: ¶¶13–18, *PS* 77.13–79.10/M 74–6; conclusion: ¶¶19–21 *PS* 79.11–81.14/M 76–9.
26 The verb 'to posit' has entirely ordinary, proper sense both in English and in German ('*setzen*'); it has the sense of 'to take a *posi*tion' by *positing*, e.g., a premise or an hypothesis. By itself this verb connotes nothing about excogitating objects into existence.
27 Wolff (1981, 35–6).
28 In a word, Hegel's "dialectical" contradictions (relations of mutual interdependence among contraposed aspects of something) are required for the very *possibility* of the phenomenon in question; in this they differ altogether from formal-logical contradictions which suffice to show the *im*possibility of something.
29 Roskies (1999), Cleeremans (2003).
30 I am deeply indebted to Harper (2002a, 2002b, forthcoming); I am very grateful to Harper for kindly sharing his MS with me prior to its publication.
31 Cassirer (1971, 2:407): "physikalischer Wesen"; Bloch (1908, 452): "L' «essence» matérielle de la lumière."
32 Newton (1952, 404–5, cf. 376). Cassirer and Bloch focus on the portentous shift from qualitative to quantitative physics, while neglecting the issue central here of how properly to interpret the quantified laws and regularities obtained by (sound) quantitative physics.
33 See Cassirer (1971, 2:405–6), Keill (1725, 8/1726, 6–7); cf. Cohen (1999) on "the Newtonian Style."
34 Much of Hegel's criticism of Newton is directed to his mathematical methods; the problems Hegel notes are resolved once Newtonian mechanics is rewritten by Johann Bernoulli, using analysis. (Some of Hegel's criticism of Newton is discussed below, chapter 5. – *Ed.*)
35 There are further subtleties to Hegel's view not developed in "Force and Understanding." Hegel expressly refers to the *Science of Logic* for thorough analysis (*PS* 101.27/M 102), though he also discusses some of these issues in "Observing Reason." (See below,

chapter 5, §1.2. – *Ed.*) Very briefly, Hegel contends that the key concepts and principles of the natural sciences require careful philosophical reconstruction. Hegel's view that philosophical demonstrations cannot be approximate is consistent with the approximative, increasingly precise quantification and explanation of the physical sciences because the philosophical point Hegel justifies concerns the legitimate natural-scientific ascription of fundamental characteristics, such as gravity, to matter. This philosophical point is unaffected by the shift from Newtonian to Einsteinian mechanics.

36 Surprisingly, Wittgenstein develops the same kind of argument in later sections of his *Philosophical Investigations*; see Westphal (2005).

37 This same transcendental and cognitive semantic support of Newton's Rule Four is provided by Kant's own cognitive semantics, as I reconstruct it in Westphal (2004). This is my belated reply to Bill Harper's (2007, 734) kind question, whether Kant's epistemology, so reconstructed, provides significant support for Newton's very rich method for natural philosophy.

38 Introduction: ¶¶1–4, *PS* 82–83.30/M79–81; Phase I: ¶¶5–10, *PS* 83.31–87/M81–86; Phase II: ¶¶11–17, *PS* 88–91.16/M86–90; Phase III: ¶¶18–30, *PS* 91.17–99.29/M90–100; Conclusion: ¶¶32–34, *PS* 99.30–102/M100–103.

39 See Plato, *Theatetus* 182; Sextus Empiricus, *PH* 1: 87, 2: 72–73; Locke, *Essay* 1.4.18, 1.8.21, 2.23.2, 2.23.28; Kant, *CPR* A251; and Putnam (1980, 475–6; 1981, chapters 1, 3, esp. 60–3; 1977, 125, 127, 133.) For illuminating discussion of Herder's views, see Proß (1994), Westphal (2008–09, §4.5).

40 The relevance of Newtonian gravitation to Hegel's analysis cannot be examined here; see Westphal (2008a).

41 The most recent explicit debate about logical identity and ontological atomism familiar to me is between Will (1940) and Church (1942). On Hegel's use of 'contradiction', see Wolff (1981).

42 The close links Hegel forges in "Force and Understanding" between epistemology and natural science are developed further in "Reason Observing Nature"; see below, chapter 5. – *Ed.*

43 Hegel thus affirms realism about the objects of natural science, whereas Brandom denies it; see Rosenkranz (2001).

44 *PS* 359–62/M 405–9; Westphal (1989, 183).

45 *PS* 359.9–23, 360.31–361.4, .22–25, 362.21–29/M 407–9.

46 For discussion, see Westphal (2009b).

47 The reader is referred to the subsequent chapters which examine each section of Hegel's *Phenomenology*. – *Ed.*

48 Einstein (2000, 314).

49 The systematic character of Hegel's examination of human knowing is at odds with the piecemeal approach to dissolving or resolving problems still predominant among analytic epistemologists. However, this piecemeal approach was undermined by Carnap (1950); see Wick (1951), Westphal (1989, chapter 4).

50 Hegel's semantics of cognitive reference appears to provide his premises for his account of thought in the second part of "Self-Consciousness"; see below, chapters 3–6. – *Ed.*

51 I gratefully acknowledge the financial support provided me by the Alexander von Humboldt-Stiftung for my research on "Perception" (1995) and on "Force and Understanding" (2007). I also wish to thank Hans-Friedrich Fulda and Martin Carrier, respectively, for hosting and so productively engaging with my research.

52 '*T.s.*' is logician's shorthand for 'to show', following which a thesis (conclusion) is stated, for which Hegel argues by *reductio ad absurdum* through internal phenomenological critique of the form(s) of consciousness espousing the opposite thesis. This chart is revised from previous versions.

Concepts are *a priori* when they can be neither defined nor learned on the basis of sensory experience alone, as understood by empiricists (Concept Empiricism); they are 'pure' *a priori* when they are required for us to learn, define, or use any concepts that are learned or defined in terms of sensory experience.

Hegel twice identifies the topic of his section on "Spirit" as "immediate spirit" (*GW* 9:240.1–4, 365.23/M 265, 413).

References

Anon. (Christian Huygens) (1673) "An Extract of a Letter Lately Written by an Ingenious Person from Paris, Containing Some Considerations upon Mr. Newtons Doctrine of Colors, as Also upon the Effects of the Different Refractions of the Rays in Telescopical Glasses," *Philosophical Transactions* 8:6086–6087 (DOI: 10.1098/rstl.1673.0034).

Berkeley, George (1975) *Philosophical Works, including the works on vision*, ed. M. R. Ayers. London: Dent; Totowa, NJ: Rowman & Littlefield.

Bloch, Léon (1908) *La philosophie de Newton*. Paris: F. Alcan. Rpt. by The Canadian Libraries Internet Archive, http://www.archive.org/details/ laphilosophieden00blo-cuoft (accessed May 8, 2008).

Bonjour, Laurence (1997) "Haack on Justification and Experience," *Synthese* 112: 13–23.

Carnap, Rudolf (1950) "Empiricism, Semantics and Ontology," *Revue International de Philosophie* 4; rev. ed. in Rudolf Carnap (1956) *Meaning and Necessity* (pp. 205–21). Chicago: University of Chicago Press.

Cassirer, Ernst (1971) *Das Erkenntnisproblem in der Philosophie und Wissenschaft der neueren Zeit*, 4 vols. Hildesheim: Olms.

Church, Ralph (1942) "Bradley's Theory of Relations and the Law of Identity," *The Philosophical Review* 51.1: 26–46.

Cleeremans, Axel (ed.) (2003) *The Unity of Consciousness: Binding, Integration and Dissociation*. Oxford: Oxford University Press.

Cohen, I. Bernard (1999) "A Guide to Newton's *Principia*," in Newton (1999), pp. 1–370).

Descartes, René (1964–). *Oevres de Descartes*, 13 vols., ed. C. Adam and P. Tannery, rev. ed. Paris: Vrin/C.N.R.S.

Descartes, René (1984–) *The Philosophical Writings of Descartes*, 3 vols., tr. J. Cottingham, R. Stoothoff, and D. Murdoch. Cambridge: Cambridge University Press.

Einstein, Albert (2000) *The Expanded Quotable Einstein*, ed. A. Calaprice. Princeton: Princeton University Press.

Evans, Gareth (1975) "Identity and Predication," *Journal of Philosophy* 72.13: 343–63; rpt. in Gareth Evans (1985), *Collected Papers* (pp. 25–48). Oxford: The Clarendon Press.

Evans, Gareth (1982) *The Varieties of Reference*, ed. J. McDowell. Oxford: The Clarendon Press.

Harper, William (2002a), "Howard Stein on Isaac Newton: Beyond Hypotheses?," in D. Malament (ed.), *Reading Natural Philosophy* (pp. 71–111). Chicago: University of Chicago Press.

Harper, William (2002b) "Newton's Argument for Universal Gravitation," in I. B. Cohen and G. Smith (eds.), *The Cambridge Companion to Newton* (pp. 174–201). Cambridge: Cambridge University Press.

Harper, William (2007) "Comments on Westphal," *Dialogue* 46: 729–36.

Harper, William (forthcoming) *Isaac Newton's Scientific Method: Turning Data into Evidence for Universal Gravity*. New York: Oxford University Press.

Hooke, Robert (1667) *Micrographia or some Physiological descriptions of minute bodies*. London (n.p.); rpt. by The University of Wisconsin Digital Collection, http://digicoll.library.wisc.edu/cgi-bin/HistSciTech/HistSciTech-idx?type=turn&entity=HistSciTech001303260108&isize=M (accessed May 8, 2008).

Hume, David (1975) *An Enquiry Concerning Human Understanding*, in P. H. Nidditch (ed.), *Enquiries Concerning Human Understanding and Concerning the Principles of Morals*, 3rd ed. Oxford: The Clarendon Press.

Hume, David (2000) *A Treatise of Human Nature*, ed. D. F. Norton and M. J. Norton. Oxford: Oxford University Press.

Kaplan, David (1989) "On Demonstratives" (1977), in J. Almog et al. (eds.), *Themes from Kaplan* (pp. 481–563). New York: Oxford University Press.

Keill, John (1725) *Introductio ad veram physicam*, 3rd ed. Oxford: Bennet.

Keill, John (1726) *Introduction to Natural Philosophy*, 2nd ed. London: Innys.

Locke, John (1975) *An Essay Concerning Human Understanding*, ed. P. H. Nidditch. Oxford: The Clarendon Press.

Newton, Sir Isaac (1673) "Mr. Newton's Answer to the Foregoing Letter Further Explaining His Theory of Light and Colors, and Particularly That of Whiteness; together with His Continued Hopes of Perfecting Telescopes by Reflections Rather than Refractions," *Philosophical Transactions* 8: 6087–6092 (DOI: 10.1098/rstl.1673.0035).

Newton, Sir Isaac (1952) *Opticks*. New York: Dover (rev. ed. 1979).

Newton, Sir Isaac (1999) *The Principia: Mathematical Principles of Natural Philosophy*, tr. I. Bernard Cohen and Anne Whitman, with assistance from Julia Budenz. Berkeley: University of California Press.

Perry, John (1979) "The Problem of the Essential Indexical," *Nous* 13: 3–21.

Plato (1997) *Complete Works*, ed. J. M. Cooper, with D. S. Hutchinson. Cambridge, Mass.: Hackett Publishing Co.

Proß, Wolfgang (1994) "Herders Konzept der organischen Kräfte und die Wirkung der *Ideen zur Philosophie der Geschichte der Menschheit* auf Carl Friedrich Kielmeyer," in K. T. Kanz (ed.), *Philosophie des Organischen in der Goethezeit. Studien zu Werk und Wirkung des Naturforschens Carl Friedrich Kielmeyer (1765–1844)* (pp. 81–99). Stuttgart: Steiner.

Putnam, Hilary (1977) "Realism and Reason," *Proceeding and Addresses of the American Philosophical Association* 50 (1976–77); rpt. in Hilary Putnam, *Meaning and the Moral Sciences* (pp. 123–40). London: Routledge & Kegan Paul.

Putnam, Hilary (1980) "Models and Reality," *Journal of Symbolic Logic* 45.3: 464–82.

Putnam, Hilary (1981) *Reason, Truth, and History*. Cambridge, Mass.: Harvard University Press.

Rosenkranz, Sven (2001) "Farewell to Objectivity: A Critique of Brandom," *The Philosophical Quarterly* 51.203: 232–7.

Roskies, Adina (ed.) (1999) "The Binding Problem," *Neuron* 24: 7–125.

Sextus Empiricus (1934) *Outlines of Pyrrhonism* [cited as '*PH*'], tr. R. G. Bury, in *Works*, 4 vols., vol. 1. Cambridge, Mass.: Harvard University Press.

Westphal, Kenneth R. (1989) *Hegel's Epistemological Realism: A Study of the Aim and Method of Hegel's Phenomenology of Spirit*. Philosophical Studies Series in Philosophy, ed. K. Lehrer, vol. 43. Dordrecht and Boston: Kluwer.

Westphal, Kenneth R. (2004) *Kant's Transcendental Proof of Realism*. Cambridge: Cambridge University Press.

Westphal, Kenneth R. (2005) "Kant, Wittgenstein, and Transcendental Chaos," *Philosophical Investigations* 28.4: 303–23.

Westphal, Kenneth R. (2006) "Contemporary Epistemology: Kant, Hegel, McDowell," *The European Journal of Philosophy* 14.2: 274–302; rpt. in J. Lindgaard (ed.), *McDowell: Experience, Norm and Nature* (pp. 124–151). Oxford: Blackwell, 2008.

Westphal, Kenneth R. (2007) "Force, Understanding and Ontology," *Bulletin of the Hegel Society of Great Britain* 57/58.

Westphal, Kenneth R. (2007–08) '*Intelligenz* and the Interpretation of Hegel's Idealism: Some Hermeneutic Pointers,' *The Owl of Minerva* 39.1–2: 95–134.

Westphal, Kenneth R. (2009a) "Philosophizing about Nature: Hegel's Philosophical Project," in F. C. Beiser (ed.), *The Cambridge Companion to Hegel and Nineteenth Century Philosophy* (pp. 281–310). Cambridge: Cambridge University Press.

Westphal, Kenneth R. (2009b). "Urteilskraft, gegenseitige Anerkennung und rationale Rechtfertigung," in H.-D. Klein (ed.), *Ethik als prima philosophia?* Würzburg: Königshausen & Neumann.

Wick, Warner (1951) "The 'Political' Philosophy of Logical Empiricism," *Philosophical Studies* 2.4: 49–57.

Will, Frederick L. (1940) "Internal Relations and the Principle of Identity," *The Philosophical Review* 49.5: 497–514.

Wolff, Michael (1981) *Der Begriff des Widerspruchs. Eine Studie zur Dialektik Kants und Hegels.* Königstein/Ts.: Hain.

Further Reading

Hegel's Introduction:

Westphal, Kenneth R. (1989) *Hegel's Epistemological Realism: A Study of the Aims and Methods of Hegel's Phenomenology of Spirit.* Dordrecht and Boston: Kluwer.

Westphal, Kenneth R. (1998) "Hegel's Solution to the Dilemma of the Criterion," rev. ed. in J. Stewart (ed.), *The Phenomenology of Spirit Reader: A Collection of Critical and Interpretive Essays* (pp. 76–91). Albany: State University of New York Press.

"Sense Certainty":

deVries, Willem (2008) "Sense Certainty and the 'This-Such'," in D. Moyar and M. Quante (eds.), *Hegel's 'Phenomenology of Spirit': A Critical Guide* (pp. 63–75). Cambridge: Cambridge University Press.

Westphal, Kenneth R. (2000) "Hegel's Internal Critique of Naïve Realism," *Journal of Philosophical Research* 25: 173–229.

Westphal, Kenneth R. (2002) "'Sense Certainty', or Why Russell Had No 'Knowledge by Acquaintance'," *The Bulletin of the Hegel Society of Great Britain* 45/46: 110–23.

Westphal, Kenneth R. (2005) "Hume, Hegel, and Abstract General Ideas," *Bulletin of the Hegel Society of Great Britain* 51/52: 28–55.

"Perception":

Westphal, Kenneth R. (1996) "Vom Skeptizismus in Bezug auf die Sinne oder das Ding und die Täuschung," in H. F. Fulda and R.-P. Horstmann (eds.), *Skeptizismus und Spekulatives Denken in der Philosophie Hegels* (pp. 153–76). Stuttgart: Klett-Cotta.

Westphal, Kenneth R. (1998) *Hegel, Hume und die Identität wahrnehmbarer Dinge. Historisch-kritische Analyse zum Kapitel "Wahrnehmung" in der Phänomenologie von 1807.* Frankfurt am Main: Klostermann.

Westphal, Kenneth R. (1998) "Hegel and Hume on Perception and Concept-Empiricism," *Journal of the History of Philosophy* 33.1: 99–123.

"Force and Understanding":

Westphal, Kenneth R. (2006) "Science and the Philosophers," in H. Koskinen, S. Pihlström, and R. Vilkko (eds.), *Science: A Challenge to Philosophy?* (pp. 125–52). Frankfurt am Main: Lang.

Westphal, Kenneth R. (2008) "Force, Understanding and Ontology," *Bulletin of the Hegel Society of Great Britain* 57/58.

Westphal, Kenneth R. (2008) "Philosophizing about Nature: Hegel's Philosophical Project," in F. C. Beiser (ed.), *The Cambridge Companion to Hegel and Nineteenth Century Philosophy* (pp. 281–310). Cambridge: Cambridge University Press.

Hegel's Epistemology in the *Phenomenology*:

Westphal, Kenneth R. (1998) "Harris, Hegel, and the Spirit of the *Phenomenology*," *Clio* 27.4: 551–72.

Westphal, Kenneth R. (2002/2003) "Die Vielseitigkeit von Hegels Auseinandersetzung mit Skeptizismus in der *Phänomenologie des Geistes*," *Jahrbuch für Hegel-Forschungen* 8/9: 145–73.

Westphal, Kenneth R. (2003a) *Hegel's Epistemology: A Philosophical Introduction to the Phenomenology of Spirit*. Cambridge, Mass.: Hackett Publishing Co.

Westphal, Kenneth R. (2003b) "Hegel's Manifold Response to Scepticism in the *Phenomenology of Spirit*," *Proceedings of the Aristotelian Society* 103.2: 149–78.

Westphal, Kenneth R. (2006) "Contemporary Epistemology: Kant, Hegel, McDowell," *The European Journal of Philosophy* 14.2: 274–302; rpt. in Jacob Lindgaard (ed.), *McDowell: Experience, Norm and Nature* (pp. 124–151). Oxford: Blackwell, 2008.

Westphal, Kenneth R. (2009) "Urteilskraft, gegenseitige Anerkennung und rationale Rechtfertigung," in H.-D. Klein (ed.), *Ethik als prima philosophia?* Würzburg: Königshausen & Neumann.

Westphal, Kenneth R. (2009) "Consciousness, Scepticism and the Critique of Categorial Concepts in Hegel's 1807 *Phenomenology of Spirit*," in M. Bykova (ed.), Сущность, Явление и Феномен. К Юбилею Нели Васильевны Мотрошиловой (*Essence, Appearance, and Phenomena. Festschrift for Nelly V. Motroshilova*). Moscow: Hermeneutics & Phenomenology Press.

2

Desire, Recognition, and the Relation between Bondsman and Lord

Frederick Neuhouser

The transition from "Consciousness" to "Self-Consciousness" is one of the *Phenomenology*'s most important turning points. It is also one of the most perplexing, perhaps because it results in not just a new object for phenomenological consideration – consciousness itself – but also a new mode of relating to the world, namely, as a practical rather than purely theoretical subject. Whereas in the previous chapter consciousness's goal was to know its object – an object it took to be distinct from and independent of itself – self-consciousness's aim seems fundamentally different: it seeks to "satisfy itself" and to do so through activity that transforms, rather than merely knows, its world.

The first of these differences is easier to grasp than the second. The various configurations of consciousness that occupy the first chapter of the *Phenomenology* are united by the belief that "the true" – the reality each form of consciousness takes to be independent, or self-sufficient (*selbständig*) – is radically distinct from, or "other than," the subject. Knowledge, on this view, consists in the subject's representing its object just as it is "in itself," without importing anything of its own into that representation. "Consciousness," of course, shows that no such relation between subject and object is possible and that in knowing the world the subject necessarily plays a role in constituting its object as an object of knowledge. The transition to "Self-Consciousness" is motivated by precisely this insight: if the object of knowledge is always an object "for" (constituted as such by) the subject, then the object of knowledge, taken by itself, is not a "true" – which is to say, a wholly independent – reality. This realization necessitates a fundamental revision in the subject's understanding of what is real and what it is to know the real: its conception of what is self-sufficient must now take into account the subject's necessary relation to its object, which means that from this point on, "the true" will be located not in an isolated object but in a subject-relating-to-an-object that, only as a whole, is self-sufficient. Self-consciousness, then, is not simply an inversion of its predecessor such that now it is the subject, conceived as wholly independent of its object, that appears as "the true." Rather, the subject now construes itself as the essential, law-giving pole of the subject–object pair and at the same time recognizes its relation to an object – its relation to some reality other than itself – as necessary and not merely incidental to it. How the subject comes to join these two descriptions of itself into a coherent conception of self and world is precisely the tale that "Self-Consciousness" purports to relate.

This account of the end point of "Consciousness" should help to clarify why self-consciousness is inherently practical. If at the end of "Consciousness" the subject regards itself as the true (as the sole source of the norms that bind it in its knowing the world) but at the same time recognizes its necessary relation to something other, then the subject must find a way of maintaining its relation to its other that is consistent with its conception of itself as self-sufficient. Precisely because it is confronted with this task, Hegel understands self-consciousness as a *movement* in which it seeks to assert its sovereign status in relation to its object:

> self-consciousness has a dual object: one is the immediate object . . . , which has for it the character of a negative; the other is *itself*, which is the true *essence* and is initially present only in opposition to the first object. Self-consciousness presents itself as the movement in which this opposition is overcome, and its identity with itself becomes for it. (*PS* 104.24–31/M 105)

It should be clear by now that what Hegel treats under the name 'self-consciousness' is quite different from what Kant means by the term. In contrast to his predecessor, Hegel sees a self-conscious subject as characterized by a *goal* – that of demonstrating its sovereignty and self-identity by overcoming the opposition between itself and its other – and the subject's drive to realize this goal accounts for its practical nature. This begins to make sense once we realize that 'self-consciousness' here refers not to the awareness of oneself as a self-identical subject of experience but instead to what could be called a *self-conception*. A subject that holds a self-conception ascribes something more to itself than the merely formal unity that defines theoretical self-consciousness for Kant: a self-conception goes beyond the purely formal thought of "an I that thinks" to include a contentful claim about *who* or *what* a subject takes itself to be. Moreover, a self-conception is a description under which a subject *values* itself; it conveys who or what a subject aspires to be, and so self-conceptions have practical implications for the subjects who hold them: conceiving of oneself as free (in the manner of the subject of "Self-Consciousness") implies that one will want to act in ways that realize, or express, the value of independent sovereignty. The self-conscious subject as Hegel conceives it, then, is practical rather than merely theoretical because it is characterized by a basic drive – the drive to be completely self-sufficient, free, or constituted only by its own autonomous activity.

Hegel often characterizes the goal of a self-conscious subject as "self-satisfaction." Taking a moment to clarify this goal is essential to understanding the philosophical project Hegel undertakes in "Self-Consciousness." The basic idea is that "true" self-consciousness requires more than simply conceiving of oneself in a certain way, or merely aspiring to be such-and-such; it also requires successfully realizing that conception, along with being aware that one has done so. Hegel's view is that a self-conscious subject cannot satisfy itself until it really "has itself" before itself as the object of its consciousness – that is, until it finds itself realized in the world just as it conceives itself to be. (Hegel sometimes characterizes both *reason* and *freedom* in precisely these terms, as the subject "re-finding itself in the world"; *Enc.* §424Z.) To borrow an example from Sartre: if I think of myself as a brilliant novelist but I write no books, or everything I write is judged mediocre by others, then I may conceive of myself as a brilliant novelist, but I cannot be truly *conscious* of myself as one. My subjective view of who I am is not confirmed in the world outside me – or, as Hegel would put it, my "certainty" fails to correspond to my "truth." Giving objectivity to my self-conception – making it true – constitutes satisfaction because in becoming what I aspire to be, I establish in reality the valued identity I claim for myself in thinking of myself as a great novelist (or a sovereign subject).

"Self-consciousness," then, aims to narrate the "experience" of a subject as it progressively uncovers the conditions under which it is possible for it to realize its conception of itself as free (or self-sufficient) and thereby find itself as such in the world. This account of the necessary conditions of a subject's realizing itself as free is not, however, a straightforwardly transcendental argument of the sort Kant offers in proving the *a priori* validity of the categories of the understanding. Hegel's argument, in contrast to Kant's, is dialectical, which means that it does not begin from a fully determinate conception of what it is for a subject to be free and then, holding that idea fixed, deduce the conditions that must be met if free subjectivity is to be possible. For Hegel, a complete conception of what a subject's freedom consists in emerges only at the end of his argument, and it comes into view only at the moment that the real possibility of self-conscious freedom is established. It is only when we see *that* and *how* free subjectivity is possible that we know precisely what it is for a subject to be free.

We can see how an argument of this sort works if we think of the *Phenomenology* as starting out with only the barest idea of what it is to be free, with what Hegel sometimes calls a "formal definition" of freedom. In both "Consciousness" and "Self-Consciousness" this bare concept of freedom is denoted by the term *Selbständigkeit*, which literally means "self-standingness," though it is often translated as "self-sufficiency" or "independence." These translations are not inappropriate, since the core idea of *Selbständigkeit* is that of a being's not depending on anything "other" than itself – on something alien or external to itself – in order to be what it is. An important part of what Hegel means by a subject's independence is its not depending on anything external to itself in its two central undertakings – its knowing and its willing. In other words, the bare concept of freedom with which the dialectic of "Self-Consciousness" begins includes the idea of a subject whose beliefs and actions are undetermined (or unconstrained) by anything – whether the world or other subjects – that is not itself. This wanting to be completely sovereign with respect to one's own will and belief constitutes for Hegel the defining aim of a self-conscious subject.

There is a further component to the idea of a subject's essential independence. This is the thought that a subject is self-sufficient, not just because it is a sovereign authority – the ultimate source of the norms that bind it – but ontologically as well: a subject depends on nothing other than itself in order to be what it is. The idea that a subject is ontologically self-sufficient is related to Fichte's central claim about the kind of existence that characterizes subjects in distinction to things: for Fichte, the subject just is – is nothing more or other than – its own spontaneous, substrateless activity of self-positing. Of course, this view is itself an appropriation of some of Kant's doctrines, especially his denial that the subject is to be understood as a substance, together with his claim that the mark of a subject is its capacity for conscious activity that is governed by norms immanent to itself rather than determined externally by the objects of consciousness. In these claims the two characteristics of the subject just distinguished – sovereign authority and ontological independence – appear to merge: if the subject is nothing but its own activities (of thinking and willing), and if the norms that govern those activities are immanent to subjectivity rather than derived from something external, then these two species of independence converge.

"Self-Consciousness," then, is Hegel's attempt to answer the question, "Under what conditions can a subject fully satisfy its aspiration to be self-sufficient, or free?," where the criterion for satisfaction is whether a subject can find a stable reflection of itself in the world that corresponds to its conception of itself as free. Accordingly, the dialectical experience observed in "Self-Consciousness" consists in three moments. The first involves a hypothetical subject (the object of our phenomenological observation) imputing to itself a specific conception of self-sufficiency. In the second, the same subject attempts to enact its self-conception, and we phenomenologists observe what realizing such a self-conception in the world entails. That is, we look to see what relations to the world a subject who conceives of itself in this way establishes in its effort to "prove" that it is sovereign in precisely the sense that figures in its self-conception. Finally, we compare what is involved in realizing a specific self-conception with the content of that self-conception in order to see whether the two match up – to see, in other words, whether that self-conception can be realized in a way that is consistent with the specific conception of self-sufficiency it ascribes to a subject. Only when we find that the first two moments are in complete accord is self-consciousness satisfied, and only then can we claim to know both in what a subject's freedom consists and what relations to the external world – both to things and to other subjects – it must have if this freedom is to be real. If, instead, the two moments fail to agree, the dialectic continues by revising the conception of freedom that takes into account what has been learned about freedom by the previous failure, and the succession of moments just described is repeated until self-consciousness's "certainty" accords completely with its "truth."

The experience of self-consciousness begins with the simplest conception of self-sufficiency a subject can attribute to itself: "I am, on my own, fully self-sufficient. Any object I have before me may appear to exist independently (and thus to place external constraints on my knowledge or will), but I am certain that my object has no independent being (and that I am therefore subject to no such constraints). Moreover, I can *prove* that my object is nothing – that I, not it, am self-sufficient – by showing its very being to depend on me (on my knowledge or will)." This attitude, Hegel claims, is best exemplified by a subject that is driven to negate – to destroy (*PS* 107.30/M 109) or consume (*Enc.* §427Z) – a living but unself-conscious "other" with the aim of making true its claim to sovereignty in relation to its dependent, inessential object. In other words, self-consciousness first appears for phenomenological consideration as "desire."

One of the most perplexing aspects of "Self-Consciousness" is Hegel's insistence that the object of desire is not just any object but "something living" (*PS* 104.38/M 106). The main import of this claim appears to be that, although desire itself remains unaware of this fact – it is apparent only to "us" phenomenologists – desire's object, life, is in truth not as different from the desiring subject as the latter takes it to be. More precisely, the object of desire can be seen by us to exhibit the same basic structure as self-consciousness itself – with the important difference, of course, that life, unlike self-consciousness, has no *awareness* of its structure or, indeed, any awareness of itself at all. To say that desire and its object share a basic structure is to say that life, too, is (in some sense) self-sufficient and, more specifically, that its self-sufficiency, like self-consciousness's, consists in its being "reflected into itself" (*PS* 104.32–33/M 106) or, equivalently, in its being a "self-developing whole that dissolves its development and in this movement preserves itself as something simple [or self-identical]" (*PS* 107.8–9/M 108). Hegel's point is that, regarded as a whole, life – the totality of living beings – maintains itself only as a self-reproducing cycle, as a process of constant movement in which individual organisms are born, interact with their environment, reproduce, and then pass away. Life, like self-consciousness (and later on *Geist*), counts as a self-identical "unity of distinguished moments" (*PS* 105.1–2/M 106) because it preserves itself as what it is only through the activity, interaction, and ultimate passing away of its distinct individual members.

That the object of desire has this complex structure is explained by the principle that earlier moments of Hegel's dialectic are not simply left behind but preserved in later ones. Desire's object has the complexity of life, then, because it takes over the complexity of the object of consciousness's final stage, "Force and Understanding." The forces that the understanding posits in explaining nature approximate the structure of life because the laws that describe those forces exhibit the same "infinity," or identity-maintained-through-difference, that characterizes life. (The law of gravitation, for example, explains motion by positing a necessary relation – by establishing an essential "unity" – between "opposing" empirical properties, such as location in space and time, or distance and velocity.)

The more important point here is that even though "we" are aware of the structural similarity between desire and its object, desire itself is not. On the contrary, the subject of desire conceives of itself as fundamentally different from life, and this distinction is central to its understanding of what makes it superior to its object. The individual desiring subject regards itself as wholly self-determining and self-contained, while it sees the living beings that are the objects of its desire as just the opposite: radically dependent for their existence on other living beings, as well as on their inorganic environment. Life is the realm of need, finitude, and dependence, and for this reason life appears to desiring self-consciousness as the antithesis of its own self-sufficiency. (From this it follows that the desiring subject will have to deny its own groundedness in life in order to maintain its conception of itself as independent. In the later struggle for recognition, this denial will manifest itself in the subject's attitude that its own life is inessential to it, while its sovereignty, in contrast, is everything.) Hegel complicates this picture by adding that the objects of the desiring subject nevertheless *present themselves* to it as self-sufficient; they in some sense – from the point of view of desire – make a claim to being self-sufficient, even though the desiring subject is "certain" they are not. Desire is driven to deny any hint of independent being on the part of its objects because, in its eyes, their being self-sufficient would contradict its own self-sufficiency. Hegel's claim is that at this early stage of self-consciousness, the subject must regard any relation to something other as a threat to its own independence. In desire, the longing for an object points to a lack in the desiring subject – a need for something other in order to achieve satisfaction – that, for it, represents a failure to be wholly self-sufficient and, so, contradicts its self-conception.

For Hegel, then, the subject of desire is a single self-consciousness that conceives of itself, and only itself, as self-sufficient. Formulated differently: the only being to which desire grants the exalted status "subject" is itself, and it regards everything that is not itself as less than a subject, a mere (dependent) thing. It is important to see, however, that desiring self-consciousness takes itself to be the only self-sufficient being not because it thinks the universe just happens to contain only one such being but rather because, given what it takes self-sufficiency to consist in, there could be only one. In other words, the conception of self-sufficiency with which Hegel's dialectic begins is one that takes a free subject to be absolute, or unconditioned (both are alternative expressions for 'self-sufficient') in the sense of being free from – unbound by – all constraints whatsoever on its doing and believing. The purely desiring subject, then, takes its sovereignty to consist in recognizing no law or authority beyond its own immediate desires.

Understanding the two reasons for desire's failure enables us to explain the next move in the dialectic of self-consciousness, the transition from desire to the search for recognition. This transition is the site of one of the most influential arguments of Hegel's entire corpus. Hegel characterizes this relation as follows:

> certain of the nothingness of [its] other, [the desiring subject] explicitly affirms that this nothingness is *for it* the truth of the other; it destroys the self-sufficient object and thereby gives itself the certainty of itself as a *true* certainty. (*PS* 107.29–31/ M 109)

Desire attempts to satisfy itself, then, by enacting the attitude: "I am the only self-sufficient being; every other being exists only 'for me'." Although Hegel describes desire as seeking the destruction of its object, this is potentially misleading. What desire seeks, more precisely, is the complete negation of every claim to self-sufficiency other than its own; it seeks to show that everything other "*counts* as nothing," "has no *true* reality," and "does not *deserve* to exist for itself" (*Enc.* §426 & *Z*; emphasis added). Desire's aim, in other words, is to show not that nothing else *exists*, but that nothing else has the kind of being that imposes constraints on it (on its will and belief).

Following our earlier account of the *Phenomenology*'s method, we should expect to find next an argument to the effect that, given its self-conception and the relation to the world that conception implies, desire is unable to satisfy itself (unable to find itself realized in the world just as it conceives itself to be). This is precisely what the following passage asserts:

> Desire and the certainty of itself obtained in desire's satisfaction are conditioned by the object, for that self-certainty comes to be through the superseding (*aufheben*) of this other: in order for this supersession to be, the other must be. Thus self-consciousness, by its negative relation [to the object], is unable to supersede the object; instead, because of that relation it produces the object again, and the desire as well. It is in fact something other than self-consciousness that is the essence of desire. (*PS* 107.34–39/M 109)

This passage suggests two distinct but compatible accounts of why desire's project is self-contradictory, that is, two reasons why what desiring self-consciousness must do in order to prove itself independent belies the conception of independence it ascribes to itself. Understanding each claim is essential if we are to grasp the necessity of the move to the next configuration of self-consciousness, in which desire becomes a subject that seeks recognition from another subject.

According to one line of thought, desire is caught in a performative contradiction: in attempting to prove itself self-sufficient, it is compelled to grant an importance to the objects it thinks itself superior to that its self-conception cannot admit. In conceiving of itself as independent, the desiring subject takes itself to stand above all other beings (whose desires and claims count for it as nothing), but in proving its exalted status it depends on the very beings it claims to be both above and independent of. The thought here is that because desire needs to make its claim for itself true – needs to find itself in the world just as it conceives of itself – it can find satisfaction only by relating to a realm of otherness (the external world) in which it must negate others' claims to independent status. In relying on these others in order to sustain its picture of itself, however, desiring self-consciousness shows itself not to possess the self-sufficiency it aspires to, since it depends on something other than itself in order to realize its conception of what it essentially is. Or, in language closer to Hegel's own: since desire's satisfaction is conditioned by its other, that other is essential to it; this, however, contradicts desire's certainty that it is absolutely self-sufficient.

The second reason desire's predicament is contradictory is that the only satisfaction available to it is temporary, or fleeting, and for this reason it is trapped in an endlessly repeating cycle that "*never*... reaches its goal" (*Enc.* §428Z). The feature of desire's situation singled out here as responsible for its failure is the purely negative character of the relation desire establishes to its object. Hegel's claim is that once desire completely negates, or destroys, its object, the very being that was to provide a reflection of its self-sufficient status no longer exists, and with the object's disappearance all worldly evidence of the subject's exalted status has disappeared as well.[1] Due to its purely negative relation to its object, then, the very moment at which Desire satisfies itself is also the moment at which it loses what it sought. This loss engenders the need to seek out a new object in relation to which self-consciousness can prove its self-sufficiency, and so, as long as it continues to conceive of self-sufficiency in the same way, it is caught in an unending cycle of satisfaction and emptiness, followed by the renewed search for another object in relation to which it can once again demonstrate its sovereignty. According to this second line of thought, then, desire is unable to achieve satisfaction because it cannot find in the world any stable reflection of the kind of independence it seeks.

This argument seems to depend on the idea that, once negated, desire's *object* ceases to exist. But if we construe the object's demonstrated nothingness less literally – as the claim that the negated object *counts* as nothing, that it imposes no constraints on desire's ends – Hegel's claim still holds: once the object is annihilated in the sense that its self-sufficiency is completely denied, there is nothing left in desire's world with sufficient standing (or "being") to reflect the value that desire takes itself to have. Desire then loses interest in its demeaned object and is compelled to seek confirmation in another, in some object that makes a credible claim to self-sufficiency and, so, is worthy of desire's negation. Hegel's thought here can be made more concrete if we think of desire's attitude as exemplified, if imperfectly,[2] by a compulsive seducer who has a conception of his own elevated standing that he attempts to express, or prove, by ruining – destroying the honor of – the victims of his seduction. The seducer's attitude to his objects parallels desire's insofar as he attempts to prove his elevated status in relation to an other that counts for him, roughly, as a thing. More precisely, the seducer's object initially presents itself as a being of a certain standing – a person of honor – and his satisfaction consists in completely abolishing that claim by destroying his object's honor; the moment the seduced succumbs to the seducer's desire, she or he ceases to exist as a subject of value. The seducer, then, embodies the attitude "I am everything (everything that counts), and my objects are nothing," but when he enacts this self-conception, he shows that his being everything – his actually proving it – depends on there being some other being with its own claim to self-sufficiency for him to negate. The seducer shows himself to be less self-sufficient than he takes himself to be – this was the first claim characterized above – but it is also the case – this is the second claim – that satisfaction for the seducer can be only momentary. Once his destroyed object stands before him, it ceases to be of use to his project of self-assertion since, completely void of any claim to standing, it can no longer serve as a being in relation to which the seducer can establish his own value; once his object has been reduced to a nothing, it is no longer suitable for the task of reflecting the value of a self-sufficient subject.

The next move in the dialectic of self-consciousness, the transition from desire to the search for recognition, contains one of the most influential arguments of Hegel's entire corpus. Its implicit claim is that intersubjectivity – standing in relations of a certain kind to other subjects – is a necessary condition of self-consciousness (of full, objectively confirmed knowledge of oneself as a self-sufficient subject). This point could also be formulated as the claim that there can be no subject without intersubjectivity or, as Hegel puts it, that self-consciousness exists only as "an I that is a we and a we that is an I" (*PS* 108.39/M 110). The essential claim here is that only another subject can provide self-consciousness with a satisfying confirmation of its own self-sufficiency; the key to reconstructing Hegel's argument lies in understanding how taking another subject as one's object remedies the dual failings of desire.

Progressing beyond the standpoint of desire requires us to ask what phenomenological experience has taught us about what an object must be like if it is to satisfy a subject. What we have learned in this regard follows directly from the two deficiencies of desire. First, we know now that a satisfied subject cannot avoid depending in some manner on something external to itself, given its need to prove its self-sufficiency in the world. This means that a satisfying object must be one that a subject can depend on in such a way that its dependence does not undermine its claim to self-sufficiency; that is, the subject must find an object it can depend on to reflect its status without degrading itself in the process, thereby losing the very status it seeks to prove. (This sounds like a *logically* contradictory demand, and so it is, until later in the dialectic the subject revises its conception of what it is to be self-sufficient.) Second, in order to satisfy a subject, an object must be capable of providing lasting, not merely temporary, satisfaction; it must be able to endure negation (to reflect the value of another) without itself disappearing or being reduced to nothing.

Hegel claims that only another subject meets both of these criteria, because only a subject is able to negate itself (*PS* 108.4–5/M 109). A subject negates itself and exists "for another" whenever it recognizes another subject as a being of value whose desires or beliefs in some way "count," or impose constraints on it. Why, though, does a subject's capacity for self-negation offer the way out of desire's conundrum? In the first place, negating oneself by recognizing another need not imply self-immolation, either literally or metaphorically. In acknowledging the standing of another subject, one does not (normally) cease to exist, and, more important for Hegel's purposes, by undertaking that negation oneself, one maintains a certain dignity or status even as one stands there negated "for another." This is because even though the self-negating subject is negated, it is also the author of its negated condition, and so in a certain sense it remains *self-determining* (*PS* 108.7, 23/M 109, 110). Clearly, this responds to the second problem the desiring subject encountered – a self-negating object can endure negation with its value-affirming capacities intact – but, less obviously, it is also relevant to the first.

It may seem that with regard to the first of desire's problems – how it can depend on something other to prove its independence without thereby undermining its claim to be self-sufficient – seeking recognition from another subject represents no advance. For in seeking recognition, a subject still depends on something other (on a numerically distinct individual) in order to achieve self-consciousness.

It appears, then, that it is impossible for such a subject both to satisfy itself and to avoid depending on something other. It is important to see, however, that self-consciousness's new object differs from the object of desire in an important respect that ameliorates the problem the desiring subject encountered in relying on thing-like objects to prove its self-sufficiency. The difference is that now, in seeking recognition, the subject implicitly acknowledges that its object – another subject – also has a standing above that of mere things. To say that a subject seeks recognition from its counterpart implies that it recognizes the latter as the kind of being that is capable of determining itself to exist "for another," and thus as having the same capacities that characterize subjectivity – and hence the elevated status – that it takes itself to have. This addresses desire's problem of reconciling dependence with self-sufficiency in that even though the subject now depends on a being numerically distinct from itself, its dependence does not degrade it as desire's did since the being it depends on is one it regards as belonging to the same honored species as itself. The subject's tacit recognition of its *generic identity* with the object from which it seeks recognition marks the beginning (though only the beginning) of the constitution of a collective subject – the consciousness of a we – that Hegel claims to be a condition of self-consciousness. The idea to be developed more fully as the dialectic progresses – an idea that has its source in Rousseau's account of how having a general will makes us free – is that once a subject begins to think of itself as part of a we, then in depending on the others that also constitute that "we," that subject depends only on itself (on a collective subject it identifies with). To anticipate the result of what will be a very long story, the problem of self-consciousness's dependence on an alien other will be solved not by retreating from the ideal of self-sufficiency, nor by eschewing all dependence on others, but instead by an *identification* with the object depended on that abolishes not the object itself but only its otherness.

The progress made thus far in the dialectic of self-consciousness yields not just insight into the kind of object a subject must relate to in order to achieve satisfaction but also a conceptual revision of the ideal the subject aspires to realize. A crucial lesson that desire's experience has taught us is that true self-sufficiency for a subject – self-sufficiency that affords full and stable satisfaction – does not consist in absolute independence from everything other but involves instead dependence on other (numerically distinct) subjects that one also recognizes as in some sense oneself. In other words, the quest for recognition counts as a step forward for self-consciousness only if one assumes a corresponding revision in its understanding of what a subject's claim to be self-sufficient requires: a subject's dependence on an other is compatible with a kind of self-sufficiency as long as that subject can see the being it depends on as sufficiently like itself (as of the same exalted type – subject rather than mere thing – that it takes itself to be). Insofar as the subject "identifies" with the object it requires for its satisfaction, it depends only on itself, which is to say: on an object of the same species as itself, the defining characteristic of which – the capacity to negate itself – allows dependence on such an object not to entail a degradation of the status the subject seeking recognition claims for itself. For us phenomenologists, however, the ideal of self-sufficiency has been expanded even further. For we can see – though the individual subjects we are about to observe in their search for recognition still cannot – that once desire has been replaced by the quest for recognition, complete self-sufficiency cannot reside in an individual subject but only in the whole ensemble of subjects, together with the relations they establish among themselves in seeking to satisfy their need for recognition. It is, in other words, the we not the I that is truly self-sufficient here, though as later developments will show, the fully self-sufficient we is one that also accords a significant measure of (relative) self-sufficiency to each of its individual I's.

In his introduction to "Self-Sufficiency and Non-Self Sufficiency of Self-Consciousness" (*PS* 109.8–110.29/M 111–12), Hegel analyzes the complicated dynamic that is always at play among subjects once there are at least two self-consciousnesses, each seeking recognition from the other. The starting point of this analysis is the realization that once a subject seeks proof of its self-sufficiency through recognition, it can no longer fulfill its aspiration without at the same time existing "outside itself," as an object for another subject. This truth about the quest for recognition is the source of the fundamental "ambiguity" – the dual significance of every action – that pervades all recognitive relationships and that generates much of the back-and-forth of the dialectic that follows.

One source of dual significance is that the subject who succeeds in finding recognition from another "has lost itself, for it finds itself as an *other* being" (*PS* 109.20–21/M 111). A recognized subject finds in the world a confirmation of what it takes itself to be, but in doing so it has (from its point of view) also surrendered its sovereignty, since insofar as it finds recognition, it cedes authority to a point of view other than its own, namely, the value-conferring gaze of its other. This relinquishing of absolute sovereignty evokes in the subject an urge to repudiate the other's authority to confer value on it (*PS* 109.24–27/M 111) – perhaps by retreating, perhaps by denying in some way the independent authority of the other – but acting on this impulse only makes it impossible for its other to provide it with the recognition it seeks, thereby precluding its own satisfaction. In other words, a subject in search of recognition seeks to be recognized by an other as self-sufficient, but in order for that recognition to count for it, it needs to see the being from which the recognition comes as possessing sufficient authority (sovereignty) to confer on it the status it seeks. This point illustrates one aspect of the dual significance possessed by every attempt to be recognized: whatever one recognition-seeking subject does to its counterpart, it in effect does also to itself. Since it is precisely in the other subject that it seeks to find a confirmatory picture of what it takes itself to be – since it "sees... *itself* in the *other*" (*PS* 109.22–23/M 111) – how it treats its other ultimately affects the kind of reflection of itself it is able to find in the world.

A second source of dual significance enters the picture when one notes the further complication that everything a recognition-seeking subject does "is as much *its doing* as *the doing of the other*" (*PS* 110.3–4/M 112). Hegel is not referring here to the fact that the being from which the first subject seeks recognition is itself a (second) subject that seeks the same thing from the first. Instead, he is drawing our attention to a feature of the quest for recognition that can be seen when viewed still from the perspective of only one subject's aim. What is at issue here is hinted at in Hegel's suggestion that everything the first subject does in seeking recognition corresponds to a demand it simultaneously makes of its counterpart that it (the second subject) also act in a certain way. This type of dual significance is said to reflect the fact that, given the aim of recognition, "a merely one-sided doing would be useless" (*PS* 110.12/M 112). And all of this, Hegel says, is bound up with the circumstance that, once recognition is its aim, self-consciousness's object is fundamentally different from the object of desire. That is, in distinction to its earlier manifestation, self-consciousness now needs to see its other as "just as self-sufficient, self-enclosed" as itself – as a being of which it is true that "there is nothing in it that is not there [through its own doing]" (*PS* 110.4–5/M 112). This second dual significance derives, then, from the familiar point that the recognition-seeking subject cannot find satisfaction merely by imposing a negated status upon its other (since doing so would violate the self-standingness it needs to find in its object so that its dependence on that other does not involve depending on something lower than itself). If the other's negated status is to count as recognition, the subject must get its other to *negate itself*; every act the first subject undertakes in seeking recognition must elicit a corresponding, freely undertaken act by the second. Any instance of recognition, then, includes at once the first subject's act of demanding recognition and the second's free acquiescence to that demand; two subjects must act in concert for even a single (one-sided) act of recognition to occur.

These points about the dual significance of recognitive interactions become clearer in the following paragraphs, where the abstract schema of recognition (*PS* 109.8–110.29/M 111–12) assumes its first concrete shape in the struggle unto death. Hegel introduces the latter by recalling that at this stage in its development self-consciousness has "doubled" since, as we have seen, a single subject "achieves satisfaction only in another self-consciousness" (*PS* 108.13–14/M 110). Each of the subjects we are about to observe begins by taking its character as pure self-consciousness – its "simple being-for-self" in "exclusion of everything other" (*PS* 110.35–36/M 113) – as its essential property, as that which it must prove itself to be in order to find satisfaction. Of course, in fact each exists as something more than pure self-consciousness as well, for the very possibility of their meeting in the world depends on their being present to each other as bodies and, so, on their immersion in life and the realm of material dependence. This fact of embodiment, together with the entirely negative conception of self-sufficiency that each maintains – where self-sufficiency is taken to consist in *not* being defined by any particular relation to an other – means that each subject is motivated to prove, both to itself and to its other, that nothing material, not even its own body (or life), is essential to it. At this point in the dialectic, seeking recognition by risking its life appears to self-consciousness as the only way of proving its self-sufficiency.

If we take seriously the dual significance of recognitive interactions described above, then each subject's risking of its life must be understood as an attempt not only to demonstrate that it has no attachment to life but also to elicit as a free response in its other an acknowledgment of its sovereign status. In addition, since whatever one subject does to its counterpart it does also to itself, each – in a single act with dual significance – both risks its own life and goes after the life of its other. This is because each participant in the struggle seeks to prove itself *as well as its other*: each "must raise its self-certainty... to truth [both] in the other and in itself" (*PS* 111.28–29/M 114). As we know from Hegel's account of the basic structure of recognition, each dueling subject must set out to risk its own life as well as to evoke the same action in its opponent, since in order to be satisfied it must be able to see in its recognizer a being worthy of conferring the sovereign status it seeks (a being willing to risk its own life in pursuit of recognized sovereignty).

It is important to note that even though every act of recognition involves some degree of reciprocity (since my seeking recognition from you implies that I regard you as sufficiently worthy for your recognition to count), *reciprocal* recognition need not be *equal*. Indeed, each participant in the struggle unto death seeks to be recognized by its counterpart not as an equal but as the only "absolute" subject. (That a self-sufficient subject must be a single individual, distinguished from everything other, follows from the negatively defined self-conception, described above, that self-consciousness possesses at this point in its development.) In other words, each subject seeks the total (self-)negation of its other, though not in a sense that involves obliterating the existence, or even the value-conferring capacity, of its other. Instead, each wants its counterpart freely to enact the attitude: "you count for everything, I for nothing." More precisely, the aim of each is to be recognized (by a being it in turn recognizes as a subject, capable of self-negation) as absolute in the sense that it – its particular desiring and believing – is the unconditional authority for the desiring and believing of any subject.

The struggle unto death can end in a variety of ways, but the only phenomenologically productive outcome occurs when, in the face of death, one of the two combatants embraces life as more essential to it than its honor and submits to the other in order not to die. The result in this case is

> two opposed configurations of consciousness: one, a self-sufficient consciousness for whom being-for-self is essential; the other, an un-self-sufficient consciousness for whom life, or being-for-another, is essential. The former is *lord*, the latter *bondsman*. (*PS* 112.30–33/M 115)

With this begins the most influential section of the *Phenomenology*, perhaps of Hegel's entire corpus: the so-called master–slave dialectic.[3]

Let us begin, as Hegel does, by considering what the lord has gained in his victory over the bondsman. The lord's most obvious achievement is that his self-conception as a self-sufficient subject is no longer merely "certain" but "true," which is to say: his status as a sovereign subject is now recognized by another consciousness that, through its obedience, continually proves the authority of the lord's desires. Less obvious but just as significant, the lord has achieved a kind of mastery over "being" – the world of things – as well. For, first, in holding out in the struggle unto death, the lord demonstrated his superiority to life (which is precisely the basis of the bondsman's recognition, since he, unlike the lord, proved unable to deny his tie to life). Second, in consuming the objects prepared for him by the bondsman, the lord achieves a mastery over things that recalls but also improves upon desire's quest for the same. Because the lord's relation to the things he consumes is mediated by the bondsman – the bondsman must work on things before they can be enjoyed – the lord is able to accomplish the pure negation of things that desire strove for, but in a more satisfying way. The reason Hegel gives for this is that since the bondsman works on the things to make them suitable for human consumption, it is he, not the lord, who must interact with and accommodate the self-sufficiency of things; the lord, in contrast, is able to "enjoy the thing purely" and "to be done with the thing and satisfy himself in his enjoyment" (*PS* 113.19–20, 23/M 116). But our previous account of the failings of desire suggests another reason the lord's relation to things is more satisfying than desire's: for the lord, unlike desire, the consumption of things does not result in the loss of a worldly confirmation of his sovereign status. The lord's satisfaction is more enduring than desire's because even when his objects have been consumed, there remains in the world another subject that continues to bear witness to his exalted standing.[4]

Despite these achievements of the lord, Hegel famously holds that the bondsman, not the lord, holds the key to the future development of self-sufficient subjectivity. His argument for this appeals to three "moments" of the bondsman's situation: fear, labor, and obedience (or service). In fact, however, there is a fourth advantage[5] Hegel mentions before any of these: the bondsman has before him "*self-sufficient . . . consciousness* as *the truth*, though it is a truth that exists *for the bondsman*, not yet *in him*" (*PS* 114.18–19/M 117). Self-sufficient subjectivity constitutes the bondsman's "truth" in that he, unlike his counterpart, has constantly before his eyes, in the lord, a concrete picture of what it is to be a sovereign subject, where one's own will and point of view carry authority for other subjects. In interacting with his superior, the bondsman experiences sovereign subjectivity – from the outside, as it were – and that sovereignty counts for him as "essential." Even though the bondsman does not yet see self-sufficiency as his own potential attribute, his relationship to the lord provides him with a living exemplar of sovereignty that, however incomplete, will function as a guiding ideal in his future spiritual development.

For Hegel the possibility of that development depends on the circumstance that, even though the bondsman does not yet regard himself as a sovereign subject, his interaction with the lord transforms him, without his knowledge, in ways that will enable him to realize a more complete form of self-sufficiency than the lord is capable of. This is what Hegel means when he says that "the truth of . . . *being-for-self* belongs *implicitly* [or potentially]" to the bondsman (*PS* 114.19–20/M 117). It is precisely his fear, obedience, and labor that explain why self-sufficient subjectivity exists already *in* the bondsman, even though he remains unaware of that potential.

The fear at issue here is not the bondsman's fear of his particular lord but his fear of the absolute lord, death. Here it is relevant to recall that the bondsman's relation to the lord is grounded in his own relation to being: precisely because he was unable to renounce his attachment to life, the bondsman emerged from the struggle unto death as the lord's servant. Yet in experiencing this fear the bondsman acquires a capacity that is lacking in the lord but essential to self-sufficient subjectivity, the capacity for "absolute negativity." This is because in confronting the possibility of his own death, the bondsman feared not just the loss of this or that particular quality but rather "for his entire being" (*PS* 114.22–23/M 117). In the fear of death everything about a person that previously seemed fixed and stable is shaken loose and dissolved; every particular property that seemed to define that person now ceases to matter in relation to one supreme, overriding value: remaining alive. What occurs in the fear of death, then, is a kind of "universal dissolution" – an absolute negating – of everything one presently is that Hegel takes to be the essence of free subjectivity. A fully self-sufficient subject – one for which "there is nothing in it that is not the result of its own doing" (*PS* 110.5/M 112) – must be able to step back from every one of its merely given properties[6] in order to ask whether it is *good* that it have such a property. The bondsman, in effect, judges all his particular qualities from the perspective of a supreme value, and in this respect he has advanced beyond the master. Insofar as he remains a bondsman, however, his criterion of the good is mere life. If he is to become truly self-sufficient, that criterion must eventually be replaced by the ideal of sovereign subjectivity – a more adequate version of it – that he now sees and values in the master but not yet in himself.

By distinguishing the bondsman's obedience from his labor, Hegel draws our attention to the fact that the bondsman's labor is undertaken *for another*, that it is activity determined by the dictates of an external will. Hegel says very little about the significance of this aspect of the bondsman's situation, but his allusion to the "discipline of service" (*PS* 115.29/M 119) makes it possible to guess the main thrust of his idea:[7] being subject to the discipline of an external authority is necessary for acquiring the capacity for self-discipline that true sovereignty requires. In serving his lord the bondsman learns to say no to his own particular, merely natural desires and to act instead for the sake of something higher, for ends that emanate from the will of a subject that he recognizes as self-sufficient and therefore as authoritative. The bondsman's obedience, then, develops in him the capacity (ultimately) to be master over *himself*, where self-mastery, or self-determination, consists in subjecting one's will – subordinating one's particular, given desires – to the authority of a higher ideal that in some sense derives from oneself. Of course, insofar as he remains a servant, the bondsman fails to achieve self-determination, for the higher ends he serves lack universality, which is to say: he labors to satisfy the merely particular and arbitrary ends of another individual, not for the sake of absolute, genuinely authoritative ends, those of freedom itself.

Hegel's discussion of the bondsman's labor is both more extensive and more celebrated than that of fear and obedience. It can be divided into two claims, one concerning the "positive" significance of labor, the other about labor's "negative" import (*PS* 115.12–14/M 118). The first of these claims is easier to locate and understand. It turns on the idea that the bondsman's labor provides him with a more satisfying relation to the realm of being than is possible either for the lord or, earlier, for desire. The bondsman's relation to being is superior to desire's because he negates (changes) the things he works on in a way that does not entail their annihilation. Labor negates things by forming them (and forming them in accordance with a subjective end), but when it has finished, its objects have not ceased to exist but instead remain standing in the world as objective testimony to the laborer's subjectivity. The bondsman refashions the given world according to his own plan (even though this plan is determined ultimately by the ends of his master), and in doing so, he inscribes his subjectivity into the world of things and finds therein an objective reflection of his sovereignty as a subject – of his authority to "give laws" to the world of objects. Since the master, in contrast, merely "enjoys" but does not work for the objects of his enjoyment, he is unable to experience himself as a fully self-sufficient subject, one with the ability to infuse the world, in all its particularity, with its own mark.

The second, negative significance of labor finds expression in Hegel's claim that labor negates, or "works away," the first moment of the bondsman's situation, his fear of death (*PS* 115.14/M 118). The key to understanding this point lies in Hegel's statement at the end of the previous paragraph that "through its labor, consciousness comes to see self-sufficient being *as itself*" (*PS* 115.9–11/M 118). Hegel's claim here is that the bondsman's labor accomplishes something more than providing him with objective evidence of his subjectivity; it also, by re-forming the world of things, makes that world less foreign to him. Instead of regarding the realm of things as hostile and alien, he comes to see it "as himself," as a realm that accommodates rather than thwarts the aspirations of subjectivity.

Still, even if labor diminishes the foreignness of being, how does that negate the fear of death? Hegel's answer is both direct and puzzling: "this objective *negative* [i.e, the form of being that labor negates] is precisely the foreign being in the face of which servile consciousness trembled" (*PS* 115.16–17/M 118). The puzzle this answer poses is why the bondsman's fear of *death* is to be equated with a fear of alien *being*. It will help to recall that at the moment in which the future bondsman first experienced the fear of death, the world of things had for him (as for the future lord) the significance of something alien. That is, both contestants in the struggle for recognition regarded membership in that world as antithetical to their aspiration to be a subject since, for them, to view oneself as connected essentially to the material world – to something "other" – was to lose one's defining character of self-sufficiency. In saying that alien being terrified the future bondsman, Hegel implies that the fear experienced in the struggle unto death is in fact twofold: a fear of dying and a fear of losing one's self (one's status as a subject). As we have seen, the bondsman's labor strips being of its alien character by demonstrating that, in receiving the form imposed on it by the bondsman, the material world can accommodate and reflect subjectivity rather than merely oppose it. But in addition to proving that self-sufficient subjectivity can be reconciled with an essential relation to things, this accomplishment negates the bondsman's fear of death. For the bondsman can see now that the material world's receptivity to his formative activity also immortalizes his subjectivity, since it enables the latter to acquire existence in a world that is more enduring than any individual self-consciousness can be. Enshrining his subjectivity in the realm of being allows what is most essential to the bondsman to survive his physical death, and realizing this makes the prospect of physical death less terrifying. This marks an important spiritual advance for self-consciousness because once a subject is no longer dominated by the fear of death, it is freer to do what a self-sufficient subject must: determine its actions in such a way that all material values – whether pleasure or life itself – are subordinated to the higher, spiritual end of freedom.

In introducing the next stage of the dialectic, Hegel picks out two moments of lordship and bondage as principal advancements in the development of self-sufficient subjectivity: first, that the bondsman has come to see an objectified reflection of his subjective activity in the things he has formed and, second, that he sees in the lord a concrete example of a consciousness that takes itself to be, and is recognized as, a sovereign subject (*PS* 116.15–17/M 119). The problem – and the impetus for future development – is that these two moments are not yet integrated. The configurations of self-consciousness that follow represent different attempts to synthesize these two moments of the bondsman–lord relation into a single consciousness. From the experience we have observed in the beginning sections of "Self-Consciousness" we know something about what such a synthesis will involve: a fully self-sufficient subject must be able to see itself – evidence of its own subjectivity – permeate the other that it necessarily relates to (both the world of things and in its relations to other subjects). One condition of achieving satisfaction in this undertaking is that individual subjects renounce their claim to absolute sovereignty (qua individuals) and instead identify themselves with a collective will (or perspective) that is universal in two senses: it is constituted by taking account of, and according equal value to, the perspectives of all individual subjects that compose it; and it takes as its ultimate authority not the given, natural ends of pleasure or life but a single, overriding spiritual value, the realization of freedom.

Notes

1 This line of argument is confirmed later, when Hegel explains why labor represents a more satisfying relation to objects than desire: "desire reserved for itself the pure negating of the object and thereby an unalloyed feeling of self. But that is why this satisfaction is itself merely fleeting, for it lacks the side of objectivity, or permanence" (*PS* 114.39–115.3/M 118).
2 One obvious disanalogy is that the seducer's object is another person, not a mere living thing. But the analogy remains enlightening insofar as the seducer in effect regards his object as a thing, as something that imposes no constraints on his own desire.
3 Since 'lord' and 'bondsman' are more accurate translations of *Herr* and *Knecht* than the familiar 'master' and 'slave', I shall use the former pair here.
4 This interpretation is supported by a later passage which emphasizes the "disappearing," or fleeting, nature of desire's satisfaction and contrasts it with the lord's experience of the thing (*PS* 114.39–115.3/M 118).

5 This talk of advantages should not be understood as implying that the bondsman is "better off" than the lord. The bondsman is better situated only from the perspective of the future developments in subjectivity that his oppressed condition makes possible.
6 This is the moment of universality ascribed to the free will in PR, §5.
7 Hegel is more explicit about the significance of obedience at Enc. §435Z.

Further Reading

Neuhouser, F. (1986) "Deducing Desire and Recognition in Hegel's *Phenomenology of Spirit*," *Journal of the History of Philosophy* 24.2: 243–62.

Siep, L. (1992) "Der Freiheitsbegriff der praktischen Philosophie Hegels in Jena," in L. Siep, *Praktische Philosophie im Deutschen Idealismus* (pp. 159–71). Frankfurt am Main: Suhrkamp.

Siep, Ludwig (2006) "Die Bewegung des Anerkennens in Hegels *Phänomenologie des Geistes*," in O. Pöggeler and D. Köhler (eds.), *G. W. F. Hegel: Phänomenologie des Geistes*, rev. edn. (pp. 109–129). Berlin: Akademie Verlag.

Westphal, K. R. (2009) "Urteilskraft, gegenseitige Anerkennung und rationale Rechtfertigung," in H.-D. Klein (ed.), *Ethik als prima philosophia?* Würzburg: Königshausen & Neumann.

3

Freedom and Thought: Stoicism, Skepticism, and Unhappy Consciousness

Franco Chiereghin

1 Introduction

Section B of the Self-Consciousness moment is subdivided into three figures (*Gestalten des Bewußtseins*): Stoicism, Skepticism, and Unhappy Consciousness. According to Hegel's intentions, they are presented as further specifications of the section's general theme "Freedom of Self-Consciousness." In Hegel's introductory outline of this theme, the word "freedom" does not appear. Rather Hegel uses the adjective "free," once to qualify self-consciousness and once to qualify thought. In effect, thought constitutes the central theme of the introduction. It may seem strange that only at this point in Hegel's phenomenological investigation is thought made an explicit theme. In reality, looking back at the phenomenological figures that have already been presented, one can find some good reasons why thought, in its specifically Hegelian sense, doesn't constitute a manifestation of figures of consciousness such as "Sense-Certainty" or "Perception." It seems rather more difficult to accept the absence of thought in a figure like "Understanding." And yet, as Hegel shows, as long as the understanding or intellect is identified with the activity that abstracts, that separates the subject from the object, that isolates parts from the whole and crystallizes them into mutually independent entities, it is correct to say that the intellect does not exactly think. The activity of thought, as conceived by Hegel, is presented as the complement to the workings of the intellect. Thought in fact aims to gather and express the unity of the being and of the knowledge of it, of the subject and the object, and the multiplicity of the parts within a totality which is articulated in itself and by itself. Even in the figures of section A of Self-Consciousness, thought is still latent, both in the more natural aspects of life and in the movement of desire and longing, as well as in the struggle for recognition, and in the dialectic of the lord and the bondsman. Yet precisely through this dialectic all these elements mature, in the experience of the observed consciousness, and once they are reintegrated, they make possible the manifestation of thought.

The elements brought into play by the dialectic of lord and bondsman are the following: on one side there is the lord as "being-for-itself," meaning a consciousness which is in immediate relation with itself while enjoying the fruits of the bondsman's labor; on the other side there is the servile consciousness which, through work, impresses its own form, "being-in-itself," on things and upon objectivity in general. The more the servile consciousness has been fearful before the lord, not for this or that particular thing but because its whole being has been seized with dread, the more its work not only deals with the individual particular thing, but concerns the whole field of objectivity and is a universal configuring. The crux upon which the fashioning of thought depends is mainly the servile consciousness. When it becomes aware that the "being-for-itself" of the lord is no longer something outside of itself, but is within itself in the form of an absolute negative (the fear of Death), and when in the "being-in-itself" of the objectivity formed by its own work it becomes aware of its own form and thus is aware of itself in a positive significance, then through this unification of the "being-for-itself" and the "being-in-itself" thought may be fashioned. For there to be thought requires that the "being-in-itself" of things and the "being-for-itself" of consciousness are no longer distributed into separate and independent entities; it requires that they are recognized as identical in the unity of consciousness. Only when "the aspect of being-*in-itself* or *thinghood*, which the form receives through work, is no other substance than consciousness," says Hegel, is a new figure of "self-consciousness . . . born" (*PS* 116.22–25/M 120).[1] The essence of this new figure does not depend on another consciousness or on thinghood in general, as is the case both with the lord and the bondsman, who depend reciprocally upon each other and on things. Since this consciousness is solely indebted to its own essence and this essence is expressed as "infinity, or the pure movement of consciousness" (*PS* 116.25–26/M 120), the consciousness which is now present is one "which *thinks*, or is free self-consciousness" (*PS* 116.26–27/M 120).

Consider the equivalences Hegel here proposes on the one hand between the infinitude of consciousness and the pure movement of consciousness, and on the other hand between consciousness which thinks and free self-consciousness. Both equivalences help clarify what for him is the essence of thought. We know that for Hegel, especially in his Jena years, infinity is a key word in his dialectic.[2] The infinite for Hegel is not "something" to be placed alongside or outside the finite, rather it is the act with which everything finite, and thus every limit, transcends itself in its being. Thus the infinite is movement, it is the absolute dialectical unrest that does not allow the finite to remain satisfied by itself, but drives it beyond itself, to integrate it with its proper opposite. This movement of self-transcendence gives the purest insight into consciousness, not as one special property among others, but as constitutive of its essence. In fact, consciousness could not possess knowledge of limits or of finitude if the unlimited and infinite were not present in it. This then is thought. It is not possible to limit thought (to paraphrase Wittgenstein 1922, Foreword), because it would be necessary to think of both sides of the limit and then go beyond the limit we have set. In as much as consciousness gains independence, this movement to overcome the limited and the finite is no longer subject to an external power; it is self-consciousness acting freely. As we can see, the key to the passage to free self-consciousness and to thought lies in the relationship of consciousness to objectivity. First consciousness must form the things, be aware of itself in those things through itself, and only then may it grasp itself as self-consciousness that thinks (see Westphal 1989, 160–2).

At this point Hegel can present the definition of thinking:

> For not as *abstract* "I," but as "I" which at once has the significance of being-*in-itself*, to be to itself the object, or to relate to the objective essence in such a way that this objective essence has the significance of the *being-for-itself* of the consciousness for which it is, is called *thinking*. (*PS* 116.27–30/M 120)

This is a very important definition, which epitomizes the result of the lord–bondsman dialectic. In thinking, the I is the object of itself, though not like the abstract "I think" that accompanies, as Kant says, all of my representations (*CPR* B131). It is an I that finds itself in objectivity and, conversely, deals with objectivity as characterized by the same movement of the "being-for-itself" which belongs to the I. This identity of the subjective and the objective, in which the form of subjectivity expresses the same constitution of objectivity, is what Hegel calls "concept" (*Begriff*). Hegel stresses both sides of this identity.

About a concept's identity with objectivity Hegel states:

> *To thought* the object moves ... in *concepts*, that is, in a differentiated being-in-itself, which for consciousness is immediately nothing different from consciousness.... a concept is at once something *extant*, – and this distinct [being], insofar as it is in itself, is the concept's determinate content, – however, in that this content is at once conceptually comprehended (*begriffen*), consciousness remains *immediately* conscious of itself in its unity with this determinate and differentiated extant being ... (*PS* 116.30–117.6/M 120)

As one can see, according to Hegel the concept is not abstract and empty, but is determined and differentiated in itself. Its differences, immediately present to consciousness, are nothing different from the concrete articulations of what *is*, what exists in the world.

Here, as in every other place of his thinking, Hegel neatly distinguishes between "concept" (*Begriff*) and "representation" (*Vorstellung*). This distinction does not imply that these two notions, concept and representation, are mutually extraneous; on the contrary, for Hegel the duty of philosophy consists essentially of the transformation of representations into concepts. It is particularly significant that he mentions this relationship precisely at the moment in which self-consciousness, being free, is raised to thought. A key characteristic of representation, according to Hegel, is that in it consciousness must especially bear in mind that a determinate representation is "its" representation (*PS* 117.6–8/M 120). Consciousness is aware of the content of a representation as "placed before" it (*Vor-gestellt*), as something other than itself, something found and external. A special mediation is necessary before consciousness takes up that content into itself as its own product. Having a representation requires connecting the internal image of something to the memory of the external, sensory intuition that occasioned its manifestation. Only by recognizing that the image, the memory of the intuition, and the process that connects one to the other belong to its intrinsic being, can consciousness repossess the representation from the external being and posit it as "its" own. Completely different from this is the way in which a concept is present in consciousness. A concept is pure thought, not mixed with representations or sensory images; it has a determinate content which constitutes its "being" distinct from consciousness. In as much as the content is grasped as a concept (and not as a representation), it is not distinct from consciousness and is immediately unified with it. In other words, with concepts consciousness has no need to institute a special reflection to recall that the representation "has the form of being something other"; a concept is consciousness's own production: "the concept is to me immediately *my* concept" (*PS* 116.30–117.8/M 120). For this reason consciousness raised to thought is not only self-consciousness but free self-consciousness. It is "free," because that which, as a determinate content of thought, is distinctive and different from consciousness, is nevertheless something that within which consciousness is aware of and is in unity with itself. Thus, according to Hegel, what is free is what is able to recognize itself in its otherness and thus to remain by itself even in that which it presents as other:

> In thinking I am *free*, because I am not in an other, but remain simply with myself, and the object, which to me is the essence, is in undivided unity my being-for-myself, and my movement in concepts is a movement within myself. (*PS* 117.8–12/ M 120)

According to this particular dialectic, which is active throughout the entire phenomenological process, Hegel takes care to underline that the identity of thought and being is manifest only *in itself* or *for us* (*PS* 116.20/M 120), which is to say, this identity is apparent for knowledge that is not a prisoner of the limitations of consciousness but which already moves at the level of absolute knowledge. The observed consciousness, on the other hand, has a long way to go before it can reach that goal and thus the identity of the being-in-itself and the being-for-itself is presented here in a very general way. Consciousness is object to itself as "*thinking* consciousness in general"; it is far from knowing how to develop its objective side in the fullness of its articulation, "in the development and movement of its manifold being" (*PS* 117.17–18/M 121). It considers thought "initially only as universal essence in general" (*PS* 117.16–17/M 121). Historically, this speculative position has been realized in Stoicism, the first phenomenological figure of this section.

2 Stoicism

The reference to the historically determinate philosophical positions of Stoicism and Skepticism is unique in Hegel's phenomenological process, which is replete with uninterrupted dialogue with traditional philosophical thought. However, even when the identity of Hegel's interlocutor is sometimes absolutely evident, Hegel generally avoids explicitly identifying philosophers or schools of thought. The *Phenomenology* is not a work of philosophical historiography, but the philosophies which appeared historically are used as examples of figures of consciousness which may appear in different epochs.

The exemplary value of Stoicism consists primarily in its principle, which announces the correct conviction "that consciousness is essentially a thinking being, and something counts for it as essential or true or good only insofar as within it consciousness relates to itself as a thinking being" (*PS* 117.21–23/M 121). However, this has as an immediate counterpoint: "to the question put to it of what is good and true, it replies by repeating the *contentless* thought, that the true and the good consist in rationality" (*PS* 118.29–31/M 121). Thus Stoic thought does not take intimately concrete form in the living world; instead it is thought in general which has abstracted from the differences among things and has withdrawn into its pure form, "in which nothing determines (or specifies) itself" (*PS* 118.32–33/M 122) and which is "*indifferent* regarding natural existence" (*PS* 118.11–12/M 122). For this reason, because it is affected by the unresolved duality between the pure form of thought and the world that actually exists, Stoicism is a form of *consciousness*; it is characterized by the dualism of subject and object, which typifies consciousness as such.[3]

Stoicism behaves negatively towards the immediately preceding figures, the lord and the bondsman. It does not in fact identify with either the lord, in the moment that he who commands finds himself in some way dependent on he who is commanded, or with the bondsman who is subjected through fear to the service of the lord. The stoic knows that to be truly free one cannot command or be commanded and he believes it possible to achieve this condition only if "it constantly *withdraws* itself out of the movement of existence, out of effects and out of passions, into *the simple essentiality of thought*" (*PS* 117.37–39/M 121). Through this withdrawal from the world, the stoic is "to be free, whether on the throne or in chains, within all the dependency of his individual existence" (*PS* 117.36–37/M 121). This does not mean that Stoicism is completely disengaged from the lord–bondsman dialectic; on the contrary, its negative behavior towards it indicates its persistence in an essential relationship with it. Just how much this is so Hegel renders explicit when he underlines this withdrawal into a pure universality of thought "that could appear as a universal form of the world-spirit only in the time of universal fear and bondage, though also universal culture which has achieved the level of thought" (*PS* 118.3–6/M 121).

Even if the phenomenological figures do not generally indicate so much of an historical pathway as a "trajectory of essence" (Sherman 1999, 104), it is evident that the epoch of general fear and slavery to which Hegel here alludes, is that age of Roman history in which, alongside imperial despotism, a rich cultural life bloomed, including philosophy. In reality it has to do with a philosophy which is imported, in a manner of speaking, because it was born elsewhere. It was born in Greece and at the moment of its formation it was in a certain way foreordained for a world yet to come. The philosophy of the great stoic, skeptic, and epicurean masters was in fact able to conform perfectly to the Roman world, and in particular to the imperial age. When the state structure became oppressive and autocratic enough that the more noble spirits felt disgust for the reality at hand, there emerged the need to search within themselves for the good and just things trampled under in real life. The harmony cultured Roman classes felt with Stoicism was based upon finding the freedom of which they had been deprived inside their own consciousnesses and in the abstract universality of thought. But this consciousness had by now lost the capacity for producing bonds in the community where they could recognize each other and also be recognized by them. What took its place was the need to withdraw into themselves in order to try to maintain their individuality by anchoring it to thought in its pure form (*PS* 261.16–33/M 290). But because pure thought lacks "the fullness of life" (*PS* 118.14/M 122), freedom of thought obtained in this manner was only the thought of freedom, incapable of actualizing itself in any concrete form.

Taking refuge from the actual world in the abstract thought of freedom constitutes the fundamental limit of Stoicism, according to Hegel. This limit was made embarrassingly evident because it fell apart when asked about the criteria of truth regarding the contents of thought. Once Stoic thought had made every content abstract, it could respond with nothing more than empty, boring platitudes (*PS* 118.27–36/M 122). The indifference to reality, the radical detachment from passions and from particular goals, in fact results in leaving things as they are and thus constitutes no genuine negation of the extraneousness of the world, though this negation is required by the essence of Stoic thought. To be genuine, this negation would have to penetrate the totality of its natural being in such a way as to eliminate every remnant of extraneousness and to allow consciousness to become filled with the wealth of concrete life. In reality, because consciousness is withdrawn into itself from its being, "it has not achieved the absolute negation of otherness within itself" (*PS* 118.38–119.1/M 122). The experience of the negativity of the thought, which presents itself in Stoicism as a unilateral and unfinished fulfillment of freedom, is brought to full expression in the second figure of this section: Skepticism.

3 Skepticism

Compared to the preceding phenomenological figures, Stoicism corresponds to the independence demanded by the figure of the lord, while Skepticism corresponds to those attitudes in which consciousness achieves a negative behavior toward otherness, in particular toward the appetites and the fashioning of the bondsman. Yet, as Stoicism in abstract thought reaches a first stage of that independence which is merely prefigured by the lord, Skepticism overcomes incapacity both in appetite and in the fashioning of the bondsman to achieve a total negation of whatever is other than consciousness. Skepticism may finalize the dissolution of otherness and the independence of things, because it does not regard them from an initial finite, limited position, but rather from what has been demonstrated to be the essence of self-consciousness: "*thought*, or infinity." To the infinity of thought, all independent existences and their differences, "are only as vanishing quantities" (*PS* 119.12–22/M 123). The expression "vanishing quantities" is taken by Hegel from Newton's lexicon of infinitesimal calculus, in which it signifies the moment in which a quantitative determination is removed: in the moment of its disappearance a quantity is, at the same time and in the same manner, nothing and not nothing; thus it is the existing contradiction or (in Hegel's lexicon) infinity, as the integration of opposites.[4] The disappearance of whatever has a determinate existence is the universal working of Skepticism. It is able to demonstrate to consciousness the effective nullity and inconsistency of every existing reality. In Skepticism, "thought achieves the complete annihilation of the being of the *manifoldly determinate* world, and the negativity of free self-consciousness achieves, in this manifold formation of life, real negativity" (*PS* 119.9–12/M 123).

In the preceding figures of consciousness, it merely "*happens* to it, without its knowing how" (*PS* 61.21/M 56) that "its true and real disappeared" (*PS* 120.1–2/M 124). Skeptical self-consciousness, however, turns its negative energy not only against the objectivity of the world as such and its relationship to it, but against itself. Thus "through this self-conscious negation it creates *for itself the certainty of its freedom*, it brings forth the experience of this certainty, and thus raises it to truth" (*PS* 119.39–120.9/M 124). From this affirmation it is easy to understand the absolute importance Skepticism has within Hegel's epistemology. Once liberated from the unilateralness and the admixture of empirical and intellectual elements that make it a figure of consciousness, skepticism constitutes a central moment of the dialectic and thus of the properly philosophical understanding of reality. In the Introduction to the *Phenomenology* Hegel takes care to neatly distinguish the skepticism which makes "spirit first able to assess what truth is" (*PS* 56.31/M 50), which is thus constitutive of philosophical science, from skepticism as a particular figure "of imperfect consciousness" (*PS* 57.5–6/M 51). This distinction has everything to do with the meaning and the role attributed to skeptical negation, which presents itself as an abstraction in skepticism as a figure of consciousness, though as a determinate negation in that special "self-completing skepticism" which Hegel identifies with his phenomenological science (*PS* 56.12–13/M 50). Skepticism, as the figure of imperfect consciousness, processes for the sake of negation. But in negating something it perceives nothing other than pure nullity, in which every determinateness disappears. That from which it abstracts, and which thus renders its negation abstract, is the fact that this nothingness "is the nothingness *of that from which it results*" (*PS* 57.8–9/M 51), and is thus "something *determinate* and has a *content*" (*PS* 57.11/M 51). If we take the result of a negation for what it is in its truth and completeness, that is to say, "as a *determinate* negation," then "thus appears immediately a new form" (*PS* 57.15–16/M 51). In contrast, "the skepticism which ends up with the abstraction of nothing, or with emptiness, cannot proceed any further from this but must wait and see whether anything new presents itself to it, and what this is, in order to cast it into the same empty abyss" (*PS* 57.11–14/M 51).

The fecundity of determinate negation is based on a fact that is for Hegel easily comprehended. In order to exist, something must be determinate: of the completely undetermined it is impossible to say or to know anything. Determination, as Spinoza teaches, is negation, "*determinatio negatio est*" (Spinoza 1995: Letter 50), because whatever individuates something distinguishes it from all others by contrast. However, these contrasting others, which are its determinate negation, may not be eliminated as inessential. On the contrary, only by including within the determination of any one thing also that which determinately negates it, can we know the thing in its entirety and truth. The fact that in the affirmation of something we must also comprehend its negation does not constitute a contradiction that results simply in nothingness. It permits us to reach a higher content where both the abstract affirmation of something and the necessary relation to that which negates it flow together in unity.[5]

This is the method gleaned from Skepticism, which already in his early Jena article, "The Relation of Skepticism to Philosophy," Hegel incorporates into the dialectic as its essential moment. In this article, Hegel deals with a skepticism epitomized in the *Parmenides* of Plato, and that in its scientific function is implicitly present, according to Hegel, within every genuine philosophical system (*Skept.*, *GW* 4:207.15–209.3). He recognizes that what originates Skepticism and guides it in every phase of its development is the principle of equipollence (*isostenia*), the equal force with which any discourse may be opposed by a contrary discourse in such a way that they annul each other. This principle is the basis of Pyrrho's skepticism and of his immediate followers; it has the typical dialectical weapons of the so-called ten tropes and is directed, according to Hegel, not so much against reason and philosophy, but against the certainties of commonsense consciousness and the finite determinations of the intellect (*Skept.*, *GW* 4:213.27–217.34). The theoretical strength of this principle, also used in the *Phenomenology*, corresponds to the so-called trope of relativity, which consists in showing how every determination, every finite existence, and likewise each of their differences, cannot be taken as anything solid and immutable because their essence is always and only found in something other than themselves. Absolute nothingness may thus be found at the level of finite determinations, because anything that is posited as distinct and separate from something other finds itself implicated by this something other precisely through the relationship of exclusion that precludes it from existing as something absolute unto itself. That which disappears is precisely the difference between absolute and relative, and this difference "*must* disappear to thinking, because that which is differentiated is just this, not to be *in itself*, but only to have its essentiality in an other" (*PS* 120.10–14; cf. 80.24–81.14/M 124, cf. 78–79).

This turning into the exact opposite, to which every determination is subject, demonstrates according to Hegel how the experience of freedom is fundamental to skepticism: "Skeptical self-consciousness thus experienced, in the change of everything that wants to be fixed for itself, its own freedom as given and retained by and through itself" (*PS* 120.16–18/M 124). Only an act of freedom can disengage consciousness from enslavement to the finite and thus bring thought into knowing possession of its essence. Hegel explicitly names "imperturbability," the "ataraxia of thinking of itself" (*PS* 120.18/M 124), as the form in which skeptical self-consciousness obtains "the unchanging and *truthful certainty of itself* (*PS* 120.18–19/M 124). Self-consciousness achieves this result without leaving behind or forgetting how it achieved it, even if this way exhibits characteristics opposed to the immutability and veracity of the certainty of itself, and instead presents itself as "*absolute dialectical unrest*" (*PS* 120.22/M 124).

Imperturbability and absolute unrest are the two movements within skeptical self-consciousness. Ataraxia constitutes the positive side of Skepticism that does not crystallize into a particular doctrine, but offers itself as an *agoghé*, a way of life. It is the absolute tranquility that contains and dominates the negative and nullifying side of the incessant self-annulling of finite determinations. This way of life does not privilege one determination over others, but reduces all of them to their finitude. This is possible because in its positive existence Skepticism expresses the freedom of reason. This aspect of Skepticism Hegel affirms in the Introduction to the *Phenomenology*, where the complement to the incessant dissolving of the experiences of observed forms of consciousness is the imperturbability of our "pure observing" (*PS* 59.30/M 54). This pure observing abstains from intervening with its findings or its particular thoughts about the experience had by observed consciousness. It leaves these aside; in exchange it obtains the power to consider the life of observed consciousness as it is in itself and for itself (*PS* 59.22–25/M 53–4).

Hegel's proposal that skeptical self-consciousness is infected by a dualism between ataraxia and the immutable certainty of itself, on the one hand, and the incessant change and absolute unrest on the other, constitutes an important moment in the development of this section, because it first announces the polarity which characterizes the final figure, the "unhappy consciousness." Skepticism of the imperfect, observed consciousness (not the skepticism that is a constitutive moment of the dialectic) is divided between these two extremes that it cannot unify: the universal consciousness identical to itself which experiences the freedom of being raised above everything incidental and finite, and the empirical side of itself which is forced to live according to everything that has for it no reality or essentiality and to busy itself with confusing mixtures of sensible representations and thoughts (*PS* 261.34–262.27/M 291–2). Hegel does not restrain his sarcasm about this form of skepticism that ends up prisoner to the inconsistency and misery of that which it negates. From the moment that negation constitutes its essence, it needs to feed and incessantly seek out incidental and inessential determinations precisely in order to continue to negate them. The skeptical consciousness "in this way counts to itself as a *singular, contingent*, and indeed animal life and *lost* self-consciousness" (*PS* 120.32–34/M 125); it "is thus this unconscious twaddle shifting back and forth between the one extreme of self-identical self-consciousness and the other extreme of contingent, confused, and confusing consciousness" (*PS* 120.39–121.3/M 125). In this way, despite being aware both of its immutable and its inessential sides, it continues to keep the poles of this contradiction separate from each other and thus cannot experience itself as a consciousness which contradicts itself *within* itself: the skeptical consciousness is contradictory "in itself," but not yet "for itself." When the two extremes that Skepticism keeps separate are connected by consciousness within a single individual experience, then this is a new kind of phenomenological figure, the "Unhappy Consciousness."

4 The Unhappy Consciousness

The two modalities of a free and unchangeable consciousness and of a consciousness which confuses and inverts itself absolutely are now recognized as aspects of one single consciousness aware of its own contradiction. Recapitulating the path followed up to now in an extremely synoptic way, Hegel puts the accent on freedom as a character of thought, to which self-consciousness is raised. In Stoicism, "self-consciousness is the simple freedom of itself" (*PS* 121.31–36/M 126), whereas in Skepticism stoic freedom emerges from abstraction and is realized as an active negating of every determinate being; at the same time, raising itself above that which it negates, the skeptical consciousness exhibits its internal duality and thus lays the ground for the duplication of self within itself: this is the Unhappy Consciousness. In the preceding figures Hegel has always distinguished the "ontological" meaning of those factors which are "in themselves" or "for us" from their "phenomenological" meaning for those who, as observed forms of consciousness, subjectively experience "for themselves" (this last presents as defective the truth values of the phenomenological figures). This same now happens for the figure of the Unhappy Consciousness. Within it has matured "in itself" or "for us" an act which "is essential to the concept of spirit" (*PS* 121.36–37/M 126), and yet consciousness experiences it as generating a contradiction that it cannot overcome. Precisely this incapacity constitutes its unhappiness.

To understand the sense in which this final figure of self-consciousness is something essential to the concept of spirit, consider how it develops. As we will see, characteristic of this figure is not merely the reunification of what in the dialectic of the lord and bondsman was distributed between two separate consciousnesses, or what in Skepticism came to be kept apart (*PS* 121.32–35/M 126). The unchangeable side and the changeable side now develop so that each of them appears *within* the other: even in their radical opposition, they become unified, because in each of them is posited its unity with the other. Now this is exactly what is necessary for the concept of spirit. Figuratively expressed, Hegel contends that spirit has the capacity to find itself in its own radical otherness. Thus it has the capacity to receive, maintain, and overcome the contradiction within itself; the contradiction is maintained and mastered when each of the two contradictory opposites is essential to fashioning the other. This formal structure of the concept of spirit also plays a fundamental role in the speculatively more important movement of Hegel's epistemology. The dialectic completely unfolds its epistemic potential when it takes the conceptual determinations of reality out of their mutual isolation in which they are maintained by an abstract intellectual consideration and is able to show how a precise, concrete understanding of the real must know how to grasp the whole development of the negativity that everything, insofar as it is determinate, includes within itself. This development now has its culminating moment, as has been said, where each of the two opposed determinations is found to be essential for fashioning the other.

Precisely because the final figure of the self-consciousness realizes this development "in itself," Hegel can affirm that with it the concept of spirit, having become vital, has come into existence (*PS* 122.5–7/M 126). Indeed, what happens in it is that, as an unchangeable consciousness, it also always has within it the changeable consciousness,

> as One undivided consciousness it is a doubled consciousness; it itself *is* the gazing of a self-consciousness into another self-consciousness, and it itself *is* both of these, and the unity of both is also to it the essence, though *for itself* it is not yet to itself this very essence, not yet the unity of both. (*PS* 122.7–11/M 126)

This persisting limitation and insufficiency, which make this consciousness as such *unhappy*, results from the development and the strengthening of the contradictions of the skeptical consciousness. The fact that it originates from skepticism should caution us against overemphasizing the role of this phenomenological figure or of overestimating its importance to the point of assuming it is a key to reading the *Phenomenology*, if not indeed to Hegel's philosophy in its entirety, *pace* Jean Wahl (1929). Consciousness is in fact unhappy because it remains a prisoner of an unhappiness of which it is the cause. This often provides reasons for those aspects of the dialectical movements which Hegel at times parodies.

Initially, the Unhappy Consciousness finds itself living in this situation: It *immediately* unites within itself the two modes of consciousness inherited from Skepticism, though they do not have equal value for it. Instead, their opposition is present as a subordination of one to the other. The simple and unchangeable side of the opposition is for it what is essential, the same consciousness of the divine, to which Unhappy Consciousness subordinates its continually changeable and accidental side, which it attributes to itself, thus condemning itself to its own unhappiness. But because an essential side is present and acts within it, Unhappy Consciousness liberates itself from what is inessential and the source of unhappiness. However, this signifies that the Unhappy Consciousness must free itself by itself. However, it is precluded from such a liberation because eliminating the inessential would be its own doing, which would be spoiled by the inessentiality and contingency that constitute it: the liberation would thus be inessential and incidental. The consciousness is unhappy, because it is torn within itself between its consciousness of the divine and its consciousness of itself as a non-essence. Thus Unhappy Consciousness

> is only the contradictory movement in which the opposite does not come to rest in its opposite; instead, it only produces itself anew as an opposite within its opposite.

> Thus there is a struggle against an enemy in which victory is instead defeat, to have reached the one is rather to have lost it within its opposite. (*PS* 122.28–33/ M 127)

Thus the way in which the Unhappy Consciousness undertakes to raise itself to the divine and unchangeable has its prospects for success spoiled in the beginning by being aware that its consciousness contains its own nullity: every attempt will be the non-attempt of a nullity that will be thrown back into its proper singularity, separated from and opposed to the unchangeable consciousness.

The Unhappy Consciousness is unaware that it has effectively within its reach the possibility of overcoming the contradiction between the two consciousnesses which constitute it. If their contrast is considered in its development, it is not difficult to discern that each of the opposites – the single individual changeable consciousness and the pure unchangeable consciousness – appears in the other as what essentially constitutes its existence. In this movement "it experiences precisely this *coming forth of individuality* WITHIN *the unchangeable*, and *of the unchangeable* WITHIN *the individuality*" (*PS* 123.5–6/M 127–8). However, so long as the Unhappy Consciousness holds firm to their inequality, this originating of the singularity in the unchangeable and vice versa will not restore unity of these opposites, but will perpetuate within each of them the unhappiness of an insurmountable division.

Hegel specifies three possible modes in which the singularity of the individual consciousness can relate itself to the unchangeable consciousness. In the first the unchangeable appears to the single individual as an external, separate, and hostile essence that judges and condemns it. In the second the unchangeable assumes the figure of singularity. Hence it is no longer distinct from it (at least in kind), even though the opposition between the two singularities remains. Finally, in the third the opposition is overcome, the observed consciousness transforms itself out of its unhappiness into a consciousness *happy* to find itself in the unchangeable "and becomes to itself conscious that its individuality is reconciled with the universal" (*PS* 123.21–22/M 127). When this happens, consciousness has made itself spirit, although to fully reach this level, as announced many times by Hegel, it must traverse a range of experiences that transcends the limits of the Self-Consciousness moment (*PS* 123.11–22/M 128).

Although Hegel provides no concrete historical indications, it is evident that the figure of the Unhappy Consciousness prima facie represents the religious attitudes of the believer. The attitudes he presents here are their defective aspects, that is to say, faith as it originates from a consciousness enclosed in its singularity and torn by the opposition between finite and infinite; certainly not faith as it is in itself in its truth. Authentic faith in the *Phenomenology* awaits the concluding phase of the moment Religion, where faith is no longer the attitude of a single individual consciousness, but originates from the community of believers. At this stage it is only possible to take the decisive step towards the divine, a step that is impracticable for the Unhappy Consciousness and yet will allow the community of believers to open the passage to absolute knowledge.

It is easy enough to recognize, in the first of ways in which the Unhappy Consciousness relates to the divine, Hegel's interpretation of the Jewish religious attitude, wherein God is conceived as an outside power that exists as the incarnation of the law that judges and absolves or condemns. In the second mode Christianity is recognized, wherein incarnation is represented by God assuming human form in the Son, who is identified with the singularity of Christ as an historical individual. Finally, in the third mode, the age of the Spirit is recognized, wherein the total reconciliation and identification of the single individual with the universal, of man with God, is actualized.

The relationship that Unhappy Consciousness establishes with these modes of divine manifestation is marked by its own unhappiness: because it is divided within itself, it reflects that division into any aspect of the divine with which it comes into contact. This is most naturally true for the first two modes, because the third is still far out of reach. Beyond forced and parodistic tones, what Hegel presents in the figure of the Unhappy Consciousness is a fundamental character of human subjectivity. In consciousness both the awareness of its own finiteness and, by virtue of this same awareness, the idea of the infinite are present. A limit, as mentioned above, may be known as such when one can look at both of sides of the limit – what it contains and what it excludes – though such knowledge surpasses that limit. This capacity for going beyond the limit, which is characteristic of consciousness, bears witness to the idea of the infinite in us.[6] Once the finite and the infinite have been identified as constitutive of consciousness, the way in which they articulate their relationship becomes crucial. One of these ways might be to take this surpassing of every limitation as an infinite characteristic of consciousness: the infinite is not something other than consciousness. It is not a kind of guest foreign to its nature, but is consciousness itself constantly transcending the limited. The transcending of every finiteness is the immutable character of the infinity of consciousness. What Hegel states in the Jena *Logic*, "this alone is the true nature of the finite: that it is infinite, that it sublates itself in its being" (*L&M* 35), might very well be extended to the ontological structure of consciousness. Yet it does not coincide with the way in which consciousness experiences itself as unhappy. Here consciousness has disavowed its own nothingness and has opposed to its own accidental nature the infinite and unchangeable, thus cutting off the possibility of transcending its own finiteness and of finding itself in unity with infinity. This makes not only the representation of itself partial and incomplete, but also its representation of the divine as well. What is manifest is not "the unchangeable *in and for itself*," but "the unchangeability as the unchangeability of consciousness, which is thus not the true, but rather is still trapped within an opposition" (*PS* 123.32–34/M 128). Hence the unchangeable and the divine are present in consciousness, though they are characterized by being divided and by opposition to the single consciousness. In this way, as the infinite opposed to the finite, it itself becomes something limited, hence here too the unchangeable acquires the figure of the singularity, the very one to which it is opposed (*PS* 123.38–124.1/M 129).

Hegel now concentrates almost exclusively on the second mode of relationship with the unchangeable consciousness, that which corresponds to Christianity and to the incarnation of Christ. That the divine assumes human form could be an essential step in the genuine reconciliation of the finite and the infinite. In reality, because this event is experienced within the unhappy consciousness, the incarnation cannot at all bring God to the single individual consciousness. On the contrary, precisely by identifying itself with an historical existence, the divine becomes even more impenetrable, distinctive, and transcendent with regard to consciousness. Furthermore, from the moment that, because it is historical, God suffers death and leaves the world, nothing but an infinite longing for a desired and indefinitely postponed reunification is left to the single individual consciousness (*PS* 124.1–19/M 129). The single individual consciousness thus comprehends that the true obstacle to overcome is its presupposition that its division from the Divine is irremediable. Hence it undertakes a series of attempts to achieve unity with the God that became man, attempts which Hegel highlights in three consecutive steps (*PS* 124.20–37/M 129–30).

The protagonist of the first step is "pure consciousness," which Hegel states is incapable of raising itself to the thought of effective identity between its own singularity and the God who assumed human form. Consequently, it seeks unity with God by entrusting itself to an unsuitable means, to the immediacy of feeling, which, in the best of cases, is not so much a thought as a movement towards thought expressed as "devotion": "its thinking as such remains the formless chiming of bells or a warm fog of satisfaction, a musical thinking that does not achieve the concept, which would be the only immanent and objective route" (*PS* 125.26–29/M 131). This incapacity to think of Christ, as an historically existing man, joined to the universality which belongs to him as man–God, insures that its attempt to join itself to his unchangeable singularity fails, because he remains an unreachable beyond: "wherever it is sought, it cannot be found, because it is to be *a beyond*, such a being as cannot be found" (*PS* 126.9–11/M 131–2). Once Christ has been sought as something that is given sensibly, as an object of sense-certainty, it has already been lost and in its place only the empty sepulcher may be present to the unhappy consciousness. Outlining the adventures of the Crusades, Hegel observes that even the sepulcher is something empirical and cannot possess any stability or assurance of anything lasting; thus "even this presence of the grave is only a toiling struggle which must be lost" (*PS* 126.15–18/M 132). On the other hand, consciousness becomes well aware of the evanescence of the empirical testaments provided by a sepulcher or by the very figure of Christ as an empirical figure. It thus abandons its attempt to join itself to the divine through mere feeling and devotion, and tries instead to learn from its experience by giving up its search for any *actual* unchangeable individuality, or its fixation upon something vanished, or its taking repose in its feeling, which in itself is its feeling of itself; it feels itself to be a pure consciousness that thinks purely of itself in its own singularity and thus posits itself as a universal and conceived (not merely felt) single individual.

In the second step, the protagonist is the consciousness which has returned back into itself. To attain the certainty of its own salvation and its own union with God it relies on its own forces or original capacities: desire and work. Developing a dialectic which in certain aspects seems to anticipate Weber's (1930) thesis in

The Protestant Ethic and the Spirit of Capitalism, Hegel shows how consciousness turns to the world, which, once God made himself flesh and assumed a mundane form, is a world consecrated in the totality of its aspects (cf. *PS* 127.5–11/M 132–3). If consciousness were not intimately torn, working, and appropriating to itself worldly reality, it would draw from the consequent success of its own work the certainty of living in unity with the divine within a consecrated reality. It would thus also be reassured about attaining its own salvation. Yet this consciousness is again thrown out into uncertainty and the misery of its own unhappiness, because everything that it achieves, like the holiness of the reality upon which it works, is for it uniquely a gift that comes from beyond. It is a generous gift for which it renders thanks and over which it has no control (*PS* 127.12–27/M 133). Thus it "forsakes the satisfaction of its consciousness of its own self-sufficiency" (*PS* 128.9–10/M 134) and its unity with the sacred and the divine "is affected by the separation, in itself it is again broken, and from this emerges again the opposition of the universal and the singular" (*PS* 128.13–15/M 134). This incapacity to realize a true unification stimulates its awareness of its unhappiness, because it understands very well that if it also refuses the fruits of its own work, it submits itself completely to the divine through giving thanks and renouncing itself and its proper essence before the divine omnipotence. In reality even these acts of renunciation continue to be works of consciousness, an individual initiative that can only replicate its misery, its separation from the divine, and the unreachability of its unity with it: in giving thanks, "consciousness feels itself as this singular individual, and doesn't allow itself to be deceived by the appearance of its renunciation, for in truth consciousness has not renounced itself" (*PS* 128.27–29/M 134).

From here begins the third and final step, through which consciousness tries to overcome effectively its own unhappiness by creating a new and radical experience of its own nothingness. It now undertakes mortification, first as the mortification of the flesh, which Hegel describes mercilessly as one of the most wretched obsessions of Christian ethics. Instead of simply fulfilling our animal functions, without exaggerating their importance, the desire for mortification makes an object of its own zeal, transfiguring those functions into an obsession. Trapped in a struggle against an enemy that becomes much larger the more it is defeated, far from being free from it, it affixes it to itself as an unessential singularity that is a continual source of pollution (*PS* 129.14–27/M 135–6). What we see is thus "just a personality restricted only to itself and its petty acts, as unhappy as it is impoverished" (*PS* 129.29–30/M 136).

In devotion, work, enjoyment, and mortification the Unhappy Consciousness has until now only experienced immediate ways to actualize its unity with the divine. Now it has the experience of inserting a mediator, a minister or priest, between itself and the unchangeable divine essence. In this way what the minister does and what he represents to the Unhappy Consciousness is the same as what he does and represents to God (*PS* 129.38–130.8/M 136). Now the Unhappy Consciousness really takes the road to a genuine and total self-abnegation. It begins by alienating *in toto* its own will to the minister, obeying solely his advice; in this way it is able to unload upon him all the blame derived from his work;

through fasting and punishments it renounces even the fruits of its own work (*PS* 130.9–24/M 136–7). At this point the Unhappy Consciousness has abandoned every vestige of independence so that, following the directions of the clergy, it does things completely alien and incomprehensible, such as using symbolic gestures or ritual language. In this deadening of itself and of its faculties consciousness "has alienated its certainty in the truth of itself, of its '*I*', and has made its immediate self-consciousness into an objective being" (*PS* 130.29–31/M 137). However, by reducing itself to a thing, by renouncing the independence of its own singularity and action, consciousness finally achieves freedom even from the unhappiness deriving from its work (*PS* 131.1–3/M 137). Even in this extreme renunciation, consciousness keeps for itself only the negative aspect of the annulment and does not realize that precisely in its capacity to sacrifice itself completely can it experience "internal and external freedom" (*PS* 130.27–28/M 137).[7] At the same time, through the mediating work of the minister, everything that it renounced has been transferred to the divine unchangeable essence (*PS* 131.3–26/M 137–8). Hence this divine being comes to have the same content which earlier belonged to the singular, individual consciousness. In this way, this is the movement in which each of the two opposed extremes, the Unhappy Consciousness and the unchangeable consciousness, having reached maturity, each finds within itself the opposite of itself: consciousness has now within its reach the experience of internal and external freedom and of the infinite power of thought; the unchangeable has taken upon itself the entire travail of consciousness. Even if consciousness persists in taking root in the negative side of its separateness and unhappiness, in reality it is now ready to approach the horizon of reason, where it is certain "in its individuality of being *in itself* absolute, of being all reality" (*PS* 131.30–31/M 138).

Notes

1 All translations from Hegel are by the editor. – *Ed.*
2 In the *Phenomenology*, "infinity" is first introduced in "Force and Understanding"; see above, pp. 22–23. – *Ed.*
3 In the Introduction, Hegel states: "consciousness *distinguishes* from itself something to which it at the same time *relates* itself; or, as this is expressed, this something is something *for consciousness*. The determinate side of this *relation*, or the *being* of something *for a consciousness*, is *knowledge*. From this being for an other, however, we distinguish the *being in itself*; that which is related to knowledge is at the same time distinguished from it and is posited as *existing* also outside this relation. The side of this in itself is called *truth*" (*PS* 58.25–31/M 52); see above, pp. 4, 193. – *Ed.*
4 For discussion of Newton's vanishing mathematical quantities, see De Gandt (1995), esp. pp. 202–44, though the whole of chapter 3, on Newton's mathematical methods, is relevant.
5 This point is first argued for in "Perception" and is argued further in "Force and Understanding" (*PS* 99.9–100.28/M 99–101); it concerns the integration of contrasting or opposed moments within or among things, which is the key to Hegel's distinction between a genuine concept (*Begriff*) and abstract universals, which are a species of *Vorstellung*; see above, pp. 10, 15–16, 23–24. – *Ed.*

6   This issue is not limited to religion or theology; consider, for example, one of Descartes's premises for his first argument for the existence of God in *Meditation* 3: "And I must not think that, just as my conceptions of rest and darkness are arrived at by negating movement and light, so my perception of the infinite is arrived at not by means of a true idea but merely by negating the finite. On the contrary, I clearly understand that there is more reality in an infinite substance than in a finite one, and hence that my perception of the infinite, that is God, is in some way prior to my perception of the finite, that is myself. For how could I understand that I doubted or desired – that is, lacked something – and that I was not wholly perfect, unless there were in me some idea of a more perfect being which enabled me to recognize my own defects by comparison?" (AT 7:45).

7   There is a significant parallel here between the Unhappy Consciousness and the servile consciousness: neither the Unhappy Consciousness nor the bondsman is able to go beyond its limit, since neither achieves, nor even attempts, the radical negation of whatever is other than consciousness. (Also, both of these figures of consciousness are self-negating; cf. pp. 48, 51. – *Ed.*)

References

De Gandt, F. (1995) *Force and Geometry in Newton's Principia*, tr. C. Wilson. Princeton, NJ: Princeton University Press.

Descartes, R. (1964–76) *Oeuvres de Descartes*, ed. C. Adam and P. Tannery. Revised ed. Paris: Vrin/C.N.R.S., cited as 'AT'.

Rauch, L. (1999) "A Discussion of the Text," in L. Rauch and D. Sherman (eds. and trs.), *Hegel's Phenomenology of Self-Consciousness* (pp. 55–160). Albany: State University of New York Press.

Spinoza, B. (1995) *The Letters*, tr. S. Shirley, with Introduction and Notes by S. Barbone, L. Rice, and J. Adler. Cambridge, Mass.: Hackett Publishing Co.

Wahl, J. (1929) *Le malheur de la conscience dans la philosophie de Hegel*. Paris: Presses Universitaires de France.

Weber, M. (1930) *The Protestant Ethic and the Spirit of Capitalism*, tr. T. Parsons, with a foreword by R. H. Tawney. London: G. Allen & Unwin.

Westphal, K. R. (1989) *Hegel's Epistemological Realism*. Dordrecht: Kluwer.

Wittgenstein, L. (1922) *Tractatus Logico-Philosophicus*, tr. D. F. Pears and B. F. McGuinness, bilingual edition with an Introduction by B. Russell. London: Routledge & Kegan Paul.

4

The Challenge of Reason: From Certainty to Truth

Cinzia Ferrini

1 What Is 'High' and What Is 'Low' in the Significance of Reason[1]

Hegel's introductory discussion of "Reason" (§C. (AA); Chapter V), which focuses on reason's "Certainty and Truth," is as important as it is brief and allusive. Careful consideration reveals that in "Reason" Hegel addresses a much broader array not only of philosophical, but also of historical and natural-scientific views and issues than has been recognized previously.

Right at the outset Hegel underscores the novelty of the new figure that has arisen for consciousness, namely reason, which contrasts sharply with the significance of the relation between self and world central to Section B, "Self-Consciousness" (*PS* 132.16–133.5/M 139–40). Up to now all the real finite world of both nature and consciousness's own action and actual doing appeared to self-consciousness as the *negative* of its free and independent essence. To affirm its own nature, it had to struggle *against* reality. It took the world's existence primarily for its will: the world was something desired, but with an independent existence of its own that had to be worked on and transformed to make consciousness self-assured of its own independent reality. In Section B, Hegel's use of the verbs to desire (*begehren*) and to work on (*bearbeiten*) indicates the realm of the practical versus the theoretical, which is indicated by the verb to understand (*verstehen*); indeed, before acquiring reason, self-consciousness does *not* "understand" the world (*PS* 132.30/M 140). In the last figure experienced – Unhappy Consciousness – the absolute essence, i.e., the being-in-itself (*das Ansichsein*), did not inhabit the earth; it was an object of faith as a *transcendent* "beyond." As consciousness that is reason, however, self-consciousness has returned into itself, and it now can convert that negative relation to otherness into a positive one: now "being" (*Sein*) means "what is its own" (*Seinen*). This implies reverting from the practical attitude of considering nature as something that it is for itself to the theoretical-cognitive approach of meaning, perceiving, and understanding, though now the perception and experience of things are no longer something consciousness undergoes, which simply *occur* (*geschehen*) to it. Rather, consciousness now makes *its own* observations; it arranges and performs *its own* experiments (*PS* 137.24–25/M 145). Therefore, the world itself constitutes the "here" and "now" of reason, though no longer according to the merely theoretical significance of being (*Sein*) as the mine that is meant (*mein, meinen*) which merely "happened" to be here and now to Sense-Certainty, which regarded nature only as *das Meinige*, devoid of any independent self. Hegel writes that self-consciousness, as reason, is certain of itself as reality, meaning that everything actual is nothing alien to it, and its thought (*Denken*) is itself *immediately* the actuality of the world (*PS* 132.27–28/M 139). At the beginning of the sub-section of Chapter V dedicated to "Observing Reason," Hegel clarifies the meaning of the observational activity of reason against the background of the positive relation to reality sketched above, by stressing that at this stage to understand the world involves *will*:

> reason *wants* to find and to have itself (*will sich . . . finden, und haben*) as an object that is (*als seyenden Gegenstand*), in an actual, sensuously present manner. (*PS* 138.11–12/M 146).[2]

This active and intended "discovery" of the world is rooted in the "universal *interest*" of reason in it.[3] This is a key point, for it *immediately* links the "changeable" (the particularities of the empirical manifold of appearances) with the "unchangeable" (the permanence and universality of reason's will to find and have herself in a sensuous way) by *understanding* the real world. It underscores that what stands before self-consciousness no longer means *an* "other" that confronted consciousness; it has become the knowing subject's *own* "other," not just for us, but *for* consciousness, which is now certain of its presence in the world.

However, this essential feature contains an inner opposition. On the one hand, it allows us to understand why, a couple years later, Hegel presents the figure of Reason as the highest unification of the knowing of the object as an "other" (that along its theoretical path was in general first meant, then perceived, and then apprehended by the understanding) and the practical knowing of the self, or consciousness of the world of the finite spirit, developed by self-consciousness in Section B.[4] Similarly, at the outset of "Spirit" (*PS*, §BB, Chapter VI) Hegel recapitulates the immediately preceding movement of the coming-to-be of spirit. Here he states: "as immediate consciousness of the *being-in-itself* and the *being-for-itself*, as unity of consciousness and self-consciousness, spirit is consciousness that *has reason*" (*PS* 239.31–33/M 264–5). On the other hand, as Hegel will say in an 1806 lecture fragment on the *Phenomenology*, reason is self-consciousness that has not yet grasped either itself or its object as spirit (Forster 1998, 610): reason is unaware of being "knowing spirit."[5] At the conclusion of "Observing Reason," indeed, Hegel states that the meaning of the result of the itinerary of reason's observational activity is recognizing the reality of self-consciousness, though as an immediate, sensuous object to be perceived. He points out, then, that the result has a *twofold* significance. The first is the 'high' one recalled above, that Hegel calls "its true meaning," because it completes the outcome of the preceding movement of the entire figure of Self-Consciousness (*PS* 190.31–33/M 208). The second is the 'low' one of observing the world aconceptually; that is, by taking and resolving the real presence (*Dasein*) of spirit into a purely objective thinghood. Interestingly enough, as we will see below (chapter 5, §2.3), in his 1762 *Emile*, Rousseau (1969, 4:526) had already warned against the danger of knowing the nature of the human spirit by principles that would *immediately* proceed from sensible to intellectual objects, thus producing an incomprehensible metaphysics, whereas one should follow only the authority of one's own experience and intellectual progress and gauge men solely by their actions, that is, from the standpoint of human history.[6] In the same vein, here Hegel claims that reason is in truth "all reality" *only in the concept*, not in lifeless objects of outer reality such as bones or brain fibers, the observation of which dispenses with the concept (*PS* 191.25–26/M 209). This final remark extends the justification of the charges of formalism advanced in the "Preface" against a certain kind of philosophy of nature (Hansen 1994, 293–307) such as that espoused, for example, by Schelling in his *Darstellung meynes Systems der Philosophie* (1801, §152), where, following Steffens, polarities of inorganic, lifeless nature were taken as "directly represented by or equal to" degrees of organic, living nature.[7] Harris (1999, 41) observes that, "the 'science of experience' is the great corrective for all varieties of 'formalism'." Indeed, in the "Preface," Hegel reacts against the violence suffered by the quiet surface of sensuous data through such associations, "which imparts to them the illusory aspect (*Schein*) of a semblance of the concept but saves itself from expressing the main thing: the concept itself or the meaning of the sensuous representation" (*PS* 37.18–20/M 30).[8]

This first observational step of reason, therefore, is characterized by the conjunction of the 'highest' and the 'lowest'; the depth which spirit brings forth from within itself is joined with the ignorance and "crude" instinct of a consciousness that observes the world, expecting to take things truly insofar as they are taken as sensuous things opposed to the "I" (*PS* 138.28–29/M 147). This will prove to be a "false manifestation." Reason's actual activity, Hegel contends, "contradicts" such a belief (*PS* 138.30–31/M 147), for in fact she "cognizes" (*erkennt*) things, transforming their empirical sensuousness into concepts. According to the paradigm of the living substance that is both being and subject, the movement of positing oneself set forth in the Preface,[9] the "becoming" of rational observing consciousness is its actual activity. This means that the path of reason is to develop what she is within herself, showing to us, through her development, her own inner nature, her *an sich*, and thus becoming for herself what she essentially is.[10]

We shall examine this "contradiction" between the belief of Observing Reason when she looks upon things seeking to possess in thinghood the consciousness only of herself, and the truth revealed to us by her activity. To understand the significance of this double characterization, however, we must understand the chapter's place in the overall economy of Hegel's book; thus we shall begin with some brief remarks concerning the phenomenological transition to "Reason."[11]

1.1 The transition to reason

As Hegel himself points out at the very beginning of "The Certainty and Truth of Reason," the dialectic of Consciousness (of meaning, perception, and understanding) had destroyed the certainty that the being-other of the thing constituted an alien, independent essence, indifferent to the knowing subject.

From the being-other of the object as something alien to consciousness we passed to the object as self-consciousness's *own other* in "Lord and Bondsman," where through service and work, external reality was transformed by obedience and by renouncing individual choice (see above, chapter 2). The freedom and universality of self-consciousness represented by Stoicism and Skepticism, in turn, achieved independence and liberation from the practical and theoretical forms of the self's bondage: affections and desires (in "Stoicism"), and reliance on sense data, on valid rational procedures and argument, and on absolute rules and norms (in "Skepticism"). In this way self-consciousness was subjectively certain of itself as being essential, as pure universal spirituality, though only *against* an internal and external reality to which it denied all value and significance (see above, chapter 3).

The final form of self-consciousness was the internal splitting of self-consciousness into a dual-natured being: on the one side, an entirely individual, changing consciousness that daily experiences what it knows as a vanishing, transient internal and external reality; on the other side, an unchanging consciousness that is projected out of the real world into a transcendent, supersensible "beyond," which appears to the changeable individual consciousness to have a different essential nature. The mediation between the consciousness of singular independent individuality and the consciousness of the supersensible unchangeable occurred thanks to the intermediation of a clergy, a Church (Hyppolite 1974, 212–15), along a confessional path of penance through renunciation, self-alienation, and negation of the individual will, though only because the individual will knows itself as conjoined to a *universal* will.[12] This turn of the singular will from waiting to be redeemed by a transcendent divinity toward "actively bringing" its subjective point of view into line with God's universal will (Pinkard 1994, 77) is a path marked by references to the Lutheran inwardness of evil and power of earthly things. Hegel's *Lectures on the Philosophy of History* make clear that the Reformation (with the doctrine of justification by individual grace and substituting consubstantiation for transubstantiation) spread the consciousness that the Host was simply a wafer, and the Saint's relics were merely bones.[13] It appears that in Hegel's reconstruction it was necessary first to defeat the superstition backed by the Church that associated superhuman virtues with material things (via magic and miracles) in order to treat *both* nature and subjectivity according to their own proper principles: to recognize that the laws of nature were the only link among phenomena and to feel at home in this new world established by the *independent authority* of the *certainty* of rational self-consciousness (cf. *VGP* 9:63.978, 64.985–88, 65.45–66.52). This was, indeed, *also* a path marked by Jesuitical casuistry which, shaking any inward fixed determination about what was evil and what was good, made the elements of the will vacillate: hence it was for spirit itself to be nothing but pure universal activity. According to the historical background retraced in the *Lectures* and presupposed in these pages of the *Phenomenology*, this path reached its climax after the religious wars with the principle of the *freedom of consciousness*.[14]

In the *Phenomenology* Hegel accounts for self-consciousness passing into an immediacy that is "Reason" (Kalenberg 1997, 61ff.) in a single, cryptic sentence.[15] Note, however, that starting from the "struggle for absolute liberation by the consciousness divided against itself," the being-other "that has become something only for consciousness," vanished also for consciousness itself (*PS* 133.20–22/M 140). In this way, the certainty has arisen for consciousness that, *in its particular individuality*, it has being absolutely within itself, or it *is* all reality: it is *reason* that comes to be the unity of thought with the other, the medium or the substantial basis of two traditionally separated extremes: consciousness and the externality of natural things.[16] What stands before consciousness is no longer a beyond with a different substantial nature, as was the case with "Unhappy Consciousness." Contrary to Kant's perspective, the realization of the concept of freedom now determines a *new* (in respect to the Understanding) cognition of nature. To underscore the meaning of inserting "Self-Consciousness" between "Understanding" and "Reason," Hegel writes that for self-consciousness "it is as if now for the first time the world had come into being."[17] Hence that which has the 'highest' significance of thought is reconciliation (*Versöhnung*) between the thinking self of reason and the natural world.[18]

2 The Standpoint of Reason: or When Certainty Is Not Yet Truth

2.1 The idealism of reason

The lowest aspect of reason is brought about by the singularity and immediacy that characterizes this shape of natural consciousness. When Hegel first introduces reason, he underscores that consciousness grasped the thought that the *single* individual consciousness is in itself (*an sich*) absolute essence (*PS* 132.1–2/M 139). A few paragraphs later he explains that this means the simple category of the "I" is the (only) pure essentiality of all there is (*PS* 134.20–24/M 142). The refrain is that individual reason is certain of being *all* reality, of being *every* "in-itself and essential being" (*Ansich und Wesen*). Nevertheless, natural consciousness experiences its new configurations as being *immediately* present, without noticing the processes of mediation that generate them. These processes constitute the truth of consciousness, and the justifications of its forms, though initially only for us. Thus, to the extent that the phenomenological path demonstrates that the immediate appearance of a new form of consciousness is nothing but an abstraction from the actual movement that was in fact present (though apparent only for us) in the experience of the preceding figure, bringing the new one into being, then reason, with her motto: "I am I, my object and my essence is I" (*PS* 134.4/M 141), appears immediately on stage

> only as the *certainty* of that truth. She merely *asserts* that she is all reality, but does not herself comprehend (*begreift*) this; for that forgotten path is the comprehension of this immediately expressed assertion... The idealism that does not exhibit (*darstellt*) that path but begins with this assertion is therefore, likewise, pure *assurance* which does not comprehend itself, nor can it make itself comprehensible to others. It pronounces an *immediate certainty*. (*PS* 133.28–37/M 141)

This passage repeats some polemical warnings against inadequate forms of intelligibility (subjective and objective idealism) of the initial appearance of a new world.[19] Hegel stresses that the phrase, "reason is the certainty of consciousness that it is all reality," is the way in which "idealism" expresses this new figure.[20] It is worth noting that the *allness* to which Hegel here refers signifies also a defective kind of cognition that typifies the initial stage of observing reason, affecting her representational way of thinking. In the way in which, for Hegel, "idealism" expresses this certainty: "all reality is I," or "I am all reality," *allness* is not a true, speculative, rational totality, but merely the abstract form of it, as we may elucidate by focusing on the *logical* form (all A are B) of this initial self-judgment of reason (cf. Chiereghin 1994, 97–100).

Beginning in the *Jena Logic*[21] Hegel treated a kind of judgment where the predicate is not a true universal, the content of the predicate is made up of particulars related only externally, and the subject, which contrasts with its object as something fixed, is thus only reflected immediately into itself (cf. *Enc.* [1817], §328). A passage in the 1804–05 *Logic* states that in the "judgement of allness" the subject is not strictly speaking a self-determining (concrete) universal incorporating all its constituent moments, as, for instance, in the speculative proposition: "the actual is the universal," where the actual as subject is *dissolved* in its predicate thus dissolving also the fixed difference between the two terms (*PS* 44.17–21/M 39),[22] but a particular which is now extended to all instances of that particular as happens with a generic predicate. Thus, it is the *finitude* of both sides, the subject and the predicate, that is, their permanent difference according to the principles of identity and non-contradiction, which typifies both representational thinking (*Vorstellungen*) and "idealism." In being certain of its singularity *directly* joined with the allness of reality, in the sense of the universal subject "I" in immediate unity with the immediacy of being, the self-consciousness that is reason in fact *logically* judges and determines itself in the lowest way, because it looks at perceived things to find *them* in the form of a universal, which turns out to be nothing but a mere act of appropriation in the form of an abstract 'mine': "idealism" with its "I am I" gives *direct expression* to reason's certainty, that, in comparison with the "I" which is an object for me, any other object whatever is a *non-being*, something inessential (cf. *PS* 133.6–14/M 140).[23] At the same time, despite its claims, "idealism" remains within the limits of the representations of a finite subject, insofar as it posits (*setzt*) the cognizant subject as dependent on this relation with finite objects. In his *Lectures on the History of Philosophy* (first delivered in 1805–06) Hegel defines the subjective idealism that arises with modernity in terms of self-consciousness or self-certainty as being all reality and truth, which he views as proceeding from Locke's appeal to experience and perception of the finite as source of truth (see below, note 37). He identifies its worst (*schlechteste*) formulation in the motto "all the objects (*Gegenstände*) are our representations" (*Vorstellungen*; H&S 3:364: "conceptions"), which he traces back to Berkeley and regards as a form of Skepticism, as he holds in the *Phenomenology* (cf. MM 20:270/ H&S 3:363–4, *PS* 136.23–30/M 144).

Though it may be useful to think of Schelling's spinozistic claim in his *Darstellung meines Systems* (§35), that no one individual thing contains the reason for its own existence, because everything is identical according to the essence,[24] interpreters agree in reading these references as drawing from Fichte's first *Wissenschaftslehre* and his *Grundlage der gesamten Wissenschaftslehre*,[25] where the form of subjectivity is the fundamental condition for the explanation of experience, the "I am" is the standpoint of the free rational agent in contrast to things, and the self is nothing more than the product of its free activity (Beiser 2002, 278–88). It is worth recalling here, however, that at the time of the polemical debate about the founders of the "newest philosophy," Fichte was regarded as an "idealist" because he knew (with the same certainty with which one knows of oneself, i.e. with the *highest certainty possible*) that no thing actually exists out of him and that all the things were his own product, which he constructed and produced through the intellectual intuition in his own pure "I" (Nicolai 1801, 4).

Here Hegel's reference to the 'lowest' status of non-being (*Nichtsein*) that idealism bestows upon all the objects of self-consciousness other than the "I" recalls the polemical note against the mistreatment of natural objects in Fichte's system, which explicitly involved Kant's transcendental idealism (*Diff.*, GW 4:8). Indeed, as noted above, at this stage the object of knowing is determined for consciousness as the thing that is also the unity of the "I" and being, which is *categorial thought* as such.[26]

Already in the *Differenzschrift* (1801), Hegel praised the significance of Kant's transcendental deduction of the categories, which Hegel esteemed as pure activities of thought that are also objective determinations. Excepting the modal categories, Kant's deduction of the forms of understanding expressed concretely "the principle of speculation," namely, the "identity of subject and object." Indeed, Hegel stressed that Kant's theory of the understanding was "baptized" by reason (*Diff.*, GW 4:6), though he further noted that when Kant conceived the rational identity of thought and otherness, of subject and object, as reason, this crucial identity vanished, because Kant analyzed it as subjective and formal. Indeed, Kant treated reason with the tools of *abstract* thought, the understanding. Confined to the practical, ideas of reason were opposed to determinate beings. According to Hegel, this was the root of the contrasting result of Kant's first *Critique*: for the understanding, objective determinations were always conditioned, though they had empirical reality; while for reason, objective determinations were absolute, but had no reality (*Diff.*, *GW* 4:6). Consequently, in the third *Critique* an immense empirical realm of sensibility and perception had to remain absolutely *a posteriori*.[27] Considering Hegel's chapter on "Reason" in the *Phenomenology* in the context of this criticism of Kant shows that "Reason," which results from the transition of the theoretical legislation of nature into the practical legislation of freedom (from "Force and Understanding" to "The Truth of Self-Certainty"), and vice versa (from "Unhappy Consciousness" to "The Certainty and Truth of Reason"), aims to fulfill the 'highest' obligation of demonstrating and justifying the *a priori*, the concept (*Begriff*), of sensuous perceived being through the self-superseding of that finitude which characterizes observing reason until her lowest and thus turning point, that is, until the reduction of the infinite nature of the spiritual self of the subject to its predicates as a finite thing in Phrenology (see below, chapter 5, §2.3; cf. *Enc.* §411Z). In his 1821/22 Lectures on the Philosophy of Nature this unification (*Vereinigung*) of the theoretical and practical consideration of nature – according to which, from the theoretical standpoint, nature is not only *das Seiende* but also *das Meinige*, and from the practical standpoint, nature is not only "the selfless" (*das Selbstlose*), but also "what it is for itself" – constitutes the task itself of philosophy, to solve the problem of the subject–object opposition.[28]

To sum up the dialectical movement of this section: although reason is in truth only the universality of things, reason tries to possess herself *in natural things* and not in their essentiality *qua talis*; because natural consciousness's knowing takes sensuous things opposed to the "I," it neglects that reason is present in her own proper shape only in the conceptual inwardness of objective thinghood. This is why, at this stage of consciousness, on the one side, reason's sensuous expression cannot be taken essentially as *concept* (*PS* 138.16–22/M 146); on the other side, reason 'naturally' moves within what in truth is the mediated unity of single individuals with their (concrete) universals (laws, species, and genera), restlessly ranging from the bad infinity of enumerating differences to "articulate conditions of empty self-identities" (Russon 2004, 122).[29]

Within this general frame, we can retrace the unifying themes of Hegel's initial assessment of a variety of issues: the Kantian merely reflective approach to determinate nature; his concept of the synthetic unity of apperception with the related theory of sensibility as a modification of the subject and the problematic, negative concept of the *Ding an sich*; the mere assertive and empty value of the immediate certainty of Fichte's "I am I" in relation to the empirical content of knowing, and Fichte's related conception of the *Anstoß*;[30] all of these points are collected by Hegel as significant articulations, implications, and consequences of the reflective, intellectual expression of the *very first* ("*erst*" is repeated three times in two lines; *PS* 136.14–16/M 144), *abstract* moment of the appearance of the figure of Reason that recognizes herself in externality. The abstract beginning of the certainty of being all reality, endorsed and fixed by idealism, dooms Reason's quest for truth, and raises the problem of how to satisfy the demands of reason and her restless claims to know the world (cf. Lumsden 2003). This is announced at the very beginning of the sub-section on the "Observation of Nature":

But when (*wenn*) reason rummages in the bowels of things and opens all the veins in them in order to be able to spring herself out of them, then (*so*) she will not attain this enjoyment. (*PS* 138.7–9/M 146)

This is an important passage: according to Hegel, reason *has* "hands and feet for digging" (contra Jacobi's quotation of Luke 16:3; *F&K*, *GW* 4:316). Therefore, the *real* ground of reason, which makes her own observations and conducts her own experiments,[31] is *not* the ground identified by Kant's account of the heuristic, merely subjectively valid judgments of the infinite natural realm in the *Critique of Judgment*, which lacks objectivity and stability, and lacks categories and subsumptive judgments. Hegel's polemics in *Faith and Knowledge* (*GW* 4:316) against Kant, Fichte, and Jacobi, for holding that because "the highest Idea does not at the same time have reality," refuge must be taken in faith *beyond* reason, pertains directly to Hegel's key issue in "Reason."[32] Hegel's account of "Reason" in the *Phenomenology* seeks to demonstrate the view of reason Hegel espouses from his early Jena essays right through the *Encyclopedia*: that human self-consciousness, permeating nature with its "veins of objectivity," can make the realm of nature "stand erect," as the king in a fairy tale by Goethe who stands up like a fixed and complete figure (*er als aufgerichtete Gestalt steht*). Indeed, in *Faith and Knowledge* Hegel charges metaphorically that Kant's formal transcendental idealism sucked these veins out of nature, out of the king, so that the upright shape collapses, thus becoming something between "form and lump" (*F&K*, *GW* 4:332).[33]

On the other hand, the passage underscores that reason's demand and quest for meeting and finding herself in the very core of otherness's objectivity and stability, when she opens the veins injected into nature by self-consciousness, is a hopelessly naive illusion. Indeed, the hopeless inadequacy of thinghood to instantiate directly the universality of thought is not yet recognized. This underscores the ways in which self-consciousness, as reason, is not yet spirit, being yet unable to take the presence of reason in the world according to the form of the concept, and to acknowledge the "impotence" of nature to realize the concept.[34]

This further implies, first, that idealism has taken "as the truth" what was only an abstract immediate appearance of our rational understanding of the natural world (*PS* 137.8–9/M 145), looking for and finding directly expressed in the world the same universality of our own thought (cf. *Enc.* §422Z), and, second, that from such a dogmatic move follows the different fates of German Idealism and of Hegel's phenomenological reason: idealism cannot allow any development and depends on an absolute, uncritical empiricism. Indeed, in order to give filling (*Erfüllung*) to a "mine" that is "void," the reason of that idealism "needs an extraneous impact, in which first lies the *multiplicity* of sensations or representations" (*PS* 136.20–23/M 144). The appearance of phenomenological reason, which for itself is forgetful of, though in itself it is brought about by, the previous dialectical movement, is thus something abstract and formal in respect to her own nature, and therefore is impelled (*treiben*) from her depth *instinctively* to raise its certainty to truth and to fill in its empty "mine" (cf. *PS* 137.13–17/M 145; Negele 1991, 80). On my view, although Hegel does not directly say here that idealism also expresses this paradoxical feature of reason, he had it in mind: recall Hegel's 1802 attitude towards Jacobi, whom he charged with giving to reason only the feeling and consciousness of her "ignorance of the true." In *Faith and Knowledge*, Hegel stressed that Jacobi viewed reason as something subjective though universal (*F&K*, *GW* 4:316), and when infinity appears affected by subjectivity, reason is nothing but an instinct (*F&K GW* 4:321). As early as 1802, Kant, Fichte, and Jacobi were already taken as examples of a notion of reason that was "simply and solely directed against the empirical," thus making infinity into something inherently dependent on its relation to empirical finitude (*F&K*, *GW* 4:321).

3 Philosophical Issues: Standard Views and Reappraisals

3.1 The idealism of empiricism

The central philosophical issue in these introductory pages is the proper significance of the idealism of reason. When reason first appears, do we really have Fichte's Ego before us, although we are not yet in Fichte's world (Harris 1997, 1:449; Kojève 1996, 99)? Or are we confronted by idealism as a phenomenon in the history of human consciousness, an idealism that subsequently appeared in abstract form in Kant's and Fichte's philosophies (Hyppolite 1974: 281–4)? Or is Hegel instead presenting the emergence of reason *as* the philosophical position of contemporaneous idealism, thus making the phenomenological development through Unhappy Consciousness *equivalent* to the first statement of Fichte's first *Doctrine of Science* (Kaehler and Marx 1992, 35, 38)? Does Hegel only aim here to come to terms with the history of German Idealism (Bisticas-Cocoves 1998, 163), exposing the weaknesses of this sort of rationalism (Stern 2001, 98ff.)? Moreover, though Hegel does not explicitly refer to Bacon or Descartes, Harris (1997, 1:468) rightly notes that, "We must expect the echoes to go back to the times of Bacon and Descartes; for otherwise there would be an inexplicable gulf between the unmistakable historical references ... to Luther ... and the appearance of Fichte's *Wissenschaftslehre* in 1794."[35]

The interpretation developed above allows us to elucidate these two related interpretive issues. Our analysis of the contradiction between reason's initial belief and her actual observational activity shows that Hegel does not regard his own appraisal of the (Kantian and Fichtean) idealistic expression of the first appearance of reason, dependent on an absolute empiricism, as equivalent to the result of the dialectic of the Unhappy Consciousness, which constitutes the nature or in itself of reason, governing her becoming. We have seen how Reason first appeared as just the certainty and assurance of being the essentiality (the *Ansich*) of things, that is, of being all reality, by clarifying the significance of her first appearance against the background of the independent authority of the individual subject, the freedom of consciousness, and the vanishing of any alien and transcendent essential nature of otherness. In the *Lectures on the History of Philosophy*, Hegel repeatedly stated that Descartes was the first to claim that thought must start from itself and that the freedom and certainty of itself are contained in the principle of the autonomy of thought, rejecting religious presuppositions, ecclesiastic authority, and conditioning from any external givens.[36] Hegel also repeatedly stated, however, that the *cogito*'s standpoint is also Fichte's own point of departure.[37] In his *Grundlage der gesammten Wissenschaftslehre* (1794), Fichte himself acknowledged continuities between his "I am I" and Kant's "I think" in the Transcendental Deduction of the Categories, together with Descartes's "*cogito, ergo sum*," while also distancing his views from theirs. If Kant failed to establish the transcendental "I" as a fundamental principle, Descartes was a forerunner, because the "*ergo*" did not conclude a syllogism but could be regarded "as an immediate *res facti* (*Tatsache*) of consciousness" (*FGA* 2:262.11–14). However, in Fichte's view, Descartes stated that if one thinks, one necessarily is, comprehending thought *merely* as a "special" determination of our being, to which other determinations external to thought were also given (*FGA* 2:262.16–19).

Hegel appears to endorse Fichte's view when he marks the difference between Descartes and Fichte using Fichte's terms. He stresses that for Descartes, after the ego, we find in ourselves also other kinds of thoughts that come from without (MM 20:392/H&S 3:486). For Hegel, Descartes assumes the content of determinate representations empirically; he does not develop determinations such as extension from the "I think," and he does not truly trace them back to thought; he wants only to think, though in fact he takes determinations such as resistance or colors as sensible things. Descartes remains within the limits of subjective, singular consciousness. According to Hegel, what predominates in Descartes is the thinking treatment of the empirical.[38] In contrast, Fichte's needs and summonses are viewed as entirely different: Fichte is the first to propound speculative knowledge as the deduction of determinate thoughts from the free development of the concept in a system of thought, where nothing empirical is taken from without.[39] Thus it is difficult to maintain that the phenomenological appearance of reason really presents "Fichte's Ego," because Hegel does not state that Reason's initial motto can be equated with Fichte's fundamental proposition that thought is the essence of our being because one thinks *necessarily* if one is (*FGA* 2:262.16–17). On the contrary, Observing Reason is defined as an *unthinking* consciousness (*PS* 139.3/M 147), though we should bear in mind a continuity in the *form* of Reason's immediate certainty and assurance between Descartes's "I think" and the theses of German Idealism, to understand Hegel's claim that "idealism" gives direct expression to reason's "I am I."

I propose that Hegel addresses a *common* ground for philosophical consciousness from Descartes to German Idealism's own empty and abstract versions of this stage of cognition, for it appears to me that their lowest common denominator is simply the *general* insight that thought progresses freely in its determinations, making these thought-determinations the intrinsic, objective substantiality of nature.[40] Furthermore, this interpretation properly includes Bacon's approach and contribution.[41] Consider Bacon's *Novum Organum* (Bk. 1, Aph. 124): "I am building in the human understanding a true model of the world, such as it is in fact." Indeed, *pace* Harris, Hegel owned the Frankfurt 1665 edition of Bacon's *Opera Omnia* (cf. Neuser 1987, 481 entry 14) and in his *Lectures on the History of Philosophy*, Hegel refers to Bacon in the same terms of independence from authority and tradition he used for Descartes, thus placing Bacon, too, against an historical background characterized by the same themes of the phenomenological transition from "Unhappy Consciousness" to "Reason," in light of the reconciliation between self and world and the new interest in reality that emerges after the Reformation (MM 20:62–6/H&S 3:158–64). Bacon, Hegel says, looked at the existing world with "open eyes," restoring and recognizing the value and dignity of its presence, showing the trust of reason in herself and in nature when reason turns to the world, thinking about and finding truth in it (MM 20:77/H&S 3:174). These features clearly fit the interpretation proposed above, and they match Hegel's sketch in the *Phenomenology* of the emergence of Reason (cf. *VGP* 9:73.77–74.96); hence they should have a proper place in Hegel's 1807 agenda (see Arndt 2006, 263).

However, this common position was expressly ascribed by Hegel to phenomenological Reason and to idealism, whereas Hegel's *Lectures* cite Bacon as the leader of the troops of every philosophy of experience (MM 20:74/H&S 3:172; cf. *VGP* 9:73.58, 75.148). At first sight, it seems that Hegel takes Bacon's empirical philosophy simply as a kind of knowledge drawn from experience which is its sole legitimate source, and therefore opposed to any kind of knowledge that derives from the concept, in other words, opposed to any principle of the autonomous generation of thought from thought, as Hegel saw in Descartes.[42] When introducing the Modern age in the *Lectures*, Hegel distinguished between a realistic form of philosophizing, for which the objectivity and content of thought arises from perception, proceeding from without, on the part of the object, and an idealistic form of philosophizing that reaches truth through the autonomy of thought, proceeding from within, on the part of the subject.[43] To stop with this division, however, would occlude how Hegel regards this prima facie contrast between experience and speculation as abstract and one-sided, as if the concept should be ashamed of empirical knowledge and empirical knowledge were devoid of conceptual elements (MM 20:78/H&S 3:175). More importantly, from the contrast between realism and idealism Hegel does *not* draw the conclusion that Bacon's philosophy depends on an absolute and abstract empiricism of the finite, whose form of activity is restricted to formal identity and which dissolves the concrete given by isolating its distinct features. It also does *not* follow that Bacon's empiricism amounts to merely recording facts as they accidentally occur. Finally, that contrast does not entail that Bacon's position is utterly foreign to idealism. Rather, Hegel underscores that experience, *as Bacon understands it*, is methodical inquiry, giving order to thought with regard to things; it is not merely observational, a simple hearing, feeling, and perceiving of particulars, because it essentially aims *to discover universals* in the form of classifications and laws.[44] Indeed, Hegel appears to ascribe to Bacon an 'understanding consciousness', which remains within the limits of finite cognition, though its method is "the concrete way of knowing"

(*VGP* 9:72.41), consisting "in leaving the concrete as *ground* and making a concrete universal – the *genus*, or force and law – stand out through abstraction from the particularities that seem to be inessential" (*Enc.* §227, cf. Hegel 1992, 184.254–59). On my view, this must not be confused with the first, simple significance of the analytical way of theoretical cognition, which starts with the isolated single being and changes it into the abstract form of a universal: this (Lockean) way takes the given immediate singularity of the perceived "sensible this" as the ground for truth (Hegel 1992, 184.245–46). On the contrary, Bacon is seen to derive *determinations* from an already conceptualized experience, mediated by observations and experiments (*VGP* 9:77.222–228). In other words, it seems to me that Hegel ascribes to Bacon the standpoint with which he opens the section on reason observing nature: observation requires advancing from perception to thought; a mere perception cannot pass for an observation because what is perceived should at least have the significance of a *universal*, not of a *sensuous particular* (*PS* 139.12–13/M 147). In this respect, Bacon's empiricism looks more advanced than the crude one presupposed and implied by subjective idealism. The counterpart to Hegel's appreciation of this concrete kind of finite cognition is his criticism of any natural history or empirical science that merely collects individual facts, extraneously determined by chance rather than reason (*Enc.* §16R). The main target of Hegel's criticism is not empirical science as such, but rather any formal and external method of collecting data, to which Hegel opposes experimental sciences that "make sense," thanks to the order given to phenomena by "insightful intuition" (*Enc.* §16R; Moretto 2004, 30). It thus appears clear how, due to this 'concrete universal' aspect of Bacon's experimental philosophy, Hegel claims in the *Lectures on the History of Philosophy* that, despite the prima facie opposition between speculation and experience, in natural science realism meets idealism, to the extent that experience seeks to draw universal laws from observations.[45]

From this standpoint, it becomes clear that Hegel's discussion of the certainty and truth of Reason not only shows us the degree of realism involved in Descartes's idealism, when, beyond the ego, he finds in himself also other kinds of thoughts that come from without; or that the abstract formalism of German Idealism depends on an absolute empiricism, namely, on a crude, uncritical, extraneous impact to give filling to its empty "mine"; rather, Hegel appears also to point out, conversely, the idealistic side of "concrete" empiricism, which includes not just Bacon, but also Kepler's laws of planetary orbits. Indeed, consistently from *De orbitis* (1801) to the *Encyclopedia* (1830), Hegel recognized Kepler's merit in his *empirical* discovery of physical *laws* through *induction*, extracting from single phenomena their own universal law, assuming in his observational activity the absolute "faith" that reason works in nature.[46] This is precisely the same instinctive force that ceaselessly drives Reason in the *Phenomenology* (cf. Hegel 1801, 31.21–25/*GW* 5:252.15–18), guiding her search for her presence in nature, though also counteracting any simple satisfaction through any direct mirroring in sensuous things in her immediate certainty, which would lead her to depend upon her relation to externality, as Hegel saw expressed by "idealism."

In sum, the essential universality to which natural things are necessarily raised insofar as they are thought has been demonstrated to be no mere subjective move of merely heuristic value for our scientific cognition. Empirical data have their own universal expression, and this is actually real in the concrete realm of nature. This was Hegel's conclusion about laws of nature in "Force and Understanding," and neglecting the significance of this conclusion was one of Hegel's central criticisms of "Self-Consciousness." This is also what Hegel indicated in the *Encyclopedia* as the *common* ground of empiricism and philosophy of nature, which can and must make use of the material that physics has developed by drawing from experience, because empirical physics, although it is not comprehending (*begreifende*), speculative cognition, is nevertheless thinking (*denkende*) cognition of nature (*Enc.* §246 & Z).

In showing us the idealistic side of concrete empiricism, the phenomenological reason that emerges from the dialectical consummation of faith in a beyond also links the principle of realism to the movement of the absolute liberation of self-consciousness: "In Empiricism there lies this great principle, that what is true must be in actuality and must be there for our perception" (*Enc.* §38R). For the *Phenomenology*, rational, judicious (*sinnige*)[47] experience, in which consciousness has its own immediate *presence*, begins by observing the world, freed from the teleological and pseudo-empirical premises of Scholasticism, from the authority of both tradition and religion, from faith in miracles, from superstition, from the uncontrolled individualism of mere argumentation, from the ambiguity and variation of chance, and from the superficiality of mere experience (cf. *VGP* 9:78.242–244). The question, then, is how reason can make good on that great principle found in empiricism.

Notes

1   Both this chapter and the following one are based on research conducted in Jena's libraries (March 2005), thanks to the substantial financial support of the Alexander von Humboldt-Stiftung and funds from the 2004–2006 Italian National Research Project, "Lo studio della 'natura umana' tra filosofia e nuovi campi disciplinari: il caso della Germania e la scienza europea 1790–1830."
2   In both this chapter and in the following all translations have been amended by the author, even when translations are cited. The Editor has provided references to H&S and to Sibree (Hegel 1963).
3   *PS* 137.29/M 145–6. The same expression, "universal interest," also occurs in parallel passages in which Hegel refers to the sixteenth century (MM 12:521/Sibree 439); cf. "The present world was once again present as worthy of spirit's interest" (MM 20:62/ H&S 3:159).
4   See *Phil. Prop.*, *Bewußtseinslehre für die Mittelklasse*, §40/G&V:63.
5   The lecture fragment is published in Rosenkranz (1844, 212–14), and reprinted in *GW* 5:473–4. The passage relevant here is *GW* 5:474.5–10. – *Ed.*
6   On the direct influence of Rousseau's *Emile* on the young Hegel's conception of human nature (1792/1793–94) and his later philosophical development see de Angelis (1995, 230–75).
7   *PS* 491, editorial note to *GW* 9:37.13–15.

8   Cf. also the polemics against the monochromatic formalism of any conception of the identity of the Absolute as principle and abstract universality versus the self-determining difference of forms in the becoming of the being-in-itself of things (*PS* 16.22–17.33/M 8–9).
9   *PS* 10.12–19, 10.34–11.4, 18.18–28, 19.28–20.25/M 2, 10, 11–12.
10 *PS* 138.35–36/M 147. McCumber (1999, 143) holds that Hegel does not really reject the Kantian concept of the in-itself: "rather, he rethinks its relation to experience . . . What he has in mind is the characteristics a thing has that are, indeed, unexperienceable – but only because they are still latent within the thing, have not yet been brought out by its development."
11 See Chiereghin (1997, 26–32); Verra (1999, 43–50).
12 Harris (1997, 1:433–6, 447–9); Kimmerle (1978, 288).
13 MM 12:522/Sibree 440; see also *VGP* 9:63.980–81. In his *Lectures on the History of Philosophy*, Hegel plays with the double meaning of *eigen*, "singular" and "proper own": the Lutheran faith, which dispenses with works, is defined in terms of the singular (individual) spirit that self-appropriates the eternal to itself: *der eigene Geist macht sich für sich das Ewige zu eigen* (MM 20:63/H&S 3:159; see also *VGP* 9:64.12–15, 70.183–89). On the new kind of human substantiality that emerges from the religious debate of the sixteenth century, see Proß (2000) (on Erasmus, Luther, and Calvin see ibid., 93–102). Hegel refers our appropriation of the external world to Bacon, and our appropriation of our inwardness to Böhme (*VGP* 9:259, editorial note to 70.184–89).
14 Note that, contrary to the view influenced also by Gaetano Filangieri that the ideas of human rights and the certainty of freedom were due to the policy pursued by the Enlightened Absolutism of the eighteenth century against religious fanaticism and feudal anarchy, at Hegel's time the emergence of freedom of thought had been retrospectively retraced to the context of Reformation and the Netherlands' revolution by Schiller's 1787 *Don Carlos*, Sc. X, Act III. An implicit issue here is whether the *Phenomenology* is and can be interpreted as a philosophy of history or as a psychology just because its dialectical movements must appeal to forms of consciousness of concrete human subjects. Peperzak (2001, 151–8) carefully distinguishes between "the story of actual individuals" and the elements, dimension or moments of human spirit.
15 Stern (2001, 95–6); cf. Pöggeler (1973), Pippin (1993, 52–7).
16 In the 1830 *Encyclopedia*'s "Anthropology" (§394Z), we find *das Vernunftige* defined as bringing together that which is separated by the understanding, although this form of the rational is not yet comprehending cognition (*des begreifenden Erkennens*). (On Hegel's account and critique of "individuality," see below, chapters 6, 7, and 10. – *Ed.*)
17 *PS* 132.29–30/M 139–40; cf. MM 12:521/Sibree 440. The point is overlooked by M. Westphal (1998, 97).
18 See MM 12:521/Sibree 439): "Spirit has now arrived at the stage of thought which contains the reconciliation in its utterly pure essentiality, for it approaches what is external with the demand that it have in it (*in sich*) the same reason as the subject has." Reconciliation (*Versöhnung*) is a central theme in Hegel's *Phenomenology*; see the index for references.
19 *PS* 15.22–18.2/M 7–9; cf. Maesschalck (2000). This passage also recalls Hegel's concern with Pyrrhonian Skepticism and *petitio principii*; see above, pp. 2–3, 9, 60–64. – *Ed.*
20 Note that already in *Faith and Knowledge* for Hegel "idealism" (Kant's task) meant that thought was objective (see Baum 1989, 198ff.). On the philosophical, essential distinction between the concept of truth and mere certainty, see *Enc.* §416Z.
21 *L&M* (*GW* 7:83): "a *one*, taken up in universality, expresses itself as allness, and the judgment 'All A are B' . . . determines the subject equally well as negative one and also

as something universal. This restoration of particularity in universality itself, however, is not a positing of what the subject as such is. The subject should be on its own account, and precisely as subject. Yet as allness it is in fact not subject but has the universality of a predicate and is something particular simply and solely in this connection with it."

22 See the entire argument of *PS* 41.24–44.37/M 35–9.
23 This self-conception echoes that of the initial forms of Self-Consciousness; see above, chapter 1. – *Ed.*
24 According to Harris (1997, 1:456), Spinoza's *Ethics* is the paradigm of the certainty of reason of being all reality, having it implicitly within itself.
25 See Kaehler and Marx (1992, 35–7), Düsing (1993, 250–6), Harris (1997, 1:449, 452–5), Stern (2001, 98ff.)
26 *PS* 190.36–191.2/M 208–9; cf. K. R. Westphal (1989, 165) and Harris (1997, 1:462–5).
27 See parallel passages in *F&K* (*GW* 4:332–3) and MM 20:376/H&S 3:476–7.
28 See Bonsiepen (1985, 9). On the point cf. Wahsner (1996, 23–4).
29 Cf. *PS* 136.6–9/M 144 and Hegel's Introduction (*PS* 54.30–55.30/M 49–50).
30 See *PS* 498, editorial notes to 133.6–9, 137.4–7.
31 This sense of a strategy really pursued by reason is overlooked by Miller's rendering of "*wenn*" with the hypothetical "even if" (M 146), which omits Hegel's attention to time in this passage. Also, he does not translate "*so*," thus missing Hegel's construction "*wenn . . . so*," which parallels the subsequent unambiguously temporal phrase "*vorher . . . dann*" (*PS* 138.10/M 146).
32 On Jacobi's rejection of the possibility of a philosophical scientific knowing that grasps the quality of natural existence, the sole genuine scientific method being the analytical one of mathematics and logic, see Verra (1976, 52–3).
33 Compare two parallel passages from *Faith and Knowledge*: "Objectivity and stability (*Halt*) derive solely from the categories . . . For the cognition (*Erkenntnis*) of nature, without the veins injected into nature by self-consciousness, there remains nothing but sensation" (*F&K*, *GW* 4:332); "But nature is not just something fixed (*fest*) and complete (*fertig*) on its own account, which could therefore subsist even without spirit" (*Enc.* §96Z).
34 See Lacroix (1997, 42–61), Collins (2000), Marmasse (2003), Ferrini (2004).
35 In Harris's view (1997, 1:470, note 8), however, this echo of Bacon would be based on second-hand knowledge.
36 MM 20:126, 130, 134–5/H&S 3:224, 227–8, 231–2. See also *VGP* 9:92.676–83.
37 MM 20:130, 132, 394/H&S 3:228, 230, 485. In Hegel's view, Descartes and Fichte share the same starting point, though only Fichte sought to develop all the determinations from the "I," from what is absolutely certain (MM 20:132/H&S 3:230; cf. *VGP* 9:93.719–21). Hegel (*Enc.* §64R) writes that Descartes's statements on the very first nature of the simple conscious intuition of the *cogito*, of the inseparability of my being and my thought, are "so eloquent and precise that the modern theses of Jacobi and others about this immediate connection can only count as superfluous repetitions." When retracing theoretical continuities between modern and contemporary thought in 1802, Hegel regards Kant's "formal" idealism as a development of Locke's empiricism (*F&K*, *GW* 4:333; see Nuzzo (2003, 83–8); cf. also *Enc.* §40). From this standpoint, it is worth noting that in his *Lectures on the History of Philosophy*, Hegel criticizes Kant's notion of experience, objecting that, in Kant's view, 'experience' or 'observation' (*Betrachtung*) of the world can have no other meaning than to state that "here is a candlestick, there a snuff-box (*Tabackdose*)" (MM 20:352/H&S 3:444–5). The same point is made, using the same word, *Tabackdose*, in *PS* 139.10–11/M 147, when Hegel writes that also the unthinking consciousness that declares observation and experience to be the ground for truth "will not let, e.g. the perception that this

penknife lies alongside this snuff-box, pass for an observation" (see below, chapter 5, §1.1).
38 MM 20:126, 130–1, 132, 146, 151/H&S 3:224, 227–8, 229, 241, 246; cf. *VGP* 9:95.784–96.802, 99.903–8, 100.956–58.
39 MM 20:132, 153, 391–2/*H&S* 3:228, 248, 485.
40 See above, pp. 55–58, for discussion of Hegel's account of thought; also see Houlgate (2005, 78). – *Ed.*
41 Pinkard (1994, 80–1, 327–73 note 6); Forster (1998, 327).
42 Endorsing what Popper called the "myth of Bacon" in his *Conjectures and Refutations* (1963), neo-positivists and epistemologists have often taken Bacon as a mere empiricist, who grounded scientific discoveries only on facts and mere observations, regarding theories as superfluous and misleading. Nisbet (1972, 26–30) has shown how this reading was anticipated by Goethe, soon after the publication of the *Phenomenology*. Rossi (1986, 98–117) strongly criticizes Popper's (and Lakatos's) interpretation, by stressing the theoretical implications of Bacon's notion of experience.
43 MM 20:77–9/H&S 3:175–6. In the post-Kantian debate, realism was a view that assigned to the intellect in itself (*an sich*) no other specific property than a pure receptivity, while idealism raised the question whether in the human intellect a pure cognition is given, and whether space and time are the forms of sensibility (see Wrede 1791, §1:6–7). Hegel also finds the finitude of cognition in representations of the material as something given and of the intellect as *tabula rasa* (*Enc.* §226Z).
44 Cf. MM 20:79/H&S 3:176; *VGP* 9:77.222–28; *Enc.* §38. Hegel's appreciation of the conceptual features of Bacon's attitude towards experience can be easily retraced in many aphorisms of Book 1 of the *Novum Organum*, such as Aph. 82 (for the notion of *experientia ordinata* and *bene condita* in contrast to *casus et experientia vaga et incondita*); Aph. 95 (for the rational aspect of a genuine experimental philosophy); Aph. 98 (for the methodical requirements of the genuine empirical inquiry: verification, enumeration, pondering, measuring); Aph. 102 (for the disposition and coordination in tables of the collected empirical material). See also Book 2, Aph. 1, where the task and aim of science is the discovery of the *Form* of nature, which in Aph. 2 is defined as the *law* according to which the qualities gather themselves in things. (Unless otherwise indicated, all references to Bacon's aphorisms are to Book 1; also see the later references to the notion of form in Book 2 elucidated in *VGP* 9:268–9, editorial note to 77.225–28).
45 MM 20:67–8/H&S 3:163–4.
46 *Enc.* §270Z, cf. §21Z and §422Z, where Hegel says that the third of Kepler's laws is to be grasped according to the internal necessary unity of its determinations (space and time) only by the speculative thought of reason (*Vernunft*); at the same time, however, he stresses that this law was already (*schon*) discovered by the "understanding consciousness" (*verständigen Bewußtsein*) in the multiplicity of appearances, for the laws are the determinations of the *Verstand* that inhabits the world itself, in which the understanding consciousness finds its own nature and takes itself as object.
47 "*Sinnig*" means "sensible," as the English say, meaning "making good sense" rather than nonsense.

References

Angelis, M. de (1995) *Die Rolle des Einflusses von J. J. Rousseau auf die Herausbildung von Hegels Jugendideal. Ein Versuch, die "dunklen Jahre" (1789–1792) der Jugendentwicklung Hegels zu erhellen*. Frankfurt am Main: P. Lang.
Arndt, A. (2006) "Idealismus," in P. Cobbes et al. (eds.), *Hegel-Lexicon* (pp. 262–64). Darmstadt: Wissenschaftliche Gesellschaft.

Baum, M. (1989) *Die Entstehung der Hegelschen Dialektik*, 2nd ed. Bonn: Bouvier.
Beiser, F. (2002) *German Idealism: The Struggle Against Subjectivism 1781–1801*. Cambridge Mass.: Harvard University Press.
Bisticas-Cocoves, M. (1998) "The Path of Reason in Hegel's Phenomenology of Spirit," in D. Köhler and O. Pöggeler (eds.), *G. W. F. Hegel: Phänomenologie des Geistes* (pp. 163–82). Berlin: Akademie Verlag.
Bonsiepen, W. (1985) "Hegels Raum-Zeit-Lehre. Dargestellt anhand zweier Vorlesungs-Nachschriften," *Hegel–Studien* 20: 39–61.
Chiereghin, F. (1994) *La "Fenomenologia dello spirito" di Hegel. Introduzione alla lettura*. Roma: La Nuova Italia Scientifica.
Chiereghin, F. (1997) "Gli anni di Jena e la *Fenomenologia*," in C. Cesa (ed.), *Hegel. Fenomenologia, Logica, Filosofia della natura, Morale, Politica, Estetica, Religione, Storia* (pp. 3–37). Roma-Bari: Laterza.
Collins, A. B. (2000) "Hegel's Unresolved Contradiction: Experience, Philosophy, and the Irrationality of Nature," *Dialogue* 39: 771–96.
Düsing, K. (1993) "Der Begriff der Vernunft in Hegels *Phänomenologie*," in H. F. Fulda and R.-P. Horstmann (eds.), *Vernunftbegriffe in der Moderne* (pp. 245–60). Stuttgart: Klett-Cotta.
Ferrini, C. (2004). "Being and Truth in Hegel's Philosophy of Nature," *Hegel-Studien* 37: 69–90.
Forster, M. N. (1998) *Hegel's Idea of a Phenomenology of Spirit*. Chicago: University of Chicago Press.
Hansen, F.-P. (1994) *Hegels "Phänomenologie des Geistes."* Würzburg: Königshausen & Neumann.
Harris, H. S. (1997) *Hegel's Ladder*, Vol. I: *The Pilgrimage of Reason*. Cambridge, Mass.: Hackett Publishing Co.
Harris, H. S. (1999) "Hegel's Intellectual Development to 1807," in F. C. Beiser (ed.), *The Cambridge Companion to Hegel* (pp. 25–51). Cambridge: Cambridge University Press (rpt. 1st ed. 1993).
Hegel, G. W. F. (1801) *Dissertatio philosophica de orbitis planetarum*. Jena: Prager.
Hegel, G. W. F. (1963) *Lectures on the Philosophy of History*, tr. J. Sibree. London: Bell & Daldy (1872); rpt. London: Routledge & Kegan Paul.
Hegel, G. W. F. (1992) *Vorlesungen über Logik und Metaphysik. Heidelberg 1817. Mitgeschrieben von F. A. Good*, ed. K. Gloy et al. Hamburg: F. Meiner.
Houlgate, S. (2005) *An Introduction to Hegel: Freedom, Truth and History*. Oxford: Blackwell.
Hyppolite, J. (1974) *Genesis and Structure of Hegel's Phenomenology of Spirit*, tr. S. Cherniak and J. Heckman. Evanston, IL: Northwestern University Press.
Kaehler, K. E. and W. Marx (1992) *Die Vernunft in Hegels Phänomenologie des Geistes*. Frankfurt am Main: V. Klostermann.
Kalenberg, T. (1997) *Die Befreiung der Natur. Natur und Selbstbewußtsein in der Philosophie Hegels*. Hamburg: F. Meiner.
Kimmerle, H. (1978). *Sein und Selbst. Untersuchung zur kategorialen Einheit von Vernunft und Geist in Hegels "Phänomenologie des Geistes."* Bonn: Bouvier Verlag Herbert Grundmann.
Kojève, A. (1996) *Introduction à la lecture de Hegel. Leçons sur la Phénomenologie de l'Esprit professéés de 1933 à 1939*. (Originally published 1947.) Italian trans. by G. F. Frigo. Milano: Adelphi.
Lacroix, A. (1997) *Hegel. La philosophie de la nature*. Paris: Presses Universitaires de France.
Lumsden, S. (2003) "Satisfying the Demands of Reason: Hegel's Conceptualization of Experience," *Topoi* 22: 41–53.
Marmasse, G. (2003) "La philosophie de la nature dans l'*Encyclopédie* de Hegel," *Archives de Philosophie* 66: 211–36.

McCumber, J. (1999) "Schiller, Hegel and the Aesthetics of German Idealism," in M. Baur and D. O. Dahlstrom (eds.), *The Emergence of German Idealism* (pp. 133–46). Washington D.C.: The Catholic University of America Press.

Maesschalck, M. (2000) "Construction et réduction. Le conflit des philosophies de la nature chez Fichte et Schelling entre 1801 et 1806," in O. Bloch (ed.), *Philosophies de la nature* (pp. 217–26). Paris: Publications de la Sorbonne.

Moretto, A. (2004) *Filosofia della matematica e della meccanica nel sistema hegeliano*, 2nd ed. Verona: Il Poligrafo.

Negele, M. (1991) *Grade der Freiheit. Versuch einer Interpretation von G. W. F. Hegels "Phänomenologie des Geistes."* Würzburg: Königshausen & Neumann.

Neuser, W. (1987) "Die naturphilosophische und naturwissenschaftliche Literatur aus Hegels privater Bibliothek," in M. J. Petry (ed.), *Hegel und die Naturwissenschaften* (pp. 479–99). Stuttgart-Bad Cannstatt: Frommann-Holzboog.

Nicolai, F. (1801) *Ueber die Art wie vermittelst des transcendentalen Idealismus ein wirklich existirendes Wesen aus Principien konstruirt werden kann.* Berlin and Stettin (n.p.).

Nisbet, H. B. (1972) *Goethe and the Scientific Tradition.* London: Institute of Germanic Studies/University of London.

Nuzzo, A. (2003) "Sinnliche und übersinnliche Erkenntnis. Das Problem des Empirismus in Hegels *Glauben und Wissen*," in K. Vieweg and B. Bowman (eds.), *Wissen und Begründung. Die Skeptizismus-Debatte um 1800 im Kontext neuzeitlicher Wissenskonzeptionen. Kritisches Jahrbuch der Philosophie* 8, pp. 75–92.

Peperzak, A. (2001) *Modern Freedom. Hegel's Legal, Moral, and Political Philosophy.* Dordrecht: Kluwer.

Pinkard, T. (1994) *Hegel's Phenomenology. The Sociality of Reason.* Cambridge: Cambridge University Press.

Pippin, R. (1993) "You Can't Get There from Here: Transition Problems in Hegel's *Phenomenology of Spirit*," in F. C. Beiser (ed.), *The Cambridge Companion to Hegel* (pp. 52–85). Cambridge: Cambridge University Press.

Pöggeler, O. (1973) "Die Komposition der *Phänomenologie des Geistes*," in H. F. Fulda and D. Henrich (eds.), *Materialen zu Hegels "Phänomenologie des Geistes"* (pp. 329–90). Frankfurt am Main: Suhrkamp.

Proß, W. (2000) "Le péché et la constitution du sujet à la Renaissance," *Rue Descartes* 27: 79–116.

Rosenkranz, K. (1844) *Georg Wilhelm Friedrich Hegel's Leben beschrieben durch Karl Rosenkranz.* Berlin: Duncker & Humblot.

Rossi, P. (1986) *I ragni e le formiche. Un'apologia della storia della scienza.* Bologna: Il Mulino.

Rousseau, J.-J. (1969) *Emile ou de l'Education*, in B. Gagnebin and M. Raymond (eds.), Jean-Jacques Rousseau, *Oeuvres Complètes*, IV. Paris: Gallimard.

Russon, J. (2004). *Reading Hegel's Phenomenology.* Bloomington and Indianapolis: Indiana University Press.

Stern, R. (2001). *Hegel and the Phenomenology of Spirit.* London: Routledge.

Verra, V. (1976) "La qualità nell'età romantica," in E. R. Lorch (ed.), *La qualità* (pp. 51–62; discussion: 63–77). Bologna: Il Mulino.

Verra, V. (1999) *Introduzione a Hegel*, 9th ed. Roma-Bari: Laterza.

Wahsner, R. (1996) *Zur Kritik der Hegelschen Naturphilosophie. Über ihren Sinn im Lichte der heutigen Naturerkenntnis.* Frankfurt am Main: P. Lang.

Westphal, K. R. (1989) *Hegel's Epistemological Realism. A Study of the Aim and Method of Hegel's Phenomenology of Spirit.* Dordrecht: Kluwer.

Westphal, M. (1998) *History & Truth in Hegel's Phenomenology*, 3rd ed. Bloomington and Indianapolis: Indiana University Press.

Wrede, E. G. F. (1791) *Antilogie des Realismus und Idealismus. Zur nähern Prüfung der ersten Grundsätze des Leibnizischen und Kantischen Denksystems.* Halle: Francke und Bispink.

Further Reading

Americks, K. (2000) "Introduction: Interpreting German Idealism," in K. Ameriks (ed.), *The Cambridge Companion to German Idealism* (pp. 1–17). Cambridge: Cambridge University Press.

Becker, W. (1971) *Hegels "Phänomenologie des Geistes." Eine Interpretation* (pp. 78–81). Stuttgart: W. Kohlhammer.

Bonsiepen, W. (1981) "Zu Hegels Auseinandersetzung mit Schellings Naturphilosophie in der '*Phänomenologie des Geistes*'," in L. Hasler (ed.), *Schelling. Seine Bedeutung für eine Philosophie der Natur und Geschichte* (pp. 167–72). Stuttgart-Bad Cannstatt: Frommann-Holzboog.

Buhr, M. (1984) "Absolute Vernunft – ein Oxymoron? Zum Verhältnis von absoluter und historischer Vernunft," in D. Henrich and R.-P. Horstmann (eds.), *Hegels Logik der Philosophie. Religion und Philosophie in der Theorie des absoluten Geist* (pp. 99–105). Stuttgart: Klett-Cotta.

Doz, A. (1993) "La distinction hégélienne de raison et entendement est-elle éclairante pour nous aujourd'hui?," in H. F. Fulda and R.-P. Horstmann (eds.), *Vernunftbegriffe in der Moderne* (pp. 237–44). Stuttgart: Klett-Cotta.

Falke G.-H. H. (1996) *Begriffene Geschichte. Das historische Substrat und die systematische Anordnung der Bewußtseingestalten in Hegels Phänomenologie des Geistes. Interpretation und Kommentar* (pp. 160–94). Berlin: Lukas Verlag.

Hartmann, N. (1929) *Die Philosophie des deutschen Idealismus*, II: *Hegel*. Berlin and Leipzig: W. de Gruyter.

Horstmann, R.-P. (2003). "Den Verstand zur Vernunft bringen? Hegels Auseinandersetzung mit Kant in der *Differenzschrift*," in W. Welsch and K. Vieweg (eds.), *Das Interesse des Denkens. Hegels aus heutiger Sicht* (pp. 89–108). München: W. Fink.

Kohl, E. (2003) *"Gestalt." Untersuchungen zu einem Grundbegriff in Hegels Phänomenologie des Geistes* (pp. 137–45). München: H. Utz.

Nuzzo, A. (1993) "Vernunft und Verstand – Zu Hegels Theorie des Denkens," in H. F. Fulda and R.-P. Horstmann (eds.), *Vernunftbegriffe in der Moderne* (pp. 261–85). Stuttgart: Klett-Cotta.

Pinkard, T. (2000) "Hegel's Phenomenology and Logic: An Overview," in K. Ameriks (ed.), *The Cambridge Companion to German Idealism* (pp. 161–79). Cambridge: Cambridge University Press.

Scheier, C.-A. (1986) *Analytischer Kommentar zu Hegels Phänomenologie des Geistes* (pp. 148–64). Freiburg and München: K. Alber.

Solomon, R. C. (1983) *In the Spirit of Hegel. A Study of G. W. F. Hegel's Phenomenology of Spirit* (pp. 301–T411). New York and Oxford: Oxford University Press.

Valenza, P. (1999) *Logica e filosofia pratica nello Hegel di Jena* (pp. 203–97). Padova: Cedam.

Vetö, M. (1998) *Etudes sur l'idéalisme allemand* (pp. 11–24). Paris: L'Harmattan.

Vinci, P. (1999) *"Coscienza infelice" e "Anima bella." Commentario alla Fenomenologia dello spirito di Hegel*. Milano: Guerini & Ass.

5

Reason Observing Nature

Cinzia Ferrini

1 The Dialectic of Reason Observing Nature

1.1 External descriptions and internal differences in the classification of nature

Hegel's basic speculative thesis is that "the true is actual and must exist" (*Enc.* §38Z).[1] This is the 'highest' justification of empiricism and of reason's drive to seek its infinite determinations *in* the world, because this is the reason for the collapse of the empty "beyond." However, this thesis also contains the unavoidable 'lowest' inadequacy of the particular sensible "this here" to be what is true, because the truth of things does not genuinely exist in external finitude, but in thought: whatever is external is merely true in itself. Therefore, although empiricism contains the principle of freedom (*Enc.* §38), one is only truly free in thinking, while in an important sense, as finite cognition that has the significance *only* of abstraction and formal identity that seizes upon isolated aspects of the concrete without integrating them, empiricism remains a doctrine of unfreedom.[2] The observed and experienced content which consciousness as Reason takes as the source of truth cannot, for consciousness itself, any longer have the form of the immediacy of sense-certainty or perception.[3] This is Hegel's first point at the beginning of "Observation of Nature," when considering the role and limits of description and classification in empirical sciences. This point has been relatively neglected by commentators, though it is extremely instructive.

Hegel's analysis starts by remarking that "observation" requires advancing from perception to thought: for consciousness itself, despite its declarations, a mere perception cannot pass for an observation because "what is perceived should at least have the significance of a *universal*, not of a *sensuous this*" (*eines sinnlichen diesen*: PS 139.12–13/M 147). The positive side is represented by the necessity to begin to distinguish in order to comprehend; initially cognition is, and must be, analytic (*Enc.* §§38Z, 227Z). When empiricism analyzes objects by distinguishing and isolating their various features, these features acquire the form of universality by being separated. Yet this highlights the first inconvenience of *description*, the *superficiality* of abstracting universals from particulars and the consequent instability and arbitrariness of these general forms under which things are merely subsumed (*PS* 139.20–24/M 147–8). Moreover, description is accompanied by the false consciousness that supposes it leaves objects as they are (Russon 2004, 119). Description appears to be passive (*Enc.* §226Z), whereas in fact reason actively transforms the sensuous being of a concrete individual existing (and perishing) lion into the particularization of a universal nature (the species *Lion*) that does not exist as such, although it persists through time (*Enc.* §24Z). Similarly, description loses the vital connection of the parts when it transforms a piece of meat into a series of its (dead) chemical components, which are nothing but abstract *thought*-determinations. In the *Encyclopedia* Hegel makes this last point by referring to Goethe's *Faust*, thus using a poetic criticism of the *absoluteness* of the standpoint of analytical division (*Enc.* §38Z).[4]

Recent scholarship has stressed that Hegel criticizes the logical procedures and metaphysical presuppositions of the working scientist's activity.[5] Unlike Schelling, who engaged in the scientific debate of the time, Hegel is thought to have confined himself to observing and judging it, demonstrating his ability to grasp its main features, on the basis of which to build his later philosophy of nature (Poggi 2000, 19–20, 45). While germane (cf. *Enc.* §246Z), Hegel's analysis seems to be more rich and complex, for in the *Phenomenology* it is also possible to retrace Hegel's objections to description and to classification in contemporaneous scientific literature, which provides examples that justify Hegel's critical remarks, elucidates his allusions in "Observing Reason," and shows how Hegel took active part in such debates by publicly siding with some strands of contemporaneous natural science against others. This last point has been neglected. Indeed, it has been claimed that, in contrast to his mature system, in the *Phenomenology* Hegel's confrontation with the natural sciences is "essentially and necessarily critical," aiming to reveal the partiality, one-sidedness, and inadequacy of various aspects or forms of the cognitive approach to the world typical of the natural sciences, as part of Hegel's dissolution of all of consciousness's forms of externality (Illetterati 1995b, 217). In some cases, however, we will show how Hegel supports a debated scientific position by providing it with speculative justification and foundation. What is more, when Hegel appreciates systems of classification based on a unified, integrated study of the living being, or questions the validity of a law-like fixed quantitative scheme, he vindicates quality, fluidity, dynamical process, purposiveness, and contingency for genuinely knowing organic existence. We will show how he does so on the anti-formalistic basis of accounting for self-differentiating and self-maintaining independent natural individuals, i.e. their being-for-self, but always in connection with up-to-date research trends in empirical sciences, relying on – and accounting for – the awareness of those working scientists who, in the years of transition from Enlightenment to Romanticism, have started to conceptualize experience, regarding themselves more as "thinking natural researchers" than "observers of nature" (cf. Bach 2001, 68–9). This is because the phenomenological standpoint allows Hegel to reconstruct the genesis and functions of scientific theories within shapes (*Gestalten*) of consciousness which are also necessary and irreplaceable advances toward the concept of absolute knowing (Verra 1997, 96).

Hegel had long studied geology and mineralogy, and in 1804 became Assessor of the Jena Mineralogical Society.[6] Founded in 1796, this Society was transformed in 1804 under Goethe's influential university policy (Müller 2001, 152), which endowed the Society with laboratories and an important scientific library. At Jena, Hegel also pursued experimental studies of nature in physiology, botany, chemistry, optics, medicine, and geology, collaborating with colleagues in each of these disciplines (Rosenkranz 1844, 220). Hegel personally owned a host of handbooks about mineralogy, crystallography, geology, geography, and fossils (Fritscher 2002, 59–60). In the Preface of one of these, *Beobachtungen über die Harzgebirge* (1789, iv), the author Georg S. O. Lasius claims to consider "only such objects which nature presents to the eye of the observer."[7] Nevertheless, Lasius considers the issue of choosing a criterion for describing not just individual mountains, but "general kinds" of mountain formations (Hegel 2002 §44), i.e. *Gebirgsarten*, famously studied by Werner's *Geognosie*,[8] which contemplated also a "principal kind": granite (Hegel 2002, *ad* §44, 129b). The choice determines the "order of observation," which in the case of the stratified sedimentary formations (*Flötzgebirgen*) forces the author to revert the typical one for rocks stratified with veins (*Ganggebirge*), which started with older and proceeded to younger formations, beginning with granite mountains.[9] Many problems confront the "determination" (*Bestimmung*) and especially in the written exposition of such *Gebirgsarten*, leaving open whether this choice depends on scholarly tradition or subjective inclination.[10]

Here we have a concrete instance of what Hegel called the contradiction between reason's belief and its actual procedure. At first, the working scientist claims to conform to mere (passive) description without adding anything subjective (à la Locke; Russon 2004, 119–20) though in fact he cannot describe without introducing order and priorities and therefore using criteria (which vary from scientist to scientist);[11] nor without converting the concrete sensuous being of a particular mountain into the specimen of a genus, a difficult conversion requiring determining the genus and finding words and names to convey its characteristics linguistically (Lepenies 1978, 34; Bach 2006, 70–1).

Hegel's strategy, which pits methodological intentions (how reason takes itself) against actual procedures (the process in which she is in fact engaged),[12] that is, perception against understanding, is not that of a passive, disengaged spectator of a scientific debate, for it was not at all obvious to contemporaneous working scientists. Consider Gren's principal definition of experience in his *Grundriß der Naturlehre*:[13]

> experiences are called perceptions (*Wahrnemungen*) through our senses of the changes in the matters of our world. Experience is called an *observation* (*Beobachtung* oder *Bemerkung* [*Observatio*]) when we leave things in the state in which they are found without our activity. (Gren 1797, §11)[14]

Another handbook of the time, found both in Hegel's private library and in the library of the Jena Mineralogical Society, begins by pointing to two well-known, central difficulties in mineralogy: the inexactness of the scientific terminology of the discipline with the consequent inconsistency and incomprehensibility of various modes of description, and, even more detrimental to scientific progress, the excessive admixture of different standpoints from which minerals can be regarded (Brunner 1803, iii). As a remedy, Brunner (1803, v) advises beginners to react against any mental laziness, dismissing "the glasses of their scholarly preconceived hypothesis and opinions," and yet the point of this warning is only recourse to what Hegel regards as nothing but the *myth* of "pure experience" (Brunner 1803, vi).[15] Unaware of this, Brunner claims in his "Preface" to have made an effort "to distribute the geognostic experiences in due order," with the hope not to have missed "any . . . important observation" (Brunner 1803, xx).

These examples help us understand what Hegel means when he writes that the *description* of things, this form of reason's observational activity, does not yet involve movement in the object itself, but consists only in the act of describing (*PS* 139.22–24/M 148), and is thus condemned to ceaseless efforts with a series of consequences that bring description to an impasse: as soon as it has been described, the object loses interest; description consumes its material but cannot extinguish itself, giving rise to an insatiable search.[16] Because the "lucky" discovery of a new species is a rare event, and lucky because it does not follow from any predictive law,[17] description must return to the same objects to further analyze their components. This is a potentially limitless activity, given the profuse particularization of sensible things, their complex nature, and overlapping among species which makes it hard to draw lines between "natural" groups.[18]

This problem is at least as ancient as Aristotle's rejection (*Of the Parts of Animals*, Bk. I) of Plato's method of dichotomy in taxonomy. Plato's method requires assigning to each species only one distinguishing mark, which results in the same group falling under several divisions and contrasting groups falling under the same division, thus cutting off "natural" groups whenever one single differentiation is taken for the division. In contrast to this, according to Aristotle, who also follows popular terminology and usage in this regard, each group is marked off by many *differentiae*.[19] He himself did not produce any formal taxonomy in the modern, regular, and systematic sense of the term according to the generally accepted five unities: classes, orders, genera, species, variety, introduced as early as 1735 by Linnaeus in his *Systema Naturae*, in analogy with the terms of the Aristotelian logic.[20] For Hegel, the confrontation with endless particularization where the universal is indeterminate shows that any classificatory system is obtained through "power and art" (*PS* 140.3/M 148). This kind of difficulty marks the end of pure description, because it becomes evident that one cannot know by mere description whether what appears to be an essential characteristic is not in fact accidental (*PS* 140.10–11/M 148).

The next, improved strategy attempts to classify the world by identifying essentially distinguishing marks. Significantly, here Hegel does not confine himself to explicating the presuppositions of scientific research, but develops his philosophical concerns by endorsing the working scientist's own criticism of the state of art in natural history. Hegel owned the fourth edition of Blumenbach's *Handbuch der Naturgeschichte*,[21] where a general description of the natural world divided into the three traditional realms of animals, plants, and minerals is initially given, drawing from Aristotle, Plinius, Buffon, Bonnet, Linnaeus, among others (Blumenbach 1791, 5), although Blumenbach warns the reader not to take it for granted, due to very recent discoveries, such as the following. Some naturalists do not want to draw any determinate borderline (*keine bestimmte Grenzen*) between the animal and plant realms, due to the discovery of sensible plants, and of so-called animal-plants (*Pflanzenthieren*) such as Trembley's famous *Hydra*. Others who support a universal and general continuity in nature (modeled by a ladder or chain) find it totally arbitrary to divide nature, not only into realms, but also into classes and orders (Blumenbach 1791, 6). Blumenbach's approach to this issue shows his awareness that this is a matter of which kind of *determinate concept* of the nature of animals and plants a naturalist adopts. His final judgment, sharing Oehme's objections to the continuity and hierarchy of the ladder (Barsanti 1992, 27–33), is that those who to join everything, even though some classes seem so isolated from certain species they should comprehend, cannot sustain the model of the ladder without effort (*Mühe*) and a visible forcing (*Zwang*). In his *De generis humani varietate nativa* (1795),[22] Blumenbach supports a taxonomy based on habit (*hexis, habitus*), that is, according to an animal's way of living, its activities, characters, parts, ways of reproduction, motion, and considering its environment. Here Blumenbach repeats the same points, this time emphasizing the limits of Linnaeus's criterion of classifications of mammals based on teeth – thus endorsing Buffon's criticism from 1749 (Barsanti 1992, 178) – which was regarded as a good tool at the time of the first edition of the *Systema naturae* (1735), though now superseded by new discoveries overseas of many exceptions to his artificial system.[23] In this context Blumenbach repeats his objections to the motto *natura non facit saltus*: this motto forces classes such as the one of birds and genera such as the one of cuttlefishes into a graduated scheme. This time he uses the expression *male et non nisi affectatione*, terms that again convey a significance very close to Hegel's use of contrivance (*Gewalt, potestas* with the connotations of *imperium, violentia*) and artifice (*Kunst*, in the sense of *artificium*).

These references provide at least part of the scientific background to Hegel's phenomenological account of the inadequacy of the experience of description and of the advent of the distinction between what is essential and what is inessential within systematic classifications, through which the concept "rises above the dispersion of the sensuous" (*PS* 140.18–20/M 148–9). What has actually been shown, on the one hand, is that reason does act as the understanding of the Consciousness section, so that the infinite truth of the concept is only something ideal and abstract, in itself (*an sich*), out of her current reach, while on the other hand, her activity is nevertheless inwardly guided by the concept, the living universality which "constitutes the inner thread" of reason's progression.[24] In considering the role of distinguishing marks (the teeth and claws of animals, sexual dimorphism of plants, according to Linnaeus's *Philosophia botanica*) in the rational cognition of nature, Hegel has then the difficult task of accounting for both sides.[25] Indeed, he has shown that, at this stage of knowing, the identity of mutually related phenomena is only an external one, for between the universality of any scheme and the singularities of the individuals remains an unresolved tension: so that the phenomena are simply not captured by any classification that analytically picks up only a single, isolated distinguishing mark, using it as the principle of difference of its artificial system.[26] This objective feature of the scientific debate of his time is viewed as the typical consequence of the separation, abstraction, and external connections of the determinations of natural phenomena set up by the understanding's logical procedures (*Enc.* §467Z). In this way Hegel prepared for the transition to the subsequent stage of seeking the *law* of the determinateness. However, Hegel has also shown the legitimacy of the quest to find essentiality and universality *in* the world,[27] testified by the instinct of reason guided by the concept as such, that is, the universal unity that particularizes itself and comprehends singular individuals as its immanent specified moment, thus maintaining itself in and through *all* its (inner, or conceptual) particular differences: the true form that produces its content from itself.[28]

For Hegel it follows necessarily from the concept of Reason that artificial classifications ought to conform to nature's own system, and he highlights the *unity* that reason – despite her merely instinctive activity – was able to reach in systems "where the objects are themselves so constituted that they have in themselves an essentiality or a being-for-self, and are not only the accident of this moment and this place."[29] In *GW* 9 there is no editorial note to those lines; on my view, examples which help clarify such a brief, cryptic reference may well be found in the *Zootomie*, or in the overcoming of the separation – unknown to the Ancients – between pure dismembering (*Zergliederung*) and physiology as put forward by M. A. Weickard's *Philosophie der Zergliederungskunde* – an approach praised and endorsed also by Sömmering (Sömmering 1791, xxv) – or in the new *Zoochemie*, which aimed to unify light, caloric, electricity, magnetism and galvanism under physiology (see note 4). In this respect, it is worth noting that in J. F. H. Abegg's transcription of Hegel's Nürnberg *Encyclopaedia*, the third part of the section "Natural Science," "Physics of Organics," is given along with the alternative title, in parentheses, of "Physiology" (cf. Hegel 2002, vii; v, editorial note). Indeed, in 1812/13 Hegel will develop this point by making explicit that "reason provides (*macht*) a basis for the fundamental determination (*Grundbestimmung*) of the animal" (Hegel 2002, *ad* §49, 143.31–32b). There he refers to the definition that rises from the animal's properties to its essential distinguishing marks to the whole (*das Ganze*) of the "general type": structuring from within *all* its single parts, *all* its bones and limbs according to its genus.[30] In this way Hegel provides with speculative significance the results of comparative anatomy for zoology (*Enc.* §368Z): he owned Blumenbach's 1805 *Handbuch der vergleichende Anatomie* (Neuser 1987, 482 entry 31), which mentions Cuvier's early works. What is more, from the standpoint of phenomenological Reason itself, "the inexhaustibility of nature" ceases to militate "against any claim to explanatory completeness on the part of a rational observation of nature" (Dahlstrom 2007, 43); rational systems of classification that conform to nature do not revert to ceaseless description, and though later Hegel will say that many specifics remain as yet unexplained, at the same time he stresses that one must trust in the possibility to know the concept within the natural variety of the sensible real (*Enc.* §353Z). From this standpoint, it is worth noting that Treviranus had already lowered the value of "descriptions" (*Beschreibungen*) of animals and plants, based on visual details and findings, pitting artificial systems regarded as "mere registers" against the higher purpose of the "science of nature" to inquire into the driving force that keeps the "great organism" that we call "nature" in eternal activity, uniting its dispersed parts into a whole (Treviranus 1802, v–vi).

Therefore, the distinguishing marks derived from the animal's essential inner *unity* of the whole, such as its means to be-for-self, cannot be regarded as something related only to our subjectivity, and pertaining only to our reason's interest. Rather, only by means of these "weapons" (such as claws or teeth, broadly used as distinguishing marks since Aristotle, see *PS* 498–9, editorial note to 140.36–37), which within the frame of the *Typus* are *determined* as *objective* weapons, an animal sets itself individually apart from others, and maintains its independence.[31] At stake is the quest to comprehend organic life according to the *unity* of its two moments of universality (genus, *Gattung*) and singularity, so that the individual parts that constitute a single animal can be entirely drawn from its inner determined, specific (*besondere*) form,[32] and for the conceptual cognition of its independence, its being-for-self (*Fürsichseyn*) which represents an appreciation of Leibniz's stress on the uniqueness of individuals, contra both Locke's model and Spinoza's global structures formed by an infinity of modal elements.[33]

That the living individual must have difference as its own immanent determination (and not merely in virtue of our modes of cognition) is something that Hegel does not fully recognize here in plants: they do not yet have in themselves the full, complete force of the individual unity and therefore they arrive only at the border of individuality,[34] where they show the "semblance" (*Schein*) of sexual dimorphism.[35] Later, Hegel will explicitly praise Tournefort's classification, contra Linnaeus's artificial system, for being more philosophical and natural, because it judges "according to the whole of the plants (*nach dem Ganzen der Pflanze*)" and not according to single marks.[36]

Moll (2004, 150) remarks that, "individuality designates the movement of the living organism both away from the universal and away from other individuals." In sharp contrast to animals, and in contrast to plants, Hegel views the chemical object as "the individual not yet determined as different" (*SL, GW* 12:149.3–6) and as what is "simply (*schlechthin*) related to what is other" (*Enc.* §200Z): chemical substances in fact have no individuality, for in empirical relation to each other they do not remain the same or maintain themselves, thus challenging any cognitive attempt to determine their proper (e.g., acidic or basic) and stable nature.[37]

When Hegel makes this epistemological point in favor of an idealism that is at the same time realism (*Enc.* §353Z; Westphal 2003, 51–5, 63), he again pursues some of his earlier anti-Kantian concerns. At the outset of his *Differenzschrift* (1801) Hegel criticized Kant's nomothetic laws of understanding for containing only the condition of the possibility of experience in general, and for being objective only in relation to the objects of experience, not for the thing-in-itself. Insofar as Hegel denies Kant's view that *particular* experience, in its multiplicity, variety, and heterogeneity can be thoroughly interconnected *only* transcendentally, Kant is a target of Hegel's criticism in "Observation of Nature" because Kant's *a priori* presuppositions, which guide our rational investigation of real, empirical nature, are only reflective maxims of heuristic and subjective judgments in the *Critique of Judgment*. Yet in the Appendix to the Transcendental Dialectic, Kant made clear two related aspects of the *Critique of Pure Reason* concerning the role and rationale of systematic unity in empirical knowledge. First, although the understanding connects the manifold of appearances through concepts by using schemata of sensibility, and brings appearances under empirical laws, nevertheless, apart from these schemata, its actions are *undetermined* (*CPR* A664/B692). Similarly, second, "the unity of reason is also in itself *undetermined* with regard to the conditions under which, and the degree to which, the understanding should combine its concepts systematically" (*CPR* A665/B693). Kant proposes an analogue of a schema of sensibility (which as such cannot be found in this case), that is, a schema of reason for the thoroughgoing systematic unity of all concepts of the understanding. Through the application (*Anwendung*) of the categories to their sensible schemata we reach a cognition of the phenomenon itself; we thus identify ("determine") something through its constitution. Through the application of the concepts of the understanding to the "idea of the maximum of division (interest in multiplicity, according to the principle of specification) and of unification (interest in unity, according to the principle of aggregation) of the understanding's cognition in one principle," we have "only a rule," a "maxim," a "merely regulative" or "subjective" kind of judgment grounded only on the interest of reason without any possible insight into the nature of the object (*CPR* A666–7/B694–5). However, in this way Kant *voids* the objectivity of any conflicting claims advanced by alternative scientific theories. By reducing their principles to maxims that express the twofold interest of speculative reason (in multiplicity and in unity), Kant contends that what naturalists assume comes from their proper insight into objects is "only" grounded *in their own mode of thought*. The scientific battle among different systems of classification of the inorganic and organic realms (Kant mentions the model of the ladder of continuity among creatures used by Leibniz and Bonnet)[38] is not merely deprived of a possible objective outcome. Rather, Kant thus makes it an objectively unjustified contrast, because the constitution of the object "lies too deeply hidden" for empirical scientists, who are unaware of the results of the first *Critique*.

Beyond this strictly anti-Kantian aspect, through the principle of individuality Hegel makes the case for the rational comprehension (*begreifen*) of actual existence. This is something more than a mere expression of confidence that there are natural categories rather than simply artificially imposed ones, or that our ordering is a matter of discovery rather than invention; this was the issue at stake in the scientific debate of the time (cf. Knight 1986). If the reference above to Kant's "Appendix" is appropriate, then Hegel affirms the objective presence of reason in experience, not as a mere guideline for our investigation of nature but *through* our genuine specification of animal species in terms of an animal's proper characteristics and determinate differences that enable it to defend and to preserve itself. As Harris puts it: "every 'thing' is *conceptually* (or 'by definition') *rational* . . . it has its own 'essence' in virtue of which it distinguishes itself from other kinds of 'thing'" (Harris 1997, 1:485). This is the deepest aspect that Hegel sees in Leibniz's principle of the identity of indiscernibles: whatever does not involve an intrinsic difference cannot distinguish itself (MM 20:241/H&S 3:333–4).

In sharp contrast to the view that "everything is equal according to the [one] essence" espoused in Schelling's *Darstellung* (1801, §§12, 35),[39] the feature of being endowed with a positive subsistence of its own that Hegel assigns to animals and to plants (though as a limiting case), i.e., to organic nature, appears to me to mark an important contrast between Hegel's view and the latent mysticism and anti-scientism of any non-dialectical, monistic, or Spinozist (*Enc.* §151Z) philosophy of nature.[40]

1.2 The laws of inorganic nature: Their theoretical inwardness and empirical outwardness

Overlaps, transitions, confusions, and reversion to mere description in classifications all invalidate the conscious intellectual quest for the alleged *essential* character of distinguishing marks, which is thus insufficient to capture the actual, categorial objectivity of sensuous reality, and thus to conform to the concrete and processual, self-determining universality proper to the concept, which is nothing but the underground, inner drive of the instinctive activity of reason itself. Hegel here recalls the nature of the *living* "substance that is essentially subject," or identity-in-difference as outlined in the *Phenomenology*'s Preface: this kind of rational universality, according to which a succession of diverse organic forms does not betoken mutual incompatibility and conflict, but rather moments of the teleological unfolding and becoming of a nascent unity,[41] this is what reason naively seeks *directly* in the world and now tries by instinct to find in the laws of phenomena (*PS* 142.4–7/M 150–1). Generally speaking, the substantial limit of observing reason rests on both natural objects resisting attempts to describe or classify them and knowing subjects' conceptual fallacies (Hoffheimer 1992): this section aims to demonstrate the empirical reality of the unconditioned (absolute) objective determinations of thought achieved by *purifying* laws derived from induction and generalization of sense-experience into concepts (examining chemistry and electricity for the inorganic realm) and the self-superseding of law-based quantitative fixed explanations for the rational comprehension of living phenomena (for the organic).[42] The significance of the movement of rational cognition is the unity of extra-conceptual being and the reflective, cognizant self: philosophical cognition shows that thought has been changed into a thought-that-is-a-being, or equivalently, that extra-conceptual being has been changed into a being-that-is-thought.[43] For observing consciousness, the truth of laws of nature lies in experience. The dialectic of this section aims to show how for consciousness it emerges that the truth of the laws lies in the concept (*PS* 142.7–14/M 151).

At first consciousness confronts the inductive derivation of a law of nature, though an empirical genesis cannot insure any *necessity* of the law, without which "it is not, in fact, a law" (*PS* 142.14–15/M 151). While we now most readily think of Hume and Kant, this problem is as ancient as Aristotle's rejection of induction for demonstrating the essence of an object. No necessity can follow from an induction based on enumerating (contingently) existing cases, by which one claims that the object in its totality must (in all cases) behave in a certain way, because no single observed case has behaved differently. Aristotle remarks that by induction one does not *prove* what an object is, but only shows that it (contingently) exists, or that it is not (*An. post.* 2b7, 92a35–92b). When Bacon, referring to Plato, proposes in the *Novum Organum* (Aph. 105) his axiomatic form of induction based on exclusions, he is well aware of Aristotle's advice, and accordingly rejects enumerative induction, which Bacon acknowledged reaches precarious conclusions that are subject to counter-instances. Through his graduated tables of affirmative, negative, and comparative instances about the form or nature of a phenomenon, Bacon aimed to insure a continuity between higher and lower axioms, where these latter "differ but slightly from bare experience" (Aph. 104). From what Hegel recalls to consciousness about what truth is for it, we learn that even if in this way experience would proceed according to "fixed law" (Aph. 100) or to "a certain method and rule" (Aph. 103), this "certainty" does not suffice for a law to be a law, and neither does analogy or likelihood (*Wahrscheinlichkeit*). Let this "likeness of truth" (e.g., the Baconian fixed law) "be as great as it may, it is nothing as against truth" (*PS* 143.10–13/M 152). In this way Hegel also rejects Newton's claim that this is the best way of reasoning allowed by nature in experimental philosophy, as Newton claims in Quaery 31 of his *Opticks* (Bk. 3, Pt. 1), when he accounts for his methodology by speaking *first* of the analytic and *then* of the synthetic method,[44] although he is well aware of the fact that to draw general principles from experiments and observations does not *demonstrate* their necessity, as is also made clear in the fourth of the *Principia*'s *Rules of Philosophizing*, where he indifferently speaks of "exact or very nearly true" propositions drawn from phenomena by induction, and of degrees of (more or less) exactness for them (cf. Newton 1999, 796).

Within this new context, Hegel's general aim to legitimate reason's quest to find essentiality and universality *in* the world – because what is universally valid is also universally effective (*PS* 142.23–24/M 151) – seeks to conjoin, *for* consciousness, the necessity of the universality of the law in the sense of the universality of reason (on the basis of its conceptual nature) with empirical observation, thus saving her cognition of laws not only from contingency – "avoiding the pitfalls of radical empiricism and conventionalism," as Lamb (1980, 103) notes – but also from alleged "necessary" demonstrations that impose categories on the world regardless of "sensible" experiences.[45] The *essential* reality of the *rational ratios* of the law,[46] *relations* which should not be confused with the mere quantitative significance of the mere numbers (see below), and their inherence in nature in a way accessible to observation (Westphal 1989, 169), is something that does not become apparent to consciousness that remains at the level of observation and believes that the universality of natural laws has nothing to do with the nature of reason, and derives solely from external nature. The first counterexample contradicting this belief concerns generalizing the law to cover *all* cases. When, despite Hume's skeptical doubts about the operations of the understanding (*Enquiry*, §4),[47] consciousness realizes that she does not make the experiment of the fall by raising a stone from the ground and then dropping it *ad nauseam* (*PS* 142.20–143.5/M 151–2), she has in experience the *being* of the law, but also its conceptual form (*PS* 143.23–24/M 152). Thus consciousness comes to acknowledge that the validity of a law lies *both* in its phenomenal manifestation and in its conceptual nature (*PS* 143.24–26/M 152).

To clarify Hegel's reference to a separation of what is purely conceptual from what is phenomenal, and his subsequent reference to the "purification" of the law and its moments as the quest for finding the pure conditions of the law (*PS* 143.27–36, cf. 91.33–37/M 152–3, cf. 91), recall the innovative twofold structure of mechanics introduced by Galileo, which provides theoretical definitions (e.g., the notions of "uniform" or "uniformly accelerated" motion) and (mathematical) proof, and also treats empirical, existing facts as additional, existential propositions that do not affect the law, as in Galileo's geometrical proof of the law of falling bodies *independent* of empirical observation of any kind. In his letter to Pietro Carcavy (June 5, 1637), Galileo states that if experiments would not confirm that the empirical motion of fall is uniformly accelerated, his proofs would lose none of their force and conclusiveness since they are only supposed to be valid for his own hypotheses. More importantly, he states that they are no more affected than are the propositions of Archimedes on spirals by the fact that no bodies found in nature exhibit a spiral movement.[48] In this way, it has been observed, Galileo divided mechanics into two methodologically *distinct*, though systematically related parts: an empirical one, "in which hypotheses about the physical world are formulated and experimentally verified or falsified," and a conceptual one, with principles that first make experiments at all meaningful, such as "equal conditions lead to equal results," which supply tools such as definitions and propositions that follow logically from these determinations.[49]

The other, sensible side of the law also undergoes a similar process of abstraction by arranging experiments (*PS* 143.29–30/M 152). Gren's *Grundriß* is paradigmatic of this (Moiso 2002, 436). Gren first defines experiment (*Versuch*) as the experience we obtain when we change the state of a thing and thus allow other effects to occur from the altered circumstances (cf. *PS* 143.33–34/M 152–3). In this way we can know forces that we may never have been able to perceive through simple observation. The experiment brings us deeper into the nature of the examined bodies (Gren 1797, §§11, 12). Experiments are conducted with instruments, which allow us to "reach the necessary requirements of simplicity, precision, and purity" (Gren 1797, §13). Inquiring into the forms of bodies and their cohesion, these experiments amount to physical, mechanical, and chemical analysis of the bodies, individuating their constituent materials and parts, and also their proximal and distal parts or elements (*Urstoffe*), which are similar in kind for the first two sciences, though dissimilar for the third (Gren 1797, §§109–117). Gren actually diagrams the progressive decomposition of "bodies" (e.g., atmospheric air) into "matters" such as heat, oxygen, carbonic acid, etc.[50] Whatever working scientists may think of it, Hegel regards this kind of research as freeing the moments of the law from any one specific being (*PS* 143.35–39/M 153).

Consider in this regard Gren's account of Riccioli's and Grimaldi's attempts to prove by experiments and a posteriori Galileo's law of falling bodies.[51] Their results, which Gren, in language strikingly close to Hegel's in the *Phenomenology*, calls seeking "to confirm the truth of the Galilean proposition through immediate experiments," perfectly satisfied the law of the acceleration, proving its 'reality' versus its alleged 'appearance', per Galileo's "strange conjecture" in the *Dialogue*, to support the Copernican daily motion of the Earth, according to which "the body really moves in nothing other than a simple circular motion . . . the true and real motion of the stone is never accelerated at all but is always equable and uniform." However, Gren comments that these measures matched the formula quite exactly despite air resistance, an empirical factor disregarded "in the theory itself." Hence he draws the lesson that "one can rightly posit mistrust in the reliability of observation" (Gren 1797, §213).[52] In this regard, Hegel contends that experiments themselves show to consciousness the inversion of her standpoint, which takes experience and observation as the source of *truth*. References to this kind of scientific awareness help us understand how and why Hegel interprets the investigation of the pure conditions of a law as *totally* (*ganz*) *elevating the law into the shape* (*Gestalt*) *of the concept* (*PS* 143.38/M 153).

After considering a further series of examples drawn from chemistry and electricity,[53] Hegel concludes this section with a joint result. On the empirical side, the "purified" matters of chemistry, as singularities that are not existing beings, are universal beings, that is, *still* beings, though consciously posited in a conceptual mode.[54] On the theoretical side, the nature of laws of nature is the simple concept that, although effectively embedded in sensuous being and thus present to observation, is also free from its spatio-temporal manifestations and our observation of them.[55] Thus concepts are not ashamed of empirical knowledge and empirical knowledge is not devoid of conceptual elements.

To highlight the meaning of the itinerary covered so far by the observational activity of reason, it suffices to recast the results sketched above against the background of the very first strategy of reason to find her own universality directly in the world, and to seek the reality of self-consciousness immediately in an individual, sensed object, thus making the conceptual infinity that defines and animates reason depend upon her relation to the finitude of a crude, abstract empiricism. The same kind of empiricism is involved in Kant's theory of absolutely real, though transcendent, inaccessible things-in-themselves, which nevertheless affect our sensibility, thus generating the *a posteriori* "immense empirical realm of sensibility and perception." It is also expressed by Fichte's original impact against an externality that is totally other than the knowing Ego, and thus void of any empirical content. The cumulative point of Hegel's analysis, from the dialectic of description and classification to the laws of inorganic nature, is to exhibit the route to fill that void and to consummate the *essential* externality of the known object. For the first time the empirical reality of matter appears in our self-conscious experience of knowing otherness as being essentially a thought-product, and the nomothetic universality of thought has emerged as the conceptual net inherently regulating the appearances of sensible things, actually existing within phenomena. Furthermore, we have here a clear example of Hegel's famous anti-Spinozist, anti-Schellingian formula of the identity-in-difference of object and subject, of real and ideal, that often seems to preach only to the converted. Take for instance the convergence of real and ideal, of natural being and concept (cf. *Enc.* §23), in chemical reactions: each side moves towards the other due to their essential unity *and* their distinction: what is outwardly sensed (the real side), though remaining a being on which to perform experiments, is posited abstractly as idealized "purified matter," constitutively related to its other, to its proper chemical complement; what is inwardly universal (the ideal side), though distinct from sensuous existence, has an empirically real content consisting in a reflected, mediated determination of singularity and universality in the form of the laws of chemical combination and affinity.

1.3 Inner and outer in (b) observation of organic life

The meaning Hegel assigns to these historical achievements of scientific experimental consciousness provides the transition to the observation of organisms, because natural consciousness, forgetful as it always is of its path and result, takes organic life as yet another kind of sensible thing to observe. Harris (1997, 1:495) observes that "the paradigm of the organism as an object of rational observation is easy to identify," for what truly characterizes rational universality is that a succession of diverse developmental stages of an organic unity does not involve mutual incompatibility and conflict among different forms, because they are moments of the unfolding of an implicit, potential unity. It seems, therefore, that here reason can actually satisfy her demand to represent in her object what she has in herself, thus mirroring herself in actual existence. Nevertheless, what in fact occurs within natural consciousness's experience is not actually grasped by it; this movement acquires such a meaning only for us, who have achieved philosophical consciousness by freeing ourselves from our natural habits of thought. From an immanent standpoint, this will be the highest peak reached by reason. However, reason fails to maintain this insight into an identity constituted only in and through the mutual determination of inner differences (i.e., of an organic mediated unity) by taking this in the form of an immediate, external being and seeking observational laws that 'link' the two separate inward and outward aspects of natural organisms. This occurs because, logically speaking, reason still falls within the "simple connection" between the understanding and its object, adopting the abstract law-based strategy of the (finite) understanding that requires 'linking' the two fixed sides of the stable inner universality and the changing outward specific expression; it immediately requires, that is, "only a quiet taking-up into the form of universality of purely *subsisting* (*seyender*) differences" (*PS* 156.29–30/M 168) as the content of our scientific theory constructions of the regularities of the natural world (cf. Hoffheimer 1992, 40–6).

Recall that in "Force and Understanding" Hegel introduced law (*Gesetz*) through the mental act of positing (*setzen*) the world of sense-knowledge and perception as superseded, as being in truth an inner world (*als innere gesetzt*). The inner world, however, filled itself out for the understanding: the truth rested on the side of a stable, internal, simple universal being, while immediacy fell to the unstable flux of appearances (*PS* 91.14–23/M 90). Law was to express this difference (*PS* 91.25–26/M 90). The realm of laws was said to be the truth of the understanding, insofar as the permanent difference between the two sides of being, theoretical and empirical, constituted the abstract nature of the law-based explanations (*PS* 91.31–32/M 91) which typify the finitude of the intellectual habit of thought. The Understanding's strategy, which has its proper sphere in the phenomena of finite mechanics, is totally inadequate for dissolving differences between these two sides in any self-regulating (natural or social) organism because of the mutual exchange and the same in-itself of inner and outer that characterizes the object (its fluidity, self-relation, freedom, its internal purposiveness and principles of development, growth and preservation)[56] and the conceptual fallacy of employing finite modes of thought to cognize the self-maintaining dynamism and the self-actualizing form of living phenomena.[57]

The point is that after electricity and chemistry, reason now no longer has as her content such an external, fixed non-identity of thought and otherness: her object is organic life, where the immediacy in which the living object exists is the inner difference or concept itself, namely, different beings (for instance bud, blossom, and fruit in a plant) are not to be comprehended as mutually exclusive, conflicting determinations, but as vanishing differences, because they are reciprocally necessary moments of an organic phenomenon (cf. *Enc.* [1817], §343): logically speaking, the *essential* opposition of inner and outer is reconciled in the categories of "Actuality" (Harris 1983, 444). In applying the finite modes of the understanding to the absolute fluidity and self-manifestation of life, reason takes sensible real finite things as representing the universal, the ideal, the infinite, and reduces human inwardness to mere physiological terms, thus entirely missing the true explanation of the *free* spiritual dimension of the self. Given the scope of the present paper, Hegel's further (and more often studied) analyses of the rational observation of organisms and the observation of the self, both in its purity (logical laws) and in its connection with external actuality (psychological laws), will be considered more briefly.[58]

An object whose key characteristic is the mutual interdependence between the whole and its parts, that is, the universal and its individual aspects, represents the universality of the concept (*Enc.* [1817], §273) *and* the kind of mediated unity that constitutes the universal nature of reason, which reason now seeks to find in organic nature. Despite these convergences, Hegel shows that there remains an insoluble tension between, on the one hand, the close analogy of the (purposive) connection between means and ends in our rational activity and the organism as an end in itself (à la Aristotle),[59] so that reason rightly expects to find herself objectively in the world,[60] and yet, on the other, the incapacity of consciousness to recognize itself *in* what it experiences. The inner, essential, conceptual unity of universality and activity does not exist for observing consciousness: since it is natural (i.e., unreflective, immediate, external to the observed objects), it seeks these moments immediately (in the form of *Sein*) and externally (in the form of *Bleiben*; cf. *PS* 149.11–12/M 159). Therefore natural consciousness either takes the essence of the thing only onto itself, as a subjective, heuristic guide to inquiry (à la Kant),[61] or it projects it outside itself and outside the thing, by holding that the laws governing a living individual's relations to its inorganic habitat have been designed by "another intellect," that of an absolutely unobservable Author of nature (*PS* 147.33–36/M 157). This is the physico-theological view already criticized by the pre-critical Kant.[62] In either case, the living being is not taken as truly having within itself the principle of its own making in an organic unity (cf. Aristotle, *Phys.* II.i.192b.25–30; Frigo 2004); instead this principle is ascribed to an *external* agent. Consciousness fails to understand organisms in proper teleological terms,[63] because by its own nature, as consciousness "of" something that separates it from what it observes,[64] it is driven to turn even the (Kantian) concept of internal purposiveness into something "subjective," merely reflective and regulative, thus always lapsing into forms of external purposiveness regarding organic beings.[65]

Following its instinct, after this failure consciousness tries to fix purposiveness and actuality in the forms of the immediate being and to seek the inner and outer aspects of the laws governing the organization of living beings from plant to animal.[66] Reason tries two strategies: one is to consider the inner side of the organic whole in relation to its own outward manifestation (Kielmeyer);[67] the other considers how the opposition of an organism's inner and outer aspects is determined throughout the multifarious actuality of forms and shapes of nature (Steffens).[68]

The first strategy takes an organism's outer aspect – a particular observable appendage or part of the body which performs a natural process – as an expression of inner purposive forces (functions, operations), through the correspondence between characteristics and organic systems. Relevant "characteristics" include sensibility (the capacity to retain representations together with the impressions that come from the nerves), irritability (the capacity of muscles to contract themselves or move under stimuli), reproduction (for the preservation of the individual and the species); relevant "organic systems" include those revealed by anatomy: nervous, muscular, and visceral systems (*PS* 149.32–151.7/M 160–1; cf. *Enc.* §§353–4). The "compensation laws" (*Kompensationsgesetze*) found by Kielmeyer were based on direct or inverse relations; e.g., the variety of possible sensations diminishes according to the descent in the ladder of organisms; irritability augments in inverse proportion to the velocity, frequency, and variety of sensations; the force of reproduction is inversely proportional to the size of the individuals, etc. (Poggi 1996, 101–21; cf. Poggi 2000, 129–45).

Regarding the outer aspect of organic forms, Hegel rejects Kielmeyer's laws because the "true" nature of an organism's system is more than the sum of its anatomical components.[69] Hegel contends that organic individuals cannot be brought under these quantitative schemes of universal relations, and the *representation* (*Vorstellung*) of a law as something that is "posited" (*gesetzt*) and is to express a stable, inert difference between the inner and the outer side of a being, in the case of the organic being, where the moments are essentially a pure transition (*PS* 156.32–36/M 168), is altogether lost (*überhaupt verloren*; *PS* 156.2/M 167). The organism is *free*, because each side of the organism is "simple universality within itself," in which all the (fixed) determinations are dissolved (qua fixed) or released, and each of them exists only as moments in their physiological processes.[70] Regarding the inner aspect of organic forms, Hegel rejects the *truth* of observational laws of this kind (*PS* 151.27–28/M 162), because they fail to conform to the inner concept of the observed object (*Enc.* §24Z2), indeed for two reasons. First, these functions are pervasive and fluid (that is, shapeless; cf. *PS* 145.5/M 154); they are interrelated and overflow into one another, and therefore cannot be restricted to "a thing" (*PS* 151.29–152.3/M 162). Rather, they should be *truly* taken as moments of mutual determination which have their reality in three systems. (Recall the model of the bud–blossom–fruit sequence for the manifestation of a plant used in the Preface to the *Phenomenology*.)[71] Second, because these functions are classified as mutually distinct and opposed (e.g., the antithesis between irritability and sensibility; cf. Steffens 1801, 292), their differences are merely qualitative and lack any fixed quantitative correlation (*PS* 153.3–28/M 163–4).[72]

Hegel writes that when the object to be observed is an organic unity, Reason has before herself in her object (unlike what happened to the Understanding; *PS* 156.14–19/M 167) the *relation* (*Beziehung*) between inward essentiality (universality) and externality (singularity). To express such a relation would require "laws which immediately possess in these differences also the unrest of the concept, and therefore at the same time possess the necessity of the relation between the sides" (*PS* 156.28–32/M 168). In the form of the immediate sensuous being, however, the difference between the sides expresses itself only as indifferent, quantitative difference, i.e., magnitude (cf. *PS* 156.13–17/M 167).[73]

On my view, these passages do not imply that a misinterpretation of Newtonian mechanics led Hegel to deny the existence of any law in organics (Borzeskowski 2006, 199) or even their possibility (Wahsner 2006, 225). From the books owned by Hegel and present in Jena's libraries we can see how he responded to a line of the natural science of his time that sought to identify the cause of the *motion* of the body parts (that is, the cause of what they called "life"; Autenrieth 1801, §§82–3)[74] within the realm of physical forces (Ackermann 1805, xvi; Neuser 1987, 480 entry 2) and to determine the laws of organic life according to fundamental physical principles (Ackermann 1805, xii). This trend denied the existence of either a "vital force" (*Lebenskraft*) or a "principle of life" (*Lebensprinzip*: Meyer 1805 §27; Neuser 1987, 489 entry 140). By following Kielmeyer's characterization of the organic forces (which draws from Tetens 1777, *Philosophische Versuche über die menschliche Natur*; cf. Bach 2001, 145–8) and rejecting their quantitative proportions, as a matter solely of experience of compensation, arranged in an arithmetical series, like the Titius–Bode astronomical formula for the distances of the planets from the sun (cf. Bach 2001, 173ff.), already criticized in his 1801 *De orbitis* (see notes 17 and 46), Hegel is publicly siding with the anti-reductionist line represented since the second half of the eighteenth century by Stahl, Alexander von Humboldt, and Brandis, among others.[75] At the turn of the century, this trend had received a significant impulse from Bichat's 1799–1800 *Recherches* (Neuser 1987, 481 entry 22; cf. *Enc.* §354Z). Bichat had eliminated the appeal to physical-chemical factors by focusing on tissues and on the interdependence and coordination of functions, claiming the systematic unity of organic life (Bichat 1995, 13). In doing so, Bichat underscored the "immense interval" separating physics and chemistry, on the one side, from the science of organized bodies, on the other side – not because the phenomena of the first two sciences were ruled by laws and the others not, but because the former were the *same* laws. Therefore "an enormous difference exists between these laws and *those* of life. To say that physiology is the physics of animals, is to give an idea that is extremely inexact; likewise, I would like to say that astronomy is the physiology of the heavenly bodies" (Bichat 1995, 83–4; my italics. See Illetterati 1995b, 201–2).

The second of reason's strategies Hegel finds represented by the principles and approach executed in two parts, inorganic and organic, by Steffens's *Beyträge*, to which he refers at length (*PS* 159.4–166.6/M 170–80). This work was dedicated to Goethe, and owned by Hegel. In it Steffens viewed the plant and animal realms in terms of progressive degrees of individuation, and, drawing from Kielmeyer's comparative physiology, as a discontinuity of forms resulting from a continuity of functions. Following Schelling's *Weltseele* (1798), *Erster Entwurf eines Systems der Naturphilosophie* (1799), and *System des transzendentalen Idealismus* (1800), Steffens held that the various configurations of inorganic and organic nature were produced through the entire organization of nature, including the force of reproduction, the water element that originates chemical mixtures, conflicts between both fluidity and rigidity and between dead residues and living matter, the systems of irritability and sensibility, etc. (cf. Poggi 2000, 369–72).

Steffens starts with the view that salts do not constitute a series on their own distinct from metals, but form two fixed and opposed parallel series of silicon and calcium. He warns that the two series always remain separate without commingling, so that all the operations of the restless inner activity of nature can be understood according to this *determinate* division (Steffens 1801, 14–15). In this way nature gives rise to figures, shapes, and products, that is, to *determinate* matters, the diversity of which rests only on the quantitative ratio of nature's inner activity. His general plan covers both inorganic and organic nature and seeks to reduce the qualitative to the quantitative (to simple numbers, sums, or ratios), analogically extending to organics the model of the laws of celestial mechanics by decomposing matters, as was just achieved by the "newest chemistry." In this way, for instance, all the component parts of plants have been reduced to *products*, their differences rest solely on the different relations of carbon, hydrogen, oxygen, and nitrogen, and this, united with the results of the chemistry of the animal, "will allow us to gaze into the most secret depth of nature" (Steffens 1801, 36–7). Steffens claims that

> as Kepler and Newton, by applying mathematics, discovered simple laws for the planetary motion, one expects (*glaubt man*) to be able to decipher the most internal secret of the formation of nature (*Naturbildung*) through mathematical formula, like Lavoisier has reduced (or has given us the hope to reduce) the infinite multiplicity of chemical processes to the mutual interaction of a few matters. (Steffens 1801, 37)

Steffens's program continues with the decomposition of the chemical and physical properties of metals,[76] attempting to reduce them to laws, always according to the schema of duality in identity as the ground of all natural configurations. Since metals were gradually arranged according to degrees of "coherence" in two parallel series, the specific gravity of metals is said to stand in inverse ratio with their coherence, so that the least coherent is nitrogen, corresponding to the maximum of expansion,[77] while the most coherent is carbon, to which corresponds the maximum of contraction, or "intension."[78] Carbon and nitrogen "represent" the two original forces of attraction and repulsion within the rigid bodies of the earth (Steffens 1801, 262). In this way, the series of metals "only" *represent* magnetism (cf. *PS* 162.34–163.2/ M 175), and "we have also, through this, established the relation of the metals with the silicon and calcium series together with animalization and vegetation... Polarity is nothing but contraposition in unification" (Steffens 1801, 193–4).

Hegel's main objections to Steffens's account are that the principle of movement falls outside the inorganic natural products: nature is not regarded as a process, but as "quiescent being" (*als ruhendes Seyn*; *PS* 161.34–39/M 174), a complex of dead, inactive products. Mere number, quantity, is an indifferent magnitude, an inessential determination,[79] which expresses no connection or transition of properties to another, but instead voids any conformity to law (*PS* 162.4–8/M 174). This recalls Hegel's point in "Force and Understanding" about the vacuity of the covering-law model of scientific explanation; neither that account nor Steffens's explains why specific individuals behave in regular, quantifiable fashion.[80] Thus Steffens's reduction of activities or material combinations to unity is nothing but the internal exposition and figuration (*Figuration*) of what is merely formal (*PS* 162.19/M 174).

In the second part of Steffens's *Beyträge*, inorganic nature is said to exhibit the inevitable organization of the inner activity of nature; hence organic life exhibits (*darstellt*) the highest peak of its producing in opposed directions, by blindly generating the degrees of animality (Steffens 1801, 265) up to the antithesis between individual and species (Steffens 1801, 310), including, e.g. – following Schelling – both face (*Gesicht*) and feeling (*Gefühl*), which "represent" the ideal and real pole of the senses (Steffens 1801, 312), and instinct and reason (Steffens 1801, 313). Only the "truest," the most individual formation, the human being, which represents the centripetal tendency of the whole of nature, is the creature that has an entire world opposed to him while carrying an entire world within him (Steffens 1801, 316). Once Steffens "proved" the *necessity* of a discontinuity in the forms of the superior animals, he rejected the images of the ladder and the net, as Blumenbach had also done. But while Blumenbach had developed a classification of his own based on *habitus*, Steffens regards the question of the criterion, of the Ariadne's thread through the labyrinth of nature, as an insoluble question. Against any continuous transition of organic shapes one into the other, Steffens speaks of "a much deeper fundament at the basis" of progressive formations, finally appealing to "an infinite, holy, mysterious abyss (*Abgrund*) of forms," into which we can only gaze in amazement (Steffens 1801, 304–6). What nature seeks in its degrees of individuation is nothing but a "creation in which her entire infinity is expressed by (*aus*) what is the most individual" (Steffens 1801, 291).

Hegel contends that this kind of Schellingian philosophy of nature only allows "reason as *life* in general (*überhaupt*)" to be observed in existing, determinate beings, though such general observations do not themselves afford any rational series or arrangement of members, nor any system of forms grounded within itself (*PS* 165.24–27/M 178). The universal individual which concludes the entire construction is only *immediately* the individual of the natural formations (*Gestaltungen*) and is not consciousness itself (*PS* 164.32–34/M 177).[81]

Steffens would not have been discouraged by the failure of his overall quest for law-likeness, for he claimed to believe to have been able nevertheless to prove the legitimacy of presupposing such a general conformity, because scientific experiments have shown "traces" of laws, thus authorizing us to draw the most important consequence (Steffens 1801, 103). Hegel concludes this section by rejoining that this kind of attempt offers on all sides "the beginning of laws, traces of necessity, allusions to order and series, ingenious and seeming (*scheinbare*) connections." Nevertheless, all of this has "nothing to do with law and necessity" (*PS* 166.18–21/M 179). To sum up, the organic unity that constitutes the universal nature of reason as the principle of identity that posits difference (negativity, separation, division) within itself – thus remaining simply self-identical within its development and articulation, in contrast to undifferentiated unity (of the kind championed by Schelling) – was not found to be reflected in such laws, where particular things were treated as abstract universalities.

Insofar as Schelling's ideas, also via Steffens, became matters for working scientists, they were accordingly criticized by working scientists, for example by the Professor of Chemistry J. B. Trommsdorff (cf. *Enc.* §328Z). Note that at least once, in Wintersemester 1799/1800, Schelling himself, then at the beginning of his career as Professor of Philosophy in Jena, lectured on a properly scientific, not philosophical subject matter: "*Organische Naturlehre*,"[82] and he influenced physics (Mende 1975; Olesko 1980; Caneva 1997) and biology (Richards 2002, 190–2 and *passim*). Once again, however, Hegel does not appear to have played merely the role of the learned and critical spectator of a scientific debate, for he clearly endorses key features of Trommsdorff's criticism of the Schellingian approach, presenting himself to the Jena academic scene not as a mere "mouthpiece" of

Schelling (as he was commonly regarded in 1801–03; Harris 2000, 273), but as someone who could provide scientific reasons with a proper conceptual, speculative ground. Indeed, Trommsdorff (1801, 194–202) criticized Schelling's and Steffens's contributions to the first volume of Schelling's *Zeitschrift für speculative Physik* because they were based on arbitrary synthesis of imagination, which substituted poetry for experimental research, mixed idealism and materialism, and thus appeared to be an extension of Spinozism, with very questionable accounts of contingency and freedom. In reviewing Steffens's account of Schelling's philosophy of nature (*Zeitschrift für speculative Physik* 1.1, 1.2), and Schelling's Appendix on Eschenmayer's *Spontaneität-Weltseele* (*Zeitschrift für speculative Physik* 2.1), Trommsdorff (1801, 201; 1802, 34) speaks repeatedly of the "spinozism" of this "objective ideal-realism" (cf. MM 20:435, 437–8/H&S 3:526, 228–9). Because Schelling taught "Philosophy of Nature" at Jena from 1798 to 1800, and lectures based on his principles were held starting in 1802 by his followers, including Krause, Gruber, Henrici (who lectured on Gall), Schelver, and eventually by Oken in 1807,[83] Steffens placed Schelling at a higher speculative level than Ritter and Arnim (Steffens 1801, 155 note 1). This highlights Hegel's double move, to criticize the main "academic" line of reasoning of Schelling's school and to demote Schelling's own philosophy of nature, with its claims to speculative truth and to absolute knowing, to the phenomenological level of Observing Reason, which "is not knowing (*Wissen*) itself, and does not know it" (*und kennt es nicht*; PS 168.16–18/M 181).[84]

2 Observing the Nature of the Self

2.1 The logical laws of the theoretical activity of the self

What results from Hegel's immanent examination of reason's attempts to find herself in outer organic life is that the opposition between universality and singularity fell outside of the essence, the in itself (*an sich*) of any individual organism. Therefore reason tries now to seek herself in the inwardness of organic life, that is, in the very element of the concept existing as concept, by looking for laws governing self-conscious thought (*PS* 167.5–15/M 180). Hegel briefly considers the logical laws of pure thought, by underlining the twofold aspect of their formality. When abstracted from all cognitive content, their formality entails their lack of truth (*PS* 167.16–24/M 180; cf. *CPR* B196–7); when not abstracted from all cognitive content, the content itself is transformed into something abstract and formal (cf. *PS* 167.20–24/M 180). Here the "low" side of reason is highlighted by two key objections Hegel makes to Kant's analysis of the understanding: Kant simply "found" the categories empirically, drawing them from ordinary logic. Kant's "finding" exhibits the unavoidable aspect of observation, which gives the laws of thought the character of something merely "given," that merely "is" in kind and number.[85] This converts their fluid nature as moments in the differentiated unity of thought into fixed determinations, without (necessarily) developing either their differences or their interrelations and genesis from the ground of their absolute totality.[86]

To this approach Hegel briefly opposes his own speculative appraisal of the laws of thought expounded in the Jena *Logic* (1804–05), "in which they show themselves to be what they are in truth, that is, single vanishing moments whose truth is only the whole of the thinking movement, the knowing itself."[87] In brief, what makes "observing" laws of thought untrue is the fluid nature of our mental processes, which is not captured by any fixed logical content. Second, this logical content appears to be a mere recollection of a number of mutually disconnected categories, simply retraced through the history of thought. Third, to account for an aggregate of de facto regularities, which as such are something merely given and externally found, fails to account for any immanent and philosophical critique of the dimensions of thought: observing laws of thought says nothing about how we should *truly* think and how our basic concepts are integrated in the unity of thought. Simply put, "observing" laws of thought cannot justify the normative and systematic nature of thought.[88] Driven by her instinct, reason therefore turns to observing self-conscious actions, to find laws for the intrinsic difference of individuals who distinguish themselves in and through their behavior.

2.2 The psychological laws of the practical activity of the self

In its reality the being-for-itself is active consciousness; hence Hegel can outline the transition from the observation of the laws of thought to reason seeking the laws of the behavior of individual consciousness in her actual being-other, that is, within her social and cultural environment, by writing that consciousness will "by the nature of the matter" be led to this new field of inquiry (*PS* 168.24–34/M 181–2). Thus the dialectic of the laws of thought provides an important transition: we pass from the theoretical activity of performing experiments and arranging observations to understand a natural world the existence of which is independent from us, and in respect to which we are passive, to a human world resulting from our social history, in which *reason takes herself as an agent*, thus paving the way to the following sections on the actualization of rational self-consciousness through her own activity and on the individuality which takes itself to be real in and for itself.[89] Turning now to the actuality of spirit overcomes the limit of a merely observational reason that is "too narrowly interested in the immediate *individuality*" both of natural objects and of self-consciousness itself. This limit is why "reason still falls short of absolute knowing" (Houlgate 2005, 78).[90] From this point of view, these pages on behavior are not at all a "repulsively long discussion of the crude physiognomic speculations of Lavater and the phrenological fantasies of Gall" (Findlay 1977, xix). Indeed, an echo of this discussion returns at the anthropological level of the corporeality of spirit, where Hegel opposes contemporaneous physiognomy by providing his own system of the somatizations of the inward content of the human soul (*Enc.* §§401, 411Z).

Once again, consciousness as Observing Reason is not aware of the spiritual content and movement of her experience. Therefore, in observing the *interaction* of the individual with his *community* and in seeking the psychological laws governing these interactions, she takes the universal modes of thought (mental faculties, inclinations, etc.) of individuals to be distinct from the "objective" or social side (habits, traditions, cultural ways of thinking etc.), which are again regarded, according to natural consciousness's wont, as something "given" and externally "found." Observing Reason's first strategy is to comprehend self-conscious behavior by beginning with the external actuality of the individual's natural and social world. This results, however, in the inversion of this standpoint: it is to be shown that the world of the individual must be comprehended through the individual him- or herself. The point of any alleged law of psychological necessity is to show the effects and influences of the individual's environment on the individual. Psychological laws miss the point and do not hold (*PS* 171.15–17/M 185), for their representation implies two sides that fall apart: a world that *an sich* is already given, and an individuality existing on its own account (*PS* 171.13–17/M 185). Hegel contends that things in truth *are* otherwise: how any individual behaves is not merely a function of his or her environment, but also of how he or she apprehends his or her given situation. Depending on how an individual regards his or her circumstances, he or she can either comply with them, or remain indifferent to them, or change – even react against – them, in various, particular, and *unpredictable* ways: "individuality is what *its* world as *its own world* is" (*PS* 171.10–11/ M 185). Thus neither environmental circumstances nor individual character alone can determine or predict individual behavior (Emerson 1987, 137–8).

Surmounting this failure requires yet another strategy. Observing reason's final strategy for understanding and explaining individual behavior attempts to determine laws that relate an individual's character to his or her bodily characteristics, by studying physiognomy and phrenology. Hegel shows how these strategies, too, fail to provide even candidates for genuine laws, in part because the relative durability of physiological characteristics cannot explain the range of an individual's often momentary forms of behavior. Rational spontaneity simply cannot be understood, explained, or predicted by observational methods. The alternative, then, is to examine how rational self-consciousness actualizes itself as an objectively real historical *world* in and through its own activity. This is the topic of the second part of Hegel's chapter on Reason, which makes the transition to the section on Spirit.

2.3 Physiognomy and phrenology

In Hegel's day, the attempt to understand a human being in terms of the outer expression of the individual inner being was the core of Lavater's very popular hermeneutic and semiotic project, a cultural enterprise also undertaken by Goethe, Herder, and Sömmering among others.[91] Lavater sought to "know the inwardness of man by means of his outwardness,"[92] by deciphering at least some[93] of the divine alphabet's characters written on the human face and the external, visible surface of the body. Physiognomy is the "science that explains the signs of the faculties," interprets supersensible (i.e., unobservable) forces, and judges the inner person via the outer body (Lavater 1782, Fragment 4 [p. 25], Addition, p. 27). Although he acknowledged dissimulation and mimicry, so that not every external feature can be taken as a genuine sign of an internal trait (cf. *PS* 176.17–25/M 191),[94] this science is "true," for it is the true and visible expression of invisible qualities (Lavater 1782, Fragment 5 [p. 29]); it has nothing to do with divining human destiny from perceptible, discernable lines (known as chiromancy).[95] As the sole uncontroverted and demonstrated proposition of his "science," Lavater offers this: "the external distinction (*différence extérieure*) of the human face and figure must necessarily have a certain relationship, a natural analogy, with the internal distinction (*différence intérieure*) of the spirit and the heart" (Lavater 1782, Fragment 5 [p. 30]). Furthermore, the tools Lavater requires to carry on his 'scientific' inquiry are personal talent, ability acquired by practice, sound inferential reasoning (Lavater 1782, Fragment 3, [pp. 22–23]), attention to details, and analytical, comparative, and synthetic skills (Lavater 1782, Fragment 14 [pp. 107–8]): in sum, a kind of "observing spirit" that Lavater himself (Fragment 14) claims is rare in Physiognomy. This "science," for which Lavater never provided a systematic code or table of proportions,[96] is thus conducted by three different kinds of experts: the natural physiognomist, who is able to formulate a true judgment on an unknown subject at a first sight, after the first impressions of his outwardness; the learned physiognomist, who classifies lineaments and external signs; and the philosophical physiognomist, who examines the reasons for determinate features, discovering internal causes of these visible effects.[97]

Referring inter alia to Lichtenberg's comments (Gray 2004, 26–7), which were also discussed by Lavater (1782, 237–90), Hegel shows how Lavater's project is a groundless blend of 'high' and 'low' traits: On the one hand spirit, individual self-consciousness, is rightly supposed to be known in its outer manifestations,[98] and this aspect meets the proper rational demand for the actual existence of the truth. On the other hand, its "language," the "visible" part of its "invisible" essence, is taken according to the low, inadequate, sensible profile to be the immediate being of a body conceived of as shaped and molded by mental forces and faculties, a passive being that is the *sign* of the inner (*PS* 173.35–174.1/M 188), an immobile reality, a mere thing (*PS* 179.37–180.3/M 195), which receives its features from an external, alien element, and lacks of any meaning on its own (Hyppolite 1974, 268–9).[99] On Hegel's view, the mutual externality of both the 'high' and 'low' aspects makes their relation something absolutely contingent for the self-conscious being (*PS* 176.1–12/M 190). Thus, the over-hasty judgment of the natural physiognomist expresses merely subjective opinion, and his required rare skills are able to grasp only a presumed being: that is to say, on the basis of modern scientific methodology alone, the laws of physiognomy lack both foundation and finality.[100]

Significantly, the followers of Gall's theory (Arnold 1805, 12–27), which became increasingly popular after Austria banned it in 1801 for its alleged materialism (Wyhe 2002a, 25ff.), raised the same kinds of objections to Lavater's enterprise, namely: its results are empty and uncertain and it establishes only a contingent, accidental connection between the "inner ground" and the "outer appearance" of human behavior ([Bloede] 1805, 106; Arnold 1805, 90). From the standpoint of Gall's *Phrenology* or *Organology* (Wyhe 2002a, 22), the main defect of Lavater's Physiognomy was to omit the brain, which was claimed to contain the "organs of spirit's development," such as the organs[101] of the sense of colors, tones, words, language, but also the sense of "circumspection,"[102] "metaphysical depth," and "theosophy," and which, by relying only on the skull, had no bearing on the construction and form of all the other parts of the human body, including the face (Bischoff 1805, 106–7, 110–14). When presenting Gall's theories of the brain and skull, on which Gall himself lectured in Jena in 1801,[103] his supporters emphasized their empiricism and certainty, in line with Cicero's and Bacon's (Aph. 36) claims to "follow nature." Phrenology was a purely empirical, though "entirely new" science, with no trace of speculation ([Bloede] 1805, v, 15). According to Hufeland, Gall was endowed with a rare degree of observational spirit and had established "truths" as a simple replication of nature (Bischoff 1805, 117–18). They all insisted that Gall's doctrine was grounded on the "observation of nature,"[104] that is, on an anatomical and physiological basis,[105] according to which innate human predispositions (mental faculties and spiritual tendencies) correspond to organs which impress themselves on the surface of the brain, where they have a proper specific localization, and, through protrusions and folds, build the apophysis and the hollows of the skull.[106]

Like Schelling in 1807,[107] Steffens (1805, 18–19) criticized Gall's doctrine as a "false hypothesis" on the basis of his theory, recounted above, of the whole of nature that expresses itself through the determinate contrapositions of two factors: in the highest form of the polar organization of nature's activity, the individual human being, whose system of bones represents passivity, while the system of sensitivity represents activity, so that the brain had no 'local' reality separated from the whole of the body, and there was no other *organ* for the soul than the body itself. In his criticism of Gall, Hegel also implicitly objects to Steffens's attempt to seek "organs" for spirit. When examining Lavater's theory, Hegel already stressed that the genuine being and essence (the in-itself) of the inner spiritual individuality of man rests on his actual voluntary intentions and conduct, in the nature of his free activity, not in his bodily shape.[108] Once again, Hegel's 1807 position against Gall's reductive physiological approach to our universal mental faculties, and against Steffens's romantic science, results neither from a common moral and humanistic philosophical attitude opposed to experimental science,[109] nor from an observational approach disengaged from debate raised by the empirical sciences' approach to the study of human nature, for it accords with another line of objection that, in Hegel's terms, "instinctively" rejected the presumptive "science" of the skull: recall Rousseau's motto in *Emile*: "*Pour connoître les hommes, il faut les voir agir*,"[110] which appeared on the frontispiece of Bergk's 1803 reaction to Gall's attempt to identify the moral and intellectual qualities of people from their (alleged) innate dispositions, organs, impressions on the brain cortex, and shape of the skull, by reducing a cultural, psychological, and anthropological question to mere physiology.[111] Against this critical background, Hegel claims that to conceive the relationship between inner and outer as a "sign," à la Lavater, which at least conveys the significance of a conscious, expressive movement, is something higher than taking what is in itself a dead object, a *caput mortuum*, a phrenological skull to convey, through mechanical cause–effect relations with organs impressed within the brain, the expression of the inner spirituality of individuals (*PS* 182.12–183.2, 184.12–29/M 198–9, 200–1). So doing takes recourse to mere thinghood, whereas the dialectic of the laws of inorganic nature exhibited the highest peak of reason's conceptualization of sensuous being (the purified matter) and the observable actualization of the nomothetic universality of thought. The very highest, the knowing of the inner human self through its outer manifestation, is joined by phrenology to the very lowest: an ossified, dead shape.

The doctrine of the skull (*Schädellehre*) thus becomes the Golgotha (*Schädelstätte*) of the spirit, which does not exist as a mere body, in the form of an aconceptual being.[112] At best this reduces the reality of spirit to the arbitrary and indifferent exhibition and connections of ossified hollows or bumps for any faculty of the soul:[113] "Thus this final stage of Reason in its observational role is its worst; but this is why its inversion becomes necessary" (*PS* 189.9–10/M 206). Thus does Hegel conclude reason's purely intellective knowing of our human intellectual and moral dispositions in their finitude. Once again, the failure rests on both an object's resistance to mechanical cause–effect explanation (spiritual freedom) and a conceptual fallacy, for "the objects of reason cannot be determined through such finite predicates" (*Enc.* §28Z). This extreme alienation creates for itself the possibility of knowing a higher, conceptual existence for the spiritual reality of self-consciousness, whose outer existence has now entirely exhausted the prospects of being taken as the mere form of a lifeless, fixed being. As Hegel says, "spirit's being active implies . . . that it manifests itself outwardly . . . It is essential that spirit be considered in its concrete actuality, in its energy, and more precisely in such a way that its utterances are recognized as being determined through its inwardness" (*Enc.* §34Z). True comprehension of concrete conscious agency requires considering the agent's perspective, his or her relationships and self-manifestation, explaining (infinite) freedom as constituting the sociality of human life with appropriate categories, passing from the intellective dimension of law as *Gesetz* to the rational dimension of law as *Recht* (see Hoffheimer 1992, 45–52).[114] This strategy is examined in the remaining subsections of "Reason."

Notes

1 Cf. *PR*, Preface: "To comprehend what is is the task of philosophy, for what is, is reason" (MM 7.26/Nisbet 21); on philosophy's necessary accord with actuality (in contrast to transient, insignificant appearance) and experience, see *Enc.* §6.

2 *Enc.* §§38Z, 227Z; Inwood (1983, 67). Only this kind of (analytical) empiricism remains opposed to speculation. See, e.g., Hegel's appreciation of Aristotle's

philosophy of nature: "Aristotle is completely empirical inasmuch as he is at the same time thinking . . . The empirical conceived in its synthesis is the speculative concept" (quoted by Ferrarin 2001, 219; cf. MM 19:146–7, 172, 246/H&S 2:131–3, 228–9, cf. 149–50).
3 Stewart (2000, 174–5, 178–9).
4 The point, however, was not entirely alien to the working scientists of the time. For instance, presenting a book by Carl Wilhelm Fuch, Trommsdorff, Professor of Chemistry at Erfurt, supports the project of a *Zoochemie* in the sense of a "vital Chemistry," as part of physiology (accounting for light, warmth, electricity, magnetism, galvanism), that has nothing to do with the representation of a chemical *analysis* of *dead* animal substances (Fuch 1800; Vorrede, viii–ix).
5 Cf. Neuser (1995, 175f.); Illetterati (1995a, 347); Ferrarin (1998, 76); Poggi (2000, 48).
6 Ziche (1997, 18–30, 40); Fritscher (2002, 60–1). A host of surviving manuscripts related to philosophy of nature (and of spirit) belongs to the series of lectures Hegel delivered between 1803 and 1806 known as the *Jenaer Realphilosophie* (*GW* 6–8). Note that Hegel became *außerordentlicher Professor* at the University of Jena only in 1805 (Müller 2006, 523f.), and he also became member of the Heidelberger Society of Physics in 1807 (Ziche 1997, 19); he was not, however, a member of the *Naturforschende Gesellschaft* (as Schelling was; cf. Ziche 1997, 18–19). (An "*außerordentlicher*" Professor is not a regular member of the faculty. – *Ed.*)
7 "Ich habe mich blos an solche Gegenstände gehalten, welche die Natur dem Auge des Beobachters darbieten"(Lasius 1789, iv).
8 Cf. Hegel 2002, 252–6, editorial notes from 128.27–129.3 to 130.3–6; cf. *Enc.* §340Z.
9 Lasius (1789, v): "Gern hätte ich die Ordnung die ich bey dem Ganggebirge beobachtete, hier ebenfalls verfolgt, allein ich fand in dem Laufe der Beschreibung so mannichfaltige Schwierigkeiten, daß ich mich genöthiget sahe, in umgekehrter Ordnung zu gehen"; cf. *Enc.* [1817] §§264, 339Z, 340Z.
10 Lasius (1789, v): "Ich weiß nicht ob es die Gewohnheit macht, daß man alle in verschiedenen Schriften beschriebene Flötzgebirge nach dieser beobachteten Folge abgehandelt findet, oder woher es kommen mogte, daß mir in der Beschreibung derselben der Uebergang von den ältern Flötzlagen zu den jüngeren nicht gefallen wollte?"
11 Cf. Emmerling (1793, V, IX) on the host of useless handbooks on mineralogy and on the comparison between Lenz's and Werner's systems. Hegel owned Emmerling's *Lehrbuch* (see Neuser 1987, 484 entry 61), and quotes Werner's mineralogy in *Enc.* §340Z. The same held for the classifications of the animal kingdom. Borowski reports at least four different classifications (by the ancients, Brisson, Linnaeus, and himself) in 6, 9, and 8 classes (Borowski 1780, 26–8).
12 See Russon (2004, 124).
13 Hegel owned the 1801 edition (Neuser 1987, 486 entry 91). In his "Preface," presenting the first section of his book on the metaphysical theory of nature, Gren (1797, vi–vii) claims to follow Kant's critical philosophy and its dynamical foundation of matter. When Hegel writes that consciousness will not let the perception that this penknife lies alongside this snuff-box pass for an observation (*PS* 139.9–11/M 147) he is likely thinking of Kant; see above, chapter 4, note 37.
14 Gren goes on to distinguish another sense of experience as experiment (see below). Moiso (2002, 436–7) underscores the typically German attitude of Gren's primacy of *Beobachtungen* over *Versuche*, the former constituting the integrated frame of reference of the latter, which counterbalances the risks of any partial or isolated experimental practice. Moiso also points out that a similar distinction between

observations and experiments within the general notion of experience is also found in the widely used, influential *Dictionary of Physics* by Gehler (1787–1796), under "*Erfahrung.*"

15 In its entirety, Brunner's passage runs: "Die Folge davon ist, daß angehende Geognosten, anstatt mit reinen Erfahrungen in ihrer Wissenschaft bekannt, und zur Vermehrung derselben angefeuert zu werden, Hypothesen und Meynungen kennen lernen, nach welchen sie aus Bequemlichkeit, oder gefasster Vorliebe nun alles entstehen lassen und ordnen; sich um fernere geognostische Erfahrungen wenig oder gar nicht mehr bekümmern, weil sie schon den Zweck erreicht zu haben glauben; oder wenn sie auch Beobachtungen mit aller vorhabenden Genauigkeit anstellen, doch alles zu flüchtig durch die Brille ihrer Schul-Hypothesen und Meynungen sehen, den unbefangenen Forscher mit zweydeutigen, oder wenigstens über die Richtigkeit derselben in Zweifel lassen" (Brunner 1803, v–vi); see Lamb (1980, 104). In his life-long controversy with Linnaeus, Buffon followed a similar line of argument, remarking that the only way to know the natural world was through sustained observation of bodies, without any "intention" (*dessin*), to the point of forbidding beginners, whenever possible, any premature deduction of lines of reasoning and connections (Buffon 1749, 6; see Barsanti 1992, 129ff.).

16 These lines probably refer implicitly to the new wealth of material supplied by the scientific journeys of discovery, beginning with de Saussure's tour of the Alps to investigate the formation of high mountains, up through Alexander von Humboldt's South America expedition (1799–1804). (This insatiable search may also echo the analogous points Hegel makes about the Lord and about the pyrrhonian Skeptic; see above, pp. 43–44, 61–62. – *Ed.*)

17 Here (*PS* 139.31–33/M 148) Hegel mentions also the case of "a new planet," referring to the "fortuitous," that is, contingent (in his eyes) discovery of Ceres by Piazzi: the final, main, controversial issue of his 1801 *De orbitis planetarum*. The acknowledgment seems to show also that in 1807 for Hegel the finding was not to be considered a scientific verification of Bode's law on the distance of the planets from the sun (Ferrini 1998). Also in this case, then, Hegel respected the rules of the empirical sciences. (For a different view see Renault 2001, 285).

18 Hegel draws examples from animals, plants, and mountain formations (*PS* 139.33–140.1–3/M 148). In his lectures of 1812/13 he will say that nature merges borders through transitions and mixes principles of difference (Hegel 2002 §50, 145.23–24).

19 *De part. anim.* I.ii–iii.642b.5–644a.10.

20 Linnaeus (1751, 98 note 155). See for instance Erxleben (1777). Consider, however, Linnaeus's warning that species and genera are always produced by nature only, whereas varieties are a cultural product of human ability, and classes and orders come from nature and art (Linnaeus 1751, n. 162, 101). Hegel owned the 1770 edition of the *Philosophia botanica* (Neuser 1987, 489 entry 129).

21 See Neuser (1987, 482 entry 28).

22 Another book owned by Hegel (Neuser 1987, 482 entry 29).

23 Blumenbach (1795, viii–x). For similar considerations regarding Linnaeus's terminology see Willdenow (1792, vi). It is therefore hard to maintain that ca. 1800 zoology and botany were "still entirely in line with Linnaeus's tradition" (Heuser-Keßler 1986, 24–5).

24 *Enc.* §226, cf. *PS* 140.18–22/M 148–9.

25 Harris (1983, 444): "The need for a double perspective itself arises from the logical necessity that every new phase in the evolution of the *Begriff* must carry all previous phases sublated within it."

26 The same holds for the problem of classifying the genera of fossils through internal (chemical, physical) or external characteristics (such as the location of the find, its

mineralogical characteristics, etc.). According to Emmerling (1793, xvi–xvii), all naturalists who do not follow Werner's oryctgonosy fall into confusing heterogeneous concepts, which is responsible for the incompleteness and uselessness of available descriptions of fossils. On Hegel and Werner's theory see Levere (1986). Hegel owned a book by Werner (Neuser 1987, 495 entry 227).

27 See Linnaeus (1751, 287): "in natural science, the principle of truth must be confirmed by observations."
28 Cf. *Enc.* §467 & *Z*; cf. *PS* 16.22–17.33/M 8–9. Cf. Hegel (2002 *ad* §50, 147.27–37b), where he mentions the classifications of the animals according to the elements of their habitat or according to their "weapons" as following the *Typus*. He says that through hoofs, horns and teeth "machen sich die Tiere gegeinander zum Einzelnen und Besonderen."
29 *PS* 140.32–36/M 149; cf. Treviranus (1802, v–vi): "Ein Werk, worin die vielen Thatsachen, die in den Schriften der Naturforscher zerstreut liegen, in Beziehung auf jenen Zweck zu einem Ganzen verbunden wären, würde einen höhern Werth haben, als alle Beschreibungen neuer Thiere und Pflanzen, die uns weiter nichts sagen, als dass diese so oder anders aussehen, und in diesem oder jenem Winkel der Erde zu finden sind."
30 *Gattung*: Hegel (2002, 281–2, editorial note to 143.17–22); cf. Breidbach (2004, 212–14, 219–20).
31 See the entire argument, *PS* 140.14–39/M 148–9; cf. Harris (1997, 1:484) and *Enc.* §353Z.
32 Cf. Hegel (2002 *ad* §14, 60.30–61.16b); *Enc.* §350 & *Z*. In the *Encyclopedia* (§§159ff.), the concept is defined as "the truth of being and essence," as "the *substantial might which is for itself*," that is, "what is *free*": a universality that remains within itself – and it is not dependent on, nor determined by, something alien to itself – in its self-differentiation. Moreover, Hegel stresses that conceptual freedom is to be (syllogistically) understood as totality insofar as *any singular moment* is the totality (the universality) that the concept is, and any moment is posited in an undivided unity with the concept itself. From the speculative and *a priori* standpoint of the determination of the concept, the systematic unity of nature's structural determination (*Enc.* §350Z) cannot be captured by analogies or similarities among single parts, marks or configurations arranged in a series of *external* transformations, as was the case with Goethe's metamorphosis (*Enc.* §345Z; Breidbach 2004, 221); see the following note.
33 Duchesneau (1998, 313–72, 121–48, respectively). See MM 20:241/H&S 3:333–4, where Hegel uses the same phenomenological instance of the animal's self-distinguishing marks to elucidate the deep meaning of Leibniz's principle. On the influence on botanical theory of Locke's criticism of essential classification, see Morton (1981, 235ff.). On Goethe's view, which oscillated between accepting Spinoza's monistic metaphysical principle that nature forms a single, unique totality within which all finite existences partake of infinity, and the reference to Leibniz's monadistic terminology whenever dealing with individual phenomena, see Bell (1984, 159–61); on Goethe's general dismissal of the concept of individuality for understanding organic nature, see Moiso (1998, 316). In his letter to C. L. F. Schulz of November 24, 1817, ten years after the *Phenomenology*, Goethe charged "numbers and signs" with "disemboweling" and "mummifying" natural phenomena, and mathematical calculus and experiments with burying "what was eternal" and immeasurable in singularities: cf. Verra (1976, 51–2). (Hegel's Lectures on the History of Philosophy in MM 20 are central to this chapter because they – like H&S – are based on Hegel's own full manuscript of these lectures from Jena 1805–06; see Hegel (1928, 17:xvii, 2–2; H&S 1:vi. – *Ed.*)
34 Hegel (2002 §45, 131.32–35, *ad* §45, 133.28–134.9a); *Enc.* [1817], §267.

35 *PS* 141.1–3/M 149, Harris (1997, 1:486); cf. *Enc.* §348 & *Z*. On Hegel's theory of plant life in the 1805/6 philosophy of nature, see Harris (1983, 451–7). On the influence of Aristotle's assessment of vegetable organisms on Hegel's view, see Illetterati (1995a, note 166, 393). It has been suggested that Hegel, in the *Encyclopedia*, refused to assign a proper, but granted only an analogical sexuality to plants, on the basis of Schelver's counterarguments: a criticism that the director of the Jena botanical garden early addressed to Linnaeus's *clavis systematis sexualis* but did not publish until 1812, on Goethe's advice (Bach 2004a, 187). Given the use of word *Schein* (semblance) in the *Phenomenology*, which suggests Hegel's distrust of Linnaeus's criterion, consider that both Schelver and Hegel may have drawn from a common source: Smellie's account of the sexuality of plants, which reports the scientific objections of Dr. Hope of the botanical garden of Edinburgh (Smellie 1791, 289ff.). This reference to Smellie does not lose its cogency even in the light of Bach's most recent publication: retracing the same orientation in an 1801 text (Hegel's first *Jenaer Systementwurf*), two years before Schelver's arrival in Jena, Bach underscores that there is no reason to speak of any immediate dependence of Hegel's position on Schelver's theories and sees the origin of the former in an independent philosophical appraisal of Linnaeus (Bach 2006, 75–6). On Linnaeus's reception in England with regard to feminine and masculine gender politics, see Schiebinger (2001, 107–33); on Smellie see ibid., 117–18. (I thank Thomas Bach for this bibliographical information.)

36 Hegel (2002 *ad* §46, 136.25–137.5b; cf. 272–4, editorial notes to 136.30–137.12).

37 At the time of the *Phenomenology*, Hegel owned the 1796 German translation of Fourcroy's *Philosophie chimique* and *Essai de statique Chimique* by Berthollet (1803; Neuser 1987, 485 entry 74, 481 entry 19, respectively). Lavoisier classified bodies according to their most characteristic chemical properties, following the relationship of composition and resolution showed by analysis and synthesis, which provided an order based on ratios of composition, in essentially static terms (*GW* 6:328–329, editorial note to 64.27–65.13). On Hegel's discussion of the chemical elements in his Jena Lectures on Philosophy of Nature, see Burbidge (1996, 20–2). Fourcroy tried to improve the order by giving it the shape of a natural series that would present the elements of the science together with their relationships, connections, and reciprocal actions (see Renault 2001, 251ff.). This was not without problems. See how Winterl sets up the problem constituted by the proper definition of what is an acid and what is a base for the host of distinguishing marks that come together. Those marks may give a likely indication of this or that nature of bodies, but do not provide anything *determinate*, for there is a borderline beyond which the acidic or basic character disappear in the same body (Winterl 1804, §1). On Winterl and Hegel's appreciation of him see Renault (2001, 231–2).

38 On Leibniz's law of continuity in the *New Essays* (1756) that leads to the modern revival of the "great chain of being," together with Bonnet's progressive scale of nature in his *Contemplation de la nature* (1764), see Barsanti (1992, 11–22).

39 See also Düsing (1988, 52).

40 See Schmied-Kowarzik (1996, 72–82); Frigo (1998, 219–29); Horstmann (2000, 127–40); Renault (2001, 45–9, 55).

41 In the case of the plant, the intellectual, abstract habit of thought confines itself to seeing in the forms of life only conflicts between one-sided incompatibilities; whereas the rational habit is able to recognize the opposites as "reciprocally necessary moments of a concrete becoming," for *die Sache selbst* "is not exhausted by stating it as an aim, but by carrying it out." Thus, in the case of the embryo, the human being is for itself only as a "cultivated Reason," which "has *made* itself into what it is *in itself*" (cf. *PS* 10.15–19/M 2; see Harris 1997, 1:488).

42 Hoffheimer (1992, note 36, 40–1), remarks that "Hegel is expanding on Kant's distinction that while nature is governed by laws, only rational creatures can act to the concept of laws . . . Kant associated this concept of the form of law, in contrast to natural laws, with freedom . . . Hegel is pushing the implications of Kant's practical philosophy back into nature."

43 Cf. *PS* 138.32–33/M 147, cf. Düsing (1993, 251). This cognitive unity should not be confused with Parmenides' identity or the idealist program (*pace* Fink 1977, 210).

44 In this Newton is close to Bacon: "For our road does not lie on a level, but ascends and descends; first ascending to axioms, then descending to works" (Aph. 103); ". . . my course and method . . . is this . . . from works and experiments to extract causes and axioms, and again from those causes and axioms new works and experiments" (Aph. 117).

45 *PS* 142.18–23/M 151. This was exactly the task that Galileo set for Aristotle in Day One of his *Dialogues on Two Chief World Systems*, defending his "truly" experimental method from Simplicio's apriorist *ipse dixit* even when confronted with new observational data that contradict an hypothesis (Galileo 1975, 63–4). By making this point, however, Hegel also pits Newton against Kepler (see the following note).

46 This point recalls and supports an early concern of Hegel's philosophy of nature. He had spoken of "true arithmetic" in the fourth of his *Theses* prefaced to his *Dissertation on the orbits of the planets* (1801), where he ascribes to the observable distances of the planets the status of not merely being a matter of experience *alone*, because "in truth the measure and number of nature cannot be alien to reason (*ratio*)" (Hegel 1801:31.19–22; *GW* 5:252.14–16). What is more, at the beginning he stated that "to be sure, the whole of mathematics must not be considered as purely ideal or formal, but at the same time real and physical. For the relations (*rationes*) among quantities exhibited by mathematics, precisely because they are reasons (*rationes*), they are inherent in nature, and if they are understood, they are laws of nature" (Hegel 1801:5.1–6; *GW* 5:238.7–10). Just a few lines before, Hegel warns the reader not to confuse purely mathematical relations with physical relations, rashly supposing that the lines used by geometry to construct demonstrations of its theorems are forces or directions of forces (Hegel 1801:4.25–5.1; *GW* 5:238.4–7). In Ferrini (1994), I have shown that, contrary to the received view, the central issue is that Hegel questions the validity of Newton's mathematical (pure and formal) demonstration of Kepler's (real and physical) second law.

47 Hegel appears to have in mind Hume's statement: "A stone or piece of metal raised into the air, and left without any support, immediately falls: But to consider the matter a priori, is there any thing we discover in this situation, which can beget the idea of a downward, rather than an upward, or any other motion, in the stone or metal?" (Hume 1975, 4.1.10). It is worth noting that Kant regards organics as a "class" of things, not as a miscellany of individual things. Postulating such a class supports our (i.e. Linnaeus's) *hope* to outline a system, bringing individual organic beings under genera or species (see *CJ*, "First Introduction," §V note, Ak 20: 216).

48 Mittelstraß (1972, 305). Recall that the famous thought experiment of the inclined plane on which is posited a "perfectly" spheric ball that presents the principle of inertia in the second day of the *Dialogues on Two Chief World Systems*, is introduced by Galileo by saying that he is sure that the effect will follow according his own (quantitative) representation *without experience*, because it is *necessary* that it follows thus (Galileo 1975, 177).

49 See Mittelstraß (1972, 306–7).

50 *PS* 144.22–32/M 153–4. Also see Gren (1797, §§829–831) on the component parts of atmospheric air and in particular on oxygen separated through heat (burning

certain quantities of either phosphorus or *gas oxicum*) from the *Sauerstoffgas* (*gas oxicum*) by Lavoisier. In §839, the *Sauerstoff* (mentioned by Hegel) is "for us a simple substance (*eine einfache Substanz*), that is to say, that we cannot decompose it further in other dissimilar matters (*Stoffe*)" (Gren 1797, 567). Dahlstrom (2007, 47) sees Hegel's reference to this process of purification in terms of "loss of the sensorily given individuality of things." In my view, Hegel contends that Oxygen, Heat, positive and negative Electricity are not ideal as if they were independent modes of a merely subjective thought, or ideas of reason according to which we question nature (see below, note 54). In the system Hegel makes clear that their significance and validity rests in being taken *from* their perceived sensuousness and their justification rests in the connection that can be demonstrated in the phenomena (*Enc.* §38).

51   See Riccioli's *Almagestum novum*, L. II, Cap. 21, Pr. 24 (Bononiae 1651; Frankfurt 1653).

52   Gren (1797, §213): "Aber diese Resultate treffen ohngeachtet des Widerstandes der Luft, auf welchen doch in der Theorie selbst keine Rücksicht genommen worden ist, so genau mit dieser selbst zusammen, daß schon deshalb mit Recht Mißtrauen in die Zuverlässigkeit der Beobachtung gesetzt werden kann." By connecting the Galilean law of falling bodies with the polemic on heliocentrism, the Jesuit Father Riccioli eventually took his experimental proof of the reality of the acceleration as invalidating the Copernican daily motion of the Earth, which would have required (according to Galileo's "strange conjecture") that falling bodies would traverse equal spaces in equal times along a circular trajectory ending in the centre of the Earth. On the issue and Riccioli's misunderstanding of Galileo's argument see Dinis (2002, 63ff.). For a recent assessment of Riccioli's and Grimaldi's experiments, performed with a more advanced instrument for the measure of time (a pendulum with a very short period of oscillation: six times in one second) see Borgato (2002). Hegel will always maintain that the "proof" of an empirical law can only be given conceptually, on a rational, speculative basis (Ferrini 2004, 86–90).

53   *PS* 143.39–144.24/M 153–4. One of Hegel's examples is to show the passage from glass- and resin-electricity (static electricity, still connected to bodies) to the abstract representations of positive and negative electricity, as self-subsisting matters which are neither things nor properties, but "beings in the *form* of a universal." Compare Gren (1797, §1297), who provides the following sequence: first du Fay, who experimentally distinguished between the frictional electricity of rubbed glass and of resin. Yet this designation (*Bezeichnung*) proved inadequate because both bodies were proven to contain in part the two kinds of electricity. Then Franklin distinguished between *plus* (for frictional electricity) and *minus* (the frictional electricity produced by the glass tool that rubs glass and resin bodies) which eventually were called positive and negative electricity. Finally Lichtenberg introduced the notation +E and −E. On this and the other points made by Hegel (the relation between acid and base, their passing into a neutral product), see Winterl (1804, §157). In Winterl's (1804, §8) terminology, "syntomaties" designate the unions of acids with acids and of bases with bases, which differ from neutralization (ibid., §8; Hegel will refer to Winterl's syntomaties in *Enc.* §327Z.). On the emergence of formal and symbolic language in chemistry and on Hegel's subsequent treatment of chemical matters, forces, and processes see Engelhardt (1976, 34–42, 89–116). On the problem of "simplicity" and "matter" in chemistry, freeing it from sensible qualities and raising it from merely empirical knowledge (as stated by Kant, *MFNS*, Ak 4:469.8–11) to the status of a natural science with a pure part, see Renault (2002, 195–235). On Schelling's appraisal around 1800 of the scientific character of chemistry as "applied dynamics" see Verra (1976, 57–8). On Hegel's later intervention in scientific debates about chemistry see Renault (2001, 225–84).

54 *PS* 144.25–26/M 154. Kant had already recognized the "influence of reason on the classifications of students of nature," but he had taken, e.g., pure earth, pure water, pure air, as ideas of reason according to which we question nature, not as concepts of objects (cf. *CPR* A645–6/B673–4).
55 *PS* 144.34–38/M 154; Harris (1997, 1:493–95).
56 In *Enc.* §343Z Hegel states that, "generally in Life all the determinations of the Understanding cease to be valid," with special reference to the cause–effect relationship. To clarify Hegel's view on how a living organism develops its shape through the relation between its inner and outer (cf. *PS* 150.18–23/M 160–1), it is worth recalling how he sees the relationship between these two aspects of an animal organism in the 1805/06 philosophy of nature. Harris (1983, 459–60) explains: "We begin now directly with the lymph (i.e. the internalized raw material for body-building and activity). This energy forms the (self-reproductive) skin, and the inward antithesis of (sensible) bone and (irritable) muscle. Bone is called 'sensible' in the minimal meaning of the word – it can feel pressure or weight. The skin 'which can be and become everything' is the 'organic activity' of both the sensible and the irritable system. Within this frame of bones, muscles, and skin is the real inner organism. This begins with the productive activity of the digestive system – fuelled through the mouth and inner skin. Through this 'the animal heat' 'assaults' the mouth's pulped intake, first 'infecting' it with organic lymph (the saliva), then subjecting it to the organically chemical complements of acid and base (from stomach and pancreas) and finally to the 'fire' of the bile. In this way the outer organism produces the *blood* whose circulation constitutes the inner organism."
57 On the distinction between finite intellective and infinite rational thought, see *Enc.* §28Z.
58 These sections are certainly the best known and most studied of the entire chapter and, in contrast to the pages discussed so far, the editors of the critical edition of the *Phenomenology* have annotated them fairly well. See the editorial notes to *PS* 500–07, which refer to Treviranus, Kielmeyer, Kilian, Brown, Schelling, Steffens, Hoffmann, Lavater, Lichtenberg, Gall, and Hufeland.
59 In the "Preface" Hegel defined reason as the "purposive activity" (*das zweckmässige Thun*), "just as" Aristotle had determined nature as purposive activity (*PS* 20.11–15/M 12; *Enc.* §245Z). In the pages considered here Hegel repeatedly makes the point that the organism has within itself the principle of its own making; it is within itself its own goal, it preserves itself and maintains its individuality in relation to otherness [i.e., its environment – *Ed.*], it returns and has returned into itself (*PS* 145.9–13, 147.37–38, 148.15–16/M 154, 157–8, 158). What first initiated an organic process is its end (*PS* 146.28–38/M 156; cf. Aristotle *Phys.* I. I. 193b.15–20). In the *Encyclopedia* (§365R) the organism is what joins itself with itself *in its external process* (see Düsing 1997; De Cieri 2001). On Hegel and Aristotle's notion of organism and internal finality see Ferrarin (2001, 209–20), and Frigo (2004, 29–31).
60 As was held by Kielmeyer, *Über die Verhältniße der organischen Kräfte* (1793), and Schelling, *Einleitung zu den Ideen zu einer Philosophie der Natur* (1797) and *Weltseele* (1798).
61 See *CJ*, §§64–66. On Hegel's appreciation and criticism of the Kantian principle of the internal finality in the Jena period see Lamb (1987, 174–6) and Chiereghin (1990, 127–75).
62 For instance, by drawing a distinction between "advantage" and "purpose" in Kant's *The only possible Argument* (1763); see Ferrini (2000, 304–11).
63 Cf. Findlay (1980), Stanguennec (1990), Illetterati (1995a). Also see DeVries (1991). – *Ed.*
64 See Chiereghin (1990, 18), Harris (1997, 1:499).
65 *Enc.* [1817], §332R; cf. Lamb (1987) and Gottschlich (2006).

66 See Harris (1997, 1:495–504) on the entire argument of *PS* 145.14–149.31/M 154–60.
67 Cf. Harris (1997, 1:504–16).
68 Cf. Harris (1997, 1:522–39).
69 *PS* 154.36–155.28/M 166; see Breidbach (1982), d'Hondt (1986), Düsing (1986), Harris (1997, 1:515–16).
70 *PS* 156.1–12/M 167; see Illetterati (1992, 427–43) and Chiereghin (1994, 102–6).
71 As Hegel will do in the Heidelberg *Encyclopedia* (§§276, 277), in the Berlin *Encyclopedia* (§353), and in the *Science of Logic* (*GW* 12:185ff.), determining syllogistically those basic functions and systems of the animal organism: sensibility as universality, irritability as particularity, and reproduction as singularity; see Düsing (1986, 285).
72 In his *Lectures on the History of Philosophy* Hegel points out how Schelling drew from Kielmeyer's work (as well as from Herder's; see Bach 2001, 284–5) on organic forces and their compensation laws (MM 20:422/H&S 3:514; the reference does not appear in *VGP* 9). Moreover, Hegel stresses that philosophy must not borrow forms from mathematical science (MM 20:453/H&S 3:529). See also MM 20:440/H&S 3:530–1 on the untruth and externality conveyed by quantitative difference as used by Schelling to express individuality. Charges of formalism against Schelling's (as well as Görres's) notion of organism as "third power of the absolute identity" also appear in MM 20:443–4/H&S 3:534–5. The *Phenomenology* here paves the way to Hegel's famous definition of the philosophy of nature as the science of the idea in its being-other (*Enc.* §18), and of the absolute idea that at the end of the *Logic* resolves to release out of itself into freedom the moment of its particularity or of the initial determining, as nature (*Enc.* §244). Indeed, in the system the idea is present in nature only as the negation of the mutual extrinsicality that characterizes nature in respect to itself, that is, it is present only as its ideal unity (see Renault 2001, 56), until the point at which, with organic individuality, nature first reaches the determination of subjectivity (*Enc.* §252). In the organic individuality's singularity, the process is present in the simple form of the concept; for the organism maintains itself in otherness, its real determinations are brought back to their conceptual unity and are the concrete moment of universality (*Enc.* [1817], §273; Ilting 1987): the animal ends with the feeling of its own individuality, the self (*PS* 147.29/M 157; *Enc.* [1817], §§279–80). On the transition from nature to spirit, see Marmasse (2002).
73 In the Jena Logic Hegel did not conceive any dialectical unity of qualitative inwardness and quantitative outwardness as the form of the continuity of an essentiality with itself in its externality. In 1804–05 he treated relations among numbers only under the category of Quantity and within the frame of the "rational negation," even in the case of system of numbers (e.g., the scale of water temperature) where the external quantitative variation of a thing comes necessarily to be considered together with its qualitative determination (cf. *L&M*, *GW* 7:22.7–23.28). Only in the 1812 Doctrine of Being of the greater *Logic* does a new category, Measure, emerge within the transition of Quality into Quantity (a double transition in the 1832 edition), as a determinate self-relating externality, thus providing a form for thinking of the unity of the inner and the outer aspects of a concrete natural thing in the immediacy of being. On this necessary logical correlation of the qualities of natural things with their magnitude for the measuring an organism, which overcomes the problem of applying indifferent and abstract numbers to life, its context and its variation in the 1832 edition of the *Science of Logic*, see Ferrini (1988). On laws and magnitudes of nature as moments of the category of Measure in its various systematic versions, see Ferrini (1998).

74 Hegel cites and discusses Autenrieth (1801) in *Enc.* §§354Z, 355Z, 362Z, 365Z, 368Z, 374Z.
75 Brandis identified the cause of the *Lebenskraft*'s action in the *Reitz* (*irritamentum*, *stimulum*: Brandis 1795 §9), emphasizing how "up to now" (*bis jetzt*) that force did not allow itself to be brought back to the known laws of the physical forces of unorganized nature (Brandis 1795 §7 [pp. 15, 23], §8). Alexander von Humboldt, following the Edinburgh school of chemical physiology, had already indicated the effect of the *Lebenskraft* (always bound to a certain part of caloric) in unbinding the chemical affinity's bonds, as well as in contrasting and mastering the proper motion of the elements of the organism. Material components which otherwise, left to themselves, would go on their own way, causing the decomposition (*Fäulniss*) of the organism itself (A. von Humboldt 1794 §2; cf. Hegel 2002 *ad* §47, 140.16–19a). Significantly, von Humboldt commended the Edinburgh school for restoring a view already advanced by the Ancients, referring to Cicero's *inclusus calor* (*De natura deorum* II.9) and to Sömmering. Indeed, Sömmering treated the same point, referring to Hyppocrates's and Galenus's *calidum innatum* and to Aristotle's *excrementum feminale* (Sömmering 1791 §33, note).
76 Properties such as coherence, cohesion (*Kohärenz*; *Kohäsion* in Schelling's – and Hegel's – terminology: *PS* 502, editorial note to 161.11–19), specific gravity, hardness, etc.
77 The "real pole," according to Schelling (Düsing 1988, 53).
78 The "ideal pole" for Schelling (Düsing 1988, 53; cf. *PS* 160.28–161.34/M 172–4).
79 *PS* 159.36–39, 160.10, 160.14–17, 162.4–9; cf. 157.13–17/M 171, 172, 174, cf. 168.
80 *PS* 94.35–95.24, 100.35–101.16/M 94–5, 101–2; cf. above, pp. 18–19. – *Ed.*
81 As to Hegel's notion of organism in the natural philosophy of 1805/6, Harris (1983, 451) remarks: "'Organism' is the concrete universal, the identity of the logical moments of universality and particularity in the singular subject who is a true individual. I say 'who' not 'which', because it is only the human organism [*sc.*: human consciousness] which properly realizes this identity."
82 Breidbach (2000), 47; cf. Neuper (2003). Thomas Bach has drawn my attention to the different ways Schelling's 1799/1800 course was advertised in the German and Latin versions of the University of Jena's public notices. The Latin catalogue is ordered by academic hierarchy, and the title of the lectures is: *Physica organica et principia philosophiae naturalis*. By contrast, the German checklist (published in the *Allgemeine Literatur-Zeitung*, n. 120 [1799], 972) is divided by subject matter. Schelling's course is entitled "*Organische Naturlehre*" and falls under the heading "*VII. Naturwissenschaften*," where the first heading is "*Wissenschaft überhaupt*" and the fifth "*Philosophie.*"
83 See Ziche (1997), Breidbach (2000), Bach (2004b).
84 See Vater (2003). On the basis of Schelling's earlier abandonment of philosophy of nature and formal constructions, Harris (1997, 1:513, 521) holds that the Schelling of 1807 is not a target of Hegel's attack, but in my view Harris fails to stress the significance of framing Schelling's positions in terms of consciousness's opposition to its object: see the entire argument of *PS* 167.33–168.16/M 180.
85 *PS* 167.33–35/M 181, cf. MM 20:346/H&S 3:439.
86 *PS* 167.35–168.20/M 181, cf. MM 20:346/H&S 3:439.
87 *PS* 168.20–23/M 181, cf. *L&M*, GW 7:123–6. Cf. Westphal (2000, §VII). – *Ed.*
88 Accounting for the normative dimensions of true and justified thought and judgment is a central task of Kant's *Critique of Pure Reason* (A261–3/B317–9). – *Ed.*
89 *Phenomenology* §§VB, C, on which see below, chapter 6. – *Ed.*

90 On the centrality of the problem of individuality for Hegel see Hyppolite (1974, 50, note 29); regarding this concluding moment of the dialectic of observing reason, see Moll (2004, 148–9, 151–5).
91 Graham (1979), Kordelas (1998), Gray (2004).
92 Lavater (1782, Fragments 3, 22, and 4, 25). Hegel refers to the first volume of Lavater's *Physiognomische Fragmente zur Beförderung der Menschenkenntiniß und Menschenliebe* (4 vols., 1775–78), which I quote from the French translation owned by the Thüringer Universitäts- und Landesbibliothek Jena.
93 This is why Lavater (1782, vii) composed his *Essay* by collecting his remarks into "fragments."
94 Gray (2004, xlvi).
95 Lavater (1782, Frag. 6, 40); cf. *PS* 174.6–19/M 188.
96 Lavater (1782, 271). Polemicizing against Lichtenberg, Lavater regrets having insufficient mathematical skill to compose a "table of proportions" to determine scientifically, through simple outlines of the skull, the measure of the intellectual faculties, or at least the degrees of human ability and talent; Lavater (1782, 247), "Remarques sur une dissertation physiognomonique de Monsieur le Professeur Lichtenberg." Tomasi (1997, 181–2, note 33), highlights Lavater's non-mathematical though scientific account of physiognomy, as the science of signs à la Baumgarten and in accord with the scientific though non-mathematical status of physics, medicine, theology and fine arts, for physiognomy partakes in all of them.
97 Lavater (1782, Frag. 3, 24); Gray (2004, xliv–xlviii).
98 *PS* 179.28–30/M 194; cf. *Enc.* §411.
99 On Hegel's criticism of the status of signs ("what passively receives the inner as an alien element into its passive existence"; *PS* 173.35–174.1/M 188) and of speech, action, and facial lineaments as outer aspects of self-conscious individuality, see Emerson (1987).
100 *PS* 177.17–178.13/M 192–3; cf. *Enc.* §411 & *Z*; see MacIntyre (1972), Verene (1985, 80–5), and Kordelas (1998, 159–64). Kant devoted the second part of his *Anthropologie in pragmatischer Hinsicht* to the ways of knowing human inwardness from its outer aspects, acknowledging that the properties of the human figure reveal tendencies and faculties of the subject under observation. Like Hegel, Kant denied that any kind of "conceptual description" (*Beschreibung nach Begriffen*) could provide scientific knowledge of human inwardness. Because it relies solely on observation and description, physiognomy does not overcome the limits of an anthropological *characteristica*. Unlike Hegel, according to Kant the scientific cognition of the properties of the human figure would be attained only through its reproduction and exposition in intuition (*Abbildung und Darstellung in der Anschauung*) or its imitation (*Nachahmung*) (Ak. 7:296).
101 For "organs" Gall intended "discrete regions of the cerebral cortex where innate universal faculties or aptitudes resided" (Wyhe 2002a, 21).
102 Drawn from J. H. Campe; cf. Wyhe (2002a, 20).
103 Gall's lectures in Jena, Weimar, and Halle were patronized by Goethe (Whye 2002a, 30–1).
104 Arnold (1805, 93). Gall's theory was criticized by Ackermann (1806) on the same basis (Illetterati 1995a, 417 note 234).
105 Drawing from Bonnet's thoughts about a theory of the forces of the soul ([Bloede] 1805, notes to §§8–9, 122–124, to §14, 127–8; to §15, 129; cf. *PS* 507, editorial note to 192.1.
106 [Bloede]1805, chapters I and II, 1–115. See Whye (2002a, 22–4) for the account of Gall's own presentation of his theory in the 1798 *Der neue Teutsche Merkur*. (A good selection of phrenological charts is included in Wyhe (2002b): http://pages.britishlibrary.net/phrenology/images.html – *Ed.*)

107 See Wyhe (2002a, 38 note 120).
108 *PS* 176.25–30, 178.21–179.24/M 191, 193–4.
109 See in this connection Bouton (2002, 189).
110 Rousseau (1969, 526); omitted from most editions; "In order to know men, consider their actions."
111 Bergk (1803), Ackermann (1806), cf. *PS* 188.22–23/M 205, *Enc.* §411 & Z. Note that, polemicizing against Lavater, Lichtenberg had also stressed that *actions* were the only reliable signs to decipher self-orienting, self-producing individual human inwardness; see Tomasi (1997, 157–8).
112 *PS* 187.6–12, 187.36–188.1/M 204–5; cf. Verene (1985, 87–91); Luft (1987, 37–8); Harris (1997, 1:582–606); Kordelas (1998, 164–75).
113 *PS* 183.11–31, 185.14–186.13/M 199, 202–3.
114 Consider that Hume (*Treatise*, 3.2.1) offered already an example of the link between actions as proper external signs to indicate the character of human inwardness and the social sense of moral qualities and justice: "It is evident that, when we praise any actions, we regard only the motives that produced them, and consider the actions as signs or indications of certain principles in the mind and temper. The external performance has no merit. We must look within to find the moral quality. This we cannot do directly; and therefore fix our attention on actions, as on external signs. But these actions are still considered as signs; and the ultimate object of our praise and approbation is the motive that produced them."

References

Ackermann, J. F. (1805) *Versuch einer physischen Darstellung der Lebenskräfte organisirter Körper*. Jena: Frommann.
Ackermann, J. F. (1806) *Die Gall'sche Hirn-, Schädel, und Organ-Lehre vom Gesichtspunkt der Erfahrung aus beurtheilt und wiederlegt*. Heidelberg and Frankfurt am Main: Mohr; Zimmer.
Arnold, J. T. F. K. (1805) *Dr. Joseph Gall's System des Gehirn- und Schädelbaues*. Erfurt: In der Henning'schen Buchhandlung.
Autenrieth, J. H. F. von (1801) *Handbuch der empirischen menschlichen Physiologie. Zum Gebrauch seiner Vorlesungen*, vol. 1. Tübingen: Heerbrandt.
Bach, T. (2001) *Biologie und Philosophie bei C. F. Kielmeyer und F. W. J. Schelling*. Stuttgart-Bad Cannstatt: Frommann-Holzboog.
Bach, T. (2004a) "Leben als Gattungsprozeß: Historisch-systematische Anmerkungen zur Unterscheidung von Pflanze und Tier bei Hegel," in W. Neuser et al. (eds.), *Logik, Mathematik und Natur im objektiven Idealismus* (pp. 175–90). Würzburg: Königshausen & Neumann.
Bach, T. (2004b) "Zur Institutionalisierung der Naturphilosophie in Jena," *Acta Historica Leopoldina* 43: 167–84.
Bach, T. (2006) "'Aber die organische Natur hat keine Geschichte...'. Hegel und die Naturgeschiche seiner Zeit," in R. Beuthan (ed.), *Geschichtlichkeit der Vernunft beim Jenaer Hegel* (pp. 57–80). Heidelberg: Winter.
Barsanti, G. (1992) *La scala, la mappa, l'albero. Immagini e classificazioni della natura fra Sei e Ottocento*. Firenze: Sansoni Editore.
Bell, D. (1984) *Spinoza in Germany from 1670 to the Age of Goethe*. Leeds: Maney & Son.
Bergk, Johann A. (1803) *Bemerkungen und Zweifel über die Gehirn- und Schädeltheorie des Dr. Gall in Wien*. Leipzig: Wilhelm Rein.
Bichat, M. F. X. (1995) *Recherches physiologique sur la vie et la mort*. Paris: Brosson, Gabou, et C.ie, 1799–1800; rpt. Paris: Gauthier-Villars.

Bischoff, C. H. E. (1805) *Darstellung der Gallschen Gehirn- und Schädel-Lehre [. . .] nebst Bemerkungen über diese Lehre von Dr. C. W. Hufeland*. Berlin: In Commission bei L. W. Wittich.

[Bloede, K. A.] (1805) *D. F. J. Galls Lehre über die Verrichtungen des Gehirns, nach dessen zu Dresden gehalten Vorlesungen [. . .] von einem unbefangenen Zuhörer*. Dresden: In der Arnoldischen Buchhandlung.

Blumenbach, D. J. F. (1791) *Handbuch der Naturgeschichte*, 4th ed. Göttingen: J. C. Dieterich.

Blumenbach, D. J. F. (1795) *De generis humani varietate nativa*, 3rd ed. Göttingen: Vandenhoek & Ruprecht.

Borgato, M. T. (2002) "Riccioli e la caduta dei gravi," in M. T. Borgato (ed.), *Giambattista Riccioli e il merito scientifico dei gesuiti nell'età barocca* (pp. 79–118). Firenze: Olschki.

Borowski, G. H. (1780) *Gemeinnüzzige Naturgeschichte des Thierreichs, darinn die merkwürdigsten und nüzlichsten Thiere in systematischer Ordnung beschrieben und alle Geschlechter in Abbildungen nach der Natur vorgestellet werden*. Berlin & Stralsund: G. A. Lange.

Borzeszkowski, H.-H. (2006) "Kann die Physik das Leben wissenschaftlich erfassen?," in A. Arndt et al. (eds.), *Das Leben Denken. Erster Teil, Hegel-Jahrbuch 2006*, pp. 197–201.

Bouton, C. (2002) "Die Theorie des Handelns in der Hegelschen Kritik der Physiognomik (*Phänomenologie des Geistes*, Kap. V)," in A. Arndt (ed.), *Phänomenologie des Geistes. Erster Teil, Hegel-Jahrbuch 2001*, pp. 184–90.

Brandis, J. D. (1795) *Versuch über die Lebenskraft*. Hannover: Hahn.

Breidbach, O. (1982) *Das Organische in Hegels Denken. Studie zur Naturphilosophie und Biologie um 1800*. Würzburg: Königshausen & Neumann.

Breidbach, O. (2000) "Jenaer Naturphilosophien um 1800," *Sudhoffs Archiv* 84: 19–49.

Breidbach, O. (2004) "Überlegung zur Typik des Organischen in Hegels Denken," in W. Neuser et al. (eds.), *Logik, Mathematik und Natur im objektiven Idealismus* (pp. 207–27). Würzburg: Königshausen & Neumann.

Brunner, J. (1803) *Handbuch der Gebirgskunde für angehende Geognosten*. Leipzig: Kleefeldsch.

Buffon, G.-L. Leclerc de (1749) "Premier discours. De la manière d'étudier et de traiter l'histoire naturelle," in G.-L. Leclerc de Buffon, *Histoire naturelle, générale et particulière, avec la description du Cabinet du Roi*, 15 vols. Paris: de l'Imprimerie Royale, 1749–67, 1, pp. 1–62.

Burbidge, J. (1996) *Real Process. How Logic and Chemistry Combine in Hegel's Philosophy of Nature*. Toronto: Toronto University Press.

Caneva, K. L. (1997) "Physics and Naturphilosophie: a Reconnaissance," *History of Science* 35: 35–106.

Chiereghin, F. (1990) "Finalità e idea della vita. La recezione hegeliana della teleologia in Kant," *Verifiche* 21: 127–229.

Chiereghin, F. (1994) *La "Fenomenologia dello spirito" di Hegel. Introduzione alla lettura*. Roma: La Nuova Italia Scientifica.

Dahlstrom, D. O. (2007) "Challenges to the Rational Observation of Nature in the *Phenomenology of Spirit*," *The Owl of Minerva* 38 (2006/07): 35–56.

De Cieri, A. (2001) "Presupposti aristotelici della filosofia dell'organico," *Atti dell'Accademia di Scienze Morali e Politiche* 111: 81–96.

De Vries, W. (1991) "Hegel's Dialectic of Teleology," *Philosophical Studies* 19: 51–70.

d'Hondt, J. (1986) "Le Concept de la Vie, chez Hegel," in R.-P. Horstmann and M. J. Petry (eds.), *Hegels Philosophie der Natur. Beziehung zwischen empirischer und spekulativer Naturerkenntnis* (pp. 138–50). Stuttgart: Klett-Cotta.

Dinis, A. (2002) "Was Riccioli a Secret Copernican?" in M. T. Borgato (ed.), *Giambattista Riccioli e il merito scientifico dei gesuiti nell'età barocca* (pp. 49–77). Firenze: Olschki.

Duchesneau, F. (1998) *Les modèles du vivant de Descartes à Leibniz*. Paris: Vrin.

Düsing, K. (1986) "Die Idee des Lebens in Hegels Logik," in R.-P. Horstmann and M. J. Petry (eds.), *Hegels Philosophie der Natur. Beziehung zwischen empirischer und spekulativer Naturerkenntnis* (pp. 276–89). Stuttgart: Klett-Cotta.

Düsing, K., ed. (1988) *Schellings und Hegels erste absolute Metaphysik (1801–1802). Zusammenfassende Vorlesungnachschriften von I. P. V. Troxler, herausgegeben, eingeleitet und mit Interpretationen versehen von Klaus Düsing*. Köln: Jürgen Dinter.

Düsing, K. (1993) "Der Begriff der Vernunft in Hegels *Phänomenologie*," in H. F. Fulda and R.-P. Horstmann (eds.), *Vernunftbegriffe in der Moderne* (pp. 245–60). Stuttgart: Klett-Cotta.

Düsing, K. (1997) "Ontologie bei Aristoteles und Hegel," *Hegel-Studien* 32: 61–92.

Emerson, M. (1987) "Hegel on the Inner and the Outer," *Idealistic Studies* 17: 133–47.

Emmerling, L. A. (1793) *Lehrbuch der Mineralogie*. Gießen: G. F. Heyer.

Engelhardt, D. von (1976) *Hegel und die Chemie. Studie zur Philosophie und Wissenschaft der Natur um 1800*. Wiesbaden: G. Pressler.

Erxleben, J. C. P. (1777) *Systema regni animalis per classes, ordines, genera, species, varietates, cum synonymia et historia animalium. Classis I. Mammalia*. Lipsiae: Weygand.

Ferrarin, A. (1998) "Aristotelian and Newtonian Models in Hegel's Philosophy of Nature," in R. S. Cohen and A. I. Tauber (eds.), *Philosophies of Nature: The Human Dimension* (pp. 71–90). Dordrecht: Kluwer.

Ferrarin, A. (2001) *Hegel and Aristotle*. New York: Cambridge University Press.

Ferrini, C. (1988) "On the Relation between 'Mode' and 'Measure' in Hegel's Science of Logic: Some Introductory Remarks," *The Owl of Minerva* 20: 21–49.

Ferrini, C. (1994) "On Newton's Demonstration of Kepler's Second Law in Hegel's *De Orbitis Planetarum*," *Philosophia naturalis* 31: 150–68.

Ferrini, C. (1998) "Framing Hypotheses: Numbers in Nature and the Logic of Measure in the Development of Hegel's System," in S. Houlgate (ed.), *Hegel and the Philosophy of Nature* (pp. 283–310). Albany, NY: State University of New York Press.

Ferrini, C. (2000) "Testing the Limits of Mechanical Explanation in Kant's Pre-Critical Writings," *Archiv für Geschichte der Philosophie* 82: 297–331.

Ferrini, C. (2004) "Being and Truth in Hegel's Philosophy of Nature," *Hegel-Studien* 37: 69–90.

Findlay, J. N. (1977) Foreword, in *Hegel's Phenomenology of Spirit*, tr. A. V. Miller (pp. v–xxx). Oxford: The Clarendon Press.

Findlay, J. N. (1980) "The Hegelian Treatment of Biology and Life," in R. S. Cohen and M. W. Wartofsky (eds.), *Hegel and the Sciences* (pp. 87–100). Dordrecht: Reidel.

Fink, E. (1977) *Hegel: Phänomenologische Interpretationen der "Phänomenologie des Geistes."* Frankfurt am Main: Klostermann.

Frigo, G. F. (1998) "Von der Natur als dem 'sichtbaren Geist' zur Natur als 'Anderssein des Geistes'. Der Ort der Natur in der Jenaer Reflexion Schellings und Hegels," in K. Vieweg (ed.), *Hegels Jenaer Naturphilosophie* (pp. 219–29). München: Fink.

Frigo, G. F. (2004) "Aristotels Einfluß auf Hegels Naturphilosophie," in W. Neuser et al. (eds.), *Logik, Mathematik und Natur im objektiven Idealismus* (pp. 23–38). Würzburg: Königshausen & Neumann.

Fritscher, B. (2002) "Hegel und die Geologie um 1800," in O. Breidbach and D. v. Engelhardt (eds.), *Hegel und die Lebenswissenschaften* (pp. 55–74). Berlin: Verlag für Wissenschaft und Bildung.

Fuch, C. W. (1800) *Ideen zu einer Zoochemie systematisch dargestellt [...] Mit Zusätzen und einer Vorrede versehen von D. Joh. B. Trommsdorff.* Erfurt: In der Henningschen Buchhandlung.

Galileo, G. (1975) *Dialogo sopra i due massimi sistemi del mondo tolemaico e copernicano*, 2nd ed. Einaudi: Torino.

Gottschlich, M. (2006) "Das Lebendige und sein Verhältnis zum Anorganischen," in A. Arndt et al. (eds.), *Das Leben Denken. Erster Teil, Hegel-Jahrbuch 2006*, pp. 213–20.

Graham, J. (1979) *Lavater's Essays on Physiognomy: A Study in the History of Ideas*. Bern: P. Lang.

Gray, R. Y. (2004) *About Face. German Physiognomic Thought from Lavater to Auschwitz.* Detroit: Wayne State University Press.

Gren, F. A. C. (1797) *Grundriß der Naturlehre*, 3rd ed. Halle: Hemmerde & Schwetschke.

Harris, H. S. (1983) *Night Thoughts (Jena 1801–1806)*. Oxford: The Clarendon Press.

Harris, H. S. (1997) *Hegel's Ladder*, Vol. I: *The Pilgrimage of Reason*. Cambridge, Mass.: Hackett Publishing Co.

Harris, H. S. (2000) *Between Kant and Hegel. Texts in the Development of Post-Kantian Idealism*, ed. and tr. G. di Giovanni and H. S. Harris, rev. ed. Cambridge, Mass.: Hackett Publishing Co.

Hegel, G. W. F. (1801) *Dissertatio philosophica de orbitis planetarum*. Jena: Prager.

Hegel, G. W. F. (1928) *Vorlesungen über die Geschichte der Philosophie*, vol. 1, ed. K. L. Michelet. Stuttgart: Frommann.

Hegel, G. W. F. (1963) *Lectures on the Philosophy of History*, tr. J. Sibree. London: Bell & Daldy (1872), rpt. London: Routledge & Kegan Paul; cited as 'Sibree'.

Hegel, G. W. F. (2002) *Philosophische Enzyklopädie*. Nürnberg 1812/13. Nachschriften von C. S. Meinel und J. F. H. Abegg, ed. U. Rameil, *Vorlesungen* 15. Hamburg: Meiner.

Heuser-Keßler, M.-L. (1986) *Die Produktivität der Natur. Schellings Naturphilosophie und das neue Paradigma der Selbstorganisation in der Naturwissenschaften*. Berlin: Duncker & Humblot.

Hoffheimer, M. (1992) "Hegel's Criticism of Law," *Hegel-Studien* 27: 27–52.

Horstmann, R.-P. (2000) "The Early Philosophy of Fichte and Schelling," in K. Ameriks (ed.), *The Cambridge Companion to German Idealism* (pp. 117–40). Cambridge: Cambridge University Press.

Houlgate, S. (2005) *An Introduction to Hegel: Freedom, Truth and History*. Oxford: Blackwell.

Humboldt, A. F. von (1794) *Aphorismen aus der chemischen Physiologie der Pflanzen*. Aus dem Lateinischen übersetzt von G. Fischer. Leipzig: Voss u. Co.

Hume, D. (1975) *An Enquiry Concerning Human Understanding*, in P. H. Nidditch (ed.), *Enquiries Concerning Human Understanding and Concerning the Principles of Morals*, 3rd ed. Oxford: The Clarendon Press.

Hyppolite, J. (1974) *Genesis and Structure of Hegel's Phenomenology of Spirit*, tr. S. Cherniak and J. Heckman. Evanston, IL: Northwestern University Press.

Illetterati, L. (1992) "Sulla posizione di Hegel nei confronti della *Naturphilosophie* romantica," *Verifiche* 21: 413–52.

Illetterati, L. (1995a) "Vita e organismo nella filosofia della natura," in F. Biasutti et al. (eds.), *Filosofia e scienze filosofiche nell'Enciclopedia hegeliana del 1817* (pp. 337–427). Trento: Verifiche.

Illetterati, L. (1995b) *Natura e ragione. Sullo sviluppo dell'idea di natura in Hegel*. Trento: Verifiche.

Ilting, K.-H. (1987) "Hegels Philosophie des Organischen," in M. J. Petry (ed.), *Hegel und die Naturwissenschaften* (pp. 349–76). Stuttgart-Bad Cannstatt: Frommann-Holzboog.

Inwood, M. J. (1983) *Hegel*. London: Routledge.
Knight, D. (1986) "Ordering the World," in R.-P. Horstmann and M. J. Petry (eds.), *Hegels Philosophie der Natur. Beziehung zwischen empirischer und spekulativer Naturerkenntnis* (pp. 401–12). Stuttgart: Klett-Cotta.
Kordelas, L. (1998) *Geist und caput mortuum. Hegels Kritik der Lehre Galls in der Phänomenologie des Geistes*. Würzburg: Königshausen & Neumann.
Lamb, D. (1980) *Hegel: From Foundation to System*. The Hague: M. Nijhoff.
Lamb, D. (1987) "Teleology: Kant and Hegel," in S. Priest (ed.), *Hegel's Critique of Kant* (pp. 173–84). Oxford: The Clarendon Press.
Lasius, G. S. O. (1789). *Beobachtungen über die Harzgebirge, nebst einem Profilrisse, als ein Beytrag zur Mineralogischen Naturkunde. Erster Theil*. Hannover: In der Helwingischen Hofbuchandlung.
Lavater, J. G. (ca. 1782) *Essai sur la Physiognomonie, destiné à faire Connoître l'Homme & à le faire Aimer. Par Jean Gaspard Lavater, Citoyen de Zurich et Ministre du St. Evangile. Prèmiere Partie. Dieu créa l'Homme à son Image*. La Haye: H. Steiner & Co.
Lepenies, W. (1978) *Das Ende der Naturgeschichte. Wandel kultureller Selbstverständlichkeiten in den Wissenschaften des 18. und 19. Jahrhunderts*. Frankfurt am Main: Suhrkamp.
Levere, T. H. (1986) "Hegel and the Earth Sciences," R.-P. Horstmann and Michael J. Petry (eds.), *Hegels Philosophie der Natur: Beziehungen zwischen empirischer und spekulativer Naturerkenntnis* (pp. 103–20). Stuttgart: Klett–Cotta.
Linnaeus, C. (1751) *Philosophia botanica in qua explicantur Fundamenta botanica cum definitionibus partium, exemplis terminorum, observationibus rariorum*. Stockholm: G. Kieswetter.
Luft, E. von der (1987) "The Birth of Spirit for Hegel out of the Travesty of Medicine," in P. G. Stillman (ed.), *Hegel's Philosophy of Spirit* (pp. 25–42). Albany: State University of New York Press.
MacIntyre, A. (1972) "Hegel on Face and Skulls," in A. MacIntyre (ed.), *Hegel: A Collection of Critical Essays* (pp. 219–36). New York: Anchor.
Marmasse, G. (2002) "Das Problem des Übergangs von der Natur zum Geist in Hegels *Enzyklopädie*, in R. Wahsner and T. Posch (eds.), *Die Natur muß bewiesen werden. Zu Grundfragen der Hegelschen Naturphilosophie* (pp. 142–58). Frankfurt am Main: Lang.
Mende, E. (1975) "Der Einfluß von Schellings 'Prinzip' auf Biologie und Physik der Romantik," *Philosophia naturalis* 15: 461–85.
Meyer, J. C. H. (1805) *Grundriß der Physiologie des menschlichen Körpers*. Berlin: Realschulbuch Handlung.
Mittelstraß, J. (1972) "The Galileian Revolution. The Historical Fate of a Methodological Insight," *Studies in the History and Philosophy of Science* 2: 297–328.
Moiso, F. (1998) "La scoperta dell'osso intermascellare e la questione del tipo osteologico," in G. Giorello and A. Grieco (eds.), *Goethe scienziato* (pp. 298–337). Torino: Einaudi.
Moiso, F. (2002) "*Experientia/experimentum* nel Romanticismo," in M. Veneziani (ed.), *Experientia* (pp. 435–522). Firenze: Olschki.
Moll, P. (2004) "The Purposive Purposelessness of Hegel's Physiognomy," in A. Arndt (ed.), *Hegels Phänomenologie des Geistes heute. Deutsche Zeitschrift für Philosophie*, Sonderband 8, pp. 145–56.
Morton, A. G. (1981) *History of Botanical Science: An Account of the Development of Botany from Ancient Times to the Present Day*. London: Academic Press.
Müller, G. (2001) "Perioden Goethescher Universitätspolitik," in G. Müller et al. (eds.), *Die Universität Jena. Tradition und Innovation um 1800* (pp. 135–53). Stuttgart: F. Steiner Verlag.

Müller, G. (2006) *Vom Regieren zum Gestalten, Goethe und die Universität Jena.* Heidelberg: Universitätsverlag Winter.

Neuper, H., with K. Kühn and M. Müller (2003) *Das Vorlesungsangebot an der Universität Jena von 1749 bis 1854,* 2 vols. Weimar: Verlag und Datenbank für Geisteswissenschaften.

Neuser, W. (1987) "Die naturphilosophische und naturwissenschaftliche Literatur aus Hegels privater Bibliothek," in M. J. Petry (ed.), *Hegel und die Naturwissenschaften* (pp. 479–99). Stuttgart-Bad Cannstatt: Frommann-Holzboog.

Neuser, W. (1995) *Natur und Begriff. Zur Theorienkonstitution und Begriffsgeschichte von Newton bis Hegel.* Stuttgart & Weimar: Metzler.

Newton, I. (1999) *The Principia: Mathematical Principles of Natural Philosophy,* tr. I. B. Cohen and A. Whitman, with J. Budenz. Berkeley: University of California Press.

Olesko, K. M. (1980) "The Emergence of Theoretical Physics in Germany: Franz Neumann and the Königsberg School of Physics, 1830–1890." PhD dissertation, Cornell University.

Poggi, S., ed. (1996) *Psicologia e scienze naturali,* vol. III, 2, in G. Bevilacqua (ed.), *I romantici tedeschi,* 3 vols. Milano: Rizzoli.

Poggi, S. (2000) *Il genio e l'unità della natura. La scienza della Germania romantica (1790–1830).* Bologna: Il Mulino.

Renault, E. (2001) *Hegel. La naturalisation de la dialectique.* Paris: Vrin.

Renault, E. (2002) *Philosophie chimique. Hegel et la science dynamiste de son temps.* Pessac: Presses Universitaires de Bourdeaux.

Richards, R. J. (2002) *The Romantic Conception of Life: Science and Philosophy in the Age of Goethe.* Chicago: University of Chicago Press.

Rosenkranz, K. (1844) *Georg Wilhelm Friedrich Hegel's Leben beschrieben durch Karl Rosenkranz.* Berlin: Duncker & Humblot.

Rousseau, J.-J. (1969) *Emile ou de l'Education,* in B. Gagnebin and M. Raymond (eds.), Jean-Jacques Rousseau, *Oeuvres Complètes,* IV. Paris: Gallimard.

Russon, J. (2004). *Reading Hegel's Phenomenology.* Bloomington and Indianapolis: Indiana University Press.

Schiebinger, L. (2001) "Das private Leben der Pflanzen: Geschlechterpolitik bei Carl von Linné und Erasmus Darwin," in M. Hagner (ed.), *Ansichten der Wissenschaftsgeschichte* (pp. 107–33). Frankfurt am Main: Fischer Verlag.

Schmied-Kowarzik, W. (1996) *"Von der wirklichen, von der seyenden Natur."* Stuttgart-Bad Cannstatt: Frommann-Holzboog.

Smellie, W. (1791) *Philosophie der Naturgeschichte [. . .] Aus dem Englischen übersetzt . . . von E. A. W. Zimmermann. Erster Theil.* Berlin: In der Vossischen Buchhandlung.

Sömmering, S. Th. (1791) *Vom Baue des menschlichen Körpers.* I. *Knochenlehre.* Frankfurt am Main: Varrentrapp und Wenner.

Stanguennec, A. (1990) "La finalité interne de l'organisme, de Kant à Hegel: D'une épistemologie critique à une ontologie speculative de la vie," in H.-F. Fulda and R.-P. Horstmann (eds.), *Hegel und die Kritik der Urteilskraft* (pp. 127–40). Stuttgart: Klett-Cotta.

Steffens, H. (1801) *Beyträge zur innern Naturgeschichte der Erde.* Freyberg: Im Verlag der Crazischen Buchhandlung.

Steffens, H. (1805) *Drei Vorlesungen des Herrn Prof. Steffens zu Halle über Hrn. D. Gall's Organenlehre.* Halle: Im Verlage der N. Soc. Buch- und Kunsthandlung.

Stewart, J. (2000) *The Unity of Hegel's Phenomenology of Spirit. A Systematic Interpretation.* Evanston, IL: Northwestern University Press.

Tomasi, G. (1997) *Significare con le forme. Valore simbolico del bello ed espressività della pittura in Kant.* Ancona: Il Lavoro Editoriale.

Treviranus, G. R. (1802) *Biologie, oder Philosophie der lebenden Natur für Naturfoscher und Ärzte,* I. Göttingen: Röwer.

Trommsdorff, J. B., ed. (1801) *Allgemeine chemische Bibliothek des neunzehnten Jahrhunderts. I.ten Bandes I.tes Stück*. Erfurt: In der Hennigschen Buchhandlung.

Trommsdorff, J. B., ed. (1802) *Allgemeine chemische Bibliothek des neunzehnten Jahrhunderts. I.ten Bandes 2.tes Stück*. Erfurt: In der Hennigschen Buchhandlung.

Vater, M. G. (2003) "Schelling in Hegel's *Phenomenology*. Verstand, Vernunft, Wissen," in A. Denker and M. Vater (eds.), *Hegel's Phenomenology of Spirit* (pp. 139–68). New York: Humanity Books.

Verene, D. P. (1985) "Phrenology," in D. P. Verene, *Hegel's Recollection. A Study of Images in the Phenomenology of Spirit* (pp. 80–91). Albany: State University of New York Press.

Verra, V. (1976) "La qualità nell'età romantica," in E. R. Lorch (ed.), *La qualità* (pp. 51–62; discussion: pp. 63–77). Bologna: Il Mulino.

Verra, V. (1997) "La filosofia della natura," in C. Cesa (ed.), *Guide ai filosofi. Hegel* (pp. 83–122). Roma-Bari: Laterza.

Wahsner, R. (2006) "Hegels ambivalenter Begriff 'Organismus'," in A. Arndt et al. (eds.), *Das Leben Denken. Erster Teil, Hegel-Jahrbuch 2006*, pp. 221–7.

Westphal, K. R. (1989) *Hegel's Epistemological Realism. A Study of the Aim and Method of Hegel's Phenomenology of Spirit*. Dordrecht: Kluwer.

Westphal, K. R. (2000) "Kant, Hegel, and the Fate of 'the' Intuitive Intellect," in S. Sedgwick (ed.), *The Reception of Kant's Critical Philosophy: Fichte, Schelling, and Hegel* (pp. 283–305). New York: Cambridge University Press.

Westphal, K. R. (2003). *Hegel's Epistemology. A Philosophical Introduction to the Phenomenology of Spirit*. Cambridge, Mass.: Hackett Publishing Co.

Willdenow, C. L. (1792) *Grundriss der Kräuterkunde zu Vorlesungen entworfen von Carl Ludwig Willdenow*. Berlin: Haude & Spener.

Winterl, J. J. (1804) *Darstellung der vier Bestandtheile der anorganischen Natur [. . .] Aus dem Lateinischen übersetzt von Dr. Johann Schuster*. Jena: Frommann.

Wyhe, J. van (2002a) "The Authority of Human Nature: the *Schädellehre* of Franz Joseph Gall," *British Journal for the History of Science* 35: 17–42.

Wyhe, J. van (2002b) "The History of Phrenology on the Web." http://pages.britishlibrary.net/ phrenology/images.html (accessed September 23, 2006).

Ziche, P. (1997) "Naturforschung in Jena zur Zeit Hegels. Materialen zum Hintergrund der spekulativen Naturphilosophie," *Hegel-Studien* 32: 9–40.

Further Reading

Observation of nature:

Bach, T. and Breidbach, O. (2001) *Die Lehre im Bereich der "Naturwissenschaft" an der Universität Jena zwischen 1788 und 1807*. Basel: Birkäuser.

Bach, T. and Breidbach, O., eds. (2005) *Naturphilosophie nach Schelling*. Stuttgart-Bad Cannstatt: Frommann-Holzboog.

Barrande, J. M. (1977) "Geo-logique (Hegel et les sciences de la terre)," *Annales publiées par l'Université de Tolouse* 13: 5–21.

Bogdandy, A. von (1989) *Hegels Theorie des Gesetzes*. Freiburg and München: K. Alber.

Bonsiepen, W. (1997) *Die Begründung einer Naturphilosophie bei Kant, Schelling, Fries und Hegel. Mathematische versus spekulative Naturphilosophie*. Frankfurt am Main: V. Klostermann.

Breidbach, O. (2005) *Bilder des Wissens: zur Kulturgeschichte der wissenschaftliche Wahrenhmung*. München: Fink.

Breidbach, O. and Ziche, P., eds. (2001) *Naturwissenschaften um 1800. Wissenschaftskultur in Jena-Weimar* Weimar: H. Böhlaus.

Ferrini, C. (2007) "Hegel's Confrontation with the Sciences in 'Observing Reason': Notes for a Discussion." *The Owl of Minerva* 55/56: 1–22.

Fink, G. L. and Klinger, A., eds. (2004) *Identitäten. Erfahrungen und Fiktionen um 1800.* Frankfurt am Main et al.: P. Lang.

Hagner, M. (1999) "Enlightened Monsters," in W. Clark et al. (eds.), *The Sciences in Enlightened Europe* (pp. 175–217). Chicago and London: The University of Chicago Press.

Heckmann, R., Krings, H., and Meyer, W. R. (1985) *Natur und Subjektivität. Zur Auseinandersetzung mit der Naturphilosophie des jungen Schelling.* Stuttgart-Bad Cannstatt: Frommann-Holzboog.

Kielmeyer, C. F. (1993) *Über die Verhältniße der organischen Kräfte untereinander in der Reihe der verschiedenen Organisationen, die Gesetze und Folgen dieser Verhältniße (1793)*, ed. with an Introduction by K. T. Kanz. Marburg: Basilisken-Presse.

Moiso, F. (1986) "Die Hegelsche Theorie der Physik und der Chemie in ihrer Beziehung zu Schellings Naturphilosophie," in R.-P. Horstmann and M. J. Petry (eds.), *Hegels Philosophie der Natur. Beziehung zwischen empirischer und spekulativer Naturerkenntnis* (pp. 54–87). Stuttgart: Klett-Cotta.

Montalenti, G. and Rossi, P. (1982) *Lazzaro Spallanzani e la biologia del Settecento.* Firenze: L. Olschki.

Salomon, J. (1990) *Die Sozietät für die gesamte Mineralogie zu Jena unter Goethe und Johann Georg Lenz.* Köln and Wien: Böhlau Verlag.

Schmied-Kowarzik, W. (1998). "Die frühen Abweichungen Hegels von der Naturphilosophie Schellings und ihre Folgen für das absolute System," in K. Vieweg (ed.), *Hegels Jenaer Naturphilosophie* (pp. 231–49). München: Fink.

Wahsner, R. (2005) *Hegel und das mechanistische Weltbild: vom Wissenschaftsprinzip Mechanismus zum Organismus als Vernunftbegriff.* Frankfurt am Main and New York: P. Lang.

Ziche, P. (1996) *Mathematische und naturwissenschaftliche Modelle in der Philosophie Schellings und Hegels.* Stuttgart-Bad Cannstatt: Frommann-Holzboog.

Physiognomy & Phrenology:

Bonfanti, E. (1997) "Il ritratto tra fisiognomica e 'semeiotica morale'," in E. Bonfanti and M. Fancelli (eds.), *Il Primato dell'occhio. Poesia e pittura nell'età di Goethe* (pp. 35–49). Roma: Artemide Edizioni.

Breidbach, O. (1997) *Die Materialisierung des Ichs: zur Geschichte der Hirnforschung im 19. und 20. Jahrhundert.* Frankfurt am Main: Suhrkamp.

Brooks, G. P. and Johnson, R. W. (1980) "Johann Caspar Lavater's *Essay on Physiognomy*," *Psychological Reports* 46: 3–20.

Campe, R. and Schneider, M., eds. (1996) *Geschichten der Physiognomik: Text, Bild, Wissen.* Freiburg im Breisgau: Rombach.

Cooter, R. J. (1976) "Phrenology: The Provocation of Progress," *History of Science* 14: 211–34.

Hagner, M. (1994) "Aufklärung über das Menschenhirn. Neue Wege der Neuroanatomie im späten 18. Jahrhundert," in H.-J. Schings (ed.), *Der Ganze Mensch. Anthropologie und Literatur im 18. Jahrhundert* (pp. 145–61). Stuttgart: Metzler.

Hall, J. Y. (1977) "Gall's Phrenology: A Romantic Psychology," *Studies in Romanticism* 16: 305–17.

Lanteri-Laura, G. (1993) *Histoire de la Phrénologie. L'homme et son cerveau selon F. J. Gall*, 2nd ed. Paris: Presses Universitaires de France.

Moiso, F. (1986) "Die Hegelsche Theorie der Physik und der Chemie in ihrer Beziehung zu Schellings Naturphilosophie," in R.-P. Horstmann and Michael J. Petry (eds.),

Hegels Philosophie der Natur: Beziehungen zwischen empirischer und spekulativer Naturerkenntnis (pp. 54–87). Stuttgart: Klett-Cotta.

Oehler-Klein, S. (1990) *Die Schädellehre Franz Joseph Galls in der Literatur und Kritik des 19. Jahrhunderts: zur Rezeptionsgeschichte einer medizinisch-biologisch begründeten Theorie der Physiognomik und Psychologie*. Stuttgart and New York: G. Fischer.

Pestalozzi, K. (1988) "Physiognomische Methodik," in A. Finck and G. Gréciano (eds.), *Germanistik aus interkultureller Perspektive*. Strasbourg: Université des sciences humaines de Strasbourg.

Renneville, M. (2000) *Le langage des crânes: une histoire de la phrénologie*. Paris: Institut d'éd. Sanofi-Synthélabo.

Sampalmieri, A. (1968) "Dalla fisiognomica di Giovanni Gaspare Lavater (1741–1801) alla frenologia di Francesco Giuseppe Gall (1758–1828)," *Medicina nei Secoli* 5.3: 10–16.

Schelling F. W. J. von (1807) "Einiges über die Schädellehre," *Morgenblatt* 74: 542–3.

6

Shapes of Active Reason: The Law of the Heart, Retrieved Virtue, and What Really Matters

Terry Pinkard

Hegel's examination of "the Actualization of Rational Self-consciousness through itself" (*PS* 193–214/M 211–35) is the second of three major sections of his chapter on "Reason." Thematically this section is closely related with the first sub-section of the subsequent third major section of "Reason," viz., "The Animal Kingdom and Humbug, or what really matters" (*PS* 214–28/M 236–52). Accordingly, the present chapter considers these sections together.

Hegel never tires of telling us that his work is a "system," a whole which can only be fully understood in its entirety; anything less, he insists, would not amount to *Wissenschaft*, "science" (or, more generally, rigorous theory). Even though saying it's so doesn't make it so, it still means that any interpreter of Hegel has to take that claim seriously. Nonetheless, Hegel does not make it easy. Each part of the system seems to demand coming to terms with some other part, and it is easy to despair of ever isolating the sense of any particular part.

The "Reason" chapter itself comes on the scene as the result of a puzzling transition. After the rather abstract discussions about "consciousness," Hegel turns to his social account of "self-consciousness," which results in the establishment and subsequent failure of relations of mastery and servitude between two individuals (obviously abstracted out of all their social relations, something Hegel stressed in his lectures on the subject; *Enc.* §432). Out of that, however, comes an obviously historically informed discussion of the ancient doctrines of stoicism and skepticism, an account of the anguish of Christianity in its early and mediaeval forms (as the promised savior failed to return for the final judgment), followed by an abrupt transition to an entirely new chapter, titled simply, "Reason," which itself begins with what can seem like some kind of once-over-lightly discussion of idealism in the philosophies of Kant and Fichte.[1] It then supposedly makes a necessary transition to an even longer chapter, titled "Spirit."

The puzzling nature of the "Reason" chapter has, however, a deeper rationale. First, the chapter advances the rather ambitious thesis that all individualist accounts of authority encounter a *partial* failure, which propels them to more social accounts. Second, it sets the stage for Hegel's equally ambitious thesis that we best understand the failure of individualist accounts only if we understand the role of reason in history, specifically, once we understand that when history is understood from the point of view of ourselves as self-interpreting animals, what turns out to have been at stake in history is the very nature of normative authority itself.[2] Third, this chapter advances the view that we have over historical time learned better how to mark what counts as normative authority, and that understanding what this requires of us amounts to "spirit's coming to a full self-consciousness," which is best characterized as an "absolute" point of view. This in turn leads Hegel to one of his most ambitious proposals of all, namely, that the best way to understand how a norm has its grip on us is to be found by looking at how accepted, "positive" norms *lose* their grip on us, which in turn leads him to his various phenomenological proposals that we examine such norms as they are *at work*, or are "actual," *wirklich* (as Hegel says), in various *practices*, which in turn leads to his thesis that reason itself must be also understood as social, and that in a very complicated, "dialectical" way, we hold ourselves responsible to the *world* only in holding ourselves in certain very determinate ways responsible to *each other*.

Hegel calls such practices "shapes of consciousness," which are themselves parts of more general practices which he calls "shapes of spirit," or what he sometimes called in his pre-*Phenomenology* writings "forms of life."[3] A "shape of spirit" is a social unity of *norm* and *fact* that shapes how people understand themselves and, equally importantly, how they envision their social existence (that is, how they see themselves as fitting together with others, what they can reasonably expect things go on among them and their fellows, how those expectations are to be normally met) and, crucially, a conception of what the *world* is like that makes those norms *realizable* (or not).[4] Equally crucially, such a "shape of spirit" constitutes an only partially articulated background understanding of this fusion of norm and fact; typically, a shape of spirit cannot be understood as a collection of beliefs but as a deeper orientation that is prior to and presupposed by explicit beliefs, giving the agents living in it a kind of unarticulated fluency which, as Hegel puts it, "consists in having the particular knowledge or kind of activities immediately to mind in any case that occurs, even, we may say, *immediate in our very limbs*, in an activity directed outwards."[5]

Modern individualism itself is such a "shape of consciousness," a picture of normative authority with its own characteristic fusion of norm and fact which therefore appears to those *within* that set of practices as a way in which the individuals in the practice see it not in fact so much as a *practice* at all but more as just the way things are: They see the world as constituted so that within it there are rational, reflective individuals who give and ask for reasons from each other; since they paradigmatically do that with great success in science, those individuals must therefore either already be doing that or be striving to do that in the practical world, and nothing but ill will, superstition, excess timidity, fear, or corruption could prevent that conception from being fully realized.

A word of caution: It is all too tempting to understand this as the view that in applying norms, extending them, specifying them in different ways, or criticizing them, we are always operating with a set of background "assumptions" which are "presupposed" in our various activities of claim-making and criticism, and that the goal of philosophical criticism is to make such presuppositions explicit so that they can be subjected to criticism. Hegel's point is different: The way in which we operate with a background understanding of the way in which the normative and the factual combine itself often involves various *contestations* about how to state just what the norm *is*, what it *means* in concrete cases, what exactly is to count as *falling under* the norm (or the concept) and how far the *scope* of certain entitlements goes. Moreover, since the understandings *at work* in these kinds of practices are almost always relatively inexplicit about these matters, it is a mistake to think of the orientation they give us as always capable of being exhaustively expressed in fully propositional terms, as "presuppositions" we could state and link up with other propositions. Indeed, the very propositional articulation of these orientations, which makes what is going on explicit in one way as opposed to another and which thus inevitably rules some things in and some things out, is often exactly *what* is contested. Particularly in cases of breakdown (which interest Hegel the most), there is no clear consensus on just what the norms *concretely mean* in the sense that it is unclear just how they are to be *taken*, or articulated, by the participants to be meaning this or that (cf. Travis 2003). In such contested situations, the participants are often themselves at odds on how best to state, or make explicit, what they are doing, about which kinds of commitments form genuine entitlements and which do not, or what constitutes the ideal or "central case" at issue. Such appeals cannot be solved by appeal to "criteria," and "settled intuitions" about the meaning will vary; there is, moreover, no contextual way of resolving the disputes that can be neutral with regard to all the competing parties.[6] In the cases that draw Hegel's attention the most – those in which a shape of normative authority is losing its grip on people – there are instead increasingly contested maneuvers about just how one best states the ideal case and what it implies.

In fact, one of the reasons why Hegel thinks that philosophy follows the Owl of Minerva is that it is almost always only after the fact that we can say with any definitiveness just how the contest was in fact finally resolved in the minds of the participants, and what it finally *came to mean* for them; and it is only after the fact that we can note whether what it finally came to mean for them marks any kind of normative success or failure – that is, whether the attempt to state the norm in "this way" and not "that way" marked, for example, only the disguised establishment of a form of coercive social power or an advance in our understanding of normative authority.

We can frame Hegel's theses against the following background. The full realization of the appeal to reason in human interactions demands that we think through what might be called the "missing antinomy" in Kant's work in practical philosophy: On the one hand, we are always completely socially constituted and our normative status is derivative from that; and on the other hand, we are free, self-originating sources of claims that no claim of social utility may override.[7] Contemporary disputes between communitarians, "identity theorists," and liberals may be seen as the ways in which this antinomy is at work in the basic practices of modern life.

Hegel begins his discussion with the most basic problem lying on the surface of any naive form of individualism: On the one hand, for the individual to be a modern individual, he must have a critical distance from his norms and must therefore in some sense elect his norms for himself by relying only on his own resources; but, on the other hand, such a choice made from within that kind of void is already itself meaningless because without any norms to bind one in the first place, there can be no meaning to "binding norms" at all.

Modern individualism is thus compelled, in Hegel's dialectical terminology, to seek its "ground" in an "other," in something other than an otherwise unconstrained act of choosing or electing. Modern individualism is thus pushed to working with some kind of conception of there being "constitutive standards" such that there are some set of non-chosen norms that "just mean" or "constitute" the activity in question, such that failure to abide by these norms simply counts as not engaging in the activity in question.[8] The most obvious metaphor to capture that view is, of course, that of a game; the rules of the game (whether that of chess, baseball, or English) constitute what counts as playing that game. This has the advantage of providing a clear-cut notion of normative judgment and obligation: a norm is always relative to some set of rules, and to say that one is obligated to do something is just to say that there is some set of rules from which it follows that one ought to do it. Such views are familiar in a wide variety of contemporary discussions, ranging from discussions about how one must simply accept certain categorical demands in order to be an agent at all, all the way up to discussions of legal positivism as resting on "master rules of recognition."[9] The idea in discussions of agency is that the "master rule" is definitive, constitutive of agency itself, such that in refusing to follow such a rule, an agent condemns himself to some kind of incoherence or even to ultimate failure in his own agency itself.

If so, then there must also be other necessary, non-chosen conditions for agency such that conforming to them would be conforming to a necessity that is *one's own*. To make it one's own, however, one cannot simply adapt oneself to a foreign necessity and "identify" with it. That would at best be a Hobbesian solution to the individualist dilemma (illustrated in Hobbes's famous metaphor of freedom as water freely flowing downhill).[10] On Hegel's reading, the emotionalist and sentimentalist reformulations of the experience of early modern Europe took this to its next logical step. The necessity must be one that corresponds to what is required to be a rational *individual*, such that in following out the demands of some ethical imperative that makes a claim on *you* as the individual person *you* are, you are doing something of great normative importance which is definitive of you as the individual agent *you* are. This view leads to the related conception of the claims of reason reaching their terminus in something like the "law of the heart," which is both a *law* (binding on all) and a matter of *personal commitment* (since it is of the "heart"). The person who obeys the law of *his* "heart" – one thinks perhaps of the line famously attributed to Luther, "Here I stand, I can do no other" – is therefore not obeying a whim but rather a binding, universal norm. However, the norm consists in the *individual* seeing where rational necessity takes him by virtue of relying only on his own resources, and there are certain material claims that put constitutive constraints on what can be rationally willed. Thus, for modern rational individuals, such subjection to the "law of the heart" seems to be the highest form of freedom since it involves subjecting yourself to a law that is both rational, that is, universal, and that is "your law." In following that law, the necessity pushing you is thus *your own* necessity.

Surprisingly (at least at first), Hegel turns to literary examples to provide the general frame for working out this view. The turn to literature is not simply a way of using literary works merely as illustrations of general principles – that would make them extrinsic to the argument – but as necessary in light of the deeper Hegelian view that we understand the true meaning of our most basic conceptions of normative authority only when we understand how they are *worked out* and *realized* in our practices, and that literature gives us a better sense of how that goes than does a more traditional theoretical alignment of principles to each other.[11] Thus, Hegel relied on several literary sources to frame his discussion of the law of the heart, in particular, Schiller's play, *The Robbers*, with its main character of Karl Moor, who, as a result of a personal injury against himself, rebels against the inhumanity and injustice of the existing social order, thus giving his personal wrong a universal significance.[12]

Nonetheless, as a "shape of consciousness" the follower of the "law of the heart" is familiar to modern sensibilities. In one mode, he or she is content with the existing order, secure in the knowledge that it is, despite its other flaws, in keeping with the demands of reason as fixed by our natural assent to certain virtues (such as benevolence, affability, humanity) and the way in which the conventional rules of society encourage and reward those natural dispositions; in another mode (such as that of Karl Moor), he is the figure of protest, the person who sees natural human benevolence being crushed or perverted by some unjust regime. In yet a third mode, a more detached philosopher caught in this picture might even attempt to come up with a philosophical account of such views; he would take the law of his heart, or, as we would now say, his "settled intuitions" about his "deepest commitments" and then see what followed from them, how they might be consistent with each other, what kinds of alternative accounts of those "settled intuitions" and "deepest commitments" would be ruled out, and so forth. Hegel, on the other hand, thinks he can show that all such appeals to "deepest commitments," "settled intuitions," to "our rules," or even to the rules given by an "ideal community" all themselves rest on something like the idea that (1) there is a constitutive standard for what counts as "the reasonable" and (2) that such a standard dogmatically rules out alternatives, claiming, in effect, that they are trying to do the equivalent of "not playing the game."

The agent following the "law of the heart" thus does not claim to be stating simply an idiosyncrasy on his part, a kind of wish list for the world that would best suit *him*. He is staking a claim as to what reason, the "universal" requires. However, as the statement only of the "law of *his* heart," *his* "settled intuitions," or "deepest commitments," his is only a *singular* claim competing against other claims made by other "hearts" that, for their part, also rest on "settled intuitions." Indeed, what is most distinctive about the "law of the heart " is its status as both a *singular* claim (a statement about one's own "settled intuitions") and as a claim to *normative*, "universal" status.[13] This holds even in the conservative case of the "law of the heart," where the existing order is almost exactly to one's liking, where what gives that order its binding force is that it agree with *one's own* deepest commitments; but, nonetheless, where the existing order does not comply with one's own deepest commitments, it follows that (at least without some further story) there can be no binding normative force to the rules that de facto make up that order as a "positive" order (that is, one that rests on some positive "master rule" or set of rules).

As Hegel notes, one can refine the picture; one might, for example, add all kinds of constraints about how the individual has to "reflectively endorse" any constraint for it to be binding, but the fact remains that its binding quality depends on its being *accepted by the individual* as being in accord with *his* deepest commitments. What interests Hegel the most in such a view is not simply the alienation that inevitably accompanies such a view (since it is always a matter of contingent fact whether the existing order fully complies with one's deepest commitments, and it is rare when it does so completely and without residue) but the way the view takes shape when the existing order is dramatically out of kilter with one's deepest commitments. As not merely an idiosyncratic wish but a demand of reason itself, the "law of the heart" must lay claim to the necessity to reform or abolish the existing order where it fails to meet the unconditional demands of "our deepest commitments." If it in fact finds that most people accept the existing order as more or less in conformity with what they take to be right and true (to be in conformity with *their* own deepest commitments), then it has to explain this away; in the extreme case, it must attribute this to some kind of subversion of the true order of things which somehow has masked, disguised or lied about the alienated, unjust reality with which it is so manifestly confronted.

At the extreme, as Hegel points out, such a view is one step away from a certain type of madness. Faced with the resistance or recalcitrance of those whom one wishes to liberate, who even seem sometimes to side or identify with their "oppressors," and who oddly seem to be unable to see the rational, compelling nature of one's views, one finds oneself not merely at odds with the world but also slightly unhinged. If, as Hegel says, madness is the substitution of unreality for reality, then at its outermost limits, the "law of the heart" provides a good example; in place of the reality confronting all the Karl Moors of the world, there is the counter-reality added by the same Karl Moors, in which all those others are duped, in which the regime's propaganda has been all too successful, or, as Hegel remarks, alluding to some views at large in the revolutionary eighteenth century, there is a widespread social deception "completely fabricated by fanatical priests and by gluttonous despots together with their lackeys, who, by lowering themselves to abjection, seek to compensate themselves for their own humiliation by humiliating and oppressing those below them" (*PS* 206.9–11/M 226).

The failure of the reformer to gain the assent of those he wishes to save – part of a larger, necessary failure of the "law of the heart" to gain a foothold in the hearts and minds of others – thus logically turns into a kind of cynicism about the "way of the world" (itself the title of a play by William Congreve, first performed in 1700) in which the person originally moved by the "law of the heart" comes to the view that, in the last analysis, it is not the claims of justice that move men's hearts; what instead moves them is their own self-interest, fairly narrowly conceived. If it is to preserve anything about itself, the "law of the heart" must therefore come to terms with the "way of the world," in which the rules of play are not those of justice and morality but those of strategy, tactics, and game-theory; the only appropriate response to the cynicism of the "way of the world" and, so it seems, the only genuinely moral response, is therefore the individual cultivation of one's own virtue. Consequently, emerging from that picture in the early eighteenth century was a renewed fascination with the virtue of the ancients and a program to "retrieve" it, interpreted as a way of finding one's true agency in the sacrifice of self-interest for a more beautiful cause.

This shape of consciousness, which Hegel simply calls "virtue," took itself to have learned from the experience of the failed and embittered Karl Moors of the world; on that view, the failure of the "law of the heart" lay in its one-sided assertion of the individual as *opposed* to the social order; "virtue," however, protests that *true* self-interest, the genuine way to realize one's agency, is not that of bending the social order to the dictates of "one's settled convictions," but that of shaping one's "heart" so that it is ready to be of service for the common good (when that good is *truly* conceived by virtue, not by the game-theorists of the "way of the world"). The agent of virtue, to be sure, is just as concerned with expressing his deepest commitments, but those deepest commitments involve (in a way that seems paradoxical at first) a commitment to sacrifice one's own interests (again, narrowly conceived) in favor of the common good, since the constitutive standards of agency require this; genuine virtue therefore consists in training and using one's various capacities so that this constitutive standard of agency and goodness will be fully realized.[14] The "way of the world," on the other hand, is a state of affairs of limited benevolence and narrow self-interest in which the actors, without knowing it, deprive themselves and others of what is really in their own interest, which is that of being better versions of what they only defectively are, such that those who play the "game" according to the rules of the way of the world are misusing the very capacities that could otherwise be put to genuine use in the pursuit of virtue.

The problem with virtually all such conceptions of *retrieving* virtue, so Hegel thought, is that it rests on a confusion of what was *really at work* in ancient conceptions of virtue – what was *wirklich*, in Hegel's terminology – with what *can be at work* in modern individualism. Ancient virtue was based in a conception of the *polis* as divided into various social roles that specified in very determinate ways how the human good was to be realized by this kind of person in that kind of situation;

and it made sense only where it could also be reasonably believed that the social whole was itself a unity that spontaneously led itself to harmony when each person fulfilled the duties of their role. Thus, one major obstacle to all such efforts at the "retrieval" of ancient virtue is that the form of life in which ancient virtue was rooted had itself collapsed under its own weight; it was a harmonious social whole only by virtue of suppressing the claims of individuality which it itself provoked and this, its strongly "communitarian" basis, became undone by the forces of individualism it itself generated.[15] Thus, the modern appeal to a "recovery" of ancient virtue has to see it as revivifying something which is already there in human nature but which has become corrupted by something else (capitalism being among the usual culprits): Virtue, so it was thought, requires allegiance to the common good, but this is an allegiance which modern market societies have turned topsy-turvy. Thus, the campaign to retrieve virtue has to campaign against such individualism that itself rests on a form of the very individualism it combats, since it appeals to the individual, relying solely on his own resources, to experience his greatest personal fulfillment in its sacrifice for and to the common good. Hegel's use of the Don Quixote image to characterize the followers of the Earl of Shaftesbury, a prime proponent of that view, is as satirically intended as was Cervantes's novel; there were, after all, no knights in the ancient world; they are a more recent – indeed, Christian – invention. The "honor" of the knight is restricted to his person, not to the *polis*, and injuries to honor can equally well be substantial and justified or just idiosyncratic and petty.

The view put forward by Shaftesbury and the like held that in fact nature had so constituted us such that only a virtuous sacrifice of *narrow* self-interest before the dictates of the common good could even count as following out one's *true* self-interest. Arguing against that view were those who (like Bernard Mandeville in his *The Fable of the Bees*) held that in the modern world of market relations, private vices (or what might look like narrow self-interest) actually lead to public benefits. In fact, the dispute over what were the supposedly constitutive standards of agency ended up being decided in favor of the moderns (represented by Mandeville), not by virtue of philosophical arguments so much as by the triumph of the modern way of life over what turned out to be only an empty challenge to it.[16]

As Hegel notes, it is not that virtue had to give way and admit that the way of the world is a wicked path; in fact, the redrawing of the spheres of virtue and vice that the modern market societies were creating themselves were not as bad as even they made themselves out to be. Individualist agency, having failed to live up to the "constitutive standards" imposed on it by an "other" (by the very nature of "being an individual," by the nature of the "heart," or just by "nature" itself), now takes itself to be *giving itself* its own standard – *as an individual.* Its choices must be, so it seems, criterionless, and its actions must therefore have "the appearance of the movement of a circle, which, freely moves itself within itself within a void ... and is fully satisfied in playing a game within itself and with itself" (*PS* 215.18–20/M 237). Normativity all the way down, so it seems, means that there is no starting point, no primordial norm fixed from without, and that the agent simply has to *give himself* his criterion for action in the very process of acting itself (a picture of agency that bears more than a passing resemblance to Sartre's famous example of the man who must decide whether to care for his mother or join the resistance).

Of course the problem of beginning, as Hegel notes, is thereby rendered acute, since at first, so it seems, there is nowhere to begin when one is confronted with such a fantastical demand for self-bootstrapping. However, the individualist picture has at least one plausible answer in reserve.[17] Even if there are no constraining metaphysical "constitutive standards" determining the rational content of any action, there are nonetheless the *factual* constraints of the individual as the specific individual he is, and thus he must begin with his own facticity, his own "thrownness" – begin with whatever interests he just finds himself to have, whatever talents he just happens to possess, and in the circumstances in which he just happens to find himself.[18] (Hegel's term for this is the individual's "original determinate nature," an unwieldy description, as are many of Hegel's choices of technical terms.)

Hegel calls what such an individual brings about in his actions his "work" (*Werk*), with its double meaning of something like an artistic or literary product and its more quotidian meaning where it simply denotes the results of what one has done (as in "that has the stamp of your handiwork all over it"). An individual's "work" therefore is the expression of who he is by virtue of what he has chosen to express as his own combination of interests, talents, and circumstances. Like the followers of the "law of the heart" and the "knights of virtue," such an individual is also concerned to express his deepest commitments but now in such a way that the expression makes a claim which demands recognition for its validity in a wholly particularist way. It is not the expression of a rebellious attitude to society (as it was with Karl Moor), nor that of a quixotic "knight of virtue" tilting at Mandevillean windmills, but somebody concerned to give voice to *himself*, to give expression to *what really matters to him*, and to be recognized and accepted for it. (I have argued elsewhere [Pinkard 1994, 119–21] that one such model for this kind of character is Rousseau in his *Confessions*.) What emerges from actions of that type bears the stamp one's own handiwork and, as such an *expression*, is supposed to *embody* one's deepest commitments. The problem, of course, is that with such "works," the same kind of issues arise as with more distinctly artistic works. Criticizing a *work* as, say, sentimental, can only be a criticism if there is something wrong with being sentimental; to say that your works are "sentimental," therefore, seems to be saying that, as expressions of you, you are sentimental, and that seems to be a criticism of you, not just your works.

On one version of this account, that would be going too far. If there are no standards other than the one the individual fashions for himself in the contingent circumstances of his own "thrownness," and if the individual has genuinely sought to bring to light those commitments he finds himself with, then the criticism of such works is beside the point since the charge of "sentimentality" would be made only from somebody else's standards. As Hegel rather sardonically notes, this is not complete relativism; there are claims to there being universal standards at work here; it is just that it is universally demanded that individuals are to express their deepest commitments, directly and honestly – one could even add, *authentically* – and that criticism can at best, so it seems, only involve charges of dishonesty or hypocrisy, not of whether those deepest commitments themselves are bad.[19]

On Hegel's view, there is a kind of logic to this form of individualism which pushes it in fairly recognizable directions. If the individual and what he is *an sich*, "in itself" (that is, what are his deepest commitments) are supposed to be displayed in his undertakings and deeds, then *he* is, as it were, the norm, the "universal," for those deeds and undertakings, and they in turn are supposed to be judged according to how well they have expressed those commitments. The demands of reason demand that such works be recognized for what they are and claim to be, not for what they cannot be. However, all such acts involve deeds, or "works," and such works are to be found in a public space where, like it or not, they are subject to, or at least open to, the judgments of others, who in turn by the very logic of such individualism need not be constrained to judge it only in terms of its expressive quality; those others can, for example, find in the work something that helps them put a shape on their own idiosyncratic interests or help them spin out their own variations on their own expressive acts. What bears the stamp of one's own handiwork therefore can mean more than just what it said about oneself; it can take on other meanings entirely depending on the contingencies of the public space and the others one shares it with.

What bears the stamp of one's own handiwork is thus a "vanishing," as Hegel describes it.[20] What seems to be a personally expressive deed is taken by others as something else. But if what counts *absolutely* are one's deepest commitments, and one's deeds and handiwork only incompletely or inadequately express those commitments, then the *absolute* importance of those deeds itself vanishes. Indeed, how could it be otherwise? That one lacks the talent for adequate self-expression is itself a contingent fact; that one is surrounded by compatriots who lack the talent or means to render a proper judgment on one's deeds is equally as contingent. That one might have chosen the wrong expression, as it were, which then led others to see one's acts as insulting, when, you assure them, nothing remotely like that was in your intention – all these could seem to be contingent matters, and the charges of dishonesty, hypocrisy, or ineptitude are always ready to fly. Hegel might well have been describing the scenario that contemporary politicians in Washington carry out almost as if reading from a script. First, they are caught short on something distasteful they said; then they deny having said it; when that is proven, they wail that it was taken out of context; when it is shown that it was not taken out of context or could not have been so taken, they solemnly declare that it was a mistake, an error in judgment, that it was not meant *in that way*, that such a thing does not express their deepest commitments, that anybody who knows them would know that; and then there's the final step, virtually never that of directly apologizing for the statement but of apologizing for any hurt that *might* have been caused on the part of somebody *misunderstanding* what it was that they *really* meant.

In light of all that, Hegel says that the next step in such modern individualism is that of a kind of normative self-withdrawal, a "reflection into self," an affirmation that one is not *just* expressing one's deepest commitments, but that in one's own self, in one's own *act of committing* oneself, one is doing one's best in the more existential sense (itself derivative from an older religious sense) of committing oneself to *what really matters* in these affairs. With this "reflection-into-oneself," that is, into the importance of the *commitment* itself, there is now, as Hegel puts it, a "vanishing of the vanishing," and what emerges out of the vanishing importance of the "work" is something more like the *authentic* individual, the "true concept," as Hegel calls it, of modern individualism, whose own handiwork may vanish but whose commitment to what really matters remains steadfast.[21] That reflection-into-self brings with it a radical split between inner and outer, between subjectivity and the way one makes one's appearance in the social world, a move which in turn introduces its own twists and turns until such modern individualism begins to sag under its own weight. The problem with such authenticity, after all, is that it repeats in a more subtle form the problems of the individualism that gave rise to it. It claims to be concerned not primarily with expressing itself but rather with *engaging itself* with *what really matters*, *die Sache selbst* (as Hegel calls it), and only then giving expression to that commitment.

Indeed, once individuals begin to mark off what each *intends* (or *means* to say) as radically or sharply set off from what each actually *does* (or really *says*), there then arises a different kind of social space in which a certain *theatricality* comes to dominate; each actor makes a claim to be concerned with this or that, and in staking that claim simultaneously judges the reaction of the audience to see how well he is doing, with each member of the audience reciprocally doing the same; each actor in the "play" begins to operate therefore with the suspicion that the whole affair really is just a "game" with its own odd rules in which all actors deceive others and are themselves being deceived, each acting out the realization of the line usually attributed to Groucho Marx: "Sincerity is the greatest thing in the world, so if you can fake that you've got it made" (cf. Sennett 1977).

That, however, threatens to bring the whole house down; what holds the "game" together is the conception that one really is supposed to be attending to what really matters, not just playing a game of pretending to do so. However, just as the actors of the "way of the world" (in *The Fable of the Bees*) were not half so bad as they made themselves out to be, it turns out that there is a truth still to be realized in this form of theatrical individuality. First, in Hegel's terminology, the theatricality of modern agency implicitly acknowledges that our being-for-others is crucial to our agency; without others, there is no audience for the role being played; and, second, the theatricality of modern life takes it that the standards for agency are themselves, after all, "roles" and are therefore self-legislated, not simply prescribed by the meaning of the terms we use nor by the metaphysical structure of the world. However, if it is all *just* theatricality, then all that can really matter is our "reflection into ourselves," our normative withdrawal of the most significant part of our lives, our deepest commitments, from that public space. We then at best become the "managers" of our interests (or even the "managers" of our lives, outfitted with self-help books and up-to-date technologies of communication).

The *meaning* of these practices thus at first seems to teeter between that of a necessary failure in our attempts to reach any genuine conception of what really matters (at least in terms of reasons that are good for others) and that of an alienated, almost nihilist conception to the effect that it really is *just* a "game" and that the only thing that really matters is who convinces whom, that is, who wins the game. Nonetheless, in playing out our roles in our managerial function – to the extent that we still commit ourselves to what really matters – we are still making claims on others, and if we are to go beyond just playing the game (in which the participants "find themselves deceiving themselves and deceiving each other reciprocally"; *PS* 226.17–19/M 250), if we are to be *really* concerned with "what really matters" (and not just pretending to be, or not just taking our own contingent success at bringing others to whatever view we happened to have landed on to be the only thing that really matters), then we have *required ourselves* to play *that* game under the constraints of and according to the demands of giving and asking for reasons from each other.

Embedded in this idea of theatricality and managerial expertise, there is after all something to the idea of authenticity, of working at getting it right about one's deepest commitments both in the sense of their being *expressive* of who one is and their being *congruent* with what really matters in life. Part of the reformulation hinted at but not determined by that practice (which continually finds itself teetering between two bad extremes) is to be found in Kant's conception of the moral will in the *Groundwork*, where the theatrical *role* is replaced by the self-legislated *rule*; or, in Kant's well-known formulation, "the will is therefore not merely subject to the law, but is so subject that it must be considered as also *giving the law to itself* and precisely on this account as first of all subject to the law (of which it can regard itself as instituting)" (*Groundwork* 4:431).[22]

To be sure, Kant's own formulation at first looks as if it just repeats the paradoxical nature of individualism that preceded it.[23] To avoid that, Kant amended it in *The Critique of Practical Reason* where he there characterized it as an expression of the "fact of reason," namely, that in playing, as it were, the "game" of giving and asking for reasons, one cannot step out of the normative realm to see if the "game" is itself in order; one always finds oneself *already* obligated by the act of looking for justification in the first place.[24]

If the conditions of agency are neither fixed by the "meanings" of the words nor by some prior, metaphysical structure of agency, then the "constitutive standards" of agency must themselves be legislated; but since they cannot be legislated individually (and indeed in one clear sense cannot be *legislated* at all), they are therefore the "substance," the social space within which the agents engage in their activities. The metaphor of the *game*, so appropriate to theatricality, itself now vanishes with reference to giving and asking for reasons. The "role playing" of modern theatricality, the *game*, thus ultimately has to become the *practice* of giving and asking for reasons, in which the various goods and reasons for belief and action – *what really matters* – are themselves *not* legislated by individuals *as* individuals. If what really matters, the *Sache selbst*, are indeed our deepest commitments, and if we are to be true to ourselves as being true to those commitments as *intelligibly* demanding our allegiance, then we are in turn required to abandon the idea of self-sufficiency in its individualist shape. The individual simply does not have the resources within himself to give shape to his agency, not because those resources are external to him and always out of reach, but because the development of modern individualism has reached the point (by 1807, so Hegel perhaps naively thought) where modern life is ready to acknowledge the truth to which it had implicitly committed itself once it had set foot on the path towards the modern ideal of individualism in the first place: *We are never self-sufficient agents*; our agency itself is a kind of social norm, indeed, one that has developed into its Kantian formulation by virtue of the very determinate failures to hold onto a conception of itself as shaped by some "other" (the constitutive standards of agency, the meanings of the terms, the metaphysical structure of agency, the rise of modern theatricality); we are who we are only within the social space instituted by the agents engaged in the practice of giving and asking for reasons, and the idea of the *individual* is *itself a social norm*, something each of us *can be* only if others *are* also individuals in that sense; and, so it turns out, that the notion of a "constitutive standard" for agency itself is a historically developing norm.

What emerges from the passage of individualism to its truth in sociality is a series of "shapes of consciousness," or characters, that are each defeated in their own terms. Yet, these characters, despite being *defeated* characters, still emerge over and over again in modern life, "shapes" that modern life seems condemned to repeat.[25] The *social* ideal of being an "individual," of taking the inward turn (an *In-sich-gehen*, as Hegel calls it), is itself possible only within a social space of certain types of very determinate *dependencies*; and part of the complexity of that social space is that it fashions within itself an idea of self-reflection and of being an independent origin of ethical and epistemic claims which itself encourages the kind of cropped picture of the *individual* as the original source of the social space instead of fostering the more intelligible picture of the "individual" as a *constitutive moment* of the shape such social space has assumed in modernity. The modern "individual" emerges out of a "reflection-into-himself" from out of that social space; and having emerged from it, the "individual" now becomes an essential participant in the self-sustaining of a modern, self-reflective culture.

Modern life had moved along a path that found its penultimate culmination in modern Kantian individualism; what was *at work* in all the contestations of meaning along that path was a conception of *Geist* as the sociality of reason, a conclusion, so Hegel thought, that we could only draw at the end of that path. But was it necessary to enter that path in the first place? Nothing in the development of modern individualism would answer that question. To answer that, so Hegel thought, one had to start again at the beginning, which in 1807 he still took to be the ancient Athenian *polis*. He wrote two longer chapters in the *Phenomenology*, "Spirit" and "Religion," detailing why the path from Athens to Paris to Berlin had to take the shape it did. But this is a story for subsequent chapters.

Notes

1. For discussion of this section, see above, chapter 4. – *Ed.*
2. This was the guiding theme in my book *Hegel's Phenomenology: The Sociality of Reason* (1994). This point is also made especially forcefully by Robert Pippin in a variety of places. In an otherwise very sympathetic assessment of Robert Brandom's reading of Hegel, Pippin (2005a) takes Brandom to task on exactly this point: The issue is not that of "administering" norms so that we correct the errors in the ways our ancestors took them but the nature of normative authority itself. Although the point was made by Pippin in his earlier work, it comes to the forefront especially forcefully in his *The Persistence of Subjectivity* (2005b). (This theme is central to Hegel's analysis of *Antigone*; see below, chapter 8. – *Ed.*)
3. In his early, pre-*Phenomenology* writings, Hegel often used "life" in contexts where he would later prefer the term "spirit," and he would speak of a "shape of life" in a way that foreshadowed his later preference for a "shape of spirit." In "The Spirit of Christianity and Its Fate," he more or less equated a "shape of life" with a "form of life": ". . . while the group's love must always have retained the form of love, of faith in God, without becoming alive, with exhibiting itself in specific forms of life (*Gestalt des Lebens*), because every form of life can be objectified by the intellect and then apprehended as its object, as a cut-and-dried fact. The group's relation to the world was bound to become a dread of contacts with it, a fear of every form of life (*Lebensform*), because every form exhibits its deficiency (as a form it is only one aspect of the whole and its very formation implies fixed limits), and what it lacks is a part of the world" (MM 1:403/Hegel 1975b, 287–8). All translations are by the author.
4. In his later, post-*Phenomenology* usage, Hegel calls this the "Idea," characterized as the unity of concept and reality. In one sense, Hegel thus seems to accept the Rawlsian distinction between ideal theory and non-ideal theory. For Rawls, ideal theory assumes that everyone acts in terms of the ideal (according to what he calls strict compliance) and that the ideal is realizable in the existing social and historical conditions. That would correspond at one level with Hegel's conception. Non-ideal theory deals with how the ideal is to be implemented in conditions where people do not act in terms of the ideal and where there are various complicating factors (racial discrimination, class bias, and the like) that prevent the ideal from being realized. On the other hand, there is another level at which it is simply not clear how much Hegel's scheme would agree with Rawls's scheme; for Hegel, the ideal must be actual, be at work in the life of the people for which it is an ideal. It is not enough that it be *realizable*, but that it be substantially already *realized*, even if the reality of the situation does not fully measure up to the ideal.
5. *Enc.* §66, emphasis added. Hegel continues: "In all these cases, immediacy of knowledge not only does not exclude mediation, but the two are so bound together that immediate knowledge is even the product and result of mediated knowledge" (ibid.).
6. These issues recall Hegel's concern with the Pyrrhonian Dilemma of the Criterion and Trope of Relativity; see above, pp. 2–6, 60–64. – *Ed.*
7. Kant certainly never put it this way, although one might see hints of it in *Religion Within the Limits of Reason Alone*, where he divides the basic "determination" of humanity into three categories – animality, humanity, and personality. "Humanity" is our constitution as social where we judge ourselves only in comparison to others, and "personality" has to do with our ability to act according to the dictates of pure practical reason (*Rel.* 6:26–8/22). (Resolving this antinomy is central to Hegel's new theory of subjectivity in the *Phenomenology*; see below, chapter 13. – *Ed.*)
8. This is a common picture (e.g., Korsgaard 2002; Stern 2001).

9 See Lance and O'Leary-Hawthorne (1997). Lance calls his alternatives the "attributive" conceptions of normativity (where for something to be a norm is to follow from some accepted set of social rules) and "transcendental" conceptions of normativity (as to what the real norm is). The reference to "master rules" is, of course, taken from Hart (1961). (Lance's use of "transcendental" to characterize his own views is, it seems to me, misplaced, but that is another story for another time.)

10 Hegel took himself to have come to terms with such Hobbesian readings in the chapter preceding this one, where he discussed other naturalist conceptions of intentions, activities, and freedom with regard to psychological laws and the great naturalist pseudo-sciences of his day, physiognomy and phrenology. (See above, chapter 5. – *Ed.*) The citation from Hobbes is from *Leviathan*, Chapter XXI, "Of the Liberty of Subjects": "Liberty and necessity are consistent: as in the water that hath not only liberty, but a necessity of descending by the channel; so, likewise in the actions which men voluntarily do, which, because they proceed their will, proceed from liberty, and yet because every act of man's will and every desire and inclination proceedeth from some cause, and that from another cause, in a continual chain (whose first link is in the hand of God, the first of all causes), proceed from necessity."

11 This thesis is well argued by Speight (2001).

12 See Speight's discussion. Hegel is reputed to have said in his lectures of Schiller's play: "A similar example is Schiller's [*Robbers* where] Karl Moor is enraged by the entire civil order and the whole situation of the world and mankind in his day, and his rebellion against it has this universal significance" (*Aesthetics*, 1224/MM 15:557).

13 "Because that autocratic divine and human order is separated from the heart, it is to the heart a *mere semblance* which ought to lose what is affiliated with it, namely, power and actuality. In its *content*, that order may contingently coincide with the law of the heart, at which point the law of the heart can acquiesce in it. However, it is not lawfulness purely as such which is the essence to the heart. Rather, it is the consciousness *of itself* in such lawfulness, its consciousness that it has therein satisfied *itself*" (*PS* 203.19–23/M 222–3).

14 "The good, or the universal as it here comes on the scene, are what are called gifts, abilities, powers. It is a mode of the spiritual in which the spiritual is represented as a universal; it requires the principle of individuality to bring it to life and movement, and it has its actuality in this, its individuality. This universal is well used by this principle insofar as it is deployed in the consciousness of virtue, and it is misused by it as far as it is deployed in the way of the world" (*PS* 210.8–14/M 231).

15 "Ancient virtue had its own determinate, secure meaning since it had its *basis, itself rich in content*, in the *substance* of the people, and it had an *actual, already existing good* for its purpose. Hence, it was also oriented neither against actuality as a *universal topsy-turvy invertedness* nor against the way of the world. However, the virtue which has been just considered has left that substance behind, and it is a virtue with no essence, a virtue merely of ideas and words which have dispensed with that content" (*PS* 212.34–213.1/M 234). (About the ancient world, see below, chapter 8. – *Ed.*)

16 "The way of the world is victorious over what constitutes virtue in opposition to it. It is victorious over that for which the essenceless abstraction is the essence. However, it is not victorious over something real but merely over the creation of distinctions which are no distinctions, over this pompous talk about what is best for humanity and about the oppression of humanity, this incessant chattering about sacrifice for the good and the misuse of gifts" (*PS* 212.23–28/M 433–4).

17 "But he thereby seems not to be able to determine the *purpose* of his activity before he has taken the action. However, at the same time, since he is consciousness, he must prior to the action have the action itself as *wholly his own*, i.e., the *purpose* in front of him. The individual who sets himself to act therefore seems to find himself caught in

a circle in which every moment already presupposes the other; it thus seems that he is incapable of finding a beginning for his actions because he only becomes acquainted with his originary essence, which must be his purpose, *from his deed*, but, in order to act, he must have *the purpose beforehand*. However, precisely for that reason, he has to begin *immediately* and, whatever the circumstances may be, without any further reservations about *beginnings, middles,* and *ends,* set himself to act, since both his essence and his nature which exist-*in-itself* are beginning, middle, and end all rolled into one" (*PS* 218.10–21/M 240).

18 "As *beginning*, the individual's nature is present in the *circumstances* of action, and the *interest* which the individual finds in some particular thing is the answer already given to the question: Whether he should act and what is here to be done? For what seems to be a merely given actuality is in itself his originary nature, which merely has the semblance of that of *being* – a semblance which lies in the very concept of a self-estranging activity but which, as *his* originary nature, is articulated in the *interest* which his originary nature finds in it" (*PS* 218.21–27/M 240).

19 "In contrast with this purely unessential distinction of quantity, *good* and *bad* would express an absolute distinction; but this does not happen here. Whatever would be taken one way or another is in the same way something the individual goes in for, an individuality's self-presentation and self-articulation; and for that reason, all of it is good; and one could really not say what would be supposed to be bad here. What would be called a bad work is the individual life of a determinate nature realizing itself in the work. It would only be debased into a bad work by the comparative thought that is itself empty since it goes beyond the essence of the work, which is to be a self-articulation of individuality, seeking and demanding who knows what" (*PS* 219.20–30/M 241).

20 "But if we look at the content of this experience in its completeness, then that content is the *work which is vanishing*. What *sustains itself* is not the *vanishing* itself, but rather it is the vanishing itself which is both actual and bound up with the work, and it vanishes with the work. The *negative*, together with the *positive* which is *its negation*, itself *perishes*" (*PS* 222.27–31/M 244).

21 "In this way, consciousness reflects itself into itself from out of its transitory works and affirms its concept and certainty as *the existing* and the *persisting* vis-à-vis the experience of the *contingency* of the act" (*PS* 223.8–11/M 246). He then adds: "Therefore, in the *thing that matters* as the permeation of individuality and objectivity which has itself objectively come to be, the true concept of self-consciousness has in the eyes of self-consciousness come to be, that is, self-consciousness has arrived at a consciousness of its substance" (*PS* 223.35–38/M 246).

22 Translation amended. In particular, I rendered "davon er sich selbst als Urheber betrachten kann" as "of which it can regard itself as instituting" rather than translating "*Urheber*" as "author." (More literally, it would be rendered as "instituter" but that seemed more awkward.)

23 Because it requires an individual to have a prior law in order non-arbitrarily to legislate for himself and since this prior law (as non-self-legislated) could in no way obligate him, it would thus render the legislation useless.

24 To Hegel's ears (and those of Fichte) that seemed more like a restatement of the problem than a solution, since, left at that, the "fact" either just restates the paradox or falls back into the idea that our wills are constrained by some "other," the metaphysical structure of practical reality. (Kant's tests of the categorical imperative are examined in chapter 7. – *Ed.*)

25 "Since these moments cannot yet possess the meaning of having been fashioned into purposes which stand in opposition to that lost ethical life, they are here valid just in their naïve, natural content, and the aim towards which they press is the ethical substance. However, since our time lies closer to the form those moments take when they appear after consciousness has forsaken its ethical life and when, in searching for that

ethical life, it repeats those forms, the better representation of those moments may be in the forms appropriate to our own time" (*PS* 197.24–30/M 216).

References

Hart, H. L. A. (1961) *The Concept of Law*. Oxford: The Clarendon Press.
Hegel, G. W. F. (1975a) *Aesthetics: Lectures on Fine Art*, 2 vols., tr. T. M. Knox. Oxford: The Clarendon Press.
Hegel, G. W. F. (1975b) *Early Theological Writings*, tr. T. M. Knox, introduction and fragments tr. by R. Kroner. Philadelphia: University of Pennsylvania Press.
Hobbes, T. (1968) *Leviathan*. Harmondsworth: Penguin.
Korsgaard, C. (2002) *Self-Constitution: Agency, Identity, and Integrity* (the Gifford Lectures, available only online): http://www.people.fas.harvard.edu/~korsgaar/Korsgaard.LL1.pdf
Lance, M. and O'Leary-Hawthorne, J. (1997) *The Grammar of Meaning*. Cambridge: Cambridge University Press.
Pinkard, T. (1994) *Hegel's Phenomenology: The Sociality of Reason*. Cambridge: Cambridge University Press.
Pippin, R. B. (2005a) "Brandom's Hegel," *European Journal of Philosophy* 13.3: 381–408.
Pippin, R. B. (2005b) *The Persistence of Subjectivity: On the Kantian Aftermath*. Cambridge: Cambridge University Press.
Sennett, R. (1977) *The Fall of Public Man*. New York: Knopf.
Speight, A. (2001) *Hegel, Literature, and the Problem of Agency*. Cambridge: Cambridge University Press.
Stern, R. (2001) *Hegel and the Phenomenology of Spirit*. London: Routledge.
Travis, C. (2003) *Liaisons Ordinaire: Wittgenstein sur la pensée et le monde*. Paris: J. Vrin.

7

The Ethics of Freedom: Hegel on Reason as Law-Giving and Law-Testing

David Couzens Hoy

The sections on "Reason as Lawgiver" and "Reason as Testing Laws" are the last two sections of Chapter V of the *Phenomenology of Spirit* (*PS* 228–37/M 252–62). This chapter is entitled, simply, "Reason." The next chapter is entitled, simply, "Spirit." However, Hegel provides another way of organizing the book. In that way there are three major divisions: "Consciousness," "Self-Consciousness," and then a third that is left blank. This third division is then divided into four parts: "Reason," "Spirit," "Religion," and "Absolute Knowing." The question is, what name should fill in the blank? "Spirit" is the most obvious answer, given Hegel's later system constructions. If that answer is right, then our sections are the point at which Reason becomes aware of itself as Spirit.

What do Reason and Spirit mean here? Reason is essentially individual reason, but it is individual reason that projects itself as universal. So it is an individual's self-certainty of knowing the truth that must obtain for everybody. It is the "I" that thinks that everybody else should know what it knows and agree with it. Spirit, in contrast, is the "We" that makes individual forms of Reason possible. Spirit is the cultural and historical background that allows one to be who one is. Moreover, Spirit is not just a matter of different cultural paradigms that flourish at different points in history, but it is the cumulative story of the development of thought up to Hegel's own historical moment.

These sections are important, therefore, because they represent the moment when individual reason becomes moral. Morality implies seeing that one's own maxims for actions can be the same for everybody else. The most famous version of this view is Kant's theory of Practical Reason. Hegel provides some counterexamples to show the emptiness of Kant's famous procedure whereby we can test our maxims to see if they can consistently be viewed as moral rules. For Kant these moral rules are then duties, which must be acted on for the sake of duty alone, whether or not they represent our natural inclinations.

This story becomes especially challenging from a philosophical standpoint when one realizes that Hegel is not simply shifting his narrative from the "I" to the "We," but that he is developing a stronger argument that there is no "I" without a "We." The question is, however, what kind of argument is he giving and how strong is it? Does a dialectical transition in the *Phenomenology* constitute a transcendental argument establishing necessity or a hermeneutical interpretation establishing possibility? This is the larger meta-theoretical question that I will be unfolding around his account of *Sittlichkeit*. This account comes up in the last paragraphs of these sections and is the starting point of the next chapter on Spirit. *Sittlichkeit* is the shared ethical life that surrounds and conditions individual moral reason. Hegel is thus not simply jumping from Reason to Spirit, but he is offering an interpretive *explanation* of the transition from Reason to Spirit. This essay will therefore examine the meta-philosophical issues as well as the dialectical plot structure at this crucial point of the *Phenomenology*. Insofar as Hegel developed these ideas in other writings, including the later *Philosophy of Right*, those texts are referenced as well.

1 John Rawls on Hegel

Interpreters of earlier philosophers have to be aware of differences between the present-day and the earlier contexts. Currently, for instance, Kant is taken as a paradigmatically deontological philosopher, and his position is standardly contrasted to the utilitarian theory of Mill. This contrast brings out some features of the Kantian theory and suppresses others. Hegel could not have read Kant in terms of the contrast with Mill, because Mill was only born when Hegel was writing the *Phenomenology*. The Harvard political philosopher John Rawls points out in *A Theory of Justice* that Kant was writing not only against teleological theory, but also against a tradition that Rawls identifies as rational intuitionism (see Rawls 1971, 30, 396). This group of theories (including Leibniz's and Wolff's perfectionism) postulated the difference between the natural and the moral orders, such that moral principles were grasped through a purely rational form of intuition of the prior and independent moral order. This view was thus "heteronomous" from Kant's point of view. As the capstone of individual reason, Kant was trying to develop an account of morality evolving from within reason rather than outside reason.

Today, however, we tend to see moral philosophy mainly in terms of the standard contrast between *teleological* theories, which start with a conception of the good and only then specify what is morally right, and *deontological* theories, where the right is not defined in terms of the good. Kant's sense of morality as duty-based rather than happiness-based leads him into the deontological camp that sees teleological theories as "heteronomous." Kant's emphasis on duty puts more weight on conscious intention than on the consequences of action. The term 'deontology' can be misleading if it suggests that Kantians entirely eliminate the relevance of consequences of action from judgments of moral worth – which, Rawls says, would be crazy.

Rawls's lectures on Hegel have not yet received the attention from Hegel scholars that they deserve. These lectures, which were eloquently compiled by the UCLA moral philosopher and Kant scholar Barbara Herman, also illuminate Rawls's own philosophy. They show how Rawls is not a strict Kantian and how he transcends the rigoristic Kantian conception of individual autonomy and rule-governed action. He recognizes that Hegel is not opposed to Kant's notion of moral principles, but instead that Hegel seeks to ground principles in the social domain of this world rather than the noumenal domain of a transcendent world. The Hegelian rejection of noumenal freedom brings moral philosophy more within the ambit of political philosophy (Rawls 2000, 330). Hegel is also replacing Kant's morality of duty with what I will call (following Foucault 1997, 284) an ethics of freedom. A morality of duty supplies rules for action and demands that these rules be followed only for the sake of duty. An ethics of freedom, however, requires reflection on the contingencies of the social and political situation. Rawls brings this out in his first of two lectures on Hegel where he explicates Hegel's dark saying, "The free will is the will that wills itself as the free will" (*PR* §§10, 27).

Rawls begins this explication by emphasizing that Hegel's goal is not to view individual persons as isolated units who are guided in some mysterious way by a part of themselves that is outside of space and time. Instead, Hegel wants us to reconcile ourselves to being who we are in space and time. He wants us to find our freedom in the best aspects of the society in which we find ourselves. However, to say that philosophy is *reconciliation* is not to say that it is *resignation*. There is much about his contemporary society that Hegel deplores. But he believes that contrasting the real world to an ideal world in the Kantian manner is counterproductive. Contemplating the ideal world tends to lead us to condemn the real social world. As Rawls puts it, "for Hegel, in contrast to Kant, the aim of the account of ethics as *Sittlichkeit* is not to tell us what we *ought* to do – we know that – but to *reconcile* us to our *real* social world and to convince us not to fix our thinking and reflection on an ideal social world" (Rawls 2000, 334).

I have more to say about *Sittlichkeit* below, but for now let me focus the contrast that Rawls sees between Kant and Hegel. Kant thinks that through transcendental freedom each person can individually rise above the contingencies of space and time and act purely from the moral law, thereby achieving a good will. Hegel, in contrast, does not think that human freedom is possible without a social framework. What we must come to understand collectively is how that framework promotes rather than stifles our freedom and therefore our capacity to lead fully rational and good lives. Rational social institutions are the necessary background for freedom.

Of course, at the same time individuals must be able to reflect on and judge their own and others' conduct. Hegel believes, however, that the kind of guidance that Kant envisions with the reflective procedure of the categorical imperative is not sufficient. The CI-procedure rules out some behavior, so Hegel is not saying that there is no content at all in Kant's account of practical reason. Rather, on Rawls's reading, Hegel is saying that the CI-procedure does not have all the content that Kant claims it has. "Moreover," says Rawls, "what it does give us are not moral conclusions that we can properly be said to know: we do not attain moral knowledge through the CI-procedure. We attain moral knowledge only in what Hegel calls *Sittlichkeit*" (Rawls 2000, 334).

Hegel also disagrees with Kant's account of the psychology of moral agency. Kant thinks that moral action should follow from the moral law itself and nothing else. In contrast to Kant's desire for what Rawls calls "radical purity" (Rawls 2000, 335), Hegel rejects the distinction between morality and prudence. Instead, Hegel sees what Kant might consider as heteronomous interests (e.g., family, friendship, and the normal involvements of everyday life) as important moments of ethical life.

In effect, then, Rawls can be read as agreeing with Hegel's transition in the *Phenomenology* from Reason to Spirit. I will have occasion to return to Rawls's Hegel lectures again below. Guided by this reading of Hegel's moral and political philosophy, let me now turn to the details of the *Phenomenology of Spirit*.

2 Legislating and Testing Moral Rules: Christine Korsgaard vs. Hegel

While there is general agreement that Hegel's section on "Reason as Testing Laws" targets Kant's moral philosophy directly, there is some disagreement about whether the section directly preceding it is aimed at Kant or not. This section, on "Reason as Law-Giver," is not a deep or sophisticated critique of Kant's texts, and as a critique of the deontological approach to morality, it is rather casual. Michael Forster is therefore inclined to say that Hegel is not targeting Kant in the "Law-Giver" section, but *Popularphilosophen* like Feder and Garve (Forster 1998, 348–50).

However, the idea of giving oneself the law is so central to Kant's moral theory that it is hard not to hear Kant in the background when reading Hegel's critique of the notion of the lawgiver. In the *Critique of Practical Reason*, Kant emphasizes that what it means for pure reason to be practical is that reason can be "*law-giving*" or, as I might translate him, *self-legislative*. I shall therefore take Hegel as targeting some basic Kantian intuitions, and as pointing out other features of ethics that are overlooked or only minimally acknowledged by deontological moral theory.

Before proceeding further, I should register a note on terminology. Translations of Kant usually distinguish 'maxims' from 'laws'. Maxims are personal, whereas laws are universal. The term 'law' can be ambiguous, and can mean a law of nature or a legal law. A legal law is prescriptive: it tells you what you have to do if you do not want to be punished. A law of nature is descriptive: one could not disobey it. Insofar as moral principles can be disobeyed, I prefer to think of the deontological program as investing heavily in the idea of moral *rules*. I use the term 'rules' because I think that it captures the action-guiding sense of prescription that is at stake in practical reason in general, and in the terms 'maxims' and 'laws' more specifically.

Hegel's critique of moral rules can be interpreted in at least three ways. One is that moral rules are too weak because they are purely formal and empty of content. Another is that they are too strong insofar as they can lead to overly rigoristic demands on action that could well result in an impoverished life. A third is that even if they are just right, they are not action guiding because they depend on interpretation and interpretations can vary. I will use the terms '*formalism*' for the charge of emptiness, '*rigorism*' for the charge of being too strong, and '*dogmatism*' for the charge of lacking a "hermeneutical consciousness," that is, an awareness of the variability of interpretation. These three levels of criticism are important moments of the present essay, as will become evident shortly.

Hegel offers three examples to show the limitations of the idea of moral rules. The first is the claim that everyone ought to speak the truth (see *PS* 229.36–230.36/M 254–5). Hegel argues that there are suppressed assumptions behind this rule, and that making these assumptions explicit shows that what seems "universally necessary" and "intrinsically valid" is in fact "completely contingent" (ibid.). His point is that individual reason thinks that it knows this rule with certainty, yet when it tries to act accordingly, it finds out that the rule must be qualified because what it thinks is true might not be true. So the rule becomes merely that everyone must speak the truth only if what is said is true. In light of the fallibility of belief, it turns out that one is no longer sure of what one believes or means to say. Reason, which was apparently self-certain, turns out to be tongue-tied and unsure of what it wants to say.

The second rule that Hegel deconstructs is the commandment to love your neighbor as yourself (see *PS* 230.37–231.27/M 255–6). Here again Hegel argues that the rules depend on the context of interpretation, such that one must know what is good for the neighbor in order to act with love. What seems to be universal and necessary (that one should love one's neighbor) thus depends on knowing the particular circumstances of the individual in question in order to know how to act toward that particular individual. Hegel then infers that the rule has only a "formal universality" (*PS* 231.30–37/M 256).[1] This demonstration of the emptiness of the rule when universalized thus leads to the charge of formalism: "For universality that lacks a content is [merely] formal, and an *absolute* content itself is tantamount to a distinction which is no distinction, i.e. to absence of content" (ibid.). The "mere form of universality" is mirrored in the "tautology of consciousness" (*PS* 231.38–232.3/M 256). The problem with tautologies, after all, is not that they are not true, but that their truth is *vacuous*.

The narrative then unfolds dialectically. From the vacuity of moral rules, universal reason learns that it has to abandon the idea of being able to give itself *substantive* moral rules. Reason therefore backs off from this overly strong conception of morality to a weaker one based purely on the idea of *procedural* rules. In other words, reason no longer sees itself as being able to specify the good concretely, but instead settles for specifying the right way to achieve the good. Hegel thus characterizes this procedural morality as reason as *testing* or *critically examining* rules, not as giving them to itself (*PS* 232.4–7/M 256). The third example that he brings up to illustrate the shape of reason as merely testing rather than legislating rules is whether there should be an absolute right to property (see *PS* 233.3–33/M 257–8). Here the question is whether property is essential to society. If so, then stealing, for instance, would seem to contradict itself, in some sense of "contradict" that remains to be clarified below. But if there could be a society without property, then, as I will explain, the actions of an "anarchist thief" would not be contradictory and the categorical imperative procedure would be disproved by counterexample.

Subtle Kant scholars have been quick to defend Kant against these Hegelian lines of criticisms. Harvard Professor Christine Korsgaard, for instance, offers rebuttals of the Hegelian charges of formalism and rigorism. (She does not address the charge that I am calling dogmatism.) Of course, she has the advantage of over 200 years of Kant scholarship to draw on, whereas Hegel had fewer than 20 years after the publication in 1787 of Kant's *Critique of Practical Reason*. Also, Korsgaard is not concerned with the role these criticisms play in the context of the *Phenomenology*. In fact, as she herself states explicitly, she is not purporting to deal with Hegel directly, but with the formulations of the criticisms by F. H. Bradley and H. B. Acton, who give arguments generally attributed to Hegel. Let me give a brief account of her defense of Kant.

Kant offered different formulations of the categorical imperative, but the first, the Universal Law formula, is the most well known: *Act only according to that maxim by which you can at the same time will that it should become a universal law*. The way that a maxim is tested is by seeing what happens if a personal maxim were like a universal law of nature. I should therefore ask if everybody could follow the principle that I would be following in a particular action without contradiction. I am to test the moral maxim (where a maxim is the personal reason that I have for doing something) by seeing whether its contradictory (the immoral maxim) could be followed without contradiction. Kant thinks that when put to this test, immoral maxims will self-destruct, or annihilate themselves, insofar as they are inconceivable or cannot be willed. In Kant's best example of making false promises, for instance, Korsgaard suggests that we are trying to imagine a situation in which someone tries to deceive by making a false promise in a world where no one accepts promises at all. By stipulation, then, making a promise in that world would be impossible.

However, as Hegel indicates, there are many other cases where what contradiction involves is not entirely clear. That is the point of Hegel's example mentioned above about whether it ought to be "an absolute law that there should be property" (*PS* 233.5–7/M 257). Hegel applies Kant's universalizability test, which involves seeing what would happen if the contradictory of the principle in question were universalized. In this case, Hegel sees no reason why there could not be a society without property. Kantians then try to save Kant by asking whether, in parallel with the case of false promising, we could *will* a world without property. Hegelians could grant that we could not will a world without promises because we require the trust that promises presuppose. However, we could will, and indeed entire nations have tried to will, a world without property. The failure of these attempts does not necessarily show the inconceivability of the principle that property is not a necessary good. The decline of world communism may simply be the outcome of an economic power struggle with capitalism, which requires property.

Although this may be the point of the argument in the *Phenomenology*, in the *Philosophy of Right* Hegel takes a more Kantian tack on private property. As Rawls points out, there Hegel does not advocate a utilitarian justification of private property on the basis of our desires and wants, but strictly on the idea of freedom, which is manifested in respect for the dignity of other persons as free beings. Rawls sums up Hegel's argument as follows:

> So it is as a free will that I have the right to own property; my needs and the fulfillment of my desires have nothing to do with it. The true position, as Hegel says, is that the system of property is justified as the most appropriate embodiment of freedom. The very system itself as expressing freedom is the substantive end. (Rawls 2000, 342)

Hegel thinks that nothing is gained by formulating the rules for action and then calling them our "duty." As I explain below, Hegel's view is that free will is expressed in the institutions of *Sittlichkeit*, so moral rules are just the reflective working out of what ethical life already calls for.

Commentators now distinguish between contradiction in conception and contradiction in the will. The latter is the more difficult to understand. Korsgaard makes an important contribution by noticing that in the Kant literature there are currently three different interpretations of contradictory willing. These include logical contradiction (whereby universalization would entail an action that was inconceivable, i.e., logically impossible), teleological contradiction (whereby universalization would be inconsistent with a systematic harmony of purposes or principles), and practical contradiction (whereby universalization would be self-defeating in that it would thwart its own purpose). Korsgaard thinks that Kant's actual texts could support each of these interpretations, so she bases her own preference for the third interpretation on philosophical considerations about what makes willing rational. Let me now take a closer look at her reasons for this preference.

Sometimes the Hegelian objections to particular moral principles can be rebutted easily. For instance, in discussing the principle of loving one's neighbor, Hegel points out that the principle is not an absolute, but a qualified one:

> I must love him intelligently. Unintelligent love will perhaps do him more harm than hatred. Intelligent, substantial beneficence is, however, in its richest and most important form the intelligent universal action of the state – an action compared with which the action of a single individual, as an individual, is so insignificant that it is hardly worth talking about. (*PS* 231.5–10/M 255)

Korsgaard takes Hegel's point that in a world in which there is no one who is poor, the maxim to aid the poor would be impossible to apply, and therefore fails by the logical contradiction test. Hegel, like William Blake and F. H. Bradley, does sometimes argue that the Kantian duties such as beneficence to the poor or pity of those less well off presuppose a world in which there are indigents and unfortunates. The critique would then be that Kantians really value beneficence and pity so much that they must really want a world in which poverty exists. Without poverty, it would be impossible to fulfill these duties and the CI-procedure would be worthless. Korsgaard then shows that the CI-procedure and the Logical Contradiction Interpretation are not invalidated by this example. She argues that in a world with no poor, the maxim to aid the poor is not self-contradictory because the maxim can still be a rule, but it is a rule "that gives one nothing to do" (Korsgaard 1996, 87).

Hegel's point here in the *Phenomenology* is somewhat different, however. He is more concerned with the efficacy of the action than its formal outcome when the CI-procedure is applied. The Kantian will find Hegel's point irrelevant to the issue of universalizability. However, Hegel's narrative at this stage in the dialectic is also to show the limitations of the individual agent, and to emphasize that ethical requirements apply to the social collectivity as well: to the "We" more so than to the "I" (although the "I" is, of course, among the "We"). In the middle of his discussion of whether there is an individual duty to relieve poverty (*PS* 231.14–19/ M 255), Hegel introduces seemingly from nowhere the point that an individual's efforts can do little for society as a whole, and that only the state can do much that is genuinely efficacious. This is not as much a leap as it might seem if one did not know about his view of social intentions that come to more than the sum of individual intentions. Whereas Reason sees only I-intentions, Spirit involves what the philosopher Wilfred Sellars called we-intentions, that is, ends that we hold as a collectivity and that do not simply reduce to the individual's aims and purposes.

The advantage of the Teleological Contradiction Interpretation is that it can accommodate this emphasis on collective willing. The Teleological Contradiction Interpretation is based on the idea of the systematic harmony of human purposes. Take Kant's example of why suicide is wrong and then imagine someone with a brain tumor or Alzheimer's disease. In order to preserve his sense of who he is, he kills himself. But this just destroys his selfhood altogether. For the Kantian (and for Kant himself), this action is contradictory. However, Korsgaard recognizes the power of the Hegelian objection here. The Hegelian objection is that there is no reason for the suicide to suppose that self-preservation is a necessary feature of the harmony of human purposes. To accommodate this objection, Korsgaard develops her own view (acknowledging its affinity with arguments developed by Marcus Singer and Onora O'Neill), which is that the contradiction in willing is neither logical nor teleological contradiction, but practical contradiction. Crucial to the Practical Contradiction Interpretation is that the agent's *purpose* be specified. The practical contradiction is that in acting on the universalized maxim, the agent's purpose will be frustrated. Korsgaard responds to the Hegelian charge of formalism and emptiness – for instance, when the Hegelian points out that there is no contradiction in a world without promises – as follows:

> The proponent of the Logical Contradiction view replies that the contradiction is not merely in a system without such practices as deposits or promises but in an agent engaging in these practices in a system without them. On the Practical Contradiction Interpretation the answer we shall give is still better. The person who tries to will the universalization of this maxim is not only thereby willing a situation in which practices like deposits and promises do not exist. He is also willing that they do exist, precisely because he is willing to *use* them to achieve his ends. (Korsgaard 1996, 95)

On her interpretation, then, the Hegelian reproach is taken into account and resolved in Kant's favor.

Korsgaard also believes that the charge of rigorism is best answered by this interpretation. To the charge that the Kantian duties are too strong and that they presuppose the existence of the social evil (e.g., poverty) in order for there to be a duty towards the afflicted, Korsgaard responds:

> One's purpose in succoring the poor is to give them relief. The world of the universalized maxim only contradicts one's will if it thwarts one's purpose. A world without poverty does not contradict this purpose, but rather satisfies it another (better) way, and no contradiction arises. (Korsgaard 1996, 95)

Consider again the case of the thief who is an anarchist and who does not believe in private property. On the Logical Contradiction Interpretation, *everyone* would have to want property to exist. But Hegelians can imagine a world without property. So does that mean that a thief who is an anarchist and who does not believe in private property would be justified in stealing? Note, however, that on the Practical Contradiction Interpretation, when the agent's purpose is included, the analysis would be that the anarchist thief must want property to exist by the very fact that he takes it for himself.

I think that Hegel would feel that none of these three interpretations of contradiction (whether logical, teleological, or practical) fully responds to what he is trying to bring out in his examples. One claim that he surely wants to make is that, stated in their most general form, moral rules would not be action guiding in the way that the moralist thinks. His point about loving others intelligently or about being able to speak the truth only when one knows the truth is to bring out that to guide action, the general principles have to be made more concrete by specifying the qualifications that are assumed in the interpretation of the situation. Students of Hegel could thus raise the following two questions about Korsgaard's defense of Kant.

(i) The first is whether the maxim is really being universalized so that everybody could will it, or whether only those with the specific purpose could will it. The more conditions that are tacked on, the more specific the law becomes. This problem reinforces the argument against Kant that if the universal law formula has some content, that content does not follow from the idea of pure duty (*Moralität*), but from more empirical practices (*Sittlichkeit*) that are tacitly presupposed by the moral point of view.

This logical problem then translates into a problem for Kantian moral psychology. Later in the *Phenomenology* Hegel says: "Since the determinate duty is an end, it has a content, its content is part of the end, and so morality is not pure" (*PS* 339.8–10/M 381; see Wood 1990, 168–72). The Hegelian charge is that the Kantian "moral point of view" depends on the possibility of saying that even when duty and inclination coincide, the agent is capable of acting because of duty and not inclination. Furthermore, the agent must be able to distinguish between acting from *pure* duty (e.g., keeping promises) and not from *empirical* duty (e.g., keeping this particular promise). Hegel's view is that agents cannot abstract their ends in this way, and that performing one's duty will always involve some empirical motives for acting on a particular duty in a particular case. The Kantian is therefore wrong to believe that agents could act from pure duty alone. Indeed, Kant himself says as much.[2] Hegel accordingly rejects the Kantian claim that the only question that is morally relevant is whether the action is motivated by pure duty. Hegelians who reject the Kantian moral psychology may even suspect that the question is not intelligible.

(ii) A second question is whether Korsgaard's rebuttal of the first two Hegelian objections (formalism and rigorism) does not take into account the third objection that I raised earlier, namely, dogmatism. This is the charge that the Kantian account is dogmatic and does not take account of the social background and the interpretive variability of the situation. Jean-Paul Sartre argued, for instance, that the principle of helping others did not tell a young Frenchman during the last world war whether to stay home and care for his ailing mother or to go off and help others by joining the Resistance. Either way of trying to help others would at the same time violate the principle. If he joined the Resistance, his mother would die and if he stayed home to care for his mother, other Resistance fighters would die.

Furthermore, if the situation depends on its description, then changing the description could very well change the situation. If, for instance, the anarchist thief really has no respect for anyone's property, including his own, he could even say that "stealing" and "thief" are appellations that should not be applied to him. Of course, then he could have no objection to anyone else taking the items that he had just stolen. The situation is thus ironic, but not necessarily contradictory.

Kant's theory tries to avoid these difficulties by lexically ordering duties so that there can be no conflict of duties because some come before others. However, this only serves to make the theory even more rigoristic. It also makes the theory seem to say that for every moral question, there is only one right answer. In the next section I will explain why Hegel's ethics of freedom challenges this apparent dogmatism of a morality of duty.

3 *Moralität* and *Sittlichkeit*: Transcendental Argument or Reflective Equilibrium?

One Kant scholar who has spotted and addressed the issue that I am calling dogmatism is Onora O'Neill. In *Constructions of Reason* (1989) she recognizes that descriptions of situations are matters of interpretation, and that they can vary even to the point of incommensurability. She thus anticipates the philosophical problem that I see behind Hegel's worries about the universality and the concomitant risk of dogmatism on the part of *Moralität*:

> But the comprehensibility of alternative descriptions of a situation and of proposed lines of action is an insufficient guarantee of a way by which agreement on one rather than another equally comprehensible set of descriptions is to be the basis for action. If we have no way in which to reason over the formulation of descriptions of situations and (proposals for) action, practical reasoning must remain local. (O'Neill 1989, 180)

By looking into late writings of Kant, including the third *Critique*, she finds a role for moral principles in what Kant calls reflective judgment, and thus her own stance is not local, but cosmopolitan and Kantian. However, she also wants to keep our appraisals of situations "open-ended" (O'Neill 1989, 186). Appraisals include our intuitive grasp of what is at stake in situations and the way that we understand our situation. Appraisals thus involve interpreting the situation a certain way, such that if this interpretation changes, the cultural understanding of what sort of situation it is could change as well. I understand her to be suggesting that reflective judgment must move between principles and appraisals so as to arrive at what Rawls called a "reflective equilibrium." Without conceding anything to relativism, she thinks that even if our appraisals of situations are guided by "considerations of coherence and interpretability to all parties (and indeed to the 'collective reason of mankind')," that will not necessarily generate only one valid way of looking at a situation (O'Neill 1989, 184). Which principles are applied will vary according to how the situation is understood and appraised. As she quips, "Principles without appraisals are empty; appraisals without principles are impotent" (O'Neill 1989, 186).

This non-dogmatic, hermeneutical way of thinking about the relation of principles to situations is helpful to keep in mind as we work through Hegel's analysis of the balancing of reflection and intuition in concrete ethical life. Appraisals involve *Sittlichkeit*'s concern with insight into concrete situations as opposed to *Moralität*'s interest in abstract principles. Given this way of thinking about the distinction, one wonders why we are faced with an either/or here. What leads to the idea that these two must be opposed? Apparently, it is only due to a certain conception of philosophy, call it the "Kantian" conception. The goal of philosophy on this Kantian conception is to discover transcendental arguments that show that one concept is *derived* from the other. If we gave up doing this kind of foundationalist philosophy, however, then we might be able to see *Moralität* and *Sittlichkeit*, if not as two sides of the same coin, at least as two interrelated features of ethical life. Let me now explore whether we can find support for this way of viewing the two less as competitors, and more as dual aspects of the ethical domain. After discussing this issue, I will conclude with a response to the charge against Hegel that what is empty and dogmatic is not *Moralität* but *Sittlichkeit*.[3]

(i) First, let us make sure that we understand what Hegel means by each of these terms. The scholarly literature on Hegel includes many excellent expositions of the differences between them. Clearly, there are contrasts between *Sittlichkeit* and *Moralität*. For instance, in *Sittlichkeit* moral obligations flow from the common life that is already there: my obligations arise in this common life and my fulfillment of these obligations sustains this common life. As Charles Taylor says,

> The crucial characteristic of *Sittlichkeit* is that it enjoins us to bring about what already is . . . Hence in *Sittlichkeit* there is no gap between what ought to be and what is, between *Sollen* and *Sein*.
>
> With *Moralität* the opposite holds. Here we have an obligation to realize something which does not exist. What ought to be contrasts with what is. And connected with this, the obligation holds of me not in virtue of being part of a larger community life, but as an individual rational will. (Taylor 1975, 376; 1979, 83)

Allen Wood makes the contrast more explicitly in terms of the difference between moral psychology in Kant and Hegel:

> ["Moral" duties in the Kantian sense] are experienced as external limits on the subject's particular desires, projects, and mode of life. Morality tells me which of my desires it is permissible to satisfy . . . Moral duties, as Kant often emphasizes, are experienced as constraints on the will . . .
>
> Ethical duties, on the other hand, are not constraints on my life; on the contrary, they are the best part of it, "the substance of my own being" (*PR* §148) . . . Ethical duties include my love for my spouse, my parents, and my children, and the self-satisfaction I get from engaging in my profession or vocation (*PR* §207, §255) . . . Morality takes, as our philosophers say, "the moral point of view." The point of view of ethical life, however, is nothing distinct from the concrete individual's total, unified perspective on the world. (Wood 1990, 210)

In contrast to the paradigm of *Moralität*, which is the stoical Kantian, the paradigm case of *Sittlichkeit* is the ancient Athenian, who acts "as it were, out of instinct" and for whom ethical action is "second nature" (MM 12: 57/Hegel 1963, 41; cited by Taylor 1979, 89). If reflection is essential to *Moralität* insofar as action done without reflection on dutifulness has no moral worth, reflection is *problematic* for *Sittlichkeit*. Historically, a breakdown in *Sittlichkeit* can be tied to heightened inward reflection that leads to alienation from the immediacy of *Sittlichkeit*. Hegel thinks that we witness this alienation both in Antigone (discussed in more detail in the next essay in this volume) and in Socrates. Socrates reflects on *Sittlichkeit*, but this is possible only because *Sittlichkeit* is already breaking down. Socrates' need to reflect is itself a sign of this breakdown. The reflective questioning of *Sittlichkeit* may contribute to the destruction of *Sittlichkeit*, but this is not to be taken as a victory of individual reason, since the destruction of *Sittlichkeit* leads in turn to the unfortunate deaths of both Antigone and Socrates.[4]

Historically the destruction of Athenian *Sittlichkeit* leads to the Roman state, which Hegel sees as a mere aggregate of atomistic individuals with no real community and with laws that are only dead vestiges of a once-living ethos. Eventually the *Sittlichkeit* that no longer existed in this world had to be projected beyond this world to another one. Kantian *Moralität* is a late variant of this process. On the one hand, it identifies the moral capacity with the rational capacity of each individual being. On the other hand, it makes moral worth less a function of how individuals relate to the world and to the consequences of actions, and more a function of how individuals relate both to their own inner wills and to the good will that is ultimately noumenal or other-worldly.

Hegel uses the word *Moralität* not as a general term, like the English word "morality," but specifically for the way of life that follows from trying to live according to the Kantian theory of morality. That is to say, Hegel does not object entirely to the deontological program. Instead, in the *Phenomenology* he sees *Moralität* as a particular "shape of consciousness," that is, as a historical and cultural phenomenon to be explained dialectically as evolving from Reason into Spirit. The philosophical explanation would suggest why *Moralität* had come about and therefore what its advantages and achievements were given the previous history of thought. But Hegel also sees Kantian *Moralität* as a response to the particular historical circumstances of modernity. So *Moralität* is a phenomenon or a practice that is not to be simply dismissed. However, the explanation can lead to seeing the limitations of the moral point of view, limitations that may not be perceived from within the point of view.

Consider, for instance, what happens in this dialectical explanation of the central Kantian idea of autonomy. Hegel is targeting Kant's conception of the rational individual who aspires to actions that are based not simply on personal maxims, but on *laws* that anyone and everyone should *give to themselves*. Insofar as everyone could act on the principle that the particular individual is about to act on, the individual thereby demonstrates autonomy. On the Kantian theory, the autonomy that is a feature of the noumenal will is not something that one could not have. We may not always live up to the autonomy of the will, but even falling short of it requires us to have autonomy. Kant's conception of autonomy is what makes his moral theory individualistic. So when Kant answers the question, "where do substantive moral laws come from?" his answer is: from the autonomous individual. The autonomous individual gives the law to him- or herself in the sense that the individual determines whether everyone could follow the particular law. This is the kernel of the Kantian stance that Hegel labels "*Moralität.*"

When Hegel asks the same question, he suggests that the Kantian has not understood the problem. For Hegel, moral intuitions are acquired through one's upbringing and acculturation, or what he calls *Sittlichkeit*. If the origin of moral principles is in *Sittlichkeit*, does that mean that there is no such thing as autonomy? Not necessarily, for autonomy need not be construed as a metaphysical feature of the individual will, but as a social achievement. That is to say, the society that makes it possible for individuals to be autonomous agents is to be preferred to the society that works against autonomous action. Hegel thus turns the tables on the Kantian in a dialectical reversal whereby individual autonomy is not possible without the requisite social conditions that enable and foster one's freedom of action.

The Hegelian's dialectical reversal may look to the Kantian less like an explanation and more like a dismissal, a misleading characterization, or, as I shall discuss shortly, an irrelevant shift from philosophy to sociology. The moral point of view claims to apply to any social state of affairs, and thus to transcend the particularity of social contingencies. That is, it claims universality for itself, and priority over any other point of view (such as the social, the historical, or the political) that might conflict with it. Morality from within itself claims not to be simply "a point of view," and for Hegel to treat it as one among others is already to reject its own sense of its necessity. It is precisely this sense of necessity, not the historical phenomenon of *Moralität* itself, that Hegel is challenging. This sense of its own necessity and universality is the internal false consciousness of the moralistic outlook of someone like Socrates who sees himself as independent of his social situation.

However, in pointing out the dangers of *Moralität*, Hegel is not denying the phenomenon. The danger is that moral principles are abstract, and they are the result of extensive meta-theoretical reflection. Hegel maintains that reflection taken to the degree of Socratic or Kantian (or utilitarian) theory can destroy the concrete moral sense of what is right. Such a result might follow, for instance, from the standard use of the Socratic method in the undergraduate philosophy classroom, which students often perceive as the professor constantly asking questions and never giving any answers. That practice could give students a sense that current ethical theories, like Kantian and utilitarian ones, never lead to a satisfactory moral resolution of a problem.

These contrasts between the moral and the ethical still do not explain why there needs to be a further (transcendental) question about which comes first. This frequently asked question suggests that Hegel is overly influenced by Kantian transcendental philosophy, despite his own abhorrence of the term. Hegel's way of expressing his dialectical critique of the Kantian account of moral practice is to contrast Kantian *Moralität* with its focus on principles and their justification, to concrete ethical practice, or *Sittlichkeit*. *Moralität* also draws this contrast, and asserts itself as "superseding" *Sittlichkeit*. That is, morality claims necessity and universality for itself, and thus to be more than the customs or *Sitten* of particular societies. Hegel's strategy is to reverse *Moralität*'s own story, suggesting ironically that *Moralität* is really *aufgehoben* or superseded by *Sittlichkeit*.

Although commentators often speak as if *Sittlichkeit* and *Moralität* were opposed to each other, the concepts may be responding to different issues and therefore may not necessarily be oppositional. Each of the two terms can be explaining different aspects of practical reason and need not require an either/or. *Sittlichkeit* is the answer to the question about the social glue that binds people together. Often pre-reflective and particular, *Sittlichkeit* involves social skills or what Aristotle called practical wisdom (*phronesis*). *Moralität* enters the picture when these skills are made the object of a reflective judgment that asks for the principles that legitimate actions. Hegel need not be rejecting Kantian *Moralität* altogether, then, but rather he is situating it differently than Kant does. Instead of grounding moral principles in a noumenal will, as Kant does, Hegel focuses on the social origins of moral activity. Considering two further examples (not from Hegel himself) will show the value of the distinction independently of the transcendental derivation argument.

(ii) The danger of an account based on custom and convention, no matter how longstanding, is that it appears to reduce morality to sociology. This reduction raises difficult questions. If the moral grows out of the social, how is one going to be able to criticize existent values? "In the name of what," it will be asked, "can one go against existing values?" Alan Donagan problematizes Hegel effectively when he reverses Hegel's critique by asking whether it is not *Sittlichkeit* rather than *Moralität* that is empty. Donagan believes that simply looking at the concrete situation cannot be the basis of a moral choice. Donagan cites the specific case of an Austrian farmer, Franz Jägerstätter, who was beheaded in 1943 for refusing induction into the German army because of his belief that the war was unjust. Donagan equates Hegel's position with that of Jägerstätter's bishop, who even after the war criticized Jägerstätter and praised instead the "heroes" of the Wehrmacht. Donagan writes:

> Hegel disparaged the point of view of morality on the ground that, being abstractly rational, it could find content for its judgments only in the mores of some actual community. The case of Jägerstätter reveals an opposite process. The moral theory of Catholic Christianity furnished specific precepts on the subject of legitimate war service . . . But, by recourse to the mores of their actual community, Jägerstätter's spiritual advisers were able to evaporate the precepts whose applicability to his case they could not dispute. For, according to those mores, apart from such fanciful possibilities as a war with the declared intention of destroying the Church as an institution, no individual citizen was deemed capable of assuring himself that any war his country proposed to wage was unjust. Here, what is exposed as empty, as lacking specific content, as allowing any filling whatever, is not *Moralität* but *Sittlichkeit*. (Donagan 1977, 17)

This response is indeed a provocative challenge to Hegel. However, the Hegelian can argue in return that it misconstrues the force of Hegel's turn to the social as the source of concrete practices. As Onora O'Neill pointed out above, the turn to the social need not relativize moral principles. So Hegel need not abandon the universal principles of morality when he rejects Kant's notion of a noumenal will that is outside space and time. Instead, Hegel's emphasis on the social serves to open the door to a different moral psychology than the Kantian one, that is, to a strictly phenomenal (historical and psychological) account of ethical behavior.

For Hegel to make his historical, sociological contextualization of morality stick, he does not need to offer a competing "moral theory," at least not in the same sense of "theory." That is, his criticisms are intended to show the limitations of the Kantian approach to moral experience that turns it into a deduction of principles. Hegel's strategy is not to offer an alternative set of principles, and, more importantly, it is not to offer an alternative "grounding" of these principles in one meta-principle like the categorical imperative or the utility principle. In our more contemporary parlance, I am suggesting that Hegel is not offering an alternative "foundational" account to Kant's (like the utility principle). Instead, he is claiming that the attempt to "ground" or justify our ethical practices in something that transcends our contingent self-interpretation is misguided. The "foundational" approach to moral philosophy gives an overly abstract account of ethical practice and moral psychology. It is also misguided in its desire for a meta-principle or a meta-point of view that transcends any and every other point of view.

In contrast, Hegel seems methodologically less like a foundationalist "theorist" and more like what is now called a holistic "anti-theorist."[5] Hegel's approach to *Sittlichkeit* is not to deduce all social and moral relations from a single principle (although these relations are said to flow from human freedom), but to construct an account in which our various practices hang together. The phrase "hang together" should not imply that these practices never conflict with one another, but only that for the most part they are integrated with one another. The Hegelian account is of course theoretical in the sense that it articulates the coherence between practices (and criticizes any incoherency in them), but it does not specify a single universal test or procedure for correct moral conduct in the way that rationalistic moral theory projects.

So understood, Hegel need not even give up the idea of moral rules. All that he needs to say is that moral rules do not flow from a noumenal or a purely rational and necessary ground, but from historically contingent practices. Rules are determined by reflecting on practices, but through critical assessment reflection can serve not only to reinforce practice but also to undermine it.

I offer a final example to gather together various intuitions about the relation of the two aspects of the ethical life and to challenge Donagan's charge that it is *Sittlichkeit* that is empty, not *Moralität*. The example is the famous case of Heinz's dilemma that was debated extensively by Kohlberg and Gilligan. The question is whether an impoverished Heinz can steal a drug that the cruel pharmacist will not give him to save the life of Heinz's wife. In an addition to §127 of the *Philosophy of Right*, where Hegel is concerned to show the limitations of "abstract right," Hegel maintains explicitly that pure duty or formal right (e.g., property rights) can be abrogated by concrete circumstances:

> Life, as the totality of ends, has a right in opposition to abstract right. If, for instance, it can be preserved by stealing a loaf, this certainly constitutes an infringement of someone's property, but it would be wrong to regard such an action as a common theft. If someone whose life is in danger were not allowed to take measures to save himself, he would be destined to forfeit all his rights; and since he would be deprived of life, his entire freedom would be negated ... The *beneficium competentiae* is of relevance here, because links of kinship and other close relationships entail the right to demand that no one should be sacrificed completely for the sake of right. (*PR* §127Z)

In contrast to the Kantian insistence on following the rule against theft, Hegel thus affirms that Heinz has ethical reason to steal the drug to save his wife's life. I know that this example will be controversial, but it strikes me as being a case where the *phronesis* of concrete ethical life trumps abstract rules. Hegel's conception of ethical life shows itself here to have action-guiding value without being formalistic, rigoristic, or dogmatic.

4 Conclusion: The Transition from Reason to Spirit

Whatever one thinks about these examples, Hegel's larger point should not be lost from sight. Kant raised the question, "why be moral?" Kant's answer depends on metaphysical views about not only the existence of God and the immortality of the soul, but also of a will that mysteriously guides action from a standpoint outside of space and time. If these theological beliefs are less than compelling in our own secular time, then Hegel's answer is an alternative that is still available today. His answer depends on seeing that morality is not just a matter for individuals to decide in isolation, but that it is embedded in a collective sense of what is right and wrong. For Hegel the "I" of individual Reason must expand into the social "We" of Spirit. Normative activity is not sufficiently accounted for by an individual morality of duty alone, but it also requires what I have called an ethics of freedom. This broader ethical framework would recognize the role of actual social institutions in determining individual duties. Given the particular historical circumstances, it would also envision the integration of individual wills with their inherent autonomy in the collective drive to maximize freedom.[6]

To understand the transition from Reason to Spirit one must realize that as the *Phenomenology* progresses, natural consciousness changes from the attempt of an individual to look inside consciousness to discover the principles for normative action. In the section on Reason, natural consciousness is at the stage of seeing itself in all others. In contrast, in the standpoint of Spirit the regard turns initially outward towards the world and others. Hegel thus turns away from the individual's decision procedure and focuses more on the actual moral claim itself. At the very end of the section on law-testing, then, he emphasizes the ethical substance more than the moral subject. As the ethical claim becomes the topic, he has to address the question of how there can be ethically compelling obligations, or in his terminology, "absolutes." That these obligations are built into individuals through the culture is to be shown in the next chapter by the analysis of Antigone and ancient Greece. That chapter then ends once again by an analysis of Kantian morality, which is accused of hypocrisy. Hypocrisy is a contradictory duplicity not just in a normative sense, but also in a metaphysical sense insofar as it posits another world as the real world and this world as merely apparent. That chapter moves from the Greeks' sense of themselves as bound to ethical absolutes to the Roman state where legal "persons" are reduced to being the bearers of abstract rights. If abstract moral principles represent a dry and thinned-out conceptualization of the individual agent who is faced with the decision about what to do, abstract legal rights are the dried-up residues of the social glue that holds a culture together. Hegel is often construed as the most conceptual of philosophers. At this point in the text, however, conceptualization is seen as dry abstraction in contrast to the richness of concrete ethical experience. How long the richness of immediate

Spirit will last, and how soon it will degenerate into an impoverished over-conceptualization of normative obligation is for the remaining essays in this volume to explain. The dialectic moves on, and the sections on law-giving and law-testing are not the last instances of Hegel's use of Kant as a stepping-stone to his own system.

Notes

1. Translations of the *Phenomenology of Spirit* by A. V. Miller have been revised without further notice.
2. *CPrR* 5:25, cf. *Rel.* 6:7 note, 36; *CJ* 5:450, cf. *CPrR* 5:32, 122–5. (My thanks to Ken Westphal for these references.)
3. Kantian morality as a shape of consciousness comes up again later in the *Phenomenology* and is a topic for chapter 10 of this volume. My task in this essay is to consider morality only as rule-following behavior, not as postulating the existence of God, an immortal soul, or a free will.
4. Cf. chapter 6 on the importance of the historical breakdown of social norms for understanding normativity. – *Ed.*
5. For the opposition between rationalistic "theory" and holistic "anti-theory," see the editors' introduction to Clarke and Simpson (1989, 10–12).
6. For a nuanced account of Hegel's emphasis on the importance of social institutions in determining duties, see Westphal (2005).

References

Clarke, S. G. and Simpson, E., eds. (1989) *Anti-Theory in Ethics and Moral Conservatism.* New York: State University of New York Press.
Donagan, A. (1977) *The Theory of Morality.* Chicago: University of Chicago Press.
Forster, M. N. (1998) *Hegel's Idea of a Phenomenology of Spirit.* Chicago: University of Chicago Press.
Foucault, M. (1997). *Ethics: Subjectivity and Truth.* New York: The New Press.
Hegel, G. W. F. (1963) *Lectures on the Philosophy of History,* tr. J. Sibree. London: Bell & Daldy (1872); rpt. London: Routledge & Kegan Paul.
Korsgaard, C. M. (1996) *Creating the Kingdom of Ends.* Cambridge: Cambridge University Press.
O'Neill, O. (1989) *Constructions of Reason: Explorations of Kant's Practical Philosophy.* Cambridge: Cambridge University Press.
Rawls, J. (1971) *A Theory of Justice.* Cambridge, Mass.: Harvard University Press.
Rawls, J. (2000) *Lectures on the History of Moral Philosophy.* Cambridge, Mass.: Harvard University Press.
Taylor, C. (1975) *Hegel.* Cambridge: Cambridge University Press.
Taylor, C. (1979) *Hegel and Modern Society.* Cambridge: Cambridge University Press.
Westphal, K. R. (2005) "Kant, Hegel, and Determining Our Duties," in S. Byrd and J. Joerden (eds.), *Philosophia practica universalis. Festschrift für Joachim Hruschka. Jahrbuch für Recht und Ethik/Annual Review of Law and Ethics* 13: 335–54.
Wood, A. W. (1990) *Hegel's Ethical Thought.* Cambridge: Cambridge University Press.

Further Reading

Hoy, D. C. (1981) "Hegel's Morals," *Dialogue* 20: 84–102.
Hoy, D. C. (1989) "Hegel's Critique of Kantian Morality," *History of Philosophy Quarterly* 6: 207–32.
Pinkard, T. (1994) *Hegel's Phenomenology: The Sociality of Reason*. Cambridge: Cambridge University Press.
Pinkard, T. (2000) *Hegel: A Biography*. Cambridge: Cambridge University Press.
Pippin, R. B. (1995) "Hegel on the Rationality and Priority of Ethical Life," *Neue Hefte für Philosophie* 35: 95–126.
Sedgwick, S. S. (1996) "Hegel's Critique of Kant's Empiricism and the Categorical Imperative," *Zeitschrift für philosophische Forschung* 50: 563–84.
Solomon, R. (1983) *In the Spirit of Hegel: A Study of G. W. F. Hegel's Phenomenology of Spirit*. Oxford: Oxford University Press.
Speight, C. A. (1997) "The *Metaphysics of Morals* and Hegel's Critique of Kantian Ethics," *History of Philosophy Quarterly* 14: 379–402.
Stern, R. (2002) *Hegel and the Phenomenology of Spirit*. London: Routledge.
Westphal, K. R. (1991) "Hegel's Critique of Kant's Moral World View," *Philosophical Topics* 19: 133–76.
Westphal, K. R. (1995) "How 'Full' is Kant's Categorical Imperative?" *Jahrbuch für Recht und Ethik/Annual Review of Law and Ethics* 3: 465–509.

8

Hegel, *Antigone*, and Feminist Critique: The Spirit of Ancient Greece

Jocelyn B. Hoy

Hegel's *Phenomenology of Spirit* seems an unlikely place for debates about sexual difference, gender roles, and family relations. But in fact, Chapter VI of the *Phenomenology*, subtitled "The True Spirit. The Ethical Order," includes Hegel's discussion of these questions in his famous account of *Antigone*, a play and a character that continue to speak to us in strange and provocative ways.

My presentation will focus on the appearance of Spirit in the world of ancient Greece (*PS* 9:238–260.23/M 263–89). My strategy will be, first, to present a brief account of the "story" of this appearance of Spirit in these paragraphs; second, to reflect on Hegel's use of dramatic form, specifically Attic tragedy, to introduce us to Spirit; and third, to examine contemporary feminist interpretations of Hegel's account of *Antigone* in this section of the *Phenomenology*. The questions I take up include the following: Why does Hegel consider the ancient Greeks as the model for emergent Spirit in ethical life? Why does Hegel resort to literary figures, in particular to dramatic tragedy, to represent this ethical life? Why focus on Sophocles' *Antigone*? Does Hegel's treatment of *Antigone* enrich our understanding of the *Phenomenology*, or simply reveal Hegel's own deep-seated patriarchal biases? Can this section of a 200-year-old text speak to contemporary social and political issues? Questions about sexist biases, literary figures, and historical examples, I hope to show, are not philosophically tangential or irrelevant. Exploring recent feminist critiques of this section gets to the heart of Hegel's phenomenological project, and may well support a general interpretation of Hegel's *Phenomenology* potentially fruitful for feminist and social theory as well as contemporary philosophy. But first, then, the "story."

In his opening remarks in Chapter VI, Hegel says that Reason becomes Spirit when it becomes "conscious of itself as its own world, and of the world as itself" (*PS* 238.4–5/M 263). We should understand 'world' here not as a separate metaphysical or natural object but as an historical, communal space organized by practical norms governing the actions of individuals and institutions. If we had previously thought of Reason as detached reflection and knowledge, transcending historical and cultural circumstances, that view of Reason has been shown to be inadequate. Reason becomes or realizes itself as Spirit when the ways of reflecting and knowing are embedded within social relations in an historical community. Spirit is the practical embodiment of Reason: Spirit is at least initially manifested in "ethical life" (*Sittlichkeit*), the customs and norms holding sway for an historical community. Spirit is the "substance" and "abiding essence" of this community by allowing people's actions to be purposeful and meaningful in terms of their communal norms (*PS* 238.8–239.39/M 263–4).

Understanding Spirit in this way, Hegel uses the ancient Greeks as his historical paradigm. Why? Importantly, the ancient Greeks were presented in Hegel's own time as an idealized example of such "spiritual" harmony: The ancient Greeks, according to this picture, understood themselves in terms of their social roles, their place in the community. This social order presented the ways things *must be*, by nature or "eternal necessity." Questions about the ultimate meaning or justification of their lives and individual actions were answered in terms of their customs and laws. Both historically and conceptually, the ancient Greek world seems the prime candidate for Spirit's unfolding as an ethical community. In keeping with his phenomenological mode of investigation, however, Hegel will probe this world with his usual critical question: Does this form of Spirit which *appears* to be perfectly harmonious actually live up to its own conception of itself – or at least to the conception of those of Hegel's contemporaries who deem it preferable to the alienated modern world? (Pinkard 1994, 137).[1]

Although the ancient Greek world appears to be a perfectly harmonious community or ethical world, it does after all contain differing institutions and laws, "a plurality of ethical moments" (*PS* 241.33/M 267). Hegel focuses on the binaries of divine law and human law, family and state, and women and men. For instance, there are governmental laws, laws of the state, "human laws" directed toward preserving the social order of the community. These laws are "known," "accepted and manifest to all" (*PS* 242.18–25/M 267–8) because they are explicitly decreed by acknowledged political authorities. However, there are also "divine laws" felt to be eternal, "unconscious," that is, not promulgated by particular rulers or regimes but understood by the community at large as what must be done (*PS* 242.26–31/M 268). These divine laws concern the "spiritualization," or making into ethical duties, of otherwise natural factors such as birth, death, familial relations, and sexuality.

Apparently closer to the concerns of divine law, Hegel identifies the family as the "*natural* ethical community," the "inner" or "immediate" or, again, "unconscious" sense of the ethical order which supports and yet differentiates itself from the broader, or "universal" public sphere of state interests (*PS* 242.32–243.5/M 268). The family belongs to the ethical order, however, not in terms of the "natural" relationships of desire, reproduction, and nurturance but primarily in terms of how *the* natural state – "*pure being, death*" – becomes "spiritualized," or included within the ethical through rituals of burial. Burial ceremonies bind individual family members to the ancestral line, allowing them to endure as members of the "spirit" of the family as an individual social-historical institution rather than merely a natural grouping (*PS* 244.14–245.17/M 270–1). Moreover, women, bound as they are to family life, are assigned the duties of burial. Men, in contrast, leave the family unit to occupy the various social – and importantly, military – positions and duties in public life. This sexual division of labor is grounded in nature, in natural differences, in the "way things *are*," yet becomes explicitly ethical in balancing the duties and roles of society's members, "the way things are *done*."[2]

With Sophocles' *Antigone* as his model of Greek ethical life, Hegel elaborates more specifically the differentiations internal to state and family. While the state depends on family members to sustain its activities and common goals, it recognizes the pull of familial ties and individual projects that can work against the common purpose. Thus, says Hegel, government has "from time to time to shake them to their core by war" (*PS* 246.15–16/M 272). In war, the ultimate "lord and master, death" intervenes in individual pursuits of happiness and wealth, reminding citizens of their dependencies on the community as a whole. On this account, war is not merely a painful necessity or intermittent calamity but, rather, a governmental institution that helps to maintain the state precisely – paradoxically, we might now say – by having its individual members die on the battlefield. The state, after all, is more than its particular members, and it benefits from their sacrifice.

The family, too, contains "differences," or diverse relations (*PS* 246.27–247.10/M 273–4). Relationships between husbands and wives, and parents and children, are certainly constitutive of family life. But, Hegel argues, duties between sister and brother have an ethical dimension that distinguishes them from the other relationships based on sexual desires or natural feelings. While husband and wife might attain "mutual recognition" within their marriage relationship, still, Hegel claims, this mutual recognition – which one might have thought to be paradigmatic of attained ethical relationship – is not strictly speaking ethical at all since it is based on sexual desire and feeling. Moreover, insofar as care of children is also based on natural affection and inequality, this relationship also fails to be ethical in Hegel's sense. Remember, Hegel has *Antigone* in mind. We find, therefore, that the relation between sister and brother, *not* based on sexual desire, is the place where a woman within this ancient society can find genuinely ethical recognition and be called to her highest ethical duty.[3] Not surprisingly, her highest duty as guardian of the eternal divine law takes its concrete form in burying her dead brother, whose loss for her is "irreparable" (*PS* 248.3–10/M 275).

We will return to examine the logic of family relations when we take up the feminist critique. For now, we have Hegel's sketch of the ancient Greek order as it takes itself to be – or, at least, as it is taken to be in its idealized form. "The whole is a stable equilibrium of all the parts, and each part is a Spirit at home in this whole, a Spirit which does not seek its satisfaction outside of itself but finds it within itself, because it is itself in this equilibrium with the whole" (*PS* 249.29–31/M 277). Man and woman, *polis* and family, human and divine: the elements are stable, balanced, "unsullied by internal dissension" (*PS* 250.20–21/M 278) – or so it would seem.

The subheading "Ethical Action. Human and Divine Knowledge, Guilt and Destiny" marks the unfolding of the tragic tension or contradiction buried in the social relations of ethical life. An action, a deed "disturbs the peaceful organization and movement of the ethical world" (*PS* 251.13–14/M 279). Actually, there are two deeds: Antigone's burial of her brother Polynices and Creon's promulgation of the law forbidding that burial. Antigone acts in accord with her familial duty to her brother, and thus fulfills her ethical obligation decreed by divine law. Creon acts in accord with his duty as ruler to promote public safety against traitors, and thus fulfills his ethical obligation decreed by human law. Their actions are not merely the collision of duties, Hegel reminds us (*PS* 251.30–33/M 279); rather, each is unwaveringly following the law assigned to them by their respective places within ethical substance, within the community. Each "sees right only on one side and wrong on the other" (*PS* 252.27/M 280). On Hegel's reading, however, both are "guilty," their deeds "criminal": in following divine law, Antigone violates human law; in following human law, Creon violates the divine (*PS* 253.31–254.37/M 281–3). Their actions thus bring into the open the internal tensions and conflicts implicitly contained within the harmonious whole (*PS* 255.1–24/M 283–4). For Hegel, "both sides suffer the same destruction" (*PS* 256.19/M 285). There is no possible reconciliation or synthesis here. Antigone, condemned by Creon to be buried alive, commits suicide. Creon loses his son, his wife, and his ruling power. But it is not merely Antigone and Creon as individuals who suffer. For Hegel they represent the dimensions of the Greek community only "immediately," or unreflectively balanced and harmonious. On these terms, they are unable to reconcile their opposing positions. The Greek community splinters from within, giving way eventually to the legal individualism of Roman imperial rule, where individuals are regarded uniformly only as "persons," merely as bearers of "rights."

This is only the bare bones of the story. Before looking more closely at some of the moments in the narrative, let's consider why Hegel uses Attic tragedy to introduce Spirit in this chapter.

Ever since Hegel's presentation of *Antigone* in the *Phenomenology* and subsequent discussions in his *Lectures on Aesthetics* and *Philosophy of Right*, his accounts have served as "the whipping boy" of later interpretations (Donougho 1989, 67). Goethe may have been one of the first to object to Hegel's alleged "reduction" of *Antigone* to an opposition of human and divine laws, but he was not the last. Some readers (e.g., Lacan 1992, Irigary 1996) insist that the play is driven by the desire and passion of both Antigone and Creon, though in different directions. Others (e.g., Reinhardt; quoted by Donougho 1989, 73) see the characters not as representatives of ethical norms or abstract principles but as "daimons" playing out their religious fates. Still others (e.g., Nussbaum 1986, 51–82) focus on the theme of vision, of practical wisdom, or lack thereof. For the moment, however, I want to consider the question not of Hegel's interpretation but of his use of tragedy as a form of philosophical argumentation.[4]

We have noted so far that Chapter VI formally introduces Spirit as a "world," a social realm of ethical norms. People's lives and actions are normatively structured by their places within this world. As we know, Aristotle defined tragedy as the imitation of action. But on the account of Spirit as normative social space, an action has meaning and purpose only by its embeddedness within the particular social community. The meaning of an action unfolds only against the larger social framework, and cannot be contained or understood in terms of a notion of individual intention or personal motivation, as we might interpret action in more modern terms. Moreover, the ethical consequences of an action go far beyond an individual's intention or character. Ancient Greek tragedy, portraying actions as inevitably entwined with the larger social fabric and transcendent fate, thereby provides a model for understanding human action and agency along the lines of the interactive, socially dependent theory Hegel propounds in his account of Spirit. Furthermore, Attic tragedy not only presents the transformation of consciousness of the actors – as in the recognition of the "mistake" or error of judgment, *hamartia* – it also, according to Aristotle, produces a transformation in the spectators. The experiential dimension in the spectators, whether of feelings of pity and fear or some other state, is a crucial aspect for Hegel's overall project in the *Phenomenology*. Each shape of consciousness he explores suffers a breakdown. His *Phenomenology* is famously self-styled a "pathway of despair" (*PS* 56.6/M 49). But the readers, or "phenomenological spectators," are not to be left unmoved: they, too, must experience the breakdown in order to understand and appreciate the move to another formation of Spirit. Dramatic tragedy, more than traditional philosophical argumentation, vividly calls for such movements. If the suffering of breakdown is essential to Hegel's phenomenological method, then his use of ancient tragedy seems appropriate, especially in this chapter on the formation of Spirit, of reason as living social space.[5]

Recall that for Hegel this introductory formation of Spirit among the ancients is marked by "immediacy," a certain level of "unreflectiveness" (*PS* 365.23/M 412–13): the ethical norms of the community strike its members as what *must* be done. The divine and human laws, in this sense, "predetermine" the moves available to individual agents. The tragic characters must enact their deeds, play out their roles, in their predestined world. Antigone, for example, is not caught in the throes of Hamlet's inaction; she *knows* what she must do, and she does it. A feature of the presentation of Attic tragedy calls attention to this "immediacy" of ethical knowing: the masks used in the actual performances can be said to reflect to the spectators this "pre-given" determination of action.[6]

If some general features of Attic tragedy fit nicely into Hegel's phenomenological schema, why did he select Sophocles' *Antigone* for his discussion of Greek *Sittlichkeit*? Aside from Hegel's personal admiration for Antigone, there are more important theoretical considerations. For example, classicists Vernant and Vidal-Naquet (1981, 9) argue that the hundred years of Attic tragedy are integral to the developing social-political thinking within the *polis* and reflect conflicts between different senses of "law" (*nomos*) emerging at the time. As for Hegel, "law" here means both the law of de facto political authority and a broader sense of sacred powers. The separation of these "laws" into human and divine allows for their conflict precisely while they are seen as inseparable. For these scholars tragedy is indeed rooted in social reality, though it is no mere reflection of it; rather, as Hegel demonstrates, tragedy calls that social reality into question. *Antigone* perhaps more than any other Attic tragedy highlights this issue of the emerging ambiguities and conflicts within social, political, and religious dimensions of law, *nomos*. Indeed, Antigone presents one of the earliest extant characterizations of what became known as (normative) "natural law," the idea that there are objective, non-statutory standards of justice (Valditara 2002, §B & note 43; Ostwald 1973), a view Hegel ultimately seeks to articulate and defend (Westphal 2003, §5). But the conflict of human and divine laws within the tragedy allows for no reconciliation, no answers. Each character clings unwaveringly to his or her sense of law, blinded to the legitimate sense of the other's use, and is thus doomed to destruction.

Vernant's reading strongly supports Hegel's account of the play as the conflict of human and divine laws. However, recent feminist critiques of Hegel's *Antigone* highlight some problematic and contentious aspects of Hegel's presentation. As suggested in my introduction, I will consider feminist critiques of Hegel not simply to expose potential sexist biases but to examine the logic of Hegel's arguments in this focal section of the *Phenomenology*. Since Hegel's presentation of Spirit in the ancient Greek world is tied up with oppositions of man and woman, public and private, government and family, religion and politics, these feminist examinations go right to the heart of Hegel's important philosophical strategies.

Rather than present individual feminist critiques, I begin by summarizing the main feminist contentions against Hegel, and then examine how they are or are not borne out in the text at hand. For the sake of clarity, I will list these criticisms as ten individual points, although they overlap considerably and are not intended to be exhaustive:

1   Hegel "essentializes" woman's nature, relegating her to private life within the family, and denying her access to the public sphere.
2   Woman "feels" or intuits what she ought to do; she is insufficiently self-conscious to reflect on and understand the complexities of her position in the community. Later in his *Philosophy of Right*, Hegel likens women to plants, but even here in the *Phenomenology* Hegel discredits women's rational capacities.
3   Because of his shortsightedness with respect to woman's role in the community, Hegel cannot explain Antigone's public defiance of Creon. Antigone as a female rebel cannot be contained by the description of femininity Hegel ascribes to her.
4   Ironically, Hegel claims that Antigone's guilt is equal to Creon's. But this attribution of guilt to Antigone is not supported by the play itself.
5   In general, Hegel misreads *Antigone*, both the play and the character, to suit his own purposes, to impose on them the logic of his own argument about the development of Spirit.
6   Thus Hegel ignores the sisterly relations between Antigone and Ismene. He claims that the sister can gain recognition only through the brother, and

denies that wives and mothers can achieve any ethical recognition within marriage and family, although they are confined to those institutions.

7 Since woman remains stereotypically tied to nature, family, reproduction, and death, Hegel allows woman to sink into oblivion rather than to become actualized in the development of Spirit. This development is thus revealed to be a masculinized process of overcoming the side of the dualities associated with woman: nature, body, family, the sacred, etc.

8 Moreover, Hegel accepts the oppositions of divine and human, nature and spirit, woman and man, family and *polis*, private and public as natural givens, rather than historical or social constructions. Hegel treats the "otherness" of woman to man, spirit, and political life as fixed by nature rather than a difference to be dialectically mediated and overcome.

9 The synthesis, mediation, or reconciliation that Hegel posits as the outcome of the *Antigone* is really just the suppression of the feminine, rather than a genuine reconciliation. While Hegel professes to be a philosopher of identity-in-difference, in suppressing the feminine, female, womanly in favor of the masculine, he subverts the core of his philosophy.

10 Yet Hegel sees womankind as "the eternal irony [in the life] of the community," somehow threatening or undermining the cohesiveness of substantive ethical life. Hegel views woman as an outsider to the progressive development of Spirit.

As noted, I will consider these objections only in relation to the *Phenomenology*, not his *Philosophy of Nature* or *Elements of a Philosophy of Right*, where they would have a different philosophical impact.

Clearly, Hegel's account of Spirit as the ethical life of the ancient Greeks depends on the binaries of man/woman, human/divine, *polis*/family, and spirit/nature. Feminists contend that binaries are notoriously suspect for at least three reasons: one, a binary is typically an oversimplification of more complex interactive factors; two, one side of a binary is typically valued higher, or much higher, than the other; and three, binaries are often supposed to be given or "natural" rather than matters of historical or social conditions. Binaries conceal yet reinforce hierarchies. So the question is, how does Hegel treat the binaries that figure so prominently in his discussion?

Let's start with the distinction between human and divine law Hegel uses to differentiate the "ethical powers" within the Greek world. As we have seen, human law is decreed, promulgated, authoritative for the particular community, and instantiated in government. Divine law, in contrast, reaches beyond or beneath the actual human laws in place in any community and concerns matters of life and death in a more general sense. The divine law is immutable and "unconscious": it is not a decree of any particular ruler or authority, and has no distinct origin to be questioned or overturned. The question is: are human and divine laws equally important? Are they equally valid?

As Hegel reads it, *Antigone* dramatizes the confrontation of *equally valid laws* represented by Antigone and Creon. Their confrontation reveals the contradictions and tensions within the Greek community. Antigone insists she *must* bury her beloved brother Polynices, not simply because he is her beloved brother, but because as her brother his burial is a matter of the divine law which *must* be obeyed. Creon as the legitimate ruler forbids that burial because he *must* protect his city against traitors, such as Polynices. For Creon, blood ties, family connections – that Polynices is his nephew, Antigone his niece – are of no consequence. He goes so far as to claim that the only genuine "ties" that he himself recognizes are those in service to the state (Nussbaum 1986, 57). Importantly, for Creon the divine law calling for the women of the household to bury their family members is also of no consequence. Initially he seems even oblivious to that divine decree, or at least he ignores it, eventually defying it. He is concerned only with the preservation of his state – and, increasingly, his own power which he identifies as the state. So, does Hegel posit a set of binaries that are questionable in their origins, and questionable in their oppositions? Does he in fact privilege one over the other?

The claim made not only by feminists but by many critics of Hegel's interpretation of *Antigone*, that Hegel imposes a reading on the play to further his own agenda, certainly seems plausible. But let's see how it works with respect to issues of binary oppositions. The binaries are said to be cleanly opposed but equally valid. As Hegel presents it, Antigone and Creon each cling to their own ethical law but do not acknowledge the validity of the other's. Their unwavering sense of being in the right is precisely what leads to their destruction. Antigone, Hegel admits, *knows* she is violating human law, Creon's law, but nevertheless "commits the crime" (*PS* 255.30/M 284). Creon's case seems different. At first he does not acknowledge the validity of Antigone's claim, that of a mere woman, but in the end comes to recognize his mistake, his *hamartia*, marking him as a tragic character doomed to destruction.

But the important point here is that for Hegel the antithesis between divine and human law, tragically portrayed by Antigone and Creon, *is itself a mistake*, a matter of what I call "false consciousness." False consciousness in the relevant sense involves instantiating a position held as true which, upon examination by the phenomenological analyst, turns out to contain a tension or contradiction which negates or undermines that position. In the case at hand, Hegel argues that the Greeks differentiate and oppose the divine and human ethical powers in merely an "immediate," unquestioning sense, i.e., as given, a matter of fact, a matter of how things stand for them, how these laws must be upheld in their different realms. But Hegel, the phenomenological observer and analyst, sees that this "immediate," unreflective sense of their opposition covers over deeper interdependencies:

> Neither of the two is by itself valid in and for itself; human law proceeds in its living process from the divine, the law valid on earth from that of the nether world, the conscious from the unconscious, mediation from immediacy – and equally returns whence it came. The power of the nether world, on the other hand, has its actual existence on earth; through consciousness, it becomes existence and activity. (*PS* 248.39–249.5/M 276)

Thus Hegel the phenomenological analyst sees what the allegedly unreflective ancient Greeks – represented by Antigone and Creon – did not see: that the binaries operative in their society were at bottom deeply connected and interdependent. The play *Antigone*, at least on Hegel's reading, shows the collapse and destruction that tragically follows precisely from holding the binaries stringently apart. It is not Hegel, then, who maintains those binaries in strict opposition but, rather, Greek ethical life itself, infected by this "false consciousness."

If we look a bit more closely at Sophocles' play, is this the story we find? Here the objection that Hegel misreads the play for his own purposes becomes pertinent. Of course we find dramatic antagonism between Antigone and Creon, but also between Creon and Haemon, Antigone and Ismene. Yes, the antagonisms unfold around Creon's decree versus Antigone's revering the sacred traditions of burial, an opposition cast in terms of gender. Creon, stubbornly insisting on his sole right to rule, refuses to listen, to be undone, to be "unmanned" by a mere woman. By the end of the play, however, Sophocles has Creon admit that the guilt is all his (*l*. 1441/1318).[7] Near the end Creon even performs burial rites on Polynices' ravaged body (*ll*. 1320–26/1197–1204), thus showing himself to be indeed "unmanned" by taking on the role of woman. In the Chorus's final words, the "moral of the story" is told in terms of wisdom and reverence toward sacred traditions. Rather than presenting Greek ethical life as the unreflective, unmediated oppositions between human and divine laws, family and state, Sophocles dramatically emphasizes the importance of recognizing precisely the *interdependence* of these realms. One might conclude, following Vernant, that as the meaning of the term "law" becomes increasingly ambiguous, unsettled, and problematic, Sophocles calls attention to the need for greater practical wisdom, better judgment, in learning how to navigate the terms of law in the increasingly complex Greek *polis* (cf. Nussbaum 1986, Chapter 3). This point supports Hegel's insight that when the interconnections and interdependencies of human and divine law are ignored, doom and destruction follow. As idealized by the Romantics, the Greeks were happily unconcerned with such difficult problems; their lives went on tranquilly, harmoniously structured by the binaries in question. On Hegel's reading, that Greek society, the romanticized one, spiritually collapses.

In what sense, or to what extent, is Antigone guilty in contributing to this collapse? Commenting on the culminating passage (*PS* 255.25–37/M 284), Pinkard (1994, 144) claims that for Hegel, Antigone's guilt is "perhaps a little greater" than Creon's, since she *knowingly* violates his law, while he apparently violates the sacred traditions out of ignorance. The end of the play, however, emphasizes that in tragedy ignorance is no excuse. Indeed, Creon's "ignorance," consisting in stubborn refusal to listen, learn, and consider larger ramifications of his actions, is itself the root of his crime and is shown to be entirely blameworthy.[8] It seems plainly wrong to say that Antigone is even *more* guilty than Creon, but is she guilty at all, and if so, of what crime?

In his text Hegel quotes a line from the play implying that Antigone *admits* her guilt: "Because we suffer we acknowledge we have erred" (*PS* 256.1/M 284).

But she actually says something quite different. Invoking the gods and divine law she claims to revere, she says:

> Very well: if this is the pleasure of the gods,
> once I suffer I will know that I was wrong.
> But if these men are wrong, let them suffer
> worse than they mete out to me –
> these masters of injustice!
> (*ll.* 1017–1021/925–928)

Antigone invokes the gods, not human powers, to judge her. If Hegel regards Antigone and Creon as equally guilty, the play doesn't bear out his allegation, not only because of the questionable line Hegel inserts, but also because the Chorus, the Theban citizens in the play, Creon's own son, and presumably the spectators, all attest to the righteousness of Antigone's act, even within the larger scheme of her life's entanglement in the fate of the Oedipal household.[9] Granted, from the standpoint of Creon's decree, Antigone *is* guilty of breaking it. But the point is that breaking this law is a "crime," as Hegel names it, only when this decree is divorced from its place within the sacred traditions, as Creon-turned-tyrant so enforces it. On this reading, Antigone's "crime" is contingent precisely on splitting law into its opposed binaries, but this split constitutes the false consciousness, or self-misunderstanding of the ancient world. We seem to be left with these alternatives: either Antigone is guilty from the standpoint of the false consciousness operating within the Greek world; or Hegel *claims* Antigone is guilty as a matter of his own logic, where both sides of the dialectical oppositions must be flawed to bring about "the negation" of the form of life in question.

However, other readings of Antigone's "crime" are possible. For example, she may be guilty of refusing to submit as a woman. "She is *autonomous*, a law unto herself," and hence disruptive to the *polis* (Sjoholm 2004, 43). Or, as Nussbaum suggests (1986, 63ff.) – closer on this point to Hegel's reading – Antigone like Creon is guilty of a lack of vision, of practical wisdom. She stubbornly refuses to see that her ethical obligation to her dead brother requires service to the state as well; one must stay alive within the community to continue to honor the dead. Her stubbornness commits her to the gods of the dead, cut off from the gods of love, procreation, and life. But here again her crime lies in not seeing that justice requires the *interconnections* of human and divine, rather than their separation. Antigone is guilty, then, not only from the standpoint of the false consciousness of her community but because she herself instantiates this false consciousness.

How do attributions of false consciousness, stubborn ignorance, or lack of wisdom correlate with the feminist criticism that Hegel underestimates the rational capacities of women? It appears that *both* male and female characters know and do not know in significant ways. They both know what they must do according to their respective laws, but do not envision how their actions will affect not only themselves but also the whole community. Judging by the consequences, Creon's lack of wisdom is far greater, more serious, and more blameworthy than Antigone's.

Antigone's impeded vision ends with her dying the "beautiful death" of the male warrior (Sjoholm 2004, 44). In contrast, Creon's error leads to the bloody deaths of his niece, his son, and his wife, and to the demise of his own state and ruling power. Why suppose Hegel relegates women to the intellectually inferior position?

A simple but important response is that Hegel's account depicts the ancient Greek world in which women are confined to home and family and are generally denied opportunities for education. Hegel does not structure that world in that way. Indeed, his phenomenological analysis calls attention to inherent tensions within those structures. As Pinkard (1994, 143) aptly comments, "It would be a mistake to take the issue here to be the incompatibility of this Greek view of the possibilities for men's and women's lives with modern, egalitarian views. For the purposes of Hegel's discussion, the only issue is whether this Greek understanding is *in its own terms* rational, not whether it fails to fit *our* modes of self-understanding." Along these lines, I am not trying to exonerate Hegel from the charge of overt or latent sexism here, but to highlight his project of phenomenology. The purpose of the dialectic is to examine critically different forms of consciousness or kinds of normative social worlds to see if their own criteria of reasonableness or integrity can escape falling into contradiction. In the context of the ancient Greek world as seen through Hegel's dialectical analysis, women's intellectual and social confinement points to a hidden source of fatal instability.

One may object, however, that even if Hegel is only describing and analyzing the Greek world, he is at the same time interpreting that world by using the terms and categories of his dialectic. It is Hegel, after all, who terms women's relation to divine law "unconscious":

> The feminine, in the form of the sister, ... has the highest *intimation* of what is ethical. She does not attain to *consciousness* of it ... because the law of the family is an *im*plicit, *inner* essence which does not lie in the daylight of consciousness, but remains an inner feeling and divine element devoid of actuality. (*PS* 247.17–21/ M 274)

Hegel's language here relegates feminine "knowing" to a kind of unknowing, presumably an irrational or at the very least an unarticulated feeling. Hegel himself employs this terminology with its derogatory connotations.[10] Therefore, we cannot overlook Hegel's blatant reinforcement of sexist biases by attributing to women inferior rational capacities.

This charge against Hegel is difficult to refute in general, but at least a partial response may be available. Granted, we have noted repeatedly that Hegel calls divine law, associated with women and family, "unconscious." Within Hegel's dialectic, generally speaking, what is unconscious, or implicit, needs to be articulated to become "conscious," or explicit. This process of articulation – through language, actions, principles, social practices, and cultural institutions – forms the basis of the development of Spirit. So Hegel's account of women's "unconscious" relation to the ethical does suggest an inferior relation. However, in terms of the differentiations of divine and human law, we have also seen that divine law is something "unconscious," merely felt or intuited, and in that sense "unknown" – as opposed to the human laws which are "known" and "manifest to all" – because the divine law has no historical origin, not having been promulgated or decreed by particular authorities. Already at the end of the Reason chapter (immediately preceding Chapter VI), Hegel quoted the *Antigone* on the status of the "*unwritten* and *infallible* law of the gods: 'They are not of yesterday or today, but everlasting / Though whence they came, none can tell' " (*PS* 236.10–11/M 261; *ll* 506–508/456–458). In this sense, the status of divine law as "unconscious" or "unknown" is not a detraction or derogation but, rather, an attribution of its ethical necessity or "absoluteness," the sense that such law *must* be obeyed. Here the binary 'conscious/unconscious' has to do with the origins, scope, and force of the laws, rather than their positioning in an epistemic hierarchy. This point helps explain, furthermore, how Hegel can claim that Antigone "*knowingly*" does what she does even when she is supposedly only darkly, "intuitively" aware of her ethical duties. Creon's decree is public, intelligible to all, so defying that law entails she knows it. Her "knowledge" of the divine law, in contrast, involves her very positioning within her world rather than a belief or knowledge claim subject to rational testing. While this interpretation does not fully address the feminist objection that Hegel derogates women's rational capacities, at least it calls attention to different senses of "unconscious" that figure in Hegel's text.[11]

Let's move on to consider the contention that on Hegel's account, Antigone's womanly role prevents her from acting publicly. Obviously Antigone does act openly and defiantly. To be sure, Sophocles also presents her as a "stranger," outside the scripted gender roles, even while she insists on her sisterly duty within the sacred traditions (*ll*. 940–43/849–852). Ismene is clearly the stereotypically feminine woman, obedient and compliant, afraid to contend with men, wanting to maintain the status quo – and in the end, showing genuine affection and solidarity with her sister. Antigone, in contrast, renounces this form of sisterhood as well as the joys of love, marriage, and children, instead to wed death. In that sense, Lacan's (1992, 281) claim that she is driven by a desire for death, for a "beyond," is well taken. In any case, we are led to the following paradox. Precisely by insisting on her sisterly duties to her dead brother, Antigone dramatizes that the ethically prescribed confinement of women to familial roles and duties is deeply flawed. She becomes an impossible outlaw, an unnatural stranger indeed, while her outlaw position dislodges her from representing woman's ethical place within the community. We come to see that she cannot be both a female outlaw *and* the womanly paradigm within ethical life. Insofar as Hegel identifies Antigone with woman, family, and divine law, he occludes her rebel role.[12]

The role of woman as disruptive outsider, however, does appear explicitly in Hegel's text. Reviewing the relationship between the public and familial – this time, near the end of his discussion, and so near the "spiritual" end of Greek *Sittlichkeit* (*PS* 258.19–260.6/M 287–9) – Hegel reveals that the "universal" public sphere of men maintains itself by "consuming and assimilating into itself the separation of the Penates, or the self-sufficient individuation of families, over which womankind presides . . ." (*PS* 258.33–35/M 287–8). Finally the suppression of women and family is openly admitted! At the same time, he reiterates that the public *depends* on the private, or familial. "In what it suppresses and yet is essential to it – womankind as such – [the community] creates for itself its own internal enemy" (*PS* 259.2–4/M 288). Immediately following, Hegel presents his famous – or infamous – passage on "womankind":

> Womankind – the everlasting irony [in the life] of the community – changes by intrigue the universal end of the government into a private end, transforms its universal activity into a work of some particular individual, and perverts the universal property of the state into a possession and ornament of the family. Woman in this way turns to ridicule the earnest wisdom of mature age which, indifferent to purely private pleasures and enjoyments, as well as to playing an active part, only thinks of and cares for the universal. (*PS* 259.4–10/M 288)

What shall we make of this depiction of "womankind"?[13] So far, I have been arguing that Hegel is not necessarily subject to the feminist criticism that he "naturalizes" or "essentializes" binaries and privileges one side over the other. I have been pointing out that Hegel the phenomenological analyst criticizes ancient Greek society for that kind of oversimplified thinking. But now, when Hegel speaks of "womankind" as the "everlasting irony" in the community, the charge of his "essentializing" woman's nature and roles returns to center stage. Let's consider a few possible interpretations relating to this charge.

First, does this passage actually refer to Antigone herself as she has prominently figured in this chapter? Given the context one easily assumes that it does. However, Patricia Mills (2002, 214) argues convincingly that "Antigone is not merely *distinct* from woman as the irony of the community, but that she is in fact the very *antithesis* of this picture of 'womankind in general'." After all, Antigone does not engage in hidden intrigue against the state by seducing its young men away from their public, military duties, or by using the state to augment family fortunes. On this reading, Hegel implicitly distinguishes Antigone, his ethical paradigm of the virginal, dutiful sister, from the typical role of woman as manipulative, sensual seductress. Despite his charges of her guilt, Hegel's Antigone somehow transcends woman's nature to become the beautiful figure he so admired.

A different reading of the passage avoids the issue of essentialism altogether. On this reading (Donougho 1989, 85), Hegel points out how women's historical suppression within Greek society reveals that society to be an individualistic warrior ethic rather than a harmonious ethical whole. Thus, the line 'Womankind as the everlasting irony of the community' refers to women in *that ancient Greek* community, not all communities over time.[14] Hegel is to be neither condemned nor celebrated for judging women's "eternal" sensual seductiveness. On the contrary, he should be appreciated for uncovering the contingent, violent, individualistic "truth" hidden beneath the idealized conception of Greek ethical life.

If the latter reading makes sense in the context of Hegel's discussion of the collapse of the Greek community, it may not settle issues about Hegel's particular word choices, namely, his use of "womankind" and "everlasting" or "eternal" irony of the community. His statement suggests a claim about "womankind" as a universal or transhistorical category, not merely the particular women within ancient Greek culture. This suggestion is often taken by feminist critics to be Hegel's own position. If we suppose him to be making a universalist claim, what follows?

On the one hand, we may applaud Hegel's insight that women have been constantly excluded by male-dominated history and culture. "Woman's irony" is thus a needed and ever-present challenge to a system bent on closure. But then Hegel's insight presumably turns against his own philosophical system aimed at mediating or dialectically overcoming the "otherness" threatening to remain excluded (Benhabib 1996). On this reading, if Woman, associated with sensuality and family intrigue, is forever ironically excluded by the "progressive" development of Spirit, that admission supports the feminist charge that that development is indeed a masculinized process of continual suppression of the feminine.

On the other hand, we may call attention to the inconsistency of Hegel's universalist claim. On his own phenomenological grounds, according to which knowledge claims are justified within a particular shape of consciousness or spiritual world, he has no justification for holding that women necessarily, "naturally," or "eternally" remain excluded from the progressive development of spirit, or – more mundanely – remain confined to private or familial realms, cut off from cultural, political interaction and recognition. That women have historically been so excluded is surely true, but this historical observation does not warrant a universalist claim that women's nature justifies such exclusion (cf. Hutchings 2003, 99). Accordingly, to render Hegel consistent with his dialectical project we would do well to read his passage about "Woman's eternal irony" as referring simply to the particular Greek world in its decline.

While offering an interpretation of Hegel's conception of *Sittlichkeit* within the *Phenomenology* by examining feminist criticisms of his account of *Antigone*, I have not yet directly addressed what follows the breakdown of Greek ethical life. Here the feminist objection that Hegel privileges a masculinist development of Spirit by siding with an individualistic, legalistic "overcoming" of the Greek spiritual world seems plausible (cf. points 7 and 9 above). After all, the next sub-section turns to "legal status," the putative next stage of Spirit in its unfolding (*PS* 260.25–264.6/ M 290–4). But is that feminist criticism upheld in this case? What sort of "overcoming" takes place in the Roman community based on laws, rights, and property?

Here we find that Hegel actually condemns this "development." "Legal Status" avoids the problem central to "immediate spirit" by omitting the non-statutory norms of customary and divine law represented by Antigone. However, this strategic advantage has its price: the Greek spiritual world has been "shattered into a multitude of separate points" (*PS* 260.22–23/M 289); it becomes a "spiritless community which has ceased to be the unself-conscious substance of individuals" (*PS* 260.27–28/M 290). Here "a mere multiplicity of individuals" are regarded equally as "*persons*," but abstracted from the normative world of interdependent social actions and institutions. Hegel reminds us that this kind of abstract independence of the self-conscious 'I' was previously examined in his critiques of

Stoicism and Skepticism: "Personal independence in the sphere of *legal right* is rather the same general confusion and reciprocal dissolution" as skepticism (*PS* 262.3–5/M 291).[15] That is, the independent citizen, as a bearer of rights, notably property rights, is not thereby *spiritually* "richer" or more developed than the participant in earlier Greek *Sittlichkeit*, but only thinks himself to be so. Put even more strongly, "to designate an individual as a 'person' is an expression of contempt" (*PS* 262.26–27/M 292). Furthermore, insofar as legal power becomes concentrated in the ruler or emperor – "the titanic self-consciousness that knows itself as being an actual god" (namely, Caesar) – the ruler's "activities and self-enjoyment are equally monstrous excesses," revealed in the "destructive power he exercises against the self of his subjects, the self which stands over against him" (*PS* 263.9–15/M 291–3).

If one claims, then, that in this section of the *Phenomenology* Hegel assigns the "victory" to Creon over Antigone – or more broadly, to a masculinist notion of individual power over a feminist conception of communal relationships – we see that such a claim is mistaken, a misconception of Hegel's conception of spirit and dialectical development. On Hegel's dismal description, legal status is tantamount to Creon's rule by pure, positive edict, without any basis in actual social practices or familial relations. This sorry development reveals the essential importance of such communal dimensions of society highlighted in the previous discussion of *Antigone*. "Legal status" is thus *not* a spiritual improvement over Antigone's world but, rather, a historical change that emphasizes, or *over*emphasizes an important but insufficient facet of the modern conception of self; it serves, after all, to introduce "the self-alienated Spirit" discussed in the second section of Hegel's chapter (*PS* 264.8/M 294; see chapter 9). We learn thereby that not all "later developments" in the *Phenomenology* are actually improvements. We need to remember a point made earlier: it is a mistake to identify as Hegel's own a view that he is instead examining and criticizing. In the case of legal status, his strongly negative language makes it clear that this configuration of spirit is sorely lacking. But his strident criticism is thus aligned *with* and not against a feminist call for a genuine overcoming of the masculinist individuality and abstract legal power that collapses under his phenomenological vision.

In conclusion, what I hope to have shown is that examining feminist contentions against Hegel, especially in this section on Spirit, is an important, helpful way of opening up and learning to read this complex text. Exploring feminist critiques of Hegel in the *Phenomenology* shows that Hegel's claims about sexual difference and gender roles need to be contextualized in terms of his dialectical strategy. Within the *Phenomenology* each shape of consciousness or spiritual world presents its own ideals or conceptions of knowledge, whether about "sense certainty," as in the opening chapter, or the relationships of normative practices to individual actions, as in the ancient Greek world. Along the way Hegel cannot rightfully be assumed to identify with any one set of claims made from within the world under examination. Granted, it is often difficult to determine when Hegel is speaking from within that world and when he shifts to the voice of the phenomenological analyst. But it is important to be aware of this interpretive shift. On my reading of this section, I have called attention repeatedly to Hegel's stance as the phenomenological analyst revealing the fragility and interdependencies of the supposedly natural or necessary binaries figuring prominently in Greek ethical life. If we suppose that Hegel is asserting the truth of the binaries or divisions in question, then we identify as Hegel's a view he is in fact criticizing.

Hegel is certainly no feminist, as his later explicitly asserted views attest. However, a feminist insistence that gender and sexuality are socially constructed, and are thus historical and variable, gets support in the *Phenomenology*, especially in this section, which explicitly confronts these issues. Hegel himself seems not to have recognized the radical import of his examination of Greek *Sittlichkeit*. From his later writings, we see that he continued to suppose that sexual difference is "natural," an ahistorical given which becomes incorporated into ethical life through social practices of family. But when we see that his treatment of divine and human laws shows them to be more interdependent and fluid than initially supposed, we can claim on similar grounds that gender categories and sexual difference are also socially, historically variable. If Hegel himself misses the radical potential of many of his analyses, readers of the *Phenomenology* may want to push his texts in that direction.[16] Emphasizing Hegel's contextualism and historicism, then, offers a reading of the *Phenomenology* that makes it closer to and more useful for feminism and contemporary social thought than one might have supposed.

Notes

1 PS 238–41/M 263–6 are discussed further below, pp. 191–92. – *Ed.*
2 PS 244.14–245.17, 251.9–24 /M 270–1, 276–7. In light of feminist criticisms considered below, it is interesting to note that prior to the *Phenomenology*, Hegel in his essay on *Natural Law* had viewed only the sacrificial act of the aristocratic soldier as constituting the ethical order. Here in the *Phenomenology* Hegel attributes ethical action to female members of the family (Speight 2001, 63).
3 The relation between Antigone and Polynices, as siblings, is the first case of genuinely mutual recognition in Hegel's *Phenomenology*, albeit an immediate, undeveloped form of mutual recognition. – *Ed.*
4 For more detailed discussions of this issue see Westphal (2003, chapters 3 and 4), Speight (2001), and Willett (1991). All three authors highlight the emotional, experiential elements in both tragedy and in Hegel's phenomenological method, a point often overlooked by those who see Hegel privileging intellect over other aspects of human spirit. Furthermore, Westphal argues that Sophocles' *Antigone*, specifically his characterization of Creon, provides a literary model for Hegel's "internal critique," or phenomenological method.
5 This point about the breakdown for forms of consciousness bears comparing with Hegel's constructive lessons from skepticism and his examination of normative authority via its breakdown; see above, chapters 1, 3, 6, 7. – *Ed.*
6 Speight (2001, 64). After quoting from Hegel's *Aesthetics* on the importance of the mask in Greek tragedy, Donougho (1989, 87) notes that for Hegel "the truth of Greek tragedy (and by extension of the Greek world-view and of art generally) is 'the truth of masks' . . . For the plastic character or ethos there is nothing behind that mask; the

agents identify themselves totally with their personae, their pathos, as do the players/dramaturges presenting them."

7   Fagles (1982), whose translation is used here, devised his own line numbering system; lines of the Greek text follow his, after a '/'. – *Ed.*

8   Countering Irigaray's charge against Hegel that he overlooks the connections between blood ties and community, Hutchings (2003, 96) writes: "there is no reason to read Hegel as if he were unaware of the irony of Creon's simultaneous dismissal of and dependence on the claims of kinship. Rather, Hegel presents Creon's treatment of human law as entirely self-legitimating, without regard to its dependence on and entwinement with the ties of blood, as being at the heart of his crime." Hutchings generally supports the line I am arguing: Hegel, the phenomenological analyst, stresses the often hidden or merely implicit *interconnections* between the divisions in Greek life.

9   Irigary (1996, 49) interprets Antigone's "guilt" in the following way: "However guiltless, she feels she bears the burden of her mother's fatal marriage, feels guilty for being born of such terrible embraces. Thus she is damned, and by consenting to a punishment she has not merited and yet cannot escape, at the least she accepts on her own account the death knell of her *jouissance – or is mourning itself her jouissance?* – by killing herself."

10 Kelly Oliver (1996, 84) develops this point in her essay on Hegel's treatment of family: "[T]he feminine element remains unconscious and unconceptualizable. Hegel's *Phenomenology* is a phenomenology of masculine consciousness that is possible only by setting up feminine 'consciousness' as the negation of masculine consciousness and then suppressing the feminine."

11 These considerations are supported by Hegel's view that it is possible "to know something falsely" (*PS* 30.36–37/M 22–3). For Hegel knowing is a process, within which "false knowledge" can contribute to our subsequently achieving true (genuine) knowledge (Westphal 1989, 102). Hence to know something explicitly does not suffice to know it either truly or justifiedly, as shown in Creon's case. According to Hegel, regardless of whether Creon and Antigone "know" their principles implicitly or explicitly, their knowledge suffers from being "immediate" because it is dogmatic and unjustified; this is central to the "immediacy" of the ancient Greek spirit. At least Antigone has the advantage of having firmly grasped a truth; no matter how implicit her grasp may be, it is correct and justifiable, even if she cannot provide its justification. – *Ed.*

12 Agreeing with other feminists that Hegel's reading does not allow for this outlaw role, Judith Butler (2000) articulates Antigone's claim to be the ever-present disruptor of familial and political arrangements. Patricia Mills (1996a, 77) – also reading Hegel against the grain – points out Hegel's failure to discuss Antigone's suicide. Mills sees her suicide as a significant, active positioning outside or beyond the female ethical ideal. For Mills Antigone can be read as the precursor of the modern feminist who proclaims the personal is the political. But Mills asserts that *this* Antigone is occluded in Hegel's interpretation.

13 Irigaray's (1996) critical meditation on Hegel's Antigone is appropriately entitled "The Eternal Irony of the Community." Irigaray plays with the ironies and tensions she discovers in this phrasing as well as within the entire passage on Greek ethical life.

14 The community that is said to suffer the eternal irony of womankind (*PS* 259.4/M 288) is the same community that is said to survive only by suppressing individuality (*PS* 259.15–17/M 288), something Hegel regards as a key defect of Greek *Sittlichkeit*. – *Ed.*

15 See above, pp. 60–64. – *Ed.*

16 Cf. especially Hutchings (2003), Ravven (2002), and Gauthier (1997).

References

Benhabib, S. (1996) "On Hegel, Women and Irony," in P. J. Mills (ed.), *Feminist Interpretations of G. W. F. Hegel*, (pp. 25–43). University Park, PA: Pennsylvania State University Press.

Butler, J. (2000) *Antigone's Claim: Kinship between Life and Death*. New York: Columbia University Press.

Donougho, M. (1989) "The Woman in White: On the Reception of Hegel's Antigone," *The Owl of Minerva* 35: 65–89.

Gauthier, J. (1997) *Hegel and Feminist Social Criticism*. Albany, NY: State University of New York Press.

Hutchings, K. (2003) *Hegel and Feminist Philosophy*. Cambridge: Polity Press.

Irigaray, L. (1996) "The Eternal Irony of the Community," tr. G. C. Gill, in P. J. Mills (ed.), *Feminist Interpretations of G. W. F. Hegel*, (pp. 45–57). University Park, PA: Pennsylvania State University Press.

Lacan, J. (1992) *The Ethics of Psychoanalysis: 1959–1960*, ed. J.-A. Miller, tr. D. Porter. New York: Norton & Company.

Mills, P. J. (1996a) "Hegel's *Antigone*," in Mills (ed.), *Feminist Interpretations of G. W. F. Hegel*, (pp. 59–88). University Park, PA: Pennsylvania State University Press.

Mills, P. J., ed. (1996b) *Feminist Interpretations of G. W. F. Hegel*. University Park, PA: Pennsylvania State University Press.

Mills, P. J. (2002) "'Hegel's *Antigone*' Redux: Woman in Four Parts," *The Owl of Minerva* 33: 205–21.

Nussbaum, M. (1986) *The Fragility of Goodness*. Cambridge: Cambridge University Press.

Oliver, K. (1996) "Antigone's Ghost: Undoing Hegel's *Phenomenology of Spirit*," *Hypatia* 11: 67–90.

Ostwald, M. (1973) "Was There a Concept of *agraphos nomos* in Classical Greece?," in E. N. Lee et al. (eds.), *Exegesis and Argument* (pp. 70–104). *Phronesis* Supp. Vol. I, Assen: van Gorcum.

Pinkard, T. (1994) *Hegel's Phenomenology: The Sociality of Reason*. Cambridge: Cambridge University Press.

Ravven, H. M. (2002) "Further Thoughts on Hegel and Feminism," *The Owl of Minerva* 33: 223–31.

Sjoholm, C. (2004) *The Antigone Complex*. Stanford, Cal.: Stanford University Press.

Sophocles (1982) *The Three Theban Plays*, tr. R. Fagles. Harrisonburg, VA: Penguin Books.

Speight, A. (2001) *Hegel, Literature and the Problem of Agency*. Cambridge: Cambridge University Press.

Valditara, L. (2002). "Scenografie morali nell'*Antigone* e nell'*Edipo re*: Sofocle e Aristotele," in L. Valditara, (ed.), *Antichi e nuovi dialoghi di sapienti ed eroi* (pp. 101–49). Trieste: Edizioni Università di Trieste.

Vernant, J.-P. and Vidal-Naquet, P. (1981) *Tragedy and Myth in Ancient Greece*, tr. J. Lloyd. Brighton: Harvester Press. (First published 1972.)

Westphal, K. R. (1989) *Hegel's Epistemological Realism*. Dordrecht: Kluwer.

Westphal, K. R. (2003) *Hegel's Epistemology: A Philosophical Introduction to the Phenomenology of Spirit*. Cambridge, Mass.: Hackett Publishing Co.

Willett, C. (1991) "Hegel, Antigone, and the Possibility of a Woman's Dialectic," rpt. in B.-A. Bar On (ed.), *Modern Engendering* (pp. 167–81). Albany: State University of New York Press, 1994.

9

Hegel's Critique of the Enlightenment in "The Struggle of the Enlightenment with Superstition"

Jürgen Stolzenberg

Hegel's most thorough and nuanced critique of the Enlightenment is in his first independent, systematic work, the creative and audacious *Phenomenology of Spirit*, in the section titled "The Struggle of the Enlightenment with Superstition" (*PS* 293–311/M 328–55). This section raises both a hermeneutic and a related systematic problem in Hegel's philosophy. My aim is to understand the core argument that underpins Hegel's critique of the Enlightenment. Hegel's central thesis is anything but obvious. It is that the Enlightenment's confrontation with faith, which it regards as superstition, is an unrecognized battle of the Enlightenment with itself, in which the Enlightenment itself is this trial.[1] How is this strange thesis to be understood, and how is it justified by Hegel? There is insufficient clarity on this question in the available literature.[2]

The systematic problem connected to our question consists in the fact that Hegel's critique of the Enlightenment is a part of his theory of spirit. With this theory, one could well say, Hegel introduced a new criterion of rationality into modern philosophy. And Hegel's self-understanding was that only on the basis of this new criterion of rationality can Modernity be brought to a clarified consciousness of itself. Accordingly, Hegel first sought to ground his new criterion of rationality in the context of his critique of the Enlightenment, through which, as we can in this respect formulate Hegel's self-understanding, the Enlightenment can be enlightened about itself. The process, which Hegel makes the Enlightenment out to be, thus becomes central to justifying his own philosophical enterprise and its main principle. This is the systematic background of the question about Hegel's argument in his critique of the Enlightenment. The core issues of Hegel's argument lie in his analysis of the concept of spirit, to which we now turn.

1 Consciousness and Spirit

"Spirit," as Hegel explains at the beginning of his chapter on spirit in the *Phenomenology*, "is the ethical life of a people" (*PS* 240.1/M 265). The expression "ethical" here does not mean "moral" in the narrow sense, but rather the mores or values expressed in the customs and form of life of a people. Hence the concept of spirit designates here the totality of various common, shared forms of life, in which a people realizes its individuality and identity. Among these forms of life are various social institutions, the spheres of economy, law, and religion, as well as forms of artistic activity, including the language and linguistic peculiarities of a people. If one introduces here the closely related concept of culture, which is entirely appropriate, then Hegel's concept of spirit designates the unity of the culture of a people. Hegel's phenomenological philosophy of spirit, it may be said, contains a philosophy of culture.[3]

In Hegel's view, the cultural forms of life just mentioned can be generally understood to be forms of the objectification of the ways in and means by which humans collectively organize and interpret the life they undertake and guide. This objectification can be described formally in the following twofold manner: first, as the relation of the individual to a universal sphere which is distinct from and independent of the multifarious life plans and conduct of individuals, to the norms of which they ascribe a trans-individual objective validity. For this reason, Hegel calls this an "objective, actual world" (*PS* 238.30/M 263). Second, the objectification can be described by saying that in their various relations to the universal sphere individuals nevertheless only relate to themselves. This is because these spheres present nothing other than the objectification of the theoretical and practical intentions of individuals, through which they collectively organize and interpret their common life. Thus this sphere is collectively produced by individuals, in which they realize their own self-given ends. Therefore, this sphere has, Hegel emphasizes, "lost all meaning of something . . . foreign" for those who live in it (*PS* 238.31–239.2/M 263–4). The fundamental structure of Hegel's concept of spirit is defined by this double relation.

Hegel's talk of spirit as the ethical life of a people also means something further, which directly pertains to the previous point. This is Hegel's concept of *freedom*. Hegel specifies freedom as being-at-home-with-oneself ("*bei sich selbst sein*").[4] This includes the idea that humans can be 'at home' in the world in which they live; this is the case when they have the possibility in that world to realize and to be what they in their own right (and hence authentically and autonomously) want and are able to be. "Man is free we say, who exists for his own sake and not for another's" (*Metaphysics* 1.2); Hegel adopts this Aristotelian definition of freedom.

He also adopts from Aristotle the thought that the Greek city, the *polis*, is the place where human freedom first found its appropriate legal form and actuality. Hegel had this historical phenomenon in mind when he speaks in this connection of the ethical life of a people as imprinted with spirit.[5]

With this a further and decisive moment of Hegel's phenomenological theory of spirit comes into view: It contains a *philosophy of history*, which can be called a history of human culture. Its aim is, via a *typology of models of world-interpretation* – as I shall call it; Hegel speaks of "forms of a world" (*PS* 240.7/M 265) – to reach an understanding, not of the history of political events, but more broadly of the intellectual and cultural changes from Antiquity to Modernity, in which the Enlightenment finds its systematic place.[6] Hegel's concept of spirit in the *Phenomenology* undergirds this typology of models of world-interpretation. It is the principle by which these changes can be grasped and understood, and at the same time it is the standard by which the actualization of freedom in the forms of life of a people can be assessed and judged. Hegel's philosophy of cultural history, as it is developed in the *Phenomenology of Spirit*, is thus simultaneously a critical theory of this history, which might better be called a *critical-structural theory of models of world-interpretation*. It can be called 'structural' because Hegel is concerned not so much with the multifarious contents as with certain fundamental relationships in which spirit in each case manifests itself.[7]

The methodological concept with which Hegel attempts to develop this theory and evaluate the capabilities of the various models of world-interpretation, without which his critique of the Enlightenment remains unintelligible, can be understood more precisely through a qualification Hegel added to the following claim. "Spirit," he contends, "is the ethical life of a people." The qualification adds: "insofar as it is the *immediate truth*" (*PS* 240.1–2/M 265). This means that the fundamental relationship of spirit, as Hegel saw it first realized historically in the ethical life of the ancient *polis*, first presents itself, conceptually considered, in an immediate way. This means that the corresponding form of life does not yet afford a recognition or construction of a conceptually articulated and rationally grounded *knowledge* of its specific constitution. As Hegel puts it, only a "beautiful ethical life" (*PS* 240.3/M 265) reigns here, one that is not yet a conceptually reflected life.

According to Hegel, this reflection is something required by the concept of spirit. The form of life in which spirit realizes and objectivizes itself is not an antecedent factual condition that can thus be immediately picked up, adopted or accepted in the form in which presents itself. Instead, it is a relationship containing a completely clarified and grounded consciousness of the connections in which spirit presents and expresses itself. This includes the consciousness that spirit, which Hegel contends is the universal principle of actuality, is *itself* the principle or architect and builder of this "objective" and "actual world." This world is to be called spirit's "work" (*PS* 239.6/M 264), because it concretizes and objectivizes itself, and because it must be able to present and to know this. This is what Hegel means by saying that these "shapes of the world" constitute the "proper being-for-self" of spirit (*PS* 239.25–29/M 264).[8]

1.1 The Principle of Consciousness

Hegel provides a minimal structural condition for a consciousness that can be regarded as a conceptually reflective and grounded *knowing* of its objects. (Here I begin analyzing Hegel's theory.) This condition consists in the fact that such a consciousness must be so related to the object that the object can be thought of as existing for itself independent of any merely subjective relation to consciousness. This is immediately obvious, for this is exactly what one means when one makes a judgment about an object or state of affairs about which one does not merely opine, which can also be false, but about which one *knows*, which involves objective grounds, so that it is not a mere subjective correlate of consciousness, but exists independently.

Hegel expresses this state of affairs in his famous "Principle of Consciousness" in the Introduction to the *Phenomenology of Spirit*:

> Consciousness *distinguishes* from itself something to which it at the same time *relates* itself. (*PS* 58.25–26/M 52)[9]

That which consciousness distinguishes from itself and to which it at the same time relates itself is an object or a state of affairs which is no mere subjective correlate of this consciousness, but is something to which a true judgment relates, of which a conceptually determinate and objectively grounded cognition is available, and of which it can be said that it exists independently of the subjective relation to it. This agrees with Hegel's express intention to use this principle to indicate how the "abstract determinations of knowledge and truth ... occur in consciousness" (*PS* 58.24–25/M 52). It also corresponds with the further explanation that that to which consciousness in the mode of cognition relates, is also *so* distinguished from it that it is "posited as *being* also outside of this relation" (*PS* 58.29–31/M 52).[10]

1.2 The Principle of Spirit

As illuminating as this explication may be, it is clear that it is insufficient for describing the basic structure of *spirit* and needs an essential elaboration. This can be easily seen from what has been said about the fundamental relationship of spirit. It was said that the object presents only the *objectification* of spirit, which, for just that reason, can be called its "work" in which it concretizes itself and in which, as mentioned, it has its "own being for self." Thus it can be said – and this is decisive – that in its relation to the object which it has brought forth from itself, spirit, in truth, does not relate something distinct from the content, but rather is identical with it. Hence in its relation to its object spirit only relates itself *to itself*.

In the Principle of Consciousness, *this* moment, the specific self-relation of spirit in relating to its object, is obviously *not* mentioned. That which consciousness distinguishes from itself and to which it equally relates itself is only an object or state of affairs that presents an objectively valid fact. Yet this of course does *not* mean that this state of affairs presents nothing other than the objectification of spirit itself. Thus the Principle of Consciousness does *not* say that the relation of consciousness to the object is identical to the relation of consciousness *to itself*. Indeed, Hegel emphasizes in the elucidation of the Principle of Consciousness that it is precisely when there is a consciousness that the object exists for itself and independently of it, when it is "posited as *existing* also outside this relation," that there is also a relation of consciousness to itself, which means that self-consciousness is present (*PS* 59.31–35/M 54); otherwise consciousness could not think of the object as *independent* of it, and there could be no knowledge of it, nor any truth of this knowledge.[11] However, this is not the crucial point here. The point is that in the Principle of Consciousness, consciousness does not grasp or conceive of the object *as the objectification of itself*, so that it would therein *relate only to itself* and in this sense would have "its own being for self" in its relation to the object. The Principle of Consciousness is silent about this.

Hence one might suggest as a complement to the Principle of Consciousness a "Principle of Spirit," which could be put as follows. Recall the minimal condition for a relation of consciousness in the indicated sense of the Principle of Consciousness:

> Consciousness distinguishes something from itself to which it at the same time relates itself.

In contrast, a relation of spirit can be expressed thus:

> Consciousness distinguishes something from itself to which it at the same time so relates itself that it relates only to itself.

This formulation aims to clarify the basic structure of Hegel's concept of spirit sufficiently for the present analysis.[12]

My thesis is that Hegel's critique of the Enlightenment can be understood in terms of the relation of these two principles and that his basic argument can be reconstructed on this basis in a way that does not get lost in the details and in extensive analyses of Hegel's operative terminology, which requires much interpretation and which tends to discourage rather than encourage even the most charitable readers. In view of the foregoing, a preliminary overview of the relation between the two principles, to explicate the methodological structure of the argument underlying Hegel's critique of the Enlightenment in the *Phenomenology of Spirit*, would be as follows:

1 One must begin from the point mentioned at the outset that, according to Hegel, the concept of spirit realizes itself at first in an *immediate* fashion. This means that initially the differences and the objective relations which are essential to spirit are not *as such* expressly present *for spirit itself* and cognized in a conceptually reflective fashion. Hence, a theory which seeks to explicate the concept of

spirit must develop the conditions under which this explicit self-comprehension is possible.

2   The basis of the development of these conditions is the basic relation of consciousness as expressed in the Principle of Consciousness. The first requirement of Hegel's theory of spirit is that the *difference* between consciousness and its object must be brought into the structure of *spirit*. Yet this must happen under the condition of the self-relation of spirit, because this is spirit's fundamental structure. This condition can be neither avoided nor superseded.

3   Hence it follows, and this is the decisive step, that spirit must first be so presented that it appears *to itself* in an objective manner and hence in the form of an object that is distinct from it and exists independently unto itself. This relation of spirit to an independent object existing unto itself must be, so to speak, a *simple* relation, for no alternative is yet available. The simplicity of this relation indicates the lack of consciousness's self-relation in its relation to its object, rather than any denial of the distinction between consciousness and object, nor of the distinction implicit in the self-relation of consciousness mentioned above in connection with the Principle of Consciousness.

In this simple relation, which is not reflected into itself, to its object, the object thus appears to spirit as a form of consciousness which spirit is not able to cognize as being *in truth* only an *objectification of itself*. Spirit is not able to do this because this relation presents itself to spirit in the form of the *simple* relation between consciousness and its object expressed in the Principle of Consciousness, and, as we've seen, this is defined precisely by the fact that the object *cannot* be comprehended as the objectification of consciousness's own achievement. Spirit, we may say, does not initially grasp the distinct and independently existing object as its own "work" in which it presents and objectifies itself.

4   Accordingly, the thrust of Hegel's theory is that spirit unavoidably falls into self-deception. It is unavoidable, because it results from the demand that spirit first present itself in the basic relation of consciousness, which means in the form of the *simple* opposition of consciousness and object. Spirit's self-deception thus consists in understanding its relation to its object as if it were related to something completely different from the objectification of its own achievement, which, in truth, is not the case.

Naturally one immediately asks how self-deceiving spirit understands itself and its object, how it is related to it, and how it can overcome its self-deception. Hegel seeks to answer exactly these questions with his staging of the struggle between the Enlightenment and Superstition, and one can already anticipate that this will be a struggle the Enlightenment fights with itself. That the Enlightenment does not understand that this is Hegel's critique of the Enlightenment.

Yet why is it a matter of a *struggle*, why is it a struggle with *superstition*, and, finally, to what extent can Hegel designate spirit as "Enlightenment"? We must clarify these matters before considering further Hegel's theory of the Enlightenment. The answers can be found in Hegel's theories of alienation and enculturation.

2 Alienated Spirit and the World of Enculturation

Hegel's remarks on the concept of alienation are easily connected to what we have said. The thesis that the logical form of the *simple* opposition between consciousness and object (in which spirit finds itself deceived about the constitution and status of the object it relates to) must be introduced into the concept of spirit is confirmed by the fact that Hegel speaks of "Self-alienated Spirit" (*PS* 264.8–9/M 294) and of "the World of self-alienated Spirit" (*PS* 266.25/M 296). The alien condition in which spirit finds itself in relating to itself is of course only another description of the self-deception just mentioned.

This also explains the second point. Hegel's talk of self-alienated spirit occurs in connection with his theory of enculturation (*Bildung*, 'education' in its widest sense).[13] It is important to see here that enculturation is not, for Hegel, the free unfolding of natural talents, but takes *work*. Work entails the loss of immediate, naturally grown and unreflective forms of life and intuition.[14] This loss is described by Hegel as alienation.[15] Only by overcoming their loss can a reflective and intersubjectively mediated and recognized relationship to self and world be achieved which can support a sustainable form of life grounded on freedom.

The *world of culture* – and here recurs the motif of history – is, for Hegel, the world of modern natural science, modern philosophy, and the consequent life-relationships which have become reflective and conscious of issues of legitimation.[16] This is the "disenchanted world," as Max Weber called it, in which the subject can no longer base its world-conception and the justification of its action on the authority of tradition or a pre-established, ultimately divine world order, but only *on itself*.[17] Modernity, we can say, is obliged to ground and support its legitimacy on its own principle, the principle of subjectivity.[18]

From this perspective Hegel tries to characterize the self-understanding of spirit more precisely by saying that spirit understands itself as the only entity which is the reliable ground and guarantor of the validity of knowledge or as the entity that prescribes objectively valid laws not only to external nature but also to a social life that can be called fair and just. On the basis of its authority and its justificatory function, spirit understands itself in the Modern era as an instance of *pure reason*, independent of the world of experience and existing for itself, which understands itself as undeniably actual and thus seeks to legitimate itself as the ground of all truth.[19] The highpoint of this development is, according to Hegel, Kant's *Critique of Pure Reason*. Clearly the model of the *simple* opposition between consciousness and object still underpins both this description and Hegel's assessment of Kant's Critical philosophy. This is confirmed by Hegel's characterization of spirit as a *duality* of the "consciousness of an objective actuality, free for itself" counterposed to the rational "unity of the self and what is essential (*Wesen*)" (*PS* 265.7–8/M 295).

Hegel's talk of an *objective actuality, free for itself* – which must be emphasized here – means in the present context not the world of objects of experience in a theoretical sense, as in the "Perception" chapter. The reason for this comes from the concept of spirit that underpins the argumentation reconstructed here. It immediately follows from the concept of spirit that an objective actuality that exists for itself also has sense and meaning only with reference to the concept of spirit. This in turn means that what is here called "actuality" can only mean spirit's "work" (mentioned at the outset), that is, a specific kind of actuality or the appearance of spirit itself.

Bearing all this in mind reveals how this kind of actuality of spirit must be formally constituted. This point augments the previous sketch of Hegel's approach to these issues. This actuality must be so constituted that the *difference* between consciousness and object, which is essential to the basic relationship of spirit, and which is a real distinction generated by the activity of spirit, does not exist *for spirit itself* and is not available to spirit *from its own perspective*. For only in this way can this actuality appear to spirit as independent of its relation to spirit, as existing for itself, which for spirit is something *foreign* and something *other* than itself. Hence to spirit this actuality will become objective and present itself as a form of consciousness which appears to spirit as something utterly foreign, not produced by spirit. This means that this actuality will also appear to spirit as an object characterized by an *immediate unity* of consciousness and object, and hence as a form of consciousness for whose self-understanding the distinction between itself and its object *as such* does not exist at all.

A further circumstance to consider arises from the fact that the unity, conceived as just indicated, arises from the world of enculturation. Hence it cannot be an immediate, natural, pre-reflective, "beautiful" unity. Instead it results from reflection generated by the *negation* of an objective, experienced actuality existing unto itself. Hence the immediacy of this unity is in truth something reflected, indeed it has *negated*, sublated, and left behind the real distinction at issue between consciousness and object. The actuality thematized here is thus a purely ideal, purely inner actuality existing only in the mode of subjective representation, and all the contentful determinations ascribed to the objects that belong to it are only products of this 'pure' consciousness.[20] Hence this is the *immediate unity* of consciousness and object mentioned previously, to which spirit relates itself: a form of consciousness for whose self-understanding the distinction between itself and its object as such simply doesn't exist.

Hegel calls such a form of consciousness *faith* (*PS* 266.20/M 296), which Hegel identifies as the modern, reflective, heart-felt piety that flees from and before the "hostile" and "evil" world, such as that of *August Hermann Francke* in Halle, the *Jansenists* and *Quietists* in France, or the *Methodists* in England. This form of faith, as Hegel characterizes it, not without irony, takes its accoutrements out of the experienced world and transports them, so to speak, into the sphere of pure, experience-free consciousness (cf. *PS* 226.20–37/M 250), which withdraws into the cloistered, presumedly "holy" sphere of an internality that leaves behind all forms of alienated life, indeed in such a way that these objects are now made into bearers of a universal, ideal significance. In this sphere of internality, therefore, the *real* distinction between consciousness and its object is sublated. This internality is the world of the heart and of religious feeling, in which the objects obtain content and actuality only in relation to this feeling. Here Hegel further points out that this appearance of faith is to be distinguished from the substantial religious consciousness familiar to us as the object of Hegel's philosophy of religion, which is thus not relevant here.[21]

What is decisive – and here we finally reach the plane of Hegel's theory of the Enlightenment – is that in this way the simple opposition between consciousness and object, in terms of which spirit has first to realize itself, has received its *first concrete interpretation*. This opposition appears here, as Hegel puts it, as an *opposition between two realms*: it is the opposition between the realm of pure, rational self-consciousness and the realm of faith, for it is true that this piety has retreated from the world of experience into the sphere of pure consciousness. This sphere, this realm of faith, is the external and foreign object for rational self-consciousness.[22]

Precisely this gives rise to the situation Hegel describes as a "struggle of the Enlightenment with superstition" (*PS* 293.22–23/M 329). For rational self-consciousness realizes itself – and here one should recall Kant's theoretical and practical philosophy and Fichte's concept of infinite striving – by endeavoring to transform every kind of object that appears to it as simply *given* into a content either of its cognitive or its practical intentions.[23] Thus it must also direct itself polemically or negatively against the figure of faith, which appears to it in the form of an alien entity independent of it and existing unto itself, all the more so because faith maintains itself in the same element as reason, namely, in pure consciousness, without, however (or so it appears to rational self-consciousness), having achieved true insight into itself and into the way it relates to its object in its world of internality and heart-felt piety. Rational self-consciousness then tries to teach it this insight. Rational self-consciousness thus emerges as Enlightenment contra faith.

3 The Struggle of Enlightenment with Superstition

Hegel's remark that the owl of Minerva flies only at dusk is also valid for his theory of the Enlightenment.[24] For the form of spirit presented by the epoch of the Enlightenment has grown old for the Hegel of the *Phenomenology of Spirit*, and, in surveying his time, he finds the old euphoria has been replaced by disillusionment and critique. However, the notion that it falls to philosophy to paint it in gray on gray scarcely holds of Hegel's theory of the Enlightenment. Instead Hegel sketches his portrait of the Enlightenment in powerful, even garish colors. It is, namely, portrayed as "sheer uproar and a violent struggle" (*PS* 296.14–15/M 332), a struggle with what appears to Enlightenment to be superstition. Hence Hegel's theory of the Enlightenment in the *Phenomenology of Spirit* concentrates primarily on its critique of religion.[25]

Here I cannot take account of the numerous concrete contemporary theories and literary sources Hegel considers in his theory of the Enlightenment. They stretch from Goethe's recently published sensational translation of Diderot's *Rameau's Nephew* – the first vagrant in world literature, who unmasks the corruption of enlightened society and its social relations in a comic confusion of its virtues and vices – to D'Holbach's critique of society and religion from a utilitarian and materialistic perspective, and Hegel's writing is replete with allusions to Voltaire's and Robinet's Deism, to Helvétius, Lamettrie, Rousseau, and others.[26] Clearly Hegel is far more sympathetic to the *siècle des lumières* than he is to the Enlightenment in his own land. We cannot, however, examine all this here. Of interest here is the fate of the Enlightenment in its campaign against faith and the question, what systematic consequences result from it.

In its attack on the broad "realm of error," in which the Enlightenment thinks faith is trapped, the Enlightenment first takes aim at the deceitful machinations of a priesthood which, as Hegel says, "conspires with despotism" (*PS* 294.14/M 330) in order to keep the people quiet through fear, while despotism seeks to preserve the power it enjoys and to achieve the "complete satisfaction of its whims and caprice" by relying on "the people's stupidity and confusion caused by the deceitful priesthood," although despotism shares "this same dull wit, the same superstition and error" (*PS* 294.14–21/M 330).[27] However, while the Enlightenment wants to open faith's eyes to this deception and to its errors, faith rejects it by replying that the Enlightenment has no idea what is at issue and simply does not understand the matter. Moreover, faith accuses the Enlightenment of a deliberate lie. For, on the one hand, the Enlightenment explains away the religious cult as a "hocus-pocus of conjuring priests" (*PS* 298.32–33/M 335), yet, on the other hand, it understands religion thoroughly and even admits that faith puts its entire trust in that religious cult and draws the certainty of its own existence from it. For that very reason, there can be no talk from the perspective of faith of any deception in which faith is embroiled; for faith, this is instead the predicament of the Enlightenment.[28]

The same holds for the enlightened destruction of the objects of religious worship. "What is holy to *faith*," as Hegel dramatically describes the impulse of the Enlightenment, is to the Enlightenment "a piece of stone, a block of wood which has eyes but doesn't see, or else a piece of dough which is grown on the field, transformed by man and returned to the earth" (*PS* 300.3–5/M 337). Even these putative clarifications and uncoverings are for faith nothing other than presumptuous lies, because what faith worships and what is holy to it, is *for it* certainly no perceptible and impermanent object, but rather an eternal being.[29] Hence it must dismiss as totally irrelevant all critical references to the problems of a contingent, historical tradition and to the interpretation of witnesses.[30]

Since the Enlightenment seeks in this way to destroy all the positive content of faith and expose it as projections of human representations, it thus presents itself *to faith* as the opposite of what it wants to be, namely, true insight. For the Enlightenment, the thought of a divine being becomes a concept of a totally contentless and indeterminate highest being, a "vacuum" (*PS* 303.7/M 340) as Hegel says; this is the basic assumption of the enlightened Deism of Toland, Voltaire, and Robinet. Correspondingly, the world of sensuous experience and the existence of finite, natural things becomes its central interest; one should think here of the *empiricism* of the English and the French Enlightenment.[31]

Now to faith the results of the enlightened interpretation of the world as well as the critique it directs against faith must be, not merely lies, but a complete "abomination" (*PS* 305.25/M 343), for just as the Enlightenment misunderstands faith's self-understanding, it reduces the world, which is to faith a creation of its God, to a collection of matter in motion, and the divine being it reveres to a totally contentless "*être suprême*" (*PS* 305.26/M 343).[32] Thus faith now seems to have all right on its side against the Enlightenment.[33]

Yet this only appears to be so. This is evident if one recalls that the religious form of consciousness at issue here comes from the world of *experience*, which is a *reflected world of enculturation*, which has saved itself, so to speak, by withdrawing from this world into the sphere of pure, experience-independent consciousness and the inwardness of the "heart." Yet because it is a form of this *cultural* world, faith must nevertheless have developed a conceptually determinate consciousness. Accordingly, a consciousness can be imputed to it of that and how it combines the two mutually opposed realms – pure consciousness or the world of the heart, and the world of experience – into the *one* religious interpretation of the world that for it is the only truth. Hence the question now arises, in what way does the *consciousness of this unity* within faith's self-interpretation find conceptually reflected expression?

The Enlightenment is guided by just this question when it places these disparate spheres to which faith adheres before the eyes of faith and when it demonstrates to faith that faith does not bring these opposed spheres together into a conceptually determinate, unitary interpretation of self and world, although it nevertheless holds, thoughtlessly and unconceptually, that there is some such unity. Faith is incapable of developing a suitable and conceptually clarified consciousness of the represented unity of the individual sensible objects with the general, ideal, religious meaning it ascribes to them, for it denies any constitutive reference to concrete, sensible objects and it posits absolutely the universal ideal significance in a religious sense. Nor does faith succeed in becoming clear that the divine being it reveres, to which it ascribes a self-sufficient existence, utterly independent of any references to the world, is inaccessible to faith without faith's own activity in particular religious practices. And finally, it is not able to account for the fact that it ties its representations of the attributes of the absolute divine being, such as wisdom, love, goodness, grace, justice, etc., to representations of finite and contingent contents. Although faith itself produces the unitary sense of these connections, it fails to comprehend this. In this way it keeps, as Hegel remarks with dry humor, double accounts, as the Enlightenment famously points out, but which the Enlightenment confuses because it brings before faith the accouterments of this world here and now, which faith wants to disavow, but which it also cannot deny because they are the requisites of its world, which it has made for itself and in which it realizes its self-consciousness.[34]

Looked at coldly, however, the Enlightenment is in no better position: It behaves only negatively toward faith; it too divides, isolates, and absolutizes, so that it is unable to bring together the separate elements as they are *for faith*. In its critique it *isolates* the concrete objects of sensible experience, such as the representations of finite and contingent contents as well as the moments of its own actions, and altogether denies these elements any ideal meaning which transcends and unifies them.[35]

This prepares the decisive step. Because the Enlightenment proceeds in this manner, it lets it be known, if indirectly, that it is equally unclear about the specific unitary sense of its own structural constitution. For what it shows to, and for which it reproaches faith, namely, that faith lacks any adequate consciousness of the specific *unity* of its opposed moments, which faith itself has produced, although as a form of enculturation faith should have some such at its disposal, this now reveals itself as the unrecognized reflection of the Enlightenment's own constitution. The Enlightenment's interpretation and critique of faith reveals itself to be a critique that, in a way the Enlightenment does not recognize, *turns against itself*. For the Enlightenment, too, cannot comprehend the unity of consciousness and object, here specifically its unity with its object, namely faith, in a way appropriate to the concept of spirit.

This means that the struggle of Enlightenment with superstition is, in truth, a struggle that the Enlightenment unwittingly *directs against itself*, since the enlightened consciousness, it now turns out, is governed by the principle of the *simple* opposition of consciousness and its object. This is revealed by how it relates to the position of faith. It relates itself to faith only as an object absolutely opposed to it, utterly foreign, and existing independently from it – which in truth is not at all the case – against which it can therefore comport itself only polemically, negatively, or critically-destructive. Thus it can be said that the Enlightenment understands the internal constitution of faith according to the same principle, namely the principle of the *simple* opposition of consciousness and object, by which it understands *itself* and by which it also understands its relation to faith. This principle, as mentioned at the outset, is formulated in the Principle of Consciousness. Since the Enlightenment now reproaches faith with still being trapped within the *opposition* of its moments, the world of experience and the sphere of internality, and with being unable to provide any rational and conceptually reflective account of the specific sense of its unity, which it nevertheless maintains and makes into the foundation of its self-understanding, the Enlightenment does not recognize and, on the basis of its own structural constitution cannot recognize, that this reproach applies equally well *to itself*. For neither is the Enlightenment able to comprehend the true sense of its connection to faith's position. Hence the Enlightenment is also unable to see that the form of faith is in truth its own inverted, negative mirror image. Hegel's thesis, which is central to the course of his argumentation, can now be understood as follows.

Both Enlightenment as well as faith, as such, each represent a *unity* of object- and self-consciousness. However, the concepts of this unity, which form the basis of their respective self-understandings, are mutually exclusive. Faith purports to be *immediately* related to its object and thus to obtain the certainty of itself. Yet in truth it owes its certainty to its *flight* from the world of experience, that is, to its negation. This, according to Hegel, is a form of mediation.

In contrast, the enlightened self-consciousness maintains – in accord with the requirement of the Principle of Consciousness – that it has its object outside itself and is conscious of itself only because it knows itself to be distinct from its object, to which it nonetheless relates. To this extent and due to this distinction it relates *mediately* to its object and to itself. Precisely what faith unjustly *denies* concerning itself, namely, the dependency of its existence and self-certainty on its relation to the world of experience, is *affirmed* by the enlightened self-consciousness. Hence neither of them can identify the true unity of both which would result from the reciprocal negation of their untrue self-descriptions. From faith's point of view this relation presents itself thus: What faith unjustly *affirms* for itself, namely, the *immediate* unity of object- and self-consciousness, is *denied* by the enlightened consciousness. Since, however, faith can in truth maintain its self-certainty only through this relation and mediation, which from its perspective it of course disclaims, in view of this mediation it exhibits within itself the same formal constitution as the enlightened consciousness.

The enlightened consciousness, however, is unable to recognize this formal identity between itself and the position of faith. If it were able to do so, then it would satisfy the criterion of the structure of spirit. It would thus see that the position of faith is in truth, so to speak, the spirit of its own spirit, and it would thus relate to it as to its object in such a way that it would know that it is indeed distinct from it, and yet at the same time that in this relation it relates only to itself. Thus it would see that its polemical behavior towards faith rests on a misunderstanding of and a failure to recognize its own constitution as well as that of faith. But the enlightened consciousness is not able to do this, because it operates only with the model of the *simple* opposition between consciousness and object and it interprets the structural constitution of faith *and* its own relationship to it with this model. However, this model doesn't anticipate the case in which consciousness relates to an object distinct from itself in such a way that it thereby relates only to itself. Consequently faith is and remains for the enlightened consciousness an alien object existing independently of it, to which it relates only polemically and destructively. Hence it also fails to recognize that what it tries to demonstrate to faith, namely, the dependence of its self-certainty on the world of experience, in fact demonstrates faith's structural identity with its own constitution. Thus the enlightened consciousness is not enlightened about itself, and its struggle with faith is an unrecognized mirror-boxing with itself.[36]

In sum, Hegel's critique of the Enlightenment in the context of his *Phenomenology of Spirit* is that the Enlightenment systematically misunderstands its own activity and maintains the contrary of what is the case. The Enlightenment maintains it knows the truth about faith and about itself. The truth, however, proves to be that it is altogether unable to know this. Indeed, is has been shown that the Enlightenment is unable to know this for principled reasons and that accordingly the Enlightenment must systematically misunderstand itself. The grounds for this lie in the circumstance that the concept of spirit must at first be explicated and presented as the form of consciousness or the simple opposition of consciousness and object. In this opposition the object appears to consciousness as something other than, external, and foreign to it. On the basis of the logic of the concept of spirit, there is no alternative to this perspective. The guiding misunderstanding here, which is a misunderstanding of the Enlightenment about itself, one can thus say, is system-dependent and unavoidable, for it is the necessary consequence of the conceptual framework which is available for explicating the concept of spirit.

From this derives the last step of Hegel's critique of the Enlightenment. Namely, since the enlightened consciousness is a form of spirit and, as has become clear, since on the basis of its own constitution, and with regard both to itself and to its object (faith), it consistently and necessarily deceives and misunderstands itself, it thus also becomes clear that the structure it does not recognize and consistently disavows – namely, the unity of spirit's relation to itself *in* its relation to its object – is exactly the form of consciousness through which the struggle of the Enlightenment with faith could be brought to an end and overcome. This would be an end in which there is neither victor nor vanquished, but rather a new insight on both sides, namely, the insight into the articulated fundamental constitution of the structure of spirit. As Hegel emphasizes, however, the Enlightenment, on its own and with its own conceptual resources, is unable to do this.[37] Therefore, the story we have told up to now about the struggle of Enlightenment with superstition is not yet the whole truth about the Enlightenment as Hegel sees it.

The struggle of the Enlightenment with faith therefore has a sequel. It leads to a new and thoroughly dramatic turn. It brings with it yet again an accounting with the Enlightenment which makes clear that the structure of spirit can be completed only at the end of a painstaking path which ultimately is the path of the entire *Phenomenology of Spirit*. Only in this sense can the critique of the Enlightenment be understood as a necessary step in the course of justifying Hegel's fundamental principle of philosophy. In closing, let me briefly sketch this perspective.

4 The End of Enlightenment: Revolution and Terror

To faith, whose realm and refuge is plundered through the attack of the Enlightenment and which sees around it nothing but hard, finite, spirit-forsaken reality,[38] the only remaining chance of survival is in reaching out beyond finitude to a totally unknown and eternally unknowable, utterly empty Beyond in the form of a pure longing, whose close affinity with a central feature of romantic consciousness is obvious. In this relation to a totally indeterminate absolute, it finally comes into accord with the positive result that the Enlightenment itself had already reached in its critique of faith: Deism. Against this background the Enlightenment appears now as *satisfied*; in contrast, in its grief over the loss of its world faith appears as *unsatisfied Enlightenment* (cf. PS 310.35–36/M 349).

For the individual consciousness, standing in the relation that enlightened consciousness bears to that contentless absolute, "everything in its immediate existence exists unto itself and is good" (*PS* 305.27–28/M 343). Upon further analysis, this is better described as the *principle of utility* (*PS* 314.25–315.11/M 353–4). This is because, put formally, the utile is that which has independent standing and is thus regarded as something essential, and yet which also exists only in a relation to a subject distinct from it which relates itself to the utile as something essential for it, and which thus understands its own life and interpretive context only in terms of this relation in which it realizes itself. Hence in realizing the utile the subject only executes its own essential intention and in so doing thus realizes itself. With that, it appears, the enlightened consciousness has achieved objectivity in the world of utilitarianism, to which it can relate in such a way that it thereby relates itself only to itself.

In truth, however, according to Hegel's last and deliberately dramatic turn, the principle of utility has effaced all fixed objectivity from the world. Since everything becomes a matter of another's will, nothing is any longer for itself. Rather, everything seems to be subjected to a general will which realizes itself in the free disposal of its world. This is the basic form of what Hegel calls *absolute freedom* (*PS* 316.10/M 355), which runs riot in the *terror* and as the *fury of destruction*, the historical substrate of which is the terror of Robespierre, who guillotined 40,000 people – the coldest and flattest death, as Hegel writes, with no more meaning than "chopping off a head of cabbage or taking a drink of water" (*PS* 320.13/M 360). This general state terror, Hegel contends, manifests the violence that lies implicit in a totally contentless, lawless, and limitless concept of freedom, insofar as it is realized. These are fruits harvested through the deeds of an Enlightenment that misunderstands itself, Hegel contends.[39]

Nevertheless, Hegel conceals the fact that in the end, the richest and most fruitful result of the Enlightenment and the French Revolution is his own philosophy. For the thought of freedom that the Enlightenment brought into the world, which the French Revolution failed to actualize in a substantive system of laws, Hegel makes into the fundamental principle of his philosophy. The experience of the downfall of the French Revolution thus enters into Hegel's concept of substantial freedom. Hegel's theory of spirit in the *Phenomenology of Spirit* is thus to be valued as a still unsurpassed framework for a critical theory of cultural forms of life and their interpretive worlds. Their principle is the thought of freedom as the foundation of a truly humane culture. Hegel's *Philosophy of Right* is the explicated theory of how to develop a social form and system of law that enables the individual to exercise his or her freedom in a sustainable manner. It is not intelligible that any era, including our century, could abandon this thought.[40]

Notes

1 This is the point of Hegel's claim that what the Enlightenment "denounces as error or lies . . . [can] be nothing other than [the Enlightenment] itself" (*PS* 9:296.28/M 333), or likewise that "the nature of the struggle of the Enlightenment with the errors [of superstition]" consists in "battling with itself in those errors and to condemn in them what it [the Enlightenment] asserts" (*PS* 9:297.10–11/M 333).

2. Hegel's critique of the Enlightenment has not yet received its due in the literature. The one exception has hardly received notice beyond the Anglophone realm, namely Hinchman (1984). Brief summaries of Hegel's chapter on the Enlightenment are provided by Siep (2000, 198–201) and Jaeschke (2005, 191–3). A more thorough presentation is provided by Kreß (1996). A systematic introduction to the method and to Hegel's theory of consciousness, including their relevance to current epistemological and social-philosophical discussions, is provided by Westphal (2003).
3. This thesis is presented by Schnädelbach (1999, 71), who states: "The chapter on spirit in the *Phenomenology* contains . . . Hegel's philosophy of culture."
4. On Hegel's view of freedom as "*bei sich selbst sein*" (being by oneself) see Hardimon (1994). – *Ed.*
5. See above, chapter 8. – *Ed.*
6. On Hegel's conception of "forms of a world," also see Wisser-Lohmann (2006).
7. On this topic, also see chapters 6, 11–13. – *Ed.*
8. The relevant passage runs: "Spirit is the *ethical life* of a *people*, insofar as spirit is the *immediate truth*; the individual that is a world. Spirit must become conscious of what it is immediately, it must sublate the beautiful ethical life, and through a series of forms achieve knowledge (*Wissen*) of itself. However, these [forms] are distinct from the previous ones because they are real spirits, proper actualities, and instead of being forms merely of consciousness, they are shapes of a world" (*PS* 240.1–7/ M 265).
9. For discussion, see the now-classic article by Cramer (1976); also Westphal (1998). On Hegel's Introduction to the *Phenomenology* see Karásek et al. (2006).
10. Cf. above, pp. 4–6. – *Ed.*
11. This is the point of Hegel's statement that ". . . consciousness is, on the one hand, consciousness of the object and, on the other hand, consciousness of itself; it is conscious of what to it is the true, and conscious of its knowledge of this truth" (*PS* 59.31–33/M 54).
12. This is not the place to discuss the systematic connections between Hegel's concepts of self-consciousness and of spirit, on which see Pippin (1989).
13. Cf. below, chapter 13. – *Ed.*
14. Cf. Hegel's discussion of the bondsman's labor; above, chapter 2. – *Ed.*
15. Cf. Hegel's summary statement, "The spirit of self-alienation has its existence within the world of enculturation (*Bildung*)" (*PS* 286.27–28/M 321).
16. On the importance of natural science in Hegel's *Phenomenology*, see above, chapters 1, 4, 5. – *Ed.*
17. Hegel analyses the demise of merely customary forms of life in his accounts of "Active Reason" and of *Antigone*; see above, chapters 6, 8. – *Ed.*
18. Cf. Habermas (1993). Cf. *infra*, chapters 7, 10. – *Ed.*
19. In this regard, the initial "certainty of reason" (above, chapter 4) flowers socially in and as the Enlightenment. – *Ed.*
20. In this regard, the present form of spirit bears comparison with the initial forms of "Self-Consciousness" and of "Reason," on which see above, chapters 2, 4. – *Ed.*
21. "Hence it is not . . . religion which is observed here, but rather *faith*, insofar as it is the *flight* from the actual world and thus is not *in* and *for itself*" (*PS* 266.31–34, cf. 287.27–288.1/M 297, cf. 322).
22. "Thus the whole is . . . a self-estranged reality; it divides into a realm in which *self-consciousness* is *actual* and has itself as its object, and another, the realm of *pure* consciousness, which has no actual presence beyond the former, but instead is in *faith*" (*PS* 265.30–34/M 295–6).
23. Cf. the proud consciousness who becomes lord over the bondsman, the initial appearance of reason, and the "Animal Kingdom of the Spirit," discussed above, chapters 2, 4, 7 end. – *Ed.*

24 "When philosophy paints its grey in grey, then a form of life has grown old and cannot be rejuvenated by grey in grey, but only known; the Owl of Minerva takes flight only at dusk" (*PR*, 1820 Preface, end).

25 The battle of the Enlightenment with superstition has a preliminary stage under the banner of the immediacy of the relation of both sides. From this perspective Hegel describes the destructive relation between Enlightenment and superstition as, so to speak, an unwitting, unnoticed, self-completing dissolution of spiritual life. After this bloodless, peaceful revolution "then only consciousness still preserves in memory, one knows not how, as a past history, the dead ways of the previous form of spirit; and the new serpent of wisdom raised high for devotion has in this way merely rid itself painlessly of a withered skin" (*PS* 296.4–6/M 332).

26 Cf. Falke (1996), Harris (1997) 2: 247–405.

27 Here we cannot examine the "three aspects of the fiend": (1) the universal "realm of error" which corresponds to the "universal masses of consciousness"; (2) the deception of the priesthood, which "carries out its envious self-conceit of retaining possession of insight, along with its sundry self-interest" and sacrifices those masses; and (3) despotism, with which the priesthood conspires, which "stands above the bad insight of the masses and the bad intention of the priests and also unites both within itself" (*PS* 294.5–21/M 330).

28 "Here, however, the Enlightenment is completely fatuous; faith experiences it as a speech which does not know what it says and does not understand the issue (*Sache*) when it speaks of priestly deception and deception of the people. . . . The Enlightenment immediately expresses as something foreign to consciousness what it proclaims to be most proper to consciousness. – How can Enlightenment thus speak of humbug and deception? Since Enlightenment is immediately the opposite of what it maintains and expresses about faith, it presents itself to faith instead as the deliberate lie" (*PS* 298.29–299.3/M 335).

29 Cf. the 'high' and 'low' meanings of "Observing Reason" discussed above, chapter 5. – *Ed.*

30 "The Enlightenment, which presents itself as pure, here makes that which is to spirit eternal life and holy spirit into an actual *transitory* thing and besmirches it with the intrinsically null viewpoint of Sense Certainty – with a viewpoint that is not at all available to devout faith, so that Enlightenment simply lies to faith" (*PS* 300.8–12/M 337).

31 See above, chapter 5 and contrast the "Unhappy Consciousness," above pp. 64–70. – *Ed.*

32 "To faith of course this positive result of Enlightenment is just as much an atrocity as its negative relation to faith. This *insight* into the absolute being (*Wesen*), which sees nothing in it but the absolute being, the *être suprême* or the void . . . is to faith a complete abomination" (*PS* 305.24–30/M 343).

33 "Faith has the divine right, the right of absolute *self-identity* or of pure thinking, against Enlightenment, from which it experiences utter injustice, since Enlightenment twists all aspects of faith and makes them into something other than what they are in faith" (*PS* 305.36–306.2/M 343).

34 "Here [the Enlightenment] confuses spirit's house keeping by bringing in the accouterments of this world, possession of which faith cannot disavow because its consciousness equally belongs to them" (*PS* 266.13–16/M 296). This corresponds to Hegel's later statement: "Thus the Enlightenment has irresistible power over faith because it finds even in its own consciousness the moments which Enlightenment validates. . . . Faithful consciousness uses doubled measure and weight, it has two eyes, two ears, two tongues and two languages, it has doubled all representations (*Vorstellungen*) without comparing their doubled sense" (*PS* 310.1–13/M 348).

35 "Yet for its part Enlightenment here isolates the *inward*, the *non-actual* from actuality, just as it holds fast to the externality of thingness against the inwardness of faith in its intuition and devotion" (*PS* 309.30–32/M 348).

36 The crucial passage runs as follows: "However, the Enlightenment itself, which reminds faith of the opposites of its distinct moments, is just as unenlightened about itself. It behaves entirely *negatively* towards faith, insofar as it excludes faith's content from its purity and takes faith to be the negative of Enlightenment. Thus it neither recognizes *itself* in this negative, in the content of faith, nor for this reason does it bring together the two thoughts, the thought which it contributes and the thought against which it contributes the former. . . . Thus it does not produce the unity of the them as their unity, that is, the concept" (*PS* 306.28–34, 307.1–2f./M 344; emphasis added). Cf. above, pp. 55–58, on Hegel's account of thought. – *Ed.*

37 "However the Enlightenment *is* only this movement [the retreat of pure insight from its other-being into itself], it is the still-unconscious activity of the pure concept, which . . . takes [the object] for an *other*" (*PS* 307.7–9/M 345). Thus Hegel can summarize: "The self-alienated concept – since here it still stands at the stage of this alienation (*Entfremdung*) – doesn't however recognize (*erkennt*) this *same essence* (*gleiche Wesen*) of both sides, the movement of self-consciousness and its absolute essence (*Wesen*), not their *same essence*, which in fact is their substance and persistence. Because it does not recognize this unity, the essence only counts to it in the form of the objective beyond, and the distinguishing consciousness, which in this way has the in-itself outside itself, counts to it as a finite consciousness" (*PS* 311.30–312.2/M 350).

38 Cf. "Unhappy Consciousness," discussed above, pp. 64–70. – *Ed.*

39 Clearly this is tied to Hegel's sharpest, unspoken objection to Fichte's philosophy and his concept of self-consciousness, which Hegel constantly criticizes for its contentless void, for which it cannot generate from within itself any substantial content. Whether Hegel's criticism is just cannot be examined here.

40 This chapter was translated by Willem deVries, Kenneth Caskie, and the editor, all of whom I gratefully thank.

References

Aristotle (1924) *Aristotle's Metaphysics*, tr. W. D. Ross. Oxford: The Clarendon Press.

Cramer, K. (1976) "Bemerkungen zu Hegels Begriff vom Bewußtsein in der *Phänomenologie des Geistes*," in U. Guzzoni, B. Rang, and L. Siep (eds.), *Der Idealismus und seine Gegenwart. Festschrift für Werner Marx*. Hamburg: Meiner. Rpt. in R.-P. Horstmann (ed.), *Seminar: Dialektik in der Philosophie Hegels* (pp. 360–93). Frankfurt am Main: Suhrkamp, 1978.

Falke, G.-H. H. (1996) *Begriffene Geschichte. Das historische Substrat und die systematische Anordnung der Bewußtseinsgestalten in Hegels "Phänomenologie des Geistes." Interpretation und Kommentar*. Berlin: Lukas.

Habermas, J. (1993) *Der philosophische Diskurs der Moderne. Zwölf Vorlesungen*. Frankfurt am Main: Surhkamp.

Hardimon, M. (1994) *Hegel's Social Philosophy: The Project of Reconciliation*. New York: Cambridge University Press.

Harris, H. S. (1997) *Hegel's Ladder*, 2 vols. Cambridge, Mass.: Hackett Publishing Co.

Hinchman, L. P. (1984) *Hegel's Critique of the Enlightenment*. Tampa and Gainsville: University Presses of Florida.

Jaeschke, W. (2005) *Hegel-Handbuch. Leben–Werk–Schule*. Stuttgart and Weimar: Metzler.

Karásek, J., Kuneš, J., and Landa, I., eds. (2006) *Hegels Einleitung in die Phänomenologie des Geistes*. Würzburg: Königshausen and Neumann.

Kreß, A. (1996) *Reflexion als Erfahrung. Hegels Phänomenologie der Subjektivität*. Würzburg: Königshausen and Neumann.

Pippin, R. (1989) *Hegel's Idealism: The Satisfaction of Self-Consciousness*. Cambridge: Cambridge University Press.

Schnädelbach, H. (1999) *Hegel zur Einführung*. Hamburg: Junius.

Siep, L. (2000) *Der Weg der "Phänomenologie des Geistes." Ein einführender Kommentar zu Hegels "Differenzschrift" und zur "Phänomenologie des Geistes."* Frankfurt am Main: Suhrkamp.

Westphal, Kenneth R. (1998) "Hegel's Solution to the Dilemma of the Criterion." In: J. Stewart, ed., *The Phenomenology of Spirit Reader: A Collection of Critical and Interpretive Essays* (pp. 76–91) Albany, State University of New York Press.

Westphal, K. R. (2003) *Hegel's Epistemology. A Philosophical Introduction to the Phenomenology of Spirit*. Indianapolis: Hackett Publishing Co.

Wisser-Lohmann, E. (2006) "Gestalten nicht des Bewußtseins, sondern einer Welt – Überlegungen zum Geist-Kapitel der *Phänomenologie des Geistes*," in D. Köhler and O. Pöggeler (eds.), *G. W. F. Hegel: Phänomenologie des Geistes* (pp. 183–207). Berlin: Akademie.

10

"Morality" in Hegel's *Phenomenology of Spirit*

Frederick C. Beiser

1 The Context of "Morality"

Sometimes, though not often, in the midst of the crabbed prose of Hegel's *Phenomenology of Spirit*, the reader will stumble across a sentence of arresting beauty. One such sentence appears unexpectedly in the depths of Chapter VI.C., "Morality": "*Die Wunden des Geistes heilen, ohne daß Narben bleiben*"; "The wounds of the spirit heal, with no scars remaining." This is what the tired reader needs to know who has followed Hegel's argument to this point. He too is battered and bruised in his attempt to scale Hegelian summits; but he is promised redemption: there will be no scars. Such a sentence also reminds the reader of the remarkable regenerative powers of spirit; it helps him understand how it constantly renews itself on each stage of its self-awareness, fresh and ready to move forward, as if all the past struggles never happened. It is no accident that Hegel makes this statement toward the close of Chapter VI.C. The reader has come a long way, and this chapter has been especially long and difficult; but now the end of his journey is in sight: absolute spirit (*PS* 361.25/M 407–8). It is absolute spirit which, despite so many self-inflicted wounds, bears no scars.

It will help the spirits of the reader of "Morality," Chapter VI.C. of the *Phenomenology*, to recall how far we have come in Hegel's phenomenological journey. Nothing gives a better overview than the table of contents.[1] There we see that Chapter VI.C. is one of the chapters of the section entitled "Spirit." This obvious point about textual topography, though banal, is significant because it shows us that "morality" is one of the stages in the development of spirit. Spirit, as readers will recall from long ago in Chapter IV.A. of "Self-Consciousness," is "I that is We, We that is I" (*PS* 108.39/M 110). Although Hegel introduces spirit as early as Chapter IV.A., the chapters of "Spirit" mark a distinct advance beyond it. All the stages in the development of spirit, Hegel tells us in the opening section of "Spirit," differ from earlier stages in the *Phenomenology* in that they are "forms of a world" (*Gestalten einer Welt*) rather than just "forms of consciousness" (*Gestalten nur des Bewußtseins*) (*PS* 240.5–7/M 265). With spirit we are no longer dealing with the individual but the collective subject, no longer with this or that self but the spirit of a people as a whole. Morality is one stage in the *self-consciousness* of spirit, one point in its long journey from being a substance toward becoming a subject, from being something purely "in itself" to becoming something "for itself."

But precisely *which* stage, *which* point is this? We need to be more precise because there are many stages of the self-awareness of spirit. The introduction to VI.C., "Morality," where architechtonic issues are discussed, is remarkably obscure even by Hegelian standards. Here Hegel describes spirit at this stage as "spirit as it is certain of itself" (*der seiner selbst gewisse Geist*). It is not simply spirit in its "truth," as it exists in the community of ethical life, but spirit in its "certainty for itself," as it exists in, and is confirmed by, the subjects who compose it. The phrase "certainty for itself" is familiar, but also troubling, because it seems as if we have already reached that point back in Chapter IV of "Self-Consciousness," which bore a very similar title, "the truth of self-certainty" (*die Wahrheit der Gewißheit seiner selbst*). Our troubles seem to grow when Hegel writes in VI.C that spirit has moved beyond all stages of consciousness, where it was opposed to its object, and that it now has only itself for its object (*PS* 323.31–39/M 364). For is that also not what he told us back in Chapter IV of "Self-Consciousness"? So it seems that spirit is not getting anywhere at all. Is it suffering from amnesia? Have all its struggles been in vain? We only need to recollect a little more about the journey of consciousness to see that this is not so, that we have indeed reached a new and higher stage of self-consciousness in "Morality." For in Chapter IV of "Self-Consciousness" we were concerned only with the *individual* subject, and only with a stage of its *theoretical* development; in Chapter VI.C of "Spirit," however, we are concerned not only with a *universal* subject – the purely rational subject of transcendental philosophy – but also with a stage of its *practical* development. Hegel marks this important shift from the theoretical to the practical dimension when he writes in the introduction to VI.C that the self-certainty of the subject now consists in its "universal will" (*PS* 323.30/M 364). What matters at this stage is not only a subject who thinks but also a subject who wills and acts.

But surely, a grumpy reader might ask, we have already seen that willing, acting subject in earlier chapters. It is not in IV.A., perhaps, but it appears often in V.B. and V.C., and indeed all throughout the earlier chapters of "Spirit," VI.A and VI.B. We can reassure our impatient reader, however, that there is indeed something new about the willing and acting subject of "Morality." Hegel tells us in the introduction to §c that we are no longer dealing with the individual self, the person who has rights and who has its being outside the ethical community. That shape of consciousness has been surpassed in the worlds of culture and faith, chapters VI.B.I. and II. We are now concerned with the self insofar as it knows itself as a universal legislator, insofar as it is a moral agent who has the power to make general laws for itself. Hegel is explicit: this is the self who knows itself as the general will (*PS* 323.27–30/M 364). Looking back over previous chapters, it is indeed noteworthy that the subject of morality has made two distinct advances over earlier stages of subjectivity. First, it is more advanced than the subject of ethical life, VI.A., "Ethical Life" (*Die Sittlichkeit*), who lived in a naive and immediate unity with its community, and who accepted its way of life on trust and faith; the new modern subject of morality is beyond this because it asks questions and demands to know the reasons for laws and customs. Second, it is also more advanced than the subject of absolute freedom, VI.B., who thinks that freedom is nothing more than doing whatever one wants, and who attempts to throw off all constraint of the law; the new subject of morality gets beyond this immature stage too, because it sees freedom as living and acting according to laws. Moral self-consciousness realizes that freedom is possible only through a society governed by laws, which impose restraints on one's wants. Its chief problem is not recognizing the validity of law, still less determining what the law is, but how to live by the law and how to apply it to specific situations.

All Hegelian concepts, by their very nature, integrate universality and particularity, substantiality and subjectivity.[2] Morality, as one phase of spirit, is no exception. It consists in a specific form or shape of that unity as it appears in spirit: it is spirit in the extreme of its particularity and subjectivity. The moment of universality and substantiality are never lost sight of in morality; but they are the lesser and dependent moments, which are dominated by particularity and subjectivity. True unity is one where both moments are given equal weight, where both are coordinate parts in a wider whole. However, in the beginning of "Morality," only the philosopher knows about this unity. Moral self-consciousness, the subject who is undergoing the experience described in VI.C., has only the vaguest intuition of it; it stumbles and fumbles in the dark, struggling to find and formulate it. Moral self-consciousness is no longer stuck in a stage of alienation, where it sees nature and the community as something hostile to itself; it wants to overcome this alienation, to achieve some living connection with nature and the community. Nevertheless, it insists that it have that unity on its own terms; it demands to be the dominant partner, to be the independent and essential moment while nature and the community are dependent upon it. In accord with this strategy, it thinks that its own self-awareness, the depths of its own subjectivity, provides a sufficient basis to reconstruct and rebuild its bonds with the community and nature. The hard and bitter experience of moral self-consciousness throughout Chapter VI.C. will be that this is not possible. Subjectivity on its own cannot be the basis to recreate the entire world, whether that is the moral order of the cosmos or the structure of the community.

"Morality," Chapter VI.C, is divided into three sections: "a. The Moral Worldview"; "b. Dissemblance"; and "c. Conscience. The Beautiful Soul, Evil and its Forgiveness." We will attempt a summary of the chief arguments of each section. To reproduce the subtlety and depth of Hegel's arguments is the task for a treatise.[3]

2 The Moral Worldview

The first section of "Morality," §a or "The Moral Worldview," is primarily a critique of the moral worldview of Kant and Fichte. The background of Hegel's discussion is Kant's theory of the highest good in the *Critique of Practical Reason* and Fichte's theory of morality in the *Vocation of Man*. Hegel never mentions Kant and Fichte explicitly in this section; but the description he gives of the moral worldview corresponds perfectly to their doctrines. This does not mean that §a is *entirely* or *only* a disguised polemic against Kant and Fichte. We have good reason to take seriously Hegel's claim that Kant and Fichte are representatives of a more general attitude toward the world characteristic of modernity. This attitude is characterized by three basic beliefs: that the highest value, and the ultimate authority, in life consists in morality rather than art or religion; that morality appears in individual reason and conscience and not in the laws and ethos of the community; and that nature is not an end in itself but exists only for the sake of moral action. Such an attitude is the result of several fundamental historical developments, discussed in earlier sections of the *Phenomenology*. First, the separation of the modern individual from the traditional community, such that the individual trusts his or her own judgment before that of law and custom; second, the secularization of the Enlightenment, which gives natural reason greater authority than any form of religious revelation, whether it be tradition, scripture, or inspiration; third, the dualism between self and nature characteristic of modern philosophy, which appears in Descartes, Leibniz, Kant, and Fichte. According to this dualism, the self is a *res cogitans* while nature is a *res extensa* or "mechanism" consisting in "dead matter."

In the very first paragraph of §a Hegel expounds the foundation of the moral worldview. His first sentence declares that, "self-consciousness knows duty as the absolute being" (*PS* 324.30/M 365). He further states that it is bound *only* by duty, and that this is "its own pure consciousness." Much here depends on what Hegel means by duty as "the absolute being" for moral self-consciousness. The phrase is very rich and the basis for much subsequent argument. Duty is "the absolute being" for moral self-consciousness in several senses: (1) it gives primacy to duty over inclination and self-interest; (2) it makes moral duty a higher authority than the laws of state and the customs of society; (3) it knows its existence as a moral agent through the moral law, which serves as proof for its own spontaneous activity; (4) it believes in the existence of God and the immortality of the soul because it is a moral duty, and not because of any metaphysical proofs or theoretical demonstrations; and (5) it sees nature only as a means for the realization of moral ends. All these propositions are characteristic of the moral worldview outlined by Kant in his second *Critique* and by Fichte in his *Vocation of Man*.

Still in the first paragraph of §a, Hegel expounds another fundamental feature of the moral worldview. He states that moral self-consciousness involves a moment of "mediation and negativity" (*Vermittlung und Negativität*), i.e., it relates to something not itself or outside itself (*ein Anderssein*). Moral self-consciousness therefore also involves a moment of consciousness (*Bewußtsein*), the awareness of an object distinct from the subject (like all stages of self-awareness in the *Phenomenology*). This stage of consciousness consists in the complete independence of subject and object; one could exist without the other and each obeys its own distinct set of laws. Moral self-consciousness looks upon the world as something alien and indifferent to itself. What Hegel has in mind here is the dualism between the moral self and nature enshrined in the Kantian–Fichtean worldview. However critical they were of the Cartesian legacy, Kant and Fichte had inherited, and indeed refined, the Cartesian dualism between self and nature: they endorsed an essentially mechanical view of nature, and they placed the moral subject beyond nature in a self-sufficient noumenal realm.

We might well ask why moral self-consciousness consists in a movement of consciousness at all. Why does it not just stay inside its moral realm and limit itself to self-awareness of the moral law? Indeed, did not Hegel already state that moral self-consciousness reaches truth within itself, and that it had overcome all forms of consciousness? Though Hegel is not so explicit, the background assumption is that the moral subject, to prove the absoluteness of its duty, must *act* in the external world or in the realm of nature. After all, the moral worldview is not simply a *contemplative* but a *practical* standpoint: it tells the agent what it *ought* to do, so that it *must* act. But if it acts, it must act in the world, it must set foot into nature. The necessity of acting in the world, rather than just contemplating it, is a fundamental trope of the *Phenomenology* – it has already appeared in "Mastery and Servitude" (IV.A) and "Skepticism" (IV.B) – and it will indeed reappear in Chapter C. of "Spirit."

The second paragraph of §a is no less fundamental for the whole argument (*PS* 325/M 265–6). Hegel now explicitly introduces the concept of "the moral worldview," which forms the section title. He states that it consists in the *relationship* between two moments: (a) "the *moral* being in and for itself" (*moralischen An- und Fürsichseins*) and (b) "the *natural* being in and for itself" (*natürlichen An- und Fürsichseins*). The purport of these obscure phrases is not hard to fathom: that the moral and natural realms are independent of one another. Hegel is simply referring to the independence of the moral and natural realm that he has already introduced in the first paragraph. But now we are told more precisely in what the relationship between these moments consists. This relationship has two aspects: it consists in the *indifference* and *independence* of morality and nature, but also in the dominance and priority of morality over nature, and therefore in the *dependence* and *inessentiality* of nature. After introducing these aspects, Hegel, in the final sentence of the paragraph, makes a statement portentous for the whole argument to come in §a. He declares that the dialectic of the moral worldview consists in "the development of the moments involved in this relation having such contradictory presuppositions." What are these contradictory presuppositions? As we shall see, they are many, and they will become clear as the dialectic unfolds. But their general form is already apparent: nature is both independent and dependent upon morality; it is both its equal and its subordinate. Or, conversely, morality is both independent and dependent upon nature; it is both its superior and its equal.[4]

Much of the subsequent argument in §a explains the various forms of this general contradiction. Since nature assumes different forms, the conflict between morality and nature differs accordingly. Already in the third paragraph of §a (*PS* 325/M 366), Hegel introduces the first and chief form of the conflict. Here nature stands for the cosmos, the whole realm of things outside moral self-consciousness.

We have already seen that moral self-consciousness regards nature as an independent realm, as indifferent to its ideals and ends; whether it realizes them depends on its own efforts alone. Now, however, Hegel stresses a new aspect about the independence and indifference of nature: that it is completely contingent whether a good moral agent achieves personal happiness in this life; no matter how strictly he follows his duty, there is no guarantee that it will make him happy; indeed, it is perfectly possible for a wicked person to prosper. We must compare this modern view of nature with the traditional Christian view, according to which the cosmos is a moral realm, governed by divine providence, which ensures that the virtuous are rewarded and the vicious punished, whether in this life or the next. Hegel's account of the modern moral worldview here embodies two fundamental Kantian–Fichtean principles: (1) that morality demands we fulfill its precepts unconditionally, regardless of the consequences, least of all any that would make us happy; and (2) that happiness belongs to the realm of nature, because it involves pleasure and personal desires and needs. These facts together mean that there is a completely *contingent* connection between morality and happiness: a happy person is not necessarily moral, a moral person is not necessarily happy. That there is such a contingent connection was a central premise of Kant's argument for the highest good in the second *Critique* (*CPrR* 5:114–19).

In the last sentence of the third paragraph, and in the first sentence of the fourth (*PS* 325.34–326.2/M 366), Hegel makes a final comment about this tragic contingency: that it gives rise to complaints about the injustice of the world. Although the moral self-consciousness believes in the primacy of duty, it still cannot reconcile itself to the fact that the just suffer while the wicked prosper. For all the importance it gives to morality, the moral subject cannot renounce its claim to personal happiness. Although its higher self insists on the principles of morality, its lower individual self still claims satisfaction. We are reminded here of Kant's critique of stoicism in the second *Critique*: that the pleasure of doing our duty is never enough, that the stoic does not recognize the importance of "personal happiness" and fails to heed "the needs of our own nature" (*CPrR* 5:127). Now we see emerging one form of the contradiction inherent in the moral worldview: that the moral self-consciousness proclaims complete independence from nature, the absolute supremacy of duty over the promptings of nature; yet it also wants nature to bring it personal happiness, to satisfy its natural needs. It holds the cosmos to be an indifferent amoral mechanical realm; but it also wants it to be governed by laws of justice that reward the virtuous and punish the vicious.

How does moral self-consciousness resolve this contradiction? Hegel sketches its response at the end of the fourth paragraph. It resorts to the standard Kantian practice of reformulating a constitutive principle in regulative terms. Rather than asserting the constitutive principle that there *is* a moral world order, it adopts the regulative principle that there *ought* to be one. "The harmony of morality and nature," as Hegel puts it, "is *thought* as necessarily existing, or it is *postulated*. For *demanding* expresses that something is thought as existing that is still not real . . ." (*PS* 326.19–24/M 367). What Hegel has in mind here is the Kantian–Fichtean ideal of the highest good, which demands that the moral subject should strive to bring into existence the perfect correspondence between virtue and happiness. This Kantian–Fichtean ideal reaffirms the old Christian conception of justice according to which the just are rewarded and the vicious punished; but it reinstates it as a goal of action rather than as a belief about a cosmic order that already exists.

Having explained the first form of the conflict between morality and nature, Hegel immediately introduces the second in the fifth paragraph (*PS* 326–7/M 367–9). Now we learn that nature is no longer something external to the moral subject, the object outside its consciousness, but that it is part of the moral subject itself. Nature is now the moral subject's *sensibility*, which appears in the shape of its drives and inclinations. These drives and inclinations are individual, Hegel writes, because they concern my *personal* happiness, what I like or need as just this determinate creature; they stand in stark contrast with the universal principles of morality, which demand that I act in a manner that would hold for everyone alike in a similar situation. Notoriously, the drives and inclinations of sensibility are indeed often at odds with the principles of morality: they often give rise to temptations that undermine moral principles; and these principles often demand that we repress our drives and inclinations.

We can now see the second form of the conflict between morality and nature. Morality both requires and forbids the opposition between reason and sensibility. It *requires* the opposition because the moral law has a point only if we have a sensibility that might not act according to it; the Categorical Imperative, as Kant taught, has no meaning for angels who are never tempted to violate it. But morality also *forbids* the opposition because it demands that we become morally perfect agents, who act morally *from* inclination, and who are not subject to the temptations to act on desires and inclinations contrary to the moral law. To resolve this contradiction, morality again resorts to a postulate: it makes the ideal of moral perfection into a goal that we should approach through infinite striving. While in reality there exists the conflict between morality and sensibility, in principle this conflict should be overcome through the infinite striving to control our sensibility and bring it under rational restraints.

The third form of the conflict between morality and nature, which is introduced in the next paragraphs (*PS* 328–9/M 369–70), is that between the moral law in general and specific duties. Nature now takes the form of the multiplicity of duties, the various kinds of content for the moral law. These belong to the realm of nature because, following Kant and Fichte, the content or object of morality must be something given in possible experience, which is co-extensive with the realm of nature. We now see a new contradiction between morality and nature where the main terms are the pure principle of morality and the multiplicity of specific duties. The pure principle of morality here is nothing less than Kant's Categorical Imperative: that we should act on that maxim that we could will as a universal law of nature. The Categorical Imperative is, as Kant argued in the *Groundwork* (4:416; cf. *CPrR* 5:27–28), essentially the form of the law, and as such it is inherently indifferent to content; in principle anything could instantiate it. But at the same time it requires some content: for moral action to be possible, we must act according to a specific maxim, and we must have some end to our action. Hence the pure principle of duty both excludes and requires content. Once again morality is both independent of nature – in the form of the law in general or in its pure universality – and dependent on nature – in the form of having to act according to specific actions and to have a specific end.

In his discussion of the third conflict Hegel introduces a distinction between two levels of consciousness, which will play an important role in the argument to come. There is an empirical consciousness that works in our ordinary experience, and for whom arise all the needs for action in the normal world. There is also a higher level of consciousness that concerns itself with the pure form of the moral law and the demands of pure duty. Although Hegel does not introduce the terminology, the distinction would be familiar to any student of Kant or Fichte: it is the distinction between the empirical and the transcendental standpoint. The transcendental level of consciousness acts as the moral law giver, and it subjects to approval or disapproval all the specific ends or goals of empirical consciousness. Hegel introduces a new factor into this distinction when he refers to "a lord and ruler of the world" (*ein Herr und Beherrscher der Welt*), who ensures the harmony between morality and nature and who blesses the multiplicity of specific duties (*PS* 329.22–23/M 370). We can detect here the Kantian–Fichtean God whose essential function is to ensure the harmony between morality and nature of the highest good. It seems to be an extraordinary jump from the transcendental to the divine; but here Hegel was only reflecting a train of reasoning that was already explicit in Fichte, and would have been very familiar to him. In his *Lectures on the Vocation of the Scholar* Fichte (*FSW* 6:310) would argue that the ideal of a pure morality culminates in the idea of God, for pure morality demands that we extinguish all our finite individual natures and become completely one.

3 Dissemblance and Displacement

Section §b, "Dissemblance" or "Displacement" (*Die Verstellung*), continues Hegel's discussion of the Kantian–Fichtean moral worldview. Whereas §a is more an exposition of this worldview, §b is a critique of it. Hegel had already formulated the main contradictions affecting this worldview in §a; but he did not claim that they are inescapable, and he did not explain them in detail. The dialectic of §b goes a stage further because it criticizes the attempt in §a to resolve these contradictions. Its explicit subject is the three postulates by which moral consciousness tried to resolve the contradictions between morality and nature. Hegel now argues that these postulates do not work and that the contradictions are indeed inescapable.

The title of §b, "*Die Verstellung*," is remarkable and has been the source of much commentary. "*Verstellung*" is the substantive of the verb "*verstellen*," which is very ambiguous. "*Verstellen*" can mean to displace something, and so to alter or change it from its appropriate place; it can also mean to disguise or conceal something, so that it has the connotation of deception. Miller translates the title as "Dissemblance or Duplicity," whereas Robinson has used "Displacement."

Both translations are correct; Hegel means the term in both senses. As all Hegel students quickly learn from the case of "*aufheben,*" Hegel cherished the ambiguities of German. What Hegel means in any specific passage, however, has to be determined by its context. Hegel himself explains what he means by *Verstellung* in this chapter. The moral worldview is a "complete nest of contradictions," he writes, misquoting Kant.[5] To avoid them it shifts back and forth, first claiming that one term is essential and then its opposite. In so doing, it deceives itself, and attempts to deceive its listener, because it thinks that it has avoided contradiction when it really has not. Toward the end of §b Hegel introduces another variation of the dissemblance motive: hypocrisy.

Just as in §a, Hegel begins §b with an explanation of the chief contradiction that afflicts moral consciousness (*PS* 332/M 374). All the contradictions in §b will be variations on this main contradiction. Hegel talks at first rather opaquely about moral consciousness creating its object, and then this object lying beyond its powers. His point becomes clearer when we place it within the context of the Kantian–Fichtean moral theory. The object here is nothing less than the ideal of the moral world order, the postulate of the highest good, as it appears in Kant and Fichte. On the one hand, moral consciousness is supposed to create the moral world order, which should be only the product of its activity. After all, the moral world order is not an object of faith, as in traditional Christianity, but a goal for our action, an ideal that we create in this life and attempt to realize here and now. On the other hand, however, moral consciousness also sees this moral world order as something beyond its powers, as an object lying far off in "a foggy distance." This is because the highest good is also an ideal that we can approach, but never attain, through a process of infinite striving. No matter how much we strive to realize this goal, it will forever elude our grasp. The postulate of the highest good is therefore stricken with contradiction: it should be something immanent, a paradise on earth, but it turns out to be transcendent, a heaven beyond it.

Hegel starts by discussing the first postulate of moral consciousness, the harmony of morality and nature in the highest good (*PS* 333/M 374–5). The heart of his first objection against this postulate is that it is self-defeating or self-destructive: if we were to act on it, we would destroy what we intend to create. The first postulate demands that we act to realize the highest good, that we strive to bring it into existence. There ought *to be*, it proclaims, complete harmony between morality and nature where happiness is received in direct proportion to virtue. Nevertheless, this postulate also presupposes that we do *not* realize it, because if we were to do so, we would destroy its status as an ideal. Rather than being perfect and ideal, it would be rendered imperfect and defective by being drawn into the realm of nature (*PS* 337/M 379–80). While the highest good demands a complete harmony between morality and nature, it also assumes that there be some disharmony between them; for it demands that we strive, and there would be nothing to strive for if there were nothing to strive against. The disharmony is the necessary incentive and challenge to moral action.

As if this were not enough, Hegel makes a second objection against the first postulate (*PS* 333–4/M 375–6). Moral consciousness demands that the ideal of the highest good be realized through moral action. The moral ideal is universal and necessary because it is prescribed by pure reason; but moral action is particular and contingent because it takes place within the natural world. Yet the moral action is supposed to realize the moral ideal, to bring it into existence in this world. How is this possible? Behind Hegel's argument here it is possible to detect the classical dilemma afflicting Plato's theory of forms. On the one hand, the world of forms is opposed to the world of sense because it is eternal and universal while everything in the world of sense is transient and particular; on the other hand, the world of forms is supposed to be the structure of the sensible world, so that sense is supposed to be the appearance of the forms. The same dilemma arises for the ideal world of morality and the particular actions that should realize it. For morality is universal, eternal, and perfect; and the actions that should realize it are particular, transient, and imperfect. Hegel captures the tension between the high demands of morality and the imperfections of action when he writes: "Because the universal best ought to be realized, nothing good is done" (*PS* 334.6–7/M 375–6). Morality, as the champion of the best, is the enemy of the good.

After battering the first postulate, Hegel turns against the second, the harmony of reason and sensibility within a person (*PS* 335/M 377–8). Moral consciousness lays down the strict and pure demands of duty, which require that we act for the sake of duty alone, and that we therefore repress all motives of sensibility. The highest ideal of morality is the holy will, where we would act immediately and necessarily according to moral precepts without any of the temptations of desire or hesitations of feeling. Nevertheless, morality cannot completely annihilate sensibility because its needs and feelings are the media of its actions. We never act from purely moral motives, but also because of our needs and desires. Insofar as morality is to be an effective force in the world, it must adopt and adapt the needs and feelings of sensibility as incentives for its actions. As Kant himself acknowledges in the second *Critique*, we are not only purely rational beings, but also sensible ones, who have a right to demand personal happiness, and he ultimately admits that human beings can only act on mixed motives (*CPrR* 5:25, cf. *Rel.* 6:7 note 36).

Finally, toward the end of the chapter, Hegel begins his assault on the third postulate (*PS* 337/M 380). Moral self-consciousness first proclaims that only the moral law in its purity – the pure form of the law – is the essence of morality. It lays down the ideal of a moral legislator, who determines the worth of the content of maxims by their suitability according to the pure form of the law, i.e., its universalizability. But at the same time morality requires some content, some specific end for action; as it stands on its own separated from all content and ends, it would be nothing more than an empty abstraction, the pure form of universality without the demand that we do anything specific or act for any end (*PS* 338/M 381). But as soon as morality adopts some end, takes on some content, it complicates its simplicity, it sullies its purity, it tarnishes its perfection (*PS* 339/M 381–2). In this predicament a variant of the general contradiction surfaces that Hegel had already stated in the beginning of §a. Morality, in its pure formality, claimed to be purely autonomous, the source of all moral laws; but in having some content, some object for its actions, it becomes dependent upon something outside itself. Hence, impossibly, morality is both independent of and dependent upon nature.

4 Conscience

Section §c marks a new beginning for moral consciousness (*PS* 340–1/M 383–4). It now attempts to formulate a new position to avoid "the nest of contradictions" that afflicted the moral worldview in section §b. These contradictions arose from the tension between the transcendental realm of morality and the empirical world, between the pure ideal of morality and the needs for action in daily life. To avoid these contradictions, consciousness now refuses to place morality in any transcendental realm, and it rejects any dualism between duty and action. It now retires into itself, and it seeks to find morality within itself alone. What is crucial now is not the self in its universality and necessity – that would be the transcendental self again, from which we are now trying to retreat – but the self in all its particularity and contingency. We are now trying to find the source of morality within the individual self, the self who exists in this empirical world in all its contingency, concreteness, and individuality. Morality, placed within the individual himself, is nothing less than conscience (*Gewissen*). Conscience manifests itself as personal conviction (*Ueberzeugung*), in the immediate certainty that what I do is right (*PS* 343/M 386–7). The connotation of certainty associated with conscience is virtually tautological in German: "*das Gewissen*" tells me "*was gewiss ist.*"

In the beginning of §c Hegel gives us a general retrospective view of the progress of consciousness so far (*PS* 341/M 384–5). The self of conscience, he says, is "the third self" to emerge out of the world of spirit. The first self is that of the ethical world; this is "the *person*" whose existence consists in recognition (*Anerkanntsein*). The person has its identity entirely in the community, of which it is only a part. The second self is that of "*absolute freedom,*" which breaks apart the bond that held the person to the community; individual and universal now oppose one another, so that the community becomes a mere object to the individual. Plainly, these earlier selves are extremes: while the first self lacks individuality, the second lacks universality. The self of conscience has neither of these shortcomings: it is the individual who has the universal within itself. With conscience we reach a new synthesis of the moments of individuality and universality that eluded earlier stages of consciousness.

The great step forward for moral consciousness with conscience is that it has overcome the separation between pure duty and moral action (*PS* 342/M 385). That was a gap between the realms of universality and particularity; and that gap is now bridged in our new synthesis of the universal and particular. Now that the third self returns into itself and finds duty in the voice of personal conviction, it does not have to consult some transcendental standard and then see how it applies to some particular case. There is no need anymore for "the testing fuss with duty" (*das prüfende Rütteln an der Pflicht*), as Hegel puts it (*PS* 343.12/M 385–6).[6] Conscience directly examines each case on its own merits; it directly sees circumstances in all their particularity, and from that alone it determines how to act. It knows from its own immediate awareness, from its infallible intuition and personal conviction, what it ought to do in any particular situation.

It is important to understand that universality still operates in the realm of conscience. Prima facie one might think that there are no general moral principles for conscience, which acts according to the demands of each case, and which has renounced the pure duty of the moral worldview. Indeed, Hegel likens conscience to "Sense Certainty" in Chapter A.I., which notoriously operates with pure intuitions and no concepts at all (*PS* 342/M 385–6). Conscience simply seems to be the moral form of the immediacy of sense certainty. Nevertheless, Hegel is very explicit that there *are* universal principles involved in conscience, and that it still abides by general principles of duty (*PS* 344/M 387–8). The important point is to see *how* these universal principles work in conscience. They are no longer standards to which the individual self must conform; rather, they must conform to the convictions of the individual self. As Hegel now puts it: ". . . it is now the law that is for the sake of the self, not that law for whose sake the self is" (*PS* 344.15–18/M 387). Universal principles are simply the expressions of individual conviction. Hegel formulates the new attitude toward universality in more technical language: duty is for conscience no longer something *in itself*, as if it were an object outside it to which it must conform, but it is also now something *for itself*, appropriated and internalized by the individual (*PS* 344.18–20/M 387).

With conscience it seems that we have left behind Kantian–Fichtean moral theory. After all, Kant warned against making conscience into the criterion of morality. Yet if Kant drops from view, Fichte is still very much in Hegel's sights. The language he uses to describe conscience, and the specific views he attributes to it, are very much those of Fichte in his *Das System der Sittenlehre* (1798; *The System of the Doctrine of Duties*), a work Hegel knew all too well.[7] In his *Doctrine of Duties* Fichte had made conscience into his fundamental criterion of morality.[8] Conscience was for him not the source of the moral law as such, which came from reason, but the means to ascertain how the moral law applied in particular cases. Conscience was the crucial mediating term between universal principle and particular cases, the means by which we determined how a general law worked in a specific case. It was therefore the source of all specific duties. Just as Hegel indicates, Fichte stressed the immediate certainty of conscience, and described it in terms of conviction and intuition.

For all its advances over early stages, conscience too has its weaknesses, its inner contradictions. The synthesis of the universal and particular within conscience soon falls apart, so that the moments of universality and particularity oppose one another in a way similar to that in the moral worldview (*PS* 346/M 389–90). Conscience claims to treat each particular case on its own merits, to know it in all its determinacy; but insofar as it also makes claims to universality, it cannot treat each case as utterly unique, as it pretends to do; for universality demands finding respects in which cases are similar to one another. The price of universality is abstraction, which removes us from the unique determinacy of circumstance. So conscience has to admit there is never a perfect fit between particular and universal. But this is only the beginning of its problems. For the more it examines particular cases, the more it scrutinizes them in all their determinacy, the more it finds them immensely complicated: ". . . this reality is a plurality of circumstances, which infinitely extends and divides itself in all directions, backwards into its conditions, sidewards in its connections, and forwards in its consequences" (*PS* 346.15–17/M 389). But the more complicated these circumstances prove to be, the more difficult it is for conscience to derive a single moral duty from them. It finds rather that it can extract a plurality of duties, each of them equal candidates for "the right thing to do," each of them as intuitively plausible as the other; but then we are left bereft of any criterion to choose between them (*PS* 346/M 390). To illustrate this, Hegel assumes that we are in imminent danger. If we choose to stand and fight, we are courageous and stand for our principles, which is admirable; but we also endanger ourselves and jeopardize our responsibilities to others. If we choose to run away, we are cowardly, which is contemptible; but at least we do not endanger ourselves and neglect our other responsibilities. Conscience could declare either course of action as correct, and so it cannot be a means to choose between them (*PS* 347/M 391–2). From this indeterminacy of conscience Hegel draws a damning conclusion: "This *pure* conviction is as such as empty as pure *duty*; it is pure in the sense that nothing is in it; there is no determinate content that is duty" (*PS* 346.34–36/M 390). Clearly, despite all our struggles, we are now back at the stage of the moral standpoint: the universal is purely abstract, having no specific content; the realms of universality and particularity stand as far apart from one another as ever (*PS* 350/M 394).

The indifference of conscience toward any specific content means that there is nothing preventing it from turning into arbitrariness and anarchy. What matters most to conscience is its own personal self-determination; something is right for it because, and only because, it wants or chooses it. "In its power of self-certainty," Hegel writes, "it has the majesty of absolute autarchy, the power to bind and absolve" (*PS* 349.26/M 393). This is clearly no basis for forming a community or state. Since conscience is indifferent to any content, there is no guarantee that one person will agree with another (*PS* 350/M 390–1). There is now even a problem in communicating with one another. Just as sense certainty lapsed into silence when asked to identify its immediate intuitions, so conscience becomes mute in the face of the demand to justify its convictions. The question "Why do you believe this?" makes no sense for conscience, because there is no higher tribunal than inner conviction (*PS* 351–2/M 395–7).[9]

5 The Beautiful Soul

The dialectical development of conscience in §c eventually leads to a new shape of moral consciousness: *moral genius* (*PS* 352–3/M 397). This shape arises when moral consciousness attempts to make a virtue out of its greatest weakness: its failure to provide specific content or definite duties. Conscience still sees itself as the source of the law; but now it thinks that it is a great strength that it need not bind itself to any specific law. Since something is the law only if conscience decides it is the law, and since it is not bound to any specific law, conscience regards its powers as divine. Like Luther's or Calvin's God, whatever it decides to be right and good is right and good just because it decides it is so. Since its voice is divine, it is the edict of genius. The moral genius does not simply subconsciously behave this way, but it self-consciously celebrates it. Turning inward, it makes a cult out of itself. It is now nothing less than "divine service within itself" (*der Gottesdienst in sich selbst*). In short, moral genius is the narcissism of the moral standpoint.

Though deeply self-centered, the moral genius still enters into a community with others (*PS* 353/M 397–8). But it is a special kind of community, one that separates itself from the corruption of the ordinary political world. This is a community devoted to the cultivation of moral purity and virtue, where everyone can be entirely honest with one another, and where everyone is sensitive to the needs of others. Since each person is a genius, if he only sheds the corruptions of ordinary society, a spirit of equality prevails. Such a society is a kind of secular monastery, though now the God to which it is devoted is the inner self.

Before he develops the inner contradictions of the moral genius and its community, Hegel informs us from his philosophical standpoint where its ultimate failure lies: it lacks all power to externalize itself in the world (*PS* 354–5/M 399–400). Since it regards any form of life or action in the world as a source of contamination and corruption, it retreats into itself and paralyzes itself. There is nothing that it can do, and so it becomes sunk in its "self-centered powerlessness." Clearly, this is the extreme of subjectivity, a self completely withdrawn into itself and refusing to act or participate in the life of the world. Hegel regards it as the inverse of the unhappy consciousness of IV.B. The unhappy consciousness felt utterly powerless because it placed all the meaning and purpose of life *outside* itself in a God who had forsaken the earth; but the moral genius feels utterly powerless too for the opposite reason: it has placed all meaning and purpose in life *inside* itself. Hegel introduces a redolent term to describe the consciousness who suffers this affliction: *the beautiful soul* (*schöne Seele*; *PS* 355.5/M 400). Because of its unhappiness, Hegel tells us, this pure and transparent beautiful soul "vanishes like a shapeless vapor that dissolves into thin air."

Who was this beautiful soul? What was Hegel talking about? The concept has several meanings, and it had a long and complex history in German culture. Hegel had already discussed the concept in some of his earlier manuscripts, especially *The Spirit of Christianity and Its Fate* (1798). Here we cannot begin to discuss this history, not even Hegel's earlier treatment of the theme.[10] Our concern is simply whom, if anyone in particular, Hegel had in mind in chapter VI.C.c. of the *Phenomenology*. The question is not of purely historical interest, because identifying Hegel's interlocutor will help us to reconstruct and appreciate his argument.

The standard assumption in most commentaries is that Hegel is attacking the Romantics, especially Novalis, Schleiermacher, Friedrich Schlegel, and even his old friend Hölderlin.[11] There is some external evidence for this view: in his *Lectures on the History of Philosophy* Hegel describes Novalis and Schlegel in terms very similar to the beautiful soul in the *Phenomenology* (MM 20:415–18/H&S 3:507). They are accused of taking Fichte's subjectivism to a radical extreme, and of making cults out of their own egos; indeed, at one point Hegel even describes Novalis as a beautiful soul (ibid.). However, there are serious problems with this interpretation. There is too great a discrepancy between Hegel's account of the beautiful soul in the *Phenomenology* and actual Romantic attitudes and doctrines. The Romantics did not adhere to an ethics of conscience; they did not preach separation from public life; and they did not hold a theory of genius, which is more characteristic of the *Sturm und Drang*. What is behind the common interpretation of Hegel's concept of the beautiful soul – it is necessary to say – is a very shopworn and stereotypical account of Romanticism, which scarcely fits historical reality. Since Hegel himself traded in these stereotypes, it is still possible that he had the Romantics in mind after all. But if that is the case, it is necessary to admit that his critique misfires entirely, directed against little more than a monster of his own making.

We need not make this assumption, however, if we consider other more likely sources for Hegel's reflections. One of these is Book VI of Goethe's *Wilhelm Meisters Lehrjahre*, "The Confessions of a Beautiful Soul." Goethe's treatment and diagnosis of the beautiful soul anticipates Hegel's chapter in many respects: in its suspicions about moral purity, in its criticisms of withdrawal from the world, and in its belief in the necessity of self-limitation (cf. *PR* §13Z). Another plausible source is Rousseau's account of the life of the beautiful soul in *Julie, or the New Heloise*. There is a remarkable similarity between Hegel's account of the beautiful soul and the main characters in Rousseau's novel, Wolmar, Julie, and Saint-Preux. They are guided entirely by their moral feelings; they believe utterly in their moral purity; they attempt to seclude themselves from society by forming their own moral community where complete honesty and openness prevail. Last but not least, their community fails for reasons very like those Hegel discusses in the *Phenomenology*: they are all victims of hypocrisy.

Hypocrisy is indeed the fatal flaw of the beautiful soul. The beautiful soul retreats from the world into the life of his small community because he does not want to compromise and corrupt himself. Rousseau recommended such an experiment in living because natural sentiments, the source of all virtue, are corrupted by general society. But the problem is that, even in this small community, the beautiful soul has to compromise his moral principles. The beautiful soul wants to lead a life that is completely honest, open, and authentic, and he wants to do away with all the dishonesty, repression, and conformity of society. For this reason he chooses to live only among his friends in a secluded community. But Wolmar, Julie, and Saint-Preux constantly find that, even among themselves, they have to conceal their convictions, repress their feelings, and embellish their opinions, if they are not to offend one another or embarrass themselves. They still claim to follow principles of openness, honesty, and authenticity; but they do not comply with them in their everyday life. In other words, they are hypocrites. Thus the beautiful soul fails by its own standards. It demands honesty, openness, and authenticity; yet its hypocrisy is nothing less than *self*-deception.

The closing paragraphs of section §c consist in Hegel's description of a dispute between the beautiful soul and common moral consciousness (*PS* 355–62/M

401–9). Each accuses the other of evil. The common moral consciousness stresses the necessity of acting in everyday life, and the need to do our duty; it charges the beautiful soul of a complete lack of responsibility because, rather than fulfilling its duties, it attempts to escape from them entirely into its own inner domain. For its part, the beautiful soul thinks that the common moral consciousness is evil because, in surrendering to the demands of everyday life, it is compelled to forfeit ideals of moral integrity. The principle of morality demands that we do duty for its own sake alone; but if we examine the real motives for actions in ordinary life, we find that their real motives are profit, power, and honor (*PS* 358/M 403–4). No man is a hero to his valet, the beautiful soul reminds us.

Hegel thinks that there is truth on both sides of this dispute. Common consciousness is right to insist that we have to act in the world; but it fails to see that the motives for our actions are indeed often selfish. The beautiful soul is right to think that the motives for our ordinary actions are selfish; but it is blind to the need to act in the world. The solution to the dispute comes when each side admits its failings, pardons the other, and recognizes that it is no better than the other. The common moral consciousness admits that there are selfish motives behind its ordinary actions; it confesses about evil: "I'm the one!" (*Ich bins*) (*PS* 359.24/M 405). While it admits that no man is a hero to his valet, it also insists that the problem lies more with the valet than the hero, because a man can still do great deeds even if our motives are sometimes selfish. The beautiful soul recognizes the necessity of acting in the world; and it admits that its insistence on purity and integrity is only a kind of vanity and *amour-propre* all its own. It now sees that it is no better than the common moral consciousness.

After admitting their failures and forgiving one another, both sides re-enter life in a community based on mutual self-respect. Although they recognize the self-interest behind human actions, this does not undermine, Hegel thinks, the possibility of a life based on mutual respect of the equal rights of others. Through mutual respect each side recognizes itself in and through the other; the self sees itself in the other as the other sees itself in the self. Hence we witness the restoration of spirit, the I that is We, the We that is I, but now on a deeper level than ever before. The act of mutual reconciliation and recognition among moral judges *is*, Hegel claims, the advent of absolute spirit (*PS* 361.22–5/M 408).[12] Since there is reconciliation and forgiveness, all wounds have been cured. And, just as Hegel promised, a little miracle has happened: there are no scars.

Notes

1 Hegel's Table of Contents appears in outline form above, p. 28. – *Ed.*
2 See above, pp. 9–10, 14–16, 23–24, 53–58, 92–116 *passim*. – *Ed.*
3 See Further Reading, below, p. 225. – *Ed.*
4 Hegel's examination of this contradiction and its implications in "Morality" continues themes first announced in "Self-Alienated Spirit: Culture," though they recall the second part of "Self-Consciousness." See above, chapters 3, 6, 8, and 9. – *Ed.*

5 Hegel refers to a passage in which Kant refers to "*ein ganzes Nest von dialektischen Anmaßungen*" (*CPR* B637), "a whole nest of dialectical presumptions."
6 Cf. above, chapter 7. – Ed.
7 He referred to the work constantly in his *Differenzschrift*, see *GW* 4:49–62.
8 Fichte, *System der Sittenlehre* §15 (*FSW* 4:163–70).
9 This recalls Hegel's paraphrase in his Introduction from Sextus, "one bare assurance counts as much as another" (*PS* 55.18–24/M 49), the struggle for a monopoly on constitutive authority which generates Lord and Bondsmanship, as well as the stand-off between Antigone and Creon; see *infra*, pp. 2–3, 25–26, 37–53 *passim*, 60–64, 178–80, 229–30, 239–40. – Ed.
10 For a good account of its meaning in the eighteenth century, see Norton (1995).
11 See, e.g., Harris (1997, 2:478–508), Pinkard (1994, 207–21), Lauer (1993, 253–7), and Taylor (1975, 193–6).
12 Cf. *infra*, pp. 25–26, 229–30. – Ed.

References

Harris, H. S. (1997) *Hegel's Ladder*, 2 vols. Cambridge, Mass.: Hackett Publishing Co.
Lauer, Q. (1993) *A Reading of Hegel's Phenomenology of Spirit*. New York: Fordham University Press.
Norton, R. (1995) *The Beautiful Soul: Aesthetic Morality in the Eighteenth Century*. Ithaca, NY: Cornell University Press.
Pinkard, T. (1994) *Hegel's Phenomenology: the Sociality of Reason*. Cambridge: Cambridge University Press.
Taylor, C. (1975) *Hegel*. Cambridge: Cambridge University Press.

Further Reading

Brinkman, K. (2003) "Hegel on Forgiveness," in A. Denker and M. Vater (eds.), *Hegel's Phenomenology of Spirit* (pp. 243–64). Amherst, NY: Humanity Books.
Gram, M. (1978) "Moral and Literary Ideals in Hegel's Critique of 'the Moral World-View'," *Clio* 7.3: 375–402.
Harris, H. S. (1997) *Hegel's Ladder II: The Odyssey of Spirit* (pp. 413–520). Cambridge, Mass.: Hackett Publishing Co.
Robinson, J. (1997) *Duty and Hypocrisy in Hegel's Phenomenology of Mind*. Toronto: University of Toronto Press.
Westphal, K. R. (1991) "Hegel's Critique of Kant's Moral World View," *Philosophical Topics* 19.2: 133–76.
Westphal, K. R. (2009) "Urteilskraft, gegenseitige Anerkennung und rationale Rechtfertigung," in H.-D. Klein (ed.), *Ethik als prima philosophia?* Würzburg: Königshausen & Neumann.

11

Religion, History, and Spirit in Hegel's *Phenomenology of Spirit*

George di Giovanni

But we are not considering here God for himself, as natural theology does, but God inseparate from the knowledge of him in religion, and hence we only have to demonstrate that religion exists. (Lectures on the Philosophy of Religion, 1831, Vorlesungen 3:353)

Dear Henriette, no word can say how I feel! Loudly could I – and would *I – confess before the whole world that I am the guiltiest among all men . . .*
What in me now lies so dead against my own self . . . is the same hard, unbending, pride . . . I shall learn humility; I shall be yours . . . Oh, do accept me! (F. H. Jacobi, Woldemar [Werke, 5:461, 476])

Spirit, in absolute certainty of itself, is master over every deed and actuality; it can cast them off and make them as never happened. (Hegel, Phenomenology of Spirit, PS 360.8–9)

Forgive our trespasses, as we forgive those who trespass against us. (Matthew 6.12)

1 Hegel and Religion

We are concerned in this essay with the experience of religion in the *Phenomenology*, or, more precisely, with the concept of religion which *we* (the philosophers) construct on the basis of that experience. Religion is the theme of Chapter VII, and there the transition is made to the concept of absolute knowledge which is the object of the concluding Chapter VIII. But the phenomenon of religion has in fact been present from the beginning, and we already witness it in full-blown form at the end of Chapter VI, in an experience which we might call 'thanksgiving', where 'confession' and 'forgiveness' play a central role. 'Confession' and 'forgiveness' entail a special social compact. Just why this compact is essentially religious, and why *we* (the philosophers) should be able to reflect on religion as such, and then move on to absolute knowledge, only after a community based on it has made its appearance, is precisely the point which we must consider. Before all else, however, it is important to be clear about a number of terms.[1]

Glaube, i.e. 'faith' (or 'belief' as the word is often translated into English) is normally associated with religion both in Hegel's language and in common parlance. But the meaning of the two is not identical, and Hegel often plays on their distinction (e.g., *PS* 266.31–34/M 297). Kant had already insisted on the distinction. Religion is always associated with cult, with some form of ritual. In the Christian tradition, it is essentially an *agere gratias*, a work of 'thanksgiving' which bonds a community together – just as *agere bellum* is a work of waging war, which in its way also brings a community together. Faith, on the contrary, entails some view or other of the universe which has direct consequence on the human situation and therefore precipitates the kind of active communal response to it that we see in cult.[2] In this broad sense, faith is theoretical in nature. Kant had no difficulty accepting a form of it; he even deemed it necessary to moral life, provided that it was based on practical reason and had the fulfillment of the law as its ultimate scope (*CPrR*, Ak 5:126). But Kant rejected all forms of cult, which he found intrinsically superstitious and, at best, a sop thrown at the poor of moral heart (*Rel.*, 6:168–170). The only cult that he accepted was moral praxis – and that was, of course, not 'cult' in any strict sense. Hegel, on the contrary, recognized the celebratory nature of cult and its social significance from very early on (*GW* 5:505, Fragments 88, 89). Religious practices are essentially an expression of the practical judgment of a community defining how each member stands with respect to all the rest. It is "the speech of the community about its spirit" (*PS* 353.34–35/ M 398), as Hegel puts it; it is knowledge about itself which is concrete and intuitive. However broadly this speech might have to be construed to embrace all cases, it reflects in each the judgment that establishes a community in the first instance. It also provides, therefore, the concrete context for discharging the moral obligations that arise within it. Religion is the celebration of precisely a community's founding judgment. Though itself a practical act, it presupposes some sort of theoretical commitment as to what constitutes human existence. This theoretical commitment is faith – with which, therefore, religion is always associated.

However, it is important to take faith in as broad a meaning as possible. According to its long-established English as well as German meaning, the term is used in contrast to 'reason'. Inasmuch as any statement of faith is necessarily made in dogmatic form (take the Nicene Creed as an example, "I believe in God, the Father almighty, creator of heaven and earth," etc.), it does indeed convey at least the impression that it offers an explanatory account of the existence and the nature of things, and this account might well be in competition with the explanation that science offers on the base of 'reason alone'. This at least apparent competition has been, and still is, the source of many conflicts between the believer and the scientist, between the authority of the Church or the Bible and that of reason. But such competition could not have, and still cannot have, any place in a culture in which reason has not yet achieved the kind of reflective awareness and autonomy of practice that it has in the modern world. For Antigone, to believe in the power of the spirit of her departed but still unburied brother was not a matter of taking a stand against science (though it was a matter of taking a stand against reason as embodied in the law of the state), but of submitting to the way things are as accepted by everyone from time immemorial, the fathers of the state included. No conflict was possible between faith and reason. The conflict only arose when reason began in modern times to claim for itself explanatory hegemony. Yet the conflict *had* to arise. This is a point that must be stressed. Explanation necessarily tends to completion; it is hegemonic by nature whether it comes, once the distinction between science and faith has been made, from the one side or the other. The many compromises between the two which were attempted in the tradition of *fides quærens intellectum* were bound to fail, as they did indeed at the time of the Enlightenment.

Now, Hegel himself thought that faith is itself a product of reason. The Enlightenment conflict between the two was in fact a family feud in which faith, despite the advantage that it had over the formalism of the new science due to the human richness of its representations, was nonetheless bound to lose by the very fact that it had entered into discourse with science. It had thereby subjected itself to critical self-reflection, and this exposed its own rationality (*PS* 295–6, 310.1–3/M 331–2, 348). But philosophy is more for Hegel than just explanatory knowledge. It is *Wissen* and not just *Erkennen*: 'wisdom', not just 'cognition'. And in the *Logic* this wisdom culminates in the 'idea of the idea', i.e. the full comprehension of the idealizing process by which thought appropriates for itself what would otherwise be just 'being' (or, in more concrete language, merely 'given nature') by turning it into a universe of meaningful intentions. Philosophy is for Hegel a matter of self-knowledge, of clarity about one's position in nature. But if religion is essential to human existence both as cult and faith, what form would these have to assume in a culture in which the sciences are the only repository of explanation and action is performed in the full apprehension of what it means to be spirit in nature? This question is just as pressing now as it was in Hegel's time. And it might well be that Hegel's supposed answer has traditionally been the object of radically different interpretations because he, in fact, never gave a definite one. He was not in a position of giving one, for the times did not allow it. They did not allow it then just as they still do not allow it now. We shall nonetheless return to the question at the very conclusion. For the moment, it only serves to motivate our way across the *Phenomenology*.

2 The Experience of Religion

2.1 Spirit and nature

I have stressed the existential character of religion and have already associated it with nature. The warrants for these moves are in Hegel. We are told at the beginning of Chapter VII that religion is the completion (*die Vollendung*) of spirit, in the sense that it is the consciousness that spirit has of itself as the absolute essence from which all the determinate forms in which it has appeared so far, and which Hegel now passes in review (consciousness, self-consciousness, reason, and spirit), originate and into which they return (*PS* 363–364.32, 366.9–13/M 409–12, 413). Religion, in other words, is a phenomenon of spirit as concrete individual. As such, it was necessarily present from the beginning as the still unspoken yet unifying substrate of all the experiences that we (the phenomenologists) have been examining so far one by one. It already made its appearance in these experiences, as Hegel now reminds us, but in forms that are conditioned by the abstractness of such experiences and as phenomena fall, so to speak, on the side of other phenomena as just one among many. Now is the time to consider it precisely as it is for itself, as the awareness that spirit had of itself from the beginning, though only implicitly (*PS* 366.14–367.26, 108.34–35/M 414–15, 110). One should not make the mistake at this point of hypostasizing spirit, as if it were some sort of cosmic personality – though that is precisely what faith does in the medium of its imaginary content. In the context of the *Phenomenology*, any such move would relapse into the standpoint of some misguided natural theology. The self-awareness of spirit at issue here is that of individuals who know themselves to be the members of a special kind of community, as we shall see. More to the point, rather, is that spirit's self-awareness is an *achievement*: spirit acquires historical reality only as engaged in nature and as transcending it. It is there, in its transactions with nature, that it suffers dispersion and is faced by the existential problems which inspire religious practices. These practices are just as unavoidable as is spirit's engagement with nature. Hegel notes that religion is absent in consciousness as 'Reason', i.e. in Chapter V, presumably because in the consciousness examined in that chapter the self assumes the attitude that is typical of science (whether rationalistic or empiricist). It distances itself from its own subjectivity – it becomes, in other words, a sort of disembodied observer or investigator for whom there can arise (*officially*, that is) no existential problem and therefore also no religion (cf. *PS* 363.17–20, 249.13–15). Nonetheless, although religion is the phenomenon that would most graphically manifest the historical 'self' which is the object of the *Phenomenology*, *we* (the phenomenologists) turn official attention to it only now, in Chapter VII, because only now, by virtue of the experience gained both by the consciousness being observed in the *Phenomenology* and by us who observe it, is the necessary concept at hand for comprehending its essence.

What is this concept? Or, more to the point, what is the experience that leads up to it? In the concluding section of Chapter VI, just before the final experience of thanksgiving which officially introduces the theme of religion, Hegel depicts a conflict which he describes with language that brings us back to the battle of prestige in Chapter IV (*PS* 344.33–35/M 388). In the course of that earlier battle self-consciousness, and with it the first profile of a 'self', made its appearance (*PS* 109ff./M 111ff.).[3] Prestige was the issue then. In Chapter VI, however, the conflict concerns opposing claims to truth which individuals advance on the exclusive testimony of their private (hence naturally conditioned) conscience in absolute certainty of their truth (*PS* 343.19–39/M 386–7). This is a conflict in which to the eye of any of the contestants the claim of any other must necessarily appear not only objectively false, but advanced on subjectively perverse grounds (*PS* 350.1–31/M 394). In alluding to the original battle of prestige, it is as if Hegel wanted to lift and expose to view the whole range of experiences that went on between the two battles – bracketed by the two, as it were. For the two battles are extreme paradigmatic instances of the human situation, namely, that it is impossible for anyone to assert a value as one's own absolutely, thus raise oneself to the status of spirit, without at the same time asserting it from some singular natural standpoint, in effect, without investing the value with an accidental content which necessarily put it at odds with other values just as absolutely asserted from equally singular standpoints.[4] In the original battle of prestige there was no question of 'evil', for there was not enough of a reflective self to make the advance of a private desire to universal status a matter of pride. Prestige is not necessarily pride. But pride, the biblical root of all evils, is at issue in the final conflict, and evil is the ultimate threat to communal life. Hegel overcomes it at the very end of Chapter VI by invoking the language of confession and forgiveness. We shall return to it. Only then, on the strength of this language which marks the transition from *agere bellum* to *agere gratias*, is a first community of concrete individuals bound together in their very individuality forged. Such a community is typically religious in nature. How did it emerge out of the original battle? Or again, what are the elements in the experiences bridging the two battles which connect conflict with religiosity, and thus make possible the transition from 'warfare' to 'thanksgiving' or the first coming to explicit self-consciousness of the religious community?

2.2 The enchanting of nature: religious attitudes

The passage in the *Phenomenology* depicting the first battle is one of the best known in the book. A conscious organism attains self-consciousness and consequently at least the beginning of selfhood in an act of reciprocal recognition with another such conscious organism. Each becomes conscious of itself in being conscious that it is the object of the other's consciousness, and that this other is itself conscious of being the object of another's consciousness (*PS* 110.1–16/M 111–12). But why *must* this act of mutual recognition take the form of a conflict, and why *must* it arise, that is, cannot be just an accident of nature? The answer is the same for both questions, namely, because through some process which is itself the product of nature, the two organisms in question have acquired the capacity to conceptualize (cf. *PS* 110.35–112.2/M 113). For to conceptualize means to abstract, and to abstract means in turn that whatever particular object each organism might happen to desire at any moment for even the most natural motives comes to be perceived as only one possible such object, the desire for it as only one possible such desire, so that in desiring any object, the desiring of it, rather than just the object itself, becomes the primary issue. Why one desires 'this' rather than 'that' (even if the 'this' were to be, physically speaking, the only option available) requires justification. In other words, what would have otherwise been just the natural desire for a thing now becomes (in principle at least) a claim to it. It is a desire which the organism, now become a subject of discourse, is ready to stand by. But a claim has no purchase except in a universe of claims and counterclaims within which what counts most for the validity of the claim is precisely that it command recognition. And prestige is, in its rawest form, the satisfaction derived from this recognition. That it should be wrested only by way of a battle, and that such a battle should necessarily occur (that is, that human history necessarily begins in conflict) follows from the fact that nature, once desires are made infinite by conceptualization, becomes necessarily a scarce quantity. I mean to say: one cannot claim to be entitled to either 'this' or 'that' indifferently, and to 'this' just as much as to 'that', and demand that the claim be conceded by someone else equally entitled to the same, without the 'this' or 'that' becoming too small a place for the two claimants to occupy at once. Their presumed equal claims cannot be pressed on that same ground without mutual interference, for each claim is in principle a claim to the whole ground. Natural animals might indeed avoid strife if they just happen to have sufficient space to share; conceptual ones cannot, for they are constitutionally responsible for making their space insufficient. Of course, limits can be established. But a limit has meaning precisely inasmuch as it staves off either actual or threatened conflict – a conflict which is presupposed. And it is only in a situation of inevitable conflict, as different individuals constitutionally tend to occupy the same space, that a true meeting (and not just an accidental aggregation) of such individuals occurs. Society for Hegel does not begin in love (though it should and might culminate there) but in strife.

Note how Hegel succeeds in the just outlined paradigm to introduce a moment of transcendence with respect to nature while at the same time retaining continuity with it. On the one hand, through the power of abstractive conceptualization an otherwise purely natural organism gains distance from its own natural past by seeing itself determined, not just by what happens to be the case but by what (conceptually) might be the case, and thus as answerable in deciding what will be the case *for it* to others in the same situation. On the other hand, its acquired abstractive capacity is itself the product of nature (a new organic complexity), and whatever course of action it might now undertake in virtue of it has ineliminable natural consequences. One cannot engage in battle to wrest recognition from the other without risking one's life, that is, without risking putting an end to the whole human project (*PS* 112.3–18/M 114–15). This risk makes the business of recognition existentially serious and not just a game of claims. One is answerable to the other while being at the same time answerable to nature. The two orders of answerability are indivisible, the one continuous with the other. To be sure, Hegel is an idealist. It is because of the abstractive power of conceptualization that nature (to use an expression now in vogue) becomes enchanted; or, in other words, assumes for us typically human significance. One engages in the battle of prestige in dread of the natural consequences the battle might have. And this dread is not just an animal fear of death, but a fear rather of what nature might have in store for us because, in forging ways that transcend it (by making prestige rather than satiety one's leading concern), we are tempting it – daring its anonymous power as it were. Nature assumes the figure of a hidden enemy because we make it to be so.

The ultimate risk that nature presents at the end of Chapter VI is that of sin, not because nature is evil – in itself, as Kant knew, nature is innocent (*Rel.* 6.34–35) – but because spirit tempts it by absolutizing the moment of singularity of conscience which depends on it. The risk now is of spiritual death, for the ensuing conflict may undercut the possibility of the mutual recognition which constitutes the life of spirit. The flowering of the religious community is the response to this risk, and religious praxis had indeed been in general, from the beginning, spirit's response to the anonymous power of enchanted nature. But it was a long way that spirit had to traverse, and many the attitudes that it had to assume with respect to this nature, before that final flowering. We can enumerate them: resignation, dissatisfaction, unhappiness, self-satisfaction, guilt – each attitude associated, as we must now see, with a different form of religious praxis.

2.3 The pathos of resignation

There is no question of religion in Hegel's mythical reconstruction of the primordial battle of prestige, unless we take the ritualization of such battles as took place before the walls of Troy in epic times as itself a form of cult, and the combatants' belief that in waging their battle they were in fact involved in a conflict between gods as its theoretical counterpart. But precisely in the ethos of such an epic society Hegel finds a first objectification of the dread that spirit experiences before nature in transcending it, i.e. in positing itself as spirit (*PS* 363.21–33, cf. 255–56/M 410–11, 283–5). On the one hand, there is the anonymous power of a now much enchanted nature, a sort of cosmic justice (δίκη) which regulates the order of all things and regularly causes the actions of individual human beings to come to grief. On the other hand, there are these actions themselves. They are the products of particular natural desires, which are raised to the status of deliberate choices by virtue of conceptualization and which, since they are at once particular and yet universalizing in intention, necessarily tend to upset the universal order of things. In this, they inevitably call for redress at the hand of δίκη. Each side constitutes a judgment – the universal judgment of δίκη which fails to accommodate the particularity of the actions upon which it is passed and therefore redresses the disorder they cause simply by undoing them; and the self-judgment which a particular action entails by being deliberate and therefore, precisely for that reason, by setting itself up against the universal order of things. Of course, both judgments are the two aspects of one judgment for which the epic individual is in fact responsible. It is a judgment that fails to reconcile the particularity of nature with the universality of spirit (*PS* 252.15–34/M 280). *We* know this; the epic individual does not. He cannot act, therefore, without perceiving his actions as overtaken by a greater order which in fact, though unintentionally, they upset. Nature threatens him in the universalized shape of δίκη, as a Fate before which only the pathos of resignation (the first of the attitudes just listed) is possible. Thus it is that Oedipus, undertaking a perfectly legitimate course of action ('legitimate' from his individual standpoint) finds himself acting out a larger plot which he had no part in scripting. And, for this, he is justly made to suffer (*PS* 256.1/ M 284).

Religious cult intervenes to redeem through celebratory acts what would otherwise be mere suffering. There is of course the cult of the gods of heaven, the city titular gods which represent reason such as has attained reflective awareness in a particular community and has been enshrined in its laws. But these gods are themselves subject to the rule of δίκη. More to the point is the care with which the family, by means of due funerary rites, humanizes (hence redeems) the otherwise merely biological event of the death of its departed members (*PS* 242–5/M 267–72). These members attain in death the only universal significance they can have as singular, natural individuals, namely by joining the family's *penates*. As such, now part of the underworld, they are still capable of influencing the living by bringing the dark forces of that world to wreak vengeance upon those who offend it. These forces represent the anonymous, unconscious, still unrationalized side of the same nature which has otherwise assumed the abstract figure of δίκη – the side by which the latter exercises its control over those in the thrall of its enchantment. In the world of epic culture, the cult of this power is assigned to the female members of the family who, for this reason, because they stand at the point of intersection of spirit and nature, are the ones most apt to effect a new creative rearrangement of the two. So it is that, as the well-known story goes, Antigone buries the body of her brother in open disregard of the king's prohibition. She does it, indeed, in reverential fear of the shadows of the underworld as would any female member of the family, but this time in the name of laws which she perceives to be above all laws, just as universal as δίκη:

> They are not of yesterday or today, but everlasting,
> Though where they came from, none of us can tell.
> (Sophocles, *Antigone*;
> *PS* 236.10–11, cf. 381:23–27)

Here we have the first reconciliation of universal and individual judgment which issues into a first explicit 'self'. Antigone, being female, belongs to the cult of the underworld. However, by deliberately contravening the law of the city, which is the voice of explicit reason, she has stepped into the realm of the latter, and now, with a universality of claim typical of reason's voice but in the name of a departed individual, she proclaims an obligation which is as pervasive as the power of δίκη. The latter is thereby transformed into the law of reason – its judgment no longer the redressing of an anonymous cosmic order but an indictment of delinquent actions, an act *by* individuals and *for* individuals.

The subject of this law is the 'legal self', the first of the three 'selves' (the self of culture and the self of conscience being the other two) that Hegel lists in a summary in Chapter VI (*PS* 341.17–342.3/M 384–5). Its voice is the one that Antigone heard. Since it spoke her particular language but was heard by her as coming from time immemorial, it already was the voice of an individual conscience.

But it was a conscience still ignorant of itself *as conscience*. The distance that separates Antigone from the final religious community is precisely the one which conscience must traverse before attaining self-comprehension. For that, the other two selves must appear on the scene.

2.4 Dissatisfaction and unhappiness

Historically speaking, the world of the legal self is that of the Roman Empire. The governing form of judgment in this world is the product of a formalism of reason, in the sense that individuals stand under it, indeed explicitly as 'selves', but in abstraction from the demands of their naturally determined individuality. They are legally empowered individuals, *they are personae granted various rights and privileges*, but, paradoxically, anonymous as persons. In this respect, the power that judgment wields over them is not unlike that of δίκη, except that it no longer lies shrouded in the unconscious but is exercised in the full light of day. The 'self' in which it is embodied as source of authority appears, therefore, like a mighty Lord of the World – one who speaks in rational human voice but, like a blind cosmic force, is impervious to individual needs. The net effect of its rational judgment is in fact to disrupt otherwise customary, natural-like ways of doing things, and thus to unleash in the world, paradoxically again, irrational forces hitherto held in check by accepted mores (*PS* 260–3/M 290–3).

The point to be grasped about this world, in order to understand the transition to the subsequent one of culture, is that the individuals who constitute it, though legally empowered, feel and act *essentially* nonetheless like slaves. They know that the world they operate within is *their* world, the product of a reason which is everyone's reason. They have freedom, but theirs is a freedom which undermines the reality of the world in which they have actual existence. The Stoics and the Skeptics knew this – the Stoics implicitly, the Skeptics explicitly. They did so as intellectuals, cerebrally, though many of them might have succeeded in translating their cosmic theories and their dialectical practices into a lifestyle of peaceful detachment from the harsh vicissitudes of life. The very fact that they needed detachment, however, was itself witness to the underlying dissatisfaction which they felt, not as thinkers perhaps, but certainly as human individuals. I choose the word 'dissatisfaction', the second of our listed attitudes, with care. This is not a matter of 'unhappiness', not at least as in Hegel's 'unhappy consciousness' (about which more in a moment). There is no alienation here, and none of the unhappiness associated with it, because the world in which the legal individuals live is the only one that exists for them. It is *their* world, and the dissatisfaction is due to their feeling that in this, *their* world, they are constrained and even dehumanized by the very self that empowers them (*PS* 121.23–39/M 126). One can understand, therefore, how the longing for a reconciliation between universal self and individual self, a 'breaking of the heart' on the part of the former (an expression about which also more in due time), would take root in this world, and why the belief would gain ground among the crowds that the Lord of the

World has assumed a body like everybody's body, and has thereby invested with a new dignity even the most natural aspects of the human individual, including the suffering and death which in the ethical world were left to the female care of the family:

> That absolute spirit has given itself the shape of self-consciousness, has given it *in itself* and therefore also for its *consciousness* – this now takes on the appearance of a *faith on the part of the world* that spirit *is present* as a self-consciousness, i.e. as an actual human being; that the believing consciousness has an immediate certainty of spirit, that it *sees* and *feels* and *hears* this divinity. *In consciousness* this appearance is not imagination but *actual*. (*PS* 404.33–405.1/M 459)

This is of course a rendition of the Christian belief in the incarnation of God. But Hegel is not doing biblical exegesis. He is rather systematically chronicling the new meanings that nature assumes, and the new possibilities made available for human action, as the work of the concept in enchanting nature becomes ever more explicitly aware of itself.

The Lord of the World had de facto already spiritualized nature by destroying whatever nature-like social arrangement existed there. His work was one of destruction, but not any the less spiritual because of that. Now culture (*Bildung*) is the process by which the already spiritual nature of this work is made explicit and its effectiveness turned into something positive. The world of culture is one in which the presently dispersed spiritual forces reorder themselves, thus creating for an otherwise still abstract spirit a visible substance (*PS* 264.10–265.4/M 294–5). It is as if, in this world, individuals *deliberately* set about enchanting nature. Of course, historically speaking, they did not see themselves in this role. *We* do. What they did, in point of fact, was to harness again all the irrational forces that the legal self had let loose by sacramentalizing every aspect of both nature and society, i.e. by interpreting all things as tokens of a glorified world yet to come. 'Faith' now comes on the scene, because the new rearrangement of universality and singularity played out in the belief of the incarnation of God is expressed in narrative form, in an imaginary medium which is alien to reason as such. So does 'alienation', because the world which faith now holds out as the true home of humankind is in fact impenetrable to reason and, by contrast, the present one takes on the aspect of an alien place, its dwellers strangers in a strange land. And with alienation there also comes 'unhappiness', the third in our list of religious attitudes. This unhappiness is not a dissatisfaction. On the contrary, there is satisfaction now in the certainty that the vocation of humankind is a glorified nature. But this satisfaction has still nothing actual to show for itself to justify it – and therein lies the unhappiness. Now, the work of overcoming this unhappiness – in effect, of bringing the transcendent world of faith to this world here, so that there will be one world again, just as there was in the state of legality but with a satisfaction now not present then – is the work of the self of culture (*PS* 265.4–266.23/M 295–6). Hegel reflects on the religious practices characteristic of this world at the end of Chapter IV, brilliantly summing up in a few pages the whole development of Western spirituality, from the *ora et labora* of the early Middle Ages Benedictines to the *ad majorem gloriam Dei* of the post-Reformation Jesuits (*PS* 122–31/M 126–38).[5] More to the point for us, to see how the explicit self of conscience arises, is the development in Chapter VI of the social arrangements with which those practices were associated.

2.5 Self-satisfaction

Because of the alienated nature of this world of culture, its structure is fraught with internal divisions (*PS* 266.26–267.5/M 296–7). On the one hand, the work that brings it into existence is directed at its transcendent element. The laborers in this field are the priests and the philosophers. Theirs is basically a work of reason governed by an overarching insight into the rationality of all things. But this insight still remains at the level of principle alone, it is still incapable of translating itself into a concrete picture of the universe and is, therefore, just as empty as it is all-comprehensive. Faith steps in to make up for the emptiness by filling it with the imagery of the glorified world-beyond. Here is where the distinction (and the possible conflict) between faith and reason becomes institutionalized. On the other hand, there is the field of day-to-day praxis, where the here-and-now is the object and the laborers are power brokers of sundry kinds (*PS* 268.18–35/M 298–9). Here too, however, the pull of the transcendent is not to be missed, and the laborers therefore divide into two classes: those for whom power means service to the state for the welfare of all – those, in other words, who apparently act not for selfish purposes but by rising above the highly particularized needs of nature – and those who, on the contrary, openly seek wealth for the sake of satisfying precisely these needs. These last are the ones who provide for the ideals of service a concrete content – not unlike what the priests do for the reason of the philosophers, except that in their case this content is actual (*PS* 270.10ff./M 301ff.).

Now the process by which the world of culture attains its culmination and at the same time dissolution is one by which these distinctions intrude on each other and finally collapse. They *have* to collapse, because they are all the alienated expressions of the one truth which motivates their world – namely that God is with us, and spiritual transcendence is to be sought, therefore, nowhere except in the naturally conditioned particularities of the here-and-now. Hegel chronicles this process in an account which is just as conceptually brilliant as it is historically surprisingly accurate. On the one hand, there is rational insight which, in its efforts to find itself realized in nature, develops into an actual science of nature in general and of natural human behavior in particular. Hegel considers this work independently in Chapter V, only to retrieve its results in Chapter VI, at the very point where the whole world of culture is ready to collapse.[6] Here is where reason, having ranged over nature and society, confronts faith in open conflict. This is a conflict which faith is predetermined to lose because, as we have already said, in arguing with science it exposes its own rationality (di Giovanni 1995, 66). On the other hand, in the sphere of praxis, the laborers in the fields of service and wealth define and redefine themselves in the medium of different social languages

– the former, in order to come clear on what constitutes legitimate authority in a society (in effect, in order to define the meaning of 'service'); the latter, in order to come to terms with their discomfort about being dedicated to the satisfaction of present natural needs, thus to justify their status in society. This also is a distinction that cannot be maintained. One cannot work at the service of the state without at the same time gaining in wealth and thereby satisfying purely natural needs. And one cannot work at amassing wealth without thereby also promoting the wealth of the whole society; in fact, therefore, doing work of service. The various languages that are devised at different times in order to institutionalize the distinction finally give place to the language of the *philosophes*, one in which all differences are relativized and any value is shown to be equally its opposite (*PS* 283.17–33/M 317).

Short of retrenching into blind faith, the cultured individual of the late Enlightenment has no choice at this point but to indulge either in the smug satisfaction of dissolving everything which is said into its opposite, or the equally smug satisfaction of the philosophers, now the new secular theologians, for whom everything in the universe is as good as it can possibly be (cf. *PS* 310.35–36/M 349). This attitude (our fourth) might appear to be a return to classical Skepticism and Stoicism. In fact, it is something totally different. For the self which is its carrier is the successor to the self of unhappy consciousness, the same who set the whole process of culture in motion. And the reason which is now presumed to pervade the world is nothing abstract, but is the successor to the Christian God, the personal God whose knowledge extends even to the hairs on one's head. The satisfaction of this new self is one that calls for a new world – not, however, a transcendent world as at the beginning of culture, but a social one *here and now* that would make visible the pervasiveness of precisely this divine reason. The philosophers have already objectified it in the idea of a cosmos where nothing happens that does not contribute to the perfection of the whole. There is no religious faith in this world, but there certainly is a religion. It is the religion of universal reason. Hegel calls it the religion of the useful, in the sense that everything and anything has meaning only as an instrument of the whole (*PS* 305.24–35, 314.8ff./M 343, 353ff.). Translated into social terms, the same idea becomes the project of a society in which each member wills as *his* individual good the good of the whole (*PS* 14–26/M 6–18). Since action necessarily implicates the individual *as* individual, thus as necessarily opposed to the universal, it is clear in this society that everyone is in principle a threat to the whole, every course of political action ultimately a betrayal of the common good (*PS* 319.18–320.33/M 359–60). The individual, therefore, fulfills his vocation as a member of the community by acknowledging that, upon acting, he has thus committed a crime, and that there is no redress for it except his own annihilation as individual. The individual must call for his own punishment. The Fate which visited the tragic Greek hero as an impersonal force is now the explicit judgment of a society. Historically speaking, this is the society created by the French Revolution. Its cult is the work of the guillotine, which is the practical counterpart of the cerebral fluidity induced by the language of the *philosophes*.

2.6 Guilt and forgiveness: the religious community

I said earlier that in the conflict between reason and faith, the latter had to lose. But there is a sense in which the reason that shaped the world of culture had also already lost. The point is that this reason was instinctively realist. Like the characters of the ethical world, the self of culture still depicted events and situations which are in fact conceptual and social achievements in objective terms, as if on a grand cosmic canvas. The cult of the guillotine made abundantly clear the danger of assuming this objectifying standpoint in matters social. But the failure of enlightened reason in this respect was already brought home by Hegel at the end of Chapter V. It is impossible to construe a social universe in which a self can truly feel at home without adopting the standpoint of an agent and defining laws accordingly, i.e. without abandoning reason's objectifying standpoint of Chapter V (cf. *PS* 193.5–17/M 211). It is not by chance that Antigone, who was the first to hear the unmistakably subjective voice of conscience, makes her first appearance in the *Phenomenology* precisely at the end of this chapter (*PS* 236.10–11/M 261). Now, suppose that the self of culture finally recognizes that the order which it has so far assumed as transcending it is in fact one for which it is itself responsible, so that any antithesis between its knowledge and the truth of it is superseded (*PS* 323.25–324.4/M 364). It recognizes, that is, that such an order is one which reason, conceived now as a system of subjective activities, itself demands for the sake of its own subjective satisfaction, so that to *know* nature means in effect to recognize the extent to which the latter conforms to this subjectively determined order, and to *act* means to impose upon it values which this order generates. The result of this assumption is what Hegel calls, with obvious historical reference to Kant, the 'moral order'.

This is a crucial move in the *Phenomenology*. It might seem at first that it reinstates a two-tier vision of reality as we had at the beginning of culture, the division lying this time between 'what ought to be' and 'what is', and that it brings faith back into play in an effort to overcome precisely this division (*PS* 325.16–24/M 366). But nothing could be further from the truth. The 'here-and-now' and the 'beyond' of the world of culture shared, so to speak, a continuous space, the one being only the pilgrimage road to the other. Enlightenment reason, however, has created a new scarcity of space. Reason is the only factor in play now; its world as generated by the 'ought' is the only one with legitimate standing. That there is (as is undoubtedly the case) an empirically apprehensible nature which resists the order of the latter is a de facto situation for which there ultimately is no explanation. Nature, as *given*, assumes the character, therefore, of appearance – not 'appearance' in the sense of the manifestation of a world-beyond, but in the sense of 'mere appearance'; not in the sense of 'revealing' but of 'hiding'. Inasmuch as there are two worlds in the moral vision, the relation between the two is not one of opposition but of outright contradiction. Moral faith is introduced precisely in an effort to meet the existential difficulties encountered in the attempt to realize intentions in the context of a nature which is inherently antithetical to them. Unlike the earlier faith, it is not already knowledge, albeit 'as if through a glass darkly' (1 Cor. 13:12), for its intended object is avowedly self-contradictory. It is rather a commitment to certain beliefs for the purely pragmatic purpose of meeting an otherwise existentially impossible situation (*PS* 341.2–6/M 383; di Giovanni 2003, 379). From Hegel's standpoint, it is another way of masking the dissemblance, the shifting back and forth from the standpoint of moral obligation and natural need without ever reconciling the two, which characterizes the moral view.

This dissemblance renders truly individual agency impossible. Significantly, Hegel refers to the moral 'I' as 'speechless', and does not include it in his list of 'selves' (*PS* 351.24, 343.19–23/M 396, 386–7). This 'I' has the virtue nonetheless of forcing the self to what might appear from an enlightened point of view to be an extreme of madness, but which is in fact the only move now existentially possible. And that is to assert together, violently as it were, the two terms which in the moral view of things stand in contradiction, namely universality of value and particularity of natural content.[7] The voice of conscience now becomes the ultimate source of judgment regarding who we are and must be; the same voice that Antigone had heard has now finally come to its own. The significance of this voice is that, though *someone*'s totally contextualized voice, it carries universal authority. The individual qua individual is the repository of universal value. We are back at the beginning, but with a huge difference, for the individual now has full reflective awareness of the importance of his or her individuality. Antigone has given way to the Romantic 'moral genius', the 'beautiful soul' for whom the inner voice is the voice of God and the intuition of it the cult of God (*PS* 352.35–353.2/M 397). What ensues is a renewed battle, for we have again a conflict of natural individuals. But the contest now is not between infinite desires for nature, such desires as make nature essentially scarce, but between competing witnesses as to what counts as nature's true meaning. In a way, the conflict is still one between claims to nature as 'mine' and not 'thine'. But the 'mine' and 'thine' have now assumed the shapes of moral visions, and the threat that nature (now the battleground of these visions) holds for each contestant is that, as he or she invests natural particularities with universal significance, he or she is sinning against the universal – in effect, cutting him- or herself off from the community of humankind. Indeed, in this renewed battle of prestige, the judgment that each contestant passes on his or her opponent is that, in standing stiff-neckedly by his or her conviction, the opponent is guilty of either evil or hypocrisy (*PS* 356.7–10/M 401). As we said earlier, the threat is no longer just death, but spiritual death.

The stage is set for the flowering of the religious community. I also said earlier that religion is the concrete speech of the community about itself. This speech is the most fundamental of all, since it is about the individual as such and therefore contains all previous judgments within itself as if in a matrix. Such judgments were all attempts at resolving the conflict of universal and individual in human experience. I say 'resolving', not 'abolishing', because on Hegel's analysis this conflict is the motor of experience and as such, though hopefully creatively contained, is never abolished. At the point now reached, however, the possibility of a community of individuals self-consciously capable of evil is at issue – of individuals, in other words, taken in their extreme form of particularity, and of a community, therefore, equally taken in its extreme form of historical concreteness. It "is in world history," Hegel (1975, 43) says, "that we encounter the sum total of concrete evil." A new scarcity of space, the most extreme of all, has been created. If the power of spirit to overcome the dispersion of nature is anywhere to be manifested in concrete form, this is the place (*PS* 359.33–360.4, 362.5–10/M 406, 408–9). We also spoke earlier of the 'breaking of the hard heart' with reference to the first judgment reconciling universal and particular. It occurred as the Lord of the World, out of mercy for the human lot, became incarnate. The world of culture was the working out of this judgment. But the universal hardened again, as we have seen, first in the shape of a social order in which the individual is only the instrument of the whole; then in the shape of the moral 'I'; and now in that of individuals who invest their singularity with universal value. It is the 'hard heart' of these individuals that must now 'break' for a final reconciliation of universal and individual. This is possible, according to Hegel, on two conditions (*PS* 357.17–37, 360.31–361.10/M 403, 407). The first is that individuals must recognize that they are not just courting evil, but actually incurring it, for it is impossible for anyone to assert one's universal value starting from a very singularized natural basis without thereby infringing on someone else's equal right to do the same, i.e. without doing violence to the other. In this, they are guilty, and must confess the fact. But, in confessing their evil, individuals must equally understand that each is just as constrained by the limitation of the human situation as any other, and must therefore be ready to forgive. This is the second condition. The judgment, in other words, by virtue of which the 'hard heart' finally breaks and reconciliation is achieved is one of 'confession' and 'forgiveness'. This is not a matter of either denying or, worse still, condoning evil. In that case, the scarcity of space which makes the power of spirit manifest would be abolished and spirit would dissolve again into an abstraction. It is a matter, rather, of containing evil by recognizing that any attempt at social order, any definition of moral obligation, is necessarily the amending of wrongs already incurred and inevitably the incurring of wrongs for which amends will have to be made. In this reconciliation, in this "reconciling YEA, in which the two 'I's let go of their antithetical *existence*" (*PS* 362.25–26/M 409), the power of spirit is intuitively experienced. But now, the community of those who self-consciously have the power both to bind and to loosen sin, thus to contain its own evil without denying it, is the religious community.

3 The Concept of Religion

Religion is for Hegel not a matter of feelings (though feelings will of course accompany it just as they accompany every human activity), but of judgment – specifically, of a judgment that establishes a social compact by defining, but in the context and in the medium of actual experience, how each of its members stand with respect to every other and all of them with respect to nature. It is a judgment expressed in a given vision of the universe and in a set of cultic acts. This amounts to saying that, in the process by which spirit asserts itself over nature, religion pertains to the mediation that nature plays in it – not, of course, in the sense that nature is actively engaged in the process (by itself, nature is powerless) but in the sense that, by establishing a purposiveness which is its own over and above nature, spirit invests the latter with a new power (henceforth typically its own) as a source of unpredictability. Nature is the realm of the irrational, and religion is there to cope with it. It therefore behooves the human mortal to revere the Lord of Nature in dread, whether its power is felt as coming from below or from above, or is projected to a beyond, or is identified with reason, or is found within, according to one or other of the religious attitudes chronicled in Hegel's text. But only when the human mortal finally comes to terms with finitude, and understands that spirit creates finitude; when he or she recognizes that it is the lot of humankind to be born in sin, and that redemption comes only by acknowledging that fact – only then is dread dissolved and, just as in the scene from Jacobi's *Woldemar* on which the conclusion of Hegel's Chapter VI heavily depends, dread gives place to thanksgiving (di Giovanni 1995, 53).

We can understand, therefore, why 'religion', although an essential dimension of human experience, is officially treated only in Chapter VII, and why in that chapter Hegel repeats the phenomenal course already traversed, now exhibiting consciousness in the form of religion starting from even its simplest and most primitive of structures. At the beginning of the *Phenomenology* there was a significant disconnect between its two protagonists – the *we*, i.e., the personification of the philosophers who reflect on the phenomena of consciousness, and the phenomenal consciousness under observation (*PS* 5–7/M xxxiii–xxxv; cf. above, p. 28). Both were abstract, but for different reasons. The *we* because, though a historical figure motivated by the certainty that the absolute is with us, it has no objective evidence to justify its belief; phenomenal consciousness because, though in principle possessing the required evidence, it is not aware of it and even manages to falsify it. As the *Phenomenology* unfolds and phenomenal consciousness is forced by the *we* to become ever more aware of itself, and the *we* for its part gains ever more objective evidence for its original certitude, the gap between the two is progressively narrowed. It is de facto bridged at the end of Chapter VI, after phenomenal self-consciousness has exhibited for the *we* all the social structures which it has generated under the inspiration of the spirit which has animated it from the start. At that point, both the adequate conceptual tools and the sufficiently concrete self-awareness are at hand for the recognition by both, the *we* and phenomenal consciousness, that the historical carrier of the experiences just examined – the one of whom the *we* and phenomenal consciousness are but abstractions – is the human individual in his self-awareness as spirit. But such an awareness, as intuitive, is the stuff of religious experience. The stage is set, therefore, for a reflection on the various forms of this experience, no longer as a phenomenon accompanying others side by side, but as the fundamental experience that defines the historical human individual as such and informs all the rest.

There is nothing immediate or simple about religious experience. Hegel passes its many forms in review, drawing connections between them and the types of consciousness of which they are the defining factor. His principal interest, however, is to demonstrate that implicit in all religion is the work of conceptualization. This work marked, in the original battle of prestige, the surpassing of mere nature and the beginning of the life of spirit. The underlying theme of Chapter VII is thus the transition to Chapter VIII, where the concept is treated precisely as such. We cannot follow here Hegel's complex dialectical moves.[8] One final comment will, however, serve both as summary and conclusion. Hegel defines spirit as "the knowledge of oneself in the externalization of oneself; the being that is the movement of retaining its self-identity in its otherness" (*PS* 405.17–19/M 459). This is a knowledge, we have seen, that comes explicitly to its own in the community of those who know that they are capable of containing their own evil, but it was already present (albeit only in principle) in the original battle of prestige. The subsequent various forms of religion are all externalizations of the self as animated precisely by it. If we now abstract from such forms as belong to what Hegel calls "natural religion" and concentrate instead on those which Hegel associates with classical antiquity – where the self is exteriorized in artistic form, whether in the medium of sculpture or drama – we find that the crucial move from this religion to the one typical of the world of culture is the belief in the incarnation of God (*PS* 405.14–16/M 459). In the figure of the God-Man, the human individual finds an immediate sense both of his transcendence over nature and of his evil, and the needed comfort for an otherwise unhappy situation. Hegel's treatment of Christian dogma, whether the doctrine of the Trinity or of creation, is in this respect Christologican in character – though in an extended and even equivocal sense, because Hegel is definitely *not* an orthodox Christian. His claim that "the divine nature is the same as the human" (*PS* 406.8–9/M 460) flies in the face of the proclamations of both the Nicea and the Chalcedon Councils and would certainly have incurred Luther's worst excoriations. But the point of Hegel's treatment is to bring out the concept of spirit, which de facto, in itself and for us, is already implicit in Christian dogma but gets lost (is dispersed, so to speak) in the variety of cultic practices and symbols of faith which are the work of the imagination. The imagination insists on the division of human and divine nature and therefore forces reason to faith – whereas already by the end of Chapter VI in principle, and explicitly in Chapter VII, both the philosopher and phenomenal consciousness should *know*, though the latter only intuitively, that the true meaning of Christian faith is the concept of spirit as defined by Hegel.

Nonetheless, this dispersion of the concept in the medium of the imagination is existentially necessary for Hegel (*PS* 409.10–25/M 464). It is part of the externalization of the self by which the latter is actualized as spirit. Now, in an allegory illustrating the birth of the new religion of revelation, Hegel pictures all the gods of classical antiquity, and all the forms of consciousness characteristic of that classical world, standing around the newly incarnate God, as if witnessing his birth, still vivid in appearance but now only background figures (*PS* 402.34–403.16/M 456-7). They have been relieved of the redeeming task that they had hitherto performed, and can therefore be relegated to memory, as objects of aesthetic admiration perhaps, but no longer of vital interest. Yet in Chapter VII the allegory could be extended to the religion of the incarnate God as well, now that the *Phenomenology* has distilled the concept which animated it – has distilled, that is, the meaning of its imagery. Hence this imagery can also be relegated to memory as object of admiration, just like the gods of antiquity once were. In Chapter VII, Hegel is in fact developing the theme of the death of God which he had initiated as early as his essay on *Faith and Knowledge* (*GW* 4:413.34–414.1).

We are back to the question with which we began. Granted that religion, both as cult and faith, is for Hegel existentially necessary, what happens to it in a culture where the concept of spirit has come to full reflective light? This is not the same question as has traditionally been raised regarding Hegel and religion – namely, whether absolute knowledge replaces Christian faith or, on the contrary, is its justification. Put that way, the question either ignores the ineliminable need of the human individual of *sensing* (not just thinking) his situation as incarnate spirit, or fails to appreciate the demythologizing power of the concept. Rather, the question is about what would count as religion in a post-Christian culture, and to this Hegel has no clearly identifiable answer. Of course, many have been the religions (as a rule, either pernicious or inane) that have tried to replace the old since the time of Hegel, and there is nowadays a revival of fundamentalism. But all these developments would have been for Hegel much too reflective, in the sense of factitious or reactionary, to be genuine expressions of the human heart. One should perhaps look for such expressions in the new iconography for which the media of communication are now the vehicle – in the images of the starving child, of the Holocaust, the homeless refugee, the polluted earth – and in the trust that spirit will eventually prevail which such images evoke. But these phenomena are still too close to us to allow speculation. As is the case with all philosophy, Hegel's can help us in posing the right questions, not necessarily in answering them.

Notes

1 The literature on the subject is vast. If I hardly refer to it, it is not because I either ignore it or dismiss it, but because of editorial constraints. All translations quoted herein are my own.
2 Hegel reviews different forms of cult in Chapter VII, beginning at *PS* 382.28ff./M 432ff.
3 See above, chapter 2. – *Ed*.
4 This paradigmatic kind of conflict traces all the way back to Hegel's engagement with question-begging (*petitio principii*) and the Dilemma of the Criterion in the Introduction to the *Phenomenology*; see above, pp. 2–3, 25–26, 37–53 *passim*, 60–64, 178–80, 219–24. – *Ed*.
5 Cf. above, pp. 64–70, 190–204. – *Ed*.
6 The apparently unanimous opinion of commentators is that Chapter V has to do with idealistic (Schellingian) philosophy of nature. But this is patently false. The chapter has to do with pre-Enlightenment and Enlightenment rationalistic as well as empiricist sciences, whether of nature or of behavior, and with the self-perception of an individual who subjectively operates on the objectifying attitudes of these sciences. On this point,

see the contributions of Cinzia Ferrini in the present volume (above, chapters 4, 5. – *Ed.*).
7   *PS* 340.30–341.16, 342.11–13, 349.25–27/M 383–4, 385, 393.
8   For a detailed and accurate account, which is singularly sensitive to the theological background of Hegel's text, see Crites (1998, Part 4, Chapter 5).

References

Crites, S. (1998) *Dialectic and Gospel in the Development of Hegel's Thinking*. University Park, PA: The Pennsylvania State University Press.
di Giovanni, G. (1995) "Hegel, Jacobi, and 'Crypto-Catholicism' or Hegel in Dialogue with the Enlightenment," in A. Collins (ed.), *Hegel on the Modern World* (pp. 53–72). Albany, NY: State University of New York Press.
di Giovanni, G. (2003) "Faith without Religion, Religion without Faith: Kant and Hegel on Religion," *Journal of the History of Philosophy* 41: 365–83.
Hegel, G. W. F. (1975) *Lectures on the Philosophy of World History* (1830), tr. H. Nisbet. Cambridge: Cambridge University Press.
Hegel, G. W. F. (1983) *Vorlesungen über die Philosophie der Religion* (1831), in W. Jaeschke (ed.), *Vorlesungen*, vol. 3. Hamburg: Meiner.
Hegel, G. W. F. (1984, 1985, 1987) *Lectures on the Philosophy of Religion*, 3 vols., ed. P. C. Hodgson, tr. R. F. Brown, P. C. Hodgson, and J. M. Stewart, with the assistance of H. S. Harris. Berkeley: University of California Press; reissue: Oxford: Oxford University Press, 2006.
Hegel, G. W. F. (1998) *Jenaer Notizenbuch* (1803–1806), ed. M. Baum and K. R. Meist. *GW* 5: 483–508.
Jacobi, F. H. (1796) *Woldemar*, in J. F. Köppen and C. J. F. Roth (eds.), *Werke*, vol. 3. Leipzig: Gerhard Fleischer, 1812–25.

Further Reading

Beiser, F. C. (2005) *Hegel*, chapter 6. New York and London: Routledge.
Desmond, W., ed. (2003) *Hegel's God: A Counterfeit Double?* Aldershot: Ashgate.
Desmond, W., ed. (2004) *Philosophy and Religion in German Idealism*. Dordrecht: Kluwer.
Dickey, L. (1987) *Hegel: Religion, Economics, and the Politics of Spirit, 1770–1807*. Cambridge: Cambridge University Press.
Dickey, L. (1993) "Hegel on Religion and Philosophy," in F. Beiser (ed.), *The Cambridge Companion to Hegel* (pp. 301–47). New York: Cambridge University Press.
Fackenheim, E. (1967) *The Religious Dimension in Hegel's Thought*. Bloomington, IN: Indiana University Press.
Hodgson, P. (2005) *Hegel and Christian Theology: A Reading of the Lectures on the Philosophy of Religion*. Oxford: Oxford University Press.
Houlgate, S. (2005) *An Introduction to Hegel: Freedom, Truth, and History*, chapter 5. Oxford: Blackwell.
Jaeschke, W. (1990) *Reason in Religion: The Foundation of Hegel's Philosophy of Religion*, tr. M. Stewart and P. Hodgson. Berkeley and Los Angeles: University of California Press.
Jamos, D. (1994) *The Human Shape of God: Religion in Hegel's Phenomenology of Spirit*. New York: Paragon House.

Kolb, D., ed. (1992) *New Perspectives on Hegel's Philosophy of Religion*. Albany, NY: State University of New York Press.

Magee, G. A. (2001) *Hegel and the Hermetic Tradition*. Ithaca, NY: Cornell University Press.

O'Regan, C. (1993) *The Heterodox Hegel*. Albany, NY: State University of New York Press.

O'Regan, C. (2001–02) "The Impossibility of a Christian Reading of the *Phenomenology of Spirit*: H. S. Harris on Hegel's Liquidation of Christianity," *The Owl of Minerva* 33.1: 45–95.

Schlitt, D. M. (1990) *Divine Subjectivity: Understanding Hegel's Philosophy of Religion*. London and Toronto: Associated University Presses.

Stewart, J., ed. (1998) *The Phenomenology of Spirit Reader: Critical and Interpretive Essays*, chapters 9, 16–19. Albany, NY: State University of New York Press.

Walker, J., ed. (1991) *Thought and Faith in the Philosophy of Hegel*. Dordrecht: Kluwer.

12

Absolute Knowing

Allegra de Laurentiis

1 Introduction

Despite its formal weaknesses – both historical tumult (Napoleon's invasion of Jena) and systematic hesitations led Hegel to send to the press an atypically disorganized text – the concluding chapter of the *Phenomenology* fulfills two pivotal functions. First, it spells out a fundamental thesis underlying all previous chapters; second, it provides a transition to the envisaged and announced "part two" of the *System of Science* containing the sciences of logic, of nature, and of spirit – what would eventually become the *Encyclopedia of Philosophical Sciences*.

The fundamental thesis common to the various types of relation of consciousness to object that have been described in the course of the *Phenomenology* consists of the following general claim: thinking must fail to obtain the truth of the object it thinks so long as it fails to recognize that the fundamental dynamic structure or substance of its object is the same as its own structure or substance. This is Hegel's modern, critical version of Scholastic realism, the mediaeval, anti-nominalist reinterpretation of fundamental theses of Platonic and Aristotelian metaphysics. This is explained in some detail below; note here that for Hegel "substance" denotes a dynamic "relation of substantiality" (*SL, GW* 11:394–6; cf. above, pp. 15–24). Keeping this in mind will facilitate understanding his fundamental claim that "substantiality" must eventually be explained in terms of "subjectivity."

In this concluding chapter, Hegel formulates the connection between the experience and the conceptual grasp of "knowing" in these terms:

> [N]othing becomes *known* unless it is in *experience* . . . because experience consists precisely in the fact that the content – which is spirit – *in itself* is substance and therefore *object* of *consciousness*. But this substance that spirit is, is the latter's *becoming* what it is *in itself.* (*PS* 429.20–26/M 487)[1]

A brief clarification on Hegel's conceptions of thinking and of spirit is in order. For Hegel, "thinking" does not refer primarily to one cognitive faculty alongside perceiving, willing, desiring, and so forth. Rather it is a much broader category: it embraces "everything human" (*Enc.* §2), thus including human perception, desire, will, and action. And because thinking has always a content (it is always thinking *of* something), it is also synonymous with knowing – though not necessarily true knowing (*PS* 30.36–37/M 22–3). Having analyzed basic forms of thinking or knowing in the course of the *Phenomenology*, Hegel is now interested in finally determining the concept of thinking as "knowing of the true" (*Wissen des Wahren*) or "true knowing" in the emphatic sense (*wahrhaftes Wissen*), as announced in the Introduction:

> [In] making its appearance, science is itself an appearance,... not yet science proper... And since the present exposition has only phenomenal knowing for its object... it can... be regarded as the path of natural consciousness pressing towards true knowing... Natural consciousness will show itself to be only the concept of knowing, not real knowing.... [T]he realization of the concept counts for [natural consciousness] rather as a loss of itself; for on this path it loses its truth. (*PS* 55.12–56.5/M 48)

Determining the concept of thinking, as of anything else, means for Hegel providing its essential logical structure. Accordingly, he views the *Phenomenology* as having paved the way to a grasp of the logical structure of thinking or knowing as such.

With regard to "absolute knowing," two features that derive from Hegel's conception deserve particular attention. First, because thinking is an activity, its structure, like the structure of substance, must be a complex of relations, and the adequate concept of thinking must reflect this. Second, since "thinking" always means "thinking something," the so-called object is thought's content, that is, the object is an integral part of thinking itself.[2]

Hegel's criticism of traditional and common acceptations of "thinking" is concisely expressed in *Enc.* §20. *Das Denken*, we read there, is often taken to refer to a subject's faculty whose activity produces a plurality of thoughts or abstract universals. Thus, thinking is called the universal faculty or the activity of universalization par excellence. This is not wrong but one-sided because, just as attributes presuppose and differ from their substances, a faculty presupposes a subject whose faculty it is and from which it differs. Accordingly, the subject of thinking would have to be a subject independently of this so-called faculty. But subjectivity and thinking are for Hegel inextricably connected. For logical reasons, there cannot be a *substratum* or *hypokeimenon* for thinking that is not thinking itself. Hence, traditional substantialist conceptions either conflate thinking with one of its guises, representation (*Vorstellung*), so that the subject of thinking is pictured as having ideas like a canvas has images; or they lead to the conversion of "thinking" into a "thinker." By taking *Denken* to mean *Denkendes*, the universal activity is transformed into a singular substance. (The most immediate expression of this transubstantiation is the Cartesian "thinking thing" discussed, inter alia, in *Enc.* §64.)

Hegel's metaphysical claim about the structural identity of thinking and its object or content has radical repercussions in his theory of knowledge. Perhaps pivotal among these is Hegel's explicit reformulation of the idealistic thesis that objects of perception, understanding, or intuition owe their unity to the nature of the subject for which they are objects. Put differently: the reason why every object must be thought of as a paradoxical oneness of multiple qualities and relations that inhere in it (and without which it would not be an object at all), lies in the fact that thinking itself consists of the permanent referral of multiplicity back to oneness – an activity that representational and psychological theories of thinking refer to as "the ego."

"Spirit" is, in Hegel's use, a noun for the activity of thinking (in the comprehensive sense given above). It is a general category embracing simple or natural consciousness, self-consciousness, reason, spirit proper, and the respective forms of each. The cognitive disappointment that concludes each phase of phenomenal or "apparent" knowing in the course of Hegel's book is but a symptom of spirit's repeated failure to comprehend its structural identity with its object. Note, however, that while every form of spirit (thus also every shape of consciousness) has exhibited this failure, the meta-phenomenological thinking that has made the description possible does not. "Consciousness" is by definition a form of spirit that implies an unresolved distinction between itself and its object; it is, as Hegel says (*PS* 431.37–432.1/M 490), spirit still caught in the medium of difference. However, "we" who investigate consciousness do not and could not do so from that same perspective.

The negative performance of each shape of consciousness vis-à-vis their common goal, namely knowledge of what is true, has an overall positive effect. Each shape's inadequacy is the reason for it to evolve into the next. In the context of an analogy, strongly reminiscent of Aristotle's *De Anima*, between knowing and feeding as kinds of assimilation, in 1820 Hegel speaks of thinking as "instinct": just as lack of food does nothing to tame hunger, repeated "abstinence" from truth does not reinforce skepticism but rather stimulates "hunger and thirst for truth" (*GW* 18:43.15–26/H&S 1:17–19).

Chapter VIII now indicates a way out of the recurring inadequacies of thinking. It paves the way for the insight that truth is not volatile in principle and knowing is not reducible to its phenomenal or apparent forms. As just mentioned, however, these judgments can only be formed from a perspective that differs from that of observed consciousness. This last chapter is intended to make just this perspective explicit.

To repeat: by definition, "natural consciousness" (*PS* 55.35, 56.1/M 49) implies at all times an incongruence between itself (or the Self: *das Selbst*) and the object it experiences as "standing opposite" (*der Gegen-stand*). Knowledge of their shared structure cannot be provided by yet another shape of natural consciousness – though the emergence of that knowledge is entirely predicated upon actualizing the powers of natural consciousness, namely through the exhaustion of all its phases. The previous chapters have proven precisely that the structural identity of thinking and object cannot be sensed, perceived, nor understood (*verstanden*). Neither can it be "produced" or "intuited" as argued – in Hegel's eyes, unsuccessfully – in other idealistic systems.[3] This identity can only be grasped or comprehended (*begriffen*). It is purely conceptual and results from reflecting upon, rather than within, phenomenal consciousness. For Hegel as for Plato, comprehending or grasping differs from understanding, opining, and believing because it involves providing the logical account of what is grasped.

Thus we glimpse the intrinsic reasons for the infamous obscurity of this chapter, the one that best embodies the "unholy confusion" that, according to one of Hegel's letters to Schelling, "dominated the handling and printing process as well as, in part, the composition itself" of the book.[4] The philosophical culprit is the epistemologically hybrid status of its subject matter. On the one hand, knowledge of thought's structural identity with its object does belong to the phenomenological investigation of forms of consciousness insofar as it has been implied by them all along – a fact that also explains why it can now emerge from the investigation itself. On the other hand, knowledge of this identity cannot itself be one of the phenomenal forms because each of these implies precisely lack of identity between thought and object. Thus, the identity has to be grasped conceptually. This, however, can only be accomplished in a theory of the "pure" structure of thinking or *Science of Logic*. It will also have to be validated in a broader account of thought's many relations to its objects, that is, in a *Realphilosophie* of nature and spirit that will include a phenomenology of consciousness as one of its parts.

The subject matter of Hegel's present chapter, absolute knowing, is not a type of psychological, moral, scientistic, aesthetic, or religious cognition. The meaning and validity of each of these depend upon its respective experiential content and the separability (in principle) of this content from its corresponding mode of knowing. In other words, since knowing is a relation, all of these types of knowledge depend upon upholding the distinction between the objective (ontological) and subjective (epistemic) poles of the relation. With regards to truth, moreover, the poles are asymmetrical: either the mode of cognition is considered valid because it adapts itself to the object, or the object is called true because it is made adequate to the mode of cognition. But "absolute knowing" denotes precisely a knowing that is "unconditioned" (Latin: *ab-solutum*) by anything alien to it. There is no "absolute experience" in the sense in which there is perceptual, scientific, aesthetic, moral, or religious experience. Absolute knowing denotes an "absolute relation" in which the ground of experience and the experiencing agent are one and the same: the object known is explicitly the subject who knows.

Though not explicitly, this peculiar epistemic constellation has already surfaced at nodal points in the *Phenomenology*. It constitutes, for example, the spiritual (*geistig*) core of the production of works of art and of religious representation. More importantly for our present concern, this peculiar relation has already appeared in Chapter IV under the title "The Truth of Self-Certainty" (see above, chapter 4). The introductory paragraphs of that chapter display the kind of paradoxical formulations that are logically required by an accurate description of its subject matter, namely self-consciousness (see *PS* 103.11–16/M 104). Self-consciousness is thinking in self-relating mode, that is, thinking as simultaneous subject and object of itself. This implies a distinguishing ("dirempting" or differentiating) of thought from itself. Self-consciousness instantiates the logical configuration of identity *with* difference. Ultimately, grasping this configuration will imply grasping the category of "identity of identity and difference." Only the *Science of Logic* will make intelligible the pure concept of the identity of thought and object.

The fact that self-consciousness is already an absolute form of knowing seems to contradict the claim just made that absolute knowing cannot be a phenomenal form of consciousness. But the double nature of the "absolute relation" central to Chapter VIII is indeed already implied in Chapter IV. Self-consciousness is only improperly called a shape of phenomenal consciousness. Hegel has referred to it in Chapter IV as a radically new constellation "that did not occur in these earlier relations" (*PS* 103.12/M 104), namely in sensation, perception, and understanding. Self-consciousness is neither only an accompanying feature nor merely a condition of consciousness's relation to the object. It is already an absolute form of spirit, though "only" at the level of consciousness. While Chapter IV has described the absolute relation as a phase in *observed* consciousness's development, Chapter VIII endeavors now to explain its dynamics independently of any phenomenal manifestations. This structure (discussed below) is said by Hegel to be "syllogistic."

To investigate the dynamic structure of an object of thinking by abstracting from its temporal or developmental features, according to Hegel, is tantamount to investigating its "logic." This is analogous to the way in which we think of an inference as opposed to the psychological event of inferring: an inference is an atemporal process despite the fact that the term does refer to a flow or "movement" of thought. If, now, the object of thinking is thought itself, their dynamic structure or logic will be one and the same.

The *Phenomenology*'s last chapter both summarizes crucial aspects of the development that has led the relation of knowing to its absolute form, and provides a sketch of the logic of the absolute relation when abstracted from that development. This sketch anticipates, in other words, the logic of spirit's form as Self, whose concept (the Concept par excellence) is analyzed in detail in the Doctrine of the Concept of the *Science of Logic*. The following three sections discuss Hegel's recapitulation of spirit's movement along with his outline of spirit's logic.

2 Apparent Knowing and Its Absolute Ground

Hegel dedicates the first half of this chapter to a selective recapitulation of the general pattern of thinking described in the *Phenomenology* up to and including "manifest" or "revealed" religion. Thus, this portion of the text consists of Hegel's own summary of pivotal configurations and transitions. He runs through this summary twice (*PS* 422.29–428.15, 430.5–431.12/M 480–6, 488–90), each time highlighting two pivotal aspects of spirit, namely its logical structure and its historical existence. In both summaries, the aim is to explain the distinction as well as the connection between phenomenal knowing and the kind of knowing it ushers in: purely conceptual comprehension.

The spiritual configuration immediately preceding our chapter is that of "revealed religion" (see above, chapter 11). This expression refers to the community-forming beliefs and practices of theistic religions (principally, for Hegel, Christianity) whose object of worship is not hidden but manifested in divine–human figures and made explicit in historical events, scriptures, and dogmas.

As in its other forms, spirit as revealed religion is unable to *grasp* the true. For Hegel, "the true" in religion refers to the actual object of faith and worship beyond its manifold physical and symbolic representations. Furthermore, Protestantism, the form of revealed religion most congenial to the spirit of modernity, also expresses a radical form of spirit's alienation. In Protestantism, consciousness takes itself to be the highest tribunal in ethical matters, all the while proclaiming its complete dependence upon the divine will. The task of philosophy is to overcome these kinds of religious antitheses or "schisms" of spirit: inborn sinfulness versus sanctity of the individual, worldliness versus withdrawal, autonomy versus absolute dependence.

Epistemically, revealed-religious alienation harbors a fundamental incongruity. While the object known through religious faith is meant to be limitless and unconditioned – the divine is the absolute – simultaneously the subject of faith is confined to forming finite representations of it. Revealed religion cannot provide an adequate concept of its object, lest it become speculative philosophy.

The transition from religious representation to philosophical comprehension follows a pattern of movement ubiquitous in the *Phenomenology*: an imbalance between spirit as knowing subject and itself as known object compels it to overcome its present state. In every instance, the gap is crossed through spirit's realization (that is, its self-conscious reflection) that the object is its own content rather than something radically alien to it. In its theistic form, the gap yawns between religion's finite representational form and its objectively infinite content. The Christian worshipper bows to a human image but means to adore God. Monotheism cannot say what it means. Judaism, its most intellectual form – "the religion of the sublime," as it is called in the *Lectures on the Philosophy of Religion* – expressly forbids such misrepresentations. The truth of the logically perplexing figure of a human son of God is that God is human or that man is divine. (Hegel's interpretation of the Protestant tradition is best understood by keeping in mind that the German term for "reconciliation," *Versöhnung*, literally means "the begetting of a son." Thus, a god that begets a human represents the reconciliation of divine and human principles.) However, this truth is not immediately available to thinking. It takes a new phase of alienation for spirit to be able to reflect upon and return to its true self – after all, this alienation is self-alienation, one that produces not a generic other but its own *proper* other (*PS* 422.10–20/M 479).

In "Absolute Knowing" Hegel presupposes his readers' familiarity with the general principle underlying all transitions of spirit, including that from revealed religion to absolute knowing. And yet this principle requires elucidation. For one, it is useful to keep in mind that Hegel's conception of spirit as activity – epitomized in the words: "the history of spirit is its *deed*, and it is only what it does" (*PR*

§343) – is Aristotelian in essence. Aristotle's dialectical conception of the relation of potency (*dynamis*) and first actuality (*prote entelecheia*) in the soul (*De Anima* 412a27) thoroughly informs the self-differentiations and self-unifications of Hegel's spirit, the distinction of its in-itself and for-itself modes, as well as (with qualifications) their further actualization in spirit's in-and-for-itself or absolute mode. In one of his most important uses of the potency–actuality dialectic, Aristotle explains how so-called matter and form, despite being logically distinct, are not ontologically separable. Every existing being, whether natural or manmade, must be a unity of both (*De Anima* 412a9). Similarly, in his conception of soul, potency and actuality are logically related in such a way that, while neither subsists without the other, they do not collapse into an undifferentiated one – just like the concavity and convexity of a curved figure. Actuality is always actualization of a potential, and potentiality exists only in actualization.[5] Aristotle himself recurs to hierarchically differentiated modes of knowing, *epistemē* and *theorein*, to illustrate different levels of actualization of the thinking soul (see *De Anima* 412a10, 22).

This background explains the general sense in which for Hegel the movement of knowing is self-necessitated. It also sheds light on Hegel's system as a whole, because the Aristotelian principle operates in it by regulating the relations intrinsic to every subordinate part as well as those of the entire system. In our context, this explains how every shape of apparent knowing can be said to be in-itself, though not yet for-itself, a moment of absolute knowing. (Hegel borrows "moment" from the physics of motion: '*momentum*' indicates an intrinsic feature of a body's position whose observable manifestation is its actual motion.) At the level of natural consciousness, for example, mere sense-certainty already implies absolute knowing in that the subjective and objective sides of sensation, the sensing and the sensed, coincide. Towards the closing of our chapter, Hegel repeats that absolute spirit's self-certainty is already present in sensibility, though only in the qualified sense in which a form of consciousness can be said to harbor absoluteness:

> Spirit that knows itself is, for the very reason that it grasps its own concept, the immediate sameness (*Gleichheit*) with itself that, in its [condition of] difference, is the *certainty of what is immediate* or *sense-consciousness* – the beginning from which we started. (PS 432.33–36/M 491)

Similarly at the more general level of spirit proper, the whole of natural consciousness implies self-consciousness. If that were not the case, natural consciousness would never experience its own inadequacy and thus never initiate correction and self-sublation. (This internal negative experience Hegel often calls the "negativity of the object for consciousness.") Precisely on account of its implicit self-reflexivity, natural consciousness can eventually reflect upon itself (be "for-itself") and become self-consciousness (become "in-and-for-itself"). The same pattern is at work in the internal and mutual relations of the three major forms of absolute spirit: art, religion, and philosophy (though in the 1807 *Phenomenology*, art is treated as a form of religion).

Applied to our present concern, this conception of spirit means that religion already has the absolute as its content but in a representational form inadequate to actualizing it. This is why revealed religion is necessarily deceitful: it must always mean something other than what it says. Thus, it turns upon itself in an epoch-making act of self-reflection and becomes sublated into speculative philosophy.

3 Discovery and Structure of the Self

The most general lesson learnt from the journey heretofore is that no one shape of consciousness or form of spirit proper has yielded, by itself, true objective cognition. This recurrent inadequacy does not, however, preclude knowledge of the true resulting from the complete series of the forms of consciousness (*PS* 422.22–423.1/M 479–80). This is indeed Hegel's claim, accompanied however by the all-important specification that the totality of phenomenal forms of knowledge cannot itself be a kind of phenomenal cognition. Instead, it is knowledge of what is true *in* apparent knowing. Hegel argues that phenomenal knowing necessarily grows into philosophical science, just as in the system he argues that nature is necessarily sublated into spirit, or natural forms of spirit into forms of spirit proper. A phenomenology "is not knowing as pure grasp of the object" (*PS* 423.5/M 480). Although its moments are indeed articulations "of the Concept proper or of pure knowing," they are so merely "in form of shapes of consciousness" (*PS* 423.8–9/M 480). Hegel's present reconstruction of the phenomenological journey aims to explain this relation between shapes of knowing and conceptual comprehension.

A reflection on the phenomenological journey as a whole shows that spirit and its object share, in every phase of their respective development, fundamental features. For example, the content of immediate consciousness (Sense Certainty) is being in its immediacy, that is, thinghood without relations; the content of mediated consciousness (Perception) is being in its mediation, that is, thinghood as a web of relations; the content of essential consciousness (Understanding) is being as essence – thinghood as both immediate and mediated (see *PS* 422.29–423.1/M 480). Each fundamental feature of objectivity depends at once upon a corresponding feature of the thinking of objectivity.

It appears then that objectivity, or object-being, is determined (*bestimmt*) by thinking. Grasping this general rule amounts to grasping that the object is "a being of spirit" ("*ein geistiges Wesen*," *PS* 422.26/M 479–80; or "*geistige Wesenheit*," *PS* 423.10/M 480). The essence of objectivity is spiritual rather than the opposite of spirit. This is Hegel's version of Aristotle's claim that the object proper of thinking is always a thought, because intelligence does not assimilate the object as such but only its intelligible form. In this sense, and in this sense alone, the intellect is always thinking itself.[6] Accordingly, the kind of adequate cognition sought in vain in the *Phenomenology* can be provided by another form of thinking, one that has its starting point in the discovery that the essence of the object is its logic. Adequate knowledge of the object of sensation, perception, understanding, and so forth will be provided by the concept of its logical structure.

Of course, the object has been in-itself (or for us, the scientific observers of consciousness) "a being of spirit" all along. But this is an insight of speculative philosophy, not of phenomenology. The spiritual nature of the object becomes known only by *grasping* that each of its determinations is a facet of the knowing Self (see *PS* 422.25–28/M 479–80). Hegel calls the logical structure of the Self "the Concept" (*der Begriff*). In "Absolute Knowing," he now claims that this structure is syllogistic. In other words, he likens the concept of objectivity (the concept of a world) to that of selfhood, and the latter to that of syllogistic inference – not to a specific syllogistic form or figure, although he considers the categorical syllogism as the paradigm of all such inferences.

Hegel's theory of the syllogism cannot be treated here in detail, nor does Hegel do so in this chapter. His theory is found in the *Logic*'s Doctrine of the Concept (esp. *Enc.* §§180–93; *SL, GW* 12:90–126). In the present context, Hegel merely highlights the way in which the notion of syllogistic inference can be used to explicate the fundamental dynamics of selfhood.

In the classical syllogisms of formal logic (collectively called "*the syllogism of understanding*," in contrast to the "syllogism of reason"; *Enc.* §182, see below) the singular, particular, and universal terms are represented by symbols for subjects, middle terms, and predicates (S, M, P) that have arbitrary referents. Hegel, however, determines the Self precisely as the activity of permanently mediating between singular, particular, and universal aspects of the world. Accordingly, the concept of Self ("the Concept" or "the syllogism of reason") reflects this mediation as effected by the Self as mediator. Hegel's preliminary or "abstract" definition of the Concept is this:

> The *Concept* . . . contains the moments of *universality*, . . . of *particularity*, . . . and of *singularity*, [whereby the latter is] the inward reflection of . . . universality and particularity. This negative unity with itself is the *in and for itself determined* and at the same time the self-identical or universal. (*Enc.* §163)

Hegel's published Remark to this section explains that the singularity of the Concept, as opposed to that of a singular being, does not depend upon other beings external to it; that is, it does not result from external causes. The Concept is not just potentially real or actual, but absolutely so: "the singularity of the Concept is *what acts* as such (*schlechthin das Wirkende*), namely . . . what actualizes itself (*das Wirkende seiner selbst*)" (*Enc.* §163R).

Put differently: Hegel's "syllogism of reason" denotes the very concept of syllogistic inference, a concept underlying not only formal-logical reasoning but also the rational aspects of reality, including the reality of selfhood. Thus a thinking subject is best described as the "*mediating ground* between the singularity and universality of what is real" (*Enc.* §180). "The Concept" refers to the dynamics of a thinking subject who, like a living syllogism, permanently distinguishes and unifies what is universal, particular, and singular. The copula in the apodictic judgment (S *is* P) that concludes the categorical syllogism (S is M, M is P, thus S is P) is the linguistic expression of the identity within difference of singularity, symbolized by the subject, and universality, expressed by the predicate. The syllogism holds the terms asunder (S, M, and P differ from one another) all the while proving their identity and stating it in the copula.[7]

If what is rational in reality is best expressed in terms of a syllogism, this applies *a fortiori* to the reality of the Self. Indeed, if the subject-term of a syllogistic inference refers to the very author of the inference, this subject can be said to be "concluding *itself with itself*" (*Enc.* §182). The Cartesian idea of a substance that in virtue of its own activity proves itself not just valid but true is the most famous expression of this self-conclusion in the history of philosophy.

At the end of the *Phenomenology*, then, the logical structure of thinking and of its object is recognized as syllogistic. And yet phenomenal consciousness per se knows nothing about this. It is "not a pure grasp of the object," although the object is in truth nothing but its concept. This truth is present in the various perspectives described in the previous chapters, but always in distorted form. One kind of distortion consists of one-sided objectifications of subjectivity. For example, when spirit as Observing Reason recognizes itself in nature, it misunderstands this identity by taking itself to be a "thing" of nature (*PS* 423.23–25/M 480–1). From this derive the most abstruse claims, as for example that the "soul" must be a thing, though not one that can be sensed. (In the *Science of Logic*, judgments expressing similar claims are classified as "infinite judgments" of the kind "spirit is not red, not yellow . . . ," that is, not false but senseless judgments; cf. *SL, GW* 12:69.12.) Conversely, other distortions of the identity of subject and object in knowing consist of one-sided subjectifications of objectivity. In these cases, thinghood is declared to be nothing in itself and only a relation in the thinker. As in culture-theoretical and utilitarian worldviews, the object ends up being simply what the subject wants it to be, a mere "construct" produced by its self-alienation, or simply what is useful to it. The world does not subsist: there is only consciousness. To these distortions belongs also, Hegel thinks, the modern worldview for which the moral value of an action resides exclusively in the kind of consciousness from which it springs, namely pure knowledge and pure will, a view that threatens to render the "beautiful soul" so transparent to itself as to "disappear into empty vapor" (*PS* 425.35–426.6/M 482–3).

Despite such misrepresentations, each major phenomenal form of knowing instantiates in its own way the syllogism by which spirit "concludes itself with itself." Real self-conscious individuality (concluding Chapter V), moral conscience (concluding Chapter VI), and religious revelation (concluding Chapter VII) are all self-conclusions of spirit, or forms of its absolute self-knowing, albeit in a still inadequate form. The only adequate knowledge of spirit's selfhood is knowledge of its logical structure, that is, conceptual comprehension. Since selfhood proper just is self-comprehension, knowing the concept of selfhood is equivalent to realizing it. Thus *knowing* this concept is *being* the Concept.

All other ways in which spirit relates to itself involve self-alienation, as when sensibility feels or reason finds itself in another, apparently spirit-less object. Only in the absolute relation does spirit know the object to be "its own *doing*" rather than the "representation of an *other*" (*PS* 427.18–20/M 485). This doing, as we have seen, consists of Self's permanent inference of itself in the syllogism of reason. Its existence consists of this inference: spirit is what it does.[8]

The *Phenomenology* has produced a series of forms of knowing (*Wissen*); with the comprehension of their totality, absolute knowing, begins philosophical science (*Wissen-schaft*). As mere observers of spirit's manifestations, we do not yet grasp absolute knowing as such. And yet we are more than familiar with its singular form of existence: the "I," which Hegel defines in these pages as "pure *being for self* of self-consciousness" (*PS* 428.5/M 486), "the *sameness of the Self with itself*" (*PS* 430.38/M 489), and "*subject* [that] is equally *substance*" (*PS* 431.1/M 489).

Thus, the phenomenological journey as a whole appears now to have been a preparatory exercise for comprehending the logic of the "I." Just like spirit in general, whose self-conscious singular existence it is, "I" is an activity of relating. Contrary to the relation that is simple consciousness, however, the "I's" relation is primarily to itself. It is the incessant activity of preserving the oneness of self and its content vis-à-vis their enduring difference (see *PS* 428.4–15/M 486). In this sense, "I" is negativity: it consists in differentiations and sublations. Yet these are self-differentiations and self-sublations. The activity is absolute. Like a Möbius strip, "I" is "spirit that traverses itself, and does so *for itself* as spirit by having, in its objectification (*Gegenständlichkeit*), the shape of the Concept" (*PS* 428.14–15/M 486). Its object has the form of selfhood, that is, its own form.

It is improper to represent the Self as an identifiable substance or as simple self-identity. It must rather be grasped as self-identify*ing* substance, that is, as active subjectivity. The sameness that characterizes selfhood is not adequately expressed in the static terms of tautologies like "I = I." It must rather be understood as a movement, a balancing act. Hegel speaks of it as the "labor" of "leveling out" (*PS* 428.18–22/M 486) the share of self-consciousness vis-à-vis that of simple object-consciousness in the advance of knowing towards absolute form. In its incipient stages, simple consciousness appears to have the lion's share in knowing, but in the course of the journey, *Wissen* increasingly involves consciousness of self. For example, the role of self-consciousness in perception is less conspicuous than in understanding; in the production of art, it is less dominant than in speculative philosophy; and in the opening lines of the present chapter, the fundamental limitation of manifest religion is located in the fact that "[religion's] real self-consciousness is not the object of its consciousness" (*PS* 422.4–5/M 479).

To recapitulate: the self-reflective, speculative dimension of knowing subtends all modes of knowledge acquisition, but it is only properly grasped once their dynamic connection, their series, is comprehended. As a whole, this movement has traced nothing less than "[spirit's] *becoming* what it is *in itself*" (*PS* 429.26/M 487). Thus, though spirit's becoming must precede its being in-and-for-itself, and acquaintance with its manifestations (in the *Phenomenology*) must precede the grasp of its concept (in the *Logic*), it is equally true that this concept is the logical foundation of those manifestations:

> Now in actuality, knowing substance is there before its form or conceptual shape, because substance is the still undeveloped *in-itself*, ... the concept in its ... simplicity, ... also spirit's *inwardness* or Self that *is* not yet *there*. What *is there* is ... the object of *representational* consciousness as such. Knowing ... has thus at first only a poor object ... [and] substance ... is the still *selfless being* ... At first only ... *abstract moments* of substance belong to *self*-consciousness; but [then] ... the latter enriches itself until it has wrested (*entrissen*) from consciousness and absorbed into itself (*in sich gesogen*) the whole substance ... Accordingly, in the *Concept* that knows itself as concept the *moments* appear earlier than the *completed whole* ... although in *consciousness* the whole is earlier than the moments, though uncomprehended. (*PS* 428.26–429.7/M 486–7)

The transition from simple consciousness, for which even the self is an object, to self-consciousness, for which even objectivity is selfhood, has exhibited "the transformation of that *in-itself* into the *for-itself*, of the *substance* into the *subject*, of the object of *consciousness* into object of *self-consciousness*" (*PS* 429.28–30/M 488). These earlier formulations describe as well the main subject matter of the present chapter, namely the progression from phenomenological consciousness as a whole to self-knowing spirit.

Hegel's further remarks about the necessarily temporal dimension of phenomenal cognition versus the timelessness of absolute self-knowing (*PS* 429.7–19/M 487) cannot be considered here in detail. (Hegel's metaphysics of time is developed somewhat in the Philosophy of Nature, *Enc.* §254–259. We will return briefly to his conception of time and space in connection with the final paragraphs of the chapter.) Here it suffices to note that the emphasis these passages give to the logical patterns of spirit's "absolute" movement ought not occlude the fact that for Hegel precisely this atemporal, purely logical movement grounds the temporal, both historical and individual developments of human thinking.[9] To give but one indication of the latter, Hegel's account of the relation of consciousness to self-consciousness provides a much-needed theoretical foundation for contemporary psychological and psychoanalytic theories of ego development, of consciousness and of the unconscious – from the notion of the initial "selflessness" of consciousness to that of its enrichment by forced separation from (*entreissen*) and imbibing (*in sich saugen*) of the substance, to that of spirit's movement as a traversing of itself.[10] Hegel's epitome of this development as "spirit's *becoming* what it is *in itself*" provides a metaphysical underpinning for Freud's summation: "Where id was, I shall become."[11] Hegel's own pressing concern, however, is with the connections between the logical and the real (both natural and historical) dimensions of absolute spirit. To these he dedicates the final passages of the *Phenomenology*.

4 Absolute Knowing as Science of the Self

As we have seen, the process by which spirit acquires self-knowledge is couched by Hegel in terms of its "becoming what it is in-itself," which in turn can be described, in broadly Aristotelian terms, as actualization (Hegel's *Verwirklichung*) of a potentiality. For Hegel, this actualization is a bi-directional process.

On the one hand, the process consists of an exteriorization (*Entäußerung*) of spirit, occasionally also called its "objectification" (*Vergegenständlichung*). This constitutes the content of spirit's outward experience. Knowledge derived from this experience is an acquaintance (*Bekanntschaft*) of spirit with itself, but is not yet knowledge proper (*Erkenntnis*). The experience, however, is an integral part of knowledge proper or, as Hegel prefers to say, it is the substance of spirit, because experience both precedes knowledge in time and is logically grounded in it: "the substance that spirit is . . . is the circle returning into itself, the circle that presupposes its beginning and attains it only in the end" (*PS* 429.25–32/M 488).

On the other hand, the becoming of spirit displays as well a contrary direction, namely inwardization (*Insichgehen*): with increasing knowledge of its own manifestations, spirit also learns its innermost workings, the logic of its Self.

Hegel's second recapitulation of the phenomenological journey (*PS* 430.5–431.12/M 488–90) centers on the connection between these two opposite and complementary developments, and on their envisaged function in the *System of Science*. The history of the ethical, legal, political, moral, and religious reality of human societies is to be understood as spirit's "labor, which it accomplishes as *actual history*" (*PS* 430.6/M 488) and through which it pursues self-knowledge. (In the *Encyclopedia*, the *Philosophy of Right*, and the *Philosophy of History*, Hegel reiterates that the Socratic command, "Know thyself!," is the intrinsic *telos*, motive force, and regulative principle of human thinking in general and of philosophy in particular.[12]) Spirit begins its existence in a crude state in which the Self is dull, and life barbaric (see *PS* 430.6–10/M 488). But this existence (*Daseyn*) is incompatible with the essence (*Wesen*) or concept of spirit: in this condition, "its own essence [is to the Self] an alien content" (*PS* 430.9–10/M 488). Thus begins the series of separations and unifications between spirit's essence on the one hand, and its modes of being on the other – the process that culminates in absolute knowing.

In this second overview, Hegel emphasizes a perspective that has surfaced only briefly in the preceding pages. According to this view, since spirit is on the way to becoming for-itself what it is in-itself, we have to understand the movement described in the *Phenomenology* as "*movement* of the Self" (*PS* 431.15–16/M 490). This movement of the Self takes place in the two contrary directions just mentioned: while the Self expands into the world as its substance, it also intensifies its inwardness. Every objectification of its activity in space and time is accompanied by a deepening of its interiority. This is a thought upon which Hegel will insist time and again in the years to come. In 1820, for example, he argues that the history of philosophic systems signifies not just the expression but equally the deepening of thinking (*GW* 18:47.19–48.4, cf. H&S 1:28).

Hegel argues now that the dual direction of the development of selfhood is necessitated by its logical structure. We have already seen that, far from being an immediate identity, the Self is a relation, that is, a mediating between its identity and its difference (or self-differentiation). The Self's identity taken abstractly, namely in isolation from its difference, consists of its spatial extension. For example, the Self exists only as an extended body; from a logical point of view, space is for Hegel nothing but simple self-identity or "pure identity with itself" (*PS* 430.36–37/M 489). In the same way, the Self's differentiation taken abstractly consists of its existence in time; logically, time is the perpetual restlessness of what self-differentiates (cf. *PS* 430.35/M 489). But these are of course only abstractions from the reality of the Self. In the concrete Self, their relation explains it as at once substance and subject, *res extensa* and *cogito*, or better yet, substance that is subject. If the Self were reducible to mere self-identity, it would have no interiority and thus no content. It would be thought without content, knowledge without object or, in Hegel's expression, "content-less intuiting" (*PS* 431.2/M 489). Similarly, if the Self were reducible to mere differentiation, there would be nothing – no Self – for it to differ from. It would be nothing at all. Only in relation to one another can self-identity and self-difference explain the existence of the Self, just as the simpler logical categories of identity and difference explain the existence of the real in general.

Selfhood, says Hegel, begins as "self-differentiating of the subject from its substance" (*PS* 431.19–20/M 490). In this "negativity" (*PS* 431.26/M 490) intrinsic to simple substance begins the series of stages of natural subjectivity that eventually issues into spirit's "form of Self" (*selbstische Form*; *PS* 432.8/M 491).

If "substantiality" and "subjectivity" are terms respectively for the "in-itself" and "for-itself" conditions of spirit, then the Self-form is spirit's condition "in-and-for-itself." And since spirit is the activity of thinking, the Self-form refers to a condition of complete transparency of thought, or spirit as absolutely known to itself. We see here that Hegel's *Selbst* signifies not just the logical self-identity of the ego but *selfhood as self-knowing*. As selfhood is the "purest" form of thinking, that is, the form in which it is only mediated through itself, it is precisely what "absolute knowing" is.

Despite being the result of a movement, the Self develops, too, but in a different "element of its existence, [namely] the Concept" (*PS* 432.1/M 490). Compared with the previous medium of phenomenal manifestations of knowing, this is an entirely new element for the unfolding of self-knowledge. It is the medium of metaphysical categories and their logical relations. Only in this medium does spirit attain its genuine actualization as Self. In these dense passages, Hegel borrows generously from Aristotle's analogy between pure intellect and light as actualization of a transparent medium (*De Anima* II,7, III,5:430a15–16). Hegel writes:

> In this knowing, then, spirit has concluded the movement of its formation, insofar as the latter is affected by the unresolved difference of consciousness. It has attained the pure element of its existence (*Daseyn*), the Concept. The content [of this knowing] is . . . the self-externalizing Self, or the *immediate* unity of self-knowing . . . [I]n this Self-*form*, in which existence is immediately thought, the content is *Concept*. Accordingly, having attained the Concept, spirit unfolds [its] existence and movement in this ether of its life, and is *science*. (*PS* 431.36–432.10/M 490–1)

In other words: thinking in the "absolute relation," freed from its manifestations and thus from difference, is a knowing that is both certain and true. It "unifies the object-form (*gegenständliche Form*) of truth with that of the knowing Self" (*PS* 432.18–19/M 491). What thinking now knows is its nature, *an sich*, or Self. It is the Concept. Yet, as we have seen in the discussion of the syllogism, the innermost workings of spirit are the innermost workings of reality. Their study is the study of metaphysics. For Hegel, *prima philosophia* is the science of the logic of Self and world: the "science of logic" as such. Getting to know the pure structure of the Self means getting to know the objective logical relations among concepts (metaphysical categories) independently of their subjective presence in a particular form of consciousness: "the [logical] moment" is "freed from its appearance in consciousness" (*PS* 432.21–22/M 491).

Up to this point in the chapter, Hegel has mostly highlighted the contrast between phenomenology and logic of spirit. He now explains their continuity, since he must give a rationale for the system as a whole, which is not only science of logic, but also philosophical science of nature and of subjective and objective spirit.

Hegel begins with what he already argued in the first recapitulation: although it is not an event in time, even the bare logical Self is a dynamic relation or a relating. As all movement, even this relating is due to internal difference. In phenomenal consciousness, this was the (apparent) ontological difference between thinking, on the one hand and its recalcitrant content on the other: despite being consciousness's content, the object always appeared to it as completely "other." In logical science, instead, this difference will be shown to be part of the very structure of the Self: "the difference [of consciousness] has gone back into the Self" (*PS* 432.12–13/M 491). The *Logic*, in other words, will account not just for the dynamic structure of thinking per se but also for its ontological difference from the object. This is the sense of Hegel's statement that, in the "medium" or "ether" of its logic, thinking is transparent to itself, or knows itself "absolutely."

Hegel argues now that every shape of spirit's appearance corresponds to a category of its logic and vice versa, that is, that phenomenological and logical moments are different guises of the same reality (thinking).[13] The *Science of Logic* discloses conceptually thought's experiences in consciousness. Sensing, for example, is a form of acquaintance with the category of pure being, namely the experience of the unity of thought and being in a primordial, unmediated manner; or the postulation of invisible forces "behind" visible phenomena is a form of acquaintance with the essence of being; and so forth. Precisely on account of the necessary relation of logical categories with their phenomenological forms Hegel justifies here the future developments of the philosophical science from logic of the Concept (or "logical Idea") to science of nature and spirit – thus announcing the systematic sequel to the *Science of Logic*: the *Realphilosophie*.

Hegel's argument for the necessity of spirit's self-externalization into nature, mind, and its creations (*PS* 432.31–434.9/M 491–2), is best understood in the light of the transitional sections between the major parts of his later system: from the *Logic* to the *Philosophy of Nature* (cf. *Enc.* §§238–240) and from the latter to the *Philosophy of Spirit* (cf. *Enc.* §§376–381). In the interest of exegesis, however, we will remain as close as possible to the claims actually made in these closing paragraphs of the *Phenomenology* – despite their merely programmatic value at this early point in the development of Hegel's system.

In the third to last paragraph, Hegel states that absolute knowing, the science of and by spirit's Self, must by inner necessity divest itself of its abstractness, that is, of its purely logical form, and make a "transition . . . into *consciousness*" (*PS* 432.22/M 491). This is at first surprising, because absolute knowing has been presented as resulting from the phenomenological form of spirit called "consciousness." The pure Self of spirit, Hegel has written, is a form of thinking "liberated" from the inherent shortcomings of consciousness. Hegel must be arguing now from a different perspective, namely the perspective of the system to come. The *Logic*, as we know, exhibits the abstract, purely logical form of the Self. This, however, is not the full reality of selfhood, because the latter *exists* only as "I" and "I" implies also extension, permanence in time, self-identity: "'I' is not only the Self, but is the *sameness of the Self with itself* . . . *a subject that* is equally *substance*" (*PS* 430.37–431.1/M 489). Thus, the Self that grasps itself as conclusion of the "syllogism of reason" grasps not only a thinking activity (a *cogito*) but also a reality (a *res extensa*). The Self knows itself as unity of thought and being. Accordingly, the science of the Self will have to be developed further than its merely conceptual exhibition in the *Logic*. It will have to account for the reality of selfhood, whose *epistemologically* first form is the most opaque, least reflected relation of knowing: "sensible consciousness – the beginning from which we started" (*PS* 432.35–36/M 491). In the *Logic*, Hegel uses the same argument to explain why both the logical and the historical beginning of philosophy must be made with the category of "to be" (*Sein*): a thinking without external presuppositions cannot but start from itself as its own object, that is, from pure being. Thus the *Science of Logic* begins in the same way as the history of philosophy: with the pure, abstract, Parmenidean "to be" (cf. *GW* 21:53–68, 76.24–34). From the perspective of the (future) system, then, phenomenal forms of spirit are grounded in the logical nature of spirit's Self. They are, in this sense, its "result." For example, sense-certainty may be understood to be a crude manifestation of the absolute self-certainty of the purely logical Self. As in all further manifestations, (potentially) absolute spirit "knows not only itself but also its own negative, its limit" (*PS* 433.4/M 492).

The role of the "limit" in the syllogistic activity that we call thinking or spirit is clarified somewhat in a passage from the *Encyclopedia* that discusses the relation of subjectivity to objectivity. Objectivity, Hegel there argues, is not the outside of subjectivity (just as my body is not outside of me), thus it is also not a content "filling" an otherwise empty subject: "on the contrary, it is subjectivity itself which, being dialectical, breaks through its own barrier, and opens itself up into objectivity by means of syllogism" (*Enc.* §192Z).

The kind of knowledge that is instantiated by thinking the limits of thinking is, in Hegel's present terminology, intuition (*Anschauung*). When thought thinks its limits, it intuits itself in space and time. The intuitions of space and time represent the limits of thinking to itself. And since, in itself, thinking is a non-spatial, atemporal activity, Hegel refers to these intuitions as forms of externalization (*Entäußerung*) of thinking. To choose an illustration from the realm of the ontogenetic development of singular consciousness: a human individual's first intuition of herself as part of a spatial–temporal continuum can be said to be her first self-externalization or, as we also say, her first "realization" of herself as existing in a world. As we know from the Preface to the *Philosophy of Right*, Hegel thinks of epochal developments of spirit as taking place according to the same pattern: an epoch's intuition of itself as part of a natural and historical continuum enables it to attain for the first time a full grasp of itself, namely in form of a philosophic system.

Just as thinking must always have a content, so intuiting is always intuiting something. The content of the spatial self-intuition of spirit is what is commonly called "nature." The content of its temporal self-intuition is "history." Nature and history are, then, objects of spirit's intuition of itself. And since Hegel has characterized this intuition as spirit's first externalization, nature and history are to be counted as second externalizations (analogous to how, for instance, acceleration is a derivative of speed and thus a second derivative of motion).

Nature subsists by constantly externalizing itself: inorganic nature becomes organic, living nature becomes natural subjectivity (the "soul" of Hegel's Anthropology), simple subjectivity becomes consciousness and mind. The production and reproduction of subjectivity in nature represents the natural aspect of spirit's "eternal" (*PS* 433.10/M 492) return to its Self.

History, on the other hand, is the object of spirit's self-intuition in time. Like nature, history consists of a perennial series of externalizations. These are the epochs of human history, replacing one another by assimilation and sublation: "This becoming presents itself as a slothful movement and succession of spirits, a gallery of pictures each endowed with the whole wealth of spirit," though none equipped with adequate knowledge of it. Spirit's movement through history is so slow "because the Self has to penetrate and digest this entire wealth of its substance" (*PS* 433.15–18/M 492).

The argument underlying the elaborate metaphors of these passages may be reconstructed as follows: The goal of spirit's movement is its completion. Completion (like the *entelecheia* of Aristotle's intellect) means the full actualization of a potency. Since spirit is knowing, its completion cannot be other than absolute knowing, that is, the knowing of knowing and its content. (The goal is a condition of spirit analogous to that in which Aristotle's intellect becomes "capable of thinking itself"; *De Anima* III, 4:429b9.) The path leading to this goal consists of transforming the external experiences of spirit into its internal contents. In other words: what absolute knowing knows is the being, *Dasein*, or substance of its Self. As it directs its gaze outward, it gains inward insight. To inwardize (*insichgehen*) means also to recollect or remember (*erinnern*) one's past being, and thus to preserve what lacks external reality (because it is now past). A known past is a state of affairs that has vanished from time and space, but nonetheless exists. It is active in that it forms the material and spiritual substrate of the present and future:

> In its inwardization, [spirit] has sunk in the night of its self-consciousness, but its vanished existence (*Daseyn*) is preserved in that night, and this sublated being – past,

but reborn in knowing – is the new being, a new world and shape of spirit. (*PS* 433.21–23/M 492)

In this new beginning, it may seem as if spirit had nothing to build upon, but in truth it is building upon the sublated forms of existence of its own past. Epistemically, experience is the content, and thus integral part, of knowing in general. Past ways of thinking, expressing, and producing human life are the historical correlative of experience in knowledge: they are the content or "substance" of the presently dominant forms of human life. Both in natural and in human history, spirit's spatial and temporal unfolding is a circular movement. But while (according to Hegel) individuals and species in nature are born and die out in a merely circular pattern, the rise and fall of historical epochs of cultural and political dominance is best represented as a spiral figure. The history of spirit's epochs ("the realm of spirits"; *PS* 433.31/M 492) forms a series in which each phase replaces by sublation the preceding one in world dominance. In the *Philosophy of Right* (§342–343), Hegel writes that history is not an irrational succession of world powers in the grip of blind fate, but rather the unfolding of spirit in the rational process of taking hold of (or grasping: *erfassen*) itself as this unfolding. In the closing passages of the *Phenomenology*, the same conception is couched in terms of an internal goal explaining the very fact of human history.[14] We can call this the entelechy of human thinking (in Hegel's comprehensive use of this term): making the Self transparent to itself, or revealing "*the absolute Concept*" (*PS* 433.34/M 492). As for the apparent contingencies of human history, the "rightfulness and virtue, wrongdoing, violence and vice, talents and achievements, passions weak and strong, guilt and innocence" (*PR* §345) of states, peoples, and individuals are realities in which the actors are altogether "unconscious instruments" (*PR* §344) of spirit's movement of self-knowing.[15] As a discipline, history may well recollect events as if their succession in time had no raison d'être except time itself. But philosophical science is able to reveal the organic order of the real succession, the logic of its being, the rational explanation of human history. Together, then, the recollection and the logic of spirit's deeds form "comprehended history" (*PS* 434.4–5/M 493): philosophical science proper.

Notes

1 All translations from Hegel are the author's.
2 This point is also discussed above in chapters 1, 3, 5, and 9. (On this topic, cf. above, chapter 9. – *Ed.*)
3 See above, chapters 4, 5. – *Ed.*
4 Hegel to Schelling, May 1, 1807 (*Briefe* 1:161/B&S 79).
5 This point is central to Hegel's analysis in "Force and Understanding"; see above pp. 15–24.
6 See *Metaphysics* XII, 7:1072b20–22; *De Anima* III, 4:430a1–9, 8:431b16–432a2.
7 On predication, thought, and conceptual comprehension of objects, cf. above, chapters 1, 3, §1, and 5. – *Ed.*
8 Cf. above, pp. 24–29. – *Ed.*

9 Cf. Wartenberg (1993). – *Ed.*
10 See for example Lacan (2002, 187 n. 14).
11 Freud (1933, 111, Lecture 31).
12 See *Enc.* §377, *PR* §343R, *Lectures on the Philosophy of History* (MM 12:272/Sibree 220).
13 These correspondences are examined in detail by Heinrichs (1974). – *Ed.*
14 Harris (1997, 2:142 n. 59, 721, 723–4, 747) argues in detail that Hegel's genuine philosophy of history is contained in the *Phenomenology*, and that it is far more historically complete and accurate than has been previously recognized. – *Ed.*
15 Hegel's philosophy of history and social theory make much use of the sociological "law of unintended consequences," that unforeseen consequences can result from the same kinds of acts executed by a large number of interacting people. Smith's "invisible hand" is one example of this law. – *Ed.*

References

Aristotle (1907) *De Anima*, tr. R. D. Hicks, with Bekker's Greek text. Cambridge: Cambridge University Press.
Aristotle (1924) *Aristotle's Metaphysics*, tr. W. D. Ross. Oxford: The Clarendon Press.
Freud, S. (1933) *Neue Folge der Vorlesungen zur Einführung in die Psychoanalyse*. Wien: Internationaler Psychoanalytischer Verlag.
Harris, H. S. (1997) *Hegel's Ladder*, 2 vols. Cambridge, Mass.: Hackett Publishing Co.
Hegel, G. W. F. (1872) *Lectures on the Philosophy of History*, tr. J. Sibree. London: Bell & Daldy.
Heinrichs, J. von (1974) *Die Logik der Phänomenologie des Geistes*. Bonn: Bouvier Verlag.
Lacan, Jacques (2002) "On a Question Prior to Any Possible Treatment of Psychosis," in *Écrits. A Selection*, tr. B. Fink (pp. 169–214). (New York and London: Norton).
Wartenberg, T. (1993) "Hegel's Idealism: The Logic of Conceptuality," in F. C. Beiser (ed.), *The Cambridge Companion to Hegel* (pp. 102–29). Cambridge: Cambridge University Press.

13
Spirit and Concrete Subjectivity in Hegel's *Phenomenology of Spirit*

Marina F. Bykova

1 Introduction

Hegel's *Phenomenology of Spirit* is rightly considered one of the most difficult and puzzling works ever written in philosophy. Though Hegel's style contributes to such a perception of the book, the main reason the *Phenomenology* is so difficult to read and comprehend lies in its complex content and the wide range of issues Hegel discusses. As his first major work, Hegel's *Phenomenology* addresses many fundamental questions: metaphysical, epistemological, logico-ontological, and philosophico-historical. Hegel recasts and reformulates problems and issues discussed by his predecessors, from the Greeks to his contemporaries. The *Phenomenology*, however, does not merely integrate the insights of his predecessors; it does so in ways designed to resolve central philosophical problems. Hegel's comprehensive, often unconventional approach to standard problems is very fruitful philosophically, though also complex and challenging. Yet all of these issues, whether traditional or new, are tied together by one central theme: the nature and development of the subject and subjectivity.

The core issue of Hegel's *Phenomenology*, and the main topic of the present chapter, is the formation of the socially developed and historically oriented universal subjects of thought, will, and action within the forms of manifest spirit. These forms appear and exist as different "shapes" (*Gestalten*) of the universal ("cosmic") spirit. Hegel aims to uncover the universal and absolute in manifest spirit and to grasp this as the truth of the concrete subjectivity of individual human beings.

The approach taken here differs significantly from the two traditional, prominent interpretations of Hegel, and especially of his *Phenomenology of Spirit*. An approach typical of German scholarship starts with the cosmic spirit (*Geist*) and tries to link this grand cosmo-historical perspective with the various stages of

Hegel's *Phenomenology*, showing how forms of consciousness devolve from the "cosmic" spirit that descends upon the world.[1] Exaggerating the "cosmic" dimensions of Hegel's *Phenomenology*, this "top down" interpretation mistakenly downplays (or even ignores) Hegel's account of the individual human being. Most of the literature supporting this view inevitably winds up assimilating what is allegedly "in" Hegel's text to whatever the interpreter presumes to be Hegel's grand story about cosmo-historical spirit.

In contrast, the second approach assigns to Hegel's phenomena of "spirit" an insignificant, secondary role. This approach focuses on the point of view of individual consciousness striving towards absolute knowledge.[2] According to this "bottom up" approach widely represented in Anglophone discussions, the *Phenomenology* appears as a ladder with numerous rungs that represent the phases of how individual consciousness evolves and progresses towards absolute knowledge. The stages of the *Phenomenology* are then associated with the stages of the development of concrete individual consciousness within various forms (*Gestalten*) of universal spirit and its manifestation in the world. This development, however, is often discussed in purely epistemological terms, while social, philosophico-historical, and other important aspects of this process are greatly discounted or neglected.

Both approaches represent incomplete, one-sided views; both occlude the most important dimensions of Hegel's book, and thus misconceive the real project of the *Phenomenology* and misunderstand how Hegel views a key task of his work. The present chapter attempts to resolve these problems by showing that in the *Phenomenology* Hegel emphasizes both the broad scale of collective and historical phenomena *and* the specific dimension of the individuals who are said to participate in those phenomena and, in Hegel's view, through whom alone broad-scale collective and historical phenomena occur. Put otherwise, Hegel's main task in the *Phenomenology* is to capture how spirit becomes embodied in the modern world in and through human history and the activity of its real agents, human individuals. Through this process, individual subjectivity becomes concrete by manifesting what is universal and absolute within itself as moments of spirit. To investigate this topic is to investigate subjectivity itself, which Hegel contends must be reconceived in a radically new way.

Hegel's account is properly called a "theory of subjectivity" for several reasons. One is that "philosophy of mind" is too embedded in Cartesian mind–body dualism, and too closely associated with epistemology. Developing a theory of "subjectivity" directly accommodates the integration of cognition and action, including moral agency, the integration of mind and body, and the integration of individual subjects with their natural and social environments. More positively, a theory of subjectivity allows focusing on the active nature of human subjectivity, a point already stressed by Kant's accounts of perceptual and judgmental syntheses, through which alone we are able to identify ourselves as self-conscious persons. In his analysis Kant emphasized that both cognition and action are normatively governed; they cannot be explained merely causally and are thus "spontaneous." These innovations are central to the German Idealists, who accordingly argued that to understand human subjectivity requires examining how human subjectivity comes to be and develops in and through an individual's interactions with his or her natural and social surroundings. This marks a radical break with the Cartesian picture of the subject. German Idealists view subjectivity not merely as active, but as consisting entirely in activity. Thus the relevant conception of subjectivity is not ontological, but rather functional: the key features of subjectivity are revealed by what it does and how it does it, not by what it is made of. Thus a subject's active involvement (interaction) with the world and its activity of self-development became the focus of philosophical analyses of subjectivity.

2 Hegel's Account of Subjectivity: General Remarks

Hegel's interest in subjectivity arose from his occupation with Fichte and Schelling in Frankfurt (1797–1800) and especially in Jena (1801–1806). His focus on the self in these periods developed in direct response to Fichte's concept of the self-posited 'I' as an unlimited and in principle unchangeable being. Conceived as a simple, original self-identity, Fichte's subject appears fixed, indifferent, and in some way external to the process of its own self-reflection. It appears to be merely formal and lacks a necessary substantive aspect and thus is empty of content and incapable of real development.

Hegel altogether rejects the notion of the self as homogenous and unalterable. Unsatisfied with "abstract" and static interpretation of the self, Hegel attempts to make the self concrete and describes it in its living dynamics. Instead of discussing the self in its original "purity," he wants to grasp it "in action," through its actual manifestations in the world. This significant shift away from Fichte's concept of the self signals a move towards an essentially new approach to the subject and subjectivity – new both for German Idealism and for modern philosophy in general. Hegel's new conception of the self and its self-presentation involves more than its "reaching out" into the real world and actual experience; such a tendency is already recognizable in Fichte's interpretation of the self as the synthesis of both positing (the 'I') and contra-positing (the 'not-I'). The novelty of Hegel's approach to the subject and subjectivity is his view that the self *results from* interacting with the world. In the *Phenomenology* he makes this point in these terms: "only this self-*restoring* identity or this reflection in otherness within itself – not an *original* or an *immediate* unity as such – is true. It [*sc.* subjectivity] is its own becoming . . ." (*PS* 18.24–26/M 10).[3]

This passage marks three key innovations and gives us a threefold sense of the radicality of Hegel's account of subjectivity. First, by claiming that the self is a *result* and not an "absolute beginning," as Descartes, Fichte, and the early Schelling understood it, Hegel states that subjectivity is the conceptual sum and unity of its own entire development. What constitutes this unity is constituted by the everlasting continuous self-determining growth of the self, the process of "its own becoming." Hegel describes this process as the "path of enculturation" (*Bildung*), which has two important dimensions: social and cognitive. From the social perspective, this is a historical process that the individual subject undergoes within the social reality and history of its culture. Yet it is equally well the epistemic process or the "route of the natural consciousness" (*PS* 55.35–36/M 49) towards true knowledge. Through this process natural consciousness continuously develops into "absolute knowing" or the self-consciousness which encompasses the entire experience that consciousness has made previously. The second idea that Hegel illuminates in the passage quoted above is the conception of the self as comprising its *whole* development. What is true is not something that we start with, nor is it a mere result of a one or another particular development.[4] Instead, it is a *whole* development taken in its entirety and integrity. In contrast to Schelling, for whom wholeness is the synonym of the totality of facts, Hegel understands this whole not as a sum of all facts but rather as a process of the entire development. Applied to the self, this is the whole process of becoming who one is. The medium of one's becoming is the world. This is the third idea delineated, perhaps indirectly, in the passage under consideration. Since the self is not something given, it must constantly form itself in interaction with the world and continuously create itself by mediating of its self-otherness within itself through this interaction. (Hegel emphasizes this especially in the Introduction to the *Phenomenology*.[5]) The self is that to whom the content "returns" as a result of its enrichment and development, the process and the product of its own becoming; it is not merely posited. One's self-relation as subject is no longer viewed by Hegel as something that exists immediately, prior to participating in an intersubjective realm of language and action, but as something that emerges from this experience. In his view, self-identity and self-relation are not originally given or imposed upon human individuals by anything external. Who one is always results from one's active interaction and mediation in and with the world, both natural and social. At the same time, the world itself becomes an essential part of the individual, not just the source, but the basis and necessary condition of its self-awareness. Hegel's *Encyclopedia* clarifies this issue in the following way:

> [The] world confronting the [individual human] soul is not something external to it. On the contrary, the totality of relations in which the individual human soul finds itself constitutes its actual liveliness and subjectivity and accordingly has grown together with it just as firmly as, to use a simile, the leaves grow with the tree; the leaves, though distinct from the tree, belong to it so essentially that the tree dies if it is repeatedly stripped of them. (*Enc.* §402Z)

This passage clearly demonstrates the major advance of Hegel's approach to the self and subjectivity over Fichte's. Like the Cartesian *cogito*, the Fichtean self is originally identical with itself through the pure and immediate act of thinking that takes place before, and independently of, any relation to the "not-I." On Fichte's view, the world (the "not-I") that lies outside the ego provides merely the occasion and the useful medium for the ego's activity, but never the necessity or condition of its self-awareness or self-recognition. In Fichte's system, the world is never absorbed into the ego. Though Fichte seeks to show that consciousness is a unified universe, his two domains of the I and not-I remain separate, and their alleged synthesis is merely a compromise and coexistence, not an integral unity.[6]

Hegel does not simply reject the original unity of the self, he seeks to grasp it as "essentially a *result*" (*PS* 19.13–14/M 11). He analyses the world as actually mediating the development, the becoming of the self; it is the realm in which any self and subject grows and develops in all its dimensions, physically, intellectually, emotionally, socially, and morally. The relation between the world and the self is not extrinsic; the totality of relations to the world that constitute the self becomes the essential element of its consciousness. The self appears as a synthesis, not merely a coexistence, but an integrated unity in opposition. Hegel thus replaces the Fichtean primal unity and synthesis of mere coexistence constructed on the basis of the principle of identity, "I = I," with a dialectical unity, which is animated by the principle of contradiction. The process of establishing this synthesis Hegel calls "dialectic."

Having its roots in ancient tradition, the term "dialectic" comes from the Greek word for "art of conversation." In Hegel, however, this ancient use of the term becomes secondary. Instead, he considers dialectic the internal process of the *self-development* of the subject and the internal "mechanism" that governs relations among two or more distinct concepts, objects, or events. It is not just a method to apply to some subject matter, but the intrinsic structure of the subject matter itself. "Dialectical" explanations explicate phenomena through analysis of their dialectical relations and specific dynamics. In Hegel's system, the process of the subject's self-development is explained by means of "dialectical contradiction": constitutive oppositions and tensions which become reconciled in a new, advanced stage of development.

It is worth considering Hegel's conception of "dialectical contradiction" a bit more fully here. The traditional (formal-logical) meaning of contradiction is when an unequivocal statement is both true and false at the same time, or when both it and its negation are true. Applied to the world of real things, contradiction is present when something is assigned properties which are not just different, but rather exclude each other so that the existence of the thing itself is jeopardized. As a matter of logical necessity, something cannot have and lack the same property at the same time or have two or more properties that are logically incompatible. Hegel knew formal logic perfectly well and used it masterfully in his philosophical construction. Yet his dialectic goes beyond the formal-logical usage of a number of notions and concepts. Hegel does not object to the formal logical law of non-contradiction; however, this law governs only synchronic relations and thus does not capture the diachronic relations involved in development.[7] Diachronic relations, in contrast, are subject to the laws of *dialectical* and not formal logic, and the contradictions they display are 'dialectical', or, as Hegel calls them, *reflective-logical (dialectical) contradictions*.[8] John Burbidge notes that this kind of contradiction "is not the end of reasoning, but rather a clue that something is wrong, pointing toward a solution that will resolve the paradox."[9]

The same dialectical process is portrayed in the *Phenomenology*, but here consciousness itself becomes a concrete object within which the dialectical transition occurs and becomes manifest. Here the self essentially becomes the synthesis of both contradiction and reconciliation. As for Fichte, for Hegel the self is self-generated activity. But while Fichte could not rationally explain what animates this self-generation, Hegel shows that the self, which is essentially reflective, necessarily displays an "internal conflict" between itself (the "I") and its object (the object of consciousness). This conflict is not a conflict between something internal and what is external. Instead, it demonstrates a dialectic-contradictory relation within consciousness, where each relatum appears initially to be irreconcilable with the other. Consciousness, serving as a substance of the self, becomes plunged into the self-contradiction that upsets the balance of its elements, leading to the loss of its original unity and conceptual identity. However, since this relation of negation within the reflective being is "just as much the non-identity (*Ungleichkeit*) of the substance with itself" (*PS* 29.35–36/M 21), it has to be "repaired" from within to regain the integrated totality or unity of the substance (consciousness) itself. Hegel thus concludes that the contradiction between consciousness and its object contains the ground of its own reconciliation. The reflective self conciliates itself and the objective world which mirrors its own structure and ultimately becomes "absorbed" into the self. This "reflection into itself" is the activity through which the self continually creates itself. Hence the "internal conflict" within consciousness (the negative as a distinction between the I and its object) becomes the source of movement in any developing self, the movement which actively creates the self. Since the self is never static and its activity never ceases, its being is a chain of reconciled contradictions; it neither stagnates nor suffers obliteration. The self is thus constantly engaged in making itself and becoming what it is. The self's engagement in its own process of becoming itself, "the actual vitality" of the self, Hegel calls subjectivity.

Approaching Hegel's account of subjectivity systematically reveals three major facets. The first facet is "logical," in the modern sense, which includes both formal syllogistic and cognitive judgment. This facet concerns our logical and cognitive capacities to form predicative judgments, e.g. to recognize that a variety of characteristics belong to some one spatio-temporal object or event. The second facet is "concrete"; it concerns the self-consciousness of a living individual. The third facet concerns subjectivity as a species; it integrates the first two facets by explaining how self-conscious individuals can make logical judgments (in the broad sense indicated), and by showing how individual self-consciousness is only possible on the basis of making such judgments.[10]

These three facets of subjectivity are reiterated in several prominent aspects of Hegel's philosophy, including his accounts of "dialectic" and "reflection." However, unlike his predecessors, Hegel uniquely integrates all three facets of subjectivity into a complex theory of subjectivity that provides the focal point of many of his writings. Hegel's theory of subjectivity contains two main parts; one concerns "pure" ("absolute") subjectivity, the other concerns "concrete" empirically given subjectivity, the subjectivity of a finite individual. While the first is fully developed in *Logic*,[11] the second is a topic of Hegel's *Realphilosophie*. Much of the literature on Hegel's theory of subjectivity, including work by leading scholars written in both Continental as well as Analytic traditions,[12] stresses Hegel's alleged commitment to some basic level of "pure thinking" or "pure subjectivity" that must somehow generate an entire logic and metaphysics out of itself. Such an interpretation reiterates yet again a huge Cartesian circle, which already reappeared in various, often-expanded forms in Locke, Leibniz, Kant, and Fichte. Hegel's approach to "pure (absolute) subjectivity" is indeed indebted to Modern philosophy, though it also transcends it by successfully working out many problems that remained unsolved in previous metaphysics.

Hegel rejects both traditional metaphysics (with its concerns about the substance of God, the universe, and the human soul) and Kant's critique of the same. Hegel's own "ontology" aims to identify and to explicate the conceptual interrelations among our basic concepts and categories, for those interrelations are constitutive of the content or meaning of those concepts or categories, which can be used in accurate and legitimate cognitive judgments only if these interrelations are well understood. For that very reason Hegel's "ontology" is combined with both his theory of subjectivity and his logic. Hegel's logic concerns not only traditional syllogistic logic, but what would now be called material principles of inference. Stressing the novelty of the procedure that Hegel adopts in his logic, John Burbidge shows that Hegel's logic clearly advances the methodology of Kant and his other predecessors. At first glance Hegel's logic "follows Kant in exploring the fundamental concepts that govern all our thinking." It is, however, not limited to the analysis of traditional operations or just finite human thoughts. Its purpose is to demonstrate internal contradictions arising from the limitation of finite human thinking, though also to overcome the finite character of this thinking and achieve knowledge of the infinite (literally, the 'non-limited') or absolute. Consequently, Hegel's logic "grasps not only our own thinking process, but the principles that ultimately govern the world as well."[13] Hegel thus significantly transcends Modern conceptions of metaphysics and shifts his interest to logic, and on this ground offers a conceptually innovative approach to the "pure" ("absolute") subjectivity that differs fundamentally from traditional concepts of the "pure" self and the Absolute.

Hegel demonstrates that only a detailed and comprehensive logic can provide a theory of "pure" subjectivity and of determinate thought. This "pure" subjectivity must be distinguished from empirically given psychological subjects because it is logical and cognitive, and is thus normative, not merely psychological. Only when viewed as "pure" can this logical theory of subjectivity shed light on the structure of self-consciousness and elucidate the relevant "pure" forms and acts of thought. These latter are interpreted by Hegel as judgments about legitimate logical relations. They are crucial to how we form, grasp, and master our own thoughts. Hegel's speculative theory of "pure" ("absolute") subjectivity thus explicates the "truth," that is, the truth conditions, of statements or judgments. Hence it must take ontology into account, although it is not itself an ontology. Rather, it determines the basis and limits of philosophical ontology.

Although Hegel's account of *pure* subjectivity may be problematic, it would be a mistake to interpret *absolute* subjectivity as a merely abstract logical or psychological phantom. Hegel insists that absolute subjectivity can be understood only in terms of its relation to individual subjects, to living human beings. And, indeed, his conception of "theoretical" or "logical" thinking is not generated by some kind of "pure" cognitive activity. It is and can only be rooted in the "real" thinking of actual, functioning human subjects, considered logically and cognitively, not merely psychologically. This closes a gap between absolute and concrete subjectivity and makes the latter the main focus of Hegel's analyses.

Consequently, investigations into the concrete subject, the real human individual, lie at the core of Hegel's theory of subjectivity. This first becomes visible in the *Phenomenology* and later reappears and is repeatedly reconfirmed in the *Encyclopedia* (especially in the 1827 and 1830 editions), in the *Philosophy of Right*, and in Hegel's courses on the various sections of the *Realphilosophie* that he taught in Berlin.[14]

In the *Phenomenology* Hegel provides a well-structured account of concrete subjectivity. Although it is elaborated and perhaps somewhat revised in numerous versions of Hegel's later *Realphilosophie*, the general account of concrete subjectivity is already formed and introduced here.[15] Some scholars tend either to dismiss, or at least to seriously discount Hegel's account of subjectivity in the *Phenomenology*. They contend that the *Phenomenology* is an early work that marks Hegel's search for a paradigm and foundation of his philosophical system, so that all concepts and ideas it introduces are preliminary and so cannot elucidate the author's real position. They point to the *Science of Logic* (or less often to the *Encyclopedia*) as the text in which Hegel first formulates his conception of subjectivity. The *Phenomenology* is then considered only as "experimental" ground, and concepts and ideas which the thinker elaborates in this work are assigned no essential significance except to serve as a kind of exploratory device used for accomplishing a greater goal, namely the goal of a systematic development of philosophy.[16] Although the *Phenomenology* is indeed the first serious philosophical work published by Hegel, that does not reduce its central role and profound significance for Hegel's philosophical system,[17] nor for historical-philosophical development in general.[18] Instead of being a "mere preliminary" work, the *Phenomenology* is a *result* of Hegel's philosophical search undertaken in the Frankfurt and early Jena periods. That was a search for a new model of a systematic theory of consciousness. Unsatisfied by those offered by his predecessors, especially by Fichte, Hegel developed a theory of consciousness capable of escaping the logical circle in which transcendental idealism was trapped by instead explaining consciousness in both its theoretical and empirical history and facticity. The *Phenomenology* is thus a project within his new theory of subjectivity which Hegel develops as the history of self-consciousness.

3 The *Phenomenology* as the Theory of Concrete Subjectivity

The *Phenomenology* is the systematic study ("*Wissenschaft*" or science) of "the *experience* which consciousness undergoes" (*PS* 29.18–19/M 21) in its real developing as it evolves from its mental roots in sense-perception, moves through its first historical beginnings in ancient civilization and growth in the modern world and modern culture, and finally reaches the full apprehension and comprehension of itself in philosophy (introduced as "Absolute Knowing"). The real steps and phases that consciousness undergoes in the process of its development are the different forms of manifest spirit (*Geist*) and how it represents itself in and to the world. For this reason Hegel conceives of the *Phenomenology* as a history of the "shapes (*Gestalten*) of consciousness" by which "spirit develops itself" (*PS* 29.16/ M 21). This relation between the forms of consciousness and "a gallery of images" of spirit is often misunderstood and even mystified. In connection with Hegel, "spirit" too often suggests some transcendent, supra-human being or some kind of presence within the world of the absolute substance. Hegel himself may be guilty of obscuring the meaning of "spirit" due to his idealism and the totalizing tendency of his system. Yet despite any expository excesses, Hegel's philosophy of "cosmic" spirit and its correlation with the development of human consciousness is very realistic and of great importance, especially for understanding Hegel's project in the *Phenomenology*. Hegel stresses the interdependence of "cosmic" spirit and individual consciousness and claims that the development of individual consciousness is nothing but the self-development of spirit. What may appear here as a purely idealistic "cosmic" construction reflects in fact a very concrete and realistic idea. This is the idea that world history concerns the progressive development of the human individual (the self, concrete subjectivity) up to the realization and comprehension of what it truly is, namely spirit (*Geist*) in various forms of its actualization in the world.

Hegel distinguishes three main aspects of spirit: subjective (individual), objective (social), and absolute (historical). This general subdivision later governs Hegel's analysis of spirit in the *Philosophy of Spirit* within the *Encyclopedia* system. Yet within the *Phenomenology* it has less a structural and more a functional significance. Each of these three aspects of spirit captures a certain sphere of human development and interaction, but only taken together do they reconstruct a human reality as a whole. Although we come to life and strive for self-determination (freedom) as individual "finite spirits" (spirit in its subjective, individual mode), our interaction with other individuals makes us who we are. Through interaction people create communities, which then rise above the particular interests and existence of their members. Through its specific social laws and regulations, communal life (the realm of objective spirit) imposes intricate restrictions on who we are and how we lead our lives, whilst also enabling many otherwise impossible forms of individual activity (e.g., via contractual exchange, genres of art, traditional or regional cuisines). But this dependence of individuals upon the community is in fact an *inter*dependence, for the real agents of communal life, namely, those who think, will, and act within the community (the communal spirit), are individuals in mutual interaction. This interaction is not only a social, but also a historical process. Its results do not disappear with time, but re-emerge in modified form through human history and the historical development of human culture. Hence through our involvement with other people within our communities we play crucial roles in achieving absolute spirit and recognizing its accomplishment. Indeed, as individual subjects we find the world full of meaningful constructs and forms which are present for us as objective and universal historical and cultural phenomena. Although those forms and constructs are at hand, we still must discover and "decode" them for ourselves; we must still make them into events and actions of our own individual conscious experience. This is why, according to Hegel, world history is the history of the development and progression of self-consciousness from its immaturity – manifest in different forms of partial, incomplete knowledge of human individuals – to its full-fledged stage, the true self-realization as universal consciousness, actualized as absolute knowing. The latter is the state of agreement of consciousness with itself when it becomes aware of and realizes its spirit as its own freedom and knowledge. Thus spirit (*Geist*) is the full realization of self-consciousness.

Nevertheless, spirit arises from and becomes real only in and through human subjects and their concrete experiences with the world. Self-consciousness is necessarily mediated through the actual forms of life of individual thinking subjects, because without this "real-life" mediation there is no self-consciousness: the advent of spirit requires encountering what is initially beyond consciousness, comprehending it and incorporating it into one's self-understanding that includes one's understanding of the natural, social and historical world in which one lives and develops. Such mediation is thus a condition of the self-realization of spirit and also the very mode of its constitution. This clarifies the meaning of Hegel's often-mystified concept of self-development of spirit, which in fact consists in the concrete historical processes in which we human beings participate. For this reason the full self-realization of spirit is reached only when a certain level of social and political development of humanity is achieved. This is thus an historical process and must be understood in the context of the historical development of human subjects both in their individual lives and in their social interactions. In Hegel's view, the progression of both individual and communal forms of human existence are "animated" and in a certain way "directed" by spirit, which is immanent in the world, and in our individual striving for our own freedom and self-understanding.

It is important to stress that despite some metaphysical overtones, Hegel's position differs from Fichte's and especially Schelling's attempt to find "the undifferentiated absolutely unconditional being behind everything."[19] Hegel's "spirit" is not something that descends upon the world from without; it is something which develops within the world, and only through our own efforts, even if we do not realize this. Consequently, Hegel's "spirit" is not a substance or a substrate underlying the concrete individual subject; it is a pure infinite activity of the conscious human individual which gives purpose to itself and to the world. This purposive activity animates all periods of human history, directing it towards the progression and advancement of rational forms of human existence, the path that, Hegel argues, leads to the manifestation of freedom. This is why the development of human individuals appears in the *Phenomenology* as a process of liberation. This process liberates the human subject from its immediacy, naturalness, and its initial forms of self-certainty, thus making its actual self-formation and self-fulfillment possible. Through this liberation, the subject reveals its universal ("cosmic") essence and its absolute self-determinations. Hegel shows that our freedom, which is the realization of our capacities as subjects in the world, is a historical and social phenomenon and is necessarily mediated through our interdependence with the "cosmic" spirit.

By examining this interdependence systematically, Hegel addresses issues central to his philosophy. They not only shed light on the project of the *Phenomenology*, but also provide genuine and highly original insights into Hegel's account of subjectivity. These issues come under four headings, according to Hegel's main division of the *Phenomenology* into consciousness, self-consciousness, reason, and spirit: (1) How we are each able to identify ourselves as (self-)conscious individuals, capable of reflection and propositional attitudes; (2) How we are to justify our legitimate sense of individuality in light of our essential mutual interdependence, our intersubjectivity; (3) How we express ourselves collectively and culturally, and how we can understand such self-expression; and (4) How we can assess the adequacy of our apparent self-knowledge, whether individually or collectively, within our social and cultural context. Each of these inquiries is essential to Hegel's central concern with the nature and development of human freedom. I shall discuss Hegel's four inquiries in the order in which they appear in the *Phenomenology*.

3.1 Conscious individuality and spirit

Hegel's epistemological interest in the first three chapters of the *Phenomenology* is not restricted to pure theoretical questions, but concerns our actual production of knowledge through inquiry and investigation.

Hegel holds the (Kantian) thesis that we can only be self-aware by distinguishing ourselves from objects and events of which we are aware. He begins his investigation into consciousness by claiming that, for us to be conscious, two important requirements must be met. Since our consciousness is intentional, there must be an object of consciousness, and a relation with this object must be established. Hegel notes that in consciousness both elements of this relation are not immediate; they are mediated by their established relation and obtain their concreteness only through each other. Hegel states:

> in the certainty, as well as in the pure being, both of the two previously mentioned *thises* separate out, one *this* as *I*, and one *this as object*. When we reflect on this difference, it is evident that neither the one nor the other is only *immediately* in the sense certainty; rather they are equally well in it as *mediated*. I have the certainty *through* an other, namely the thing; and this is just as well in the certainty *through* an other, namely through 'I'. (*PS* 64.6–11/M 59)

This mediation of the I through "the extant object" gives rise to consciousness, which ultimately "becomes to itself comprehending consciousness (*begreiffenden*

Bewußtsein)" (*PS* 83.2–3/M 80). Thus both the I's "mere implicit awareness" and its ability to have propositional attitudes (conceptually structured consciousness) are possible only through engagement with extant reality, with objects and events of the material world.

The fact that consciousness evolves only by relating to its objects poses a difficulty. Both the "I" and the object originally appear as independent, unrelated entities. Furthermore, the object which is present as "a mere extant fact" in its immediate, determinate particularity appears alien to consciousness, which in its essence is a reflective activity of universalization and thus necessarily mediated. Nevertheless, the "I" (as the locus of consciousness) "ignores" all the discrepancies, "sacrifices" its independence, and establishes a relation to the object. At the same time, the "I" remains in this unavoidable relationship to the otherness of the object. This situation introduces three difficulties. First, it is not enough simply to postulate a relation between consciousness and its object. It must be explained how this relation is established and what "power" draws consciousness to the object. Second, the object always stands in only one *determinate* relation to consciousness, yet in order to achieve conscious comprehension of the object (to be capable of conceptual consciousness), the "I" must grasp the object in its universalities and thus must be able to know the object in the unity of *all* its relations. Hence, there should be an explanation of this synthesizing ability of consciousness. And finally, third, it must also be explained what gives consciousness the power to remain itself (substantially self-identical) in the face of the relation to the object.

Hegel examines these three issues in the first section of the *Phenomenology*, "Consciousness." His examination results in a highly original account of the role of spirit in the development of human consciousness. Hegel's attention to the three difficulties just noted is indebted to his German predecessors. Kant's account of the synthetic unity of apperception, Fichte's concept of the *Anstoß*, and Schelling's notion of the Absolute (as a pure homogenous entity enclosed within and mediated only by itself) are different attempts to explain the possibility of consciousness. However, none of these satisfied Hegel, who found them one-sided and limited.

According to Hegel, the "power" that draws consciousness to the object is not a single chimerical act or a temporal action. Instead, this is an unconditionally universal phenomenon, the essential activity that is immanent within consciousness. In the first three chapters of the *Phenomenology*, Hegel discusses this force as the "power of the understanding," which is able to penetrate into "the true background (*Hintergrund*) of things" (*PS* 88.12–13/M 86) and to reveal this concealed content to consciousness. This force of inquiry is always present in Hegel's *Phenomenology*, though in later chapters Hegel discusses it in terms of self-consciousness, reason, and spirit. What Hegel has in mind here is the power of enculturated reason, which "*makes* itself into what it is *in itself*" (*PS* 20.6–7/M 12). This kind of purposive activity not only posits a goal for itself, but also perseveres in its activity as the essential determinant of its being. This activity and an understanding of its constitutive power is not imposed externally; consciousness discovers it *within* itself. The relational "I" is also the reflective "I." It creates itself through its activity directed towards the world, through which it engages with the world and then absorbs its worldly experiences into itself.

Hegel contends that this ability of individual consciousness for rational activity links it to spirit. Only spirit guarantees the universal character of this activity and the striving towards rational understanding exhibited by each individual consciousness. According to Hegel, spirit animates all periods of human history, articulating successively more rational forms of human existence as it finds expression in the thoughts and actions of human individuals and their societies. In this way, spirit is essential to human life, which Hegel describes as a process of an individual becoming a rational being. Spirit does not determine this process of becoming. Hegel's "I" is a self-generating activity through which it continually creates itself. The principle that animates this process of self-creation is contradiction and the reconciliation of what was initially opposed. Spirit provides a medium and also a universal criterion or standard of the progress the individual makes in this developmental process. Hegel emphasizes that any individual is constituted by mediation and reflection, because these are the acts through which any entity is able to put whatever it encounters into relation with itself: "mediation is nothing but self-moving self-identity, or it is reflection within itself" (*PS* 19.29–31/M 11). This means that the mediated and reflected self is not the opposite of "cosmic" spirit, but the very mode of its constitution.[20] In this way, Hegel makes two important points. First, he again reaffirms the link between the process of becoming of an individual rational being and the self-development of spirit. Second, through their activity of mediation and reflection, human individuals have both an inside and an outside, and only this duality constitutes their "actual livingness and subjectivity."

Hundreds of pages later Hegel writes that, "only the self is to itself its proper object, or the object only has truth in so far as it has the form of the self" (*PS* 289.18–20/M 324). This statement represents Hegel's understanding of the whole realm of spirit as described in the *Phenomenology*. Hegel here confirms that there is no such entity as the "cosmic" spirit that could be assigned an absolute power and independent existence. Not spirit as such, but the human individual is the real agent acting in the world. The world is then opened to us as the object and context of our own desire for and striving towards self-development. For this reason, the individual self is reflected in every manifestation of "cosmic" spirit. The universality of spirit is only the expression of the historical character of human life and the processes in which we human beings participate. Our consciousness and ability to identify ourselves as beings capable of reflection is a product of our own activity, which requires a great effort on our part. Hegel shows that our inquiry and investigation into the world not only provide genuine knowledge of the world; they also supply self-knowledge concerning what we are able to know and how we are able to know it. However, our independent inquiry as well as our ability to be aware of our own limits require establishing our legitimate sense of individuality and affirmation in view of our mutual interdependence. This issue becomes Hegel's focus in the phenomenological section on "Self-consciousness."

3.2 Subjectivity as intersubjectivity

At the stage of self-consciousness, consciousness finds itself divided. On the one hand, "peering into itself" and relating to itself as to its own object, consciousness acquires a more real form, the form of life. This is the life of the individual consciousness in all its particularity. On the other hand, consciousness also encounters another world, the objective reality in its universal forms of life. According to Hegel, the two worlds – the internal realm of consciousness and the realm of external reality – are not distinct and must be conceived as one integrated world. The unity resulting from the subject's "desiring" relation to the object sustains life itself. The issue Hegel here formulates has great significance for our topic. This is the idea that one's self-certainty can be achieved only by establishing one's real unity with the objective world. By reconciling what is subjective and what is objective, Hegel contends that this unity is nothing other than *freedom* itself. The reconciliation that Hegel has in mind here is not a momentary act; it is a long and complex process. Freedom is a practical achievement; it occurs within the time and on the basis of the living world. Hegel links the realization of freedom with the development of spirit, though by linking it with the phenomenon of *Bildung*, which may be rendered in English as "formation" or "enculturation." The spirit as an infinite activity of self-development and self-contemplation is used by Hegel as equivalent to freedom. In Hegel's view both the "self-development" of spirit and freedom are not only worldly, but also human achievements. They occur in and through human activity over historical time. However, they are not results of an individual enterprise, but rather a collective human undertaking that must be understood as the universal activity of enculturation (*Bildung*). This is an intrapersonal, intersubjective activity which marks a transition to the socio-cultural dimension of individual life.

In "Self-consciousness" this transition only begins to take shape; individual particularity still prevails here. Yet already at this stage of self-consciousness the structures of "universal *Bildung*" appear as essential elements of individual consciousness in its striving for self-certainty (cf. *PS* 118.16/M 122). Hegel makes clear that *Bildung* is a concrete universal process in which we human beings necessarily participate and through which we become aware of ourselves and our natural and social environment. This process can occur only if an individual interacts with other individuals collectively pursuing their own goals. Hence the self can acquire its subjectivity (its sense of self-certainty and individuality) only in and through its own activity, activity that is not only directed towards the world, but is also mediated through relations with other people.

Consequently, Hegel contends that individual self-consciousness is fundamentally linked to intersubjectivity. At the level of self-consciousness, consciousness is defined in negative relation to its object: the "object" of self-consciousness is consciousness itself. This "negative relation" is one's desire for self-certainty, for one's sense of individuality. A difficulty arises from the fact that, in pursuing desire, consciousness tends to destroy (negate) its object, e.g., by consuming it, though so doing thwarts its own sense of self-certainty. To be both self-conscious and self-certain in relation to an object thus requires an object that retains its independence through negation. The only object that meets this requirement is another self-consciousness. The desire that a self-consciousness has and needs to satisfy in order to obtain a sense of its existence as an individual subject is a desire to be desired by others, namely, a desire for *recognition*:

> Self-consciousness exists *in-itself* and *for-itself*, since and thereby it is in and for itself for another [self-consciousness]; that is, it is only as something recognized. The concept of this unity in its duplication, of infinity realizing itself in self-consciousness, is a manifold and ambiguous limitation, so that its moments must in part be strictly kept distinct, and in part in this distinguishing they must also be taken and known always in its contraposed significance, or as not distinguished. The double significance of what is distinguished lies in the essence of self-consciousness, its infinitude, or its being directly the opposite of the determinateness in which it is posited. The detailed exposition of the concept of this spiritual unity within its duplication presents us the movement of *recognition*. (*PS* 109.8–18/M 111)

For self-consciousness there is another self-consciousness; it has come *out of itself*. This has a double significance: *first* it has lost its own self, for it finds itself as an *other* essence; *second*, it has thereby sublated the other, for it does not regard the other as essential, but sees *itself* in the other (*PS* 109.8–23/M 111).

Recognition comes about through a dramatic struggle that arises from the encounter of two self-consciousnesses. Hegel describes this life-and-death struggle in terms of the dynamic master–slave relationship. The ultimate lesson of the master–slave dialectic is that the realization of our capacities as subjects in the world requires the mutual recognition of ourselves as members of a community.

Here Hegel indicates one very basic feature of human subjectivity: that its reality lies not in solitary existence but in interaction with other selves. This interaction is mediated not only by "externality" (the objective world), but also by others and is "an infinite relation of myself to myself... *in the being of other persons*" (*Enc.* §490). According to Hegel, someone acquires the characteristics of subjectivity (Hegel often uses in this context the term "personality") only in the *fact of being recognized* by other people. For Hegel the very phenomenon of recognition is the most important methodological instrument for socializing the self. The process of recognition is a process of establishing important relations between single individuals, relations that are then reflected in their interactions with each other. In these interactions, an individual consciousness becomes aware of its own individuality and also appropriates its universal content and its freedom as the result of its dependence on others. This dependence is not one-sided. The individuals "*recognize* themselves as *mutually recognizing themselves*" (*PS* 110.29/M 112). This mutual interdependence is the real framework in which the formation and enculturation (*Bildung*) of the human individual takes place. Hegel shows that the self cannot exist as a solitary individual nor even as an ego that merely coexists with others. The individual self must be engaged in specific relations with others characterized by mutual interest and involvement. Yet relating to other selves is not relating to oneself; it necessarily is and must be recognized as relating to *others* who are not only distinct from, but are also opposed to oneself. The process of recognition is thus a dialectical progression towards the unity of conflicting entities in which the otherness of what is opposed is not simply consumed, but rather is appropriated in a way that allows development to higher stages of the (historical) involvement and development of consciousness.

The key theme of Hegel's discussion of a struggle for recognition is that subjectivity is mediated through relations with other people. This involves recognizing a very basic feature of our mutual interdependence, even as thinkers, namely our intersubjectivity. Hegel's insight here is that subjectivity is always intersubjectivity, because our subjectivity is necessarily mediated through our relations with others. Our intersubjective life and activity, including our knowledge, he calls "spirit." Hegel points out that in the struggle for recognition, where "one self-consciousness exists for [another] self-consciousness," the "concept of *spirit* is already available for us" (*PS* 108.29–35/M 110). He continues:

> What further becomes for consciousness is the experience of what spirit is, this absolute substance, which, in the perfected freedom and self-sufficiency of its opposition, namely various different self-consciousnesses which are for themselves, is their unity, the *I* that is *we*, and the *we* that is *I*. Consciousness first has its turning point in Self-consciousness, as in the concept of spirit, at which it steps out of the colorful show of the sensuous here and out of the empty night of the supersensible beyond into the spiritual day of the present. (*PS* 108.35–109.3/M 110–11)

In this passage Hegel reconfirms that the formation of the individual subject is inconceivable without its involvement in the subject–subject relation and interacting with other individuals who are also interested in such interactions. The specifics of mutual interdependence lie in the fact that, although it results from our individual activity, it necessarily has within it fundamental universal elements. This universality is determined by the very character of social connections. Although intersubjective relations are heterogeneous, they always have something in common, viz. common ways of behaving, both bodily and linguistically, without which interaction among individuals cannot occur. What is common in each of us, without which our life would be impossible, is our communal and social nature. This Hegel designates "spirit."

In later chapters of the *Phenomenology*, Hegel further explains the idea of intersubjectivity by highlighting its centrality to human social life in the various forms of its appearance. By examining social dimensions of human individuals, including the customs, practices, and institutions within which individuals become who they are, he shows that individuals and social institutions are mutually interdependent; neither exists nor has the character it does without its proper complement. Yet already in the chapter on self-consciousness, Hegel shapes and underlines the whole concept of intersubjectivity.[21] Hegel's concept attempts to overcome the atomistic view of the isolated individual who is essentially self-contained and complete prior to his engagement with the world and entering into any relations with other rational beings. The other becomes an indispensable condition for the consciousness and the actualization of one's own freedom. At the same time,

Hegel makes clear that the coexistence of free agents and their interaction presupposes as an *a priori* condition the idea of *community* of individuals that is, not historically, but transcendentally prior to these individuals. A "we" grounds the "I"; not only is my freedom possible only by my agency being acknowledged by my community, but the very concept of individuality is a reciprocal concept and can be thought only in relation to another self. Making recognition a crucial element of the progression of the "I" for its sheer self-awareness, Hegel demonstrates that individuals are conscious of themselves only as participants in collective values, endeavors, and institutions, not as atomic individuals, bearers of independent selfhood unto themselves. Unlike Descartes or Fichte, whose approaches to subject and subjectivity can be described in terms of "atomistic individualism," Hegel develops a position of "moderate collectivism."[22] On this view, epistemic justification cannot depend simply on the single individual subject. Each epistemic principle must be developed in a justificatory process that must obtain not merely individual but collective validity. It is not sufficient to assess someone's judgment individually; epistemic justification requires mutual assessment of many rational individuals. Thus although individual autonomy and the epistemic conditions of the individual subject are necessary for rational justification, only collective ("universal") autonomy can fully achieve such justification. The same point holds regarding the social practices and principles that govern communal life, which likewise can be justified only in and through interrelations among individuals.

In contrast to Fichte, who also stresses the importance of intersubjective relations for the self's development, but whose understanding of intersubjectivity remains abstract, Hegel contends that intersubjectivity is an active and necessary engagement with concrete communal and social life. He views intersubjectivity as a crucial element of the life of any individual. The self-awareness and the sense of individuality of any subject are mediated by relations to other people. If one's free agency is not acknowledged by other rational subjects, one can not become properly conscious of oneself and one's personality. The relations between self and other are fundamental to human awareness and activity. The otherness that consciousness first experiences as a barrier to its goals is the (apparent) external reality of the natural and social world. This apparent externality blocks individual freedom and independence. Yet this otherness cannot be destroyed without destroying oneself, so there must be some reconciliation between the other and the self so that consciousness grasps itself through the other. This stage of reconciliation involves and requires reciprocal recognition. Through acknowledging the other as another and likewise as a self, one comes to recognize oneself as a free and conscious being. One's consciousness or self-awareness is possible only through mutual recognition by other subjects; this justifies our collective and social nature.[23] This is why the intersubjective activity that animates our spiritual, that is, our communal life takes place in a broad context of social reality and is a crucial part of the process of enculturating the self. The mechanisms of this enculturation as well as the ways we express ourselves collectively and culturally Hegel analyzes in the sections on "Reason" and "Spirit."

3.3 Subjectivity and the social world

Concluding that individual self-understanding is dependent upon a communal understanding, Hegel logically shifts his narrative to overtly historical and social considerations. The main theme of the chapter on "Reason" is the self-realization and self-actualization of the individual in the social realm. Hegel's central question here is how and to what degree we express ourselves collectively. The basic theme of "Reason" is thus the objectification of the subjective. Since this objectification takes place in social reality, Hegel focuses on *socially* objectified, mutable forms of self-realization of individual subjects.

Hegel begins his analysis with an historical excursus into the concept of social reality. He shows that modern understanding of social reality is built upon the concept of "impersonal" universal reason which finds its roots in the idea of the Christian God. In Christianity, God appears as the bearer of the highest truth to which we human beings willingly submit. Human life is thus not just fully dependent on, but gains its meaning only through God and His "pure" existence. Applied to human affairs this idea is reflected in recognition of the fundamental, constitutive role of the "impersonal" (supra-individual) reason for social life.[24]

Hegel points to the Greek *polis* as the first and perhaps the most striking example of a form of life built on the principle of reason. The ancient city-state displays a social form that is recognized by its participants as constituted by a rational system of law. Thus reason is implicitly identified as the substance of this form of life: in a *polis*, people live bonded by an ethical substance (*sittliche Substanz*), a set of shared practices and standards that undergird Greek social life. The rationality in question has no justificatory value, although it has a practical significance, because it is rational to do things in the customary way. Hegel, for whom the Greeks and the Greek way of life always serve as a positive background for discussion, praises the Greek *polis* as a form of social life in which the individual could achieve his fulfillment in public roles. However, Greek culture counts as "immediate spirit" because it lacks sufficient rational resources to resolve fundamental normative conflicts. Its "substantive unity between the self and the world" is indeed temporal and soon becomes an opposition between the community and individuals. The "ethical *power of the state* . . . as *actual universality* is a power opposed to individual being-for-itself" (*PS* 242.27–30/M 268). This leads to neglecting individuality: "*this* [particular] *individual* counts only as an *unactual shadow*" (*PS* 251.12/M 279).[25]

According to Hegel, not only the Greek *polis*, but also other pre-modern models of social life neglect individuality, for their social realities are built without regard to individuals' intentions and their own ideas of what is good and right.[26] Thus even though individuals are already conscious of themselves as participants in social institutions, no social actualization of rational individuality is possible here. Not only are the individual and the world split, but the social forms of life appear in unreconciled conflict with its individual forms. The capacity to recognize autonomous individuals as the bearers of collective and social values is the distinguishing mark of modern culture and politics. The basic concepts of law, morality, and religion in the modern age rest on the claim that individuals may act according to their own rationally determined convictions and that social institutions respect these convictions.

Yet, as Hegel shows, Modern culture initially fails to develop a model of social reality that can give appropriate expression to these claims. Neither a Faustian attempt to reconstruct the "true" reality in terms of the "full human life," nor a sentimental belief in the "law of the heart," nor an appeal to "virtue" and altruism is able to provide a model that can explain the self-actualization of individuals in and through social actions and judgments. Hegel argues that Modern culture cannot succeed in principle, for the opposition between individual action and universal ("impersonal") reason is irreconcilable, at least in the form in which it appears in the Modern culture. Hegel interprets this as a sign of a deep crisis in reason, and therefore in modern culture itself. The essence of this crisis he sees in the "individualism" of Modern culture. He explains that in its concern with actualization of individuality within social life, Modern culture focuses on private interests and claims of individuals instead of focusing on social institutions which represent a collective consciousness and universal will. In this way, Modern theories take the individual and its quest for self-actualization individualistically. Even Kant, who comes to the rescue of Modern culture and seems to respond to the challenge of "impersonal" reason by his concept of the "kingdom of ends," which consists of spontaneously acting, self-legislating individuals, does not fully appreciate and consider the manifold mutual dependencies among interacting individuals. For this reason, Hegel argues, although it is important in terms of Modern intellectual development, Modern culture is not able to provide a coherent model for the self-actualization of individuals and thus it cannot serve as an actual guide to action.

The main lesson of Hegel's brilliant if sometimes obscure series of portraits of European life and his critique of Modern models of social reality is that individual self-actualization fails when it uses as its starting point its own individualistic convictions. In real society, the self-actualization of the individual always occurs not only in the context of one's mutual interdependence with other people, but within collective forms of life. As Hegel puts it,

> The *single* consciousness . . . is only 'this' extant one, in so far as he is conscious of the universal consciousness within his own being as his [very] being, since his action and existence are the universal custom.
> In the life of the people the concept of the actualization of self-conscious reason has in fact its completed reality, to view in the self-sufficiency of the *other* its complete *unity* with it, or to have as my object this *free thingness* of the other which I find before me, which is the negative of myself, as *my* being for *myself*. (*PS* 194.14–21/M 212)

Thus individual self-actualization depends not only on desires and decisions of this concrete individual but also on intentions and actions of other practical agents and is necessarily influenced by law, customs, and other social factors.

By conceiving of social reality in this way, Hegel accomplishes several things. First, he reaffirms the idea of intersubjectivity, but now as a medium of self-realization of the individual. The individual self that is real "in and for itself" "presents" or "expresses" itself in the social world through intersubjective activity. Second, in this way Hegel also stresses the social dimensions of human individuals. Social life is the crucial element of any individuality and subjectivity:

> [Individuals] are conscious of themselves as being these individual self-sufficient independent beings through their sacrifice of their particularity and by this universal substance being their soul and essence, just as this universal again is their own *doing* as particular individuals, or is the work they have brought forth. (*PS* 194.26–29/ M 212–13)

Only in social reality and through participating in social institutions and practices do individuals become who they are. This occurs only when they "sacrifice" their particularity, "give up" their pure individual needs and desires and "dissolve" themselves in the universal, making communal and social goals their own.

The idea of "dissolving" the individual in the universal is often taken as a sign of Hegel's universalism and his emphasis of the universal over the particular. I grant that Hegel is indeed guilty of sometimes not avoiding such a problem, which is due to the absolute character of his idealism. Yet in this particular context Hegel is absolutely right to stress the universality of the social subject. Here he clearly grasps that the practical agent acting on the scene of social reality is not a single subject or a separate individual, but rather an associate within an association of individuals, or, more precisely, individuals organized into a community. This "universal agent" that Hegel calls "a people" bears a "communal" self-consciousness.

Hegel does not claim that institutions or collective organizations like civil society or the state have their own consciousness in the sense of having subjective representations or ideas. Although he argues that the community's self-understanding can sometimes be embedded in special individuals who represent the values and goals of a community, he stresses that communal self-consciousness is not the same as individual self-consciousness. They are, however, linked to each other in a specific way. "Communal" self-consciousness, though distinct from individual self-consciousnesses, emerges and develops through interplay among individuals in their conscious interactions within the social sphere. Furthermore, we human beings are not just "situated" in social reality, but rather are immanent in the social world and *produce* the socio-political context which is the theater of our own actions. Communal spirit does not descend upon the world and upon us from without, but emerges from *within* as a product of our own intersubjective (communal) activity through our sustained interactions. This is true even of the individualists' favorite example of individual economic initiative:

> The *labor* of the individual for his needs is equally a satisfaction of the needs of others as of his own, and the satisfaction of his own needs he obtains only through the labor of others. – As the individual in his *individual* work already *unconsciously* performs a *universal* work, so again he also performs the universal work as his *conscious* object;

the whole becomes, *as a whole*, his work, for which he sacrifices himself and thereby receives himself back from it. (*PS* 195.1–7/M 213)

This "whole," however, is not something separate from or alien to the individual. Although the individual "sacrifices" its singularity for the universality of the whole, the person's individuality does not simply disappear into communal spirit; it retains its "essential particularity" and independence within the social sphere. This retention of singularity and individuality is guaranteed by the universality of communal spirit itself. In Hegel's own words, "that even the most common functions [of the particular individual] are not for naught, but have actuality, occurs through the universal sustaining medium, through the *might* of the entire people" (*PS* 194.32–35/M 213).

In this way Hegel stresses that individuals and social institutions are *mutually interdependent*; neither exists nor has its character without the other. Thus, contrary to widespread misunderstanding, Hegel does not subordinate individuals to their communities; both aspects are necessary for each other and dependent upon each other. Just as an individual self cannot achieve its full self-realization without manifesting and actualizing itself in and through social and communal forms of life, the (self)-development of the universal ("communal") self, which *is* spirit, is not possible without individuals' participation in concrete historical and social processes. To appreciate this kind of development is the point of Hegel's philosophy of history, which in the *Phenomenology* is laid out as the philosophy of "cosmic" or world-historical spirit. The exposition of self-development of spirit reveals the communal nature of humanity.

In the chapter on "Reason," Hegel clearly shows that the self-actualization of individuals must be understood in terms of human production of the social context and collective forms of human existence. It would be mistaken, however, to understand this claim as confirming the idea that only collective forces are real and individuality has no independent reality. Quite the contrary, what makes the social world real for Hegel is the individual and his action. Hegel argues that

> this universal substance speaks its *universal language* in the customs and laws of its people; yet this extant unchanging essence is nothing other than the expression of the apparently opposed particular individuality itself; the laws express what every individual person *is* and *does*... (*PS* 195.11–15/M 213)

The true agent of the world is not a disembodied universal reason or communal spirit, but the individual in his concrete subjectivity. Social or communal reality is produced by the individual as a manifestation of his own individuality and subjectivity. This is, however, not an automatic but a conscious social activity of the individual subject. Hegel stresses that the individual can be "real" only when he becomes aware of the social order and manifests this awareness in his own social role. According to Hegel, the only sphere where the individual can actualize himself is the sphere of living culture. Historical discussion of culture and its role in self-development of the human individual and humanity is the central theme of Hegel's chapter on "Spirit."

3.4 "*Bildung*" as a link between individual and universal

Hegel's chapter on "Spirit" is rich in content and examines a broad range of important philosophical issues and concepts. Here I focus on an idea rarely discussed, though essential to our topic, namely Hegel's concept of *Bildung* and its significance for his account of concrete subjectivity. This discussion sheds light on Hegel's response to the issue of how we can discern the adequacy of our apparent self-knowledge (both individual and collective) within our social and cultural context.

In his analyses of social reality, Hegel points out that the social world is not simply a result of our collective enterprise, but is also our *historical* product. Although any individual at any given time participates in this production, we create our social context collectively through our historical actions. The social world is not a making of one individual or any single group; neither is it an outcome of only one (even most noble and commonly esteemed) particular action. It is instead a creation of mankind, the result of generations of activity of human beings through history. This history is a concrete process of human development which itself occurs in social and cultural reality. Each single generation, each historical period, leaves its unique individual traces in this grand process. These traces are depicted in human culture, which, according to Hegel, is never static, but always constantly developing, moving, and changing.

We human individuals stand in complex relations to this spontaneous element. As single subjects we seem to be thrown into a certain social environment and thus encounter the culture as a world that is given to us as "ready-made." Yet in our encounter we necessarily establish relations to what we encounter and thus become engaged in certain activities within our culture. This is the discovery of what we find as "ready-made." This process of discovery is not just a cognitive, but concurrently a practical activity of internalization of what is external. In this way, the individual decodes the meaning(s) of what he encounters. Yet by engaging practically with cultural phenomena, he also produces new objects, situations, and meanings that themselves become events within the culture. These events appear as such not only to the individual agent, but also to other individuals; thus their interactions are mediated by social and cultural objects and events. Hence culture penetrates all spheres of human reality and affairs, and is a collective human undertaking.

In his section on "Spirit," Hegel offers a grand panorama of the historical process of culture, though by focusing on a specific aspect that he considers crucial for the development of human subjectivity. This he calls '*Bildung*', meaning the *process of enculturation* mentioned above. By focusing on *Bildung*, Hegel follows many of his great contemporaries,[27] yet his approach is novel. The novelty lies in a new meaning assigned to the term by Hegel. In contrast to his contemporaries, Hegel interprets *Bildung* not as an education narrowly construed as what takes place on the individual level, but rather as a universal historical process in which we all are collectively involved and in which we necessarily participate.

Hegel clearly distinguishes between *Kultur* and *Bildung*. While "culture" (*Kultur*), in his view, generally designates whatever is in one's social environment, "enculturation" (*Bildung*) designates whatever one has internalized or (better yet) mastered from and within that environment. Hegel's distinction marks an advance over his predecessors and contemporaries, including Kant and Fichte. Hegel builds on this distinction by emphasizing the process of enculturation, which provides him with the context for addressing distinctions between and the integration of, e.g., subject and object, individual and universal, or inner and outer. These processes do not occur or unfold of themselves, but require and occur in actual, historical work by individuals, groups (e.g., production or research groups), or even peoples.

In the *Phenomenology*, Hegel shows that *Bildung* is a multifaceted phenomenon. Several of Hegel's insights into *Bildung* are especially germane here. The first and most easily identifiable role of *Bildung* in Hegel's work is to label the process of individual cultural (or spiritual) development. The path of the *Phenomenology* as a whole (including its internal transitions) represents the *Bildung* of the individual consciousness, the transformation from its purely natural or unenlightened standpoint of sense-certainty and its lack of self-awareness to the concluding philosophical standpoint, where the individual becomes fully aware of himself through rational reflection on his knowledge and his social role. This is a process by which the "I" develops into concrete subjectivity. This transformation is not a natural biological process, nor is it mere growth, like natural organic growth. *Bildung* necessarily assumes the active involvement of the individual as well as his full conscious commitment; it is an individual's *self*-overcoming of the naturalness and sense-certainty and his *self*-development towards full awareness of himself. Because the individual is not solitary, because his relation to the world is mediated through his relations with other people, *Bildung* is a conscious activity of interdependent individuals.[28]

The second role of *Bildung* in Hegel's *Phenomenology* concerns how the individual's *Bildung* occurs through his *recapturing* and *appropriating* the "history of the cultural development of the world" (*PS* 25.7/M 16), which represents the "stages" of the process of enculturation (*Bildungstufen*) of the "world spirit." Thus the single individual, in the process of his self-enculturation, goes through the stages which the "cosmic" spirit has traversed and in which it has left its traces. So the individual discovers these stages as the great spiritual "conquests of the past." Hegel writes:

> This past existence is already acquired property of universal spirit which constitutes the substance of the individual or his inorganic nature. – In this regard the individual's process of enculturation (*Bildung*), considered from his side, consists in the individual appropriating what thus lies before him, to nourish himself upon his inorganic nature and to take possession of it for himself. (*PS* 25.7–12/M 16)

The individual, who is "thrown" into and brought up in the culture, is already influenced and constituted by existing culture and its traditional values, norms, and standards. Thus tradition appears as the individual's substance, the constitutive foundation of his subjectivity. Yet from the start the individual views that tradition as something external and foreign; although in itself, as a social substance, it is a spiritual essence, it does not appear to fit the individual's own spirit and his urge for spiritual independence and freedom. The solution to this real conflict lies in the individual *appropriating* tradition and making it his own, internalized content: what was "inorganic" now becomes part of an individual's "organic" nature. In these terms Hegel discusses the very important issue of individual *internalization* of cultural history. Hegel contends that this process involves a special relation between the single individual and the "cosmic" spirit. Hegel points out that

> the task of guiding the individual from his uncultivated standpoint to [the standpoint of] knowing had to be grasped in its universal sense, by considering the universal individual, the world spirit, in its enculturation. (*PS* 24.13–15/M 16)

Seen from the perspective presented in the *Phenomenology*, the individual views and internalizes cultural history as the *Bildung* of spirit itself. Thus the single individual depends upon the universal spirit both as the source from which individual persons derive much of their identity (in the sense of culturally elaborated values and norms), and also as the framework for evaluation of their achievements. Hegel stresses, however, that there can be no "cosmic" spirit separate from the particular individuals: the former exists, thinks, and acts *only in* concrete individuals, and the spirit's "self-development" is due to the dynamic development and continuous transformation of these individuals. This is why Hegel demands that tradition and cultural history receive their import not merely from the process of the *Bildung* of spirit itself, but rather from the individual's *making* this tradition his own. In this way, the immanent critique of tradition is not only possible; it is for Hegel a crucial source of progress in culture and in human history. Thus the individual remains the ultimate measure and the "absolute form" of the process of enculturation.

At the same time, Hegel warns that the process of *Bildung* is not merely a biographical but a historical human undertaking. It unfolds itself as a social process, on the basis of which alone individuals can reinvestigate various topics and issues to advance our collective knowledge and understanding by better identifying the genuine characteristics of any specific natural or social phenomenon (cf. *PS* 10–12/M 1–3). In *Bildung*, human individuals not only become knowledgeable about the natural and social world, but also conscious of themselves and their own place within the world.

Fundamental to Hegel's conception of *Bildung* is that it is not automatic, nor is it the mere unfolding of pre-formed potentials. Instead, whatever potentials are realized through *Bildung* are general ones; whatever specific forms they acquire are literally constructed by us, whether individually or collectively, in working through whatever problems we confront or puzzles we seriously investigate. Through this alone do we acquire our essential "second nature" – in this Hegel agrees with both Aristotle and Marx (cf. *PS* 267.26–37/M 298) – as educated, effective rational agents capable of expressing ourselves in our own actual activities.²⁹ Such ability for self-expression, either in thought or action, is a vehicle of self-awareness and self-knowledge, when we recognize, assess, and respond to what we have in fact done. This process, diligently pursued, develops our genuine freedom, our intellectual and practical command of ourselves and of our world, both social and natural.³⁰ Thus the process of enculturation (*Bildung*) is central to and provides the basis for both our self-realization and knowledge of our social and natural environment. Furthermore, we are not mere observers nor disinterested, disengaged thinkers. Instead, we are active, effective agents, actual vehicles and loci of that process. This is why both our failures and our successes become part of the context of our further actions, inquiries, or experiments and thus an essential part of our collective (universal) and individual (empirical) subjectivity.

Three very important points directly follow from this discussion. First, it is impossible to understand Hegel's account of concrete subjectivity (and his conception of selfhood) without grasping his concept of *Bildung*. The process of enculturation requires and guarantees conscious activity of the self in Hegel's philosophy, since without this activity there is no *Bildung* and, therefore, no subjectivity at all. Furthermore, *Bildung* appears as a constitutive element of human subjectivity. It is not some kind of additional activity we undertake in order to satisfy some individual desire or to achieve a determinate and temporal goal. Instead, this is the most important mode of our existence in the world. Second, it is a misinterpretation of Hegel's account of *Bildung* to reduce it either to a merely individual intellectual event (education, narrowly construed) or to economic production.³¹ Hegel contends that *Bildung* is a real historical process occurring within the life of any individual, any culture, and (in principle) even the human race. It is a concrete universal process in which we human beings necessarily participate and through which we become aware of ourselves and our natural and social environment. Third, *Bildung* provides a conceptual bridge between distinct and conflicting notions of subject and object, individual and universal, internal and external. The link Hegel forges between the process of individual enculturation and the *Bildung* of "cosmic" spirit indicates the essential interdependence of individual and universal in social, cultural, and historical life. Just as there is no individuality without the individual's participation in universal social and cultural life, there can be no such universal cultural life without activity of individuals. In the process of enculturation, the individual, both as concrete subject and as a collective historical subject, humanity at large, creates culture and at the same time creates himself through culture.

4 Conclusion

Hegel's *Phenomenology* offers a great panorama of the development and embodiment of spirit within the real world. Accomplished in and through the activity of human individuals over historical time, this process exhibits the progression of human self-understanding and freedom. What is described from the perspective of "cosmic" spirit, at the same time takes place and should be understood from another perspective, as a real development of human individuals. In the *Phenomenology* we observe a double movement: the embodiment and realization of "cosmic" spirit in individuals and the development of individuals raising themselves to "cosmic" spirit. Both movements, though opposite in direction, coincide historically and practically; only taken together can they reconstruct the real process of the historical development of human spirit captured in Hegel's *Phenomenology of Spirit*. We must read this movement in both directions at once. The individual self becomes who he is by absorbing spirit – in the variety of all its forms and appearances (*Gestalten*) in the world – into his own specific structures, and conversely, spirit reaches its self-realization in and through its embodiment in individuals who interact with each other and the world. According to Hegel, this complex process of mediation between collective spirit and individual spirits is human history.

Grounding his social ontology in the concept of spirit, Hegel presents human history as the history of human community and communal forms of life. He shows that individuals are *communal, social* agents. As a natural creature, conditioned by its biological and physiological configurations, the individual develops all his abilities, skills, and characteristics through his engagement with the culture and community which fosters and educates him through the process of *Bildung*. Yet this dependence of individuals on their community is not one-sided. Just as individuals cannot become who they are without engaging in communal life, there is neither communal life nor human communities without their real agents, human individuals who think, will, and act, and through whose actions alone human history occurs and becomes real. Thus individuals and their communities are mutually interdependent and their developments reciprocally condition and complement each other. This is what Hegel analyzes in the *Phenomenology* in terms of the interrelation of spirit and concrete subjectivity. Hegel maintains that only taken as a mutual process of individual and communal development can we understand universality within human history and preserve the autonomy of its social agents.

Notes

1 Cf. Löwith (1991), Theunissen (1970, esp. 59–62), Schmidt (1974), Henrich and Horstmann (1984).
2 Cf. Pippin (1999), Rosen (1974), Taylor (2000), Pinkard (2000).
3 This statement directly concerns "cosmic" substance as subject. However, Hegel holds the same view about individual subjectivity. This view clearly pervades Hegel's Introduction; it is formulated most directly in these two sentences: ". . . consciousness is for itself its own *concept*, hence it immediately transcends what is limited, and, since this limitedness belongs to it, it transcends itself" (*PS* 57.25–27/M 51); "This *dialectical* movement, which consciousness exercises on *itself* – on its knowledge as well as its object – *insofar as the new, true object emerges to consciousness* as the result of it, is precisely that which is called *experience*" (*PS* 60.15–18/M 55).
4 In the Preface, Hegel points out that the result does not represent the "actual whole"; the latter is "the result together with its becoming" (*PS* 10.35–36/M 2).
5 Cf. above, pp. 2–6. – *Ed.*

6   For detailed analysis of Fichte's concept of individual subjectivity see Bykova (2008, 131–39).
7   Westphal (1998, 139–40). Cf. above, pp. 10, 14. – *Ed.*
8   One of the best treatments of Hegel's notion of "dialectical" contradiction and its distinction from the formal-logical concept of contradiction is in Wolff (1977, esp. 35–57, 102ff.).
9   Burbidge (2006, 38, Footnote 2; cf. 65–6, 72–3).
10 For detailed analysis of all three facets of Hegel's account of subjectivity, see Bykova (1991).
11 For an extended analysis of the *Science of Logic* as a theory of absolute subjectivity, see Düsing (1984).
12 Cf. Horstmann (1990), Fulda (1990), Hösle (1998, esp. vol. 1), Pinkard (2000), Pippin (2005, esp. 27–56); Seigel (2005, 391–423).
13 Burbidge (2006, 24).
14 Perhaps the most interesting in this regard is Hegel's course on the *Philosophy of Spirit* taught in the Winter semester of 1827/1828 (Hegel 1994).
15 Some of Hegel's central ideas about "pure" or "absolute" subjectivity also find their roots in the *Phenomenology*, which was originally shaped as a paradigm and first part of Hegel's philosophical system and only later gave way to logic and the *Encyclopedia*.
16 Such a position is especially well articulated in Hösle (1998, vol. 1). Cf. Habermas (1999).
17 One clear indicator of this is that in both editions of the *Logic*, Hegel states that the *Phenomenology*, uniquely, is the "justification" and "deduction" of the standpoint of the *Logic* (*GW* 11:20.5–18, 21:32.23–33.3; 11:20.37–21.11, 21:33.20–34.1).
18 In his detailed commentary on Hegel's *Phenomenology*, Henry Harris points out that Hegel's genuine philosophy of history is in the *Phenomenology* and not in the *Philosophy of World History*, as is traditionally assumed. Harris argues that, "the Science of Experience is properly the speculative philosophy of history as applied to and perfectly exemplified in the history of Western Europe as one self-constituted, and self-conscious (i.e. universally recognized) community. Seen thus, in its *proper* perspective, the *Phenomenology of Spirit* is a far more interesting essay in the speculative philosophy of history, than the *Philosophy of World History* as conceived and executed at Berlin in the context of Hegel's mature system. . . . The *Phenomenology* shows us what the *Weltgeist* is; the *Philosophy of World History* appears to take it for granted that we already *know* that" (Harris 1997, 2:732–3). Coming to agree with Harris's intention to stress the actual significance of the historic development presented in the *Phenomenology*, I still think that its main objectives do not coincide with the aim of the *Philosophy of World History*. In my opinion, Hegel's main concern in the *Phenomenology* is the history of self-consciousness, which purpose lies in the systematic genesis of cognitive capacities of the human mind. In contrast to Fichte and Schelling, who conceived the history of self-consciousness as a development of cognitive capacities as such, Hegel takes this to be a historical process, by which natural consciousness advances in justification of our claims, both cognitive and practical.
19 Zöller (2000, 208).
20 The same point, though in connection with Hegel's *Philosophy of Right*, is stressed by Kenneth Westphal, when he explains Hegel's statement that substance is nothing but interrelation of its accidents (and vice versa): "Hegel stated his view in easily misunderstood metaphysical terms. He states that individuals are related to the ethical order and its powers "as accidents to substance" (§145). This certainly can sound like individuals are subservient to a social whole. However, Hegel held that "substance is in essence the relation of accidents to itself" (§163R). This is to say, substance is essentially the relation among the 'accidents' (properties or members) of something. More

briefly, he stated that "substance is the totality of its accidents" (§67R). This doctrine is part of Hegel's holistic metaphysics, and it is stated in the section of the *Encyclopedia* to which Hegel refers in §163R, *Enc.* §150" (Westphal 1993, 265 n. 5.) Also see Westphal's (1994) annotated excerpts from Hegel's *Phenomenology*, in which he explicates this point in the *Phenomenology*.

21 Here, however, he *only explains* the concept, while still setting the stage for a "real performance": a proof that this concept is true of us human beings. This proof is outlined in the chapter on "Spirit" and then further detailed, bringing in more factual historical material, in the *Philosophy of Right*. In the *Philosophy of Right* Hegel develops his proof for intersubjectivity in terms of the concept of a community of free agents. This community is not just an association based on reciprocal recognition, but requires a kind of supra-individual identity that is distinct from and logically prior to the individuals. This supra-individual identity is warranted by intersubjective relations. In the case of a more abstract community of right (at the beginning of the *Philosophy of Right*) the exponent of subjectivity is right itself as the universal substance of the will of the individuals.

22 In ascribing this position to Hegel, I follow Kenneth Westphal (2006) who calls Hegel's unique social ontology 'moderate collectivism'. He argues that Hegel "undercut the sterile debate between [atomistic] 'individualism' and 'holism' in social ontology" (ibid., 555) by showing the social character of human individuals and the mutual interdependence of individuals and their communities. For more detailed discussion of this topic, especially in relation to epistemological issues, see Westphal (2003, esp. chapter 10).

23 In one important sense, the German term '*das Bewußtsein*' means being conscious or aware of oneself.

24 See above, chapter 3, especially regarding "Unhappy Consciousness." – *Ed.*

25 Hegel discusses this idea in the *Philosophy of Right*, showing that the issues of subjective freedom and the right of the subject's particularity were missing in antiquity and came into life only in modern times, with the advent of Christianity (cf. *PR* §§124R, 46R, 185). Commenting on Hegel's view, Allegra de Laurentiis (2000, 73) explains that, "Hegel's thesis is not a sweeping claim about antiquity's lack of concern for individual differences. He does not deny that the ancient world was able to discern or even acknowledge individual personality or the idiosyncratic character of people's particular existence.... Hegel's point is rather more specific: the ancient world could not tolerate, by penalty of its own disintegration, 'the *autonomous development* of particularity' (*PR* §185; emphasis by de Laurentiis). It is the *freedom* or *right to* personal subjectivity, not its contingent *Dasein*, that is ancient philosophy's foe."

26 In the *Philosophy of Right*, Hegel analyses in detail the failure of the ancient Greek and other pre-modern societies to acknowledge a right or freedom of subjectivity. He shows that personal subjectivity first becomes recognized only in the modern *politeia*, because, contrary to the Greek *polis*, "the principle of the modern state requires that the whole of an individual's activity shall be mediated through his will" (*PR* §299). Thus the subject must be not just engaged in social actions, but must engage in them voluntarily; the action must be "willed" to account for individual autonomy and freedom of subjectivity. This "intentional" character of subject's action was lacking in all pre-modern models of social life.

27 It is worth noting that the notion of *Bildung* was central to the German intellectual discourse of the eighteenth and nineteenth centuries. German romantics, great educator reformers as well as philosophers, each in his own manner, profoundly worked on the concept of *Bildung*; cf. Schmidt (1884–1902, esp. vol. 6).

28 *Bildung* is not construed by Hegel as a self-conscious goal of an individual's activity. Although the path of self-formation and self-fulfillment is one that each individual necessarily follows, *Bildung* is not originally set as one's own end or a self-assigned

collective goal of the community of individuals. It would perhaps be better described as an example of a positive "unintended" consequence, like the one illustrated by Adam Smith's (1904, 4.2.9) metaphor of the "invisible hand." Smith argues that each individual, seeking "only his own gain, . . . [is] led by an invisible hand to promote an end which was no part of his [original] intention." The same is true of *Bildung*: acting from "their own self interest" (of gaining their own self-awareness and determining themselves), individuals also promote the end that is the collective (public) interest in becoming enculturated within culture and community. As an instance of Hegel's use of the sociological "law of unintended consequences," *Bildung* is construed as an unanticipated result of individuals' actions. To guarantee its progressive character, Hegel suggests that it must constantly undergo mutual assessment of its principles and occur under the scrutiny of the community.

29 As Frederick Neuhouser (2000, 149) notes in this connection, "although it is the essential nature of human beings to be free, freedom does not come naturally to [us]."
30 The same idea is more clearly articulated in the *Philosophy of Right*, where Hegel claims that in its "absolute determination" (*Bestimmung*), *Bildung* "is liberation and the work of higher liberation, . . . the absolute transition to a no longer immediate and natural, but a spiritual ethical substantiality." For the individual this process means "hard work against the mere subjectivity of behavior, against the immediacy of desire, as well as against the subjective vanity of feeling, and the arbitrariness of suiting oneself" (*PR* §187R).
31 For an interpretation of Hegel's notion of *Bildung* in terms of a narrowly construed education, see Munzel (2003, esp. 120–2, 124–6). Even Gadamer (1989, 9–12) tends to this misunderstanding.

References

Burbidge, J. W. (2006) *The Logic of Hegel's Logic. An Introduction*. Peterborough, Ont.: Broadview.
Bykova, M. (1991) "Einige Gedanken zum Geheimnis der Subjektivität bei Hegel," in B. Tuschling et al. (eds.), *Psychologie und Antropologie oder Philosophie des Geistes* (pp. 462–89). Stuttgart: Klett-Cotta.
Bykova, M. (2008) "Fichte's Doctrine of Self-Positing Subject and Concept of Subjectivity," *Fichte-Studien* 32: 129–39.
Düsing, K. (1984) *Das Problem der Subjektivität in Hegels Logik. Systematische und entwicklungsgeschichtliche Untersuchungen zum Prinzip des Idealismus und zur Dialektik*. Bonn: Bouvier.
Fulda, H. F. (1990) "Spekulatives Denken und Selbstbewußtsein," in K. Cramer, H. F. Fulda et al. (eds.), *Theorie der Subjektivität* (pp. 444–79). Frankfurt am Main: Suhrkamp.
Gadamer, H.-G. (1989) *Truth and Method*, tr. J. Weinsheimer and D. G. Marshall. New York: Crossroad.
Habermas, J. (1999) "From Kant to Hegel and back. – The Move towards Detranscendentalization," *European Journal of Philosophy* 7.2: 129–57.
Harris, H. S. (1997) *Hegel's Ladder: A Commentary of Hegel's Phenomenology of Spirit*. Cambridge, Mass.: Hackett Publishing Co.
Hegel, G. W. F. (1994) *Vorlesungen über die Philosophie des Geistes. Berlin 1827/1828. Nachgeschrieben von Johann Eduard Erdmann und Ferdinand Walter*, ed. F. Hespe and B. Tuschling, in Hegel, *Vorlesungen. Ausgewählte Nachschriften und Manuskripte*, vol. 13. Hamburg: Meiner.

Henrich, D. and Horstman, R.-P., eds. (1984) *Hegels Logik der Philosophie: Religion und Philosophie in der Theorie des absoluten Geistes.* Stuttgart: Klett-Cotta.

Horstmann, R.-P. (1990) "Gibt es ein philosophisches Problem des Selbstbewußtseins?," in K. Cramer, H. F. Fulda et al. (eds.), *Theorie der Subjektivität* (pp. 220–50). Frankfurt am Main: Suhrkamp.

Hösle, V. (1998) *Hegels System. Der Idealismus der Subjektivität und das Problem der Intersubjektivität*, 2 vols. Hamburg: Meiner, 2nd ed.

Laurentiis, A. de (2000) "Silenced Subjectivity. Remarks on Hegel's View of Plato's World," *Studies in Practical Philosophy: a Journal of Ethical and Political Philosophy* 2.1: 64–79.

Löwith, K. (1991) *From Hegel to Nietzsche: The Revolution in Nineteenth-Century Thought*, tr. D. E. Green. New York: Columbia University Press.

Munzel, G. F. (2003) "Kant, Hegel, and the Rise of Pedagogical Science," in R. Curren (ed.), *A Companion to the Philosophy of Education* (pp. 113–39). Oxford: Blackwell.

Neuhouser, F. (2000). *The Foundations of Hegel's Social Theory: Actualizing Freedom.* Cambridge, Mass.: Harvard University Press.

Pinkard, T. (2000) *Hegel. A Biography.* Cambridge: Cambridge University Press.

Pippin, R. (1999) *Hegel's Idealism. The Satisfactions of Self-Consciousness.* Cambridge: Cambridge University Press.

Pippin, R. (2005) *The Persistence of Subjectivity. On the Kantian Aftermath.* Cambridge: Cambridge University Press.

Rosen, S. (1974) *G. W. F. Hegel: An Introduction to the Science of Wisdom.* New Haven, CT: Yale University Press.

Schmidt, E. (1974) *Hegels System der Theologie.* Berlin: deGruyter.

Schmidt, K. A. (1884–1902) *Geschichte der Erziehung von Anfang an bis auf unsere Zeit*, 6 vols. Stuttgart: J. G. Cotta.

Seigel, J. (2005) *The Idea of the Self: Thought and Experience in Western Europe since the Seventeenth Century.* Cambridge: Cambridge University Press.

Smith, A. (1904) *An Inquiry into the Nature and Causes of the Wealth of Nations.* London: Methuen.

Taylor, M. C. (2000) *Journeys to Selfhood: Hegel and Kierkegaard.* New York: Fordham University Press.

Theunissen, M. (1970) *Hegels Lehre vom absoluten Geist als theologisch-politisher Traktat.* Berlin: deGruyter.

Westphal, K. R. (1993) "The Basic Context and Structure of Hegel's *Philosophy of Right*," in F. C. Beiser (ed.), *The Cambridge Companion to Hegel* (pp. 234–69). Cambridge: Cambridge University Press.

Westphal, K. R. (1994) "Community as the Basis of Free Individual Action," in M. Daly (ed.), *Communitarism* (pp. 36–40). Belmont, Cal.: Wadsworth.

Westphal, K. R. (1998) *Hegel, Hume und die Identität wahrnehmerer Dinge. Historisch-kritisch Analyse zum Kapitel "Wahrnehmung" in der Phänomenologie von 1807.* Frankfurt am Main: Klostermann.

Westphal, K. R. (2003) *Hegel's Epistemology: A Philosophical Introduction to the Phenomenology of Spirit.* Cambridge, Mass.: Hackett Publishing Co.

Westphal, K. R. (2006) "Spirit," in J. Protevi (ed.), *The Dictionary of Continental Philosophy* (pp. 555–6). New Haven, CT: Yale University Press; also published as: *The Edinburgh Dictionary of Continental Philosophy*. Edinburgh: Edinburgh University Press.

Wolff, M. (1977) *Der Begriff des Widerspruchs. Eine Studie zur Dialektik Kants und Hegels.* Bodenhain: Hain Verlag.

Zöller, G. (2000) "German Realism: the Self-limitation of Idealist Thinking in Fichte, Schelling and Schopenhauer," in K. Ameriks (ed.), *The Cambridge Companion to German Idealism* (pp. 200–18). Cambridge: Cambridge University Press.

Further Reading

Kaufmann, W. A. (1965) "The Preface to the *Phenomenology*: Translation with Commentary on Facing Pages," in W. A. Kaufmann, *Hegel: Reinterpretation, Texts, and Commentary* (pp. 363–459). London: Weidenfeld & Nicolson.

Kaufmann, W. (1966). *Hegel: Texts and Commentary*. New York: Double Day. (Self-standing edition of Kaufmann 1965.)

Schacht, R. (1975) "A Commentary on the Preface to Hegel's *Phenomenology of Spirit*," in R. Schacht, *Hegel and After* (pp. 41–68). Pittsburgh: University of Pittsburgh Press.

Stepelevich, L. S., ed. (1990) *Preface and Introduction to the Phenomenology of Mind*. New York: Macmillan, London: Collier Macmillan. (Includes extensive editorial introduction, pp. 1–56.)

Yovel, Y. (2005) *Hegel's Preface to the Phenomenology of Spirit*. Princeton, NJ: Princeton University Press. (Translation with extensive annotations.)

General Bibliography

This brief bibliography includes mainly recent works in English. References on specific chapters or sections of Hegel's *Phenomenology* may be found in the chapter References. Comprehensive bibliographies are listed below, §7.

1 Introductions to Hegel

Beiser, F. C. (2005) *Hegel*. London: Routledge.
Burbidge, J. (2007) *Hegel's Systematic Contingency*. Basingstoke: Palgrave Macmillan.
Fulda, H.-F. (2003) *Hegel*. Munich: Beck.
Hartnack, J. (1986) *From Radical Empiricism to Absolute Idealism*. Lewiston, ME: Mellen.
Houlgate, S. (2005) *An Introduction to Hegel: Reason, Truth and History*. Oxford: Blackwell.
Pinkard, T. (2000) *Hegel: A Biography*. Cambridge: Cambridge University Press.
Plant, R. (1973) *Hegel*. London: Routledge (rpt. 2007).
Taylor, C. (1979) *Hegel and Modern Society*. Cambridge: Cambridge University Press.

2 Introductions to Hegel's *Phenomenology of Spirit*

Lauer, Q. (1993) *A Reading of Hegel's Phenomenology of Spirit*, 2nd rev. ed. New York: Fordham University Press.
Marx, W. (1975) *Hegel's Phenomenology of Spirit, Its Point and Purpose: A Commentary on the Preface and Introduction*. New York: Harper & Row.
Shklar, J. N. (1976) *Freedom and Independence: A Study of the Political Ideas of Hegel's Phenomenology of Mind*. Cambridge: Cambridge University Press.
Stern, R. (2001) *Hegel and the Phenomenology of Spirit*. London: Routledge.
Westphal, K. R. (2003) *Hegel's Epistemology: A Philosophical Introduction to the Phenomenology of Spirit*. Cambridge, Mass.: Hackett Publishing Co.

3 English Translations of Hegel's *Phenomenology of Spirit*

Baillie, J. B. (1949) *The Phenomenology of Mind*. London: George Allen & Unwin; New York: Humanities, 2nd rev. ed.
Miller, A. V. (1977) *The Phenomenology of Spirit*. Oxford: The Clarendon Press.
Pinkard, T. (forthcoming) *Hegel's Phenomenology of Spirit*. Cambridge: Cambridge University Press.
Walker, N. (in preparation) *Hegel's Phenomenology of Spirit*. London: Routledge.

Also see:

Hegel, G. W. F. (1978) "The Phenomenology of Spirit (Summer Term, 1825)," German transcript with English translation in M. J. Petry (ed. and tr.), *Hegel's Philosophy of Subjective Spirit* (pp. 271–357). Dordrecht: Reidel.
Hegel, G. W. F. (1981) *The Berlin Phenomenology*, ed. and tr. M. J. Petry. Berlin: Springer. (English edition of previous item.)

Partial translations:

Kainz, H. (1994) *Hegel's Phenomenology of Spirit: Selections*. College Park, PA: Pennsylvania State University Press.
Kaufmann, W. A. (1966) "The Preface to the *Phenomenology*: Translation with Commentary on Facing Pages," in W. A. Kaufmann, *Hegel: Reinterpretation, Texts, and Commentary* (pp. 363–459). London: Weidenfeld & Nicolson.
Rauch, L. and Sherman, D. (1999). *Hegel's Phenomenology of Self-Consciousness*. Albany: State University of New York Press.
Shannon, D. E., ed. (2001) *Spirit*, tr. The Toronto Translation Group. Cambridge, Mass.: Hackett Publishing Co.
Stepelevich, L. S., ed. (1990) *Preface and Introduction to the Phenomenology of Mind*. New York: Macmillan; London: Collier Macmillan. (Includes extensive editorial introduction, pp. 1–56.)
Yovel, Y. (2005) *Hegel's Preface to the Phenomenology of Spirit*. Princeton, NJ: Princeton University Press.

4 Advanced Studies of Hegel's *Phenomenology of Spirit*

Forster, M. (1998) *Hegel's Idea of a Phenomenology of Spirit*. Chicago: University of Chicago Press.
Harris, H. S. (1997) *Hegel's Ladder*, 2 vols. Cambridge, Mass.: Hackett Publishing Co.
Hyppolite, J. (1974) *Genesis and Structure of Hegel's* Phenomenology of Spirit, tr. S. Cherniak and J. Heckman. Evanston, IL: Northwestern University Press.
Kojève, A. (1969) *Introduction to the Reading of Hegel*, ed. A. Bloom, tr. J. Nichols. New York: Basic Books.
Pinkard, T. (1994) *Hegel's Phenomenology: The Sociality of Reason*. Cambridge: Cambridge University Press.
Stewart, J. (2000) *The Unity of Hegel's Phenomenology of Spirit: A Systematic Interpretation*. Evanston, IL: Northwestern University Press.
Westphal, K. R. (1989) *Hegel's Epistemological Realism*. Dordrecht and Boston: Kluwer.

5 Hegel's *Science of Logic*

Burbidge, J. (2006) *The Logic of Hegel's Logic*. Peterborough, Ont.: Broadview.
Butler, C. (1996) *Hegel's Logic: Between Dialectic and History*. Evanston, IL: Northwestern University Press.
Hartnack, J. (1998) *An Introduction to Hegel's Logic*, ed. K. R. Westphal, tr. L. Aagaard-Mogensen. Cambridge, Mass.: Hackett Publishing Co.
Houlgate, S. (2005) *The Opening of Hegel's Logic: From Being to Infinity*. West Lafayette, IN: Purdue University Press.

6 Handbooks

Burbidge, J. (2008) *Historical Dictionary of Hegelian Philosophy*, 2nd rev. ed. Lanham, MD: Scarecrow Press (Rowman & Littlefield).
Cobben, P. G., Cruysberghs, P., Jonkers, P., and de Vos, L. (eds.) (2006) *Hegel-Lexikon*. Darmstadt: Wissenschaftlichen Buchgesellschaft.
Inwood, M. (1992) *A Hegel Dictionary*. Oxford: Blackwell.

7 Bibliographies

Harris, H. S. (1997) *Hegel's Ladder* (op. cit.), 2:784–868.
Steinhauer, K. (1980) *Hegel Bibliographie*, vol. 1. Munich: K. G. Saur. (Lists editions of Hegel's works and secondary materials world-wide from 1802 to 1975, with indices.)
Steinhauer, K., with H.-D. Schlüter and A. Sergl (1998) *Hegel Bibliographie*, vol. 2. Munich: K. G. Saur. (Lists editions of Hegel's works and secondary materials world-wide from 1980 to1989, with indices.)

8 Additional References

Beiser, F. C. (ed.) (2008) *The Cambridge Companion to Hegel and Nineteenth-Century Philosophy*. Cambridge: Cambridge University Press.
Houlgate, S., and Baur, M. (eds.) (2009) *The Blackwell Companion to Hegel*. Oxford: Blackwell.
Kainz, H. (1986) "Some Problems with the English Translations of Hegel's *Phänomenologie des Geistes*," *Hegel-Studien* 21: 175–82.
Malabou, C. (2004) *The Future of Hegel: Plasticity, Temporality and Dialectic*. London: Routledge.
Moyar, D., and Quante, M. (eds.) (2008) *Hegel's Phenomenology of Spirit: A Critical Guide*. Cambridge: Cambridge University Press.
Riley, P. (1981) "Introduction to the Reading of Alexandre Kojève," *Political Theory* 9.1: 5–48.
Rockmore, T. (1995) "Hegel as a 'French' Master Thinker," in T. Rockmore, *Heidegger and French Philosophy: Humanism, Anti-Humanism and Being* (pp. 27–39, 200–6). New York: Routledge.

Index of Names

References to authors of secondary literature are provided where their work is discussed, not merely cited.

Abegg, J. F. H. 130
Ackermann, J. F. 107, 126n104, 127n111
Acton, H. B. 158
Antigone xxi, 149n2, 164, 169, 172–87
    passim, 205n17, 228, 233–4,
    238–9
Archimedes 102
Aristotle xxiv, 30n9
  animals, differentia of 98
  De Anima 248, 252
  excrementum feminale 125n75
  form and matter 253
  induction, enumerative, rejects 101
  intellect 259, 262
  On the Parts of Animals 95
  method of dichotomy, Plato's,
    rejects 95
  motion, physical, 121n45
  nature: as purposive activity 123n59;
    philosophy of 116–17n2; realms of
    96; second 288
  organisms, unity of 106;
    vegetable 120n35
  phronesis (practical wisdom) 166
  polis, locus of freedom, 192
  potency and actuality 252
  thought, object of 253
  tragedy 176
Arnim, J. v. 111

Arnold, J. T. F. K. 114–15
Autenrieth, J. H. F. 107, 125n74

Bach, Thomas 120n35, 125n82
Bacon, Frances 81–4, 86n13, 88n42,
    88n44, 101, 115, 121n44
Benhabib, S. 185
Bergk, J. A. 115
Berkeley, George, Bishop 31n19, 78
Berthollet, C. L. 120n37
Bichat, M. F. X. 108
Bischoff, C. H. E. 115
Bisticas-Cocoves, M. 81
Blake, William 159
Bloch, Léon 17, 31n32
Bloede, K. A. 115, 126n105
Blumenbach, D. J. F. 96–7, 110
Bode, J. E. 86, 108, 118n17
Böhme, J. 86n13
BonJour, Laurence 2, 30n8
Bonnet, C. 96, 99, 120n38, 126n105
Borowski, G. H. 117n11
Borzeskowski, H.-H. 107
Bradley, Frances Herbert 158
Brandis, J. D. 108, 125n75
Brandom, Robert 23, 32n43, 149n2
Brisson, M.-J. 117n11
Brown, J. 123n58
Brunner, J. 95, 118n15

Buffon, G.-L. Leclerc de 96, 118n15
Burbidge, J. W. 269, 271
Butler, J. 188n12

Calvin, 86n13, 121
Carcavy, P. 102
Cassirer, Ernst 17, 31n32
Cervantes, Miguel 143
Christ 67–9
Cicero, 115, 125n75
Congreve, William 142
Cuvier, G. L. 97

D'Holbach, Baron 198
Dahlstrom, D. O. 122n50
Descartes, René 71n6, 81–4, 87n37, 212, 267, 281
  theory of light 16, 24
  wax 11
  see also cartesianism
Diderot, Denis 198
Donagan, Alan 167–8
Donougho, M. 184, 187n6
du Fay, C. F. 122n53

Einstein, Albert 18, 27, 32n35
Emmerling, L. A. 117n11, 119n26
Erasmus 86n113
Eschenmayer, A. C. 111

Fichte, Johann Gottlieb 79–82 *passim*, 222, 287
  Anstoß 79, 103, 276
  conscience 219–21
  Grundlage der gesammten Wissenschaftslehre 78
  idealism 78, 136
  'I = I' 79, 81, 82, 87n37, 103, 267, 268–9
  individualism 281
  intersubjectivity 281
  moral world view 211–17 *passim*
  not-I 267–9
  self-consciousness, history of 291n18
  striving 198, 215, 217
  subject, self-positing 40
  subjectivity 267–72
  unconditioned 274

Vocation of Man 212
Wissenschaftslehre 78, 81
Filangieri, G. 86n14
Findlay, J. N. 112
Forster, Michael N. 156
Foucault, Michel 155
Fourcroy, A. F. de 120n37
Francke, August Hermann 197
Franklin, Benjamin 122n53
Freud, Sigmund 257

Gadamer, Hans-Georg 293n31
Galenus 125n75
Galileo, Galilei 102–3, 121n45, 121n48, 122n52
Gall, F. J. 111, 112, 114–15
Gehler, J. S. T. 118n14
Gilligan, Carol 168
God 67–9, 75, 149n3, 150n10, 169, 199, 212, 216, 221–2, 226–39 *passim*, 242–3, 251, 271, 282
Goethe, Johann Wolfgang von xxiii, 80, 108, 120n35
  on *Antigone* 175
  on Bacon 88n42
  Faust 93
  metamorphosis 119n32
  phrenology, patronage of 113, 126n103
  quantified science, opposed 119n33
  Rameau's Nephew, translation of 198
  university policy 94
  Wilhelm Meisters Lehrjahre 223
Görres, J. 124n72
Gren, F. A. C. 94, 96, 102–3, 117n13–14, 121–2n50, 122n52–3
Grimaldi, F. M. 103, 122n52
Gruber, J. G. 111

Habermas, Jürgen 205n18, 291n16
Harper, William, 17, 18, 32n37
Harris, H. S. 74, 81, 83, 87n24, 87n35, 100, 104, 105, 111, 118n25, 123n56, 125n81, 125n84, 264n14, 291n18
Helvétius 198
Henrici, G. 111
Herder, J. G. 113
Herman, Barbara 155

Hobbes, Thomas 139, 150*n*10
Hoffmann, F. 123*n*58
Hölderlin, 222
Hooke, Robert 16–18
Hufeland, C. W. 115, 123*n*58
Humboldt, Alexander von 108, 118*n*16, 125*n*75
Hume, David 6, 10, 12, 13, 14, 15, 27, 31*n*19, 101, 102, 121*n*47, 127*n*114
Hutchings, Kimberly 185, 188*n*8
Huygens, Christian 16–18
Hyppocrates 125*n*75
Hyppolite, Jean 81

Illetterati, L. 93
Irigaray, Luce 188*nn*8 and 13

Jacobi, Friedrich Heinrich 80–1, 87*nn*32 and 37; *Woldemar* 226, 241
Jansenists 197

Kaehler, Klaus E. 81
Kant, Immanuel 198, 287; Kantian 98
  Anthropology from a Pragmatic Viewpoint 126*n*100
  animality *vs* humanity *vs* personality 149*n*7
  apperception, 'I think' 38, 57, 82, 275, 276
  behavior, human, science of 126*n*100
  categories, transcendental deduction of, objective 22, 29, 78–9, 82; subjective 26, 29
  cause, causality 20; causal interaction 16
  Categorical Imperative 153–70
  Categories of the Understanding 111
  chemistry 122*n*53
  Critique of Practical Reason 147
  Critique of Pure Reason 78–9, 125*n*88, 196
  Critique of the Power of Judgment 79–80
  ends, realm of 283
  freedom, laws of, *vs* laws of nature 121*n*42
  Groundwork of the Metaphysics of Morals 147
  'I think' *see* Kant, apperception
  idea (*Idee*) *see* judgment, reflective; principle; reason
  idealism 81, 136; formal 87*n*37; Refutation of 20, 25; transcendental 6, 20, 25, 27, 78; *vs* realism 88*n*43
  individualism 148
  judgment: moral 29; reflective 79–80; teleological 121*n*46
  logic 271
  matter, dynamic theory of 117*n*13
  metaphysics, critique of 271
  Metaphysical Foundations of Natural Science 16, 122*n*53
  moral philosophy 121*n*42, 138–9, 147–8, 153–70, 211–20; innocence of 232; knowledge of 76, 80; laws of 101; observation of 87*n*37, 99; regulative use of principles 99, 106, 123*n*54
  noumena(l) *see* supersensible, thing in itself
  Only Possible . . . Proof of the Existence of God 123*n*62
  perception, synthesis in (binding problem) 15, 266
  phenomena(l) *see* appearance
  physico-teleology, critique of 106
  proof, transcendental 39
  purposiveness, internal 106
  reason 81; idea (*Idee*) of 80, *see also* judgment; schema of 99; theoretical 78–9
  religion 175–6, 227
  Religion within the Bounds of Reason Alone 149*n*7, 227, 232
  self-consciousness *see* apperception
  semantics, cognitive 6, 18, 32*n*37
  subjectivity, theory of 40, 266, 271
  substance, concept of 15
  thing-in-itself (*Ding an sich*) 22, 86*n*10, 103
  understanding, laws of 98–99
  will, moral 147; *see also* autonomy, morality
  world order, moral 183, 211–18, 238
Keill, John, 17

Kepler, Johannes 84, 88*n*46, 109, 121*nn*45–6
Kielmeyer, C. F. 106–8 *passim*, 123*nn*58–60, 124*n*72
Kilian, J. K. 123*n*58
Kohlberg, Lawrence 168
Kojève, A. 81
Korsgaard, Christine M. 149*n*8, 156–62
Krause, K. C. F. 111

Lacan, J. 175, 183, 264*n*10
Lakatos, I. 88*n*42
La Mettrie, J. O. de 198
Lasius, G. S. O. 94
Laurentiis, A. de 292*n*25
Lavater, J. G. 112–16
Lavoisier, A. L. 109, 120*n*37, 122*n*50
Leibniz, G. W. 21, 98, 99, 100, 119*n*33, 120*n*38, 154, 212, 271
Lenz, E. 117*n*11
Lichtenberg, F. D. v. 114, 122*nn*53 and 58, 126*n*96, 127*n*111
Linnaeus, C. 95–6, 98, 117*n*11, 118*nn*15 and 20, 119*n*27, 120*n*35, 121*n*47
Locke, John 13, 21, 31*n*19, 78, 84, 87*n*37, 94, 98, 119*n*33, 271
Löwith, K. 266
Luke 80
Luther, M. 75, 81, 86*n*13, 140, 221, 242

Mandeville, Bernard 143, 144
Marx, Groucho 146
Marx, Karl 288
Marx, Werner 81
Matthew 226
Methodists 197
Meyer, J. C. H. 107
Mill, John Stuart 154
Miller, A. V. 87*n*31, 216
Mills, P. J. 184–6
Moiso, F. 117*n*14
Moor, Karl 140–2 *passim*, 144, 150*n*12
Munzel, G. F. 293*n*31

Newton, Sir Isaac, Newtonian 15–24, 27, 61, 101, 107, 109, 121*nn*44 and 46

Nicolai, F. 88
Novalis 222–3
Nussbaum, M. 175

O'Neill, Onora 160, 162, 167
Ockham 27
Oedipus 233
Oehme, K. J. 96
Oken, L. 111
Oliver, Kelly 188*n*10

Parmenides 9, 121*n*43, 261
Piazzi, G. 118*n*17
Pinkard, T. 173, 180, 182
Pippin, R. 149*n*2, 266, 271
Plato 95, 101, 218, 246, 249; *Parmenides* 62, 162
Plinius 96
Poggi, S. 93
Popper, K. 88*n*42
Protagoras 21
Putnam, Hilary 21
Pyrrho 62; *see also* skepticism, pyrrhonian

Quietists 197

Rameau 198
Rawls, John 149*n*4, 154–6, 159, 163
Reinhardt 175
Riccioli, G. B. 103, 122*n*52
Ritter, J. W. 111
Robespierre 204
Robinet 198, 199
Rosen, S. 266
Rousseau, Jean-Jacques 46, 74, 198; *Confessions* 144; *Emile* 115; *Julie* 223
Russell, Bertrand 6, 7

Sartre, Jean-Paul 39, 144, 162
Saussure, H. B. de 118*n*16
Schelling, F. W. J. v. 110, 249, 267
  absolute, the 276
  Darstellung meines Systems 74, 78, 100
  identity-in-difference 104
  intuition, intellectual 2
  natural science, engaged in 93, 125*n*82

nature, philosophy of 110–11, 115, 124*n*72, 125*n*84, 243*n*6
poles, ideal and real 109, 127*nn*77 and 78
self-consciousness, history of 291*n*18
unconditioned, the 274
Weltseele 108
whole, the 268
Schelver, F. J. 111, 120*n*35
Schiller, Friedrich 86n14, 140
Schlegel, Friedrich 222
Schleiermacher 222
Sellars, Wilfrid 160
Sextus Empiricus 2, 4, 21, 225*n*8; *see also* skepticism, pyrrhonian
Shaftesbury, Earl of (Lord Anthony) 143
Singer, Marcus 160
Sjoholm, C. 181
Smellie, W. 120*n*35
Smith, A. 264*n*15, 293*n*28
Sömmering, S. Th. 97, 113, 125*n*75
Sophocles 172, 174, 176, 180, 183, 187*n*4, 233
Spinoza, B. 62, 87*n*24, 98, 119*n*33
Stahl, G. E. 108
Steffens, H. 74, 106–11, 115
Stern, Robert 81, 139

Taylor, Charles 164, 222, 266
Tetens, J. N. 107
Theunissen, Michael 266
Titius (Tietz, J. D.) 108
Toland, John 199
Tournefort, J. de 98
Trembley, A. 96
Treviranus, G. R. 98
Trommsdorff, J. B. 110–11

Vernant, J.-P. 176, 177, 180
Vidal-Naquet, P. 176, 177, 180
Voltaire 198, 199

Wahl, Jean 65
Wahsner, R. 107
Weber, Max 68–9, 196
Weickard, M. A. 97
Werner, A. G. 94, 117*n*11, 119*n*26
Westphal, M. 86n17
Willdenow, C. L. 118*n*23
Winterl, J. J. 120*n*37, 122*n*53
Wittgenstein, Ludwig 32*n*36, 56
Wolff, Christian 154
Wolff, Michael 14
Wood, Allen 164
Wrede, E. G. F. 88*n*43

Subject Index

Several key topics (e.g., 'consciousness', 'self', 'world') are discussed repeatedly throughout this volume. In such cases, index entries refer to specific issues or to discussions falling outside the indicated sections, followed by references to relevant sections of Hegel's *Phenomenology*. Titles of Hegel's sections are capitalized. Discussions of sections of Hegel's *Phenomenology of Spirit* are indexed in the Table of Concordances. Where more than one section is indicated, they are listed in the sequence of Hegel's *Phenomenology* rather than in alphabetical order.

a posteriori 69, 79, 103
a priori
   categories *see* concept
   concepts xviii, 10, 14, 18, 24, 25, 29,
      79, 119n32, *defined* 33
   criticism 25
   knowledge 6–28, 121n47
   principles 281
   proof 6–28 *passim*, 121n45
absolute
   a posteriori 69
   being 72, 76, 200, 206n32, 207n37,
      229
   essence (*Wesen*) *see* being
   knowing, *defined* 1, 30n15, 58, 66, 226
   relation 259
   -spirit *see* spirit
   the 8, 271, 276
   undifferentiated 86n8, 203, 274, 276
action, activity
   basis for judging character 74
   causal 16, 21–2
   ethical 172–87
   justification of 196; *see also* morality
   of understanding 99
   observation of 111–16
   observational 92–116 *passim*; *see also*
      observation
actual, "at work" in practices, 137, 149n4,
   150n15, 191–2
agency 116, 136–48, 176, 239, 266,
   281
   constitutive standard of, 139, 140–4
      passim, 147–8
   see also autonomy; collectivism;
      individual; intersubjectivity;
      morality; practice; subjectivity
agere bellum 227, 230
   gratis 227, 230; *see also* thanksgiving
agoghé (way of life) 63
alienation 181, 182
   ancient Greece 164, 234
   cognitive 27
   Modern 190, 195–6, 205n15, 207n37,
      211, 251
   religious 235, 251
   self-alienation 27, 255
   and skepticism 27

of spirit 251, 255; *see also* spirit
social 141
unhappy consciousness 75
amour-propre 224
analysis
   chemical 102, 117*n*4, 120*n*37
   mathematical 18
anatomy 97, 106, 107, 115; *see also* physiology
angel(s) 215; *see also* will, holy
anthropology 112, 116, 126*n*100, 262
antinomy *see* freedom
antiquity, classical 58–64, 172–87 *passim*, 192, 242–3, 292*n*25; *see also* Greece; Rome
appearance
   manifestation of force 21
   mere 1, 184
   realm of 30
   vs reality 23–4
   of spirit 197; *see also* spirit
   of transcendent 184, 238
   see also nature; observation; Plato; supersensible
art, aesthetic appreciation 243, 249
   Lectures on Aesthetics 175
   artifice 95
   of conversation 269
   fine 144, 191, 212, 242, 249, 252, 256, 273
ataraxia 63
atomism
   ontological 8, 15, 23–4
   social 164–5, 280–1
Aufheben (sublate, supercede) 43, 217; *see also* consciousness, self-critical structure of
authentic, authenticity 145–7, 191, 223
authority 40–53 *passim*, 74, 76, 81
   divine 234
   normative 137–8, 140, 149*n*2, 178, 183, 212, 239
   political 173, 176, 178, 212, 237
   to judge 25; *see also* judgment, autonomy of
   ecclesiastical 82, 227
   independence from 83
   of tradition 83, 85, 196

autonomy 38, 138–9, 191, 228, 251, 273, 281, 290, 292*nn*25–6
Antigone 181
collective 273, 281, 283
Kantian 155, 165, 169, 218
of thought *see* freedom; judgment
see also morality; self-determination

bad
   good *vs* 151*n*19
   infinite 79
   moral 143, 145, 146
   intentions 206*n*27
beautiful soul 211, 221–4, 239, 255
becoming 267–70, 277, 290, 293
   process of 268, 270, 277
   of self 39, 269
   of rational observation 74, 81
Begriff see concept
being, absolute *see* absolute
being-for-self
   individuality 93, 97; *see also* individual, self
   as self-sufficiency 49
   simple 48
   of spirit *see* spirit
believer 66, 227; *see also* faith
Benedictines 235
Bible 227, cf. 212, 251
Binary, binaries 173, 178–81, 183–4, 187
body
   Christ's 235
   human 48, 178, 261
   vs mind 266
   Polynices' 180, 233
   organic 106, 107
   planetary 103
   see also concept; identity; Physiognomy; Phrenology
bondage, stoicism 75; *see also* bondsman; slave
bondsman (*Knecht*) 70
   discipline 51
   labor 50–2, 60
   obedience 51
   spiritual promise of 50
   see also death, fear of; Lord and Bondsman

Cartesian(ism) 19, 27, 266–7
  anti-cartesianism 17, 19, 27
  circle 271
  cogito 82, 87*n*37, 255, 259, 261, 268
  dualism 213, 266–7
  see also skepticism
Categorical Imperative 155, 158, 167, 215; cf. 139
  Formula of Universal Law 158, 215
  Logical Contradiction
    Interpretation 159–61
  Practical Contradiction
    Interpretation 159, 160–1
  Teleological Contradiction
    Interpretation 159, 160
  see also criterion, moral; duty; morality; Self-Certain Spirit: Morality
category, categories 25–6, 29, 76, 78, 99–100, 105, 112, 116, 182, 259–61, 271
  deduction of (Kant), objective 25, 26, 29, 78, 82
  deduction of (Kant), subjective 26, 29
  gender 185, 187
  humanity 149*n*7
  quantity 124*n*73
  thinking 247–8; *see also* Kant, thinking
cause, causal(ity) 11, 123*n*56, 150*n*10
  concept of 24–5
  dispositions 24, 27, 29
  laws 15–27, 92–116, 232
  mechanical 116
  necessity 15–24
  organic 114, 125*n*75
  powers 24, 27, 29
  realism about 15–27, 35
  triggering conditions 16, 21, 22; cf. 24
certainty (*Gewißheit*) 6, 60, 68–9, 101, 157, 235, 241, 252; *defined* 3
  absolute 87*n*37, 229
  commonsense 62
  self-certain(ty) 42–3, 49, 62–3, 72–85 *passim*, 153, 157, 199, 201–2, 210, 221, 226, 261, 275, 278–9
    vs truth 39, 40, 49, 61, 70, 72, 76–81; cf. 259
  uncertainty 69
  see also conscience
Chalcedon, Council of 242

Christian(ity) 67, 143, 214, 217, 227, 242–3, 251, 282, 292*n*25
  Catholicism 167
  early 64–70, 136
  ethics 69
  incarnation *see* divine, God
  justice 215
  see also Bible; church; divine; God; priest; salvation
church 75, 167, 227; *see also* authority, ecclesiastical
classification, systems of 93–9, 105–10, 113–15; *see also* concept; description
cogito see Cartesian
cognition, cognitive 1–29, 72–116, 193, 198, 228, 246–63, 266, 268, 270–72, 286, 291*n*18
  active 14, 55, 247–63; cf. 73, 81, 84, 92–116; *see also* knowing, justification
collectivism 46, 53, 155, 160, 163, 169, 191, 210, 266, 275, 278, 281–6, 288–90, 292, 293
  moderate x, *defined* 281; *see also* community; subjectivity
commitments, as settled intuitions 138–42; *see also* conviction
communism 149
communitarianism 135, 143
community 60, 113, 164, 167, 172–87, 210–12, 219, 221–4, 227, 229–30, 237, 242, 273, 279–82, 284–5, 290–3
  concrete speech of 239
  ideal 140
  religious 66, 232, 234, 238–40, 251
  traditional 212
  see also collectivism; polis
concept(s), conception(s), 4–27 *passim*, 68, 74, 83–4, 96–7, 100, 138
  a priori 6–28 *passim*; *defined* 33; *see also* a priori
  Begriff 10, 31*n*22, 79, 118*n*25, 248–9, 254; *defined* 10, 57–8
  classification 24, 25, 29, 83, 92–111 *passim*, 255; *see also* classification, systems of concept empiricism 10, 12, 14, 24, 27, 33; *defined* 6

conceptual scheme 5
determinable 7
demythologizing power of 243
identity, numerical 12, 13
of physical object 10–15
self-concept(ion) 4–6, 38–46, 48–9, 173
of substance, equivocal 15–16
confession 75, 144, 223–4, 226–7, 230, 240
of evil *see* evil
conscience 211, 219–21, 223, 229, 232, 233–4, 236, 238–9, 255
consciousness 56, 59, 248, 266–81, 283–4, 287, 290–2
as apparent, phenomenal knowledge 252–3; *see also* consciousness: natural, observed
collective *see* collectivism; community; spirit
forms (or shapes, figures) of, xvii–xx, 28, 59, 61, 96, 109, 186, 253, 256; *defined* 3–4; *see also* Table of Concordances
in-itself, for-itself, in-and-for-itself 56, 57
individual, concrete 266, 273, 277–9, 287; *see also* collectivism; individual(s); subjectivity
moral *see* morality
natural 76, 79, 104, 106, 113, 169, 247–8, 252, 268, 291n18
observed 40, 47, 53, 56, 58, 63–4, 76–7, 179, 229, 241, 248, 250, 254, 256, 290
pure 68, 197, 198, 200, 212
Principle of 4, 193–5, 201, 202; cf. 248
romantic *see* Romanticism
self-consciousness *see* Self-Consciousness
self-critical structure of 2–6, 11, 13, 228; cf. 252
unchangeable *see* Unhappy Consciousness
universal 63, 274, 283
contradiction
dialectical 14, 23–4, 61, 62, 269–71
non-contradiction, law of 14, 24, 77, 269
objectively valid 14
performative 43
see also Categorical Imperative; logic

conviction(s) 25–6, 59, 142, 239, 283; *see also* commitments; conscience
copula 254–5
cosmos 211, 213–14, 237
criterion (*Maßstab*), criteria 2–5, 12, 17, 40, 45, 139
Dilemma of 2, 27
of good 51
of justice 177, 282, 287
of justification 17
moral 138–48, 153–70, 192, 212–24
of rationality 190
of reasonablensss 182
of spirit 202, 277
of theoretical adequacy, Newton's 18
of truth 2–5, 12, 60
see also concept, classification; Linnaeus
Crusades 68
cult
Christian 242
of God 239
of guillotine 237
of moral genius 222, 223
religious 199, 227–8, 233, 241, 243
of underworld 233
warrior 232
culture (*Bildung*), enculturation 59–60, 169, 185, 191–2, 226–43 *passim*, 267–9, 273, 278–9, 281–3, 285–90
Attic Greek *see* Greece
German 222
modern 148, 204, 273, 283
philosophy of 191
post-Christian 243
self-alienated *see* Self-Alienated Spirit
world of 196, 210, 235–40, 242
see also self; subjectivity
custom *see* justification; practice

death 50–3, 56, 164, 173, 178, 182, 183, 231, 235
as absolute lord 50–1, 174
biological 233
of God 68, 243
by guillotine 204
spiritual 232, 239
struggle unto 48–51, 279
warrior's 182

description(s)
  definite 9
  of moral action 223–4
  of moral circumstances 162–3, 220–1
  of nature 17, 92–116
  see also classification, concept
desire 28, 41–52, 55, 68, 69, 72, 75,
    150*n*10, 230, 232, 239, 247,
    283–4, 289
  for death 183
  Kant on 156, 159, 164, 214, 215, 218
  natural 173, 230–1
  problems confronting 43–4
  for recognition 44–53, 279
  for self-certainty 278–9
  for self-development 277
  sexual 174, 175
  see also ataraxia; drives; needs; self-
    interest; stoicism
despotism 59, 141–2, 199
destiny 114, 175; *see also* fate
destruction
  divine, of world 235
  of ethical life (*Sittlichkeit*) 164
  fury of 204
  of icons 199
  of object 41–3, 278–9
devotion 68, 69, 206*n*25, 207*n*35, 222
dialectic(al) 269–70, 279–80, 290, 291
  argument 39: contradiction *see*
    contradiction; identity *see* identity;
    logic 269, 291
  Aristotle 252
  skeptical 62; *see also* criterion, Dilemma
    of
δίκη (dikē) 232–4; *see also* justice
discipline 51; *see also* labor; obedience;
    self-discipline
dissatisfaction 203, 232, 234–6
dissemblance, displacement
    (*Verstellung*) 28, 211, 216–17, 239
divine, divinity 221–2, 235
  alphabet 113–14
  being, essence (*Wesen*) 199, 200, 251
  incarnation 68, 251
  knowledge 28
  law 28, 173–87
  manifestation 67

nature 242
omnipotence 68
providence 214
transcendent 75
will 251
world order 150*n*13, 196; *see also* moral
    world order
see also God; Unhappy Consciousness,
    Self-Certain Spirit: Morality,
    Religion
dread 56, 149*n*3, 231, 232, 241
drive(s) 38, 41, 42 56, 84, 92, 100, 112,
    169; *see also* desire
dualism
  Cartesian mind/body 213, 266
  self/nature 212–13
  subject/object 59
  within skepticism 63
  see also subjectivity
duty 174, 175
  absolute 157, 169, 183, 212, 213, 214
  absolute *vs* conditional 159
  circumstances of 168, 220–1
  determinate 161–2
  familial 175
  and happiness 154, 214
  and inclination 161, 212
  intentions *vs* consequences 154
  multiple 221
  morality of 155
  of philosophy 57
  poverty relief 160–1
  pure 161–2, 168, 216, 218, 220, 224
  sisterly 183
  sole moral motive 153
  specific (content of) 221
  supremacy of 212, 214
  see also conscience; criterion, moral;
    morality

ego *see* I, self; *see also* Descartes, Fichte,
    Kant
empiricism 16, 17, 81–3, 85, 92, 101,
    103, 199
  absolute 79, 81, 83, 84
  concept *see* concept
  uncritical 80, 103
  see also Bacon; Hume; Locke

enculturation (*Bildung*) *see* culture
enjoyment (*Genuß*) 50, 52, 56, 69, 80, 184, 186, 199; *see also* happiness; pleasure
Enlightenment 28, 86*n*14, 93, 199, 212, 228, 237, 238–9
   Hegel's critique of 190–204
   satisfied *vs* unsatisfied 203
epistemology 88*n*42, 148
   Hegel's, in *Phenomenology* 2–29, 61, 64–5, 98, 192–6, 246–9, 251–2, 261, 263, 265, 266, 268, 281
   see also knowing
epoch(s) 3, 59, 198, 253, 262–3; *see also* history; modernity
equipollence (*isothenia*) 2, 62; *see also* petitio principii
essence, trajectory of 59
ethics of freedom 155, 169; *see also* morality
ethos 165, 212, 232
Etre suprême see divinity; God
evil 25, 28, 75, 76, 161, 211, 224, 230, 239, 240, 242
   confession of 224, 240
   pride 230
   social 161
   world 197
examples, Hegel's
   black 31
   cell, electrolytic 31
   danger, imminent 221
   electricity 23, 31, 97, 100, 103, 105, 122*nn*50 and 53
   here 15
   house 15, 41*n*19
   knight of virtue 144
   magnetism 31
   matters, free 19, 21, 94, 103, 104, 108–9
   Moor, Karl 140–4
   needs, biological 33
   night 14
   now 14
   polarity 23, 31
   poverty relief 159–61
   property rights 158–9, 161–2, 168
   salt 18

   sour 31
   suicide 160
   sweet 31
   tree 15, 41*n*19
   truth-telling 157, 161
   white 31
   wood block 199
   see also beautiful soul; Categorical Imperative; conscience; duty; gravity
experience 4–5, 239, 246
   inner and outer 25
   moral 167, 169, 211; *see also* morality
   in natural science 92–116
   phenomenological *see* observation, phenomenological
   pure, myth of 95
   religious *see* Religion
   subject of *see* I
   transitory 7, 9, 61, 63
   unsensed causes of 21, 260
   see also Bacon; empiricism; Hume; Locke; observation; Force and Understanding; The Certainty and Truth of Reason; Observing Reason
explanation
   dialectical 165–6, 269
   interpretive 154, cf. 165
   natural-scientific 17–20, 23–4, 92–116, 227–8
externalism
   mental content 20, 27
   re: justification 30*n*10
   see also epistemology; justification; knowing

Fable of the Bees, The (Mandeville) 143, 146
faith (*Glaube*) 72, 85, 210, 211, 217
   beyond reason 80
   blind 237
   Christian 66, 190–204, 227–43, 251
   in God 143*n*3; *see also* God
   Lutheran 86*n*13
   in miracles 85
   moral 238
   vs reason *see* reason
family 156, 172–87, 233, 235

fear 50–3, 56, 59, 138, 176, 199, 231, 233; *see also* death; dread; Lord and Bondsman
feeling(s) 68, 81, 83, 109, 177, 182, 218, 223, 226, 234
　at home 75, 238; *see also* freedom
　moral 223
　natural 174
　of self 69, 255
　pity 160
　pity and fear 176
　religious 197, 235, 240
　see also sentiment
fides quærens intellectum 228
figure *see* consciousness, forms of
finite 63, 242
　and infinite 2, 10, 56–7, 61, 66, 67–71, 72–84 *passim*, 200–1, 251, 270–1, 279
　understanding 10, 62, 104–5
finitude, human 5, 27, 42, 216, 241
force(s)
　cosmic 234; *see also* fate
　essential to matter 15
　essentially relational 15–22
　gravity 18–19, 23
　laws of 19, 22, 84; *see also* cause; nature
　potential *vs* actual 21, 22
　vs powers 16
　solicitation 21–2
　see also cause; Force and Understanding; Observing Reason
forgiveness 226, 230, 238–40; *see also* Evil and Forgiveness
formal
　identity 83, 92
　logic *see* logic
　unity 38
formalism 74, 84, 86*n*8, 111–12, 267
　moral 157–8, 160, 218
　legal 234; *see also* Legal Status
free(dom) 115, 234
　absolute 39–41, 204, 211, 219
　as absolute end 51; cf. 53
　antinomy of, and social constitution 138–9, 149*n*7; cf. 169
　Aristotle 191–2
　as autonomy *see* autonomy

being at home with oneself 191; cf. 174, 238
　of consciousness, as historical achievement 76, 86*n*14
　ethics of 153–70
　as finding oneself in the world 39, 191; *see also* alienation; reconciliation
　as lack of constraint 139, 211
　moral *see* morality
　noumenal 155
　as self-sufficiency 39–40; *see also* Lord and Bondsman; self-sufficiency
　of spirit 273, 274–5, 278–81, 288–9, 292, 293
　of thought 55–8, 86*n*14, 92, 104, 259–60; *see also* Freedom of Self-Consciousness
　see also Self-Consciousness, The Actualization of Rational Self-consciousness Through Itself, Individuality which is Real In and For Itself, Self-Certain Spirit: Morality
fundamentalism *see* religion

Geist see spirit
God
　ad gloriem majoriam Dei 236
　Christian 67–70, 75, 169, 200, 212, 216, 222, 251, 271, 282
　death of 68, 243
　deism 199, 203; cf. 222
　Father Almighty 227
　incarnation 68, 69, 235, 242–3, 251
　Judaic 67, 251
　see also Calvin; divine; faith; Luther; Religion; Struggle of Enlightenment with Supersition
gods, Attic Greek 181, 183, 233, 242–3
good 60, 147, 154, 237
　vs bad, absolute distinction 151*n*19
　common 142–3, 237; *see also* utility
　criteria of 51, 59, 76, 157, 204, 218, 222; *see also* morality; utility
　highest 212–18
　human 142–3, 155
　individual 282; *see also* desire; happiness; needs; pleasure; satisfaction

gravity, gravitation(al)
  essential to matter 18–19, 23
  motion 19, 23; cf. 108
  specific 109
  universal 15, 18–19, 22–4, 41
Greece, Greeks, Attic 15, 59–60, 166, 169, 172–87, 192, 232, 237, 265, 269, 282
  see also Antigone; Aristotle; Plato; polis; Rome; Socrates; Sophocles; True Spirit: Ethics
guillotine 208, 237
guilt 175–87 passim, 226, 232, 238–40, 263

happy, happiness 66
  personal 174, 214–18
  see also good, criteria of; inclination; unhappiness; utility
heart 114, 197, 200, 227, 243
  breaking of 234, 240
  law of 136–42, 283
heaven 217, 227, 233
Hegel, works:
  Difference between Fichte's and Schelling's Systems of Philosophy 78, 98
  Encyclopedia of Philosophical Sciences 19, 39, 41, 42–3, 77, 79, 80, 84, 85, 92, 93, 97, 136, 246, 258, 261, 268, 272, 273, 291, 292
  Faith and Knowledge 80, 81, 243
  Jena Logic (ms) 67, 77, 112
  Lectures on Aesthetics 175
  Lectures on the History of Philosophy 78, 82–4 passim, 222
  Lectures on the Philosophy of History 75–6, 258
  Lectures on the Philosophy of Religion 226, 251
  Philosophy of Nature 79, 257, 260
  Philosophy of Right 154, 159, 168, 175, 177, 178, 204, 258, 262, 263, 272, 291, 292, 293, 294
  Philosophy of Spirit 1, 260, 273, 291
  Realphilosophie 249, 260, 270, 272
  Science of Logic 228, 249, 250, 254, 255, 256, 260–1, 270, 272, 291, 293

  Spirit of Christianity and its Fate 149n3, 222
hero(es) 167, 224, 237
history
  actual 3, 59, 74, 76, 81, 83, 113, 198, 204, 212, 236, 240, 258
  comprehended 263
  dimensions of knowledge 26, 29, 148; see also history, philosophy of
  historia, see knowledge
  modern see modernity
  natural 84, 96
  of philosophy 58–9; see also Hegel, works
  philosophy of 136–7, 153–4, 164–70, 172–3, 191–2, 235–7, 241, 250–63, 266, 268, 272–4, 277, 285–8, 290–1
  and philosophy of science 15–24, 72–116
  reason in 137; see also history, philosophy of
  of religion 26; see also Religion
  Roman 59, 185–6, 234
  social 112; see also history, philosophy of
Holocaust 243
hypocrisy 145, 169, 217, 223, 239

I (Ich) 57, 58, 70, 74, 77, 153, 181, 185–6, 226, 227, 240, 256, 259, 261, 268, 275–6, 279, 281, 287
  beautiful soul 224
  I = I 72–85 passim
  I and We 26, 45, 46, 154, 160, 209, 279; see also intersubjectivity; spirit; subjectivity
  indexical expression 8, 10; cf. 24
  Luther 140
  self-generating 267, 277, 293
  see also Descartes; Fichte; individual; Kant; self; self-conception; we intentions
idea (Idee)
  absolute 124n72, 149n4
  of God 216
  of the idea 228
  logical 260
  regulative 99; see also principles

idealism 77–9, 88
　absolute 179, 284
　and empiricism 81–5
　Hegel's xx, 231, 248
　German 80, 81, 82, 84, 136, 266, 267, 272, 273, 284, 293, 294
　and realism xx, 55–8, 83, 84, 98, 273; *see also* realism
　of reason 76–81
　Refutation of 20, 25
　subjective 78, 84
　transcendental 6, 20, 27, 78, 80, 272
identity
　conceptual 270
　conditions 23–4, 25
　cultural 139, 191
　in difference 100, 104, 109, 110, 178, 242, 250, 255, 258, 267–70, 277, 288, 292
　formal 83, 92, 202; cf. 97, 259
　of indiscernibles 100
　'is' of 7, 9
　law of *see logic*
　numerical 12
　of perceptible things *see* Perception
　self-identity of subjects 38, 39, 219
　subject-object 78, 248–57, 261
　of thought and being 46, 57–8, 76, 78, 100, 104, 247–50, 255, 260, 261; *see also* spirit, Principle of
　see also unity
illusion, transcendent 9, 19
image, imagery
　cultural 243
　perceptual 58, 247
　religious 236, 243, 251
　of spirit 262, 273
immortality 169, 212
immutable, unchangeable 9, 27, 62–70, 73, 75
　'I' 267 *see also* I
　unwritten law 178
impact (*Anstoß*) *see* Fichte
imperturbability (*ataraxia*) 63
incarnation *see* divine
inclination(s) 94, 113, 150*n*10, 153, 162, 212, 215; *see also* drive

individual(s) 48–53, 184–5, 241, 243, 265–94
　individualism 137, 139, 145–8, 281, 283, 292
　individualist accounts of agency 137, 139, 143, 144
　particular objects 7–9, 41, 45; *see also* Consciousness; Observing Reason
　see also collectivism; community; I; self; subjectivity
infinite, infinity
　Abgrund (Stephens) 110
　bad 79
　concepts *vs* representations 10, 55–8, 60–1; *see also* concept; representation
　content of religion 251
　and finite 61–2
　as identity in difference 41; *see also* dialectic; identity
　judgment 255
　longing 68
　reason 96
　striving 198, 215, 217
　thinking 271, 274, 278–9
innocence 263
　of nature 232
instinct 109, 115, 164, 248
　observational 74
　of reason 80–1, 84, 97, 100, 106, 112, 238
　see also drive; inclination
intellect (*Verstand*) 55, 61, 62, 65; *see also* understanding
　active (Aristotle) 253, 259, 262
　intellectual objects 74; *see also* supersensible
　divine 106
　priority of 187*n*4
　women's 182
interaction 25, 29, 41, 113, 138, 185, 267–8, 273–4, 279–81, 284, 286, 292
　causal 16, 21–2, 109
　recognitive 25–6, 48; *see also* recognition; Lord and Bondsman
　social, as historical process 273
　with world 267; *see also* labor

intersubjectivity 44–5, 196, 275, 278, 280–1, 284, 292
    intersubjective realm 268
    see also interaction; recognition; spirit; subjectivity
intuition(s) 227, 259, 261–2; cf. 196
    intellectual 2, 78, 248
    intuitionism 2, 154
    moral 156, 163, 165, 168, 177, 183, 219, 220–1, 239
    religious 240, 241, 242
    self-intuition of spirit 262
    sensory 58
    settled 138, 140–1
    see also cogito
is, identity vs predication 14, 16
isostenia (equipollence) 62

Jena, invasion of 246
Jesuits 236
    casuistry 76
judgment 212, 255–6
    autonomy of 74; cf. 212 see also autonomy
    cognitive 5, 18, 25–7, 77, 80, 193, 270–1; see also epistemology; knowing
    of community 227, 239–41, 283
    error in 145, 176
    final 136
    infinite 255
    legalistic 234
    normative 139; see also morality
    of others 5, 26, 145, 281
    reflective (Kant) 79, 99, 163, 166; see also principle, regulative vs constitutive
    moral 232–3, 237, 239; see also criterion; morality
    self-judgment of reason 77
    see also logic; syllogism; wisdom, practical
justice 142, 177, 181
    δίκη (dikē) 232–4
    divine 200, 215; cf. 214
    injustice 140, 181, 214
    see also property; punishment

justification
    by grace 75
    circularity, vicious 5
    coherentism 2–3
    criteria of 2–6, 25–9; see also criterion
    customary 196, 282; see also True Spirit: Ethics
    deductivism (*scientia*) see infallibilism
    determinate negation 4–6, 24–9, 61–2; cf. 76
    Dilemma of the Criterion 2–6, 187n4
    empirical (*historia*) 2, 16–20
    epistemic 281
    externalism 30n10
    fallibilism 5
    foundationalism 2–3
    infallibilism 2, 17, 19
    internal critique see determinate negation
    interpretive 1
    logical vs cognitive gap 19, 27
    moral see criterion, morality
    mutual criticism 5, 25–6; see also judgment of others
    petitio principii (questions-begging) 2, 17; see also *petitio principii*; Criterion, Dilemma of
    rational 3, 196
    self-criticism 4–5

knight(s) 143
    of virtue 144
knowing, knowledge 266, 271, 274–5, 277, 280–1, 286, 288–9, 292
    by acquaintance 6–9, 24, 74; see also Sense Certainty
    absolute 1, 26, 94, 111–12, 137, 175, 243, 246–63, 266, 268, 271, 273, 274; *defined* 1, 262
    alienation from 27
    apparent, phenomenal see consciousness, forms of
    divine see divine, God
    genuine (true) 247
    Hegel's analysis of see epistemology, Hegel's
    moral see criterion, moral; morality
    presentation, singular sensory 9, 24

knowing, knowledge (*cont'd*)
  self-knowledge 192–4, 275, 277, 286, 289; *see also* self; Lord and Bondsman; Spirit
  skills, know-how 137, 157; *see also* labor
  Wissen vs Erkennen 228; cf. 247
  see also empiricism; epistemology; justification; perception; sensation; thought; Kant
Kulturkritik 27

labor, work 37, 50–3, 56, 69–70, 72, 75, 144–6, 184, 196, 235, 236, 284–5, 287, 288
  cognitive 5; *see also* Observing Reason
  division of 174
  natural-scientific 93–7, 103, 110
  philosophical 256
  spirit's 192, 193, 195, 197, 235–42, 258
  of thanksgiving 227
  of war 227
law
  biological 93, 96–8, 104–11
  divine and human 67, 173–87
  free fall 102–3
  of gravity *see* gravity
  of the heart *see* heart, law of
  Kepler's 84, 88*n*46
  legal 139, 156, 169, 175, 185–6, 191, 192, 196, 204, 228, 233–5, 258, 273, 282–3, 285; *see also* justice; law, divine and human
  legislated by individuals 38, 42, 52, 238; *see also* autonomy; conscience; heart, law of; individualism; morality
  logical 111–12; *see also* logic
  moral *see* duty; morality
  of nature 18–25, 41, 75–6, 79, 83–5, 99–104; *see also* cause; force
  phrenological 113–16
  physiognomic 113–16
  pyschological 113–16
  of unintended consequences 264*n*15, 284–5, 293*n*30; cf. 143
liberation 141
  absolute 76, 85
  of self-consciousness 61, 65, 75, 85

  of spirit 261, 274–5
  see also freedom
life 49–53 *passim*, 55, 59–63 *passim*, 98, 104–11
  family 174, 177
  social *see* collectivism; ethical life; modernity; morality
  of spirit 232, 242, 259
  see also biology; physiology
limit and unlimited 10, 56–7, 67, 261, cf. 271
  see also finite; finitude; infinite
logic(al) 77, 247, 269, 282, 287, 290–3
  Aristotle 95
  circle 272
  dialectical 269; *see also* contradiction, dialectic
  exclusion relations 23
  formal 269, 291
  identity, law of 24, 77
  Kant 111
  non-contradiction, law of 24, 31*n*28, 269; *see also* contradiction
  proper names 7
  syllogism 254–6, 260–1, 271
  Science of Logic see Hegel, works
longing
  for the divine 68
  see also desire
lord
  of the world (Ceasar) 186
  of the world (God) 216, 234, 235, 240, 241; *see also* divine, God
  of nature 241
  see also death; Lord and Bondsman

master(y) *see* Lord and Bondsman
  of desires *see* ataraxia; inclinations; Kant; self-discipline; Stoicism
  of injustice 181
  rules 139, 141
mathematics 61, 124*n*72
  quantified laws of nature 17–19, 102, 109, 121*n*46
matter(s) 94, 104, 108–9, 116
  dead 212, cf. 74
  essentially heavy 27
  force essential to 15, 18, 19, 23

free 11, 13, 103, 104
living 108
in motion 200
what really matters (*Sache*) 136–48
Matthew 226
maxim
   Kant 153–70 *passim*, 215, 218
   reflective 99
mechanics 102
   mechanical explanation 116, 200, 212–14
   physics 19, 102, 105, 107, 108
mechanism *see* mechanics
metaphysics 18, 19, 23, 74, 93, 144, 172
   of agency 146, 147, 148, 165
   Aristotle 191, 246
   Hegel 247–8, 257, 259, 260, 265, 271, 274
   Kant 169; *see also* idealism, transcendental
   pre-Critical 18, 212
   terms 17
   traditional 271
modernity 136–48 *passim*, 165, 173, 176, 182, 186, 190–2, 197, 198, 204, 211, 212, 214, 228, 251, 255, 266–73 *passim*, 282–3
   see also history; morality; philosophy, modern; science, natural
moment (aspect) 10, 41, 77, 98, 111, 112, 173, 201; *defined* 252
   of spirit 266, 279
moral(ity) 142, 153–187, 191, 209–24, 227, 238–40, 255, 258, 283
   action, circumstances of 168, 220–1
   agency, agent 266, 269
   character 115–16
   commonsense 223–4
   duties, obligations 176; *see also* criterion, moral
   faith *see* faith
   genius 184
   judge, judgment 25–6; *see also* autonomy
   motivation 218; *see also* good; self-interest; selfishness
   perfection(ism) 154, 215, 218

   visions, competing 184
   see also conscience; criterion; ethical life; Kant, Law of the Heart; Law-Giving Reason, Law-Testing Reason; morality; Self-Certain Spirit: Morality; True Spirit: Ethics
mortification 69
movement
   dialectical 64–5
   pointing out (ostension) 8
   reason 79–80, 100, 113
   of recognition 279; *see also* recognition
   of self 270; *see also* self
   self-consciousness 38, 41, 56–8, 63, 65–6, 68, 70, 77, 207n37, 213
   spirit 73–4, 77, 224, 250–3, 256–60, 262–3, 290
   thinking 112, 250

nature, natural 25–9, 59, 60, 72–4, 78, 143, 172–3, 196, 199, 212–13, 262–3, 267–8
   as alien 27, 39, 52, 213; cf. 276
   dispersion of 96, 98, 240
   enchanted 172, 230–2, 235; cf. 196
   female (woman's) 177–8, 184–5, 187
   history 84, 96
   innocence of 232
   laws of *see* cause; force; science, natural
   lord of *see* lord
   mechanical *see* mechanism
   natural human relations 173–4
   natural scarcity 238, 240
   particularity of 232
   phenomena 15–24, 73, 88n46, 99, 103, 104, 238; *see also* Force and Understanding; Observing Reason
   philosophy of *see* Hegel, works
   reason in *see* reason in nature
   second- 164, 288; cf. 293n29
   and spirit *see* spirit and nature
   qua sensibility (Kant) 214–15
   see also consciousness, natural; desire; science, natural; Force and Understanding; The Certainty and Truth of Reason; Observation of Nature

need(s) 42, 43, 82, 159, 214–15, 218, 222, 234, 236, 237, 239, 243, 284
  biological 25, 29
  see also desire; drives; inclinations; recognition
negation, negativity 212, 252, 254, 256, 259, 269, 270, 279
  absolute 51, 56, 60
  determinate 61–2; cf. 4–6, 24, 27
  determinatio negatio est 62
  see also Lord and Bondsman; Stoicism; Skepticism, Absolute Freedom
Nicea, Council of 242
norm, normative 191, 266, 271, 287–8
  actual (*wirklich*) 137
  authority, source of 38, 40, 75, 112, 137–48, 169–70, 172–80, 185–7
  factual basis 137
  objectivity of 3, 25, 167
  see also criterion; justice; morality; practice; relativism
nothing(ness) 42–4, 48–51
  see also negation, determinate; Unhappy Consciousness

obey, obedience 49–51, 75, 179, 183, 212
  see also autonomy; discipline, self-discipline; law; service; Unhappy Consciousness; Law of the Heart
object 269, 270, 273–9, 283–4, 286–90
  of consciousness 3–6, 193–4, 249, 270, 275; see also consciousness, forms of
objectification, objectify 53, 191–5, 232, 237, 238, 255, 256, 258, 282
objective, objectivity 3, 39, 45, 52, 57, 58, 68, 80, 82, 99, 253–7, 261
  natural law 177
  objective deduction (Kant) see category
  in sensation 252
  of social order 113, 191–2, 238, 273–4
  of spirit 195–7, 273–4, 278–9
  see also Observing Reason, morality
observe, observation
  of nature see science, natural; Observing Reason
  phenomenological 3–4, 6, 53, 61, 63, 64, 74, 104, 176, 226, 229, 258, 262–3, 268, 272–3; cf. 280
  scientific 73–4, 80–5, 92–116 *passim*
  terms 10, 29
Ockham's razor 27
ontology, ontological 64, 249, 252, 260, 265, 271, 290, 292
  conception of truth see truth, Paramenidean
  of forms of consciousness 3–4
  relational, Hegel's 15–24
  self-sufficiency 40
  see also cause; collectivism; idealism
ora et labora 235
organic, organism (biology) 31, 52, 74, 93, 97, 99–100, 104–11, 230–1, 262
  nature as organism 98
  see also life; physiology
ostension 6–9, 33
other, otherness 43, 46, 58, 60, 64, 72, 78, 80, 104, 178, 185, 242, 267–8, 273, 275–6, 278–81, 283–5, 287

patriarch(y) 172
perception 9–15, 24
  binding problem 9–10, 15
  perceived object 11–12
  perceptual understanding 21
  presentation, singular sensory 9, 24
  see also observation; Perception; Observing Reason
person 139
  of honor 44,
  inner 114
  legal 169, 175, 185–6, 234
  persona 176
  -al commitment 139; see also commitments
  -al expression 145
  personality 96, 266, 279, 281, 285, 288, 292
  self-conscious 266
  see also collectivism; individualism; knight; morality; Law of the Heart
petitio principii 2–4, 16–17, 25–6, *defined* 30n5, cf. 37–53 *passim*, 60–4, 77, 139–42, 145, 178–80, 198–200, 204, 219–24, 229–30, 239–40

phenomena, natural *see* nature
philosophy
   modern 9, 11, 12, 15, 78, 83, 196, 212, 267
   speculative 78, 83, 84, 92, 253, 254, 256, 271
   as science 253
   starting point of 261
   system of, Hegel's 1, 246, 252–3, 258, 260–1, 263, 272
phrenology 79, 112–16, 150n10
physiognomy 112–16, 150n10
physiology 94, 97, 105, 107–8, 113–16, 290
   neuro- 15
pleasure(s) 53, 214
   of the gods 181
   of performing duty 214
   private 184
   see also desire; good; inclination; need; satisfaction
pointing out *see* ostension
polis 142, 143, 148, 174, 176, 178, 180, 181, 192, 282
posit (*v*) *defined* 31n26
postulates, moral (Kant) 214–18
practice(s), practical 278
   customary 25, 29, 166–7, 172–87, 191, 211–12, 234, 280–90
   experimental, scientific *see* observation; Force and Understanding; Observing Reason
   - character of self-consciousness 38, 72–3, 112–13
   - norms 25; *see also* criterion, moral
   - reason *see* Kant, morality
   religious 200, 227, 229, 234–6, 242, 251; *see also* cult; faith; Unhappy Consciousness; Religion
   social 137–48, 172–87, 226–40 *passim*; *see also* morality
   and theoretical standpoints 78–9
   wisdom 166, 175, 180–1, 184, 228; *see also* Wissen
predicate, predication 7, 9, 10, 24, 77, 79, 116, 254, 255, 270
presentation, singular sensory 9, 24

prestige, battle for 229–32, 239, 242
   see also pride; recognition; Lord and Bondsman
pride 226, 230
   root of sin 230
   see also prestige
principle(s) 41
   of aggregation 99
   of assessment of *see* criteria; Criterion, Dilemma of
   cognitive, epistemic 3–6; *see also* epistemology; justification; knowing
   of Consciousness 4, 193–5, 201–2
   constitutive *vs* regulative 99, 106, 214; *see also* judgment; reflective
   first 3
   indiscernibles, identity of 99–100, 119n33
   Kiss 7
   logical *see* logic
   moral *see* Categorical Imperative; morality; utility
   of forms of consciousness 3–6
   practical 3; *see also* morality; practice
   of specification 99
   of speculation 78
   of Spirit 193–4, cf. 246–7
   reflective *see* principle, regulative; judgment, reflective
   of utility *see* utility
   see also autonomy; criteria; freedom; judgment; Ockham's razor
properties
   intrinsic *vs* relational 15–18, 23, 82
   monadic 16
   natural *see* Force and Understanding; Observing Reason
   perceptual *see* Perception
   tropes 13
prosperity, of wicked 214; *see also* wealth
Protestantism 69, 251; *see also* Calvin; Luther
providence, divine *see* divine; God
psychology 86n14, 105, 112–13, 116, 150n10, 248, 249, 250, 257
   moral 156, 161–2, 164, 167–8
   neuro- 30n10

punish(ment) 66, 67, 70, 156, 175, 188*n*9, 214–15, 237

question-begging (logical fallacy), *see petitio principii*

realism 11, 25, 83–5, 98, 111, 238, cf. 273
  causal 15–20, 27
  critical 246
  epistemological 3, 5, 25–7
  internal 21
  naive 6, 24; *see also* Sense Certainty
  scholastic 246
  transcendental proof of 20; cf. 24–9
reason (*Vernunft*) 265, 269, 275–6, 281–3, 285; *see also* Reason
  activity of 74; *see also* observation, morality
  actuality of 196; *see also* The Certainty and Truth of Reason, Observing Reason, Absolute Knowing
  fact of (Kant) 147
  freedom of 63; *see also* Freedom of Self-Consciousness
  vs faith 182, 183, 184; *see also* Struggle of the Enlightenment with Superstition
  in history 137, 192, 262–3, 266; cf. 113; *see also* spirit
  integrative function of 10; *see also* concept, Begriff; dialectic
  in nature 39, 80, 92, 99–100, 106; *see also* cause; force; nature, law of
  practical *see* morality
  reasons, giving and asking for 109, 116
  reflective, regulative *see* judgment; principle, constitutive *vs* regulative
  sociality of 15–19, 117, 224, 276
  theoretical *see* epistemology; knowing, justification; Consciousness, Observing Reason, Absolute Knowing
recognition, mutual 25–6, 178; *see also* Lord and Bondsman
  genuine 25–6, 224, 268, 279–82, 292
  reciprocal 49, 56, 230, 281, 292

self-recognition 58, 106, 207*n*36, 224, 255, 268, 281
reconciliation 178, 270, 272, 278, 281, cf. 283
  between moral judges 26, 224, 240, 281
  of cognitive self and nature 76, 83, 270, cf. 27
  of dependency with self-sufficiency 46, 52
  of divine and human 251; *see also* divine incarnation
  of individual and universal 66–8, 185, 233, 234, 240; *see also* spirit
  impossibility of between Antigone and Creon 175, 177, cf. 232
  of moral self and nature 155, cf. 214, 239
  as stage in dialectic 269
  Versöhnung 251
redemption 75, 185, 233, 241–3
reference, cognitive 6–9, 18, 24
reflection, reflective 192–201 *passim*, 228, 238–9, 243, 251, 267, 270, 275, 277, 287
  arm-chair 24, cf. 172–3
  cognitive 247, 254, 256, cf. 9–10; *see also* dialectic
  endorsement 141
  equilibrium 162–9
  judgment *see* judgment, reflective
  moral *see* criterion, morality
  Hegel's readers' 6, 26, 175–6, 227, 241, 249, 271
  Self- 146, 148, 155, 164, 228, 251, 253, 256, 267, 270, 277, 287; *see also* self
  of self in world 40, 43–4, 47, 52–3, 104, cf. 277
Reformation 75, 83, 86*n*14
  Post-Reformation 236
  see also Calvin; Luther
relation(s)
  conscious *see* consciousness
  ingredient/product 32
  one/many 20, 32
  relational characteristics *see* properties
  set membership 32

of spirit *see* spirit
thing/property 18, 20, 22, 32
whole/part 20, 32
religion, religious 26, 66–7, 146, 175, 177, 191–200, 212, 226–43, 249, 251
   art-religion 242, 249, 252, cf. 256
   Christianity *see* Christ; Christianity; God
   concept of 226, 240–3
   community, concrete speech of 239
   experience 241–2
   feeling *vs* judgment 240
   fundamentalism 243
   imagination *vs* reason 242
   Judaism 67, 251; *see also* God, Judaic
   natural 242
   philosophy of *see* Hegel, works
   manifest 250
   revelation 212, 241, 250–3, 255
   of the useful 237
   wars 76
   see also authority, ecclesiastical; cult; faith; Unhappy Consciousness; Self-Alienated Spirit: Enculturation; Religion
representation(s) (*Vorstellung*) 17, 57–8, 77–8, 105–6, 197, 247
   perception, indirect theory of 12, cf. 78
   religious *see* religion
   see also concept, Begriff
res cogitans 212, 247, 259; *see also* cartesian, cogito
   extensa 212, 259, 261
   factum 82
resignation 155, 232–4
revelation *see* religion
revolution
   French 203–4, 237, cf. 141
   Netherlands 86n14
   scientific *see* Galileo; modernity; science, natural
right(s)
   divine *see* God
   human 86n14
   legal *see* law; True Spirit: Ethics
   personal 191, 210, 218, 224, 292nn25 and 26

property 158–9, 168
   see also criterion; justice; morality
Rome, Roman
   Empire 186–7, 234
   history 59, 60
   state 164, 169, 175, 185
Romanticism 93, 115, 180, 203, 222–3, 239, 292n27
rule(s) 75, 142, 233, 253
   of empirical inquiry 99, 101
   games 139
   inferential 3; *see also* logic; syllogism
   master 139, 141
   moral *see* criterion; justice; morality
   Rule 4 (Newton) 17–27, 101

salvation 68, 69, 136, cf. 200
satisfaction 56, 68, 69, 84, 104, 143, 174, 199, 203, 214, 235, 237, 238, 279, 284, 289
   self- 37–52 *passim*, 104, 164, 179, 183, 214, 232, 236–7, 279
   see also desire; happiness; inclinations; prestige; pride; utility; Lord and Bondsman
science
   vs faith 228; *see also* The Struggle of the Enlightenment against Superstition
   natural 183, 187n6, 229, 236; *see also* cause; force; nature, law of; Force and Understanding, The Certainty and Truth of Reason, Observing Reason
   of human behavior 183; *see also* phrenology; physiology; psychology
   observational *see* observation
   philosophical 6, 61, 124n72, 227, 246, 247, 272–5; *see also* Absolute Knowing
self 265–70, 272–5, 277–82, 286, 289–90, 292–4
   Fichte 267–8
   form of 250, 259
   free *see* freedom
   interaction with world 267; *see also* bondsman; intersubjectivity; labor; Observing Reason; practice; subjectivity

self (cont'd)
  intersubjectivity of *see* intersubjectivity, recognition
  legal 180, 182; *see also* Legal Status
  managerial conception of 116
  self-alienation 151n18, 196–8, 251, 255, 258; *see also* alienation
  self-awareness 229, 241, 268, 278, 281, 287, 289, 293; *see also* self-knowledge, self-understanding
  self-certainty 78, 79, 153, 157, 202, 210, 221, 249, 252, 261, 275, 278–9; *see also* certainty; Lord and Bondsman; Morality; Spirit
  self-conception 4–5, 38–49; *see also* concept; self-understanding; Lord and Bondsman
  self-consciousness 268, 270–2, 274–80, 284, 291, 294; *see also* Self-Consciousness, Spirit
  self-criticism *see* consciousness, self-critical structure of
  self-deception 12, 147, 195, 196, 203, 217, 223
  self-determination 41, 45, 46, 51, 53, 77, 100, 165, 221, 267, 273, 275, cf. 238; *see also* autonomy; morality
  self-development 39, 41, 53, 73–4, 250, 258–9, 269–70, 273–8, 281, 285, 287–9
  self-discipline 51, 271, cf. 287
  self-externalization 193, 195, 222, 232, 242, 258–9, 260, 262; *see also* labor
  self-identity
    of objects 93, 100; *see also* Perception; Force and Understanding; Observing Reason
    of subject 19, 206n33, 242, 254, 256, 258–9, 267–8, 276–7
  self-interest 142–3, 206n27, 212, 224
  self-knowledge 228, 255, 257–9, 268, 275–7, 286, 289; *see also* spirit
  self-legislation *see* autonomy; Categorical Imperative; self-determination
  self-movement 258–60
  self-otherness 261, 268
  self-positing *see* Fichte
  self-preservation 160

self-realization 38–40, 43, 46, 50, 53, 69, 142, 191, 204, 236, 255, 262, 274–5, 282–5, 289–90, cf. 173; *see also* spirit
self-recognition *see* recognition
self-reflection *see* consciousness, self-critical structure of; reflection
self-regulation, organic 105
self-respect 224
self-satisfaction *see* satisfaction
self-sufficiency 37–40, 148, 283–4; absolute 42–3, 46, 49, 280, 283; of objects 22–3; *see also* substance, concept of; Sense Certainty
selfhood 230, 254–7, 259, 281, 289
selfishness 224, 236; *see also* self-interest
self-understanding 132, 168, 182, 196, 197, 200, 201, 274, 282, 284, 289
  structure of, logical 253–7
  see also subjectivity
selves, list of 184
  of absolute freedom 219; *see also* Absolute Freedom
  of conscience 180, 219 233, 234; *see also* Conscience
  of culture 180, 233, 235, 238; *see also* Self-Alienated Spirit; Enculturation
  of ethical world 219, 233; *see also* True Spirit: Ethics
  of unhappy consciousness 237; *see also* Unhappy Consciousness
  individual 234; *see also* individual, collectivism
  legal 180, 182, 233, 234, 235; *see also* Legal Status
  transcendental 219
  universal 234; *see also* spirit; subjectivity
semantics of cognitive reference 6–7, 16, 26
sensation 15, 69, 252
  sense data 13
  sensibility 15, 215
  presentation, singular sensory 9, 24
servant, servitude *see* Lord and Bondsman
service, state 182, 183; *see also* knight
sex(uality), gender 120n35, 172–4, 186–7
  dimorphism 96, 98
  sexism 172, 177, 182

sexual division of labor 174
see also patriarchy
sin 179, 185, 251; *see also* pride; vice
Sittlichkeit (ethical life) 154–68, 173, 176, 183, 185–7, 211; *see also* morality; spirit
skepticism 75, 78, 136, 186, 213, 234, 237, 248
   Cartesian 27
   causal 19, 21
   Humean 102
   Pyrrhonian 2, 4, 9, 60–5
   skeptical hypotheses 27
slave(s), slavery 59, 63, 234, 279; *see also* Lord and Bondsman
society 231, 235–7, 283, 284
   Greek *see* Greece
   modern *see* modernity
   scientific societies 94, 95
   social space 146–8, 176
   sociality 116, 148, 153–4
   see also collectivism; community; intersubjectivity; morality; *Sittlichkeit*; spirit
soul 112, 115, 116, 169, 252, 255, 262, 268, 271, 284
   see also The Beautiful Soul
sovereignty *see* state; Lord and Bondsman
spirit 25, 73, 175, 248, *defined* 186, 242
   absolute 34, 209, 235, 251–2, 257–9, 265–90, 280; *defined* 26; consists in reconciliation of rational judges 26, 224, 240; immanence of 277, cf. 229
   absolute within 253, 265, 266
   activity of 116, 192, 251–2, 256, 263; *see also* knowing; labor; practice; self-externalization
   actuality of 197, 226, 235, 242, 246–90 *passim*
   alienated *see* self, alienated
   as concrete individual 177, 290
   being-for-self of 192; *see also* spirit, self-consciousness of
   communal 25–6, 172–6, 273, 284, 285
   concept of 64–5, 191–5, 201–3 *passim*
   corporality of 112; *see also* desire; bondsman; labor
   development of xvii–xxvi, 24–9, 50, 53, 67, 73, 153, 156, 160, 169–70, 176, 209–11, 241, 246, 253, 256–8; *see also* chapters 11–13 *passim*
   externalization of 242, 259–62; *see also* self-externalization
   history of 251, 266; *see* chapters 11–13 *passim*
   immediate 33, 40, 261; *see also* True Spirit: Ethics
   inwardization 258, 262–3
   manifest 265, 273
   and nature 177–9, 185, 228–30; *see also* nature
   objective 260, 273
   Philosophy of *see* Hegel, works
   Principle of 192–5, cf. 172, 246, 251, 253, 254, 257
   self-awarenesss of *see* self-awareness
   self-certainty of 210, 226, 252
   self-consciousness of 210, 235, 256
   self-deception of 195–6, cf. 253
   self-knowing of 195–8, 210, 243, 251–2, 257, 258, 262
   self-relation of *see* spirit, Principle of
   shapes (*Gestalt*) of 28, 109, 137, 265, 266, 273, 290; *see also* Table of Concordances
   speech of community 227
   subjective 260, 273
   as substance 173, 210, 235, 246, 256–7, 258–63, 280
   universal 75, 179, 232, 265–6, 273, 275, 277, 287–90
   see also Absolute Knowledge Religion; Spirit; subjectivity
spirituality, Western 235
state 173–84 *passim*, 221, 228, 263, 284, 292n26
   action 159–60
   power 282
   Roman 164; *see also* Rome, Legal Status
   service to 236–7
   terror 204
   see also polis; virtue, knight of
stoicism 58–60, 64, 75, 136, 186, 214, 234, 237, cf. 164
Sturm und Drang 223

subject and substance *see* spirit
subjectivity 265–9, 272, 274–5, 278–81, 284, 286, 289–90, 292–3
   absolute, pure 270, 271–2, 291
   concrete, individual 266, 272–3, 282, 285–6, 289–91
   as species 270
   theory of 266, 267, 270–2, 275, 291
   unity of own development 267
   vitality of 270
   see also I, intersubjectivity, self, spirit
substance 164, 270–1, 273–4, 280, 282, 288, 290–92
   absolute 273, 280; *see also* absolute; spirit
   accidents of 291n20
   chemical 98
   ethical 147, 169, 173, 175, 185, 282–8, cf. 204; *see also* ethical life
   Hegel's concept of 10–24, 211, 246, 291n20; *see also* identity, dialectical
   physical 10–24, 104
   and spirit *see* spirit
   see also chapters 1, 5, 12, 13 *passim*
supersensible, transcendent realm 22–3, 72, 75, 103, 114, 155, 217, 235, 236–7, 273, 280
   see also divine; faith; thing in itself; unchangeable
superstition 75, 85, 138, 190–203, 227
syllogism *see* logic
system(s)
   classificatory *see* classification
   organic *see* physiology
   philosophical *see* philosophy

temptation 215, 218, 232, cf. 231
terms
   demonstrative *see* terms, indexical
   indexical 14, 17, 18
   name, logically proper 14–15
   observation 17
   scientific *see* Observing Reason
   type/token 14, 15
terror 204
thanksgiving 69, 226, 227, 229, 230, 241
theatricality 146–8
theology 169, cf. 237
   natural 226, 229

thing in itself *see* Kant
thinghood 11, 14, 56, 74, 79, 80, 116, 253, 255
thinking, thought 55–8, 246–9, 253, 263, 268, 271, 272, 274, 277, 281, 289, 294, cf. 16, 26
   identity with being *see* identity
   pure, logical 271–2
time 15, 41, 93, 155, 167, 169, 258–63 *passim*, 278
   concept of *see* a priori, concept
   historical 137, 262, 273, 278, 289; *see also* history
   the now *see* Sense Certainty
   temporality 250, 257, 262–3, 282
tragedy 172, 175–80, 237, cf. 214
Troy 232
truth
   and certainty 38–9; *see also* certainty
   correspondence 4–5, 193, cf. 271
   criteria of *see* criterion
   Parmenidean 9, 27, cf. 37; *see also* unchangeable
   of philosophical views 1–6
   as result 1, 2–6, 76, 140, 247–8, 253
   speculative cf. 14, 92, 249, 259–60
   the true 37
   see also absolute; justification; knowing; thought

unchangeable 9, 27, 63, 73, 75, 105, 267, 285; *see also* supersensible; Unhappy Consciousness
understanding (*Verstand*) 55, 248–50 *passim*, 253–4, 276–7
   perceptual 21
   vs reason (*Vernunft*) 10, 88n46; *see also* reason
   see also Force and Understanding; The Certainty and Truth of Reason; Observing Reason
unhappiness 222, 232–5, 234–6, 242; *see also* dissatisfaction; Unhappy Consciousness
unify, unity 267, 269–70, 273, 276, 278, 280, 282–3
   of being-for-itself and being-in-itself 56, 58, 73, 196, 258–9; *see also* faith; spirit; subjectivity; Unhappy

Consciousness; Religion, Absolute Knowing
  of form and matter 252
  in multiplicity 14, 41, 62, 201, 211, 248, 254, 269; *see also* identity, dialectical; logic, syllogism
  of subject and object 76–8, 197, 259–61; *see also* thought, identity with being
  see also classification, systems of; explanation; identity
universal 10, 21, 53, 79–80, 92, 153, 173, 191, 210, 265; *see also* morality; representation; subjectivity; Consciousness, Observing Reason
  abstract 21, 60, 77, 247
  see also spirit; Religion
unrest, dialectical 56, 63, 107
use(ful), utility 255, 268
  Principle of 167–8, 204
  religion of 237
  social 139
  utilitarianism 154, 159, 166, 199, 255

valet 224
value
  absolute 212, 230, 239
  collective 281, 283, 284, 288
  conferral of 38–53, 75, 83, 238–40, 255, 288
  customary 191, 287
  relativity of 237
  see also morality; patriarchy; Lord and Bondsman; Religion
vanity 224, 293*n*30
Versöhnung 251; *see also* reconciliation
vice, vicious 143, 199, 214, 215, 263; *see also* bad; morality; self-interest; selfishness; sin
virtue 136–46 *passim*, 214, 215, 217, 221–3, 263, 283; *see also* morality

war(fare) 76, 167, 174, 184, 227, 230
wealth 174, 236, 237; *see also* Virtue and the Way of the World

wicked(ness) 143, 214; *see also* bad; evil; vice
will 25, 39, 43, 73, 75–6
  autonomy of *see* autonomy
  divine *see* divine, God
  free *see* freedom, Kant, morality
  general 46, 204, 210; *see also* will, universal
  holy 218
  ill 138
  individual 75, 165, 169; *see also* individual; Lord and Bondsman; Self-Certain Spirit: Morality
  noumenal 165, 166
  pure 255; *see also* duty; pure
  renunciation of 69
  universal 75, 210, 283; *see also* criterion, moral; Kant
  see also autonomy; desire; drive; duty; good; inclination; labor; morality
work *see* labor
world 23, 40, 43, 57, 266–71, 273–5, 277–82, 284–91
  ancient *see* Greece; polis; Rome
  disenchanted 196
  forms, shapes of 192, 209
  interpretation 192
  inverted *see* Force and Understanding
  historical *see* Greece; history; modernity; Rome
  lord of *see* God; lord
  modern *see* modernity
  natural *see* cause; force; nature; science; Force and Understanding; The Certainty and Truth of Reason; Observing Reason
  objective 137, 270, 278, 279
  order, moral *see* morality; Self-Certain Spirit: Morality
  social 27, 143, 146, 281–2, 284–6, 288; *see also* chapters 6–11, 13 *passim*
  supersensible, transcendent 23, 155, 235, 236; *see also* faith; Religion
  under 179–80, 233
  way of *see* Virtue and the Way of the World
  see also consciousness, forms of

Table of Concordances

This Table indicates where in this commentary the various parts, chapters, sections and sub-sections of Hegel's *Phenomenology of Spirit* are discussed. Discussion of any sub-section is included within discussion of its superior section heading.

PREFACE xvii, 1, 30*n*14, 74, 100, 107, 116*n*1, 123*n*59, 290*n*4
INTRODUCTION xvii, 1, 2–6, 61, 63, 70*n*3, 176, 188*n*11, 193, 225*n*8, 243*n*4, 241, 247, 248, 266, 268, 290*n*3
CONSCIOUSNESS xvii, 6–29, 37–8, 39, 55, 73, 96, 153, 229, 248, 276, 280, cf. 210
    Sense-Certainty xviii, 1, 6–9, 13, 24, 27, 32, 55, 68, 73, 74, 75, 92, 105, 186, 206*n*30, 220, 221, 250, 252, 253, 254, 261, 275, 287
    Perception xviii, 9–15, 24, 55, 75, 92, 105, 196, 250, 253, 254
    Force and Understanding xviii, 15–25, 41, 55, 73, 75, 76, 79, 85, 94, 96, 105, 107, 109, 248–50, 253, 254, cf. 88*n*46
SELF-CONSCIOUSNESS xvii, xix 25, 33, 37–70, 72–6, 103, 153, 209, 210, 229, 248, 250, 275, 277–81, cf. 136
    The Truth of Self-Certainty 43–9, 79, 210, 249, 278
    Self-Sufficiency and Self-Insufficiency of Self-Consciousness; Mastery and Servitude xix, 25, 49–53, 55–9, 60, 64, 75, 136, 213, 279
    Freedom of Self-Consciousness xix, 25, 33, 55–70
        Stoicism 58–60, 62, 75, 136, 186, cf. 234, 237
        Skepticism xix, 60–4, 75, 86*n*19, 118*n*16, 136, 186, 213, cf. 9, 27, 199, 234, 237
        Unhappy Consciousness 64–70, 72, 76, 79, 81, 83, 222, 234, 237, cf. 203, 282
REASON xvii, xix–xxi, 25, 72–170, 172–3, 183, 229, 238, 275, 276, 281–3, 285
    The Certainty and Truth of Reason xx, 25, 72–85, cf. 196
    Observing Reason xx, 25, 73, 77, 79–80, 82, 84, 92–116, 255
        Observation of Nature 92–111
        Observation of Self-consciousness 111–16
          Logic and Psychology 112–13, 150*n*10
          Physiognomy and Phrenology 79, 113–16, 150*n*10
    The Actualization of Rational Self-consciousness through Itself xx, 25, 136–70
        Pleasure and Necessity

Law of the Heart and the Insanity of Conceit 139–42
Virtue and the Way of the World 142–5
Individuality which is Real In and For Itself 146–8
The Animal Kingdom of the Spirit and Humbug 147–8
Legislative Reason xxi, 153–70
Law-testing Reason xxi, 153–70

SPIRIT xvii–xviii, xxi, xxii–xxiii, 6, 25–6, 73, 136–7, 153–4, 165, 169–224, 228–30, 242–3, 248, 265–90, cf. 64, 66, 148, 253
True Spirit: Ethics xxi, 25, 164, 169, 172–87, 192, 228, 233–4, 238, 239, 282
The Ethical World: Human and divine law; man and woman
Ethical Action: Human and divine knowledge, guilt and fate
Legal Status 175, 185–6, 233–5, cf. 169
Self-Alienated Spirit; Enculturation xxi–xxii, 25, 27, 186, 190–204, cf. 267–8, 276–81, 286–90
The world of self-alienated spirit 195–98
Enculturation and its Actuality
Faith and Pure Insight
The Enlightenment 198–203, 238
The Struggle of the Enlightenment with Superstition 198–203
The Truth of Enlightenment 202–3
Absolute Freedom and the Terror 203–4, 211, 219
Self-Certain Spirit: Morality xxii–xxiii, 25, 207–24, 238–9, 240, 255
The Moral Worldview 211–16
Dissemblance 216–18
Conscience 219–21
The Beautiful Soul 221–4
Evil and Forgiveness 25–6, 223–4, 226–7, 230, 240

RELIGION xviii, 26, 66, 153, 197–8, 226–43, 250, 251, 253, 256
Natural Religion
The 'Light-being'
Plants and Animals
The Artificer
Art-Religion 252
The Abstract Work of Art
The Living Work of Art
The Spiritual Work of Art
Manifest Religion xviii

ABSOLUTE KNOWING xviii, 6, 26, 31n22, 94, 153, 226–7, 243, 246–63, 266, 268, 273, 274